THE EFFECTIVENESS OF INTERNATIONAL DECISIONS

THE EFFECTIVENESS OF INTERNATIONAL DECISIONS

Papers of a conference of

The American Society of International Law,

and the

Proceedings of the conference

edited by

STEPHEN M. SCHWEBEL

A. W. SIJTHOFF—LEYDEN

OCEANA PUBLICATIONS, INC.—DOBBS FERRY, N.Y.

1971

ISBN 90 218 9041 0 (Sijthoff)

Library of Congress Catalog Card Number: 76 140513
© A. W. Sijthoff's Uitgeversmaatschappij N.V., 1971

PREFACE

The papers and proceedings contained in this book flow from the third conference of official legal advisers convened by the American Society of International Law. The first conference brought together the legal advisers of a dozen foreign ministries with a number of scholars and other interested officials in Princeton, New Jersey, in 1963. The second brought together legal advisers of international organizations and scholars who study their work. It met in the Rockefeller Foundation's splendid Villa Serbelloni, in Bellagio, Italy, in 1965.

The first conference primarily concerned the role and functions of legal advisers of national foreign ministries. It concentrated on the organization of offices of the legal adviser and the ways in which they influence or fail to influence decision-making by governments. The conference of legal advisers of international organizations embraced a comparable discussion, but also considered the legal capacity and personality of international organizations, and the subject of consensus: its formation and effects. It also opened the question of compliance with decisions of international organizations.

These conferences, the first of the kind to be held, aroused considerable interest. The former Executive Vice President of the Society, H. C. L. Merillat, produced two valuable books which contain certain of the papers submitted to those conferences as well as a summary of their proceedings.[1]

A measure of their contribution and interest is evidenced by two review articles concerning them by Sir Gerald Fitzmaurice, Judge of the International Court of Justice, which were published in the *American Journal of International Law*.[2]

The third conference of which this volume is the product concentrated on the subject of the effectiveness of decisions of international organizations in member states. It met at the Villa Serbelloni under the chairmanship of John R. Stevenson, then President of the Society, and now The Legal Adviser of the U.S. Department of State. A list of the participants and the agenda are printed at pages 357 and 359-361.

This volume is much larger than its predecessors for two reasons: first, it contains all the papers submitted (together with a few submitted to the 1965 conference on the theme of effectiveness), and a number of those papers are lengthy. The latter in particular contain much fresh and hitherto unpublished material on the functioning and effectiveness of international organizations. Second, rather than containing a summary of the

---

[1] Merillat, *Legal Advisers and Foreign Affairs,* Oceana Publications, 1964; *Legal Advisers and International Organizations,* Oceana Publications, 1966.
[2] Fitzmaurice, "Legal Advisers and Foreign Affairs," 59 A.J.I.L. 72 (1965), and "Legal Advisers and International Organizations," 62 A.J.I.L. 114 (1968).

discussion, this volume contains a transcript of it. The transcript is an edited one. Remarks are not quoted; it should not be thought that the words reproduced were precisely those spoken by the participants. But what is found is substantially what they said. Relatively little has been omitted: largely an occasional repetition, obscurity, or an arguable indelicacy. I ventured to change the order of remarks a few times in the interest of coherency. The result, while long, is, it is hoped, the more valuable, for it preserves the substance and nuances of an exchange which at times had its subtlety more fully than a summary record could have done.

Miss Catherine Wassey, who served as the Society's deputy librarian during the summer of 1970, was good enough to review the papers to correct an occasional error of reproduction or expression, to put the footnotes and other stylistic matters in standard form, and to counsel me on the format of the volume. She has also prepared the index. I am most grateful for her skillful and cheerful assistance.

I should also like to thank Miss Editha Fuchs, who, as the conference reporter, took notes and, with the aid of them and tape recordings, produced the transcript of discussion from which the edited record has been drawn. I wish to thank as well Mrs. George B. Goba for her excellent typing of the record.

Finally, may I express the Society's profound appreciation to two foundations: to the Ford Foundation for financial assistance which has permitted the convening of these conferences and a great deal more, and to the Rockefeller Foundation for its exceptional and repeated hospitality at the Villa Serbelloni.

I should add that the Society sponsored a fourth conference of national and international legal advisers, again at the Villa Serbelloni, this on the subject of legal problems of foreign public lending and assistance. A report on its proceedings and papers is in preparation.

One final word of acknowledgement: I deeply appreciate the patience of the participants in the 1967 conference in bearing with my belated editing of the transcript. To take account of the time which has elapsed since 1967 and the initial writing of the conference's papers, a number of them were revised and updated in the spring of 1970.

Washington, D. C.   Stephen M. Schwebel
July, 1970

6

TABLE OF CONTENTS

5   Preface

PAPERS

9   Towards a Theory of International Obligation—*Oscar Schachter*

32   Compliance with United Nations Decisions on Peace and Security and Human Rights Questions—*Rosalyn Higgins*

51   Procedures Developed by International Organizations for Checking Compliance—*Louis B. Sohn*

57   Implementation of Decisions of International Organizations through National Courts—*E. Lauterpacht*

66   Application and Enforcement of International Organization Law by National Authorities and Courts—*Eric Stein*

71   Certain Aspects of the Law and Practice of the International Monetary Fund—*Joseph Gold*

100   Certain Aspects of the Law and Practice of the International Bank for Reconstruction and Development—*Lester Nurick*

129   The Inter-American Development Bank—*Elting Arnold*

134   The International Labor Organization—*Nicolas Valticos*

156   The International Civil Aviation Organization—A Case Study in the Implementation of Decisions of a Functional International Organization—*Gerald F. FitzGerald*

206   Some Aspects of the Law and Practice of FAO—*Jean Pierre Dobbert*

277   Notes on Decisions of the World Health Organization—*F. Gutteridge*

285   Decisions and Other Measures Taken by the International Atomic Energy Agency—*Werner Boulanger*

290   Decisions of the Universal Postal Union—*Z. Caha*

304   Note on the Effectiveness of Decisions Adopted by the Contracting Parties to the General Agreement on Tariffs and Trade—*Eric Wyndham White*

309   The European Communities—*Michel Gaudet*

340   The Council of Europe—*H. Golsong*

346   Applying, and Effecting Compliance with, Decisions (with Reference to the European Convention on Human Rights)—*A. H. Robertson*

351   Binding Decisions in the Inter-American System and the Central American Common Market—*F. V. Garcia-Amador*

PROCEEDINGS

357   The Participants in the Bellagio Conference

359   The Agenda

363   The Transcript of the Discussion, edited by *Stephen M. Schwebel*

TOWARDS A THEORY OF INTERNATIONAL OBLIGATION

by *Oscar Schachter* *
United Nations Institute for Training and Research

I. THE PRACTICAL IMPORT OF THEORY

It seems especially fitting to devote this essay to some reflections on a basic—some would say meta-juridical—question that appears to be at the heart of some of our present intellectual perplexities in international law. As a subject, the "foundation of obligation" is as old as international law itself; it had a prominent place in the seminal treaties of the founding fathers—Suarez, Vittoria, Grotius, Pufendorf et al—and it remained a central issue in the great controversies of the nineteenth century.[1] In our century it has had a lesser place; it was largely overtaken by the discussion of "sources" and evidence, centered around Article 38 of the Statute of the International Court.[2] Although subordinated, it was not neglected and each of the leading scholars of the twentieth century found himself impelled to advance a fresh analysis. No single theory has received general agreement and sometimes it seems as though there are as many theories or at least formulations as there are scholars. We can list at least a baker's dozen of "candidates" which have been put forward as the basis (or as one of the bases) of obligation in international law:

(i) Consent of states [3]
(ii) Customary practice [4]
(iii) A sense of "rightness"—the juridical conscience [5]
(iv) Natural law or natural reason [6]

---

* Mr. Schachter is the Deputy Executive Director and the Director of Research of the United Nations Institute for Training and Research (UNITAR), an associate of the Institut de Droit International, an editor of the American Journal of International Law, and was the President of the American Society of International Law 1968-1970. He wishes to express his appreciation to the Virginia Journal of International Law for permission to reprint much of this paper.

[1] See P. Corbett, *Law and Society in the Relations of States* 17-90 (1951).

[2] C. Parry, *Sources and Evidence of International Law* (1965); M. Sorensen, *Les Sources du Droit International* (1946).

[3] Corbett, *"The Consent of States and the Sources of International Law"*, 6 Brit. Y. B. Int'l L. 20 (1925); Tunkin, *"Coexistence and International Law"*, 95 Hague Academy Recueil des Cours 5, 32-49 (1958).

[4] H. Kelsen, *Principles of International Law* 564 (2d ed. R. Tucker rev. 1966). *See also* G. Schwarzenberger, *The Inductive Approach to International Law* 22-38 (1965).

[5] For a discussion of this position, especially as expressed by Krabbe, *see* J. Brierly, *The Basis of Obligation in International Law* 59-64 (H. Lauterpacht & H. Waldock ed. 1958).

[6] H. Wheaton, *Elements of International Law* 20 (1866); *see* Lauterpacht, *"The Grotian Tradition in International Law"*, 23 Brit. Y. B. Int'l L. 1 (1946).

9

(v) Social necessity [7]

(vi) The will of the international community (the "consensus" of the international community) [8]

(vii) Direct (or "stigmatic") intuition [9]

(viii) Common purposes of the participants [10]

(ix) Effectiveness [11]

(x) Sanctions [12]

(xi) "Systemic" goals [13]

(xii) Shared expectations as to authority [14]

(xiii) Rules of recognition [15]

On looking at this wide array of ideas concerning the "true" or "correct" basis of obligation in international law it may be wondered, on the one hand, whether the choice of a "basis" has any great practical significance and, on the other, whether the diversity of opinion does not reveal a radical weakness in the conceptual structure of international law.

For some pragmatically-inclined international lawyers, the issue is not likely to be regarded as important. As long as the obligation itself—the legal norm or prescription—can be identified in one of the so-called formal sources—treaty or custom or in general principles of law—it seems to matter little what the underlying basis of the obligation may be. It is, therefore, understandable that most contemporary treatises and textbooks on international law pass quickly and lightly over the problem of the "foundation." Like the chaplain's opening prayer at public meetings, it has little effect on what is said afterwards. The practical international lawyer is supposed to be concerned not with the foundation of obligation but with the so-called "sources," formal and material. [16]

---

[7] G. Scelle, *Droit International Public* 13-14 (1949).

[8] C. Jenks, *The Common Law of Mankind,* ch. 1 (1955); C. Jenks, *Law, Welfare and Freedom* 83-100 (1963); H. Lauterpacht, *The Function of Law in the International Community* 421-423 (1933).

[9] Stone, *"Problems Confronting Sociological Enquiries concerning International Law",* 89 *Hague Academy Recueil des Cours* 65 (1956).

[10] C. de Visscher, *Theory and Reality in Public International Law* 122, 133 (P. Corbett transl. 1957; Hoffman, *"International Systems and International Law",* in 2 *The Strategy of World Order* 135, 162 (R. Falk & S. Mendlovitz ed. 1966).

[11] J. Brierly, *The Outlook for International Law* 4-5 (1944); W. Friedmann, *The Changing Structure of International Law* 86-95 (1964).

[12] J. Austin, *The Province of Jurisprudence* 133, 193 (1954 ed.).

[13] M. Kaplan & N. Katzenbach, *The Political Foundations of International Law* 56-80, 341-54 (1961). *See also* M. Kaplan, *System and Process in International Politics* (1957).

[14] M. McDougal, *Studies in World Public Order* 1-41 (1960); McDougal, *"International Law, Power and Policy",* 82 *Hague Academy Recueil des Cours* 137 (1953). *See also* works cited note 41 *infra.*

[15] H. Hart, *The Concept of Law* 77-107, 231 (1961).

[16] Bishop, *"General Course of Public International Law",* 115 *Hague Academy Recueil des Cours* 151, 214-50 (1965).

But this is more easily said than done. Somehow conceptions as to the basis of obligation arise time and again, and not only in theoretical discussion about the binding force of international law. They come up in concrete controversies as to whether a rule of law has emerged or has been terminated; whether an event is a violation or a precedent; and whether practice under a treaty is accepted as law. They are involved in dealing with situations in which solemn declarations, couched in legal terminology, are adopted by official bodies which have no formal authority to lay down prescriptive rules. They come up when there is substantial variance between what is preached and what is practiced; or when consensus (or expectations) are limited in geographical terms or in duration. These are not, of course, new problems and over the years they have been the subject of much jurisprudential writing. But in the last few years the general problem has assumed a new dimension. The peculiar features of contemporary international society have generated considerable normative activity without at the same time involving commensurate use of the formal procedures for international "legislation" and adjudication.

It may be useful to recall the main factors which have emerged in international life in the last few years to give enhanced importance to problems of indeterminancy of obligation.

First, there has been the much-discussed "quasi-legislative" activity by the General Assembly and other United Nations bodies purporting to lay down, expressly or by implication, requirements of State conduct or to terminate or modify existing requirements.[17]

Second, there has been a recognition of so-called "rules of the game," based on implicit understandings or unilateral actions and acquiescence. This has been a notable feature of Great Power behavior in regard to their use of armed force.[18]

Third, there have been the social revolutions which have overturned traditional orders and have challenged the assumptions on which prior conceptions of authority were based.[19]

---

[17] R. Higgins, *The Development of International Law through the Political Organs of the United Nations* 1-10 (1963); Bailey, *"Making International Law in the United Nations"*, 1967 Proceedings, Am. Soc. Int'l L. 233; Falk, *"On the Quasi-Legislative Competence of the General Assembly"*, 60 Am. J. Int'l L. 782 (1966); Jennings, *"Recent Developments in the International Law Commission: Its Relation to Sources of International Law"*, 17 Int'l & Comp. L. Q. 385 (1964); Schachter, *"The Relation of Law, Politics and Action in the United Nations"*, 109 Hague Academy Recueil des Cours 171 (1963).

[18] E. McWhinney, *Peaceful Coexistence and Soviet-Western International Law* 92-100 (1964); T. Schelling, *The Strategy of Conflict* 260-64 (1960); Henkin, *"International Law and the Behaviour of Nations"*, 114 Hague Academy Recueil des Cours 171, 200-01 (1965).

[19] T. Taracouzio, *The Soviet Union and International Law* (1935); Hoffman, *supra* note 10, at 152 *et seq.*; McDougal & Goodman, *"Chinese Participation in the United Nations"*, 60 Am. J. Int'l L. 671 (1966); Tunkin, *supra* note 3.

11

Fourth, the growing interdependence of States—especially in economic and technological activities—has vastly increased patterns of cooperation and reciprocal behavior which have not been institutionalized in the traditional modes of lawmaking.[20]

Fifth, the increased "permeability" of national States has resulted in a diminishing barrier between matters of international concern and those of domestic jurisdiction.[21] Related to this is the fact that the United Nations Charter—particularly its articles relating to respect for human rights and self-determination of peoples—has brought domestic activities before collective organs for appraisal on the basis of international criteria.

Sixth, the expansion of science and technology with international impact both beneficial and harmful has given rise to informal means of setting standards and exercising supervision without entering into tight and tidy legal instruments.[22]

The mere statement of these trends indicates how extensive and far-reaching are normative processes which cannot easily be placed into the categories of treaty and customary law, at least as these terms have been applied traditionally. Lawyers are made uncomfortable by this and they ceaselessly endeavor to pour the new wine into the old bottles and to market it under the time-honored labels. They will treat many of the cases as problems of treaty interpretation; others will be dealt with on the assumptions applicable to traditional customary law. But when we examine the arguments and the grounds for decision, we find more frequently than not that the test of whether a "binding" rule exists or should be applied will involve basic jurisprudential assumptions. Even the International Court of Justice, which is governed expressly by Article 38 of its Statute as to the sources of law, has demonstrated time and again that in their deliberative process the judges have had to look to theory to evaluate practice.

We can readily illustrate this by brief references to judicial opinions which have employed criteria such as the will of the community, customary behavior, the sense of "rightness," reason, necessity, natural law, major purposes and so on. In the 1966 *South West Africa Cases,* the opinions of Judges Jessup and Tanaka provide good examples.[23] Judge Jessup found that the accumulation of expressions of condemnation of apartheid especially as recorded in the resolutions of the General Assembly

---

[20] W. Friedmann, *The Changing Structure of International Law* 275-94 (1964); Schachter, *supra* note 17, at 238-49.

[21] M. Kaplan & N. Katzenbach, *The Political Foundations of International Law* 94-108 (1961). For a suggestive sociological analysis of trends on the "general erosion of the nation state" *see* Galtung, *"On the Future of the International System",* [1967] *J. Peace Research (Oslo),* No. 4, at 305-33.

[22] Schachter, *"Scientific Advances and International Law Making",* 55 *Calif. L. Rev.* 423 (1967).

[23] [1966] I.C.J., 6, 325-442 (Jessup, J., dissenting), 250-324 (Tanaka, J., dissenting).

was "of decisive practical and juridical value" in determining the "international community" standard to be used in the interpretation of the requirement in Article 2 that South Africa promote the well-being of the inhabitants.[24] In effect, this meant that the Assembly resolutions established a conclusive, not merely a rebuttable, presumption as to the meaning of well-being. Judge Tanaka took a different ground. He concluded that, while a single resolution is only recommendatory, the repetition by overwhelming majorities of condemnation of apartheid has established a customary rule of law.[25] He also found the rule against apartheid to constitute a "general principle of law"—not because it is a principle common to diverse legal systems, but as a rule *jus naturale,* "valid through all kinds of human societies" and derived from the concept of "man as a person." Its validity therefore rests on a basis that has a "supra-national and supra-positive character." [26]

In other I.C.J. cases we can find reliance on "major purposes,"[27] on the necessity of a sense of rightness,[28] and on humanitarian values.[29] In the *Anglo-Norwegian Fisheries* Case,[30] the factor of strong economic interest of one State directly affected supported a judgment that practice of that State should be accepted as law; and in the Corfu Channel judgment,[31] the majority rejected the British claim to "self-preservation" on the ground that it was a manifestation of a policy of force such as "has in the past given rise to serious abuses." These are all criteria not easily discoverable in the text of Article 38.

When we look beyond the judicial arena to the political bodies and to the diplomatic arena, we find, not surprisingly, an even greater number of situations in which the distinction between "binding" and "non-binding" is not easily determinable. Perhaps the most important group of such situations falls into the second category of developments mentioned above, namely, the "rules of the game" or tacit understandings. In this category one might include what is often described as the *modus vivendi* between the two major powers not to use or introduce armed force in the sphere of influence of the other or to upset the existing balance between them in any significant way. Some observers have referred to the "line" accepted by the major powers, running through the divided countries and between other critical areas as if it had been laid down in treaties.[32] The

---

[24] *Id.* at 441.

[25] *Id.* at 291.

[26] *Id.* at 298.

[27] Advisory Opinion on Certain Expenses of the United Nations, [1962] I.C.J. 151.

[28] Colombian-Peruvian Asylum Case [1950] I.C.J. 266.

[29] Advisory Opinion on Reservations to the Convention on the Prevention and Punishment of the Crime of Genocide, [1951] I.C.J. 15.

[30] [1951] I.C.J. 116.

[31] [1949] I.C.J. 4.

[32] *See, e.g.,* Rostow, *"The Great Transition: Tasks of the First and Second Post-War*

Cuban quarantine and missile crisis is said to exemplify the operation of that general rule.[33] Other such rules of the game have been posited in more limited situations. For example, some would say there has been a tacit rule on the part of the two major powers not to give nuclear weapons to third parties, including their respective allies. These rules or tacit agreements are generally not characterized by lawyers as legal obligations; their violation would not be thought of as ground for legal liability and they are presumed to be terminable at will. On the other hand, their termination may well give rise to sanctions in the form of public condemnation (as in the violation of the Nuclear Test Moratorium) or, more important, to counter-action by the other party. In some cases, these "rules of the game" constitute the most crucial international obligations of our time.

As we go down the list of the six categories mentioned above, other situations come to mind. Consider, for example, the effect of anticolonialism (expressed in declarations of the General Assembly and in other supposedly "non-binding" assertions) on the meaning of domestic jurisdiction and self-determination.[34] Or consider the changing conceptions regarding the taking of private property and their effect on the existing "rule" concerning compensation for expropriation.[35] In the field of economics and technology, there is uncertainty as to the legal authority of emerging principles of international trade and economic assistance for the benefit of the developing countries which have not yet assumed conventional legal form; yet they exhibit some measure of practical efficacy and give rise to widespread expectations as to their future application.[36]

In all of these cases the traditional sign-posts of legal obligation have limited utility, at the very least they call for further analysis and possibly, as Richard Falk has suggested, for a more adequate theory of the

---

Generations", 56 Dep't State Bull. 491, 492, 494 (1967). See also Lissitzyn, "International Law in a Divided World", Int'l Conciliation, No. 542 (1963).

[33] E. Abel, The Missile Crisis 104-09, 192-93 (1966) (statements of President Kennedy). See also Chayes, "The Law and the Quarantine of Cuba", 41 For. Aff. 552 (1963); Henkin, supra note 18, at 254.

[34] Castañeda, "The Underdeveloped Nations and the Development of International Law", 15 Int'l Org. 38 (1961); Emerson, "Colonialism, Political Development and the United Nations", 19 Int'l Org. 484 (1965).

[35] Banco Nacional de Cuba v. Sabbatino, 376 U.S. 398 (1964); The Aftermath of Sabbatino (L. Tondel ed. 1965). See also, O. Lissitzyn, International Law Today and Tomorrow 75-85 (1965); Hyde, "Economic Development Agreements", 105 Hague Academy Recueil des Cours 271, 332-55 (1962); Schwebel, "United Nations Declaration on Permanent Sovereignty over Natural Resources", 49 A.B.A.J. 463 (1963).

[36] Metzger, "Development of Rules Relating to International Trade", 1965 Proceedings, Am. Soc. Int'l L. 20; Lasswell, "The Relevance of International Law to the Development Process", 1966 Proceedings, Am. Soc. Int'l Law 1; Friedmann, "The Relevance of International Law to the Processes of Economic and Social Development", id. at 8; Remarks of F. Feliciano, id. at 15, and of A. Fatouros, id. at 18; Schachter, supra note 17, at 233-49.

basis of legal obligation in international society.[37] The observations that follow will attempt to suggest some of the considerations relevant to a more adequate theory.

II. AN APPROACH TO A THEORY OF INTERNATIONAL OBLIGATION

Hardy Dillard, in a recent, typically felicitous essay, expressed concern over the emphasis on certain modes of inquiry to the exclusion of others. To know the "why" of things, we need, he suggested, a "perspective that looks both forwards and backwards. It may well elude a mind bent exclusively on fact-finding or one geared to solving specific problems." [38] It will also elude—and I know Dean Dillard will agree—a mind exclusively geared to the *a priori* and intuitive approach. If we are to snare so elusive a quarry as international obligation, we may need several nets and to spread them all wide.

The trouble with nets—or "conceptual frameworks" as they are now called—is that we can easily get tangled in the net and lose sight of the quarry. The wider the net, the greater the risk. We have seen the entanglements in the grand "top down" systems that work their way from all-embracing concepts on high through intermediate hypotheses to more specific assertions which sometimes are verifiable and sometimes are not. Hegel and Marx provide classic examples; Talcott Parsons is a good contemporary example.[39] Still, a system or framework seems to be essential if we are to organize a vast amount of material and relate it to our purposes.[40] And for the kind of problem with which we are now concerned I believe the most pertinent framework is that developed by Harold Lasswell and Myres McDougal for inquiry into the "global process of authoritative decision."[41] No other scheme that I know of provides as complete a set of tools for examining the interplay of law and the other social processes. It can enable us to discern with sharpened awareness the connections be-

---

[37] Falk, *"New Approaches to the Study of International Law"*, 61 *Am. J. Int'l L.* 477 486 (1967).

[38] Dillard, *"Minds and Moods"*, 44 *Va. Q. Rev.* 51, 58 (1968).

[39] T. Parsons, *The Structure of Social Action* (1937). For a summary and criticism of Parsons from a "juristic standpoint" see J. Stone, *Social Dimensions of Law and Justice* 16-28 (1966). An application of Parsonian theory to international law is found in K. Carlston, *Law and Organization in World Society* (1962).

[40] A conceptual framework may give a scholar a needed sense of security and also make it easier for his assistants and graduate students to get on with their research —a practical advantage not to be scorned. See MacKenzie, *"The Conceptual Framework and the Cash Basis"*, 10 *Pol. Studies* 36, 41 (1962).

[41] M. McDougal, H. Lasswell & J. Miller, *The Interpretation of Agreements and World Public Order* (1967); M. McDougal, H. Lasswell & I. Vlasic, *Law and Public Order in Space* ch. 1 (1936); McDougal, *supra* note 14; Lasswell, *"Toward Continuing Appraisal of the Impact of Law on Society"*, 21 *Rutgers L. Rev.* 645 (1967).

tween rules and behavior and—equally important—can give us strong solvents to dissolve longstanding intellectual obstructions to understanding. Not the least of its merits is its heuristic property; it sets one searching into neglected strata to uncover unsuspected correlations and explanations. The remarks that follow owe much to the Lasswell-McDougal approach; I attempt both to build on that approach and to raise questions about it. However, I shall use more conventional language—perhaps at the cost of some exactitude—in order to make my points clear to those not familiar with their special terminology. Nor shall I try to apply their various sets of categories in the prescribed manner. That apparatus seems too heavy for this essay and my own ideas might sink under its weight.

The Process of Establishing Obligatory Norms

Recent analysis in logic and scientific method has given much importance to "definitional policy" and to the variety of modes of definition appropriate for different forms of inquiry.[42] Even a superficial acquaintance with that literature warns us against dogmatism and finality in definition and suggests that different types of definition serve different purposes and subject matter. Having said that, I shall venture to put forward a definitional hypothesis for our key concept of "obligatory norm" that goes beyond the more cautious stipulative and operational definitions sometimes favored. That hypothesis will be stated in terms of process (that is, steps taken) rather than outcome. It will suggest that five processes constitute the necessary *and* sufficient conditions for the establishment of an obligatory legal norm. (This is the kind of definition which in logical theory has at various times been characterized as "real," "structural", or "theoretical," though these terms tell us little.) The definition is intended to apply to obligatory norms in their most generalized sense—whether in treaty, custom, statute, decision, or resolution; whether international or national; whether specific or highly general, concrete or vague. The component terms are intended to be empirical and not merely nominal (stipulated verbal equivalencies) and they are not merely operational indices but (as already stated) necessary and sufficient conditions. In other words, they purport to tell us how to recognize an obligatory rule or principle when we see one; and, by the same token, to reject a proposed candidate on the basis of identifiable data.

The five processes are similar to those suggested by Lasswell and McDougal in their own vocabulary—but I do not know whether my formulation will meet with their approval. Stated summarily, the five processes required for the establishment of obligatory norms are:

---

[42] A. Edel, *Method in Ethical Theory* 111-38 (1963); C. Hempel, *Fundamentals of Concept-Formation in Empirical Science* 2-14, 39-50 (1952).

16

(i) the formulation and designation of a requirement as to behavior in contingent circumstances

(ii) an indication that that designation has been made by persons recognized as having the competence (authority or legitimate role) to perform that function and in accordance with procedures accepted as proper for that purpose

(iii) an indication of the capacity and willingness of those concerned to make the designated requirement effective in fact

(iv) the transmittal of the requirement to those to whom it is addressed (the target audience)

(v) the creation in the target audience of responses—both psychological and operational—which indicate that the designated requirement is regarded as authoritative (in the sense specified in (iii) above) and as likely to be complied with in the future in some substantial degree.

Each one of these features points to the kind of material (data) which would—if available—validate or refute a characterization that a given proposition should be regarded as an obligatory norm. Moreover, it enables us to discover underlying factual assumptions that have not otherwise been noticed and to look beyond words to the realities of obligational phenomena.

In the comments that follow I shall concern myself with three aspects of this definition which are especially relevant to the practical problems raised in Part I in regard to the international legal process. One, the problem of the authority to "prescribe," that is, to designate obligatory norms; two, the response (or acceptance) of those to whom the norm is addressed (the target audience); three, the question of the relation between that response on a descriptive level and the purposes and values of the community. These three aspects have an ascending order of complexity and difficulty. My remarks on each will attempt some clarification and suggest questions.

Competence and Authority

Under our hypothesis, whether a designated requirement is to be regarded as obligatory will depend in part on whether those who have made that designation are regarded by those to whom the requirement is addressed (the target audience) as endowed with the requisite competence or authority for that role. This issue—who are the "legislators"—may, and frequently does, raise problems for any type of legal enactment, even those highly formal and explicit. But the issue is more likely to be raised and to be more critical when the supposed requirement arises in an unorganized informal interaction or when it emanates from persons lacking the formal *indicia* of authority to perform the law-making function. As we have seen in part I of this article, such issues arise sharply in the context of "practice" or other informal interactions which involve indeterminancies as to the appropriate role of the participants. They also arise with increasing frequency as a result of the activities of supposedly recommendatory organs such as the General Assembly, expert groups like the International Law Commission, or legal scholars. And one can add to this list national military officials, international civil servants, even private businessmen and scientists—all have taken part in some degree as formulators of rules which have come to be accepted as legally binding. This fact suggests the difficulty of finding general criteria to enable us to classify who—and under what circumstances—will be regarded as authoritative for designating international obligatory norms.

There are, however, some useful correlations that can be suggested for investigation. One has to do with the relation of the putative "prescribers" and the arena or context in which they have acted. A government official, operating within the national administration, may have no authority to participate in the formulation of rules of international conduct, but when he becomes a representative to the United Nations and takes part in formulating a resolution explicitly interpreting a provision on the Charter, he may come to be considered as possessing the requisite authority. As I have said in another connection:

When an organ applies a Charter principle or any other rule of law to a particular set of facts, it is asserting, as a matter of logic, a new rule of a more specific character. This is a law-creative act, even though the members of the organ maintain (as they often do) that their decision is confined to the specific facts and they do not intend to establish a precedent. It may be that the "rule" of that case will not be followed in other situations and that its applicability will prove to be limited. But the contrary may also prove true, since, once a decision is rendered by an authoritative body, it has entered into the stream of decisions that will normally be looked to as a source of law. Considerations of equity and equal treatment will tend to favor its application in "equivalent" situations; moreover, the reasons which impelled its adoption in the one case are likely to have some influence in other cases.[43]

Similarly, diplomats engaged in official correspondence asserting rights and duties, or generals engaged in hostilities and entering into truce arrangements will have a measure of authority and will be regarded as exhibiting state practice. In fact, several recent international arbitral decisions have recognized as authoritative the practice of private airlines and oil companies when their conduct was carried out in pursuance of international agreements.[44]

Another relevant aspect may well be the degree to which the "prescribers" are able and willing to employ means to render their policy pro-

---

[43] Schachter, *"The Quasi-Judicial Function of the General Assembly and the Security Council"*, 58 *Am. J. Int'l L.* 960, 961 (1964).

[44] Air Traffic Rights Dispute (United States v. France) (1963), 3 *Int'l Legal Materials* 668 (1964), 58 *Am. J. Int'l L.* 1016 (1964); Air Traffic Rights Dispute (United States v. Italy) (1965), 4 *Int'l Legal Materials* 974 (1965); Saudi Arabia v. Aramco (1958), 27 *I.L.R.* 117 (1963).

jection effective and controlling. An organ which dispenses funds, supplies and services may lack formal authority to lay down binding rules but its resolutions and practice on the disposition of its resources will clearly be a factor in enhancing its authority in respect of rules governing the use and distribution of those resources. Examples can be found in the experience of United Nations technical aid and development programs.[45]

The acceptance of the authority of a group may also depend on its procedures and linguistic symbols. For example, a body like the International Law Commission will have its product—a body of rules—more easily accepted as authoritative after it has devoted a long period in careful study and consideration of precedent and practice; the authority will be greater if the result is a codification and so designated than if it were presented as a "development" (that is, as new law).[46]

Of significance as well is the extent to which the "prescribing" group represents the principal participants among the intended audience. On the global level this becomes apparent in the greater acceptability of normative declarations which are unanimous or nearly so.[47] The fact that divergent political and ideological viewpoints have been harmonized in an agreed draft is widely treated as persuasive evidence that that draft has an enhanced authority.[48] Nor would this be immaterial for regional or other less-than-universal norms; the circumstance that the participants have had varied—and even conflicting orientation and basic objectives— is an element in adding to their authority.

As I have already observed, the critical test is the response of the target audience to the assertion (whether express or implied) of authoritativeness. Thus, if the tacit rules of the game developed by the major powers are perceived by themselves and by other segments of the community as "state practice" carried out by entities which are appropriate decision-makers for that purpose and in accordance with procedures which are considered as appropriate, that practice would be authoritative (le-

---

[45] G. Feuer, *Les Aspects Juridiques de l'Assistance Technique* (1957); Schachter, *supra* note 17, at 236.

[46] H. Briggs, *The International Law Commission* 276 (1965); Hoyt, *"The Contribution of the International Law Commission"*, 1965 Proceedings, Am. Soc. Int'l L. 2; Jennings, *supra* note 17; Lauterpacht, *"Codification and Development in International Law"*, 49 *Am. J. Int'l L.* 16 (1955); Stone, *"On the Vocation of the International Law Commission"*, 57 *Colum. L. Rev.* 16 (1957).

[47] *See* Castañeda, *supra* note 34, at 44-48; South West Africa Cases, *supra* note 23, at 441; Lachs, *"The Law in and of the United Nations"*, 1 *Indian J. Int'l L.* 429, 439 (1961).

[48] This point has been strongly made in the UN Special Committees on Principles of International Law Concerning Friendly Relations and Cooperation among States. *See* International Law Comm'n, Report 21 UN GAOR, UN Doc. A/6230 (1966) (New York Session); International Law Comm'n, Report, 19 UN GAOR, UN Doc. A/5746 (1964) (Mexico City Session). *See also*, Houben, *"Principles of International Law concerning Friendly Relations and Co-operation Among States"*, 61 *Am. J. Int'l L.* 703 (1967).

gitimate) in the sense in which I have used the term. This does not imply that the practice of two or three states "imposes" obligations on others; it means that such practice may be viewed as authoritative by those "others." And, if that practice is also perceived as likely to be complied with, it would then appropriately be characterized as "practice accepted as law." Our test, in brief, is an empirical one on both scores; legitimacy and effectiveness.

This—as we said earlier—is a general point applicable to all law, whether statutory, treaty, decree or customary. For we would all recognize that some "laws," though enacted properly, have so low a degree of probable compliance that they are treated as "dead letters" and that some treaties, while properly concluded, are considered "scraps of paper" or, in more elaborate language, as having been terminated by desuetude. As to the requirement of authority, we recognize that the orders of a gangster, though widely obeyed, would not be legal since he would not be regarded as endowed with legitimate authority to give them. Conceivably such legitimacy may in time come to be recognized as it has for countless military dictators and in that event, whatever its cause, the test would be met. In sum, the perception of legitimacy is a psychological as well as a political event; it refers to a state of mind or of awareness. When applied to the social level it is a highly complex phenomenon and it presents formidable questions when carried into the context of the nation-state relations. We shall turn now to some aspects of that problem.

The Psychological Factor and its Complexities

International lawyers have generally accepted the requirement of a psychological component of obligation, though they have had divergent views as to its specific character and as to the indices of its presence. For the most part they have dealt with the problem in relation to customary law (distinguishing usage from custom) and particularly with reference to the *opinio juris sive necessitatis.*[49] However, as we saw in part I, the same kind of issue (involving the perception of authority and effectiveness) may be presented in the context of treaty law as, for example, in regard to interpretation (the significance of practice) or termination (desuetude) or acceptance (in the case of the less formal types of accords). The basic issue is also raised, as we observed, in respect of the resolutions or declarations articulated by governments in international bodies or by tacit understandings. The three categories—custom, agreement, and international institutions—exhibit differences which are significant in drawing inferen-

---

[49] C. de Visscher, *supra* note 10, at 148-56; H. Kelsen, *supra* note 4, at 450-51; M. Sorensen, *supra* note 2; McDougal, *"The Emerging Customary Law of Space"*, 58 *Nw. U.L. Rev.* 618 (1963).

20

ces as to the psychological response, but the same requirement applies, in my view, to the three areas of normative activity and my general remarks will apply accordingly to all of them.

In the literature of international law, and in the cases as well, we find three main tendencies in characterizing the psychological factor: one stresses consent (or recognition) of the states; another, state conduct; the third, the "will" or consensus of the international community. (All three obviously relate to the posited "bases" of obligation.) In my view, each of these tendencies reflects a valid, though partial, insight which should be taken into account. The difficulty with all three arises in so far as they move away from experience and thereby tend toward a "reductionism" which blocks factual inquiry.

We can see this in regard to the notion of "consent." The idea of "consent" may be applied in the sense of "recognition" so that practice becomes law for the state concerned when that state "recognizes" it as obligatory—a conclusion which is *not* essentially incompatible with our submission that a necessary condition is a perception on the part of the target audience that the norm is authoritative and reasonably effective.[50] Thus, it may be that the psychological response which our hypothesis requires (whether expressed as perception, expectation or recognition) can be treated as constituting in a broad sense a form of tacit agreement. On the other hand, the use of so elusive a concept as tacit agreement carries with it the risk that an established rule of law—long sustained by a recognition of its authority and effectiveness—will be viewed as subject to rejection by a particular state on the ground that it no longer agrees to it or has never expressly manifested its agreement.[51] A view of this kind would run counter to the actual experience in the acceptance of law through practice.[52] The perception that certain conduct or certain articulated standards of behavior are authoritative and effective does not necessarily involve an act of consensual acceptance. One may perceive or recognize authority and control without accepting it in the sense in which a party accepts an agreement. *Opinio juris* involves the former, but not necessarily the latter, element.

---

[50] C. de Visscher, *supra* note 10, at 148-56; Tunkin, *supra* note 3, at 12-21.

[51] Professor Tunkin emphatically disagrees with the position that a norm established by long practice of a great number of States may be binding on other States irrespective of their attitude to that norm. However, he does not suggest that a customary norm which has been recognized by a State may be rejected by that State on the ground that it no longer agrees with it. *See* Tunkin, *supra* note 3, at 12-21. *See also* Tunkin, *"Remarks on the Juridical Nature of Customary Norms"*, 49 *Calif. L. Rev.* 419 (1961).

[52] C. de Visscher, *supra* note 10, at 148; W. Friedmann, *supra* note 11, at 191; Fitzmaurice, *"Law and Procedure of the International Court of Justice: General Principles and Sources of Law"*, 30 *Brit. Y.B. Int'l L.* 1 (1953); Kunz, *"The Nature of Customary International Law"*, 47 *Am. J. Int'l L.* 664, 667 (1953); MacGibbon, *"Customary International Law and Acquiescence"*, 33 *Brit. Y.B. Int'l L.* 115 (1957).

A reliance on behavior, rather than on a state of mind or of will, is the mark of another tendency, especially associated with some followers of the "pure theory of law." Kelsen, for example, accepts the *opinio juris* in theory but observes that it can only be inferred from conduct; hence it is the conduct and not the state of mind that is legally decisive.[53] There is obviously substance to this position; subjectivities are only ascertainable to an onlooker through overt behavior and one necessarily relies on conduct to infer the perceptions of others. But it would be misleading to conclude that this implied the elimination of a psychological test. It is one thing to use conduct as an indicator of *opinio juris:* it is another—and quite different a process—to evaluate conduct independently of *opinio juris.*[54] The difference might not be of great significance in relatively standardized legal procedures, such as those involving claims of rights, invocation of precedent and recognition of the claims. In these cases, state behavior—repetition, duration, legal claims and the like—require little reference to perceptions or other psychological conditions. International law is rich in examples of practice in which state behavior provides adequate grounds for inferring *opinio juris* without any need to look beyond the overt and obvious procedures.[55] However, the kinds of situations listed in the first portion of this article do not present issues that can easily be fitted into the more traditional processes of customary law. For most of these situations, one cannot identify certain types of conduct as decisive or even to accord priorities. The social and psychological elements that would associate the idea of obligation with regularities of behavior or verbal declarations of purpose are far too varied and complex for *a priori* criteria. We need the basic touchstone—the perception of authority and effectiveness to guide the selection of the behavioral features that will bear significantly on this.

A few general observations may be ventured even though they fall short of criteria. The first relate to terminology. The use of the word "perception" is probably not quite adequate from a psychologist's point of view. Perhaps a better term would be that used by Lasswell and McDougal as well as others, to wit, expectations, since the perception of authority and effectiveness must have reference to the future, not the past, or even the immediate present. The question with regard to any given possible norm

---

[53] H. Kelsen, *supra* note 4, at 450-51.

[54] Guggenheim, Jenks and Kopelmanas appear to eliminate the requirement of *opinio juris* but this seems to apply only in the context of decisions by competent judicial organs. *See* W. Jenks, *The Prospects of International Jurisdiction* 263-64 (1964); Guggenheim, *"Les principes de droit international"*, 80 *Hague Academy Recueil des Cours* 327 (1952); Kopelmanas, *"Custom as a means of the Creation of International Law"*, 18 *Brit. Y.B. Int'l L.* 127 (1937).

[55] *See* Colombian-Peruvian Asylum Case, [1950] I.C.J. 266; MacGibbon, *supra* note 52; MacGibbon, *"Some Observations on the Part of Protest in International Law"*, 30 *Brit. Y.B. Int'l L.* 307 (1953).

or practice is whether the target audience *will* regard it as authoritative and effective, not simply whether it has done so in the past.

In mentioning the target audience again, we see the advantage in using a "communications" model for considering the relation between the designated norm and the participants. If the articulated norm is viewed as a communication to an intended addressee, we can see more clearly that the norm (whether in resolution or practice) evokes varied responses in the different addressees. In contrast, the usual questions, for example, whether practice has become binding or whether a resolution has legal effect, leave this key issue in obscurity or mystery.

There are of course several other substantial issues to consider. For example:

(i) whose expectations are relevant or decisive;

(ii) how can one reliably ascertain such subjective elements, especially on a global scale, embracing a wide variety of social systems and many closed societies as well as "folk" societies;

(iii) what if no shared expectations can be found, and only divergence among the target audience.

While these questions are formulated in general terms, each would present a somewhat different aspect to persons differently situated in the decision-process. An advocate, a judge, an international official, a legal scholar—among others—would have to consider the questions from diverse points of view. From the standpoint of an "impartial" observer, the following responses are indicative of the kinds of problems that have to be considered.

With regard to the first point, the answer must relate both to the states and to groups or individuals within states. On the international level I would note only that there would be a considerable range of variations in the number and composition of the states whose perceptions and expectations were relevant. De Visscher, in speaking of custom, has noted that the "sedimentation of international practice forms strata of unequal importance." [56] He goes on to remark

If there are basic elements in the customary rule which, owing to their exact correspondence with the common needs of the great majority of States, call for general application, there are others, of a secondary character, which can only be applied with differentiations adapting them to particular situations. The malleability of custom here enables it spontaneously to achieve the individualization of the rule which must elsewhere be the deliberate work of an international convention.[57]

As this comment suggests, the issue of whether the relevant addressees or target audience are to be the great majority of states, or a regional or other type of group, or perhaps only one or two states directly concerned will vary with the subject and the situation. An important factor will be

---

[56] C. de Visscher, *supra* note 10, at 153.
[57] *Id.*

the extent to which the subject-matter is of concern to the actors. If a controversy about the obligatory effect of practice has a local geographic focus, then the subjectivities of the parties would be of overriding significance ("local custom," "historic rights"). A useful distinction may be drawn between subjects that are normally within the exclusive competence of states (for example, trade) and those which fall within the area of shared or inclusive interests (such as the high seas). In the latter category, one would expect that the relevant expectations would include those of the great majority of states, even if the particular case in issue involved only two or three participants. What this suggests is that the question of when a "general consensus" should be decisive as against the attitude of a particular state will depend on fundamental policies of the community, in a way analogous to the notion of *jus cogens*.[58]

If we look below the facade of the nation-state to ask "whose expectations are relevant," a realistic reply would probably be that the relevant expectations would be essentially those held by persons with effective authority in the national state. This may not seem satisfactory; one might perhaps prefer a more democratic dimension or at least some inclusion of non-governmental groups.[59] There may also be examples of prescriptions where the most relevant group would be non-governmental, for example, scientists or businessmen, may be religious leaders, in some cases inter-governmental officialdom. A large and interesting area of inquiry is opened up by this problem.

In regard to the second question, one must recognize the enormity of the task of ascertaining global "community" expectations over the whole range of continuously-generated putative "norms." This difficulty is magnified by the deep ideological and political divisions in the globe and the concomitant clash of objectives and demands.[60] If one thinks in terms of aggregate data and workable techniques for measurement of attitudes

---

[58] *See* K. Venkata Raman, *International Customary Law and World Public Order*, ch. II (1967) (unpublished J.S.D. dissertation at Yale Law School Library). Dr. Venkata Raman's study is an outstanding contribution, particularly in its analysis of the processes and functions of customary law in relation to the major policies and goals of the world community. On *jus cogens, see* Schwelb, *"Some Aspects of International Jus Cogens"*, 61 *Am. J. Int'l L.* 946 (1967).

[59] *See* W. Coplin, *The Functions of International Law* 176-78 (1966). For general discussion of the varied influences in foreign policymaking, *see* B. Cohen, *The Political Process and Foreign Policy* (1957); J. Rosenau, *Public Opinion and Foreign Policy* (1961). For the Marxist view as to the "will of the ruling class", *see* Tunkin, *supra* note 3, at 33, 47.

[60] *See* A. Bozeman, *Politics and Culture in International History* (1960); E. McWhinney, *Peaceful Coexistence and Soviet-Western Law* 15-61 (1964); Anand, *"Attitude of the Asian-African States Toward Certain Problems of International Law"*, 15 *Int'l & Comp. L.Q.* 55 (1966); Bozeman, *"Representative Systems of Public Order Today"*, 1959 *Proceedings, Am. Soc. Int'l L.* 10; Lissitzyn, *supra* note 32; Wright, *"The Strengthening of International Law"*, 98 *Hague Academy Recueil des Cours* 74 (1959).

about subtle and nuanced questions of international law, the practicality of the test seems remote. On the other hand, the issues do arise; claims are made, positions taken, responses given, collective views expressed in both organized and unorganized arenas. Diplomatic correspondence, international agreements, judicial decisions, scholarly studies, public statements of leaders, national legislation are all pertinent in some context. They may at some later period be supplemented by newer methods such as content analysis of state papers, memoirs, newspapers and the like.[61] Interviews, participant observations, perhaps simulation techniques may someday be developed on a scale and with such refinement as to enable them to be used.[62] It is to be hoped especially that new theoretical constructs will be invented, especially in the area of social psychology, so that the distortions and prejudices of the actors directly involved can be subjected to corrective analyses. These hopes for more scientific and comprehensive techniques for ascertaining the perceptions and attitudes of the national decision-makers and other key groups are perhaps not as far-fetched as they seem today. There is room for the view that the social sciences are entering a period of revolutionary development in conceptual and empirical aspects and it is not unreasonable to conceive of a vast and continuous network of data-collection and evaluation that some day will provide means of determining and verifying the expectations relating to authority and effectiveness.[63]

In the meanwhile, however, other discipline techniques and rational

---

[61] On content analysis *see* R. North, O. Holsti, G. Zaninonich, D. Zinnes, *Content Analysis: A Handbook with Application to the Study of International Crisis* (1963); P. Stone, D. Dunphy, M. Smith, D. Ogilvie, *The General Inquirer* 2-264 (1966); Lasswell, *"The Qualitative and Quantitive in Political and Legal Analysis"*, in *Quantity and Quality* 103 (Lerner ed. 1958). Communications theory and research are also highly relevant; *see* K. Deutsch, *The Nerves of Government*, chs. 5, 9 (1953); R. Fagen, *Politics and Communication* (1966).

[62] *See* L. Free and H. Cantril, *The Political Beliefs of Americans* (1967); H. Guetzkow, C. Alger, R. Brody, R. Noel, R. Snyder, *Simulation in International Relations* (1963); Alger, *"Personal Contact in Intergovernmental Organizations"*, in *Int'l Behavior* 523 (Kelman ed. 1965); Alger, *"United Nations Participation as a Learning Experience"*, 27 *Pub. Opinion Q.* 411 (1963). For a valuable discussion of multinational comparative social research, *see* Szalai, 10 *Am. Behaviorial Scientist* No. 4 (1966).

[63] *See* Deutsch, *"Towards an Inventory of Basic Trends and Patterns in Comparative and International Politics"*, 54 *Am. Pol. Sci. Rev.* 34 (1960); Retzlaff, *"The Use of Aggregate Data in Comparative Political Analysis"*, 27 *J. of Politics* 797 (1965). For broad surveys, *see* especially H. Lasswell, *The Future of Political Science* (1963); W. MacKenzie, *Politics and Social Science* (1967).

Of particular interest to the international lawyer is a publication prepared under the auspices of the American Society of International Law by Professors Wesley L. Gould and Michael Barkun on the new approaches in international law with special reference to developments in the social sciences. W. Gould and M. Barkun, *International Law and the Social Sciences* (1970).

analysis must be utilized. The international lawyer need not be unduly modest as to his contribution. In a number of situations, especially in international adjudication, we can find that the data as to perceptions (expressed often in terms of consensus, implied consent, acquiescence, etc.) have been put forward with a high decree of relevance and disciplined reasoning. Examples of recent interest are the pleadings of the counsel for Ethiopia and Liberia in the *South West Africa Cases* and the dissenting opinion of Judge Jessup, referred to earlier.[64] Less well-known but also instructive are such cases in the International Court as that on *Rights of Passage*[65] or *U.S. Nationals in Morocco*[66] (which concentrated on the attitudes relating to practice manifested in a local context) and arbitral proceedings between the United States and France in 1963[67] and between the United States and Italy in 1964,[68] both involving the expectations created by practice under air transport agreements. The sophistication and realism exemplified in these proceedings in respect to the "subjectivities" of the parties is somewhat more reassuring than the vague concepts suggested by some social scientists for ascertaining attitudes. True, international lawyers may at times resort to myth and symbol in their advocacy or reasoning. But this should not obscure the toughminded and realistic approaches to factual evidence and its appraisal which have been exhibited over and over again in international jurisprudence.

The third question posed above is: "What if no shared expectations are found, and only divergent subjectivities are evidenced in the relevant target audience?" This question opens up a highly complex range of problems. First, we can think of relatively familiar tests used in law to resolve conflict and ambiguities relating to the views of the parties as to what the "law" is. One can, without much difficulty, translate these tests (as evidenced in litigation) into appropriate indexes for determining what should be regarded as "shared expectations" as to authority and control. Examples of such indicators are found particularly in controversies as to the significance of "practice" under treaties or otherwise. They include factors such as duration, frequency, geographic extent, consistency, and continuity.[69] As one penetrates slightly below the explicit indi-

---

[64] Southwest Africa Cases-I.C.J. Pleadings (1966); [1966] I.C.J. 325-442 (Jessup, J., dissenting). *See* Gross, *"The South West Africa Case"*, 45 *For. Aff.* 36 (1966); Higgins, *"The International Court and South West Africa"*, 42 *Int'l Aff.* 599 (1966).
[65] [1960] I.C.J. 33.
[66] [1952] I.C.J. 176.
[67] *See* note 44 *supra*.
[68] *Id.*
[69] *See* I.C.J. Judgments—Asylum Case, *supra* note 28, Rights of Passage Case, *supra* note 65; Anglo-Norwegian Fisheries Case, *supra* note 30; Temple of Praah-Vihear Case, [1962] I.C.J. 3. *"Arbitration*—Island of Palmas Arbitration", 22 *Am. J. Int'l L.* 867 (1928). Articles, notes 49, 52, 54 *supra*; Silving, *"Customary Law: Continuity in Municipal and International Law"*, 31 *Iowa L. Rev.* 614 (1946).

cators, it is possible to locate other indicators, as, for example, whether the parties have expended resources in support of a position, whether they have special interests and responsibilities, whether the "practice" occurred in an "organized arena" or not, whether it took place in a context of crisis and so on.[70] These indicators among others, can be empirically evaluated in terms of their use and likely use by judicial tribunals and by legal advisers to resolve issues of divergencies in expectations.

We cannot, however, ignore the evident fact that the divergencies may not be resolvable through such techniques—especially when they reflect basic differences in conceptions of authority and likely effectiveness. There are, in the words of Lasswell and McDougal, diverse systems of public order, or, in Tunkin's terms, different social systems. From a more juristic standpoint, we may find conflicts about the operative "rules of recognition" (to use Hart's concept) [71] and about some of the main features of the "world constitutive process" (in the Lasswell-McDougal sense).[72] But I would emphasize that the extent and obduracy of such difficulties are subjects for investigation, not for surrender. They involve questions of fact; they change in time and in relation to changing environmental factors and to new perceptions of needs, interests, and values. I have elsewhere attempted to suggest how in the multipartisan arena of the United Nations, points of consensus and perceived common interests have emerged out of divergent attitudes and how collective judgments as to what is obligatory and permissible are being generated to meet felt necessities.[73] One might even conclude—in paraphrase of Whitehead—that the clash of doctrine and views should be seen, not as a disaster, but as an opportunity.

Obligation and Value: a three-storied approach

I should have liked to conclude on that last ringing note. However, I have just introduced a reference to needs, interests and values and it is hardly possible to discuss a theory of obligation without facing the hot issue of policy orientation. Up to this point—or rather two paragraphs back—the issue was avoided largely because my analysis was centered on the

---

[70] For the significance of "practice" within international organizations ("organized arenas"), see writings cited note 17 *supra*; W. Jenks, *The Proper Law of International Organizations* (1962); Gross, *"The United Nations and the Role of Law"*, 19 *Int'l Org.* 537 (1966). The relevance of the expenditure of resources is discernable in such cases as the Air Transport arbitration between the United States and France, *supra* note 44, and the arbitration between Saudi Arabia and Aramco, *id.* Dr. K. Venkata Raman has analyzed numerous cases to ascertain the extent to which the decisions appear to reflect factors such as those mentioned above. *See* note 58 *supra*.

[71] H. Hart, *supra* note 15.

[72] M. McDougal, H. Lasswell & J. Miller, *supra* note 41, at 27 *et seq.*

[73] Schachter, *supra* note 17, at 180-84.

meaning and conditions of obligation and obligatory norms. Although I had suggested a "processive" definition of the formation of obligation, I did not discuss the role of obligatory norms in the actual decision-process until I reached the problem of divergent expectations and the criteria of decision in that contingency. Once we take obligatory norms into real life and view them as operative in claims, advice, and adjudication, the issue of values and preferences is squarely raised. This is not an issue that arises only in the "penumbral" case as H.L.A. Hart seems to suggest; it is far more central and common, at least on the international level, than that. "Obligations" are employed—one can say they are marshalled and deployed—in the legal process to achieve ends and realize values; and their operational meaning is a function of that use. Thus viewed, they are expressions of policy and contain in themselves purposive as well as prescriptive elements. The whole process is purposive, directed to the satisfaction of interests and demands, hence pervasively "value-oriented."

This, as we know, raises endless problems for analysis, description and role-clarification. It is not resolved simply by asserting the distinction between the function of description (*i.e.* factual reporting of past decisions, causes, attitudes and expectations) and the function of expressing preferences and values whether on an individual or community basis. Consider the issues faced by the International Court in the *South West Africa Cases* [74] or the *Expenses* Case [75]—in fact in almost any one of its cases—and try to separate out the descriptive and the valuational functions. Or reflect on the different categories of norms as analyzed by Hardy Dillard in his Hague Academy lectures [76] and the implication for the judge or scholar who wishes to relate fact, norm and value. It is true of course that one commits a fallacy by deducing the "ought" from the "is" but this seems to me only a logical error which is not as portentous as some would make it. [77] What is more important and interesting are the relationships

---

[74] [1966] I.C.J. 6.

[75] [1962] I.C.J. 151.

[76] Dillard, *"Some Aspects of Law and Diplomacy"*, 91 *Hague Academy Recueil des Cours* 445, 477-86 (1957).

[77] When it is said that what ought to be cannot be derived solely from what "is", we mean only that we need a premise which includes the normative term—that is, one which relates the "ought" to the "is". If we do not have that premise, we cannot reach from what is to a conclusion as to what ought to be. Obviously this logical requirement does not mean that one cannot establish a relationship between the normative and the factual. That is a question of fact, or in some cases of definition. In national law it is quite clear that a legal obligation will arise from the fact of a statutory enactment when we have the basic premise of a relationship between "binding" authority and legislative acts of a defined type. Similarly, we have sought in the previous sections to establish a broad relationship between international legal obligation and certain factual propositions relating to perceptions of authority and compliance. Our premise consisted essentially of a series of empirical assertations (it also included a definitional element) linking facts and obligation. In the present section of this paper we are raising the question of the relationship between legal norms (viewed as "facts")

between what is and what ought to be; in our context, between the existent norms (accompanied by expectations of authority and control) and the major purposes and values of the community or its various parts.

For this massive problem, it seems to me that some helpful insights can be obtained through the metaphor of a three-storied building—in other words, by applying a multi-level frame of analysis. The use of levels to express functional relationships has been productive in economics and has been suggested in other social sciences and philosophy.[78] For the present purpose, I shall sketch the general idea in the hope that it will stimulate further reflection and application.

The three main levels (we might later wish to add a mezzanine, possibly a basement) would be:

First, on the ground floor we would place behavior and its associated "subjectivities" (demands, purposes, expectations). In our context this would include activities of governments, organizations, groups in their pursuit of interests, needs and goals of international consequence. Of course, such behavior is not simply "observed." It can only be studied with the aid of theoretical constructs and investigatory methods of considerable sophistication. Our focus would be on patterns of behavior in areas of international concern.

Second, on the next level, we would place the obligational phenomena— the legally normative patterns—and the associated activities such as prescribing, invoking, and applying. On this level, we would find the relatively well-mapped field of international legal rules and processes.

Third, on the highest level, we would place the phenomena of general policy-making and articulation of major aspiration with its accompanying doctrinal formulas. This "upper-class" floor is easily distinguishable, we believe, from the busy ground floor of conduct and from the second floor of distinctive legal phenomena. It is on this third floor that we would expect to find the formulations of national interest and goals of wide generality and also such transnational principles of basic public order that we can identify.

I suggest that there are several advantages in this three-storied approach. First, it gives us a frame for a strictly factual or descriptive analysis (in current fashion, we might say for phenomenological analysis) of activities which need to be distinguished to understand the relationships of conduct, law, and policy.

Second, we can see that each level of activity has its own purposes, goals, and values. I believe that is a significant point which is often obscured in other frameworks relating to law. Conduct manifests its own

---

and the values and policies of the participants. Here too the problem is one of ascertaining—through empirical inquiry—precisely what connections appear to exist.

[78] *See* Edel, *"The Concept of Levels in Social Theory"*, in *Symposium on Social Theory* Part IV, no. 6, at 167 (Llewellyn Gross ed. 1959).

striving, and on its own level it exhibits concrete values and preferential choices. And, as we stressed above, "obligational activity" (our second level) is purposive and value-oriented throughout. However the goals and values on this level would be distinct from those manifested on the lower level of behavior and on the higher level of doctrine and general policy Each has its own values though we might discover that in some cases values move from one floor to another.

That movement may be up or down. This suggests a third merit of our image. We become more easily aware of the escalators or staircases that go in both directions, thereby avoiding analyses in which "values" and aspirations are given one-way routes (as when legal norms are viewed as a function of behavioral goals, without reciprocal influence). An awareness that the traffic between the second and third floors can be a two-way affair enables us to avoid the pitfalls of a "top-down" approach to policy formation.

Finally this metaphor may provide as useful corrective to the heavy emphasis on specific decision-making (which made Hardy Dillard somewhat uncomfortable). Our understanding of behavior, law, and policy cannot be restricted to mere what-to-do's in particular cases; we need to have wider perspectives and see relationships in aggregates as well as in concrete choices. Whether we have the role of spectator (critic) or participant, we benefit from looking over each of our three floors and moving upwards and downwards. I can think of suggesting a mezzanine or two for some mixed phenomena or possibly a basement (for biological phenomena), but these are architectural aspirations that I shall have to leave for another occasion.

Concluding Remarks

By way of conclusion I shall anticipate some objections to the main tenor of my thesis and offer a brief defense.

First, there is the criticism of those who will consider that "legal obligation" may be dissolved by having it depend on expectations, perceptions and probable compliance. In their view "legality like virtue is not a matter of degree"[79] and while we may have compassion we should have no uncertainty when the fallen damsel has indeed fallen. But actually most of us will view virtue as a matter of degree and we should recognize that legal obligation—whether national or international—also may involve "degrees" and that it will depend on attitudes, expectations and compliance. True, these factors will in turn depend on law. The circularity is

---

[79] Leo Gross, *"Problems of International Adjudication and Compliance with International Law"*, 59 *Am. J. Int'l L.* 48, 56 (1965). *See also* Hoffman, *supra* note 10, at 161.

there, but it is not vicious; it simply takes account of interactions and influences. To be sure, at a given point one may have to decide in a concrete context whether or not an obligation exists (this can also be stated in operational terms) and that judgment will have to be made on the basis of the relevant variables. The more serious risk is to live in a "make-believe" world where the "law is always the law" and as a consequence in cynical reaction to reject a large body of normative phenomena that are actually operative in international behavior. To impose hard-and-fast categories on a world filled with indeterminancies and circularities can only result in a pseudo-realism which does justice neither to our experience nor to our higher purposes.

A second objection may come from those who believe that diverse political and cultural determinants preclude any truly international obligations in today's world. But this is a question of empirical fact, not of *a priori* judgment, and, as we indicated above, our experience provides enough evidence to indicate that divergent systems and beliefs exhibit concordances on a wide array of international norms. We have ample proof that mankind shares common characteristics and needs and its efforts to satisfy those needs provide a realistic basis for an international normative structure. In our view the specific features of that structure must be identified and validated in terms of shared expectations and attitudes, rather than in trans-empirical terms.

A third line of objection could come from contemporary "activists" who may view theories of obligation as intellectualism, removed from life and from immediate action. But action implies choice, and choices are not made in a vacuum. They have determinants and these determinants will include the perspectives of the actors with regard to authority and its effectiveness. Even if one posits "interest" or "power drives" as basic or decisive, conceptions about who is endowed with legitimate power —that is, who may decide what and under what circumstances—are a pervasive element of political life. Our understanding of that element and the related phenomenon of obligation can help to clarify the choices to be made and to evaluate them on a realistic basis. Theory is no more than an instrument to that end, a means of answering the questions "why this and why not that." It provides no final answer, but it may reveal alternatives and give us a fresh view of an age-old problem.

COMPLIANCE WITH UNITED NATIONS DECISIONS ON PEACE AND SECURITY AND HUMAN RIGHTS QUESTIONS

by *Rosalyn Higgins*
The Royal Institute of International Affairs

This paper is concerned with one particular facet of the Conference's theme of *Effectiveness of the Decisions of International Organizations*. It focuses on the decisions of the political organs of the United Nations in respect of major human-rights and peace-and-security cases. The paper seeks, for the purpose of Conference discussion, to identify some of the variables and to pose some questions. It purports to nothing more. For occasional illustration, the cases of South African radical policy, Rhodesian claims to independence, and Arab-Israeli conflict, have been drawn on.

When one speaks of the "effectiveness" of United Nations decisions one is, of course, speaking ambiguously, for the term may refer either to compliance by member-states, or to the achievement of certain objectives. Insofar as compliance by all members entails the achievement of the purpose of the decision, these two meanings fuse: thus if a resolution were to call for the release of political prisoners everywhere, and were all nations to comply, then all political prisoners would be free men. However, it is possible to conceive of certain situations—infrequent though they may be—where compliance does not necessarily correspond to full achievement of the purpose of the resolution: thus a resolution directed only to UN members, requiring them to cease all trade with Ian Smith's régime, would possibly not, even if fully complied with, bring about the overthrow of the illegal government of Rhodesia. This would be a resolution which has been given effect (i.e. complied with) but is not effective.

Any International Organization must inevitably be concerned both with compliance and effectiveness. The legal adviser will be, to some degree, involved in each, for though in the final analysis it is the majority of members in the relevant organ which will determine most decisions made in the name of the Organization, the views of the legal office will be a relevant factor in their decision making process. So far as concern with effectiveness is concerned—that is to say, whether a given decision, if carried out, will achieve a particular end—it may well be that the legal adviser's role is more limited than that of his colleagues in the political and economic departments: he will, however, be advising on substantive matters. So far as concern with compliance is concerned, the advice of the legal advisers is likely to be important, on matters of form, procedure and technique, as well as substance.

Professor Louis Henkin has perceptively noted:

"One may accept the cynic's formula that nations will violate when it is to their advantage to do so, when the cost of observance is greater than the cost of violation. But that, of course, is the beginning of the enquiry, not the end of it." [1]

The appreciation by a government (and the advice which a Legal Adviser can give) of whether the cost of observance is greater than the cost of violation depends upon a cluster of variables; and from each one of them flows a further set of variables.

VARIABLES

1. *The purpose of the decision*

(i) Broadly speaking, all UN decisions must be to promote the purposes and principles enumerated in Chapter I of the Charter. At a lower level of abstraction, however, decisions may be perceived as (i) for the purpose of permitting the organizational machine itself to continue e.g. decisions relating to seating on particular organs, to staff or financial matters. Such decisions will usually occur within a well defined framework of "rules": that is to say, there will be a decision to seat states A, B & C on the Security Council; but the decision as to *whom* to seat operates within the clear rule that only 5 non-permanent seats come up for election at any one time. Compliance with such decisions is normally not a relevant issue, because they call for no action beyond the vote itself. Once taken, a decision to seat State A on committee Y requires no action from either the supporters or the dissenters of the proposition. Indeed, it is difficult to see any method by which a dissenting state can not "comply". The most that it can do is to refuse to be party to the events that flow from the decision—as did Indonesia when it withdrew from the UN in protest at the seating of Malaysia on the Security Council. The legal adviser, when asked to provide guidance as to the status of the "Gentleman's Agreement" on Security Council representation, is not faced with a possible problem of compliance—though he will probably have to consider the question of effectiveness. Equally, because such decisions are taken within the framework of "rules", the Legal Office will not normally be required to advise on *alternative methods* to achieve organizational ends.

(ii) A decision may be taken in order to set out certain paths by which the Organization believes that some of its goals may be achieved. Sometimes this may involve the setting up of machinery—such as UNCTAD. Here "compliance" is not a real problem, because the costs of non-compliance (i.e. refusal to participate) are very high indeed; and also because

---

[1] Henkin, "International Law and National Behaviour", *Recueil des Cours,* 1965 vol. i, p. 170.

the setting up of major organizational machinery is normally subject to stiff bargaining prior to the decision. Proposals will not normally be put to the vote unless they have the support of a substantial majority, and unless they—or at least the whole package in which they are contained—are known to be acceptable to all the major actors. But "standard-setting" or "path-pointing" decisions are frequently declarations of principles—such as the belief that there should be nuclear-free zones, or that indirect subversion should not take place, or that colonialism should end. One can point to certain typical characteristics: they frequently are, or purport to be, "law-declaring".[2] They are addressed to all members. They will not normally emanate from the executive organ i.e. the Security Council. The required course of action is not spelled out in any detail. And they usually command very large voting majorities. Indeed, these large majorities are in part achieved because the requirements of the decision have deliberately been left imprecise. It will readily be seen that these varying characteristics pull in different directions, so far as compliance is concerned.

(iii) Decisions may be made in order to seek to control and rectify a particular situation which appears to deviate from the norms prescribed by the Charter. The decision may identify the situation as unacceptable to the Organization, without condemning the parties. Such a decision may be addressed either to the parties, or to others, or to both. Thus, after an outbreak of fighting, there may be, without identifying an "agression", a call for ceasefire; equally, other nations may be asked not to send arms or to take any action which would aggravate the situation. Though these may be directives addressed to particular nations, they are not "sanctions".

(iv) The decision may be taken to seek to alter the behaviour pattern of certain nations, when such behaviour is regarded as incompatible with the aims of the Organization. Where decisions calling for certain conduct are backed by the initiation of action against the addressee by the Organization or its members, these decisions may be termed "sanction". Sanctions are thus one method (among many) of seeking compliance. The real addressees of a decision on sanctions are those who are required to operate it, and not the deviating state. Thus a secondary compliance problem arises, between the Organization and its members, in addition to the compliance problem between the Organization and the deviating state. This situation has, of course, arisen in the case of Rhodesia. In theory, yet further layers of compliance problems, could arise—if, for example, the UN were to decide to order sanctions against South Africa for its failure to implement sanctions against Rhodesia. It is apparent that the variables are different in each of these layers of the compliance problem, and

---

[2] See Asamoah, *The legal significance of the Declarations of the General Assembly of the United Nations*, 1966.

that there is no necessary relationship between the degree of compliance achieved in each. One may also note that only one method—compulsion—is being used to obtain compliance by the state against whom sanctions are directed; while a much broader spectrum of factors are in play in seeking to achieve the compliance of members with the decision to apply sanctions.

2. *The addressee of the decision*

A decision may be addressed to all UN members, or—perhaps without naming them—a group of members, or to an individual member. (Resolutions on race relations in South Africa have run through each of these stages.) It is, of course, not possible to say that resolutions addressed to one member are more or less likely to secure compliance than resolutions addressed to the membership at large—it is the interplay of all the variables which determine compliance. Specific states are usually addressed when the decision has been taken to deal with the matter in terms of Charter obligation, and it has been noted elsewhere that the record of compliance in this category is not very impressive, partly no doubt because these problems are particularly intractable, and partly because, at least where the threat of sanctions does not seem very real, the "naming" of a specific state is likely to lead to a stiffening of resistance.[3] In any event, the legal adviser may well have to consider whether, in any particular set of circumstances, a general law-declaring decision is preferable to a more specific, law-applying one.

Distinctions must also be drawn between resolutions addressed to the state whose behaviour the UN seeks to alter; and to states who are asked to assist in controlling a situation or achieving a change in the behaviour of another state. Again, resolutions may be addressed to non-members: thus the resolutions on Rhodesian sanctions seek to bring non-members within their bounds. These nations will have less reason to comply through fear of possible sanctions, but (unless isolated, like China) will be unlikely to be seen to flout the wishes of the UN. Each of these non-member entities will have its own relationship with the UN which will be a factor in determining its decision. The response of western Germany and Switzerland to the call for economic sanctions against Rhodesia has been interesting. Germany has been faced with the difficulty, as a non-member, of requiring its nationals (and not just the government) to heed a UN decision: this dilemma was acutely revealed in respect of the litigation over the printing of Rhodesian banknotes in Germany. Switzerland has declared that neutrality will not permit it to participate in sanctions, but that it

---

[3] Schachter, "The Quasi-Judicial role of the Security Council and the General Assembly" 58 *AJIL* (1964), p. 960.

will keep trade with Rhodesia at the "normal" level. The most recent figures show that both Germany and Switzerland have increased their trade with Rhodesia in spite of the imposition of sanctions.[4]

UN resolutions addressed to individuals are comparatively rare,[5] though both the Congo, and the Rhodesia resolution of December 1966 afford examples. These undoubtedly present the governments concerned with additional compliance problems, especially in countries where there is no "automatic reception" of UN decisions into national law, or where constitutionally further national action is needed. If either legislation or statutory instruments need to be approved, further opportunity is given to the voicing of domestic opposition.[6] And, even if a government wishes to comply, constant vigilance may be required to ensure that individual firms and companies comply.

Resolutions may, of course, be directed to other UN organs (asking them to consider certain matters, or prepare certain proposals); to the Secretary General (asking him to carry out certain tasks); and to Specialized Agencies. These addressees will have an extremely high rate of compliance.

3. The form and status of the decision

Decisions of the Security Council are, of course, binding on all members under the terms of Article 25 of the Charter. Recommendations of the Security Council are not covered by the terms of Article 25. The seriousness with which this distinction is taken is evidenced by the arguments in Britain over the status of the earlier resolutions on sanctions against Rhodesia,[7] and by the domestic campaign mounted against "escalation" to mandatory sanctions. Opponents of sanctions did not argue that the resolution of December 1966 should simply be ignored; rather they argued

---

[4] This must not, of course, necessarily be taken to indicate non-compliance, for only a limited number of goods—arms, oil, vehicles and spare parts—are prohibited exports under Resolution 232 of 16 December 1966. What is interesting, however, is that two non-members appear among the list of five nations whose trade has increased with Rhodesia since December 1966, whether because of non-compliance or whether through diversification into permitted goods.

[5] Although individuals may occasionally be addressed in resolutions seeking to control situations, there has been no attempt to direct sanction—decisions to individuals: at no time has the UN called on Ian Smith to take any action—the addressee has been the UK, and, to a lesser degree, the community at large. For a comment on individual directed sanctions, see Galtung, "On the Effect of Economic Sanctions", *Journal of World Politics*, April 1967.

[6] This has, of course, been a relevant factor in the United Kingdom in result of UN resolutions on Rhodesia. Heated parliamentary debate preceded the adoption of the Southern Rhodesia (Prohibited Trade and Dealings) Order 1966 (Statutory Instrument 1595).

[7] See *Hansard* vol. 721, cols. 248-259.

that the resolution was invalid (on the grounds that a permanent member had abstained and that there was no *bona fide* threat to the peace under Article 39 of the Charter.[8] Nations find it marginally easier not to comply with Security Council recommendations than decisions; and easier still not to comply with decisions made by the Assembly. Further, the Organization's "decision" is likely to be tempered to meet the basic needs of the addressee if it is taken in the Security Council, because (a) the veto obtains; (b) the addressee is likely (though not invariably) to have its supporters among the Permanent Members of the Security Council; and (c) the other Security Council members may have an interest in the addressee.

Not only the organ is of relevance here, but also the form of the decision. In peace and security matters, the necessity for speed allows little choice in the method of decision—a resolution will be the usual form employed. However, the Armistice Agreements of 1949 between Israel and her four Arab neighbours, may be seen as a UN "decision", flowing from proposals made by the UN and elaborated by Dr. Bunche. Again, the resolution format may be the vehicle for detailed proposals—such as the Partition Plan of 1947. Occasionally "standard setting" or law declaring declarations are made on peace and security matters, such as the Assembly's Declaration on Offences against the Peace and Security of Mankind, or the approval of the Nuremberg Principles. In the field of human rights the treaty-form has been felt one appropriate method for attaining compliance; but in the peace and security area, where comprehensive participation and compliance may be vital, the use of resolutions and recommendations is more appropriate.

4. *Factors operating in favour of compliance*

(i) *In respect of internal, organizational decisions:*
The very availability of detailed rules removes a certain ground for controversy. *Bona fide* differences of interpretation are less likely to occur and respectable legal argument will be less available for the dressing up of political disputes.[9] Further, the community of interest in respect of the subject matter of such rules is very marked—virtually all UN members

---

[8] For a resumé of the arguments on these points, and a response to them, see Higgins, "Rhodesia, the UN and International Law", *World Today*, March 1967, pp. 94-106.
[9] Myres McDougal has convincingly suggested (*Journal of Conflict Resolution*, September 1960, pp. 337-354) that norms are in reality matching pairs of opposites between which the decision-maker has to choose. But Schachter has pointed out (*Recueil des Cours*, 1963, vol. ii) that an exception to this lies in "rules". The norm that a state may not use force is "matched" by the norm which permits self defence. But there is no "matching opposite" to the rule "15 Members shall sit upon the Security Council".

wish to see the UN machine ticking over without undue delays. Indeed, the achievement of many of their diverse aims is dependent upon the availability, and proper functioning, of the UN's machinery.[10] Moreover, many of the UN's internal or administrative decisions are taken without the express consent of those bound by them—they are not debated, or put to the vote,[11] and no occasion arises for militant positions to be taken. Given the nature of the decisions, there is no obvious way for a state not to "comply".

(ii) *In respect of standard-setting decisions and declarations*

Decisions which state a preferred course of behaviour generate certain pressures in favour of compliance. Insofar as they claim to be normative, any state considering non-compliance will be obliged to furnish legal arguments refuting the law-declaring character of the UN resolution or decision. The fact that such decisions have been reached by a collective process in which many states of diverse views and principles have participated, emphasizes the common interest.[12] The wish not to be isolated politically in this collective process makes states unwilling, unless they have very major interests at stake, not to vote for "standard-setting" declarations. Resolutions adopted by overwhelming majorities provide an additional factor towards compliance by those whose enthusiasm for it may be limited. And there are at least a group of countries who would regard an affirmative vote, even on a non-binding resolution, as a moral obligation to comply with the terms of that resolution. When a standard-setting resolution is not an isolated event, but is part of a reappearing pattern through time, then a further element in favour of compliance is generated, by virtue of the development of a customary norm.[13] These resolutions also represent a standard for which sympathetic domestic groups may press compliance, through the various means available to them. Thus MP's in England have used Question Time to urge acceptance by the Government of the Conventions on Human Rights, the ILO recommendations for equal pay for women, and so forth. Decisions whereby general reports are required from all nations on the general subject-matter, provide some yardstick by which public opinion, and the Organization, may judge compliance with the promulgated international standards. The annual reports to the Commission of Human Rights are a case in point.

---

[10] Evidence of this may be seen in the *modus vivendi* arrived at during the nineteenth session of the Assembly, whereby Assembly "decisions" were privately taken in the President's room to avoid putting to the test the Soviet Union's voting rights in the context of Article 19 of the Charter. Only Albania dissented from the consensus.
[11] For examples of "non-consented" decisions on internal matters, see Detter, *Law Making by International Organizations* (1965).
[12] A point made by Schachter, "Law, Politics and Action in the United Nations", *Recueil des Cours* (1963), vol. ii).
[13] Higgins, "The Development of International Law by the Political Organs of the UN", Proc. *ASIL*, 1965, pp. 116-124.

(iii) *In respect of decisions made to control situations*

In this category it is possible for the decision not only to refer to broad objectives of the Charter, such as the maintenance of peace, or the promotion of human rights, but to refer to specific obligations under the Charter. A resolution which incorporates reference to a specific Charter obligation will not be lightly disregarded by the government officials, who will be aware that a failure to uphold the obligation may weaken international respect for a Charter commitment which they may wish to rely on in the future.[14] Domestic political pressures for compliance will also be generated by this collective process; and the stakes must be very high for a government to disregard official warnings of caution, and public support for upholding international commitments.[15] Insofar as decisions in this category may be made without designating the addressee as "guilty", or a "violation", then the option is given to it of complying without losing face, "for the sake of international peace". Further, the Charter reference chosen may carry the implicit threat of an escalation to decisions directed against a party,[16] if the present decision is not complied with. Ceasefire orders under Article 40 may be cited as an example. Where questions of Peace and Security are concerned, and where there is a clear majority consensus that the situation must be contained, important allies of the addressee state may bring pressure to bear upon that state, citing the importance of the long term benefits of compliance with specific Charter obligations. If the decision is made by the Security Council, the reference to its mandatory nature, and the commitment under Article 25 of the Charter, as well to the substantive Charter obligation to desist from threatening the peace, or violating human rights, is an additional factor generating pressures for compliance.[17] The phrasing of a directive in terms of Charter obligation is also a factor which confirms world opinion in the

---

[14] See Schachter, "The Quasi-Judicial role of the Security Council and the General Assembly", 58 *AJIL* (1964) p. 963.

[15] Roger Fisher, "Bringing Law to bear upon Governments", 74 *Harvard Law Review* (1961), p. 1130.

[16] Occasionally, the threat is made explicit, as in the Security Council's ceasefire resolution on Palestine, S/902, 15 July 1948, which envisaged action by the Security Council if the parties declined to comply.

[17] The resolution of November 20, 1965, called upon all states to refrain from action which would help the illegal regime in Rhodesia, to desist from sending arms and military equipment, and to "do their utmost" to break all economic relations, including the export of oil. The Opposition Front Bench asked the Prime Minister whether this resolution was, to be considered mandatory. The Prime Minister, torn between appealing to both a Commonwealth and a British audience (and thus needing to appear both "in control" at the UN, and yet determined to end UDI, replied "The resolution can be interpreted as something between Chapter VI and Chapter VIII'. For comments on the relationship between questions of International Law and British domestic politics over the earlier stages of the Rhodesia crisis, see Higgins "Britain at the United Nations—A demand for Results" *Round Table* No. 222 (March 1966) 132-141.

desirability of compliance, a factor which may be brought to bear upon the addressee. This influence of world opinion—and the strength which domestic opinion in the addressee state may draw from it—may be formalized by a "scrutiny" procedure, whereby the addressee is required to report upon what measures he has taken to comply with the decision. This method has, of course, been used in respect of the resolution calling for mandatory sanctions against Rhodesia. A variation on this procedure is instead of asking states to submit reports the Secretary General is asked to go to the area and report on the status of compliance: it was in fulfilment of this role that Hammarskjöld visited the Middle East, and presented his reports, in May 1956. (In other Organizations, such as the EEC, where the Secretariat [Commission] has a very active role as "guardian of the Constitution" the checking-procedure is likely to be directed less to the activation of public opinion, and more to direct pressure by the Commission upon member governments. Thus the stream of unpublished inquiries and observations which the Commission had directed to Holland on the compatibility of that Government's regional development policy with the non-distortion provisions of the Rome Treaty, has had no public impact, but rather a direct impact upon the on-going decision making in Holland). There are, of course, a variety of "follow-through" arrangements in different Organizations operating at different legal levels. The procedure may be built into the Constitution itself (such as the duty to submit reports in respect of Non-Self-Governing Territories under Article 73e); it may be requested, for a particular case, in a resolution (such as in Security Council resolution 232 on Rhodesia); or it may have become part of the body of general organization law (such as the submission of reports on political, as well as economic and social, advance in Non-Self-Governing Territories).

(iv) *In respect of decisions directed at altering the behaviour patterns of particular states*

Many of the same factors apply. Where directives are issued to a specific state, based on its duty under the Charter and perhaps also under general international law, pressures are generated for compliance. Its allies (unless they are participating in the same behaviour pattern) may seek to use their influence, and domestic critics of the government will press for compliance. The fear of possible sanctions will also be present. However, we shall suggest below that, within this category, there are considerably more factors militating against compliance, than in the case of Section iii above.

Once the decision has taken the form of a sanction, it is reasonable to assume that all the other factors militating in favour of compliance have failed. The government concerned has, in effect, already decided that this factor does not weigh sufficiently with it. In theory at least the imposition of sanctions may conceivably cause an increase in domestic agitation in

40

favour of compliance. But henceforth the main pressure on the government will be coercive.

5. *Factors militating against compliance*

The hesitation with which a state will decide not to comply with a UN decision depends upon a variety of factors. The optimal situation, from the point of view of encouraging compliance, is for the decision to be taken by the Security Council, by an impressive majority, on unimpeachable legal grounds, for purposes clearly specified by the Charter, and running counter to no major interests of the addressee. When one or more of these variables are absent, factors militating towards non-compliance have been introduced. It seems not overly cynical to suppose that the last listed— the appreciation of the national interests of the addressee—will be the most important. But non-compliance for these reasons is made more likely when a government feels that the directive in question does not command widespread support, and that there are weighty legal arguments with which it may be attacked. To refuse compliance in the absence of such supporting factors will be comparatively rare, and is likely to occur only when the question is felt, for international or domestic political reasons, to go to the vital interests of the addressee. One may here point, by way of illustration, to the present positions of Portugal and Israel in respect of two resolutions. Portugal, in seeking not to comply with Security Council resolution 232 calling for mandatory sanctions against Rhodesia notes that the resolution was invalid, because a permanent member abstained on the voting;[18] and that its purpose was *ultra vires* the Charter, as rebellion is not *per se* illegal under international law. So far as Israel is concerned, an Assembly resolution has been addressed to its government calling on it to annul the annexation of Jerusalem; and reference has been made in the UN to the principle of the non-acquisition of territory through war. Israel has not been able to call upon legal arguments comparable to Portugal's; but is unlikely to comply because no government would survive which did comply. Instead, an attempt is made to mobilize public

---

[18] This argument is hardly impressive in the light of some 120 precedents, whereby Security Council decisions have been taken with the abstention of a Permanent Member. It is by now clear that the Permanent Members shall be deemed to "concur", within the meaning of Article 27 (3), if they abstain. This argument, however, found much favour both in the British Parliament and in the letter columns of the Press. More interesting was Portugal's point that, since the enlarging of the Security Council non-permanent membership from 6 members to 10, with the need for a substantive resolution now to receive 9 affirmative votes, it is possible on the old voting practice for a substantive resolution to be passed with all 5 of the Permanent Members abstaining. The Secretary General has declined to give Portugal an opinion on this observation, stating that legal advice is given at the request of a UN organ, and not at the request of an individual member.

opinion to sympathy with non-compliance, by showing the beneficial effects, to the community at large, of non-compliance by Israel, viz. the peaceful mingling of Jew and Arab in Jerusalem.

One could list the following factors as relevant to a determination not to comply with a UN decision:

(i) the view that one's interests would be vitally, and adversely, affected by compliance.

(ii) The fact that the decision in question is not an isolated one, but is part of a well-established series, on which a pattern of non-compliance has already been established. (South Africa has less and less need to deliberate, in Cabinet, its response to UN decisions in the field of race-relations: the pattern is already set.) Similarly, if a pattern of non-compliance by other members has already been established (such as in respect of declarations on human rights) an individual government will feel less hesitation in not complying.

(iii) A government will also be more likely not to comply if it knows that many of its allies share the same intention. This phenomenon stems as much from psychological needs as from the realisation that there will be available fewer "enemies" who might call for, and obtain, sanctions for non-compliance. This point is obviously closely related to, though not the same as

(iv) The size of the majority by which the decision was taken. (iii) and (iv) were obviously extremely relevant factors in respect of the decisions which Britain, isolated from the United States and many Commonwealth countries, had to take with regard to complying with the Assembly calls for a ceasefire and withdrawal from Suez in 1956.

(v) The company in which a nation is likely to find itself may also affect its voting, at least on matters not of vital interest. And there are at least a core of nations who are very reluctant not to comply with decisions once they have voted for them. This has been a relevant factor in British policy making at the UN on colonial issues which are of less than vital concern. Britain has been reluctant to find herself in the sole company of Portugal and South Africa, and has sought ways in the Assembly to vote with the majority—or at least to abstain—unless it was regarded as totally impossible to comply with the resolution.

(vi) The more imprecise the "decision" contained in a resolution, the more leeway is available for non-compliance. And we have already noted that decisions are often made imprecise in order to achieve substantial majorities in the Assembly, or Big Power unanimity in the Security Council. This is thus an element in the growing disparity between the passing of resolutions and the achievement of compliance with their terms.

(vii) Another, related, factor would seem to be the growing use of Assembly resolutions to state an objective or aim in the form of a decision, where it is known that there is little reality of executive action by the Security Council. This practice is occasionally rationalized in intellectual terms: the Security Council is the "practical" arm of the UN; its failure, for Big Power political reasons, to act on certain issues makes it all the more necessary for the Assembly to take upon itself the role of "standard-pointer", stating what it is that the Organization should be doing. Be that argument as it may, states are unlikely to comply with Assembly decisions which do not in their view take account of practical realities. The response of certain western nations to the Assembly decision terminating South Africa's mandate over South West Africa is a case in point.[19]

(viii) There are a cluster of legal arguments relating to the validity of the decision which may prove relevant to compliance—either because a state has *bona fide* doubts about the legality of the UN's call, or, more frequently, because this provides respectable clothing for a strong political inclination not to comply. It may thus be argued that the resolution is invalid because of improper voting practices (as South Africa and Portugal have argued in respect of the Security Council's demand for mandatory sanctions in December 1966); or because the resolution violates other Charter requirements (most commonly, Article 2(7), as the United Kingdom contended, before UDI, in respect of Assembly resolutions regarding Rhodesia—and as France has continued to contend, on behalf of the UK, even since UDI the UK's effective waiver notwithstanding); or because the resolution is violative of general international law. (Portugal let it be known in the context of the Beira oil resolution of April 1966, that she regarded it improper that the UN should authorize action directed essentially against her, in the event of her not complying with a UN resolution which was in any event not mandatory, and which was aimed at altering a state of affairs—constitutional rebellion—not prohibited by international law).

(ix) States may also point to domestic requirements as a relevant factor. Where the Organization's decision is perpetrated in the form of a treaty, governments may show their basic approval by signature, but if their domestic procedures so require, full "compliance" will depend upon ratification. The UN has, of course, adopted various devices where-

---

[19] The United Kingdom, while indicating that it favoured the mandate being withdrawn from South Africa was unwilling to vote for a resolution which merely "declared" that this was done, without actually achieving it. Lord Caradon observed "Some people say that the wording of our resolutions is of no great consequence, that no one any longer expects United Nations resolutions to mean what they say, or say what they mean ... that we need not worry about capacity or about methods any means. Others suggest that all that is necessary is to wish a result, incorporate it in a resolution, pass it by a big majority and then the wish will be some miraculous process come true ... (But) if we pass resolutions which we know are likely to be inoperative or ineffective we debase the currency of the United Nations. The archives of the Assembly will become overcrowded repositories of rotting resolutions". *GAOR* 20th sess., plen. mtg. of Oct. 19, 1966.

by the hazards of this method may be minimized.[20] The extent to which UN acts in other forms are directly binding depends to a great extent upon the constitutional requirements of members. These may well be harder to satisfy in the case of mere "recommendations" than "decisions", given the fact that UN members have agreed, under Article 25 of the Charter, to be bound by decisions of the Security Council.[21]

(x) A state may, domestic procedures apart, point to the fact that a particular resolution is not "legally binding"—being in the form of a recommendation. This is obviously not an option available, however, if one has voted for the decision concerned in the Assembly, and *a fortiori* in the Council.

(xi) The efficacy and particular mode of operation of any "check-up" procedures may also be a relevant factor. Information being returned in an annual report procedure is unlikely to make the same public impact as information on compliance gathered by the Secretary General himself; or provided in respect of one particular resolution. Public impact may also depend upon whether the information is distributed in mimeographed form, as it is provided, or whether it is published as a comprehensive collective document, with a foreword by the Secretary General. Whether or not the appropriate organ automatically convenes to consider the results of its "follow-through" procedures may also be a relevant factor.

(xii) The degree of compliance with a UN decision may also be affected by the existence or otherwise of procedures for adjudication. This adjudication may be of a judicial or quasi-judicial nature. State to State judicial adjudication clauses [22] in a UN sponsored multilateral convention may be an additional incentive to compliance by a participating party. The Mixed Armistice Commission procedure of UNTSO in the Middle East—based on observation, investigation and the use of a casting vote by the M.A.C. Chairman—has been of itself a contributing factor to the limiting of violations of the Armistice Agreement of 1949.

---

[20] One may cite the practice whereby ceasefire agreements are not deemed subject to ratification; whereby UN status of Forces Agreements enter into effect from the date of entry of UN Forces, and not from the date of ratification: and, in treaty matters, the advantages of the so-called Triple Option Clause.

[21] Holland indicated that the November 1965 resolution on sanctions against Rhodesia presented it with grave constitutional problems so far as the legal requirements of a common trade policy with its Benelux partners was concerned. In the United Kingdom domestic legislation is required before a UN decision under Article 41 can be implemented. However, the international obligation upon Britain flowing from Article 25 of the Charter already exists, even before enacting legislation. This point was used to advantage by some 20-30 Conservative MPs, known to be sympathetic to the imposition of mandatory sanctions, to persuade the Opposition Front Bench not to call a vote against the relevant Statutory Instruments, even though the Opposition had voted against oil sanctions as such.

[22] Though one may be sceptical as to the value of state-to-state adjudication procedures, especially in the field of human rights, it is likely not to be used as between allies, but only as between political opponents.

(xiii) If a state perceives its interest as similar in principle to those of a nation against whom a resolution is directed, it will have a strong motive for opposing such a resolution. (The psychological fear of precedent-setting—inspite of the variables that can serve to make any subsequent case "not on all fours" is a phenomenon deserving further study). *A fortiori,* it will be disinclined to comply with a call for sanctions against a nation whose interests and behaviour pattern are similar to its own. This is so in spite of a factor pulling in the other direction—namely, the fear that if it does not comply by participating in sanctions, it too will shortly become the object of UN sanctions. The respective weight given to these two competing factors will obviously depend upon the state's assessment of the likely effectiveness of the sanctions program. All this seems well illustrated by the South African response to the UN's decision to impose mandatory sanctions against Rhodesia under Chapter 7 of the Charter. South Africa, being in theory at least a potential addressee of economic sanctions, has had an interest in ensuring that they be seen "not to work" even against small, land-locked Rhodesia. At the same time, South Africa is known to have discouraged Ian Smith from declaring independence and to be displeased with the fact that he has effectively put South Africa in another "non-compliance" posture.[23]

(xiv) States may be unable or unwilling to comply with a call for sanctions against another state if they suffer substantial economic loss. Obviously all Rhodesia's normal trading partners suffer some economic loss, if only the loss of forfeited opportunities, from complying with the call for sanctions. Business interests within those countries bring pressure to bear upon their governments not to comply, or make business comply, with the UN decision. This will be particularly true where alternative markets are not readily available (as in the case of Dutch reliance on Rhodesian tobacco: the outcome is frequently that such goods find their way to their traditional purchaser through a non-complying "middleman") or where the economy of the country concerned is already under strain (such as the case of Britain).[24]

The availability of Article 50 in these circumstances may be a relevant factor. Zambia's non-compliance with the call for economic sanctions stems from economic necessity. Britain has been unwilling to propose (no

---

[23] It is commonly said that the optimal solution, from South Africa's point of view, would be for sanctions to be seen not to work, but for South Africa itself to bring pressure to bear upon Smith to make a settlement with Britain: and this was the path tried at the "Tiger" settlement. A weak African leadership in Rhodesia, beholden to South Africa, would also be an acceptable solution in southern African eyes: the buffer protection of the client-states of Malawi, Lesotho and Botswana could then be further extended.

[24] For examples of the constant stream of Parliamentary Questions, designed to point out to the Prime Minister that sanctions are hurting Britain more than Rhodesia, see *Hansard*, vol. 729, cols. 229-30.

doubt because the international community would be unwilling to support) financial alleviation for Zambia under Article 50 of the Charter. This Charter proviso, which was undoubtedly meant to be a factor militating in favour of compliance with a call for enforcement measures, has become inoperative because (a) Zambia would regard as politically unacceptable the spotlighting of her inability to comply (b) most African and Asian nations regard Britain, and not the UN, as responsible for Zambia's financial difficulties.[25]

Legal advice has also been required on the status of Article 50 of the Charter in the light of Portugal's request for compensation for losses incurred due to UN sanctions against Rhodesia.

(xv) So far as the state against whom sanctions are being directed is concerned, a whole new set of variables is relevant to the question of compliance. We have already suggested that, for a state to find itself facing sanctions by the UN, it must already have effectively decided that the disadvantages of compliance with the UN's preferred pattern of behaviour outweigh the advantages. By sanctions the UN is seeking to raise the costs of non-compliance. Whether it will be able to do so sufficiently depends upon many factors. Internal, political factors will obviously be extremely important: that is to say, the degree to which the ruling party represents the wishes of its community, or at least that part of its community which is permitted to participate in the nation's political life; what opportunities are available for expressing dissent with the government's non-compliance; how well organized the domestic political opposition is. The universality of the sanctions—and even more important, the participation of those who are important as existing, or potential, trading partners with the sanctioned nation—is obviously another relevant factor. The adaptability of the receiving economy, especially to diversification and to economic self sufficiency, is a further highly important variable; [26] as is the moral and political effect of sanctions upon those in the domestic community capable of making their voice heard. The significance of each of these in the case of Rhodesia needs no spelling out. Galtung has pointed out that sanctions differ from other forms of compliance—techniques by virtue of the fact they are *punishment;* and, as such, the evidence seems to be that they create a unity among the domestic population which might not otherwise exist, and present a common external foe against whom a wide range of the population will rally.[27] The Rhodesian experience would

---

[25] This point emerged clearly from the 1965 Commonwealth Prime Minister Conference where the continued existence of Smith's regime and hence Zambia's problems —was laid firmly at Britain's door, and a suggestion for Commonwealth aid to Zambia (similar to the international aid envisaged under Article 50) was rejected.

[26] For a detailed analysis of these, and related, economic factors upon the efficacy of sanctions, see Galtung, *Journal of World Politics*, April 1967.

[27] The Rhodesian experience seems to confirm this: for data, see Galtung, *op. cit.* For an analysis supporting the view that this is valid as a general proposition, see

indicate that the populace views as the cause of its "punishment" not the unacceptable behavioural pattern of its government, but the instigator of the sanctions program—Britain and the UN. In short, there is little reason to doubt that more white Rhodesians support Ian Smith than they did three weeks before UDI. This factor appears to weigh more heavily than the question of the resilience of the population: the widely expressed sentiments made soon after UDI that the average white Rhodesian was only interested in his material comforts and would soon desert a leader unable to provide them, proved wide of the mark. It is, of course, also true that his comforts have not been substantially reduced, because of the favourable operation (from the Rhodesian point of view) of the variables noted above.[28]

There are, of course, sanctions available other than those of economic coercion and diplomatic isolation. But there is a very considerable reluctance to use them. For repeated violations of the United Nations Charter, expulsion under Article 6 is possible. The strength of this sanction is in its threat: at the moment one uses it one knows that the objective of compliance has been forfeited. Article 6 is a marginally useful weapon in the armory against South Africa's refusal to obey UN decisions on apartheid; there appears to be a general realization, however, that if South Africa were expelled from the UN, there would be even less chance of securing her compliance with required race-relations behaviour. To expel South Africa from the United Nations would, in effect, be to allow the sanctioners the gratification of punishment, with the knowledge that punishment for this purpose bears little relationship to techniques aimed at securing compliance.[29] The disparate practice between the Specialized Agencies and the UN on the expulsion of South Africa appears as an attempt to indulge this desire to punish within technical Agencies, while retaining the vestiges of hope for compliance within the parent political Organization.[30]

Nations have been equally reluctant to employ the sanction in Article 19, whereby members more than two years in arrears on their budgetary dues are liable to lose their vote in the Assembly. The reluctance was initially due to the fear that a major power—Russia—would leave the Organization if it were applied. When it became evident that the availability of

---

Mudge "Domestic Policies and UN Activities", XXI *International Organization* (1967), p. 55.

[28] This has led Galtung to observe that serious consideration must be given to the possible chances of negative (i.e. punitive) sanctions in these circumstances. He suggests that further study be given to "positive" (i.e. reward-providing) sanctions, even at the risk of seeming to "reward blackmail and intransigence". *Journal of World Politics*, April 1967.

[29] Galtung, *op. cit.*

[30] For details of the constitutional problems that were faced by the WHO and ILO over demands for South African expulsion, see Higgins, "South Africa's Standing in International Organizations" *World Today*, December 1963, p. 507.

through collective processes, of the common interest is in itself a factor in favour of compliance; and "when we speak about the common interest today, it must above all relate to the threat of nuclear disaster and the demands for the effective recognition of the dignity of all human beings". But one might also add that these two pillars of community interest are often in conflict with each other, with the former dominating. When client states are diplomatically protected by nuclear powers, it becomes harder, rather than easier, for the UN to exert pressure for compliance. With the nuclear powers musclebound, it has become comparatively easy for nations in the Middle East to fail to comply with certain directives. And, in the final analysis, the membership of the UN has been more interested in world security than in the resolution of the particular problem.[37] Equally, western belief in the undesirability of major violence in Southern Rhodesia and South Africa militates against the promotion of human rights aims in those countries. Moreover, it has now become a common place to observe that the very success of the UN in obtaining "compliance" in the area of peacekeeping has often led to the "freezing" of the situation, and a failure by the parties to look beyond the temporary, UN-supported peace, to long-term political solutions.

To measure compliance is an exceedingly difficult task. Research is needed to discover who, in what circumstances, and for what reasons, signifies approval of a UN decision but then does not comply with it. The disparity between conference votes approving the text of a treaty and ratifications thereof, and between UN voting on financial questions and the actual pattern on arrears, would both be fruitful fields of study.[38] Even less is known about the circumstances, in the UN, in which nations who have voted against decisions nonetheless feel obliged to comply with them.[39]

Even if a nation does not comply with a UN decision, its action may have caused domestic opposition or international problems, which may make compliance on a subsequent resolution more likely.[40]

The task of measuring compliance, and of understanding the variables which set the pattern, must necessarily go hand in hand.

---

[37] For work suggesting that giving a high priority to the maintenance of peace necessarily means no resolution of problems which arise from the dissatisfaction of one party with the *status quo*, see Burton, *International Relations*.

[38] Some preliminary, and useful work on the arrears compliance problem has been done by Catherine Senf Manno "Majority Decision and Minority Responses", *Journal of Conflict Resolution, March 1961*.

[39] Louis Henkin has noted that Bolivia, Chile and Uruguay complied with the OAS resolution calling for severance of relations with Cuba, although they had voted against it. Mexico, claiming that the resolution contravened the UN Charter, refused to act upon it. *Hague Recueil*, 1965, vol. 1 p. 177.

[40] An observation made by Schachter, *58 AJIL* (1964), p. 960.

PROCEDURES DEVELOPED BY INTERNATIONAL ORGANIZATIONS FOR CHECKING COMPLIANCE

by *Louis B. Sohn*
Harvard University Law School

I. PERIODIC REPORTS

The International Labor Organization has developed an elaborate system of periodic reports to check on compliance with a variety of constitutional obligations and decisions. Other international organizations (for instance, WHO, UNESCO and FAO) have tried to do the same, not always with success. The United Nations has now adopted this procedure in the field of human rights.

One of the main activities of the International Labor Organization is to prepare common social standards in the form of international conventions or recommendations, and the Constitution of the ILO requires that Members submit these instruments to the competent authorities for the enactment of legislation or other action. After ratifying a convention, a Member often has to modify its legislation, issue regulations, and provide for uniform interpretation of the Convention. All these steps are monitored by the ILO through a system of reports. In the first place, each Member is obliged to report details as to the submission of a particular instrument to its competent authorities. Secondly, each Member has to report annually on steps taken to implement each Convention which it has ratified. Thirdly, each Member has to report periodically on the effect given in practice to an unratified Convention, whenever the Governing Body requests such information.

The replies are examined annually by a Committee of Experts and at each International Labor Conference by a special Committee. These Committees examine national legislation for conformity to international obligations, and study the manner in which the relevant national laws are applied in practice. Comments by organizations of workers and employers are considered, whenever available, and governments are often asked for explanations. The reports of the Committees point out inconsistencies in legislative texts or practice, and usually are accepted by the Governments concerned.[1]

It has been suggested that this system, though useful, is not sufficient, and that an international system of labor inspection should be established to supplement it.

The Constitution of the *World Health Organization* requires annual re-

---

[1] For a survey of the effectiveness of the observations made by the two committees, see International Labour Conference, 37th Session, Report III, Part IV, pp. 72-86.

ports from each Member on "the action taken and progress achieved in improving the health of its people," and on action taken with respect to relevant recommendations, agreements, conventions and regulations adopted by the Organization. While the reports have been found useful in providing a store of information for the Organization and have helped Members to understand more clearly what their health problems were and what needs to be done to meet them, the WHO had found it rather difficult to prepare a meaningful summary and analysis of Members' reports. Starting in 1956, however, these reports became the basis of the Director-General's quadrennial reports on the world health situation.

A system adopted by the *United Nations Educational, Scientific and Cultural Organization* is somewhere between the systems of the ILO and WHO. Annual reports are presented by Members on "laws, regulations and statistics relating to educational, scientific and cultural life and institutions." Periodical reports on recommendations and conventions and special reports on particular educational or cultural problems are also required. A special committee examines these reports, and presents its comments to the Conference.

The provisions in the *Food and Agricutural Organization* Constitution are similar to those in the UNESCO and WHO Constitutions, requiring in particular reports on the progress made by Members "toward achieving the purpose of the Organization." Though most Members have complied with the obligation to submit reports, the Secretariat of the Organization has not succeeded in analyzing them in an effective manner; the requirements with respect to the reports were, therefore, relaxed in later years.

The *United Nations* has experimented with requiring periodic reports in various areas. Early attempts to obtain comprehensive reports on the implementation of recommendations in the economic and social field,[2] were abandoned after a while. On the other hand, an effective system of reporting was developed with respect to trusteeship areas and non-self-governing territories. Since 1956, an elaborate procedure for periodic reporting has evolved with respect to human rights.

Questions:
    (a) What are the main advantages of periodic reporting?
    (b) What difficulties have arisen in connection with periodic reports?
    (c) What improvements in the system of periodic reporting should be introduced?

---

[2] See, for instance, UN Doc. E/1117, 3 February 1949.

II. PROCEDURES FOR INTERPRETING INTERNATIONAL AGREEMENTS

Most international organizations have the customary provisions for the reference to an international tribunal (usually the International Court of Justice) of disputes relating to the interpretation or application of the constitution of the Organization and, in some cases, also of the conventions or regulations adopted by the Organization. In practice, almost no use has been made of these provisions for judicial interpretation, except for a relatively large number of arbitrations under the Universal Postal Conventions and under the conventions relating to the transport of goods and persons by rail. On the other hand, Members of international organizations resort frequently to procedures of administrative interpretation which find no mention in constitutional instruments.

Such a procedure is used frequently at the ILO, where the International Labor Office furnishes to Members information relevant to the interpretation of international labor conventions, making it clear, however, in each case that it really has "no special authority under the provisions of the Constitution of the ILO to interpret the provisions of an international labor convention, authority to give an international binding interpretation being reserved to the International Court of Justice." [3] Nevertheless, the view has been expressed by the Office that "when an opinion given by the Office has been submitted to the Governing Body and published in the Official Bulletin and has met with no adverse comment, the Conference must, in the event of its subsequently including in another Convention a provision identical with or equivalent to the provision which has been interpreted by the Office, be presumed, in the absence of any evidence to the contrary, to have intended that provision to be understood in the manner in which the Office has interpreted it." [4]

The ILO Constitution provides also for investigation of complaints by one Member against another with respect to violations of labor conventions, and this procedure was used with success in 1962 and 1963 in two cases relating to the Forced Labor Convention, one involving a complaint by Ghana against Portugal, and one relating to a complaint by Portugal against Liberia.

In *WHO* the International Sanitary Regulations provide expressly for the reference to the Director-General of "any question or dispute concerning the interpretation and application of these Regulations." [5] Where a settlement is not reached, the dispute may be referred to the Committee on International Quarantine, either by the Director-General on his

---

[3] 33 *ILO Official Bulletin* 305 (1950).
[4] 23 *idem* 30-33 (1938); Jenks, "The Interpretation of International Labour Conventions by the International Labour Office", 20 *British Year Book of International Law* 132, at 133 (1939).
[5] 37 *WHO Official Records* 352-53 (1951).

own initiative or at the request of the State concerned.[6] The procedure before the Committee resembles that used in a contentious case before an international tribunal.[7] Many questions have been submitted to the Director-General and the Committee on International Quarantine but none of them has assumed the proportions of a "dispute", and only one case (relating to yellow fever provisions) had to be referred to the World Health Assembly for solution.

The agreements establishing the *International Monetary Fund* and the *International Bank for Reconstruction and Development* have given the power to interpret them to the Executive Boards of these institutions, and large numbers of decisions have been issued by them.[8]

The Convention on International Civil Aviation conferred on the Council of the *International Civil Aviation Organization* the jurisdiction to decide in the first instance disagreements relating to the interpretaton and application of the Convention. The Council was confronted in 1952 with a dispute between India and Pakistan before it developed any rules on the subject. An elaborate set of rules was finally adopted in 1957.[9] Many interpretative decisions have been adopted by the Council apart from actual disputes between Members.

Questions:

(a) Why is there no resort to the International Court of Justice for the settlement of disputes relating to the interpretation of the Constitutions of international organizations or conventions adopted by such organizations?

(b) What role should be played in international organizations by the various means for non-judicial settlement of disputes?

(c) What are the advantages and disadvantages of "administrative" interpretation?

(d) Can a set of model rules of administrative procedure be drafted for the benefit of international officials engaged in administrative interpretation?

III. COMPLAINTS BY NON-GOVERNMENTAL ORGANIZATIONS AND INDIVIDUALS

The ILO Constitution allows industrial associations of employers and workers to submit "representations" reporting that a Member "has failed

---

[6] *Ibid.*; 48 *idem* 23 (1953).
[7] 55 *idem* 70, 72-73 (1954).
[8] See Hexner, "Interpretation by Public International Organizations of Their Basic Instruments", 53 *American Journal of International Law* 341-70 (1959).
[9] ICAO Doc. 7782-C/898.

54

to secure in any respect the effective observance within its jurisdiction of any Convention to which it is a party." Some ten cases were presented to the ILO under this provision, and most of them were settled in a satisfactory manner.

Special procedures were also developed by the ILO to deal with complaints relating to freedom of association of workers and employers, and several hundred cases were examined under these procedures.

In the *United Nations* the right of examining petitions from individuals and organizations was established by the Charter only in the trusteeship area. Large numbers of such petitions were examined by the Trusteeship Council and the Fourth Committee of the General Assembly. In 1962 the Special Committee on the Situation with Regard to the Implementation of the Declaration on the Granting of Independence to Colonial Countries and Peoples, which was authorized by the General Assembly "to carry out its task by employment of all means which it will have at its disposal," decided to hear petitioners and accept written petitions. Many petitions were examined by it, and formed one of the bases for the Committee's recommendations for granting the right of self-determination to various territories. The Special Committee on Apartheid has also, since 1963, accepted memoranda from organizations and individuals, and heard persons or representatives of organizations who were "in a position to provide it with information." [10] Proposals have been made that the United Nations should develop similar procedures for dealing with violations of human rights throughout the world. Both the Convention on the Elimination of All Forms of Racial Discrimination of 1965 and the Optional Protocol to the International Covenant on Civil and Political Rights of 1966 contain optional provisions on communications from individuals.

Regional precedents for such procedures exist in Europe and, to some extent, in Latin America. The *European Convention on Human Rights* has conferred on the European Commission of Human Rights jurisdiction to receive petitions by individuals, and authorized the Commission to bring such petitions before the European Court of Human rights. Ten countries have accepted the jurisdiction of the Commission with respect to petitions and eight accepted the jurisdiction of the Court as well. An *Inter-American Commission on Human Rights* established in 1959 has ingeniously developed procedures enabling it not only to study human rights in general but also to discuss concrete situations and to receive petitions to hold hearings and to make investigations on the spot.

---

[10] UN Doc. A/5497, pp. 13-25, 16 September 1963.

Questions:

(a) Should there be a broadening of the power of international non-governmental organizations to call a specific violation of an international convention to the attention of the appropriate international organization?

(b) Should that power be conferred also on some national non-governmental organizations?

(c) In what categories of cases should individuals be granted the right of petition?

(d) What procedures should be developed for dealing with such complaints and petitions?

IMPLEMENTATION OF DECISIONS OF INTERNATIONAL ORGANIZATIONS THROUGH NATIONAL COURTS

by *E. Lauterpacht, Q. C.*
Trinity College, Cambridge University

The purpose of the present paper is to investigate the possibility of using the machinery of national courts as a device to secure compliance with the decisions of international organizations. Normally, of course, the problem of implementing decisions of international organizations need only be considered at the level of State or governmental behaviour. This is because in most cases the burden of carrying out the decision falls only on States or Governments—as is shown by the other papers printed in this volume. There are, however, certain decisions of international organizations which wholly or partly fall to be carried out by individuals. It is in relation to such decisions that there is room for considering recourse to national courts and legal systems with a view to procuring enforcement.

The matter may perhaps be most conveniently approached in terms, principally, of the current Rhodesian situation. Among the resolutions adopted by the Security Council is one imposing so-called "mandatory sanctions" upon Rhodesia. The relevant operative parts of the resolution [1] call for quotation:

> "... 2. *Decides* that all States Members of the United Nations shall prevent: (a) the import into their territories of asbestos, iron ore, chrome, pig-iron, sugar, tobacco, copper, meat and meat products and hides, skins and leather originating in Southern Rhodesia and exported therefrom after the date of this resolution; (b) any activities by their nationals or in their territories which promote or are calculated to promote the export of these commodities from Southern Rhodesia and any dealings by their nationals or in their territories in any of these commodities originating in Southern Rhodesia and exported therefrom after the date of this resolution, including in particular any transfer of funds to Southern Rhodesia for the purposes of such activities or dealings;
>
> ...
> "3. *Reminds* Member States the failure or refusal by any of them to implement the present resolution shall constitute a violation of Article 25 of the Charter;
>
> ...
> "6. *Calls upon* all States Members of the United Nations to carry out this decision of the Security Council in accordance with Article 25 of the United Nations Charter."

In terms, the obligation created by the resolution is imposed only on States Members of the United Nations. It is they who are required to prevent the import into their territories of the prohibited commodities and to prohibit those activities of their nationals which might promote the export of such commodities. However, in contrast with most other Securi-

---

[1] Resolution 232 (1966), 16 December 1966.

ty Council resolutions, the degree of effectiveness of this resolution is entirely dependent upon the extent to which individuals comply with it. Although many Member States have taken the necessary administrative or legislative steps to carry out their obligations, there is evidence of evasion of the resolution on a considerable scale.[2] This is primarily a matter of individual, rather than ot State or governmental, conduct—though certain cases no doubt reflect some measure ot State acquiescence or even complicity. In these latter situations—and wherever the legislative or administrative arrangements of a Member State may be shown to be at fault—the international responsibility is the State's, and is primarily a matter of concern to the Security Council.

However, this does not mean that the British Government need not or cannot show any individual or additional concern with the enforcement of mandatory sanctions. Accordingly, the idea which this paper seeks to canvass is that it may be open to the British Government to make use of the national legal systems of other countries to secure compliance in at least some cases with the objective of the Security Council resolution.

The starting point in this procedure is the consideration that the United Kingdom remains the *de jure* sovereign over Rhodesia. Furthermore, no other government has been recognized by any State as exercising *de facto* authority. Indeed, the Security Council resolution of 20 November 1965 expressly called upon all States not to recognize the illegal regime of Rhodesia. In terms of British constitutional law, the British Government is em-

---

[2] There have been three reports by the Secretary-General on compliance with the Security Council's resolution: 21 February, 9 March and 27 July 1967 (S/7781 and Adds. 1, 2 and 3). In the latest report the Secretary-General states.

". . . Since the available trade statistics relate only to the first few months of 1967 and since several of Southern Rhodesia's trading partners and, in particular, some of its immediate neighbours, have not responded to the Secretary-General's request for information about their trade with Southern Rhodesia, it is still not possible to make any definitive conclusions on the progress of the implementation of the resolution adopted by the Security Council on 16 December 1966. At this stage it could only be said that, according to available statistics, while there has been a significant decline in the trade between Southern Rhodesia and many of its trading partners in most of the commodities listed in the resolution of the Security Council, *there has been continuing traffic in certain important commodities*" (emphasis supplied).

It may be noted that the national reports of the measures which they have taken pursuant to the Security Council Resolution, and referred to in the Secretary-General's Reports, demonstrate that States were concerned fairly generally to reflect in precise statutory terms within their own legal systems the various measures specified by the Council. Only one example was given of measures specifically taken against a particular Rhodesian cargo. The Government of Cameroon reported on 9 February 1967 (see S/7781, Annex 2, p. 6) that it had just seized a cargo of 800,300 kg. of Rhodesian tobacco consigned from Rotterdam to the *Société des Tabacs Bastos* of Cameroon, discharged at the Cameroonian port of Douala by the steamship "Lake Bososutive". No further details of this action were given, and in particular nothing was said as to how the cargo in question was ultimately to be disposed of.

powered to enact legislation controlling persons, things and transactions in Rhodesia. The enactment in November 1965 of the Southern Rhodesia Act by the United Kingdom is evidence of the existence of this constitutional authority.[3] As a matter of English constitutional law, the matter may be regarded as beyond controversy.

It is, therefore, open to the British Government to vest in itself[4] title to any of the goods sold for export in violation of the Security Council resolution. Such vesting would require legislation[5] which would need to be worded so that the vesting would operate regardless of whether under the contract of sale title to the goods were to pass to the purchaser in Rhodesia or outside. At the same time, the legislation would need to be designed to bite upon goods intended to be exported and it would need to take effect to achieve the vesting of title in the Crown while the goods were still situate in Rhodesia and were thus under British sovereignty.

The purpose of thus transferring ownership of the goods to the Crown would be to enable the British Government, as owner, to sue for their recovery or value in the courts of the various States through which the goods might pass or to which they might ultimately be delivered. It need hardly be said that this situation would imply that the Crown would remain owner notwithstanding the attempt of the Rhodesian vender to pass title to an overseas purchaser.

One can, of course, only speculate upon the effect which the prospect of such actions might have upon trade in the prohibited commodities. But it would not seem unreasonable to contemplate a sharp down-turn in such trade if prospective purchasers foresaw the risk that the purchase of such goods would lead them into protracted litigation which, at the least, would be a nuisance; which would in any event lead to the public identification of the nature of their commercial activities; and which, if the procedure was fully successful, could also lead to the loss of the money invested in

---

[3] Section 1 of the Act provides: "It is hereby declared that Southern Rhodesia continues to be part of Her Majesty's dominions, and that the Government and Parliament of the United Kingdom have responsibility and jurisdiction as heretofore for and in respect of it."

[4] In technical terms, the legal person in whom title would vest would be "Her Majesty", sometimes otherwise referred to as "the Crown". "The British Government" or "Her Majesty's Government" are not persons in English law; and to speak, within the framework of that law, of the "Government" as acquiring or owning rights or property is simply a loose way of referring to "Her Majesty".

[5] The legislation could be either principal legislation, i.e. a statute enacted by Parliament at Westminster, or it could be delegated legislation, i.e. a statutory instrument made by the Executive on the basis of legislative powers already granted by Parliament. The Crown would appear to possess the powers necessary for this purpose under Section 2 (1) of the Southern Rhodesia Act, 1965:

> "Her Majesty may by Order in Council make such provision in relation to Southern Rhodesia, or persons or things in any way belonging to or connected with Southern Rhodesia, as appears to Her to be necessary or expedient in consequence of any unconstitutional action taken therein."

the purchase. Certainly, we have in this procedure, if it can be made to work, something which could operate as a sanction for the enforcement of at least this category of decision of international organizations.

Apart from the specific and direct contribution which this device might make to the implementation of the decision of the organization, one aspect of it could also play a significant political role. In describing the device so far, reference has been made only to action which the United Kingdom, as the party principally concerned, would need to take. Its success would depend exclusively upon the willingness of the United Kingdom to pursue it and of the adequacy of the legal systems of the States in which actions were pursued to enable the procedure to be implemented. This latter aspect of the matter will be considered presently. There remains, however, the possibility that the procedure here being considered could be introduced and made more effective if some specific reference were made to it in a relevant organizational decision, in this case, say, a decision of the Security Council. Thus a resolution could, in addition to placing an embargo upon the purchase of Rhodesian strategic commodities, call upon all members of the U.N. to assist the United Kingdom in any measures it sees fit to take to secure compliance with the resolution and, in particular, to ensure that the content of their national legal systems was such as to enable the United Kingdom to proceed in the way here contemplated.[6] The willingness of States to support or carry out the terms of such a resolution would also provide a good measure of their true, as contrasted with their proclaimed, attitude to sanctions. It is, of course, one thing to call publicly for measures to be applied by, and bear economically upon, others; it is a different matter to be obliged, by a requirement of this kind, publicly to identify oneself as a State willing or unwilling, as the case may be, seriously to participate in the sanctions procedure.

We can now turn to consider some of the more technical legal questions which may arise in connection with this procedure.

There is, first, the problem arising from the reluctance of many legal systems to recognize or give effect to foreign confiscatory legislation. That the legislation would be confiscatory, there can be no doubt. Otherwise the whole procedure would be frustrated. The idea is that those who knowingly trade in prohibited goods should be exposed to an uncompensated loss of their investment. To some extent, a way round this obstacle may be found in the argument that the deprivation of title is more properly classified as punishment than as confiscation. But there are many

---

[6] The present wording of the Security Council resolution already goes some way towards this in deciding that "all States Members ... shall prevent ... any activities by their nationals ...". (See text at p. 57 above, for fuller quotation of the resolution.) But it is questionable whether the wording goes sufficiently far to impose upon Members a duty to assist the British Government in recovering wrongfully exported goods; and clearly it would be advantageous that language should be used which puts the matter beyond doubt.

States whose laws are no less opposed to the enforcement of foreign penal laws than they are to foreign confiscatory legislation. In terms of the existing law of many States, one could well predict the failure of proceedings of the kind here contemplated.

By way of elaboration of this and comparable difficulties, let us assume for the moment that the United Kingdom had by now vested in the Crown title to a particular consignment of a prohibited commodity. This consignment is traced, let us say, to the territory of Ruritania, a member of the United Nations. The Crown commences proceedings in the Ruritanian courts, against the purchaser or possessor of the goods, to secure their recovery or their value. On the assumption that Ruritanian law is in this respect comparable with, say, the American or English legal systems, there are likely to be two principal legal defences (as opposed to defences of a practical nature, which will be considered presently). They are, first, that it would be contrary to Ruritanian public policy to participate in giving effect to foreign legislation of a confiscatory or penal character; and, second, that in any event, the British Government is not in *de facto* control of Rhodesia, so that British legislation cannot be treated as effective to change title to property situate there.

Now, in a situation unaffected by the community interest of the United Nations which exists in relation to the Rhodesian problem, one can recognize that both these points would be, to say the least, arguable. Admittedly, as against the challenge based on the confiscatory or penal character of the legislation, it could be said that as it had taken effect on the goods while they were in Rhodesia, and was thus part of the *lex situs* of the property at the time of the purported transfer, the Ruritanian courts were not being asked to "enforce", but only to recognize a transfer validly effected in another jurisdiction. At the same time, the possibility cannot be excluded that the Ruritanian courts might regard their public policy as thrusting more deeply and as being opposed to assisting in the implementation in any way of this category of legislation, notwithstanding that it was part of the *lex situs* at the relevant time.

The argument based upon the lack of *de facto* control by the British Government in Rhodesia could perhaps be more strongly pressed. There are now some observations by Lord Wilberforce in the *Carl Zeiss* case,[7]

---

[7] See *Carl Zeiss Stiftung* v. *Rayner & Keeler Ltd.* (*No. 2*) [1966] 3 W.L.R. 125, at pp. 177-8. Lord Wilberforce said:
". . . if the consequences of non-recognition of the East German 'government' were to bring into question the validity of its legislative acts, I should wish seriously to consider whether the invalidity so brought about is total, or whether some mitigation of the severity of this result can be found . . . [i]n my opinion, there is nothing in those English decisions, in which recognition has been refused to particular acts of non-recognized governments, which would prevent its acceptance or which prescribes the absolute and total invalidity of all laws and acts flowing from unrecognized governments."

reflecting and lending contemporary support to important decisions of the United States Supreme Court, to the effect that the legislation of an unrecognized *de facto* authority cannot be completely disregarded simply because the authority from which it emanates is not recognized officially by the State of the forum. And so, it might be contended, notwithstanding the *de jure* entitlement of the United Kingdom to legislate for Rhodesia, evidence of the absence of accompanying effective *de facto* control would entitle the Ruritanian courts to treat the British legislation as incapable of changing title to property in Rhodesia.

There is no need to pursue these arguments further here. Suffice it to say that for present purposes they might, with prospects varying according to the national system in whom they were pressed, enjoy some measure of success. This, however, is by no means the end of the story— for it is just at this point that it is proper to expect positive assistance from the legal system of the State concerned—either on the basis of the general obligation of States to ensure that their municipal law is adequate to implement their international commitments or, better still, on the basis that the relevant Security Council resolution has expressly called upon them to ensure that barriers of this kind could not be raised against the class of action here being discussed. In other words, the resolution imposing the prohibition upon the export of the goods should itself look forward to the prospect of municipal enforcement and should call upon States to ensure that the procedures will succeed—even, if necessary, by enacting legislation which will negative such defences as those just mentioned. To ask this of States is not unreasonable. It is really doing no more than setting up the public policy of the international community as a counterpoise to the public policy of particular States.

The relative ease with which legislative change of public policy can be secured should not be overlooked. Scholars of private international law throughout the world have in the past attached great weight to, for example, the so-called "act of State" doctrine and the associated "principle" that the courts of one State may not review the legality of foreign legislation, whether by reference to international law or the relevant foreign constitutional law. Yet within eighteen months of the decision of the United States Supreme Court in the *Sabbatino* case, the United States Congress had enacted legislation which effectively reversed the Supreme Court and laid down a new rule for future application in such cases. And it is noteworthy that many of the States reporting to the Secretary-General on their measures to implement the Security Council Resolution of 16 December 1966 indicated that these measures took the form of legislation.

It is of course possible to contemplate other difficulties, more of a practical than of a legal character. Thus success in any civil proceeding for the recovery of a given consignment would depend upon showing that the consignment in question originated from Rhodesia after the enactment of the legislation. This is a question of fact and a matter of evidence in any given case. To some extent the inherent physical structure of a commodity serves to identify its origin—as is true of long-staple asbestos or of certain types of tobacco. But it is always possible to conceal the origin by changing the physical structure of the goods, e.g. by breaking down the long staples of the asbestos or by mixing the tobacco with leaf of comparable quality from another source, or by partially processing it in some territory friendly to Rhodesia. Again, there are commercial devices which may be used to reduce consumer resistance to the use of prohibited commodities. Thus the goods could be sold on the basis that the purchaser would not be obliged to pay for the goods until they had been safely delivered, used and re-sold. The risk would thus be carried entirely by the vendor.

The assessment of the impact of these practical problems is not a task for lawyers, though they can properly suggest legal techniques for diminishing the impact of these difficulties. Thus, if there is a serious intention to implement the policy of economic sanctions, there would be room for recourse to the techniques developed in the context of prize law during the First and Second World Wars. For example, it would be possible by suitable enactment to shift the burden of proof in certain cases so that the purchaser of a commodity which might have been exported from Rhodesia in breach of the prohibition would be obliged to demonstrate that the cargo was not of Rhodesian origin, rather than that the Crown should be obliged to show that the cargo was of Rhodesian origin.

To suggest that such devices are available to diminish or circumvent the practical difficulties is not to say that they must necessarily be used. But it is right that, in seeking to assess whether available procedures for the enforcement of international decisions and, in particular, sanctions against Rhodesia are really being pushed as far as is practicable, regard should be paid to some of the possibilities which exist but are not yet being employed.

The theme of this paper has so far been presented in terms of the Rhodesian problem. This is because the Rhodesian situation has prompted the idea and because it represents the most immediate occasion on which use can be made of these procedures. Nevertheless, it is possible to conceive other situations in which the same techniques may be employed—for example, in relation to South-West Africa—though the legal basis for its application may perhaps be more controversial. One would need to start from the proposition that South Africa's rights as administering authority of South-West Africa have ended. This would be based, first, on the General Assembly Resolution of 22 October 1966 (2145 (XXI)) in which it declared that South Africa had failed to fulfil its obligations under the Mandate for South-West Africa and had "in fact, disavowed the Mandate". The Assembly decided that the Mandate "is therefore terminated, that South Africa has no other right to administer the Territory and that henceforth South-West Africa comes under the direct responsibility of the United Nations". To this must now be added General Assembly Resolution 2248 (S-V) of 19 May 1967 in which the Assembly established a United Nations Council for South-West Africa

"(a) to administer South-West Africa until independence. . ."

"(b) to promulgate such laws, decrees and administrative regulations as are necessary for the administration of the Territory. . ."

These resolutions appear to lead to the position that South Africa has now ceased to be the *de jure* authority in South-West Africa (at least so far as the United Nations is concerned) and that such authority has now been vested in the United Nations Council for South-West Africa. On this basis, it would be upon the Council to pursue the same kind of initiative in relation to South-West African exports as has been suggested for the United Kingdom in relation to prohibited Rhodesian exports. Thus the Council could enact that no valid title to certain important South-West African exports, such as diamonds, could be acquired save from the United Nations authority; and the United Nations authority would have the right to sue to recover such commodities in the courts of Member States. If it should be argued that South-West African diamonds are indistinguishable from other African diamonds, then additional techniques of identification could be introduced, e.g. a statistical approach. This is a technique of contraband control for which there are precedents in the First and Second World Wars. Thus if it could be shown that a given percentage of the world's supply of diamonds, or of a particular dealer's supply of diamonds, customarily came from South-West Africa, the burden would be placed heavily upon the defendant in any litigation to show that at least that percentage of diamonds involved in the case did not come from South-West Africa.

It might also be necessary in a further General Assembly resolution to call upon Members of the United Nations to ensure that their national legal systems did not hinder the United Nations in the pursuit of these processes and, in particular, that the consideration of South Africa's continuing *de facto* control of the Territory should not be treated by national courts as the basis for treating South African administered law as the *lex situs* controlling title to exportable commodities.

Again, to point to this possibility is not to say that it is necessarily advisable, in political or economic terms, to pursue it. There is the risk that interference with South-West African exports might do greater harm to the population of the territory than the pursuit of other modes of persuasion. This, however, is not a matter that needs to be taken further.

In conclusion, it may be recalled that the idea of recourse to national courts for the enforcement of international obligations is not new and should not be surprising. In a way, the situation is comparable to the enforcement of the international laws of war through war crimes trials conducted by national tribunals. Or again, a comparison may be drawn with the *Rosemary* or *Sabbatino* type actions in which an owner deprived of property by foreign expropriatory decrees violative of international law seeks to recover his property in the courts of whatever State that property may reach. The difficulties which arose in the cases just cited should, it may be hoped, be made to disappear much more readily when the decisions to be enforced are specific ones adopted by international organizations rather than general ones existing under customary international law at large.[8]

---

[8] A third type of precedent may be found in the case of *Banco de Brasil, S.A.* v. *A.C. Israel Commodity Co. Inc.* (12 N.Y. (2d) 371, 190 N.E. (2d) 235, 239 N.Y.S. (2d) 872 (1963); 84 S. Ct. 657 (1964), where the Banco de Brasil sought the assistance of the United States courts in the implementation of the provisions of Article VIII, Section 2 (b) of the Articles of Agreement of the International Monetary Fund. The Bank sought, in effect, to recover from an American purchaser of a Brazilian export the difference between the price properly payable if the lawful rate of exchange had been used and the price actually paid by reason of the fact that an unlawful exchange rate had been used. The United States courts adopted a somewhat restrictive view of Article VIII, Section 2 (b), in that they said that it simply required that contracts which it rendered unlawful should be unenforceable, not that the conduct associated with such contracts should give rise to a positive cause of action. Here, then, the difficulty arose from the narrowness of the international obligation. The case still serves as a precedent for an attempt by a State authority, i.e. a national Bank, to enforce in a foreign court its own understanding (albeit held to be wrong) of the terms of an international obligation. And there is no reason why, if the international obligation is sufficiently clearly stated, a comparable action should not succeed in another case.

APPLICATION AND ENFORCEMENT OF INTERNATIONAL ORGANIZATION LAW BY NATIONAL AUTHORITIES AND COURTS

by *Eric Stein*
University of Michigan Law School

It is *not* the purpose of this outline to bring about a discussion of the monist-dualist theories, or a detailed examination of national constitutional practices, or a systematic consideration of interaction between international and national law in the context of international organization. On the contrary, it is hoped that the outline may help to identify specific problems which legal advisors have encountered in their work or which they consider relevant from the viewpoint of ensuring more effective application of international organizational law and that the discussion would focus on these problems.

The material in *Section I* of the outline dealing with "self-executing" rules concerns primarily the more integrated organizations such as the European Communities which face the need of ensuring uniform application of their law by national agencies in the member states. It might be interesting to explore, however, whether and to what extent somewhat similar problems may have arisen with respect to other organizations.

Section II, on the other hand, is of obvious general concern in that it raises in broadest terms the question of obtaining compliance—in the form of adjustment of national law with rules of international organization law which do not have "self-executing" effect in national law and thus necessitate action by the national law maker.

Section III raises four general questions which may provide a basis for discussion.

I. APPLICATION AND ENFORCEMENT OF "SELF-EXECUTING" OR "DIRECTLY APPLICABLE" PROVISIONS OF TREATIES ESTABLISHING INTERNATIONAL ORGANIZATIONS AND OF LEGAL ACTS OF SUCH ORGANIZATIONS

The effect of these provisions in national law is generally determined by national constitutional practices with respect to treaties, which vary from country to country.

1. Selected national constitutional patterns providing for application of these provisions in national law:

(a) The Netherlands Constitution represents the most "advanced" pattern in that it includes all the following elements:

(i) Authorization to delegate legislative, administrative and judicial powers by treaties to international organizations;

(ii) Exclusion of application of any national law which is incompatible with "self-executing" provisions of any prior or subsequent treaty or act of an international organization;

(iii) Authorization to deviate from the Constitution by treaties;

(iv) Exclusion of treaties from judicial reviews for constitutionality. (Arts. 60, 66, 67 of the Netherlands Constitution.)

(b) Other modern constitutions contain variants of one or more of the above elements. Thus the French Constitutional pattern prescribes superiority of all treaties over national law and excludes judicial review for constitutionality (Art. 55). The German Basic Law (Art. 24) and the Italian Constitution (Art. 11) authorize transfer of "sovereign powers" to international organizations without providing explicitly for superiority of treaty law.

(c) Under the U.S. Federal Constitution a treaty prevails over prior or subsequent state law, over prior federal law but *not* over subsequent federal law (Art. VI, paragraph 2). Treaties are subject to judicial review for constitutionality.

(d) In the United Kingdom, treaty-making is exclusively within executive power and as a consequence there can be no "self-executing" treaty; a national judge can only apply an act of Parliament embodying the rules of the treaty and the "latest" act of Parliament binds the national judge.

2. What problems arise in connection with the application of "self-executing" or "directly applicable" provisions of international organization law?

(a) In *"non-integrated"* organizations such as the UN and its specialized agencies, *e.g.*

(i) Articles 104 and 105 of the UN Charter providing that the UN shall enjoy legal capacity and necessary privileges and immunities in member territory. Both articles were held self-executing by lower courts in the US;

(ii) Art. VIII 2b of the International Monetary Fund Agreement providing that exchange contracts involving member currency which are contrary to certain exchange control regulations of other member states shall be unenforceable in member territory. Many cases have arisen under this provision in national courts;

(iii) European Convention for the Protection of Human Rights and Fundamental Freedoms in those member states of the Council of Europe which have taken steps to make this Convention applicable in national courts or agencies. Some members did not take such steps and with respect to these latter members the Convention is enforceable only through the European Commission and—upon acceptance of its jurisdiction—also through the Court of Human Rights. Do difficulties arise from the divergence?

(b) In case of "integrated" organizations such as the European Communities:

(i) The Court of Justice of the European Communities defined the Community as "a new legal order of international law" whose "subjects are not only the member states but their nationals as well" and construed very broadly the concept of "directly applicable" provisions of the EEC Treaty which national courts must apply.[1] The same Court ruled that the Treaty makes it "impossible" for member states to accord superiority to a prior or subsequent national law over the Community legal order.[2]

"Regulations" enacted by the institutions of the European Economic Community and Euratom are by the terms of the two Treaties "directly applicable in each member state" (Arts. 189 EEC Treaty and 161 Euratom Treaty) upon publication in the Official Journal of the Communities. Three types of issues have come before courts: What provisions of the Community Treaties and regulations accord rights to individuals which the national courts and agencies must enforce? Can Community Treaties and acts be attacked before national courts for unconstitutionality (in Italy and in Germany)? Are national courts bound to accord superiority to Community law over national law even if the latter is subsequent in time?

(ii) Are there "directly applicable" provisions in the Central American Integration Treaties and if so what sort of questions have been raised in this connection?

II. APPLICATION AND ENFORCEMENT OF INTERNATIONAL ORGANIZATION LAW WHICH IS NOT "SELF-EXECUTING" OR "DIRECTLY APPLICABLE," BUT REQUIRES MODIFICATION OF NATIONAL LAW IN MEMBER STATES

1. Application of non-self-executing provisions of *treaties* establishing international organizations which call for modification of national law.

2. Application of *legal acts of organs* of international organizations requiring modification in national law, *e.g.*

(a) decisions of the UN Security Council (such as decision prohibiting direct delivery of arms to the Congo—the US executive orders implementing the decision); decisions of the OECD Council;

(b) recommendations of the UN Security Council or of the General Assembly (the problem here is to obtain acceptance *and* implementation);

(c) "directives" adopted by the institutions of the European Econo-

---

[1] Case 26/62, *Van Gend & Loos* v. *Netherlands Fiscal Administration.*
[2] Case 6/64, *Costa* v. *E.N.E.L.*

mic Community and Euratom which bind every member state to which they are addressed "as to the result to be achieved," but leave domestic authorities free to determine "the form and means" of enforcement (Arts. 189 of the EEC Treaty and 161 Euratom Treaty); [3]

(d) judgments of the International Court of Justice; judgments of the Court of Justice of the European Communities declaring that a member state has failed to fulfill its obligation under the Treaty in enacting (or failing to enact) a national legal measure; [4] judgments of the European Court of Human Rights.

3. "Transformation" into national law of normative acts of UN specialized agencies, e.g.

(a) conventions and recommendations of the International Labor Organization;

(b) technical regulations of the International Civil Aviation Organization which under certain circumstances become "automatically" binding upon member governments;

(c) Codex Alimentarius prepared jointly by the Food and Agriculture Organization and the World Health Organization.

(A separate category for this type of acts which might include also U.N. sponsored conventions may be justified on practical rather than systemic-logical grounds.)

Some general questions:

(1) To what extent do international organizations—regional or universal —rely on national courts and administrative authorities for the application and enforcement of international organization law? In the past, has this means proved appropriate essentially only on the regional level, where broad consensus exists, or are there any lessons of more general application to be learned from past experience? Are there any trends on a regional or worldwide level that should be encouraged?

(2) To what extent do divergencies of national constitutional practices concerning treaty-making and the effect of treaties in national law pose difficulties in obtaining compliance with international organization law? What means could be devised to reduce these difficulties?

(3) Where national courts or administrative authorities interpret, apply and enforce international organization law, do divergencies in interpretation pose problems? What are the means—if any—to ensure uniform interpretation, uniform application? Is this exclusively a problem of inte-

---

[3] In certain respects "directives" are quite unique. It may be argued for instance that member states are not free to change their law in the general area covered by a directive without prior consultation with the appropriate Community institution.

[4] Judgments of the Court of Justice of the Communities rendered against individuals or enterprises and imposing monetary obligations are enforceable in national courts.

grated regional organizations? Are reports of national decisions readily available to practitioners and scholars?

(4) Where compliance with a rule of international organization law requires modification of national law by the national law-maker, do difficulties arise in ensuring national action? What devices of coordination, supervision or compulsion are available or could be developed, considering the growing interdependence of states?

CERTAIN ASPECTS OF THE LAW AND PRACTICE OF THE INTERNATIONAL MONETARY FUND

by *Joseph Gold*
General Counsel and Director of Legal Department, International Monetary Fund*

INTRODUCTION

These notes deal with certain aspects of the first five topics in the Agenda circulated for the Second Conference on Legal Advisers and International Organizations convened in August 1967 to deal more particularly with the decisions of international organizations and their effectiveness in member states. In the interest of uniformity the titles of the topics are taken from the Agenda although they are not always appropriate for the Fund. This paper does not purport to be a systematic or comprehensive study of the law and practice of the International Monetary Fund in relation to the five topics but concentrates on those aspects that carry the special stamp of the Fund and are therefore not part of the common law of international organizations, if indeed there is any such common law.

The kinds of decision that the Fund takes are multifarious, but the attempt to classify them *per genus et per differentiam* would serve no purpose that would not be better served by describing the complex activities of the institution. It is impossible to do that in detail within the limits of this paper, but a brief prefatory comment is unavoidable. The Fund is an international regulatory agency which administers a code of obligations binding on its states members, of which there are 106 at present. It is also an international financial agency which owns and administers revolving resources in gold and the currencies of all members. These resources are increased from time to time by increases in the quotas of members, and they now amount to the equivalent of almost 21 billion US dollars. In addition, the equivalent of another 6 billion US dollars in ten currencies is available to the Fund in accordance with the terms of the standing loan arrangements called the General Arrangements to Borrow. The Fund makes these resources available to members in order to give them temporary assistance while they cope with present or threatened balance of payments difficulties. In the course of its regulatory activities, the Fund adopts general policy decisions on the way it would like members to behave under the code of obligations. The Fund takes decisions applying these general policies to individual members and other decisions that deal with the special problems of particular members or groups of members. In performing its regulatory task, the Fund decides whether to give ap-

---

* The views expressed in this contribution to the Conference are not necessarily those of the Fund.

proval to or withhold it from the various actions that members can take consistently with the Articles only if they get that approval. As part of its financial activities, the Fund again adopts general policy decisions on the ways in which it will make its resources available and other decisions under which these policies are applied in financial operations with individual members. Both the Board of Governors, the senior organ of the Fund, and the Executive Directors, the executive organ in continuous session, have rule-making authority for the purpose of conducting the business of the Fund, and also the power to interpret the Fund's Articles authoritatively. It must be said again that these decisions are a sampling, and they by no means exhaust the categories that could be devised by a patient dissection of the business of the Fund.

There is considerable diversity in the form of decisions. They may take the form of general statements of Fund policy for the guidance of members and contain recommendations or suggestions on the actions or measures that will carry out the policy. Decisions with respect to the policies of individual members may be in language that urges a particular course of action, expresses the hope that the member will act or continue to act in a certain way, welcomes a particular policy or measure, or suggests consideration of certain policies or programs. Decisions on requests for approval of certain practices that are temporary departures from the code of obligations usually grant express approval for a limited time only. The denial of approval is usually indicated by silence, that is to say, by the fact of withholding approval, and not by a decision explicitly refusing approval. Decisions on requests for financial operations are usually formulated in terms of accepting the request but in some cases will be in terms of no objection because of certain legal niceties based on the Articles. Most decisions expressly state that they are decisions, but sometimes they may not be identified in this way. For example, certain decisions, even of major legal or economic importance, have been embedded in a sentence or two of an Annual Report, or some other report, of the Executive Directors to the Board of Governors.

1. *The choice of techniques to carry out an agreed course of action*

(i) *Sanctions and decisions that may be considered censorious*

One approach to the question of the effectiveness of the decisions of an international organization is from the standpoint of the sanctions that the organization can impose. The character of the sanctions and the willingness of the organization to employ them are relevant to this approach and in particular to the assessment of the deterrent effect of the sanctions. This justifies some statement of the main formal sanctions available to the Fund as well as those other formal actions that it can take for which the word "sanctions" is not wholly appropriate. These other actions do not seek to punish a malefactor but are intended to achieve certain other purposes, such as the protection of the Fund's resources. The use of the word "formal" should be noted. The fact that both the sanctions and the other actions are formal, in the sense that they are referred to in the Articles and (except for paragraph 8 below) require a decision of the Fund, justifies their consolidation in a single list, because members tend to regard decisions singling them out in these ways as adverse judgments passed upon them.

1. The Fund has the right to communicate its views to any member on any matter arising under the Articles, but it may also decide to publish a report regarding the member's monetary and economic conditions and developments which tend directly to produce a serious disequilibrium in the balance of payments of members (Article XII, Section 8). The Fund has published no report of this kind.

2. In exceptional circumstances, the Fund may make representations to a member retaining exchange restrictions under the "transitional arrangements" of the Articles that conditions are favorable for the withdrawal of some or the abandonment of all restrictions (Article XIV, Section 4). The Fund has made no formal representations under this provision.

3. If the Fund finds that the demand for a member's currency seriously threatens the ability of the Fund to supply that currency, the Fund may formally declare that currency to be scarce, whereupon other members, after consulting the Fund, may impose limitations on the freedom of exchange operations in the scarce currency (Article VII, Section 3). In the negotiation of the Articles, this possibility of discrimination by other members was considered the main sanction against a member in persistent surplus, but the Fund has made no declaration of scarcity.

4. The Articles establish the circumstances in which a member may maintain or impose exchange restrictions consistently with the Articles. One consequence which flows from the maintenance or imposition of exchange controls that are not consistent with the Articles is that the courts of other members will not be bound by the duty to treat as unenforceable exchange contracts that are contrary to those controls (Article VIII, Section 2 (b)). It is possible that there may be other effects under the domestic law of members of measures that are not consistent with the Articles. Exchange rates are an obvious example, but so far there is little jurisprudence on the extent to which courts will refuse to apply rates that are invalid under the Articles. One case which considers the problem, *Adriática Venezolana de Seguros S. A. v. The First National City Bank of New York,* decided by a Venezuelan court, is discussed in Joseph Gold, *"The Fund Agreement in the Courts—IX"* in the July 1967 issue of IMF *Staff Papers* (Vol. XIV, pp. 369-400, at pp. 369-377).

5. If a member requests an exchange transaction, the Fund may challenge the correctness of any aspect of the representation that the member

must make in its request, including consistency of the request with the Articles, and the Fund may postpone or reject the request or accept it subject to conditions (Article V, Section 3 (a)) and *Selected Decisions of the Executive Directors and Selected Documents,* 3rd issue, 1965, p. 19). The challenge relates only to the request that has been made and does not amount to ineligibility (see paragraph 6 below), so that the Fund would have to consider other requests if the member submitted them. The Fund has not formally challenged any request.

6. The Fund may declare that a member is ineligible to use the Fund's resources if:

(a) the Fund finds that a member persists in maintaining restrictions that have been the subject of the representations referred to in paragraph 2 above (Article XIV, Section 4); or

(b) a member fails to comply with a request by the Fund to apply appropriate controls to prevent use of the Fund's resources to meet a large or sustained outflow of capital (Article VI, Section 1); or

(c) the Fund is of the opinion that a member is using the Fund's resources in a manner contrary to the purposes of the Fund (Article V, Section 5); or

(d) a member fails to fulfill any of its obligations under the Articles (Article XV, Section 2 (a)).

The Fund has made only one declaration of ineligibility, under (d) above, and has initiated the procedure leading to ineligibility in only one other case.

7. In any circumstances in which the Fund can declare a member ineligible to use the Fund's resources, the Fund may refrain from making the declaration and may indicate the circumstances in which or the extent to which the member may use the resources (Article V, Section 5 and Rule K-2 of the Rules and Regulations). The Fund has adopted no decision limiting the use of its resources under this power.

8. In one situation, a member can become ineligible automatically, that is to say without the need for any declaration of ineligibility by the Fund. This is the case in which a member makes an unauthorized change in the par value of its currency. Ineligibility follows unless the Fund adopts a decision to the contrary (Article IV, Section 6). One member became ineligible on one occasion under this provision.

9. Members using the Fund's resources pay periodic charges that increase in proportion to both the amount in terms of quota and the duration of use. If a member makes an unduly prolonged use, the Fund has the power to impose penalty rates of charge (Article V, Section 8 (d) and Rule I-4 (g) of the Rules and Regulations). There have been two cases in which a penalty rate was charged.

10. The ultimate sanction is, of course, compulsory withdrawal from the Fund. If, after the expiration of a reasonable period, a member persists in its failure to fulfill any obligation under the Articles, or a difference of

74

opinion continues with respect to an unauthorized change of par value, the Fund may require the member to withdraw from the Fund (Article XV, Section 2(b)). There has been one case of compulsory withdrawal, following the declaration of ineligibility referred to in paragraph 6 above.

The Fund possesses, therefore, a considerable number and variety of powers, including powers that provide for the publication of reports, representations, the challenge of requests to use the Fund's resources, penalty rates of charge, the limitation of use, ineligibility, and compulsory withdrawal. It may seem remarkable that the Fund has shown itself so reluctant to exercise these powers as a technique for deterring non-compliance with the obligations of the Articles or the decisions taken under them.

In those cases in which a decision is necessary for the application of a sanction, which is true for most of the sanctions, the decisions are taken by the Executive Directors, or by the Board of Governors under reserved powers. It became apparent at an early date that a decision to impose almost any sanction on a member or to take any action that it might regard as critical was thought to subject it to public stigma. The Fund has been hesitant even about such a decision as formal representations to remove restrictions, which might seem quite mild to some observers. In part, the explanation is that the Fund hesitates to embark on a course that could lead to the more obviously censorious action of ineligibility. But another reason, to which great weight is attached in Fund thinking, is that formal action would reduce the scope for informal persuasion. Sovereign states do not enjoy being singled out for disciplinary action and they may react fractiously against it. Ineligibility in its turn has been avoided because it has the appearance of being a station on the road to compulsory withdrawal. When it comes to that sanction, many believe that there is little logic in expelling a member from the Fund for failure to fulfill one obligation and freeing it thereby from all obligations. The Fund would certainly be less ready to consider the procedures leading to compulsory withdrawal if the member violating an obligation, even an important one, were to remain in close contact with the Fund and amenable to such arts of persuasion as the Fund could deploy.

It has been seen that almost all of the sanctions are discretionary. Without any formal decision, but as the result of a tacit practice for which even the word understanding might be too strong, the Fund has elected to encourage compliance by means others than sanctions. One characteristic of these other means has been informality. Often, the views communicated to a member will be those of the Managing Director and staff whose comprehension of the policies of the Executive Directors enable them to feel that they can communicate views based on those policies without the necessity for specific instructions. If, however, the member's non-compliance involves a breach of obligation, the Managing Director, who is the chief of the operating staff and who conducts the ordinary business of the Fund under the direction of the Executive Directors, must bring the case to their notice. "The Managing Director shall report to the Executive Board any case in which it appears to him that a member is not fulfilling obligations under the Fund Agreement" (Rule K-1 of the Rules and Regulations). Moreover, regulations have been adopted under which a member may complain to the Executive Directors that another member is not complying with its obligations, and the Executive Directors must make arrangements for prompt consultation with the members directly involved (Rules H-2 and H-3 of the Rules and Regulations).

A second characteristic of the means that have been worked out for ensuring compliance is that when views are communicated under the express authority of the Executive Directors, those views are adopted by the Executive Directors under powers not directly related to the sanctions and other actions referred to above. Thus, there is greater play for persuasion than would be possible if negotiations were conducted under the express or implied threat of sanctions or what might be regarded as sanctions. A third characteristic is reliance on techniques that protect the Fund's resources without publicity in most cases if a member's use of the resources must be interrupted while informal consultations are conducted to bring the member's policies into conformity with its obligations and the decisions of the Fund. All of this leads to a discussion of the Fund's financial operations.

(ii) *Financial operations*

Section I of the Agenda refers to the techniques that are available for ensuring that a member of an international organization observes the general policies of the organization or any particular undertakings that the member may have assumed in its relations with the organization. The international financial organizations are in a special position as the administrators of huge resources, although this does not mean that they have developed the same techniques. Certainly, those that have evolved in the Fund are unique in many ways.

Article I of the Fund's charter sets out, in general language, the purposes of the Fund. The following are included among them:

(ii) To facilitate the expansion and balanced growth of international trade, and to contribute thereby to the promotion and maintenance of high levels of employment and real income and to the development of the productive resources of all members as primary objectives of economic policy.

(iii) To promote exchange stability, to maintain orderly exchange arrangements among members, and to avoid competitive exchange depreciation.

(iv) To assist in the establishment of a multilateral system of payments in respect of current transactions between members and in the elimination of foreign exchange restrictions which hamper the growth of world trade.

The last sentence of Article I declares that the Fund shall be guided in all its decisions by the purposes set forth in that provision.

In various other Articles, the purposes of Article I have been extrapolated into a code of obligations binding on members. For example, a member must establish a par value for its currency in agreement with the Fund and see that exchange transactions in its territory involving its own and another member currency are within certain margins around this par value. Other examples are the obligations to avoid such harmful practices as multiple rates of exchange, restrictions on payments and transfers for current international transactions, and discriminatory currency arrangements. These, though important components of the code of obligations, are only a small proportion of those that make up the full code.

It is doubtful that a viable international monetary system could have been created simply by enacting the purposes of the Fund and the obligations of members that flow from those purposes. It was necessary, in addition, to help members to pursue international and domestic economic policies that would make it possible for members to observe their obligations. Therefore, the Fund was provided with considerable financial resources, as well as the means to expand them; and another of the purposes stated in Article I is:

(v) To give confidence to members by making the Fund's resources available to them under adequate safeguards, thus providing them with opportunity to correct maladjustments in their balance of payments without resorting to measures destructive of national or international prosperity.

The legal relationship between the availability of the Fund's resources to a member and the member's observance of its obligations is obvious on the face of the Articles. The practical management of this relationship has been a dominant concern of the Fund throughout its history. A member can supplement the monetary reserves with which it defends the stability of its currency by purchasing foreign exchange from the Fund in return for its own currency, but when it does this it also buys a limited amount of time in which to introduce or persevere with policies that will enable it to correct or avoid a maladjustment in its balance of payments without resorting to measures that would harm itself or fellow members. If this effort succeeds, the member's position and its monetary reserves will improve, or not deteriorate, and it will then be able not only to avoid retrogression in the observance of its obligations but also to reverse the financial transaction with the Fund. The management of the relationship between the Fund's resources and the code of obligations has required the Fund to determine the policies that it wishes members to pursue. In the main, these are not spelled out in the Articles but are derived by implication from the Articles in relation to national and international economic conditions as these develop and change. For example, if inflation is permitted, it becomes practically impossible for members to perform their obligations with respect to exchange stability, and therefore the Fund has made great efforts to induce members to control inflation even though there is no direct mention in the Articles of a duty to maintain internal financial stability. In addition, the process of managing the relationship between obligations and resources has given impetus to the invention and adaptation of financial practices that enable the Fund to make its resources available with maximum effectiveness.

Two features of these financial practices that must be mentioned for the purpose of these notes are the Fund's tranche policies and its stand-by arrangements. Both came into existence largely as the result of an accident of history. In the postwar economic conditions of the early years of the Fund it was thought that most members would be unable to pursue policies that would permit them to make that short-term use of the Fund's resources which the Articles require. Moreover, some countries were receiving adequate balance of payments assistance under the European Recovery Program. By the time that these conditions had disappeared, many members had ceased to think in terms of a possible use of the Fund's resources when framing the policies that they intended to follow. The Fund sought to change this attitude by a series of actions designed to encourage members to have confidence that its resources were really available and that members could take this into account in determining their economic policies. The Fund's tranche policies were evolved so as to give them this confidence by establishing, in a general way, the criteria for use of the Fund's resources in various successive and cumulative amounts (tranches) in terms of a member's quota. Under these policies, a member could have the assurance of virtually automatic access to a specified initial amount ("gold tranche"). For the next tranche ("first credit tranche"), the Fund's attitude would be a liberal one in examining the member's policies. For succeeding tranches, the Fund would adopt more rigorous standards and require greater conviction that the member's policies would enable it to observe the obligations of the Articles. Over the years, the Fund has tried to give more and more precision to the standards that it applies in each of the tranches beyond the gold tranche. But in a world of change and diversity there are limits on the extent to which a procrustean system is possible or desirable, and this explains the other financial practice about which something must be said.

The basic financial operation expressly provided for in the Articles is the purchase from the Fund by member A of the currency of member B in return for an equivalent amount of the currency of member A. This is an immediate purchase and sale. In order to enable members to plan ahead and in order to allay any apprehensions that a request to purchase exchange at a future date might be refused, the Fund established the technique of the "stand-by arrangement". This imaginative technique was not inspired by any express mention in the Articles. One of its basic features is an assurance to the member to which the stand-by arrangement is granted that the member will be able to purchase exchange from the Fund within a prescribed period, which hitherto has not exceeded twelve months. Indeed, the original concept of the stand-by arrangement placed most of the emphasis on the analogy of a confirmed line of credit.

78

Over time, the emphasis has moved greatly towards the conditional aspects of the stand-by arrangement as it became increasingly clear that it was a supple and versatile instrument for assisting members to observe the Fund's tranche policies in all of the many varieties of balance of payments problems that may overtake members.

Present practice with respect to stand-by arrangements involves the presentation to the Fund by a member, often after negotiations with the Managing Director and with a Fund staff mission, of a "letter of intent" in which the member's monetary authorities (usually its Minister of Finance and Governor of the Central Bank) describe the policies they intend to follow during the period of the stand-by arrangement. The choice and definition of policies will depend, of course, on the kind of balance of payments problem that the member is facing but they will also depend on the particular tranche that the stand-by arrangement provides for. The policies may be described in general terms or they may be defined with the utmost statistical precision. The decision to grant the stand-by arrangement is taken by the Executive Directors after a debate in which they discuss the letter of intent, the mission's report, and the Managing Director's recommendation. The Fund never publishes these stand-by arrangements because of the confidential character of its relationship with members. It is left to the member to decide what publicity it wishes to give to the content of a stand-by arrangement granted to it.

Continued access to the Fund's resources under a stand-by arrangement is made conditional on the member's observance of certain specified policies ("performance criteria"). These invariably have an objective character so that observance of them is readily ascertainable by the member. In this way, the member should know at all times whether it can exercise its privileges under the stand-by arrangement without the fear of challenge by the Fund on the basis of performance criteria for reasons that are not objective in character because they depend on evaluations about which opinions might differ. It has already been said that it is often important for members to know what resources are available to them. The technique of objective performance criteria protects a member against the surprise, and also the international embarrassment, of a challenge or even rejection of its request by the Executive Directors for any reason that was not defined with precision in advance.

It is impossible to exaggerate the importance of the role of performance criteria in stand-by arrangements. They protect the Fund as well as members. It has been explained that the Fund has been reluctant to use its formal powers to challenge requests to use the Fund's resources or to declare a member ineligible. The incorporation of performance criteria in stand-by arrangements is the practical substitute for these formal protections and sanctions. They are not only more private in their operation, but they also involve little or none of the stigma that is thought to attach to a member as a result of the employment of the formal procedures. Thus, although stand-by arrangements provide that a member's ability to purchase exchange under the stand-by arrangement may be suspended by the application of the formal procedures of the Articles as well as by the operation of performance criteria, the Fund has not resorted to the former on any occasion so far.

Procedures are established under which the member supplies the data that show it is observing the performance criteria that have been established in the stand-by arrangement. If one of them is not being observed, the member will have to consult with the Fund before any further purchase can be made. These consultations will examine the effectiveness of the member's policies to achieve the objectives of its program and the reasons why it has not observed the performance criteria. A revision of policies may be the outcome of these consultations. The revision will then be transmitted to the Fund in the form of a supplementary letter, and the Executive Directors will be asked to approve the attachment of this letter to the stand-by arrangement in modification of the earlier letter of intent.

If performance criteria are being observed, it is likely that the member's economic program is making good progress; if they are not being observed, this is an indication that the program should be discussed with the Fund. However, there may be other policies that are important for the success of the program but that cannot be formulated in objective terms. In addition, there may be policies that are less vital for the success of the member's program but are nevertheless useful contributions to its effectiveness. Then again, policies of whatever character may be fully observed but may turn out to be inadequate because of changing circumstances. Considerations such as these have induced the Fund to develop and adapt other "protective clauses" that seek a fair balance between assurance to members that they can use the Fund's resources and assurance to the Fund that any use will be consistent with the Articles. These clauses do not automatically suspend a member's privileges under its stand-by arrangement but they normally call for consultation with the Fund. Members usually refrain from making further purchases, even though there is no legal obligation to show such restraint, until the outcome of the consultation is known. If the consultation were not successful, the Fund would have to face the question whether to take action in accordance with the formal procedures of the Articles in order to protect its resources.

The stand-by arrangement as a financial instrument has succeeded to the extent that most of the exchange transactions of the Fund are now conducted under them, and this success can be attributed in large part to the fact that the stand-by arrangement is a balanced technique for encouraging members to observe appropriate policies with the support of the Fund's resources. It must not be thought that in the evolution of the stand-by arrangement the Fund has been its only advocate and that the Fund has had to face the opposition or passivity of members. The stand-by arrangement could not have developed as it has without the support of the Fund's membership. It would be naive to suggest that there are never problems in arriving at a program that is both acceptable to the member and considered by the Fund to be compatible with the Articles and tranche policies, but this does not mean that the stand-by arrangement as a technique is contested as too rigorous. On the contrary, members sometimes request a stand-by arrangement when there is no strong prospect of economic difficulties, and stand-by arrangements sometimes follow each other at annual intervals over a period of years.

A brief excursus on the subject of period may be useful at this point. The period for which any single stand-by arrangement is granted has never exceeded one year. Even this was evolved by the Fund with some trepidation in former years from an earlier maximum period of six months. The relatively short-term character of stand-by arrangements is explained by the difficulty of foreseeing developments in relation to the balance of payments, and basing precise policies on forecasts, for more than a brief period ahead. By limiting the period of stand-by arrangements, the Fund and its members can review programs, and ascertain that they remain realistic, at yearly intervals even when a stabilization effort requires several years for its success and is supported by successive stand-by arrangements. Even within the year of any one stand-by arrangement, it may be provided that there shall be consultations at stated periods. An obvious example of the need for this is the case in which the member introduces a new budget during the life of the stand-by arrangement.

What are the reasons why members support the technique of the stand-by arrangement and do not regard it as an unacceptable form of international surveillance? Sometimes, the government or the monetary authorities may want to make it known domestically that the policies they have chosen to follow have the backing of the Fund, although in some instances this may call for delicacy in presenting the role of the Fund. In these and other cases, the member may want a stand-by arrangement for a different reason. The stand-by arrangement has now become the leading international certificate of the soundness of the member's balance of payments policies. The cogency of this testimony should be assessed, of course, in relation to the tranches that are covered by the stand-by arrangement. It has been said above that for a smaller cumulative use of the Fund's resources in terms of quota, the Fund's criteria are less severe. Other potential lenders, whether international, governmental, or private, often refrain from lending to a country until it has been granted a stand-by arrangement by the Fund, and they will urge a member to enter into negotiations for this purpose. It is now quite clear that most countries will more readily discuss their policies and reach understandings on them with an international organization such as the Fund than with other countries. This is true even though other lenders may be able to offer larger amounts of financial assistance than the Fund itself. There are many cases in which the financing made available to a country by other lenders because the Fund is willing to grant a stand-by arrangement far exceeds the amount of the stand-by arrangement. Sometimes, it may be necessary for the Fund to know that the member will be able to recruit these additional resources because the success of the member's program will depend on larger resources than the Fund can supply. Moreover, it is understood that lenders often incorporate provisions in their loan agreements under which the obligation to make advances is contingent on the continued ability of the member to make purchases of exchange from the Fund under the stand-by arrangement. The Fund holds the view that each lender must decide for itself the terms on which it is willing to lend.

The effectiveness of the stand-by arrangement has led to the application of some of its features to the immediate sales of exchange that are referred to in the Articles. Obviously, a technique under which a member's ability to purchase further amounts of exchange depends on the observance of performance criteria cannot be fully adapted to a spot transaction. One important feature that is now common to both types of operation is the transmission to the Fund of a letter of intent signed by the member's authorities outlining current and future policies, even though an immediate sale cannot be made contingent on the observance of future policies.

Finally, it is germane to the question of technique to dwell on the legal character of the stand-by arrangement. This is not the same issue as the question of legal authority to impose conditions on the use of the Fund's resources. The attitude of the Fund to the legal classification of the stand-by arrangement has been influenced by the desire to avoid any obfuscation of the fact that the program as stated in the letter of intent is the member's own program, and, in addition, by the desire to avoid the predicament of having to look upon the member as violating international obligations if, for whatever reasons, performance is not in accordance with stated policies. The Fund may not wish the member to have continued access to the Fund's resources if those policies are not observed, but for this purpose it is not necessary or desirable to treat the member as if it were violating international obligations. Accordingly, the Fund has not classified stand-by arrangements as international agreements. The language, form, and other incidents avoid treaty connotations. Neither the Fund nor a member has ever registered a stand-by arrangement with the United Nations under Article 102 of the Charter. This is not because of the short term character of each stand-by arrangement but mainly because of the considerations that have been mentioned. None of this means that a stand-by arrangement is devoid of legal character. Obviously, the grant of a stand-by arrangement is an action by the Fund in which the Fund makes it clear that in certain circumstances the use of its resources will or will not be in accordance with the Articles. It is an action which produces legal consequences in making the resources available or in withholding them. The Fund has the legal authority to produce these consequences without entering into treaties or agreements, and no amount of theoretical speculation should obscure the fact that the practice of the Fund has been to avoid these classical pigeonholes for its stand-by arrangements.

2. *Legal effects of member states' approval of decisions*

This section of the Agenda poses a number of questions related to the legal effect and practical significance of a state's vote for a decision through its representative in an international organization.

The powers of the Fund are vested in a Board of Governors consisting of one governor and one alternate appointed by each member (Article XII, Section 2 (a)). All but certain reserved powers may be, and have been, delegated to the Executive Directors, who function in continuous session at the headquarters of the Fund and meet as often as the business of the Fund requires (Article XII, Section 2 (b) and Section 3 (g), and Section 15 of the By-Laws). At the present time, there are twenty executive directors, of whom five are appointed by the five members having the largest quotas (United States, United Kingdom, Germany, France, and India), three are elected by the American Republics, and twelve are elected by the other 82 members (Article XII, Section 3 (b), (c), (d) and Schedule C).

In the Board of Governors, each governor casts the number of votes allotted to the member appointing him (Article XII, Section 2 (e)). Each member has a uniform number of non-quota votes as well as votes proportional to quota (Article XII, Section 5(a)). For two categories of decisions, voting power is not only weighted in this way but is also adjusted for the Fund's net sales of a member's currency and the net purchases by the member of other currencies (Article XII, Section 5 (b)). In short, a member can gain votes if the Fund has given net assistance to other members with the member's currency, and the member can lose votes if it is a net recipient of assistance from the Fund. In the Executive Directors, each executive director casts as a unit the number of votes allotted to the members appointing or electing him (Article XII, Section 3 (i)). The only choices open to an Executive Director are to cast all of his votes as a unit or to abstain from voting, but in either event nothing prevents him from placing on record the reactions of each of the members that elected him even though, when voting, he cannot divide his votes in accordance with those reactions.

When the Executive Directors take a decision, it is their decision as an organ of the international person called the International Monetary Fund; it is a decision of the Fund and not of individual members or even of the collectivity of members. Therefore, if an executive director votes for a decision, the Fund does not hold that the member appointing him or the members electing him are bound because of his action, nor does the Fund hold that they are not bound if he abstains or votes against the decision. Moreover, there are circumstances, although exceptional, in which no executive director casts the number of votes allotted to a particular member. This does not enable that member to say that a decision of the Executive Directors does not apply to it or does not bind it. A member is bound by a decision taken with respect to it and all members are bound by general decisions because the Executive Directors as an organ of the Fund take the decision in accordance with the appropriate procedures and the statutory voting majority, and not because of the way in which votes are cast or not cast by individual executive directors.

The status of executive directors under Fund law is constituted by the specific rights, duties, and privileges that are to be found in the Fund's body of law, and they add up to a status which is *sui generis*. In particular, the word "representative" is scrupulously avoided in the Articles, although it appeared in some earlier drafts. There is a feeling that the duty to cast votes as a unit gives executive directors, although not international civil servants, a status as officials of the institution that they would not have if they could divide their votes.

The Articles prescribe that, in the discharge of their functions, the Managing Director and the staff shall owe their duty entirely to the Fund and to no other authority. There is no similar requirement with respect to executive directors. This enables an executive director to maintain the kind of relations with the members appointing or electing him that he sees fit. In debates, executive directors frequently make it clear that they are expressing their personal views or the views of the member appointing them or any of the members electing them. However, the legal situation will not be changed even if the executive director purports to express the views of a member. That is to say, the member will be bound because, and only because, of the decision of the organ. If the decision creates an option for a member to act or not to act, it will not be bound to act because the executive director appointed or elected by the member voted for the decision and expressed the member's views in favor of it. This can be illustrated most clearly in connection with the adjustment of a member's quota. The Executive Directors recommend a form of resolution to the Board of Governors for this purpose, and decide to make the recommendation by a majority of votes cast. The Board of Governors adopts the resolution by a special majority of the total voting power. However, the adjustment cannot take effect without the consent of the member whose quota is to be adjusted (Article III, Section 2). The fact that the executive director appointed or elected by the member and the governor appointed by the member both voted in favor of the recommendation and resolution will in no circumstances bind the member to give its consent.

It has been said that the relations between an executive director and the members appointing or electing him are not prescribed by the Articles but are left to individual arrangement. It must be assumed that these arrangements vary considerably in view of the fact that executive directors may cast the votes allotted to a single member, as the result of either appointment or election, whereas other executive directors may be elected by a very large group of members. At the moment, one executive director casts the votes allotted to as many as fifteen members, but this is not a legal limit and even this number could be increased as the result of an election.

I am aware of very few cases in which a member's legislation prescribes procedures for determining the way in which the governor or executive director appointed by the member is to vote. One such case is Section 4 of the United States Bretton Woods Agreements Act (59 Stat. 512 (1945), *Selected Decisions,* pp. 146 *et seq.)* which provides, *inter alia,* for the establishment of the National Advisory Council on International Monetary and Financial Problems, and declares that the Council, after consultation with the "representatives" of the United States in the Fund, shall recommend to the President of the United States general policy directives for the guidance of those representatives. There are other detailed provisions governing the relations of the governor, executive director, and their alternates with the Council.

Another feature of the decision-making process of the Fund that deserves a brief mention is the right of a member not entitled to appoint an executive director to send a representative to attend any meeting of the Executive Directors "when a request made by, or a matter particularly affecting, that member is under consideration" (Article XII, Section 3 (j)). The Board of Governors has adopted regulations under which a member can exercise or waive this right (Section 19 of the By-Laws). In practice, the right is exercised only occasionally.

Finally, it must be said that voting is extremely rare in the practice of the Fund, notwithstanding the elaborate provisions of the Articles on voting, special safeguards, and vetoes. A regulation adopted in September 1946 declares that "The Chairman will ordinarily ascertain the sense of the meeting in lieu of a formal vote..." (Rule C-10 of the Rules and Regulations). In accordance with the spirit of this regulation, maximum efforts are made to avoid voting and to reach a consensus on any important decision of the Fund. Even when the decision is of less importance, voting is avoided, and an executive director who feels that he cannot concur in the decision merely records his abstention, but even these occasions are rare. The adoption of decisions by this process of general collaboration, involving as it does a reasonable give and take among all executive directors whatever their voting strength, is an important factor in the high degree of compliance by members with Fund decisions.

3. *Internal legal effects of decisions of international organizations*

The Fund is one of the few international organizations that has a power to interpret its own Articles authoritatively. Article XVIII provides as follows:

(a) Any question of interpretation of the provisions of this Agreement arising between any member and the Fund or between any members of the Fund shall be submitted to the Executive Directors for their decision. If the question particularly affects any member not entitled to appoint an executive director it shall be entitled to representation in accordance with Article XII, Section 3(j).

(b) In any case where the Executive Directors have given a decision under (a) above, any member may require that the question be referred to the Board of Governors, whose decision shall be final. Pending the result of the reference to the Board the Fund may, so far as it deems necessary, act on the basis of the decision of the Executive Directors.

(c) Whenever a disagreement arises between the Fund and a member which has withdrawn, or between the Fund and any member during liquidation of the Fund, such disagreement shall be submitted to arbitration by a tribunal of three arbitrators, one appointed by the Fund, another by the member or withdrawing member and an umpire who, unless the parties otherwise agree, shall be appointed by the President of the Permanent Court of International Justice or such other authority as may have been prescribed by regulation adopted by the Fund. The umpire shall have full power to settle all questions of procedure in any case where the parties are in disagreement with respect thereto.

The Fund has adopted no more than ten interpretations under this provision so far, and has been content to take the rest of its very numerous interpretative decisions without resorting to the provision. Of course, the existence of the provision has made it possible for the Fund to adopt interpretations in this informal way. The interpretations adopted under Article XVIII have been taken in that way because it was desirable for some special reason to give them maximum solemnity. In view of the subsequent discussion of the binding effect of interpretations on tribunals, it should be noted that one reason has been the desire to ensure that courts in member countries would regard the Fund's interpretation of Article VIII, Section 2 (b) as authoritative (see Appendix A). There was evidence of widespread neglect of the impact of this provision on private international law even though it was likely to be relevant to much litigation between private parties in the courts of many members.

In discussing the binding effect of Article XVIII interpretations a distinction can be made between the executive, including the monetary authorities, and the courts of a member. When a member signs the Articles, it must deposit an instrument setting forth that the member "has accepted this Agreement in accordance with its law and has taken all steps necessary to enable it to carry out all of its obligations under this Agreement" (Article XX, Section 2 (a)). There is another provision with respect to privileges and immunities, which seems to have been adopted as a further precaution because of the prospect that privileges and immunities may give rise to special problems of compliance. This provision declares that:

Each member shall take such action as is necessary in its own territories for the purpose of making effective in terms of its own law the principles set forth in this Article and shall inform the Fund of the detailed action which it has taken. (Article IX, Section 10)

Nothing has arisen in the practice of the Fund to suggest that any member will argue that the "obligations" of its executive mentioned in Article XX, Section 2 (a) are not the obligations as interpreted under Article XVIII if they have been the subject of interpretation under that provision. The binding effect of these interpretations on a regulatory agency of the United States, the Federal Communications Commission, was established in a proceeding before that agency, *International Bank for Reconstruction and Development and International Monetary Fund v. All America Cables and Radio, Inc., the Commercial Cable Company, Mackay Radio and Telegraph Company, Inc., R.C.A. Communications, Inc., The Western Union Telegraph Company* (F.C.C. Docket No. 9362). The State Department submitted two letters in the course of that proceeding which declared forcibly that the "United States" and "the United States Government" was bound, in the opinion of the Department, to conform to the provisions of the Articles as interpreted. This interesting case is not discussed further here, because as indicated in its title, it involved the International Bank as well as the Fund and is treated more fully in Mr. Nurick's memorandum for the Conference. (See also *The Fund Agreement in the Courts* (Washington, 1962), pp. 20-26, 55-59.)

It is possible, of course, that a member may conclude that it needs additional legislative authority to be able to perform an obligation as interpreted notwithstanding the declaration it made when signing the Articles. If that were to happen, the Fund would undoubtedly hold that the member was required to see that the necessary legislation was adopted. There has been no occasion on which the Fund has needed to make this approach to a member, even in connection with the interpretation of the Fund's privileges on telecommunications that was an issue in the F.C.C. case.

The question of the binding effect of Article XVIII interpretations on the courts has been thought by some commentators to arise when a court is faced with the interpretation of a provision in the Articles which has been the subject of an Article XVIII interpretation but only the provision and not Article XVIII has been given the force of law domestically. Presumably, this problem will not arise in any member country in which the Articles as a whole have been given the force of law. I am not aware of any case in which Article XVIII has been singled out for inclusion among selected provisions that have been given the force of law.

The suggestion that an Article XVIII interpretation may not be binding in the circumstances described by the commentators would seem to be answered by the reflection that the provision which has been given the force of law is a provision of the Articles and therefore should carry with it any interpretation of the provision that is adopted under the Articles. If a court were to reject an Article XVIII interpretation in favor of a different interpretation of its own, this would not carry out the legislative intent to give the force of law to the provision of the Articles. [1] Of course, it is hardly likely that courts in member countries will fail to follow Article XVIII interpretations whatever may be their views on the binding force of those interpretations on them as a matter of strict legal obligation. They are likely to regard those interpretations as having the highest degree of persuasiveness and they are likely to be influenced, in addition, by the desirability of a uniform jurisprudence in the courts of all members. This is perhaps the reason why the English Court of Appeal in *Sharif v. Azad,* (1966) 3 W.L.R. 1285, (1966) 3 All E.R. 785, the first case in which an English court has taken a close look at Article VIII, Section 2 (b), made no mention of the Fund's interpretation of June 10, 1949 of that provision. The court's decision was consistent with the interpretation and perhaps it was thought unnecessary to raise the question of its binding force. This is mere surmise, and it may be wrong in view of the late date at which the provision itself was raised as an issue in the proceedings.

All of the cases in which the courts have referred to an interpretation by the Fund have involved the interpretation of Article VIII, Section 2 (b), and in all of these cases the opinions have been consistent with the binding force of the interpretation. The cases are *Société "Filature et Tissage X. Jourdain" v. Epoux Heynen-Bintner,* [2] *Southwestern Shipping Corporation v. National City Bank of New York,* [3] *Banco do Brasil S.A. v. A.C. Israel Commodity Co., Inc.* [4] and *Theye y Ajuria v. Pan American Life Insurance Co.* [5]

Whatever argument there may be for the view that an interpretation under Article XVIII is not binding on a member's courts must rest on the

---

[1] See, for example, Section 11 of the United States Bretton Woods Agreements Act: "The provisions of article IX, sections 2 to 9, both inclusive, and the first sentence of article VIII, section 2 (b), of the Articles of Agreement of the Fund, and the provisions of article VI, section 5 (i), and article VII, sections 2 to 9, both inclusive, of the Articles of Agreement of the Bank, shall have full force and effect in the United States and its Territories and possessions upon acceptance of membership by the United States in, and the establishment of, the Fund and the Bank, respectively."

United Kingdom S.R.O. 1946 No. 36, Section 3: "To enable the Fund and the Bank to fulfill the functions with which they are respectively entrusted, the provisions of the Fund Agreement and the Bank Agreement set out in the Schedule to this Order shall have the force of law ..."

[2] *Pasicrisie Luxembourgeoise* (1957), pp. 36-39 (*Tribunal d'Arrondissement de Luxembourg (Civil)*.

[3] 173 N.Y.S. 2d. 509 (New York Supreme Court).

[4] (1963) 12 N.Y. 2nd 371; 190 N.E. 2d 235; 239 N.Y.S. 2d 872 (New York Court of Appeals).

[5] (1963) 154 So. 2d 450 (Court of Appeal of Louisiana, Fourth Circuit).

necessity for the member to give the interpretation the force of law under its domestic law and its failure to perform this duty. No comparable necessity could be argued for public international law, and there is no room therefore for any doubt about whether an international tribunal would have to apply Article XVIII interpretations as part of public international law.

Suppose, however, that the issue which an international tribunal has to resolve requires the interpretation of some provision of the Articles. If a domestic court is faced with this problem, it must make its own interpretation when it is applying a provision that has been given the force of law. Obviously, it cannot ignore any part of its own law. In 1948, Lord Justice Evershed (as he then was), in an English case, expressed reluctance to interpret Article VIII, Section 2 (b), which has been given the force of law in England, on the ground that it had not yet been interpreted by the Fund.[6] But when the Court of Appeal in *Sharif v. Azad* was faced with the necessity to interpret certain features of the provision, some of which have not yet been the subject of Article XVIII interpretation, the court had no hesitation in making its own interpretations, and this has been the experience throughout the world wherever the necessity to interpret has arisen. Once again, however, an international tribunal is in a different position. Article XVIII is part of the law which the tribunal must apply, and the provision declares that any question of interpretation of the Articles arising between members or between the Fund and a member "shall be submitted to the Executive Directors". The effect of this language was one of the questions in the *Case Concerning Rights of Nationals of the United States of America in Morocco.*[7] The parties to that case before the International Court of Justice, the United States and France, engaged in a vigorous and detailed debate of the meaning of various provisions of the Articles which they took to be relevant to the issues in the case. The parties readily agreed that questions of interpretation of the Articles must be remitted to the Fund, but disagreed as to the party on which the burden rested to request an interpretation. In effect, the United States argued that the burden was on the party advancing an argument based on the meaning of the Articles which was controverted by the other party. France argued that the burden was on the complainant in the proceedings. The Court found it unnecessary to settle any of the issues involving the Articles, including this one.

---

[6] *Kahler v. Midland Bank, Ltd.* (1948) 1 All E.R. 811, p. 819.
[7] *I.C.J. Reports*, 1952, pp. 176-233.

4. Compliance: Measures to help assure that member states' commitments or obligations are carried out

Consultations

The provision of information by members and consultation between members and the Fund are among the main techniques for ensuring compliance with the obligations and commitments of members. Article VIII, Section 5 deals with the provision of information, but reference to any legal basis for this practice tends to give a false impression of the scope of the information which flows into the Fund and the willingness of members to supply it. Consultations take place under various provisions and on a number of occasions but in the development of Fund practice the consultation under Article XIV has had the greatest influence.

The legal framework in which Article XIV consultations operate is as follows. Article VIII establishes certain obligations for a member which in sum can be described as the duty to maintain the convertibility of its currency. However, it was recognized that some members might have to proceed towards convertibility by easy stages. Therefore, Article XIV, Section 2 provides that members may maintain and adapt certain practices (restrictions on payments and transfers for current international transactions) that are not consistent with the obligations of convertibility. Article XIV is entitled "Transitional Period" and Section 2 speaks of "post-war transitional period." This period is not defined, although Section 4 is sometimes misunderstood as performing this function. Section 4 provides that three years after the Fund begins operations [8] and in each year thereafter, the Fund shall report on the restrictions still in force under Section 2; and five years after the Fund begins operations and in each year thereafter, any member still retaining restrictions inconsistent with the convertibility of its currency as prescribed by Article VIII must consult the Fund as to their further retention. It has already been seen that the Fund may make "representations" to a member that conditions are favorable for the withdrawal of some or the abandonment of all such restrictions.

Although the Fund began operations on March 1, 1947, consultations under Article XIV are still being held with 75 members. The transition is now tacitly understood to be a transition from inconvertibility to convertibility, and "post-war" is understood literally and without limitation of time. This change in the attitude to Article XIV has been deliberate. The Fund faced a choice. Some years after the war, it could have encouraged all members to give up the privileges of Article XIV and undertake to observe the obligations of convertibility, but in that event the Fund would

---

[8] The Fund decided to begin financial operations on March 1, 1947.

have had to exercise its authority to permit derogations from convertibility for the benefit of many members. These members would have found it too burdensome to establish the full convertibility of their currencies under Article VIII, so that the Fund would have had to authorize derogations from the very date of the acceptance of convertibility. Moreover, the uncertain economic condition of other members might have made it necessary for them to introduce or reintroduce derogations fairly soon after they were induced to institute the full convertibility of their currencies. There is no way back to Article XIV from Article VIII, and a member's currency remains "convertible" in the legal sense once the member undertakes convertibility. It follows that if the Fund had adopted the first possible course, convertibility might have become largely a legal fiction. The alternative course for the Fund was to refrain from urging members to give up their status under Article XIV until they could eliminate any measures inconsistent with convertibility without the apparent need to reintroduce them in the foreseeable future. The Fund chose the latter course, and did so in order to give as much substance as it could to the concept of convertibility. It preferred to keep this as free from derogations as it could and thus to defend the reality of convertibility by discouraging widespread departures from the ideal. The issue was resolved in a decision of June 1, 1960[9] taken at a time when it was obvious that many European members were about to undertake the obligations of *de jure* convertibility under the Articles. In accordance with the choice thus made, the Fund declared in that decision that it would not readily approve derogations from those obligations once they were undertaken.

Consultations under Article XIV, therefore, continue to be prominent among the activities of the Fund and continue to take up much of its time. What is the scope of those consultations? It has been seen that the jurisdictional basis for them is the further retention of measures inconsistent with convertibility. The consultation certainly deals with that feature of a member's exchange system, but in some cases there are few measures, or even no measures, that are inconsistent with Article VIII convertibility. In the course of time, however, the scope of the consultation has broadened far beyond the retention of these measures so as to embrace almost all aspects of a member's economic and financial position. Originally, the justification for this survey was that the member's case for the further retention of measures inconsistent with convertibility could be sensibly assessed only in relation to the economic context of which they were part. Now, however, the broad survey is recognized as having a usefulness in itself.

This recognition did not occur overnight, and in earlier years there was much debate of the extent to which the Fund could properly comment on trade matters or on such domestic matters as fiscal and monetary po-

---

[9] *Selected Decisions*, pp. 81-83.

licies. In order to understand why the breadth of the survey is now established, something must be said of the procedural aspects of an Article XIV consultation. Almost invariably a consultation involves discussions in the member's own territory between a group of Fund staff officials and representatives of many ministries and of the central bank. The staff prepares a detailed and often lengthy report consisting of two parts: Part I is a report of the discussions and an analysis and critique of the member's economic position, policies, and prospects, and it includes a decision drafted by the economic and legal staff; Part II is a detailed descriptive and statistical economic survey. The discussions in the field are usually terminated with a summary of the mission's findings which is the forerunner of the draft decision to be included in Part I. The member therefore has an opportunity to react to the findings, although the text as circulated to the Executive Directors is not an agreed text. The report is brought to the agenda of the Executive Directors after an interval which permits it to be considered by all member governments. The Executive Directors discuss the report with the assistance of the mission and other members of the staff and adopt a decision. The report is not amended, except to eliminate any errors of fact, but the decision may involve certain modifications in the staff draft as the result of amendments proposed by the executive director appointed or elected by the member which is the subject of the report or by other executive directors. The decision is not published by the Fund but may be published by the member if it wishes.

There are a number of reasons why a member tends to regard its Article XIV consultation as useful and important. The consultation involves a searching inquiry, which may be the only inquiry of the kind that is conducted with the member, and the only opportunity to provide it with informed and impartial advice. Even when the member has all the expert knowledge and governmental apparatus to make its own economic analyses, the opportunity to discuss them with experienced international officials is valuable. Whatever the country, Fund opinion and advice may help the authorities to persevere with correct but not necessarily popular policies. Sometimes, the consultation may be the prelude to a financial operation with the Fund or the basis for a finding which the Fund communicates to the *Contracting Parties* to GATT under its agreement with them, but even in the absence of these circumstances the tone and content of the decision are taken seriously by the member. In the last analysis, this is because the decision is technical and not political in character, is arrived at by an expert organization after full examination, and reflects the views of its widespread membership.

For members other than the one with which the consultation is conducted, the consultation is useful as a source of information. The report is often more comprehensive and more up to date than any other available report, and it is the result of penetrating discussions that can be conducted by an international organization but not by other countries without the charge of unwarranted intrusion. The value of these reports as a source of information is endorsed by the arrangements made by the Fund at the request of a growing number of regional and other international organizations for the transmission of Part II to them. Another advantage for other members is that the discussion of the report by the Executive Directors and the drafting of the decision concluding the consultation give them the opportunity, through the executive directors appointed or elected by them, to state their views on the member's policies or practices and to voice any complaints about them. There is no reluctance to take advantage of this opportunity, and what is said in the course of debate is reported promptly to the member by the executive director it appoints or elects. The Fund communicates the decision of the Executive Directors at once, and in due course the member sees detailed minutes of the debate.

The Article XIV consultation is useful to the Fund, not only because it is endorsed by the membership at large, but also because it has become one of the main procedures that enable the Fund to determine the extent to which members are complying with their obligations and commitments and with the decisions of the Fund. Often, when it is thought that a member may have acted in disregard of its obligations, or when a member requests the approval of some new exchange practice, the Executive Directors defer action so that the matter can be discussed with the member within the broad context of the next Article XIV consultation.

There is attached to this paper as Appendix B a fictitious decision concluding an Article XIV consultation so as to give some impression of the content of this kind of decision. One paragraph will be devoted to the exercise by the Fund of its jurisdiction with respect to those practices that a member cannot introduce or adapt consistently with its obligations unless it obtains the approval of the Fund. If the decision is silent on these practices, this means that approval is withheld, and they are then inconsistent with the Articles. The Fund may encourage a member to withdraw or abandon certain practices, even though the Fund has approved them at one time or the member is authorized to have them, if the Fund thinks that they no longer serve the interests of the member or of other members. It has been seen, however, that in such cases the Fund will apply a pressure gentler in form than the use of "representations". Other paragraphs will deal with the member's observance of certain policy decisions of the Fund and will comment on the policies that the member is pursuing or should be pursuing. It should be added that Article XIV consultations are not only a procedure for determining compliance with established Fund policies, but are also a procedure by which the Fund can assess the effectiveness of those policies in achieving the purposes of the Fund. Consultations are thus a source from which new Fund policy may emerge. It is not only the member that is enlightened by these consultations.

This brief account of Article XIV consultations will be concluded with one last testimonial to their effectiveness. The Articles do not prescribe any similar consultation with a member that is no longer availing itself of Article XIV arrangements because it has undertaken to perform the obligations of Article VIII. In an earlier paragraph there was some mention of the concerted move to Article VIII by a number of European members in 1960 and to the decision adopted by the Fund as a prelude to that development. The members of the Fund, including those that had already moved to Article VIII and those that were contemplating this action, agreed that consultations with the Fund should not cease because there was no legal obligation to conduct them. The Executive Directors embodied this willingness in their decision of June 1, 1960, which declared that:

"... the Fund is able to provide technical facilities and advice, and to this end, or as a means of exchanging views on monetary and financial developments, there is great merit in periodic discussions between the Fund and its members even though no questions arise involving action under Article VIII. Such discussions would be planned between the Fund and the member, including agreement on place and timing, and would ordinarily take place at intervals of about one year."

In accordance with this decision, annual consultations are held with members that have undertaken to perform the obligations of Article VIII, and these are indistinguishable in all but one respect from those that are conducted under Article XIV. That one respect is interesting because it confirms the moral force of a consultation decision even though no legal consequences may flow directly from it. The distinguishing feature of the Article VIII consultation is that it does not conclude with the adoption of a decision by the Executive Directors. Members are willing to engage in these consultations but not to be subjected to formal judgments as a result of them. Nevertheless, Part I of the staff report contains the normal assessment by the staff, and this is debated by the Executive Directors with no less vigor than under Article XIV. The debates concluding the Article VIII consultations with members whose currencies are important in world trade and payments are among the great occasions of the Fund's activities. Although no formal decision will be communicated to the member, conclusions will be implicit in the debate and these may not lack influence merely because they are not formulated in a decision.

5. *The special problems of federated states*

The section of the Agenda that bears this title deals with the so-called federal problem, but this is not a problem that arises directly in connection with the obligations of members as set forth in the Articles. A federal state has a single currency and the powers over that currency are vested in the federal government. Problems may arise, however, in the formulation of a program for which a member seeks the Fund's financial assistance when the member has limited powers over certain economic activities of its political sub-divisions. The tendency will be to work within the limits of established powers but to encourage their employment to the maximum if this would be useful.

In the case of the Fund, something resembling the federal problem might possibly arise in connection with the obligations of the Articles and as a result of Article XX, Section 2 (g):

"By their signature of this Agreement, all governments accept it both on their own behalf and in respect of all their colonies, overseas territories, all territories under their protection, suzerainty, or authority and all territories in respect of which they exercise a mandate."

The effect of this provision is that a government signing the Articles undertakes that it will perform all of the obligations of the Articles and see to it, in addition, that the obligations will be observed in the territories enumerated in Article XX, Section 2 (g). This provision completes a universal design of the Articles, which apply not only to members but also to their dependent territories and in addition to the relations of members with non-members (Article XI). It must be made clear that dependent territories do not themselves become members by virtue of Article XX, Section 2 (g). The principle followed by the Fund is that membership is open to a political entity only if it conducts all of its foreign relations and if it can be shown that the obligations of the Articles can be performed if it were to join the Fund. One characteristic of the territories listed in Article XX, Section 2 (g) is that they do not conduct all of their foreign relations. But if membership is not available to these territories, this must not be taken to mean that they have no more than footnote importance in the economic order. Their economies can be sizable and their currencies important. One recognition of this is to be found in the provisions of the Articles dealing with the establishment of par values for the separate currencies of these territories and permitting the divergence of these par values from the par value for the metropolitan currency (Article XX, Section 4 (g) and Article IV, Section 9).

The diversity of the territories covered by Article XX, Section 2 (g) suggests the possibility of a compliance problem. Can a government readily ensure that the monetary authorities of all of its dependent territories will observe the obligations and decisions of the Fund? In practice, very little difficulty has been encountered. Even the leading case was resolved with no great complications. This was a case involving observance of the Fund's law and policy on the payment of subsidies to domestic gold producers [10] in a colony of a member. An executive director raised the question whether the payment by the colonial authorities of the subsidy contemplated by proposed legislation, which was later enacted, would be consistent with the Fund's law and policy. The issue which was then posed was the responsibility of the member for its colony in circumstances in which the member had interceded with the colony to seek com-

---

[10] *Selected Decisions*, pp. 14-15.

pliance but in which the colony, as a self-governing territory, seemed to have constitutional authority to pay a subsidy on domestically produced gold.

It was pointed out that the member might have some authority to control the action of the colony in this matter because of a provision in the colonial constitution which declared that there should be no assent to any law the provisions of which appeared to be inconsistent with the treaty obligations of the member unless the views of the member's government were first obtained. However, it was argued that even in the absence of control under such a provision, the member's responsibility under Article XX, Section 2 (g) was not curtailed because of the constitutional arrangements between it and its colony.

The member did not contest this view. Arrangements were made for discussions to be held by the Fund with representatives of both the member and the colony in joint session. As a result of those discussions, it was agreed that the form of subsidy would be changed so as to make it compatible with Fund law and policy, and new legislation was introduced and passed in lieu of the legislation that had already been adopted.

AFTERWORD

This paper was written for presentation at the Conference held in August 1967 and has been scrutinized in May 1970 for publication. In that interval, there have been fundamental developments in the international monetary system and in the Fund. It was necessary to decide, therefore, whether to bring the paper up to date, but if that had been done it would have been full of anachronisms as a document of the Conference. The alternative was to confine revisions to the elimination of those features of the original paper that had become obsolete. I have chosen the second course, but these notes are added as clues to the more contemporary Fund.

The paper did not deal with the sixth item on the agenda because at the date of the Conference there had been no amendments of the Articles. On July 28, 1969 the Articles were amended in order to enable the Fund to call into being, and to allocate to participating members, the new supplement to reserve assets called special drawing rights. The opportunity was taken to introduce a small number of changes in provisions of the Articles that were not related to special drawing rights; some of these changes merely "codified" existing practices. The original operations and transactions of the Fund are conducted through the General Account and those involving special drawing rights through the Special Drawing Account. Of the present 115 members of the Fund, 105 have exercised their option to participate in the Special Drawing Account. The resources of the Fund held in the General Account may increase to the equivalent of almost 29 billion US dollars as a result of the fifth general review of quotas.

The list of sanctions and decisions that might be regarded as censorious is now longer because of the actions that the Fund may take under the provisions that deal with special drawing rights (e.g., Article XXV, Sections 3 and 5 (a) (ii); Article XXIX, Section 2). Under the amended Articles, the assetlike quality of the gold tranche has been enhanced by a provision which declares that the Fund may not challenge a member's representation when it requests a gold tranche purchase (Article V, Section 3 (d)).

One of the "codifying" amendments has been the insertion of the word "temporarily" before "available" in Article I (v). It is still true that the Articles do not refer expressly to the policies that members should pursue but the amended Articles now recognize explicitly that the Fund will have policies on the use of its resources and that requests by members to use the Fund's resources will be examined in relation to those policies (Article V, Section 3 (c) and (d)). It has been noted already that gold tranche purchases which were "virtually automatic" under the Fund's tranche policies have become automatic under the amendments in the sense that a member's representation when requesting a gold tranche purchase cannot be challenged.

The Fund decided on September 20, 1968 that "performance criteria" would apply only to those purchases under a stand-by arrangement that exceeded the first credit tranche. That decision settled many aspects of policy involving the use of the Fund's resources. In addition, it formally established the principle that a stand-by arrangement is not to be regarded as an international agreement between the Fund and the member for which the stand-by arrangement is approved.

On matters pertaining exclusively to special drawing rights, governors or executive directors cast only the number of votes allotted to the members appointing or electing them that are participants in the Special Drawing Account (Article XXVII (a)).

Article XVIII (b) has been amended and now reads as follows:

"In any case where the Executive Directors have given a decision under (a) above, any member may require, within three months from the date of the decision, that the question be referred to the Board of Governors, whose decision shall be final. Any question referred to the Board of Governors shall be considered by a Committee on Interpretation of the Board of Governors. Each Committee member shall have one vote. The Board of Governors shall establish the membership, procedures, and voting majorities of the Committee. A decision of the Committee shall be the decision of the Board of Governors unless the Board by an eighty-five percent majority of the total voting power decides otherwise. Pending the result of the reference to the Board the Fund may, so far as it deems necessary, act on the basis of the decision of the Executive Directors."

Of the 115 members of the Fund, 34 have now notified the Fund that they are prepared to accept the obligations of Article VIII, Sections 2, 3, and 4, and 81 are still availing themselves of the transitional arrangements of Article XIV.

APPENDIX A

Unenforceability of Exchange Contracts: Fund's Interpretation of Article VIII, Section 2(b)

The following letter shall be sent to all members:

The Board of Executive Directors of the International Monetary Fund has interpreted, under Article XVIII of the Articles of Agreement, the first sentence of Article VIII, Section 2(b), which provision reads as follows:

Exchange contracts which involve the currency of any member and which are contrary to the exchange control regulations of that member maintained or imposed consistently with this Agreement shall be unenforceable in the territories of any member.

The meaning and effect of this provision are as follows:

1. Parties entering into exchange contracts involving the currency of any member of the Fund and contrary to exchange control regulations of that member which are maintained or imposed consistently with the Fund Agreement will not receive the assistance of the judicial or administrative authorities of other members in obtaining the performance of such contracts. That is to say, the obligations of such contracts will not be implemented by the judicial or administrative authorities of member countries, for example by decreeing performance of the contracts or by awarding damages for their non-performance.

2. By accepting the Fund Agreement members have undertaken to make the principle mentioned above effectively part of their national law. This applied to all members, whether or not they have availed themselves of the transitional arrangements of Article XIV, Section 2.

An obvious result of the foregoing undertaking is that if a party to an exchange contract of the kind referred to in Article VIII, Section 2(b) seeks to enforce such a contract, the tribunal of the member country before which the proceedings are brought will not, on the ground that they are contrary to the public policy (*ordre public*) of the forum, refuse recognition of the exchange control regulations of the other member which are maintained or imposed consistently with the Fund Agreement. It also follows that such contracts will be treated as unenforceable notwithstanding that under the private international law of the forum, the law under which the foreign exchange control regulations are maintained or imposed is not the law which governs the exchange contract or its performance.

The Fund will be pleased to lend its assistance in connection with any problem which may arise in relation to the foregoing interpretation or any other aspect of Article VIII, Section 2(b). In addition, the Fund is prepared to advise whether particular exchange control regulations are maintained or imposed consistently with the Fund Agreement.

Decision No. 466-4
June 10, 1949

(See *Selected Decisions*, pp. 73-74)

APPENDIX B

Article XIV Decision

1. This decision is taken by the Executive Directors in concluding the 1967 consultation with Patria, pursuant to Article XIV, Section 4 of the Articles of Agreement.

2. Two consecutive good crops have led to a sharp recovery in economic activities. However, government expenditures in the year under review increased at a greater rate than revenue, resulting in a large deficit which was financed mainly by borrowing from the Central Bank. Money supply increased sharply, in part because of government borrowing but also in part because of the relaxation of the credit restraint in the private sector. The balance of payments was in substantial deficit and international reserves continued to fall for the third straight year.

3. The Government has taken steps to reduce the budgetary imbalance and to limit the deficit in the budget for the next fiscal year to an amount which can be financed without inflationary consequences. It has also taken measures to restrict credit and keep the increase in money supply consistent with the increase in gross national product. The Fund welcomes these measures but believes that the goal of sustained economic growth under the present development plan is attainable only if further measures are adopted that would bring about domestic and external balance and enhance efficiency in the use of resources.

4. The Fund welcomes the intention of the Government to work towards the elimination of trade and exchange controls and to relax restrictions, especially those of a discriminatory character, as the balance of payments position improves. In the meantime the Fund urges that the member simplify its exchange system and give consideration to a lessening of reliance on bilateralism, particularly with Fund members.

5. The introduction of the regulation that importers must purchase varying proportions of their exchange requirements for certain imports in the special market gives rise to multiple currency practices. The Fund notes the assurances of the government that this is a temporary measure and does not object, on a temporary basis, to these multiple currency practices.

CERTAIN ASPECTS OF THE LAW AND PRACTICE OF THE INTERNATIONAL BANK FOR RECONSTRUCTION AND DEVELOPMENT

by *Lester Nurick*
Deputy General Counsel*, International Bank for Reconstruction and Development

I. INTRODUCTION

1. This paper discusses certain aspects of the topics on the Agenda to be discussed at the Second Conference on Legal Advisers and International Organizations, August 1967, relating to the law and practice of the International Bank for Reconstruction and Development (commonly known as the World Bank).

2. It should be made clear at the outset that this paper deals primarily with the legal effect of actions and agreements of the World Bank, principally as they are reflected in the Bank's lending agreements, but also in certain other respects as well. The paper is thus somewhat broader in scope than the Agenda. However, since the main area in which the acts of the Bank affect or are affected by local law is in connection with its lending agreements, it was thought useful to include a discussion of those agreements in this paper. The paper will also discuss the one proceeding which has arisen where an interpretation by the Bank of its Articles of Agreement has been given effect in a member country by decision of an administrative body.

3. In order to understand the significance of the World Bank's lending practices and agreements for purposes of this paper, it is first necessary to describe briefly the nature of the Bank and its operations.

Nature of the Bank and its operations

4. The World Bank is an international intergovernmental institution whose primary purpose is to promote the economic development of its members. One hundred and six governments are now members of the Bank. To achieve its objectives, the Bank makes loans to its members or to borrowers other than members with the guarantee of the member concerned.

5. The Bank is set up in corporate form and its members subscribe to shares of its capital stock. The total subscribed capital of the Bank is approximately the equivalent of $ 22.5 billion. However, only a relatively small part of this capital is actually paid to the Bank in a form which can

---

* The views expressed in this paper are personal and do not necessarily represent those of the International Bank for Reconstruction and Development.

be used for lending. The great proportion of the capital (90%) is not paid at all, but is in the nature of a guarantee which can be called on by the Bank if necessary to meet its obligations. One of the main consequences of this capital structure is that in order to operate the Bank must borrow most of the funds it needs from private sources.[1] This in turn means that the Bank must conduct its affairs in a business-like way so that private lenders will have enough confidence in the Bank to lend to it the very large sums of money it needs.

6. To avoid the errors which had characterized much of the international lending of the past, and particularly of the inter-war period, the Articles of Agreement contain certain protective provisions. The Articles provide that loans must be for productive purposes, that, except in special circumstances, they must be for specific projects, that the merits of all projects must be carefully studied and that arrangements must be made to assure that proceeds of each loan are used only for purposes for which the loan was granted. Aside from these rather general provisions, however, the Articles are silent as to the conditions on which the Bank should make its loans, and, in fact, for the most part it is the policy of the Bank, not the requirements of its Articles, which determines these conditions.

7. The World Bank wants to be assured that its loans are made for productive purposes of high priority, that its loans are used only for the purposes of the project and that the projects are carried out efficiently—all to the one basic goal, the economic growth of the Bank's member countries. In seeing to it that these objectives are realized, the Bank has worked out fairly elaborate procedures which have evolved over the years as the Bank has become increasingly familiar with the problems of development.

8. The first major consideration of the Bank is the country itself. Aside from the merits of particular projects themselves, the Bank realizes that projects should be planned with due regard for their place in the economy as a whole. Thus, before making a loan, a careful assessment is made by the Bank to analyze the economic position of the member state and to consider the relationship of individual projects to the member's development needs. These recommendations consider not only the effect of increased amounts of capital on the country, but also the important question of the possibility of improvement in the use of its resources.

9. The Bank has developed a practice of organizing missions of experts to visit individual countries and to draw up comprehensive recommendations that serve as a basis for the working out by countries of a detailed development program. Increasingly, the Bank is engaging in consultations about the fundamental economic policies of its members.

10. The second major consideration is the particular project being financed. It has become evident that in many developing countries if the Bank

---

[1] In this and many other respects the Bank differs from the Fund.

were to finance any considerable number of projects it would have to offer advice about how to prepare them. The Bank, therefore, not only closely examines proposals through studies of documents and visits to the field; as expert it has also developed the practice of suggesting modifications or further study whenever necessary. It thus plays an advisory role of considerable scope and variety, concerned with economics, engineering, administration and other factors bearing on project execution. The Bank discusses with the borrower what kinds of technical services are needed, advises on how best to obtain these services and, if necessary, draws up terms of reference for consultants.

11. The Bank has evolved a set of policies to guide itself in evaluating projects of different kinds. Each of the different kinds of projects the Bank finances (e.g. power, transportation, industrial, agricultural, education) must satisfy standards prescribed by the experts in those fields on the Bank staff in evaluating the soundness of the projects.

12. The culmination of these efforts is of course the making of a loan. But it must be recognized that this step, the signing of the legal documents, is only the final step in a lengthy process of analysis and negotiation. Much of what is done during this lengthy process may ultimately be reflected in changes in local law and administration. But the causal relationship, that is, the relationship between a Bank position taken on a matter and the effect of this on the local law, may not be apparent since basically the process is one of consultation, advice and negotiation, not of fiat. Nevertheless, there still remains a wide area where the making of a loan specifically involves certain consequences in local law and these are examined below in Section III.

13. It should be noted that the activities of the World Bank are supplemented by another international institution which is affiliated with it, the International Development Association (IDA), which makes loans for essentially the same purposes as the Bank, but on much softer terms of repayment.[2] The Bank makes loans to private and public entities but only with the guarantee of a member. IDA, on the other hand, makes loans only to members; if the project is for the benefit of a private or public entity, the member will usually relend the proceeds of the IDA loan to such entity under agreements satisfactory to IDA. As far as the nature of the understandings reached with the recipient of the loan is concerned to carry out and implement the project, the Bank and IDA follow essentially the same policies and consequently the effect of these undertakings on local law is essentially the same. In this paper, references to the IBRD can be taken to include IDA, unless the context otherwise requires.

---

[2] There is still another international institution affiliated with the Bank, the International Finance Corporation (IFC), which deals only with the private sector. This paper does not discuss the IFC.

II. THE CHOICE OF TECHNIQUES TO CARRY OUT
AN AGREED COURSE OF ACTION

14. As has been seen, a substantial part of what may be called the "course of action" agreed between the World Bank and a borrower arises as a result of the evaluation and negotiation process described above. The agreement may be merely the decision of a member (reached in agreement with the Bank) to construct one type of project rather than another or not to proceed with a particular project at all. These "decisions" or agreements are not usually to be found in a formal document as such, but are reflected as a position taken by the Bank and an action taken by the member followed by a loan from the Bank. This type of process is probably one of the most far-reaching of all those in which the Bank is involved.

15. During the next stage in the process, more formal and more obvious techniques are used, including informal understandings, letters of representation and formal agreements.

1. *Informal understandings*

16. As mentioned above, before the Bank decides to extend a loan in a member country, an evaluation will be made by the Bank of the economic policies and performance of the member. It may be that this evaluation will lead the member to decide that certain economic policies which affect development should be changed before a loan would be fruitful. The Bank and the member may then, in consultation, reach an informal understanding as to the nature of the action to be taken. These understandings involve the general economic policies of a government (e.g., the desirability of raising taxes in a case where public savings are too low to justify a Bank investment; the composition of a development plan, taking into account the availability of resources; the desirability of affording agriculture a higher priority in the allocation of resources; the desirability of encouraging certain kinds of imports and exports; the desirability of liquidating unnecessary and wasteful statutory corporations). This type of understanding, while it may result in substantial changes in a member's law, is not reflected in a legal document and must be distinguished from the cases referred to below where legal commitments are entered into.

2. Letters of representation

17. Occasionally a borrowing member may furnish to the Bank a letter of representations in connection with a particular loan that it "intends" to take certain legislative or administrative action which is regarded as desirable for purposes of the loan. This technique of the member's describing an intention rather than furnishing a clear contractual commitment may be used where the member may not be able to give such a commitment or where the Bank may feel it is not necessary for its purposes to obtain one. Nevertheless, this type of representation may well involve the enactment of legislation.

3. Formal agreements

18. The main formal agreements used by the Bank in its lending operations are as follows:

(a) Loan Agreement (between the Bank and the borrower to which the Bank agrees to make the loan);

(b) Guarantee Agreement (between the Bank and the member state, in case the borrower is not a member state, under which the member agrees to guarantee the loan);

(c) Project Agreement (between the Bank and the entity carrying out the project if such entity is not the borrower);

(d) Supplementary letters (exchanged between the parties amplifying, when necessary, the above agreements);

(e) Additional contractual arrangements, when necessary, evidencing specially agreed matters (e.g. security arrangements such as trust deeds, mortgages, take-or-pay contracts);

(f) In addition, in certain cases, there may be a complex of agreements between a government and a private party (e.g., a concession) which the Bank, although not a party to the agreements, will rely on in making a loan.

19. These documents embody, in legal form, the agreements reached between the Bank and other interested parties to a loan. The content of these agreements is the legal reflection of the Bank policies and decisions for a particular type of loan operation. These agreements are the cornerstone of the Bank's legal relationship with its borrowers, as far as lending is concerned, and they are examined in some detail in Section III below.

20. It is evident that as far as its formal documentation is concerned, the Bank follows practices which are similar to those of private financial lenders. This is not to say that the contents of the Bank agreements are the same as those of the private institutions; they are not, since Bank agreements, among other things, contain covenants regarding the execution of projects and standards of performance which are not generally found in

104

private agreements. But the Bank does rely to a large extent in the carrying on of its business on formal contractual arrangements, unlike the Fund which does not.

4. Conditions to be fulfilled for effectiveness of agreements; legal opinions

21. The Bank's loan and guarantee agreements provide that they shall not become effective until evidence satisfactory to the Bank shall have been furnished that the execution and delivery of the agreements on behalf of the borrow and guarantor, if any, have been duly authorized or ratified by all necessary governmental action. They also provide that such evidence shall include a legal opinion satisfactory to the Bank showing that this condition has been satisfied and that the agreements constitute valid and binding obligations of the borrower or guarantor in accordance with their terms. In addition to these standard clauses, the Bank's agreements also often contain additional conditions precedent to effectiveness. While these conditions vary greatly they concern those elements of a project which are considered important to the achievement of the purposes of the agreement. Accordingly, for example, the Bank may wish to be satisfied that under local law funds are available to complete the project, the entity carrying out the project shall have been given adequate powers, and the like.[4] In effect, these provisions mean that before the Bank declares itself bound under the agreements, it wants to be satisfied, among other things, that they can be carried out under the relevant municipal law.

22. This may require a borrowing country to enact new legislation or amend existing legislation permitting the project to be carried out in accordance with the terms of the agreement. One example of this arises occasionally in cases where under local law a member state can only borrow up to specified amounts authorized by law; in such cases it may be necessary to enact special legislation increasing the amount so authorized in order to cover the amount of the loan from the Bank. Another example is where existing local law may not authorize a member state to guarantee loans to private corporations; in such a case such legislation would have to be enacted before the Bank agreements were made effective.

---

[4] There may also be conditions regarding other types of action which have to be taken to permit the project to go forward; e.g., the purchase of necessary land, the conclusion of specified contractual arrangements.

23. In addition to examining the general economic policies of a government, the World Bank examines the economic justification and consequences of the particular project it is interested in financing. In order to be assured that the project will be efficiently carried out and will yield the returns which will make it an economically justified project, the Bank requires various governmental assurances designed to achieve those ends. These assurances, unlike those referred to above, are contained in formal agreements reached in connection with a loan. From a legal viewpoint, these assurances may call for the taking of legislative or administrative action as a condition for the loan. This is what may be called the positive aspect of the Bank's course of action. In many cases, however, the Bank's course of action takes the form of negative covenants restricting the administrative or legislative freedom of the country involved or its agencies in order to make certain that the conditions considered as essential to the success of the loan will not be subsequently put in question by governmental action contrary to both the borrower's and the Bank's interests. The particular assurances which the Bank may seek in a loan depend on the nature of the loan and the circumstances of the particular case. Accordingly, these assurances take a wide variety of forms and deal not only with relatively minor technical aspects of a given project but also with more basic problems arising from the relationship between the economy of a country and the project. Although the assurances are very varied in form and scope, nevertheless in a particular type of loan they tend to follow a similar pattern. Examples of some of these assurances, broken down into categories, are as follows:

1. *Economic considerations relating to projects*

(a) *Rate adjustment*

24. It is the policy of the World Bank to obtain assurances that a public revenue-producing entity (e.g., electric utility, port authority, railroad corporation) will be allowed to earn a reasonable return on invested capital. An assurance of this kind may have a particularly significant effect on local law since it may require legislative changes to permit the entity to raise its rates; and the making of this change may be required as a condition of the loan. In any event, the Bank takes care to try to see to it that the rate covenant in the loan agreement is consistent with local law. Sometimes this consistency is achieved by a member state's making changes in its law or by the enactment of new legislation. In addition, there may be a requirement in the agreement that the relevant law will not be changed. For example, in the loan for the construction of the Volta

Dam in Ghana, the loan agreement provides (Loan No. 310 GH) that the Volta River Authority, a governmental utility authority, will charge rates in accordance with the requirements of the Volta River Act, 1961. This Act specifically provides for the fixing of power rates according to certain prescribed standards and was worked out in consultation with the Bank. In the Guarantee Agreement for the loan, the member state has agreed to guarantee the performance by the borrower of all of its obligations under the loan agreement; this in effect means that that member government has agreed to take no action which would interfere with the borrower's being able to act in accordance with the Volta River Act.

(b) *Elimination of rate subsidy*

25. In some cases, the rate structure of a utility has been such as to give preferential rates to certain groups (e.g., the military, government employees, students). The Bank may regard this as unsound financial administration and provide, in the loan agreement, that such subsidized rates be eliminated.

(c) *Limitation on new expansion program*

26. In some cases the Bank believes that execution of the project imposes such demands on the borrower's financial and manpower resources that the successful completion of the project might be endangered by the borrower's dividing its energies. Accordingly, a limitation may be imposed on any new expansion program in that particular field until a project being financed by the Bank is completed.

27. Occasionally the Bank considers that once the project which it helps to finance is completed, the goods or services produced may for some considerable time to come meet the demand of the area in which the project is located or of the member state as a whole and that it would be imprudent further to expand production in that field without a careful review.

28. In the guarantee agreement for the Volta Dam Project (Loan No. 310 GH), the member state (Ghana) has agreed not to finance an additional major power project in the country unless the project would not materially interfere with the Volta Dam Project and "there is adequate economic justification for such project, taking into account not only the said project standing by itself but also the effect of such project on the obligations assumed by the Borrower and the Guarantor in connection with the Project."

29. Sometimes the agreement is simply to consult, rather than to obtain the Bank's approval, before embarking on the program. For example, in an education credit made to Pakistan (Credit No. 87 PAK), the Province of East Pakistan undertakes to furnish to IDA "its general programs

for the construction of new, and the expansion of existing, education institutions," and to "afford the Association an opportunity to exchange views with respect thereto."

(d) *Reduction of number of employees*

30. The Bank sometimes finds that a government corporation desiring to borrow from the Bank is overstaffed, resulting in inefficient and wasteful operations. In such a case the Bank and the borrower may agree that the borrower should reduce the number of its personnel.

(e) *Distribution of costs*

31. In order to maximize the production expected under a project, the Bank may seek to allocate among the interested parties the costs of maintenance of the project in such a way as to benefit one group in particular. For example, in a loan to Malaysia (Loan No. 500 MA), the member state has agreed, in the loan agreement, to:

"make suitable arrangement for the recovery, by means of charges for the use of irrigation water and by means of increased taxes on land in the Project Area, of all operating and maintenance costs and of as much as practicable of the moneys invested in the Project together with reasonable interest thereon. The Borrower shall cause such water charges and taxes on land in the Project Area to be assessed and shared between landlords and tenants on such a basis that tenant-cultivators will have an incentive to maximize production."

(f) *Price and export controls*

32. In certain agricultural projects the Bank may want to be assured that the government will not take measures which would adversely affect the economic benefits expected to result from the project, such as, price and export controls on commodities related to the project. In that event it may be agreed that a government will remove existing controls on such commodities or that it will not impose any additional such controls.

2. *Organization and management of the Bank's borrower or the beneficiary of the proceeds of the loan*

(a) *Establishment of a new entity*

33. The World Bank considers that the soundness of the entity which is to carry out the project (whether it be the borrower or the beneficiary of the loan) is important to the success of a project. In many cases, the Bank has required that a new entity be established to carry out the project. This is particularly true with respect to multi-purpose projects where

existing forms of organization may not be readily adapted to the complications of a project of that kind. It is the practice of the Bank not to make the loan until the legislation or other instrument under which the entity is created has been enacted and the entity is properly organized.

(b) *Setting up a special section within a ministry or department to carry out the project*

34. If a loan is made to the member state and the project is to be carried out by a ministry or department of the government, the Bank will, when appropriate, want a special section or unit in the ministry or department to be established to discharge special functions or to carry out the project. Such an undertaking by the government usually would not require legislative action. Nevertheless, budgetary allocations have to be made, and more often than not, administrative responsibility has to be reallocated in the ministry or department concerned.

35. In most of the education projects, the agreements have provided that a special project unit be set up to carry out the project. A typical example is the education project in Pakistan (Credit No. 87 PAK) where the Province of East Pakistan has undertaken to appoint a project director who would be in charge of a project office to carry out the project.

36. In agricultural credit loans, a growing activity of the Bank, elaborate governmental machinery has often been set up for the handling of both the financial and agricultural aspects of the project. These cases may involve extensive changes in both law and administration.

(c) *Maintenance of the existence of the entity*

37. In lending to a governmental entity, the Bank is concerned to see that the entity maintains its existence and proper organization. Usually the Bank agreement provides that the charter, the articles of association or the act under which the entity is created shall not be amended without the prior consent of the Bank.

38. Or, alternatively, the loan agreement may provide that any material change in the instrument under which the entity is created shall be an event of default.

(d) *Management*

39. The Bank considers that competent and experienced management is essential to the success of a project and before making a loan will want to be assured that such management is or will be available.

40. Accordingly, the Bank's agreements often contain provisions regarding the appointment of the personnel who will carry out the project. For example, in some cases it is provided that the borrower will appoint a project manager only if acceptable to the Bank or in consultation with it.

109

41. This may mean in the cases of loans to public corporations that special requirements of the Bank in this regard will have to be reconciled with civil service and personnel laws of a generally applicable nature.

3. *Financial and technical considerations*

(a) *Provision of funds to complete the project*

42. In loans made either to a member state or to a non-member borrower, it is usually provided that the borrower and sometimes also the guarantor will provide funds to complete the project.

43. In loan agreements, sometimes the provision simply states that the borrower shall carry out the project, which necessarily includes the obligation of providing sufficient funds to complete the project. In other cases, explicit provision is made stating that the borrower shall provide "promptly as needed, the *funds,* facilities, services and other resources" required for the purpose of carrying out the project. In guarantee agreements it is often provided that:

"The Guarantor specifically undertakes, whenever there is reasonable cause to believe that the funds available to the Borrower will be inadequate to meet the estimated expenditures required for carrying out the Project, to make arrangements, satisfactory to the Bank, promptly to provide the Borrower or cause the Borrower to be provided with such funds as are needed to meet such expenditures."

Provisions of this kind may require special budgetary and appropriation legislation.

(b) *Debt limitation*

44. In most loans to autonomous revenue-producing public entities, a debt limitation covenant is provided in the loan agreement restricting the right of the borrower to incur additional debt. There are various formulas to set such limit, the purpose of which is to maintain the financial soundness of the entity which is to carry out the project. While this kind of restriction would not usually be inconsistent with local law, it may serve to impose an additional restriction on the right of a public corporation to borrow beyond that found in local law.

(c) *Exemption from taxes on payments under loans*

45. There are standard provisions in loan and guarantee agreements for tax exemptions with respect to the payment of principal, interest, and other charges on the loan, and on the execution, issue, delivery or registration of the loan and guarantee agreements and the bonds called for thereunder. These provisions may require reconciliation with the general tax

110

laws of the member countries. If the Bank's requirements in this respect conflict with local law and it would be impractical to insist on a change in local law, the Bank is willing to adapt its requirements if it can get substantial protection of its own interests in a way which would not conflict with local law. For example, where payments on the bonds received by the Bank from its borrowers would not be exempt from local taxes under local tax law, the Bank may accept, instead of a clause providing for such exemption, an agreement on the part of the Bank's borrower to pay the taxes if such taxes are imposed.

(d) *Taxes affecting project*

46. In a few cases, the Bank takes an interest in the incidence of local taxes on the construction of a project or its subsequent implementation; where appropriate in special cases the Bank's agreements may provide that the tax regime in a particular country as it affects a particular project will not be changed or that certain taxes will not be imposed.

47. For example, in a credit made to Kenya for a tea development project (Credit No. 64 KE), Kenya has agreed in effect that tea processed under the program financed by the IDA credit shall be free from local taxes except taxes in effect at the time of the signing of the agreement.[5]

48. Such undertakings may require changes in the tax law and regulations of the member state.

49. When there is a concession or establishment convention between the borrower and the guarantor government providing for tax or customs duty protection, the Bank may provide in the loan documents that the concession or convention shall not be amended without the Bank's consent or to make such an amendment an event of default. This is a situation which has obtained in several loans for projects in African countries (e.g., Mauritania, Gabon and Congo Brazzaville).

(e) *Auditing requirements*

50. In loans to a revenue-producing public entity, the loan agreement normally provides that the accounts of the entity must be audited by an independent auditor or by an independent accounting firm satisfactory to the Bank. Existing law is not always consistent with such a provision; in such a case, special action may have to be taken to give effect to the provision in local law.

---

[5] In connection with a loan made to the Republic of the Philippines for the benefit of the College of Agriculture of the University of the Philippines (Loan No. 393 PH), special legislation (R.A. No. 3854) was enacted providing that the University shall be exempt from all taxes, duties, fees, imposts and other charges of the Republic of the Philippines on items imported for the use of the University in the development program for the College of Agriculture.

(f) *Procurement method and procedures*

51. One of the important areas where Bank agreements may have considerable impact on local law and administrative regulations is the field of procurement. It is Bank policy to insist on international competitive bidding for procurement under most of its loans. This means that if, say, a government corporation is a borrower from the Bank it must issue tenders on an international basis and must be prepared to award the contract to the lowest evaluated bidder. In many cases government corporations are bound to adhere to special rules regarding procurement under local law which may be in conflict with the principles of international competition. If so, local laws and procedures must be changed so as to permit the borrower to conform to the Bank competitive bidding requirement.

52. One of the problems that sometimes arises is the effect to be given to local laws which provide for certain preferences to local manufacturers. Here again, the member government concerned must see to it that these preferences do not conflict with the award of a contract to the lowest evaluated bidder.[6] This area of procurement is of particular importance since it involves very large sums of money and it is one in which the member governments of the Bank, both on the capital exporting and the capital importing side, have expressed great interest. In order to standardize the procedure as much as possible, the Bank has published a document entitled "Guidelines relating to Procurement under World Bank Loans and IDA Credits" which borrowers agree to follow in the preparation of tender documents and the award of contracts.

53. The Bank normally reviews contracts which are being financed under its loans to see, among other things, whether they comply with the principles prescribed in the Procurement Guidelines and are satisfactory to the Bank in other respects as well.

54. While the Guidelines do not provide that the contract documents must contain provisions for settlement of disputes between a government and a contractor, nevertheless in cases where the absence of a satisfactory provision for settlement of disputes has led to difficulties between a contractor and a government in the past, the Bank may require any future loan to be conditioned upon a government's providing for a satisfactory method for settling disputes with foreign contractors. This is not because the Bank is committed to any particular method of settling disputes but because it may conclude that without such a satisfactory procedure foreign contractors will not want to bid on a contract or that they will put in bids which are unduly high. A requirement of this kind by the Bank may

---

[6] In recognition of the legitimate interests of borrowing countries in promoting the growth of sound industries, the Bank will, in appropriate cases, allow a margin of preference to domestic over foreign suppliers in the comparison of bids to supply material and equipment being procured for purposes of a Bank financed project.

involve the enactment of legislation in a member state allowing disputes between the government and a foreign contractor to be settled on a basis satisfactory to the Bank.

(g) *Standards and specifications*

55. The Bank takes an interest in the standards and specifications of the goods or construction being financed by its loan and the agreements may provide that such standards and specifications shall be subject to the approval of the Bank. In some cases the Bank will examine and approve the standards and specifications before the loan is made. In any event existing government regulations, if inconsistent with the agreed standards, would have to be reconciled with them.

(h) *Non-interference by the government*

56. The Bank believes that when an autonomous public entity or a private corporation agrees with the Bank to carry out a project the member state (which is the guarantor of the loan) should agree not to interfere with the carrying out of the project. For example, guarantee agreements will generally provide that the member state

"will not take, cause or permit to be taken, any action which would prevent or materially interfere with the carrying on by the Borrower of its operations and affairs in accordance with sound financial and investment standards and practices, or with the performance by the Borrower of its obligations under the Loan Agreement."

57. This is an important provision and one which might well help insure satisfactory completion of a project. Questions have arisen as to whether or not this so-called non-interference clause would prevent a government from enacting legislation of a general nature which, incidentally and as a by-product, might interfere with the Bank-financed project and conflict with this clause. The Bank prefers to treat this question in the context of a particular case, rather than to deal with it as a general problem. But one example may be of interest.

58. In a loan made to a government corporation, the loan agreement provided that any suspension, repeal or amendment of the Act under which the borrower was set up which would affect adversely the ability of the borrower to carry out its obligations under the loan agreement would be an event of default. The Act had been reviewed with the Bank in detail before it was enacted and it provided, in effect, that the government would not interfere with the corporation's general financial and business policies. In 1966, another act was enacted which provided that:

"notwithstanding any provision of any enactment, the Minister of Finance may give to such Corporation, such directions with regard to (a) the Corporation's general financial policy; (b) any specified items of the Corporation's estimate of revenue or expenditure as he may think fit and the Corporation shall give effect to such direction."

113

59. The Bank considered that the provision of the second act had, in effect, amended the first and that such amendment would adversely affect the ability of the borrower to carry out its obligations under the loan agreement, which requires the borrower to carry out the project with due diligence and efficiency and in conformity with sound financial practices. After discussions with the government concerned, a decree was made to exempt the corporation from the application of the second act.

IV. COMPLIANCE

1. *Default provisions of loan and guarantee agreements*

60. The loan and guarantee agreements of the World Bank give it the right, if the borrower or guarantor defaults under those agreements, (i) to suspend future disbursements under the loan or cancel the remaining balance of the loan or (ii) in certain cases to premature payment of the loan, that is to call on the borrower to make payment in full of the entire amount of the loan outstanding.[7] Provisions of this kind are normally found in both private and public loan agreements.

61. The events which permit the Bank to suspend disbursements or premature a loan are two kinds (a) failure by the borrower or guarantor to comply with any obligations under the agreement, or (b) events which make it impossible or improbable that the purposes of the loan will be achieved. Attached hereto as Appendix A is an excerpt from the form of loan agreement normally used by the Bank listing the events which permit the Bank to take such action. In addition to these events, others may be added, depending on the circumstances of the case.

62. In this connection a technique used by the Bank calls for comment. As noted above, often the Bank wishes to be assured that a member state will not enact legislation which will adversely affect the project or will change the basis on which a loan is made. In most of these cases, a covenant to this effect would not be feasible. It is, however, feasible to provide in the agreement that any such legislative enactment constitutes an event of default, and this is sometimes done.

63. There have been cases where, because of a default by the borrower, the Bank has suspended disbursements on a loan or cancelled the remaining balance of a loan. This, however, has happened infrequently and, as discussed below, is a remedy which the Bank hopes not to have to exercise.

---

[7] No doubt under general principles of law the Bank would also have other rights in certain circumstances; e.g. it could rescind an agreement or sue for damages if there had been a material misrepresentation made to the Bank in connection with the obtaining of a loan.

64. The Bank in fact has never prematured a loan and the question may be raised whether a provision entitling the Bank to premature a loan is useful. There are several reasons why the Bank has decided to include these provisions in its loans. In the first place, in the case of a private borrower the right to premature gives the Bank a better position in a bankruptcy or reorganization than it otherwise would have. Secondly, since the Bank wants to sell participations in its loans and since this kind of provision is common in loan agreements generally, it probably makes it easier for the Bank to sell participations under an agreement set up in a form to which participants are accustomed. Finally, as far as governmental borrowers are concerned, including both a government entity and the government itself, while it is unrealistic to think of a bankruptcy or reorganization in a normal commercial sense, nevertheless, in case of default, the right to premature would permit the Bank to make a claim for the full amount of its outstanding loan in any debt rescheduling if other lenders were to make such a claim.

2. *Arbitration*

65. The loan and guarantee agreements provide (Section 7.03 of the Loan Regulations) that any controversy between the parties to the agreement or any claim by either party against the other arising under the loan or guarantee not determined by mutual agreement is to be submitted to arbitration.[8] It is also provided that arbitration is to be in lieu of any other procedure for determining such controversies and claims. Detailed provisions are included as to the appointment of arbitrators, the procedure of the arbitral tribunal and the rendering of the award, which can be by default. Each party agrees to abide by and comply with any award rendered by the arbitral tribunal.

66. The agreements provide no special means for enforcing an award against a borrowing country unwilling to comply with it. In fact it is specifically provided that "the Bank shall not be entitled to enter judgment against the borrower upon the award, to enforce the award against the Borrower by execution or to pursue any other remedy against the Borrower for the enforcement of the award, except as such procedure may be available against the Borrower otherwise than by reason of the provisions of this Section." On the other hand, it is specifically provided that if the Bank does not comply with the award the borrower may take any such action for the enforcement of the award against the Bank.

67. No arbitration has ever been had under a loan or guarantee agreement of the Bank.

---

[8] A brief statement regarding the law applicable to Bank's loan and guarantee agreements is set forth in Appendix B.

3. *Informal action to obtain enforcement of obligations*

68. The ultimate purpose of action by the Bank to enforce its agreements is to see that the project is carried out properly and that the loan is repaid. The Bank does not seek to enforce provisions of its loan agreements solely because there has been a default; it first looks to see what the nature of the default is and to determine how the difficulties which have arisen can be best resolved.

69. Almost all the projects financed by the Bank have given rise to problems of one kind or another, some serious and some not. It seems to be almost axiomatic that in development lending problems will arise, the only question being what they will be. For that matter, the same would probably be true if in more conventional financing agreements between private investment bankers and borrowers it was tried to cover so many details of the execution of the project and the conduct of the borrower's affairs. The problems cover a wide spectrum. The main problems of this kind have been: (i) engineering and technical problems arising in the course of construction, (ii) inadequacy of management, including difficulties arising from the exodus of expatriates, (iii) inability of the borrowers to obtain local financing (iv) inability to cope with the consequences of inflation, (v) inability of the borrower to obtain proper rates, and (vi) chronic failure by the borrower to comply with its obligations. Sometimes, they may be ascribed to circumstances within the control of the Bank itself, including cases in which covenants in loan agreements have proved to be unworkable and unrealistic and amortization schedules have proved to be unrealistic.

70. These types of problems and many others have become familiar to the Bank and the Bank has a special procedure set up to obtain current information about the functioning of a project, including field trips to the site to try to anticipate these problems before they become serious and to try to solve the problems as they arise. This kind of supervision of projects represents a very substantial part of the Bank's activities. In other words, once the Bank decides to make a loan and enters into a loan agreement, this is only the first step in a lengthy process by which the Bank assures itself that the purposes of the loan are being achieved.

71. It should be emphasized that this process has over the years developed into a standardized activity which has become well known to the Bank's borrowers. The legal basis for this process rests in provisions of the loan agreements under which a borrower furnishes information to the Bank about the functioning of the project and the Bank is entitled to send missions to the site of the project to see how it is functioning and, if necessary, to make recommendations as to changes in the project. This kind of consultation is one in which the major results are achieved by understandings reached between the borrower and the Bank which may or may not be reflected in a change in the loan agreement or in local law.

116

72. The Bank does not normally insist on strict compliance with its agreement to the point of using the legal remedies available to it until it is first satisfied that there is no practical alternative. The rationale is that the principal objective of the Bank is to get a healthy project functioning and the Bank has therefore preferred to try other ways of obtaining compliance, the particular method depending on the circumstances. Generally speaking the Bank usually first tries to use its persuasive powers before it attempts stronger methods. This is not to suggest that the Bank does not expect its agreements to be carried out. It does; and when violations do occur the Bank requests and receives an explanation. But the Bank would generally rather try to get a project functioning well than to use its sanctions. Probably the most effective remedy the Bank has is to refuse to make further loans to a borrower who deliberately defaults to the Bank. This is a powerful lever, especially where a member and the Bank expect to maintain a pipeline of loans. For the Bank to stop lending in such a case means that the member will have to look elsewhere to meet its development needs and this may not be easy to do.

73. The drastic legal sanction available to the Bank to premature a loan would most likely be used only in case of flagrant misbehavior or possibly to protect the Bank's legal position, and these cases are likely to be rare. Essentially the Bank expects and does obtain compliance because it is in the interest of borrowers, as well as the Bank, to comply and because the Bank and the borrowers expect to maintain a continuous cooperative relationship.

4. *Articles of agreement*

74. In addition to these rights under loan and guarantee agreements, the Articles of Agreement of the Bank provide that if a member country fails to fulfill any of its obligations to the Bank, the Bank may suspend its membership and the member so suspended shall automatically cease to be a member one year from the date of its suspension unless restored to good standing (Article VI, Section 2). This provision means that if a member defaults on its obligations to the Bank under a loan or guarantee agreement the Bank could suspend its membership. In fact the Bank has never taken action under this section against such a member.

V. SPECIAL PROBLEMS OF FEDERATED STATES

75. The World Bank has sometimes been faced with the problem of seeing to it that an obligation under a loan is binding upon the constituent units of a federal state. Some of the cases in which this problem has arisen and the method by which the Bank has dealt with it are as follows:

76. The Bank has made loans in a federal state for a purpose which is primarily within the competence of a region or political subdivision of that state. The problem may be complicated by the fact that some aspects of a particular project may be within the competence of the federal government whereas the balance will be within the competence of the region or political subdivision. An example of this arose in connection with a $ 20 million credit by IDA to the Federal Republic of Nigeria to finance the construction and equipping of a number of schools in the Northern, Eastern, Western and Mid-Western Regions of Nigeria and in the Federal Territory. Education in the regions was largely within the constitutional competence of the regional governments. On the other hand, foreign borrowing was a federal subject; for this reason and in order to coordinate various aspects of this project it was thought desirable to make the loan directly to the Federal Republic which, in turn, would relend the proceeds to the various regions. In order to obligate both the Federal Republic and the regions to carry out the project the following complex of agreements was entered into:

(a) IDA and the Federal Republic entered into a credit agreement under which the Federal Republic agreed to "exercise every right and recourse available to it to cause" the regions to carry out the projects applicable to each of them. If Nigeria had not been a federation and had full authority to control education throughout the country, the quoted words would have been omitted from the agreement; in the normal Bank loan agreement the borrower agrees to cause the project to be carried out, and the quoted words will not be included. The addition of the quoted words makes clear that the Federal Government must exercise only such rights and recourses as are constitutionally available to it to cause each region to carry out its project. It does not purport to bind the Federal Republic to take action which would be unconstitutional.

(b) IDA entered into so-called "project agreements" with each of the regions under which each region agreed to "carry out or cause to be carried out," the project applicable to it. Thus each region is bound by agreement to IDA to carry out the project.

(c) The Federal Republic entered into so-called "subsidiary loan agreements" with each region which provided for the relending of the proceeds of the IDA credit to each region and for the undertaking by the region to carry out its obligations under the project agreement.

77. A somewhat similar problem arises in connection with the so-called negative pledge or *pari passu* clause in Bank agreements. Under such a clause (which is a normal clause in loan agreements) the borrower agrees that if any lien is created on any governmental assets, including assets of a political subdivision, such lien shall equally and ratably secure payment of the loan. Constitutional limitations may make it difficult or impossible for a member state to undertake a negative pledge commitment on behalf of its political subdivisions. In such cases, various methods have been used

to give the Bank the substance of the protection it needs, while recognizing the constitutional limitations of a government. In some cases, regardless of direct constitutional powers, government control of foreign exchange or specific legislation respecting public external borrowing gives the member state sufficient power to give effect to the negative pledge clause insofar as political subdivisions are concerned. In these cases it is the Bank's practice (i) to acknowledge in its agreements the existence of the constitutional issue by providing that the member will make the clause effective "within the limitations of its constitutional powers" with respect to liens on the assets of its political subdivisions and (ii) to rely for the implementation of the commitment upon the authority vested in the government to control foreign exchange available to the political subdivision. (See Loan Agreement between the Government of Australia and the Bank, Loan No. 156 AU). In other cases, where governmental control of foreign exchange does not exist and the member government therefore would be unable to make the clause effective, the member state may nevertheless undertake to give to the Bank an "equivalent lien satisfactory to the Bank" if a political subdivision creates a lien which would fall within the scope of the negative pledge clause.

78. The agreements make clear that, as far as the Bank is concerned, while it recognizes the constitutional limitations on the federal government in a federated state, it may obtain the protection it needs either by obtaining separate agreements from the units of the federation or by obtaining special assurances from the federal government.

VI. AMENDMENT OF THE ARTICLES OF AGREEMENT OF THE BANK

79. The Articles of Agreement of both the World Bank and IDA contain provisions for their amendment. While these provisions differ in certain respects, they both provide that, except as stated below, an amendment may be approved by a qualified majority. Under both charters, certain amendments can become effective only by affirmative vote of all members; these cases are the right to withdraw from the institution, the preemptive right to subscribe to additional shares or subscriptions and the limitation on liability of each member in connection with its subscription.

80. Article VIII of the Articles of Agreement of the Bank provides as follows:

"(a) Any proposal to introduce modifications of this Agreement, whether emanating from a member, a governor or the Executive Directors, shall be communicated to the Chairman of the Board of Governors who shall bring the proposal before the Board. If the proposed amendment is approved by the Board the Bank shall, by circular letter or telegram, ask all members whether they accept the proposed amendment. When three-fifths of the members, having four-fifths of the total voting power, have accepted the proposed amendments, the Bank shall certify the fact by formal communication addressed to all members.

119

"(b) Notwithstanding (a) above, acceptance by all members is required in the case of any amendment modifying
(i) the right to withdraw from the Bank provided in Article VI, Section 1;
(ii) the right secured by Article II, Section 3(c);
(iii) the limitation on liability provided in Article II, section 6.
"(c) Amendments shall enter into force for all members three months after the date of the formal communication unless a shorter period is specified in the circular letter or telegram."

81. It is thus provided that, except in the three cases mentioned, the Articles may be amended, after approval by the Board of Governors, by a vote of 3/5 of the members having 4/5 of the total voting power. The same qualified majority is required in a case of an amendment to the Articles of IDA.

82. The Bank has amended its Articles only once. This amendment was designed to permit the Bank to make loans to its affiliate, the IFC. (Article III, Section 6 added by amendment effective December 16, 1965.) A corresponding amendment was made to the IFC Articles.

VII. EFFECT OF DECISIONS AND OTHER ACTIONS RELATED TO BANK'S PRIVILEGES AND IMMUNITIES

83. Under its Articles the World Bank, like many other international organizations, enjoys certain privileges and immunities. The question of obtaining proper recognition in local law of these privileges and immunities is largely a problem of interpretation of the Articles; in that sense the only "decision" of the Bank involved is its "decision" that it is legally entitled to a given privilege or immunity and then to take whatever action may be required locally to try to get whatever it is entitled to. Except for the Federal Communications matter referred to later, this area of activity is not discussed in this paper, except for the following few comments which indicate the substantial nature of the problems encountered.

1. *Borrowing by the Bank in the markets of a country*

84. A vital part of the Bank's operations is its borrowings in the markets of some of its member countries. Except for the effect in local law of its special status and its privileges and immunities, and of any special local legislation which may be relevant to it, when the Bank borrows in the private markets of a country it does so as a private person subject to local law.

85. When the Bank first sold a public bond issue in the United States the question arose whether or not the Securities Acts were applicable to the Bank and to that sale. The Bank decided not to contend that under its

120

Articles of Agreement it should be regarded as exempt from those Acts [9] and in its first two public issues registered its securities under the United States Securities Act of 1933. Thereafter special legislation was passed in the United States exempting bonds of the Bank from the Securities Act of 1933 and the Securities Exchange Act of 1934 (22 U.S.C. 286). Similar legislation was also passed relating to the bonds of the Inter-American Development Bank.

86. Problems of this kind have arisen under the so-called "blue sky" and "legal investment" laws of the United States and of other countries and on many occasions special laws have been passed giving the Bank and its bonds special status or privileges under that kind of legislation.

2. *Tax immunities*

87. In the charters of most international organizations, the privileges and immunities to be accorded the organization are dealt with in general terms only, leaving the handling of the specific details to subsequent agreement.[10] The charter of the Bank, however, spells out its privileges and immunities in detail. It is thus provided in the Articles of Agreement of the Bank that the Bank and its operations and transactions shall be immune from all taxation (Article VII, Section 9 (a)). Implementation of this provision may have a substantial effect on local law.

88. The Articles provide that each member "shall take such action as is necessary in its own territories for the purpose of making effective in terms of its own law the principles set forth" in the Articles (Article VII, Section 10) and in accepting membership a member must deposit an instrument stating that it has accepted the Articles "in accordance with its law and has taken all steps necessary to enable it to carry out all of its obligations" thereunder (Article XI, Section 2 (a)).

89. The way in which this tax immunity (as well as other privileges and immunities) afforded the Bank has been made effective under the local law of the member states has varied, depending on the way in which the particular member makes treaties effective under its own law. Thus in some cases the tax immunities have been given the force of law solely as a result of the legislative act ratifying acceptance of the Articles without further special enabling legislation. In other cases legislation has been enacted specifically incorporating the tax immunities into local law and,

---

[9] The Articles provide (Article VII, Section 6) that the property and assets of the Bank shall be free from restrictions, regulations, controls and moratoria of any nature to the extent necessary to carry out its operations.

[10] Detter, *Lawmaking by International Organizations*, p. 181 et seq. (1965); Broches, "International Legal Aspects of the Operations of the World Bank", 98 *Recueil de Cours*, 1959, p. 311.

sometimes, specifically amending existing tax law which may be inconsistent with the tax immunities accorded the Bank.

90. A few examples may be of interest. The United States accepted membership in the Bank pursuant to the Bretton Woods Agreements Act which expressly incorporates into United States statutory law the provisions conferring privileges and immunities upon the Bank [11] by simply providing that such provisions "shall have full force and effect in the United States. . ." [12] France accepted membership in the Bank pursuant to similar legislation. [13] In the United Kingdom, where a treaty is not regarded as self-executing without implementing legislation, the United Kingdom accepted membership in the Bank pursuant to a statute [14] which provided (Section 3(1)) that "His Majesty may by Order in Council make such provision as He may consider reasonably necessary for carrying into effect any of the provisions of the . . . Bank Agreement relating to the status, immunities and privileges of the . . . Bank." Pursuant to such provision the "Bretton Woods Agreements Order in Council 1946" was issued [15] which provided that the provisions of the Bank Agreement set out in the Schedule to such Order "shall have the force of law" and in such Schedule there was specifically set forth the tax immunities, among others, accorded to the Bank under its Articles of Agreement. Ceylon and Ghana specifically following the example of the United Kingdom, accepted membership in the Bank by statutes similar to that of the United Kingdom. [16]

Most other countries on the other hand accepted membership in the Bank pursuant to the legislative action ratifying acceptance of the Articles of Agreement without further specific enabling legislation. Germany, Guinea and The Netherlands are examples of this procedure. [17]

---

[11] 59 Stat. 516 (1945); U.S.C. § 286 (h) (1946).

[12] This procedure should be contrasted to that followed by the United States under the International Organizations Immunities Act (59 Stat. 669 (1945); 22 U.S.C. § 288 (1946)). Under that Act public international organizations in which the United States participates (when designated as such by the President of the United States by Executive Order) are entitled to certain specified privileges and immunities. That Act specifically amends the tax laws of the United States (the Internal Revenue Code and other tax laws) in order to confer tax immunities upon international organizations coming within the scope of the Act. That Act was designed, among other things, to accord privileges and immunities to international organizations whose charters, unlike those of the Bank and Fund, do not contain detailed provisions spelling out their privileges and immunities; and, for such organizations, it was therefore not regarded as sufficient merely to incorporate their charters into United States law.

[13] Law No. 45-0138 of 26 December 1945; *Journal Officiel de la République Française*, December 27, 1945.

[14] Bretton Woods Agreements Act, 1945, 9 & 10 Geo. 6, Ch. 19; 20 December 1945.

[15] Statutory Rules and Orders, 1946 No. 36, 10 January 1946.

[16] Ceylon, Bretton Woods Agreements Act No. 20, of 1950, 22 August 1950. Ghana, International Bank, Fund and Finance Corporation Act, 1957, No. 17 of 1957.

[17] Germany, Law of July 28, 1952; *Bundesgesetzblatt,* Part II, No. 13, August 1, 1952. Guinea, Law No. 77/AN/62 of November 23, 1962.
The Netherlands, F 318, Law dated December 20, 1945.

91. On many occasions questions have arisen as to the scope of the Bank's tax immunities and its effect on local tax law. When questions of this kind have arisen they often have been handled simply by way of interpretation by the local tax authorities of their tax laws so as to afford recognition of the Bank's tax immunities. This has been done either by regulations issued by the tax authorities or by an informal exchange of letters between the tax authorities and the Bank. For example, a question has arisen whether the Bank or other party to the transaction is subject to payment of stamp tax on the delivery of an indenture in connection with security arrangements under a loan. The Bank has taken the position that a stamp tax, being a tax on a transaction, cannot be imposed even on a party to the transaction other than the Bank.[18] This position has been recognized by the tax authorities in several countries where the question has arisen. The question has also been raised whether the United States Interest Equalization Tax Act applies to sales by the Bank of portions of its loans out of portfolio to a private person. The Bank took the position that the Interest Equalization Tax, being an excise tax and therefore being a tax on the transaction, could not be properly imposed on such a portfolio sale. This position was also recognized by the United States tax authorities.

92. In some cases a country may enact general tax laws which could be interpreted in such a way as to conflict with its obligations to the Bank under the Articles. The general tax law may specifically recognize the immunity of the Bank in order to avoid any possible question of conflict between a treaty obligation and a later statute. For example, under the United States Interest Equalization Tax Act which provides for a tax on obligations issued by a foreign obligor to a United States person the Act provides, in effect, (Internal Revenue Code; Section 4920 (3) (A) (i)) that it shall not apply to bonds issued by an international organization of which the United States is a member (e.g. the Bank, the Inter-American Development ment Bank).

3. *Effect in Local Law of Interpretation of Bank's Articles of Agreement; The Federal Communications Commission Case*

93. The Articles of Agreement of the Bank and Fund contain provisions setting up a procedure for the interpretation of the Articles by the Executive Directors of the respective institutions. Under these provisions any question of interpretation of the Articles arising between any member and

---

[18] Article VII, Section 9 (a) of the Bank's Articles provides that "The Bank, its assets, property, income and its operations and transactions authorized by this Agreement, shall be immune from all taxation and from all customs duties. The Bank shall also be immune from liability for the collection or payment of any tax or duty.

the Bank or the Fund or between any members of the Bank or the Fund are to be submitted to the Executive Directors for their decision.[19] Once the Executive Directors have duly rendered a decision, that interpretation is binding on all the members of the Bank and Fund subject to the right of appeal to the Board of Governors whose decision is final.

94. The Bank has adopted a number of interpretations involving various provisions of its Articles. However, except for the interpretation discussed in this section, none of the interpretations involved the effect of the Articles on private persons under local law. The only proceeding in which the question has been raised as to the binding effect of an interpretation in a local forum arose in connection with an interpretation by the Bank of the provisions of Article VII, Section 7 of its Articles. In this proceeding the Bank and the Fund filed a complaint with the U.S. Federal Communications Commission claiming that they were entitled to the same "treatment" as governments for their cables, that the Executive Directors had interpreted the word "treatment" to encompass treatment with respect to rates and that therefore they were entitled to special governmental rates. The Federal Communications Commission rules in favor of the Bank and the Fund.[20] The case squarely holds that an interpretation by the Bank and the Fund of their Charters is binding on their member governments and that the charter provisions so interpreted must be given effect in the territories of members even against private persons. The case is an extremely interesting and important one which surprisingly has been neglected by the commentators.

95. Briefly, the facts were as follows: In 1949 certain United States cable companies, which had hitherto been charging special governmental rates for cables sent by the Bank and the Fund from the United States to other countries, filed revised tariffs under which the Bank and Fund would be charged full commercial rates. The Bank and the Fund filed a complaint with the Federal Communications Commission asserting that the revised tariffs were unlawful because the cable companies were required to charge only governmental rates because of various provisions of law. The Bank's case was based primarily on the following argument: [21]

(a) Article VII, Section 7 of the Bank's Articles provides as follows:

"Section 7. *Privilege for communications*
The official communications of the Bank shall be accorded by each member the same treatment that it accords to the official communications of other members."

(b) This provision was interpreted by the Executive Directors of the Bank to mean in effect that member governments are required to see to it that the Bank is charged rates for its cables no higher than those rates

---

[19] Bank Articles of Agreement, Article IX, Fund Articles of Agreement, Article XVIII.
[20] 17 FCC 450 (1953).
[21] The discussion of this case applies equally to the Fund.

accorded cables of other member governments and that if a member exercises regulatory powers over rates, it is not relieved of its obligation by reason of the fact that the communications facilities are privately owned. (c) Under the US Bretton Woods Agreements Act (the act pursuant to which the United States accepted membership in the Bank), these provisions have "full force and effect in the United States." The Bank argued that consequently the United States was obligated to accord the Bank governmental rates for its cables and that accordingly the United States, acting through the Federal Communications Commission, was obliged to insure that the cable companies filed tariffs according the Bank such rates. It is interesting to note that during the proceedings before the Commission the United States State Department wrote two letters to the Commission stating that the United States Government was obliged to carry out the Articles of Agreement as interpreted in accordance with the provisions of the Articles and that since the Bank had interpreted the Articles to relate to the treatment to be accorded to official communications, including governmental privileges with respect to rates, the State Department was of the opinion that the United States Government was committed to support that interpretation.

96. The cable companies argued that the interpretation was not binding on the Federal Communications Commission; that the Commission could not enforce the provision of the charter of the Bank against a private cable company, and that the cable companies were not parties to the interpretation and that therefore they could not be bound by it.

97. On the major issue, the Commission held that the interpretation was binding on the United States Government and therefore on the Commission. In this connection it stated as follows:

"We believe that the question as to the application of the term 'treatment' in the Bank and Fund Articles to rates has been conclusively determined by the Bank and Fund Executive Directors' interpretation, by unanimous vote, that the language in question applies to rates charged for official communications of the Bank and the Fund. Under the terms of the Bank and Fund Articles of Agreement, this interpretation, in effect, is final. This procedure for issuing interpretations binding member governments does indeed appear novel; but it also appears to point the way toward speedy, uniform and final interpretations. This procedure is not only an integral part of the Bank and Fund Articles, which have been accepted by the United States, but its use was specifically invoked with respect to questions of interpretation by sections 12 and 13 of the Bretton Woods Agreements Act; and the United States Congress, by directing that an amendment of the Articles be sought if the requested interpretations were not satisfactory, appears to have recognized in these two sections that the United States is bound by the results of the interpretations. The United States Government is therefore bound by the Executive Directors' interpretation of the term 'treatment' and is under an international obligation to act in conformity therewith."

98. It is also interesting to note that the cable companies argued that the interpretation was unreasonable and *ultra vires*. The Commission rejected this argument and stated as follows:

125

"... assuming for purposes of argument, that if the interpretations of the term 'same treatment' by the Executive Directors of the Bank and Fund were so unreasonable, arbitrary or capricious as to constitute in fact an amendment of the Articles of Agreement rather than interpretations thereof we should not have to give effect to them, we think it clear that the interpretations made in this case cannot be so categorized. The language of the Articles of Agreement appears to be sufficiently broad and general to include rates, and nowhere is there any exclusion of the matter of rates, either expressed or implied, or any words of limitation."

99. Finally it should be noted that the Commission specifically stated that it was bound to consider in determining whether a particular rate schedule was legal not only the Federal Communications Act but also the impact of special legislation on international agreements.[22]

100. The case was decided on the ground that the United States was bound to observe its obligations under an international agreement irrespective of any local law; and, as has been noted, the case squarely holds that the Articles of Agreement of the Bank, as interpreted by the Executive Directors, must be given effect under local law, even as against private persons.

APPENDIX A

Provisions in loan and guarantee agreements relating to sanctions

A. In loans to borrowers which are guaranteed by a member government, the loan and guarantee agreements in their normal form entitle the World Bank to suspend the right of the borrower to make withdrawals from the loan if the events listed below occur. If the right to make such withdrawals is suspended for thirty days, the Bank may then cancel the unwithdrawn part of the loan.

(a) A default shall have occurred in the payment of principal or interest or any other payment required under the loan agreement or the bonds.

(b) A default shall have occurred in the payment of principal or interest or any other payment required under any other loan agreement between the Bank and the borrower or under any loan agreement or under any guarantee agreement between the guarantor and the Bank or under any bond delivered pursuant to any such agreement.

(c) A default shall have occurred in the performance of any other covenant or

---

[22] An interesting aspect of the decision is that the Commission saw fit to interpret the interpretation of the Bank. One of the issues in the case was whether the United States was bound to insure that in all circumstances the cable companies should extend to the Bank the same standard of rate treatment as prevailed for other member governments or whether the cable companies were required to do so only when their foreign correspondents observed certain conditions of reciprocity such as division of tolls or reduced rates. The Commission held that if the United States cable companies were required unilaterally to give reduced rates to the Bank without reference to the reciprocity of their corresponding companies they would not be giving the Bank the "same treatment under Article VII, Section 7", but better treatment. The Commission therefore held in effect that the obligation on the United States cable companies to extend governmental rates to the Bank should prevail only where the foreign correspondent also accorded governmental rates for their part of the toll.

agreement on the part of the borrower or the guarantor under the loan agreement, the guarantee agreement or the bonds.

(d) An extraordinary situation shall have arisen which shall make it improbable that the borrower or the guarantor will be able to perform its obligations under the loan agreement or the bonds.

(e) The borrower shall have been unable to pay its debts as they mature or any action or proceeding shall have been taken by the borrower or by others whereby any of the property of the borrower shall or may be distributed among its creditors.

(f) The guarantor or any other authority having jurisdiction shall have taken any action for the dissolution or disestablishment of the borrower or for the suspension of its operations.

(g) The guarantor shall have been suspended from membership in or ceased to be a member of the Bank.

(h) The guarantor shall have ceased to be a member of the International Monetary Fund or shall have become ineligible to use said resources under Section 5 of Article V, Section 1 of Article VI or Section 2(a) of Article XV of the Articles of Agreement of said Fund.

(i) After the date of the loan agreement and prior to the effective date any event shall have occurred which would have entitled the Bank to suspend the borrower's right to make withdrawals from the loan account of the loan agreement and the guarantee agreement had been effective on the date such event occurred.

B. The events listed in (a), (b), (c), (e) and (f) also entitle the Bank, after specified notice, to premature payment of the full outstanding amount of its loan.

APPENDIX B

Note regarding law applicable to IBRD's loan and guarantee agreements

It seems to be generally accepted as a matter of law that the loan and guarantee agreements between the World Bank and a member state are international agreements and governed by international law. This concept is given expression in the agreements between the Bank and its member states which provide that "the rights and obligations of the Bank and the Borrower under the loan [guarantee] agreement and bonds shall be valid and enforceable in accordance with their terms notwithstanding the law of any state, or political subdivision thereof, to the contrary." (Section 7.01 of the Loan Regulations which are incorporated in each loan and guarantee agreement.) [23]

The rule set out in Section 7.01 establishes the duty of the member state to give effect to the terms of the loan or guarantee agreements to which it is a party and this provision has the effect of insulating the loan or guarantee agreement from the member state's own law, either existing at the time of the signing of the agreements or later enacted.

In the case of a loan agreement entered into between the Bank and a non-member borrower, the question has been raised as to whether the parties can validly insulate the loan agreement from the provisions of municipal law. In this connection the General Counsel of the Bank has stated:[24]

---

[23] The parties may provide that provisions of the agreements relating to security arrangements (e.g. mortgages) are made subject to a specific municipal law. See, Delaume, *Legal Aspects of International Lending and Economic Development Finance*, pp. 138-140.

[24] Broches, "International Legal Aspects of the Operations of the World Bank", 98 *Recueil de Cours* 1959, p. 352.

"... while the borrower could not contract itself out of the applications of municipal law, the Bank and the guaranteeing member may do so in respect not only of their relationship but also (with the borrower's consent evidenced by the borrower's acceptance of Section 7.01) of that between the Bank and the borrower."

"The importance of the problem should not be overestimated since, even if the borrower's obligation could be impaired or affected by municipal law, the guarantor's obligations could not, and it would appear that the Bank could proceed against the guarantor, who is in a position of a joint co-debtor, independently of municipal law."

THE INTER-AMERICAN DEVELOPMENT BANK

by *Elting Arnold*
General Counsel of the Inter-American Development Bank

In general, the Inter-American Development Bank is not confronted with the problem of making effective, with respect to its members or others, decisions which are legally binding in themselves. The work of the Bank, whether with member countries or other entities, basically takes form in contracts and agreements which are the product of negotiation and which the other party is at complete liberty, legally, to reject if it wishes.

In the process of authorizing contracts, and other agreements, the Board of Executive Directors adopts of course numerous policy decisions and many interpretations, express or otherwise, of the Agreement Establishing the Bank, but these are directly binding only to the extent they are accepted by the other party.

It may be noted that the policy questions with which the Bank deals cover a wide range. On one hand, it is concerned with broad aspects of country performance, in which it maintains close liaison with the Inter-American Committee of the Alliance for Progress (CIAP), which under Resolution 1-M/63, adopted at the Second Annual Meeting of the Inter-American Economic and Social Council (IA-ECOSOC) is charged with review of the actions in this respect of the members of the Organization of American States. A related concern of the Bank is reflected in the annual reports on *Socio-Economic Progress in Latin America* which the Bank publishes annually pursuant to Section 5.04 of the Social Progress Trust Fund Agreement signed with the United States on June 19, 1961. On the other hand, the policy determinations may deal with specific matters such as the appropriateness, for example, of the financing by the Bank of municipal transport systems, which it has been concluded should not receive its attention for reasons of relative priority in the use of resources.

There is, however, one important field of relationships with member countries in which the Bank expressly has the power of making conclusive determinations and it is believed that a brief indication of experience in this respect may be of interest. This field is the determination of the value in terms of gold, or in practical consequence, the United States dollar, of the currencies of other members held by the Bank, a matter of great significance in view of the substantial and often continuing depreciation of their currencies suffered by some of the member countries since the creation of the Bank. Article V of the Agreement provides:

"Section 2. Valuation of Currencies
"Whenever it shall become necessary under this Agreement to value any currency in terms of another currency, or in terms of gold, such valuation shall be determined by the Bank after consultation with the International Monetary Fund."

129

"Section 3. Maintenance of Value of the Currency Holdings of the Bank

"(a) Whenever the par value in the International Monetary Fund of a member's currency is reduced or the foreign exchange value of a member's currency has, in the opinion of the Bank, depreciated to a significant extent, the member shall pay to the Bank within a reasonable time an additional amount of its own currency sufficient to maintain the value of all the currency of the member held by the Bank in its ordinary capital resources, or in the resources of the Fund, excepting currency derived from borrowings by the Bank. The standard of value for this purpose shall be the United States dollar of the weight and fineness in effect on January 1, 1959.

"(b) Whenever the par value in the International Monetary Fund of a member's currency is increased or the foreign exchange value of such member's currency has, in the opinion of the Bank, appreciated to a significant extent, the Bank shall return to such member within a reasonable time an amount of that member's currency equal to the increase in the value of the amount of such currency which is held by the Bank in its ordinary capital resources or in the resources of the Fund, excepting currency derived from borrowings by the Bank. The standard of value for this purpose shall be the same as that established in the preceding paragraph.

"(c) The provisions of this section may be waived by the Bank when a uniform proportionate change in the par value of the currencies of all the Bank's members is made by the International Monetary Fund."

Similar clauses relating to initial subscriptions of members appear in Article II, Section 4 (b), and Article IV, Section 3 (e). Provisions to the same basic effect are also to be found in the earlier Articles of Agreement of the International Bank for Reconstruction and Development.

It will be noted that these provisions give the Bank full formal power to establish the pertinent currency value, or in practical terms, the rate of exchange, which is highly important in the disbursement of the Bank's loans since an unduly low rate will result in the receipt by borrowers of real values inconveniently lower than the estimated needs of the project. However, exchange rates are such a basic aspect of the sovereignty of members that the Bank has not found it desirable to apply Section 3 exactly in its own terms, just as the International Monetary Fund does not literally apply its Articles in this field.

Instead, borrowing from a technique developed by the International Bank at an early stage of its operations, but applied by it, so far as I know, only to administrative expenses, the Bank adopted the procedure outlined below. As a preliminary point, it may be noted here that the establishment of this procedure has resulted in a lack of necessity for the consultations with the International Monetary Fund referred to in Article V, Section 2.

The Board of Executive Directors approved in 1960, the first year of the Bank's operation, Resolution DE-20/60, which after quoting the texts of Article II, Section 4 (b), and Article V, Section 3 (a), provides:

"*Whereas* several member countries have made payments under Article II, Section 4(b), and Article IV, Section 3(e), at rates of exchange below the free market exchange rate against the United States dollar for private capital transactions actually existing in those countries; and

"*Whereas* it is desirable to establish principles applicable not only to these instan-

130

ces but to any comparable circumstances which might arise in the future with regard to any of the foregoing sections,

"The Board of Executive Directors

"Resolves:

"That whenever the effective free market exchange rate with respect to the United States dollar for private capital transactions existing in any member country differs by more than five per cent from the rate at which such member's currency has been paid to the Bank, the President shall request adjustment and payment in accordance with whichever one or more of Article II, Section 4(b); Article IV, Section 3(e); and Article V, Section 3(a); of the Agreement Establishing the Bank, may be pertinent."

Simultaneously, the Board adopted Resolution DE-21/60, as follows:

"Whereas appropriate account should be taken of the practical effect of Article V, Section 4, of the Agreement Establishing the Bank, providing for the issuance of noninterest-bearing notes with respect to amounts in member's national currencies not required by the Bank for the conduct of its operations.

"The Board of Executive Directors

"Resolves:

"That when the President deems it appropriate, after having requested of any member country the payment of the amounts required by virtue of Resolution DE-20/60, he may enter into arrangements with the member country for the issuance of a letter substantially in the form attached hereto."

The form of letter reads:

"Dear Sir:

"In its letters of . . . acknowledging the payments which your country had made on the first installments of its subscription to the capital of the Bank and of its contribution quota to the Fund for Special Operations, the Bank drew to your attention the provisions of Article II, Section 4(b), and Article IV, Section 3(e), of the Agreement Establishing the Bank, which provide in substance that amounts paid in a member's currency shall be subject to such adjustment as the Bank shall determine to be necessary to constitute the full dollar value equivalent of the installments. Reference is also made to the closely related provisions of Article V, Section 3(a), of the Agreement.

"[If at the time the letter was to be issued only Article V, Section 3(a), was applicable, the following initial paragraph would be used:

"Reference is made to Article V, Section 3(a), of the Agreement Establishing the Bank which provides in substance that: 'Whenever the par value in the International Monetary Fund of a member's currency is reduced or the foreign exchange value of a member's currency has, in the opinion of the Bank, depreciated to a significant extent, the member shall pay to the Bank within a reasonable time an additional amount of its own currency sufficient to maintain the value of all the currency of the member held by the Bank in its ordinary capital resources, or in the resources of the Fund, excepting currency derived from borrowings by the Bank.']

"We believe that further attention should now be given to this subject in view of the fact that there exists in your country a free market exchange rate with respect to the United States dollar for private capital transactions which considerably exceeds the rate at which local currency was credited to our accounts. On the date of this letter, this free exchange rate was understood to be about . . . , to one United States dollar.

"The Board of Executive Directors has considered the application of these provisions and has adopted resolutions establishing principles which should be followed thereunder. In accordance with these resolutions, copies of wich are enclosed, the following procedure is proposed with regard to the holdings of the Bank in your currency, to be effective until notice to the contrary is given either by you or by the Bank. The Bank will request . . . , its depository in your country, to establish special accounts on its books from which all actual disbursements in the currency of your country will be made. From time to time, as the Bank anticipates that funds will be needed for such disbursements, it will request the [depository] to sell to the Bank United States dollars against debits to existing accounts of the Bank at the rate at which your currency was credited to those accounts. Simultaneously, the Bank will resell the dollars to the depository for your currency at the then prevailing free market rate applicable to private capital transactions and will deposit the proceeds in the appropriate disbursement account.

"It will, of course, be understood that the Bank shall be solely responsible for determining the time and amount of each transaction under the foregoing procedure although we shall be glad to advise you in advance of our intentions to convert any amount in excess of one per cent of the original balance in the account to be debited.

"Amounts in the currency of your country held in accounts other than the disbursement accounts will of course continue to be valued in dollars at the rate at which they were received by the Bank.

"It should further be understood that this letter does not constitute a waiver of any of the rights of the Bank under the Agreement, including the right to require the maintenance of value under Article V, Section 3(a), of any currency held in or loaned through a disbursement account.

"If this procedure is agreeable to your Government, will you please so advise us.

Sincerely yours,"

In some instances countries have readjusted their official rates with sufficient frequency that it has not been necessary to apply this system, at least beyond making informally the representations provided for by Resolution DE-20/60. In other instances the letter contemplated by Resolution DE-21/60 has been sent, usually adjusted to meet local conditions. To date, the Bank has received a substantially favorable response in all such cases, though sometimes after certain delay and with certain qualifications.

The Bank's loan contracts of course contain a currency clause consistent with this system, reading in its present form as follows:

"Whenever it is necessary to compute in dollars disbursements made in other currencies, then computation shall be based on the equivalent determined for this purpose by the Bank in accordance with the following principles:
"(i) When disbursements are made in the currencies of member countries of the Bank, the rate of exchange applied shall be that at which, on the date of the disbursement, the Bank carried such currencies among its assets, or if necessary, the rate of exchange on which the Bank had agreed with the member country concerned for the purposes of maintaining the value of that country's currency held by the Bank.
"(ii) When disbursements are made in currencies of countries not members of the Bank, the rate of exchange to be applied shall be that at which the Bank carried such currencies among its assets on the date of the respective disbursements."

It may be of interest to note that repayments of amounts loaned in the currency of the borrower are required under the loan contracts to be made on the basis of the dollar equivalents in the free market.

It will be seen that in practical operation this approach employs a system of agreement in place of the formal enforcement of a power of deci-

132

sion. Of course, the Bank does possess in the negotiations the ultimate ability to refuse further loans, especially those involving the use of local currency or conversion of foreign exchange into such currency, but the Management and Board of Executive Directors have never found it necessary or appropriate to resort to this step in order to bring about agreement on the use of the procedure.

It may be said that the system works quite acceptably in cases in which the country follows a true free market policy for exchange transactions generally, whether or not the nominal par value is moved from time to time. When the country has no legal free market in addition to the nominal par value, the system by definition is not applicable, even if an active black market exists, but in general the member countries subject to severe depreciation have established a free market in one way or another. However, this market in turn has sometimes been subjected to rigidities, becoming a sort of unofficial par value, and making the operation of the adjustment system unsatisfactory in some periods. Also, in some countries there have been several "free" rates different from the nominal par and difficulties have arisen from time to time in obtaining agreement on the use of the most realistic of such rates. Despite the existence of such difficulties from time to time, the system has proved to be in general an effective means of dealing with the problem at which it is directed, as well as being one much more conducive to good relations between the Bank and the members affected than a literal application of the provisions of the Agreement.

THE INTERNATIONAL LABOUR ORGANIZATION

by *Nicolas Valticos*
Chief, International Labour Standards Department, International Labour Office

I. THE CHOICE OF TECHNIQUES TO CARRY OUT AN AGREED COURSE OF ACTION

1. Since its establishment in 1919, the International Labour Organization has regarded it essential that one of its main courses of action should be the formulation of standards on labour policies which would be embodied in legal instruments of an international character.[1]

2. The following main reasons can be given for this approach. The first was the problem of international competition: as proposals for the introduction of national legislation on labour matters were often objected to on the ground that such legislation would increase the production cost and would jeopardize the relative position of the country concerned vis-à-vis its competitors in the world markets, it was hoped that the adoption of international labour standards would minimize the kind of unfair competition described as "social dumping". A more general objective for the adoption of international labour standards was to establish universal and lasting peace upon a firm internationally defined basis of social justice. Still more widely, it is felt that social progress should be promoted through concerned international action for reasons of justice and humanity, and that this could best be done on the basis of clearly defined standards of policy.

3. International labour standards are contained in two different kinds of instruments: Conventions, which, following ratification, become binding on ratifying States, and Recommendations which are not designed for the creation of obligations but are essentially guides for national action. As will be seen below, although Recommendations do not entail an international obligation for States to fulfill their provisions, they give rise, as well as Conventions, to two series of obligations under article 19 of the Constitution of the ILO: they have to be submitted to the competent authorities of each member State (normally the legislature) within 12 or 18 months of their adoption and member States have, as in the case of unratified Conventions, to report at appropriate intervals, at the request of the Governing Body of the ILO, on the position in their countries and on the extent to which effect has been given to them.

4. The relative appropriateness of Conventions and Recommendations

---

[1] For a detailed study of international labour standards, see N. Valticos, *Droit international du Travail*, vol. VIII of *Traité de droit du travail* edited by Prof. G. Camerlynck, Paris, Dalloz, 1970.

respectively to deal with a given question depends in each case on the subject-matter and the degree of maturity of the question. Recommendations may be adopted, in particular, when the complexity of the subject and wide differences in the circumstances of different countries make it impossible to provide for a universal and uniform mode of application of international standards, or where this is an exploratory measure, with a view to the subsequent embodiment of the standards in a Convention, or where a more detailed Recommendation aims at supplementing a Convention drafted in more general terms. While Recommendations thus are playing an important role in the work of the ILO, Conventions remain "the backbone" of the system established by the ILO and the only means of creating "legally binding obligations between States".[2]

5. International Labour Conventions have been adopted to a wide extent, as will be seen below, firstly because such devices are specifically provided for and dealt with in detail in the Constitution of the ILO since 1919 as one of the principal methods whereby the Organization may reach its objectives, but secondly because universally accepted standards contained in Conventions may have—and do have—a greater impact than other more informal techniques, especially through their formal ratification and the follow-up action through supervisory machinery. Such international standards may also have an indirect bearing even as regards States which are not formally bound by ratified Conventions, as they constitute, together with standards contained in Recommendations, a generally accepted code in the labour field which is a source of inspiration for governments in framing their social policy as well as a solid basis for the technical assistance work of the Organization.

6. Before dealing in greater detail with the Convention technique, it should also be pointed out that, on the basis of the Preamble of the Constitution of the ILO and of the 1944 Declaration of Philadelphia which was embodied in it, a number of basic principles enunciated in them have come to be considered as entailing certain general obligations for States Members of the ILO, in view of the fact that they have ratified the Constitution and are bound by its terms, and in spite of the fact that they may not have ratified the specific Conventions dealing with these principles in more precise terms. It is thus on the basis of the principle of freedom of association that the ILO, in agreement with the UN, has established a procedure for the international protection of trade union freedom which applies even to States which are not parties to the Freedom of Association Conventions.[3] It is also on the basis of the principle of equal opportunity and treat-

---

[2] See *The International Labour Code*, 1951, Vol. I, Geneva, 1952, pp. LXVIII-LXXV.
[3] See C. Wilfred Jenks, *The International Protection of Trade Union Freedom*, London, 1957, Stevens and Sons, and "The International Protection of Trade Union Rights", in *The International Protection of Human Rights*, edited by Evan Luard, London, Thames and Hudson, 1967.

ment, irrespective of race, that the International Labour Conference considered that the Government of South Africa had, by its policy of *apartheid,* violated its undertaking under the ILO Constitution, and that the Conference condemned this policy.[4]

7. The Convention and Recommendation techniques have been used very widely by the ILO as the two forms of its regular standard-setting activities—which, together with technical co-operation, educational and promotional programs and information media, constitute its various methods of action. In the course of its 55 sessions, from 1919 to 1970, the International Labour Conference has adopted 134 Conventions and 142 Recommendations.[5] On 1 June 1970, the total number of ratifications of Conventions was over 3,600. Apart from these ratifications, there are now in force some 1,000 declarations of application of Conventions, without modifications,[6] to non-metropolitan territories and some 120 declarations with modifications as authorized by article 35 of the Constitution of the ILO. In accordance with general practice, new member States, which had previously the status of non-metropolitan territories or which constituted part of a member State, recognize that they remain bound by the obligations under Conventions which were accepted on their behalf by the State previously responsible for their international relations. Thus, in the course of the last 25 years, 686 ratifications of Conventions in the name of 46 new member States were registered following such confirmation and on the basis of the principle of State succession.[7]

---

[4] International Labour Conference, 48th Session, 1964, *Record of Proceedings,* pp. 484-500 and 825-827.

[5] These instruments relate to the most varied fields of labour policy. They can be grouped into three main categories. The first group in which Conventions and Recommendations were adopted, in particular during the first part of the activity of the Organization, related to the traditional and most urgent fields of labour protection, especially at that time, such as conditions of work and living (hours of work, weekly rest, holidays with pay), work of women and children, social security, industrial hygiene and safety, etc. The second group of instruments dealt with basic machinery and institutions without which the labour protection cannot be made really effective: labour inspection, employment service, labour statistics and minimum wage-fixing machinery. Finally, after a beginning in this field in the Thirties, the Conference has since the Second World War adopted a series of instruments aimed at promoting and ensuring the human rights and fundamental freedoms of workers, that is freedom of association, freedom from forced labour and freedom from discrimination in employment and occupation. In framing these standards an increasing effort is made to develop devices so as to allow the necessary flexibility for Conventions designed to be ratified by countries which have very different economic and social conditions and legal traditions, while maintaining the necessary firmness in regard to basic standards.

[6] The total number of declarations registered was much larger but it has progressively decreased as former territories become independent States and, on obtaining membership in the ILO, the declarations of application are confirmed by them and are registered as ratifications on their behalf (see below).

[7] On this practice and its importance, see C. Wilfred Jenks, "State Succession in Respect of Law-Making Treaties", *The British Year Book of International Law,* 1952,

8. The ratification of International Labor Conventions subject to reservations has always been regarded as inadmissible. The practice of the Organization on the subject was summed up in a Memorandum by the International Labour Office prepared at the request of the International Court of Justice in connection with the *Genocide Case*.[8] This principle is based on the fact that International Labour Conventions are adopted by a procedure which differs in important respects from the procedure applicable to other international instruments.

9. The general reasoning which led to the elaboration of the principle was essentially that the underlying concept on the basis of which customary international law recognizes that reservations to the ratification of international Conventions may be regarded as admissible in certain circumstances is that such Conventions are simply an expression of the will of, and in a sense the exclusive property of, the States which are parties to them, and are subject to modification at any time if the consent of all the States concerned can be obtained. This underlying principle has no application to international labour Conventions, as such Conventions are not the exclusive property of the parties thereto but are governed by special rules and in particular by the Constitution of the ILO which provides, *inter alia,* for their adoption by a Conference with a tripartite composition by a special procedure provided for in the Constitution of the ILO for their submission to the national competent authorities, in the form in which they were adopted by the Conference, and for their ratification when the consent of the competent authority is obtained. The Constitution of the ILO grants to employers' and workers' organizations rights to invoke and to initiate procedures in connection with the application of the provisions of the Conventions and gives their representatives an important place in the international organs entrusted with the supervision of the Conventions. Moreover, International Labour Conventions are designed to promote uniformity of conditions among the parties. On the other hand, the Constitution of the ILO provides a procedure for the modification of the provisions of Conventions to meet special circumstances.

10. The International Court of Justice found it unnecessary to comment on the matter for the purpose of the *Genocide Case*, but the International Law Commission subsequently included in its report[9] to the General As-

---

pp. 105-144; Francis Wolf, "Les conventions internationales du travail et la succession d'Etat", *Annuaire français de droit international*, 1961, pp. 742-751, and "L'Organisation internationale du Travail, sa compétence et les transformations étatiques", *Communicazioni e Studi*, Milan, vol. 9, 1957, pp. 47-71; O'Connell, *State Succession in Municipal Law and International Law*, Cambridge, 1967, vol. II, pp. 202-204.

[8] See *I.C.J. Pleadings*, "Reservations to the Convention on the Prevention and Punishment of the Crime of Genocide", pp. 216-282; International Labour Office, *Official Bulletin*, Vol. XXIV, 1951, pp. 274-311; International Labour Office, *The International Labour Code, 1951*, Vol. I, Geneva, 1952. pp. XCIX-CIV.

[9] See General Assembly, *Official Records*, Sixth Session, Supplement No. 9 (A/1858), p. 4.

sembly of the United Nations on the Work of its Third Session a reference to the fact that "Because of its constitutional structure, the established practice of the International Labor Organization, as described in the Written Statement dated 12 January 1951 of the Organization..., excludes the possibility of reservations to international labor Conventions".

11. While reservations are thus inadmissible in the case of International Labor Conventions, varying degrees of legal obligations may be assumed by States which ratify a number of Conventions, as a result of various devices aiming at achieving the necessary degree of flexibility to take account of the variety in national conditions which is recognized in the Constitution itself.[10] Among such devices the following can be mentioned: clauses laying down different standards for specific countries [11] (such clauses, used in some early Conventions, are no longer employed); adoption of a Convention laying down basic principles [12] in broad terms, sometimes with a supplementary Recommendation dealing with technical details of implementation; division of Conventions into several separate parts, only a minimum number of which need be accepted at the time of ratification,[13] thus permitting the gradual extension of its obligations; division of Conventions into alternative parts, with varying levels of obligations; [14] clauses permitting the acceptance of specified lower standards by certain countries,[15] for example, where the economy and medical facilities are insufficiently developed; permissive exclusions, for example, of specified categories of occupations or undertakings or of insufficiently populated or developed areas,[16] clauses permitting lower standards for countries which, prior to ratification, had standards falling short of the general requirements (such lower standards might [17] or might not [18] be limited

---

[10] Article 19, paragraph 3 of the Constitution provides: "In framing any Convention or Recommendation of general application the Conference shall have due regard to those countries in which climatic conditions, the imperfect development of industrial organization, or other special circumstances make the industrial conditions substantially different and shall suggest the modifications, if any, which it considers may be required to meet the case of such countries."

[11] For example, the Hours of Work (Industry) Convention, 1919 (No. 1).

[12] The Equal Remuneration Convention, 1951 (No. 100); the Discrimination (Employment and Occupation) Convention, 1958 (No. 111); the Social Policy (Basic Aims and Standards) Convention, 1962, (No. 117); the Employment Policy Convention, 1964 (No. 122).

[13] The Social Security (Minimum Standards) Convention, 1952 (No. 102); the Plantations Convention, 1958 (No. 110); the Equality of Treatment (Social Security) Convention, 1962 (No. 118); the Labour Inspection Convention, 1947 (No. 81); the Convention concerning Statistics of Wages and Hours of Work, 1938 (No. 63); the Wages, Hours of Work and Manning (Sea) Convention (Revised), 1958 (No. 109).

[14] The Fee-Charging Employment Agencies Convention (Revised), 1949 (No. 96).

[15] The Social Security (Minimum Standards) Convention, 1952 (No. 102).

[16] To be found in many Conventions, subject to the previous consultation of workers' and employers' organisations.

[17] The Night Work (Women) Convention (Revised), 1948 (No. 89).

[18] The Night Work of Young Persons (Industry) Convention (Revised), 1948 (No. 90).

in time); clauses specifying that national legislation should be adopted in a certain field, but leaving it to the legislation to determine the precise level of the standard of social protection (for example, the minimum age to be prescribed).[19] In many of these cases, States wishing to avail themselves of flexibility clauses must do so in a statement to be included in or to accompany their ratification, and must report regularly on progress towards the establishment of a higher standard.

12. A Convention can be revised if the revising instrument is adopted by the International Labor Conference by the same two-thirds majority which is required for the adoption of a Convention. Under the standard clauses used since 1929, the effect of the ratification and entry into force[20] of a revising Convention is that the ratification by a country of the revising Convention involves the automatic denunciation by it of the earlier Convention from the date on which the new Convention comes into force, and that the revised Convention ceases to be open to further ratifications from the date of its coming into force but remains binding for the States which are bound by it and have not ratified the revised Convention.

II. LEGAL EFFECTS OF MEMBER STATES' APPROVAL OF DECISIONS

13. To be adopted by the International Labor Conference, a draft Convention or Recommendation has to obtain two-thirds of the votes cast by delegates present (either government, employers' or workers' delegates). Once the Convention or Recommendation is thus adopted, it has, in accordance with article 19 of the Constitution of the ILO, to be submitted by each State to its national competent authority, normally its legislature,[21] for the enactment of legislation or other action.[22] If the State obtains the consent of the competent authority, it has to communicate its formal ratification of the Convention to the Director-General of the ILO and take the necessary action to make it effective.

14. The obligation to submit Conventions and Recommendations to the competent authorities and, if the latter give their approval, to communicate the ratification of a Convention to the Director-General of the ILO is of a general nature and does not depend in any way on the nature of the votes cast by government delegates of the State concerned in favour of or against the adoption by the Conference of the Convention in question. In

---

[19] The Minimum Age (Underground Work) Convention, 1965 (No. 123).

[20] As in the case of most other Conventions, the entry into force of a revising Convention generally is subject to its ratification by two States.

[21] In this connection, see N. Valticos, "The International Labor Organization and National Parliaments", *Inter-Parliamentary Bulletin*, 1969, No. 1, pp. 16-31.

[22] In submitting an instrument, the government remains free to make any proposal it considers appropriate in respect of the effect to be given to the Convention or the Recommendation.

fact, it often happens that States vote in favour of Conventions which they do not feel in a position to ratify immediately but which they consider useful as establishing an objective. In other cases, as the United States Government delegation has stated more than once, although, under the national constitutional system the subject-matter of a Convention was not suitable for a treaty and the Convention could therefore not be ratified, the government representatives voted in favour of the Convention because it supported its objectives and because it was given effect to in national legislation.[23] Conversely, States which have not voted in favour of given Conventions, in particular States Members which were not represented at the time of their adoption, very often ratify them after admission to the Organization.

15. Under the above system of adoption of Conventions by the International Labour Conference by a two-thirds majority, their submission to the national competent authorities and their ratification if the consent of the authorities is obtained, there is no formality of signature of the Convention by States' representatives, as in the case of diplomatic treaties, nor is there room for approval of Conventions *ad referendum*.

III. INTERNAL LEGAL EFFECTS OF DECISIONS OF INTERNATIONAL ORGANIZATIONS

16. For States Members of the ILO obligations arise, on the one hand, from the Constitution of the ILO and, on the other hand, from the Conventions adopted within the framework of the Constitution

17. The obligations arising from the Constitution of the ILO are, in the standard-setting field, of two kinds: firstly, as indicated above (paragraph 6), it has been considered that some basic obligations derive from the general standards defined in the Preamble of the Constitution and of the Declaration of Philadelphia which set out the objectives which member States should strive to attain. Secondly, from a formal point of view, governments are, under the Constitution of the ILO, obliged to submit Conventions and Recommendations to their national competent authorities within a prescribed period, to inform the International Labour Office of the measures taken for this purpose and of their results, to submit annual reports on the measures taken to give effect to the provisions of ratified Conventions and to report on their legislation and practice, etc. in the field covered by unratified Conventions and Recommendations, at the request of the Governing Body of the ILO. However, from a substantive point of view, obligations of States mainly derive from Conventions which they have ratified. In these cases, the content of the obligation of each

---

[23] See International Labour Conference, 40th Session, Geneva, 1957, *Record of Proceedings*, Geneva, 1958, p. 352.

State and consequently of the rights of the persons concerned is defined in the terms of the relevant Convention and in the general terms of article 19, paragraph 5 (d), of the ILO Constitution, which provides that the Member which ratifies a Convention "will take such action as may be necessary to make effective the provisions of such Convention".

18. The question as to whether the ratification of a Convention is regarded as directly creating rights and obligations for nationals of the ratifying country—in other words, the question whether, by virtue of the act of ratification, a Convention becomes the law of the land—is of course a matter which depends on national constitutional law.[24] The question has often arisen in respect of International Labor Conventions, and the forms for reports by ratifying countries, which were adopted by the Governing Body of the ILO, contain the following standard clause in this connection:

"If in your country ratification of the Convention gives the force of national law to its terms, please indicate by virtue of what constitutional provisions the ratification has had this effect. Please also specify what action has been taken to make effective those provisions of the Convention which require a national authority to take certain specific steps for its implementation, such as measures to define its exact scope and the extent to which advantage may be taken of permissive exceptions provided for in it, measures to draw the attention of the parties concerned to its provisions, and arrangements for adequate inspection and penalties."

19. Four types of questions have arisen in this connection and have been examined both by national courts in the ratifying countries and by the international bodies entrusted with the task of supervising the application of ratified Conventions.

20. The first question is whether, under the constitutional law of a given country, a ratified treaty—International Labor Conventions being considered as treaties in this connection, in spite of their special features[25] —is in principle incorporated in internal law and, in that case, is effective as municipal law or even, under some constitutional systems, has a force superior to that of national law.[26] In many cases, national courts have ruled in the affirmative. Thus, in the United States, the Supreme Court held without dissent on 26 February 1951 that the Shipowners' Liability (Sick and Injured Seamen) Convention, 1936 (No. 55) became part of the domestic law of the land by virtue of its ratification evidenced by the President's Proclamation and that certain provisions

---

[24] See N. Valticos, "Conventions internationales du travail et droit interne", *Revue critique de droit international privé*, 1955, No. 2, pp. 251-288.
[25] See C. Wilfred Jenks, "Some Characteristics of International Labour Conventions", *Canadian Bar Review*, Vol. XIII, 1935, pp. 448-462, and "Are International Labour Conventions Agreements between Governments?", *ibid.*, Vol. XV, 1937, pp. 574-578.
[26] See, in this connection, N. Valticos, *Droit international du Travail, op. cit.*, 1970, paragraphs 627-628.

thereof were self-executing.[27] In France, the Cour de cassation as well as Courts of Appeal have decided more than once in the same way and have recognized the rights which were claimed by individuals on the basis of ratified Conventions.[28] In a number of cases, governments have explicitly stated in their reports or statements on the application of ratified Conventions that, in virtue of their constitutional systems, ratified Conventions become the law of the land and repeal all contrary provisions. This was in particular the case of Mexico,[29] as well as of other Latin American States. It should however be added that in other countries where ratified Conventions are not automatically incorporated in internal law as a consequence of their constitutional systems, a similar result[30] is obtained when the Act of Parliament which authorizes the ratification of a Convention also provides that the said Convention shall be executed as a national law. This is the case in certain European countries, such as Belgium, Italy and Greece. In such cases, the International Labor Conventions ratified by the countries concerned often constitute the national legislation applicable in the field covered by the Convention (e.g. hours of work, minimum age for admission to employment, holidays with pay, weekly rest) and the courts apply them in individual cases as municipal law.

21. In all the cases where ratified Conventions are thus considered as directly incorporated in municipal law, a second question arises, as was seen from the question contained in the report form quoted above (paragraph 18). It relates to the steps taken to implement the provisions of ratified Conventions which are not self-executing (e.g. provisions requiring certain matters to be prescribed by national laws or regulations or decided by the competent authorities, provisions requiring certain administrative arrangements) or calling for the prescription of penalties. The bodies entrusted with the supervision of ratified Conventions, and in particular the Committee of Experts on the Application of Conventions and Recommendations, have repeatedly found it necessary to draw attention to the non-self-executing provisions of Conventions which require more specific measures of application in the form of laws, regulations or other action.[31]

---

[27] *Warren v. United States*, 1951, 340 US 523.

[28] See, more recently, in this connection, the decision of the *Cour de cassation* of 28 March 1962 commented upon in the *Revue critique de droit international privé*, 1962, pp. 41-72, (N. Valticos, "Les conventions internationales du travail devant le juge français").

[29] See, in particular, as regards the Mexican situation on the basis of article 133 of the Mexican Constitution, International Labour Conference, *Record of Proceedings*, 35th Session, 1952, p. 492, and 36th Session, 1953, pp. 372-373.

[30] Apart from the fact that the Convention is then considered as being on the same footing as national laws and does not take precedence over them as is the case in constitutional systems like that of France and the Netherlands.

[31] See, in particular, a general review of the question in the 1963 Report of that Committee (International Labour Conference, 47th Session, Geneva, 1963, Report III (Part IV), *Report of the Committee of Experts on the Application of Conventions*

22. A third question may arise in the case of conflict between a ratified Convention which was incorporated in municipal law and subsequent legislation. While in a few countries, as said above, legislation subsequent to and inconsistent with the previously ratified Convention may be invalid by virtue of a specific constitutional provision, such is not the case in countries where—as noted by a Commission of Inquiry appointed to examine a complaint filed by the Government of Portugal concerning the observance by the Government of Liberia of the Forced Labor Convention, 1930 (No. 29) [32]—"it is well established that subsequent inconsistent legislation does override an earlier treaty in its operation as municipal law". In such cases, legislative steps have to be taken by the country concerned to eliminate the discrepancies which have arisen.

23. Finally, a fourth question, both legal and practical, relates to the need to avoid uncertainty as regards the legal position and to enable all persons concerned to be aware of the standards laid down in ratified Conventions incorporated in municipal law. The question has mainly arisen in cases where a Convention which was automatically incorporated in municipal law by virtue of its ratification conflicts with earlier national law containing standards lower than those provided for in the ratified Convention. The governments concerned have pointed out on occasion that the ratification of the Convention has had the effect of implicitly repealing the earlier provisions of national law. The position of the bodies entrusted with the examination of the application of Conventions [33] has been that it would be desirable in such cases—in particular in view of the fact that in certain cases judicial decisions did not appear to take into consideration ratified Conventions which were deemed to have been incorporated in municipal law—to bring the national law formally into conformity with the Convention by expressly repealing or amending the earlier laws or codes on the points covered by the Convention, so as to leave no doubt or uncertainty as regards the position in law or to take appropriate measures so that all persons concerned (judges, labour inspectors, employers and workers) can be informed of the incorporation of the Convention in municipal law and of its effect on pre-existing legislation. The governments concerned sometimes expressly agreed with the proposed

---

and Recommendations, General Report, pp. 8-12). See also the 1970 Report of that Committee (pp. 7-8, paragraphs 18-19) and the Report of the Commission appointed under Article 26 of the Constitution of the I.L.O. to Examine the Complaint Filed by the Government of Portugal Concerning the Observance by the Government of Liberia of the Forced Labor Convention, 1930 (No. 29), International Labor Office, Official Bulletin, Vol. XLVI, No. 2, Supp. II, April 1963, paragraphs 401-403, pp. 159-160.

[32] See Report of the Portugal-Liberia Commission quoted in the footnote above, paragraphs 405-406, pp. 160-161.

[33] See Committee of Experts on the Application of Conventions and Recommendations, 1963, op. cit., General Report, paragraphs 31-34, pp. 10-11.

course and took action in this connection. Thus, one government indicated that the Labor Code had been published with references to the provisions of ratified Conventions,[34] other governments set up committees to consider the measures needed in order to consolidate the provisions of international Conventions[35] or printed in an *Official Review* the texts of ratified Conventions as well as of related provisions of the (Mexican) Federal Labor Code, "to establish clearly that the relevant provisions of these Conventions had acquired force of law in the country in virtue of . . . the Constitution".[36]

IV. COMPLIANCE: MEASURES TO HELP ENSURE THAT MEMBER STATES' COMMITMENTS OR OBLIGATIONS ARE CARRIED OUT

24. The ILO has sought to establish machinery and procedures permitting the implementation, on the widest scale, of obligations arising out of the Constitution and ratified Conventions.[37] As was said above, these obligations relate to the submission of Conventions and Recommendations to the competent authorities and reporting thereon, to the implementation of ratified Conventions and reporting annually on the measures taken to this effect, and to reporting, at appropriate intervals, on unratified Conventions and on Recommendations. Various procedures, based either on the regular examination of governments' reports or on the presentation of complaints, have been devised in this connection.

1. *General procedure based on the regular examination of governments' annual reports*

Reports on ratified Conventions

25. The general procedure of supervision of the application of ratified Conventions is based on the obligation of governments, under article 22 of the Constitution of the ILO, to supply annual reports on the measures taken

---

[34] See International Labor Conference, 46th Session, 1962, *Record of Proceedings*, p. 690 (Guatemala).

[35] See International Labor Conference, 47th Session, 1963, *Record of Proceedings*, p. 742 (Argentina).

[36] See International Labor Conference, 50th Session, 1966, *Record of Proceedings*, p. 582.

[37] For the supervision machinery established by the ILO, see E. A. Landy, *The Effectiveness of International Supervision—Thirty Years of I.L.O. Experience*, Stevens, London, and Oceana, New York, 1966, pp. 9-52; N. Valticos, *Un système de contrôle international: la mise en oeuvre des conventions internationales du travail, Recueil des Cours de l'Académie de droit international*, Sijthoff, Leiden, vol. 123 (1968-I), pp. 311-407.

by them to give effect to Conventions which they have ratified. By virtue of the same article, these reports must be made in such form and contain such particulars as the Governing Body requests in the report forms adopted to this effect. Under arrangements introduced as from 1960, "detailed" reports on the application of ratified Conventions are normally due from States only every second year, except where, on account of the importance of the discrepancies noted or the long time during which they have been outstanding, the supervisory bodies request that a detailed report be also supplied in the intervening year.

26. States are required to communicate copies of their reports to the representative organizations of employers and workers in their country (article 23 (2) of the Constitution). These organizations may make observations on the application of the provisions of a Convention, and States are requested to supply information in their reports on any such observations received and to add any comments that they may consider useful.

Reports on unratified conventions and on recommendations

27. The Constitution of the ILO has also provided, in article 19, paragraphs 5, 6 and 7, that States Members must at the request of the Governing Body submit reports indicating the position of their law and practice in regard to the matters dealt with in Conventions which they have not ratified or in Recommendations, showing the extent to which effect has been given or is proposed to be given to their provisions. In the case of a Convention, States Members must also indicate the difficulties which prevent or delay ratification. In the case of a Recommendation, they must indicate the modifications which have been found necessary in applying the instrument. Copies of these reports also must be communicated to representative organizations of employers and workers. In application of the provisions of article 19, the Governing Body chooses each year a limited number of Conventions and Recommendations of current interest and requests States to supply reports on them.

Examination of reports

(a) Summary of reports

28. The Director-General is required by the Constitution (article 23, paragraph 1) to lay before each annual session of the International Labor Conference a summary of the information and reports which have been communicated to him by member States.

(b) The Committee of Experts on the Application of Conventions and Recommendations

29. The reports supplied by governments have been subject, since 1927, to technical examination by the Committee of Experts on the Application

of Conventions and Recommendations. This Committee is composed of independent members who are appointed in their personal capacity and not as representatives of governments by the Governing Body of the ILO, on the proposal of the Director-General. The requirements of impartiality and independence, and of eminent qualifications in the legal or social fields, have remained the basic criteria in the appointment of members of the Committee. Accordingly, the experts are at present drawn mainly from the judiciary, from academic circles (professors of international or labour law) and from amongst persons with considerable experience in public administration. The spirit in which the Committee carries out its activities was described by the Committee itself on several occasions. Thus, in 1957 and again in 1967 and in 1969, the Committee stated that its fundamental principles "call for impartiality and objectivity in pointing out the extent to which it appears that the position in each State is in conformity with the terms of the Conventions and the obligations which that State has undertaken in virtue of the Constitution of the International Labor Organization. They must accomplish their task in complete independence as regards all member States". At present, the Committee is composed of five experts from Western Europe, four from Asia and the Middle East, three from Eastern Europe, three from Latin America, two from Africa, and one each from North America and the Caribbean.

30. The experts are appointed for an initial period of three years and these appointments may be renewed for further three-year periods. Under the practice followed by the Governing Body, the mandates of the experts have generally been extended for successive periods, as it has been found that continuity of membership not only enables the experts to become thoroughly familiar with the often complex standards for which they are responsible, but that such continuity also facilitates discussion within the Committee which must rely on the cumulative experience of its members in shaping and formulating its views on a collective basis.

31. In order to comply with its terms of reference, the Committee of Experts examines the situation of the States by consulting, in the first place, the reports supplied by governments, official journals, compilations of legislation, etc., and also any available information on practical application and data contained in any comments made by employers' or workers' organizations.

32. The comments made by the Committee of Experts on the basis of this examination take various forms. In the case of ratified Conventions, the comments are normally made in the form of observations drawing attention to a divergency existing between the national legislation and practice, on the one hand, and the provisions of the Convention, on the other hand. The aim of these observations is not to condemn, but to try to persuade governments to ensure fuller compliance. The observations are incorporated in the printed report of the Committee and communicated both to governments and for discussion to the Conference (see below). Howe-

ver, since 1957, in order that the Committee's report and the discussion at the Conference may be centred on the more important points, the comments adopted by the Committee of Experts have, in a large number of cases, taken the form of requests; this is done when the point at issue is technical or involves a discrepancy of relatively minor importance, or when the object is to obtain more detailed information. These requests are communicated directly to governments on behalf of the Committee, without being reproduced in extenso in its report.

33. Apart from the cases of discrepancies, the Committee of Experts also reports and lists, each year, the cases of progress made as a result of its previous comments (see paragraph 41).

34. In 1967, the Committee of Experts put forward a proposal concerning the possibilities of *direct contacts* with governments in certain cases where, in addition to its customary procedure based on the examination of reports and legislative texts, a fuller assessment of all aspects of a particular situation might prove useful. Such contacts have taken place, in 1969, in three countries and led to positive results. Requests for similar contacts have since been received from further countries.

35. The Committee follows the same procedure in matters relating to the obligation on States to submit Conventions and Recommendations to the competent authorities.

36. In the case of reports requested on unratified Conventions and on Recommendations, the Committee presents a detailed over-all survey indicating, in regard to the Conventions and Recommendations selected for reporting, the situation in the various member States, whether or not the latter have ratified the Conventions in question.

(c) *The Conference Committee on the Application of Conventions and Recommendations*

37. The International Labor Conference, at each session, appoints a special committee comprising government, employers' and workers' representatives, which is called on to examine the question of the application of Conventions and Recommendations. This committee bases its work on the observations made by the Committee of Experts. It invites the governments concerned to participate in its work with a view to providing additional information with regard to the discrepancies noted and to the measures which they have taken or contemplate taking to eliminate these discrepancies. During the Committee's discussions, employers' and workers' representatives can express their views on the manner in which Conventions are applied, whether in their own country, or in other countries. The Conference Committee summarizes its discussions and any conclusions which it may reach in a report which it submits to the Conference and which is discussed by the latter in plenary session. In recent years, the Conference Committee has in its report drawn the special attention of the Conference to cases in which governments appear to have encountered

serious difficulties in fulfilling certain of their obligations under the Constitution of the International Labor Organization or ratified Conventions.

General characteristics of the procedure based on the examination of governments' reports

38. The supervision procedure described above thus has the following general characteristics:

(a) in the first place, the procedure is characterized by its periodicity: on the basis of reports (annual or bi-annual) requested from governments, the supervisory bodies (the Committee of Experts and the Conference Committee) are able at regular intervals to evaluate the situation and, in cases where discrepancies have been noted in the application of Conventions, to review and note at each session the extent to which progress has been made;

(b) the procedure is also characterized by the existence of two distinct bodies, one of which is composed of independent persons (the Committee of Experts), the other of government, employers' and workers' representatives (Conference Committee);

(c) the procedure is also characterized by flexibility: thus, the comments of the Committee of Experts may, according to the importance of the case, take the form either of a published observation or of a request addressed directly to the government; similarly, according to the importance of the case, reports are requested from governments at yearly or two-yearly intervals.

Results of the procedure

39. The results of the procedure can be considered from a formal and from a substantive point of view.

40. From a formal point of view, the proportion of governments which fulfill their reporting obligations is very high, as it has varied between 80 and 95 per cent in the last decade.

41. From a substantive point of view, the position can be considered as being, on the whole, relatively satisfactory, given the present stage of international organization. In the course of the seven years ending in 1970, the Committee of Experts was able to indicate 520 cases, of varying degree of importance, in which over 80 States and 30 territories in all parts of the world have taken action to eliminate discrepancies to which it had previously drawn attention.

42. In a more general examination of the effectiveness of this system of international supervision,[38] it was found that out of 3,422 cases examined

---

[38] E. A. Landy, *op. cit.* See, in particular, pp. 63-66.

by the Committee of Experts in 30 years, in 72 per cent. of the cases it was not found necessary to make any observations. Out of the remaining cases (approximately 1,000), 32 per cent. of the observations have led to full action by governments, directly or by stages, 29 per cent. to partial action, 2 per cent. to denunciation of the Convention, and in the remaining 37 per cent. (i.e. approximately 10 per cent. of all the ratifications considered) no result has thus far been achieved.

2. Procedures based on the presentation of complaints

(a) General procedure for complaints and representations

43. Apart from the above procedure based on the regular examination of reports from governments, the ILO Constitution (articles 24 to 34) provides for more formal procedures based either on complaints or on representations.

44. Complaints can be filed by one State Member against another on the ground that the latter does not secure the effective observance of a Convention which both have ratified. The Governing Body of the ILO can also adopt the same procedure either of its own motion or on the basis of a complaint from a delegate to the Conference.

45. In recent years, three such complaints were received. The first (in February 1961) originated from the Government of Ghana and was directed against the Government of Portugal (as regards Angola, Mozambique and Portuguese Guinea) and the second, a few months later, originated from the Government of Portugal and was directed against the Government of Liberia. Both concerned the ILO Forced Labor Conventions (the 1957 Convention in the first case and the 1930 Convention in the second one). In the two cases, the Governing Body appointed Commissions of Inquiry, each constituted of three independent members of high standing acting in a quasi-judicial capacity. These Commissions examined the submissions from the parties, gave an opportunity to non-governmental organizations to express their views, heard witnesses who appeared both at the request of the parties and at the request of the Commission itself and, in the case of the Commission appointed to examine the complaint of Ghana against Portugal, travelled extensively in Angola and Mozambique to supplement the evidence it had received by on-the-spot inquiry. The recommendations made by the two Commissions were accepted by the parties, which thus did not avail themselves of the possibility to refer the matter to the International Court of Justice, which is open to a party which does not accept the recommendations of the Commission. Various measures were taken by the governments concerned to give effect to the recommendations of the Commissions of Inquiry and the examination of the further measures to be taken was entrusted to the regular machinery described above (Committee of Experts and Conference Committee on the Ap-

149

plication of Conventions and Recommendations). A third complaint was submitted in June 1968 by a number of Workers' delegates at the International Labor Conference and was directed against the Government of Greece in relation to the observance of the Freedom of Association and Protection of the Right to Organize Convention, 1948 (No. 87). It is being examined by a Commission of Inquiry consisting of three independent members appointed by the Governing Body.

46. Apart from these complaints, representations can also be made by an employers' or workers' organization that any State has not effectively applied a ratified Convention. Seven such representations were received and examined between the two World Wars and more recently a representation received from a Brazilian civil servants' organization in São Paulo, alleging that Brazil did not fully apply the Labor Inspection Convention, 1947 (No. 81), was examined first by a tripartite Committee, then by the Governing Body of the ILO in March 1967 and the matter was followed up since through the regular machinery described above. More recently, in March 1970, a representation was received from an Italian employers' organization alleging that Italy did not observe a provision of the Employment Service Convention, 1948 (No. 88).

(b) *Special Procedure relating to Freedom of Association*

47. In view of the particular importance attaching to freedom of association for trade union purposes, the ILO established in 1950, in agreement with the Economic and Social Council of the United Nations, special machinery for the examination of complaints of alleged infringements of trade union rights, which may be submitted by governments or by workers' and employers' organizations.[39] This machinery supplements the general procedures relating to the application of the Freedom of Association Conventions. A striking feature of this machinery is that the submission and examination of complaints is not dependent on the ratification of the ILO's Freedom of Association Conventions by the country involved. The machinery is based on the importance attached to the principle of freedom of association, which is stressed in the Preamble of the Constitution of the ILO and in the Declaration of Philadelphia, which is part of the Constitution.

48. The procedure involves two bodies: in the first instance, a Committee on Freedom of Association, established by the Governing Body of the ILO on a tripartite basis and which follows a quasi-judicial procedure. During the first ten years of its existence, this Committee had as its Chairman Paul Ramadier, former President of the Council of Ministers of France, and since then its Chairman has been Mr. Roberto Ago, Professor of International Law at the University of Rome. Rules have been

---

[39] See C. Wilfred Jenks, *The International Protection of Trade Union Freedom*, London, 1957, Stevens and Sons.

established for the working of this procedure, particularly as regards the receivability of complaints, communication with complainants and governments, and the non-participation in the Committee's deliberations of representatives or nationals of States against which a complaint has been made or of persons occupying an official position in the organization which has made the complaint. A more rapid procedure is provided for to deal with urgent cases. The Committee has examined, since its establishment, over 600 cases of alleged infringements of trade union rights (anti-union legislation or practice, arrests of trade unionists, government interference in trade union activities, dissolution of trade unions, prohibition of strikes, etc.). The Committee's reports have been unanimous in practically all cases. In a number of cases, the recommendations made by the Governing Body on the Committee's suggestion were acted upon by the governments concerned.

49. The second body which has been established under this machinery is the Fact-Finding and Conciliation Commission on Freedom of Association. This Commission consists of independent persons of high standing acting in a quasi-judicial capacity. The referral of a case to the Commission is subject to the consent of the Government concerned. While in the earlier cases the governments which were requested to do so by the Governing Body did not give their consent, in the course of the last three years, two governments gave their consent to the referral of cases concerning their countries to the Commission. Thus, in the case of Japan, which involved persons employed in the public sector, the three-member Commission followed a procedure similar to that of the Commissions of Inquiry. It requested information from the parties and from international and Japanese employers' and workers' organizations, it heard witnesses at the request of the parties and at its own request, and it went to Japan, where it held discussions with representatives of the Government and of the complaining organizations as well as with persons in the various circles involved. The conclusions and recommendations made by the Commission in 1965 were accepted by the Government and the complaining organizations as the basis for the development of labor relations in the public sector of Japan, and, following this procedure, the Government of Japan ratified the Freedom of Association and Protection of the Right to Organize Convention, 1948 (No. 87) and repealed certain legislative provisions which appeared contrary to trade union rights.

General characteristics of the procedure based on the presentation of complaints

50. In spite of their diversity, the procedures relating to the presentation of complaints have a certain number of common features. The main one is that the examination of complaints is, as a general rule, entrusted to bodies composed of independent members working in accordance with quasi-

judicial principles and procedure (Commission of Inquiry set up in virtue of article 26 of the Constitution of the ILO and the Fact-Finding and Conciliation Commission on Freedom of Association).[40] This stress on impartiality is designed both to ensure the objective examination of the complaint and to obtain the confidence and co-operation of the parties to the complaint by guaranteeing that political considerations are excluded from the procedure. It should also be borne in mind that these procedures, if they are to be brought to a successful conclusion, necessitate appropriate diplomatic consultations at various stages, under the responsibility of the Director-General of the ILO.

Main features of the supervisory machinery

51. The two major systems described above, i.e. the system based on the regular examination of governments' reports and the system based on the presentation of complaints (see, for their general characteristics, paragraphs 38 and 50 above), are complementary in character. Whereas the system of complaints (except as regards the special procedure before the Committee on Freedom of Association) is exceptional, the system of periodical and routine supervision on the basis of reports from governments has become the general rule and constitutes, by its very regularity, the essential machinery for the supervision of the application of Conventions and Recommendations.

52. The characteristics common to all these procedures are the safeguards with which they have been surrounded to ensure the highest degree of thoroughness and objectivity, the distinction made between the quasi-judicial phases entrusted to independent bodies and the political phases of consideration by the legislative and administrative bodies of the Organization, diplomatic preparation at appropriate stages, the participation at certain stages of employers' and workers' organizations, the utilization of a qualified secretariat, and, finally, recognition that these

---

[40] The different practice established in regard to the composition of the Committee on Freedom of Association of the Governing Body, which comprises representatives of governments, employers and workers, is due, on the one hand, to the fact that originally the task of this body was envisaged as being simply to carry out a preliminary examination of complaints in order to decide whether they called for further examination, and, on the other hand, to the fact that, as it was dealing with questions of trade union rights which concern closely governments, employers and workers, the tripartite structure of the Committee made it possible to ensure a certain balance in the examination of complaints regarding the exercise of such rights and to formulate conclusions of such a nature as to command general acceptance. Furthermore, the functioning of the Committee has been attended by certain guarantees of a judicial character and it is open to any government which so desires to ask for a case in which it is concerned to be referred to the Fact-Finding and Conciliation Commission on Freedom of Association.

procedures do not operate in isolation, that they are interdependent and complementary parts of complex machinery, all pursuing a single aim: to ensure—objectively and impartially—the full respect of the rule of law and the maximum effectiveness of international labor standards.

Other measures to help member States to carry out their obligations (technical assistance, promotional action)

53. Apart from the quasi-judicial methods described above, which mainly aim at assessing the degree of compliance of member States with their obligations, other measures also are used to help them overcome the difficulties encountered in carrying out such obligations or in reaching the level which would permit them to ratify the relevant Conventions. These measures involve technical assistance supplied to governments in various forms, either in helping them in the drafting of labor legislation which would take account of the international standards, or in establishing or developing the institutions provided in the standards (social security, employment service, labour inspection, etc.). Seminars on national and international standards are also organized every year in a different region to acquaint labor officers of the governments of the region with the obligations under the ILO Constitution and Conventions and to discuss difficulties encountered. Finally, in the field of discrimination in employment and occupation a special promotional program has been established by the ILO.

V. THE SPECIAL PROBLEMS OF FEDERAL STATES

54. The special problems of federal States have been a matter of particular interest and concern on the part of the International Labor Organization [41] because of the division of legislative and administrative authority as regards the effect to be given to the provisions of Conventions and Recommendations. As a result, the number of ratifications by federal countries has generally been small. The rules which govern this problem, as contained in article 19, paragraph 7, of the Constitution of the ILO, are the following. In respect of Conventions and Recommendations which the federal government regards as appropriate under its constitutional system for federal action, the obligations of the federal State are the same as those of other Members. In respect of Conventions and Recommendations which the federal government regards as appropriate, in whole or in part, for action by the constituent States, provinces or cantons, rather than for federal action, the federal government is required: (a) to make effective arrangements for the reference of such Conventions and Recommendations

---

[41] See *The International Labour Code, 1951*, Vol. I, pp. LXXIX-LXXI.

to the appropriate federal, State or provincial authorities; (b) to arrange, subject to the concurrence of the State, provincial, or cantonal governments concerned, for periodical consultations between the federal and the State, provincial, or cantonal authorities with a view to promoting within the federal State co-ordinated action to give effect to the provisions of such Conventions and Recommendations; (c) to inform the Director-General of the action taken to bring such Conventions and Recommendations before the appropriate authorities, with particulars of the action taken by them; and (d) to report to the Director-General at appropriate intervals, as requested by the Governing Body, on the position of federal and State, provincial, or cantonal law and practice in regard to unratified Conventions and Recommendations.

55. It is to be noted that the division of powers between the federal government and the constituent units varies from one country to another according to their constitutional system, and that the matters covered by International Labor Conventions and Recommendations may accordingly fall to a varying degree within the jurisdiction of the federal government or of the constituent units, or of both.[42] Moreover, while a number of the federal States have certain powers to accept and implement treaty engagements on matters which for municipal purposes are within the jurisdiction of their respective States and provinces, such powers are, in the case of most of the countries concerned, largely ineffective in practice owing to political and administrative difficulties. On the other hand, some federal States found it possible to ratify Conventions dealing with matters primarily within State or provincial jurisdiction on the basis of the concurrence of the State or provincial authorities in ratification.[43]

56. The special problems of federal States were considered by the ILO not only in the general provisions of its Constitution, but also in the drafting of a number of more recent Conventions. The question of including in Conventions, in appropriate cases, clauses designed to facilitate ratification by federal States as such by qualifying the obligations of such States upon ratification had been discussed on a number of occasions. More generally, several Conventions[44] adopted in recent years were drafted in flexible terms providing that action to implement the relevant standards should be according to "methods appropriate to national conditions and

---

[42] This is reflected to a certain degree in the great difference in the number of Conventions ratified by various countries with a federal system (Argentina: 57; Australia: 28; Austria: 37; Brazil: 51; Canada: 24; Federal Republic of Germany: 40; India: 30; Mexico: 51; Switzerland: 31; USSR: 40; United States: 7; Yugoslavia: 56).

[43] This was in particular the case of Australia for several Conventions dealing with agricultural workers. A similar trend is beginning to appear as regards Canada which recently ratified the Discrimination (Employment and Occupation) Convention, 1958 (No. 111).

[44] E.g., the Equal Renumeration Convention, 1951 (No. 100), Article 2, and the Discrimination (Employment and Occupation) Convention, 1958 (No. 111), Article 3.

154

practice", and such provisions are capable of implementation to the extent made possible by the constitutional system and practice of each federal State.[45]

VI. AMENDMENT OF CONSTITUENT INSTRUMENTS THROUGH METHODS OTHER THAN EXPLICIT APPROVAL BY ALL MEMBERS

57. Since the establishment of the ILO in 1919, it has been provided in its Constitution that amending its constitutional provisions should not be subject to the approval of all member States. At present, the relevant rules, contained in article 36 of the Constitution, read as follows:

"Amendments to this Constitution which are adopted by the Conference by a majority of two-thirds of the votes cast by the delegates present shall take effect when ratified or accepted by two-thirds of the Members of the Organization including five of the ten Members which are represented on the Governing Body as a Member of chief industrial importance."

58. The original text of the Constitution, established in 1919, has been amended several times: in 1922 (amendment entered into force in 1934); in 1945 (amendment entered into force in 1946); in 1946 (amendment entered into force in 1948); in 1953 (amendment entered into force in 1954), and in 1962 (amendment entered into force in 1963). Moreover, three amendments were adopted by the required majority of the Conference in 1965 but have not yet received the necessary number of ratifications or acceptances for their entry into force.

Geneva, 1 July 1970

---

[45] See, in this connection, the *Report of the Committee of Experts on the Application of Conventions and Recommendations*, 1963, Report III (Part IV), Part Three, paragraph 109, p. 226.

THE INTERNATIONAL CIVIL AVIATION ORGANIZATION—A CASE STUDY IN THE IMPLEMENTATION OF DECISIONS OF A FUNCTIONAL INTERNATIONAL ORGANIZATION

by *Gerald F. FitzGerald*
Senior Legal Officer, International Civil Aviation Organization
Lecturer, Institute of Air and Space Law, McGill University, Montreal

FOREWORD

This paper describes the experience of the International Civil Aviation Organization in the implementation of its decisions and is entitled: "The International Civil Aviation Organization—A Case Study in the Implementation of Decisions of a Functional International Organization".*

The subject is examined under three broad headings: (1) Technique of making decisions legally binding and practically effective; (2) Techniques available in ICAO to encourage compliance with decisions, and (3) Specific topics and questions. Item (1) is concerned with the theories underlying the effectiveness of decisions of international organizations working in the functional field. Item (2) examines the methods of adoption of ICAO regulatory material and the process followed in its implementation. Item (3) discusses various topics and questions posed by the sponsor of the conference for which the paper was prepared; it gives a sampling of ICAO experience in the implementation of a wide variety of decisions, including decisions other than those concerned with the adoption of regulatory material.

Briefly, ICAO is a specialized agency in relationship with the United Nations, established under the Convention on International Civil Aviation (Chicago, 1944),** with some 119 Contracting States now belonging to it and having jurisdiction over matters pertaining to international civil aviation. One of the important tasks of ICAO is to adopt technical regulatory material and regional plans with a view to ensuring the safety, efficiency and regularity of international civil aviation. Much of the technical regulatory material is found in Annexes to the Chicago Convention which are adopted by the 27-Member ICAO Council. ICAO is also active in the economic field, prepares draft conventions on air law and also performs a substantial amount of work under the United Nations Development Programme.

---

* This paper was written in a private capacity; responsibility for the opinions expressed is the author's. Unless otherwise indicated, references to documents are to those of ICAO.
** 34 U.N.T.S. 295 (1948).

I. TECHNIQUE OF MAKING DECISIONS LEGALLY BINDING AND PRACTICALLY EFFECTIVE

1. *Preliminary comments*

The theme of the Conference is: "Decisions of international organizations: effectiveness in Member States." This theme may be examined in relation to the decisions classified in different ways and the classifications may vary from organization to organization. The decisions of a functional international organization like ICAO may be classified and examined under various headings of which the following are examples:

(1) *Form*

Treaty, organizational decision, resolution, recommendation and consensus.

(2) *Subject-matter*

Constitutional, administrative, technical, economic, legal and technical assistance.

(3) *Terms*

Hortatory: Such decisions do not impose legal obligations; but the extent to which they influence the behaviour of a State is important.

Binding: Such decisions impose legal obligations.

Mixed: Such decisions contain both hortatory and binding provisions.[1]

The decision of an international organization will be effective to the extent to which it can be implemented. The prospects of implementation will be affected by such variable factors as the following: Time of adoption of decision; issues involved; nature of size of majority, unanimity, States voting for and against, abstentions; language in which decision framed; methods and means available for implementation; extent to which expectations of Member States of organizations are raised by decision[2] and sanctions.

No attempt is made here to comment on the foregoing items in detail; but some of them will come up for consideration in the discussion below.

2. *Extent to which decisions are binding*

There has been much discussion concerning the extent to which decisions of international bodies are to be considered to be legally binding upon

---

[1] For a discussion of the different kinds of resolutions of the United Nations General Assembly, see Skubiszewski, Krysztof, "The General Assembly of the United Nations and Its Power to Influence National Action", (1964) *Proceedings of the A.S.I.L.*, 153-162; also in Falk Richard A. and Mendlovitz, Saul H., *The Strategy of World Order*, Vol. 3, *The United Nations* (hereinafter cited as "FM-3"), 238-247.

[2] Lande, Gabriella R., (1964), "The Changing Effectiveness of General Assembly Resolutions", *Proceedings of the A.S.I.L.* 167-173; also in FM-3, 230-236.

Member States of international organizations. One commentator writes of "the rather indefinite line that separates *binding* from *non-binding* norms governing international behaviour".[3] Much depends on whether the decisions are concerned with the internal operations of the organizations (States will usually accept financial obligations under the regular budget for regular operations)[4] or with important substantive issues in respect of which the constituent instrument gives certain powers to the decision-making body. The form of the decision, the variables applicable to it and the sanctions for non-compliance are important factors in assessing the extent to which a resolution is binding. Many resolutions are of a dual nature. While they are couched in hortatory terms which clearly put them into the class of recommendations in relation to States, they may, at the same time, contain binding instructions for subsidiary bodies of the organization.

A distinction can be made between "law-creating" and "law-applying" resolutions of an international organ.[5] There are relatively few of the former in international bodies if constitutional and internal housekeeping resolutions are left aside. As to the latter, there is authority for the proposition that resolutions dealing with the internal operations of the United Nations have the status of law.[6] But even if resolutions are not backed up by legal sanctions, i.e., sanctions expressly stated in the constituent instruments of the organization concerned, they could nevertheless be called "law-making" in a broad sense. The ground for this assertion is that reasonable community expectations with respect to the behaviour of States in conformity with these resolutions are a much more important indication of the existence of law than is the formal language accompanying the standard-setting act.[7]

In the light of the foregoing considerations, it may now be of interest to examine the varied language used in some of the resolutions of the 15th Session of the ICAO Assembly[8] and then to consider typical Council resolutions and decisions. From this examination, it will be seen that few ICAO decisions have binding force.

Decisions of the ICAO Assembly run the gamut from hortatory resolutions addressed to States, through instructions to subsidiary organs of

---

[3] Falk, Richard A., "On the Quasi-legislative Competence of the General Assembly", (1966) 60 *A.J.I.L.* 784.

[4] Skubiszewski, Krysztof, *op. cit.*, note 1 *supra*, 158; also FM-3, 243.

[5] Vallat, Sir Frances, "The Competence of the United Nations General Assembly", (1959) 97 *Recueil des Cours* 211.

[6] Skubiszewski, *op. cit.*, note 1 *supra*, 154; also in FM-3, 239.

[7] FM-3, 248, referring to the views of Professor Myres McDougal.

[8] Doc 8528 A15-P/6. In 1968, the Assembly, at its 16th session, specified the resolutions (or parts thereof) of preceding sessions that were no longer in force. The material which remained in force is published, together with resolutions of the 16th session, in Doc 8770, Assembly Resolutions in Force (as of 26 September 1968).

ICAO, to resolutions binding on States and concerned with the adoption of the budget and scale of assessments on States. By way of example, here are varied terms taken at random from the resolutions of the 15th Session of the Assembly:[9] "urges the Governments" (A15-1); "reiterates its request... to recipient States" (A15-4); "draws the attention of recipient States" (A15-4); "reminds recipient States" (A15-4); "reaffirms the validity of Resolution..." (A15-4); "reaffirms the need for user and provider Contracting States to give serious consideration" (A15-5); "invites States to examine" (A15-5); "strongly condemns" (A15-7); "requests all nations and peoples of the world" (A15-7); "urges South Africa to comply" (A15-7); "declares that the Appendices... constitute the consolidated statement of continuing air navigation policies" (A15-8); "resolves" (A15-8 and Appendices which contain sub-resolutions; but the various sub-resolutions to the main resolution are mostly hortatory); "encourages Contracting States" (A15-21); "resolves that the Contracting States should continue to review periodically their national procedures and practices" (A15-23) and "that the Contracting States should report to ICAO" (A15-23); "resolves that... there is hereby authorized for expenditure..." (Budget Resolution) (A15-26); "resolves that the budget appropriations shall be financed as follows:... by assessment on Contracting States" (A15-26); "directs the Council" (A15-1); "requests the Council" (A15-1) and "requests the Secretary General" (A15-1).

Save for the budgetary resolutions, it could hardly be said that merely because resolutions of the Assembly include such words as "resolves" and "declares", they are binding on Member States of ICAO. Many resolutions of the Assembly are directed to the Council and "request" it, "instruct" it, "invite" it to do certain things or "approve" action taken by the Council. States could be indirectly affected, though not necessarily bound by, some of these resolutions which, for example, might bind the Council to procure certain information from States.

It may also be observed that many decisions of the Assembly will be found in reports of its various committees and commissions as approved by the Assembly in plenary meetings and will not be in the form of a resolution.

The practice of the ICAO Council (a 27-member body) in making decisions is to adopt formal resolutions only rarely. When formal resolutions or declarations are adopted, they are intended to have a considerable moral effect. For example, the Council has adopted formal resolutions in relation to the interpretation of Article 5 of the Convention,[10] the elimination of burdensome insurance requirements, the elimination of double taxation

---

[9] For a reference to various operative words used in resolutions of the United Nations General Assembly, see Sloan, B., "The Binding Force of a Recommendation of the General Assembly of the United Nations", (1948) 25 *B.Y.I.L.* 3.
[10] Doc 7188-C/828 Proceedings of the Council, 11th Session (1950), 36-38.

in relation to certain aspects of international air transport [11] and the use of international airports by many types of international civil aviation without any unnecessary restrictions. [12]

Of specific interest are the Council resolutions used for the adoption of Annexes to the Convention. These resolutions are founded on provisions of the Convention which spell out the procedure for the adoption of Annexes. They have changed but little since their original pattern was established in 1948. The extent to which they are binding will be discussed later.

3. *Sanctions and the question of practical effectiveness of a decision*

The sanctions for non-compliance with, or non-implementation of, a decision by States greatly influence its practical effectiveness.

On the national level, a powerful inducement to a citizen to comply with a law is the sanction stipulated for non-compliance, the sanction often being in the form of a fine or imprisonment or both. Since the members of functional intergovernmental international organizations are sovereign States, relatively few written sanctions are found in the constituent instruments of these organizations.

Much of the writing on the subject of practical effectiveness of the decisions of international organizations has been about the effectiveness of the resolutions of the United Nations General Assembly where the political content is high and effective sanctions, apart from power considerations, low. [13] A number of authors, however, have examined the effectiveness of decisions of functional international organizations, e.g., those concerned with communications and welfare. [14] Here, the international sanctions will reside in the non-participation of the non-conforming Member State in the benefits flowing from observance of the norms stipulated in decisions of the organization. [15] In writing of the International Monetary Fund, one

---

[11] Doc 7346-C/855 Proceedings of the Council, 12th Session (1951), 33-39.
Doc 7241-C/838 Action of the Council, 14th Session (1951), 47-48.
Doc 8665-C/970 Action of the Council, 59th Session (1966), 17-18; C-WP/4457.
[12] Doc 8662-1 C/969-1 13/3/67.
[13] Mrs. Rosalyn Higgins has pointed out that "the particular 'sanction system' built into international law is simply the sanction of reciprocity. It is not, by and large, sanctions in the sense of physical compulsion or physical punishment." She then goes on to point out the lack of "a centralizing process" and indicates that "international law as it applies to a multitude of questions . . . is widely heeded because its breach would incur a reciprocal response". See Higgins, Rosalyn, *The Development of International Law through the Political Organs of the United Nations* (London, 1963), 8; also FM-3, 46. This statement could apply to a sanction system involving normative activities of functional international organizations.
[14] For an example, see Friedmann, Wolfgang G., "National Sovereignty, International Co-operation, and the Reality of International Law", (1963) 10 *UCLA Law Review* 748-750; also FM-3, 517-519.
[15] *Idem.* See also FM-3, 507 for a commentary on Friedmann's view.

author draws the distinction between *legal* sanctions (e.g., those which the organization itself may impose or which other member countries may take) and *natural* sanctions which, through the nature of the activity in question, will result from non-compliance with its laws.[16] In the technical field, a breach of the laws governing air navigation may lead to a disastrous accident.

Sanctions other than the above would include the following: direct retaliation by governments concerned; adverse reaction of governments other than those immediately concerned; political criticism from non-complying government's own constituents; the sense of having breached the moral norm inherent in the law-maker (i.e., the organization) as the representative of the community expectations.[17]

One may now consider what has been called the "normative function of the organized international community".[18] If this community established an international organization to enact norms for the performance of a particular activity (e.g., international civil aviation), enactment of these norms will, depending on the clarity of their definition and the form in which they are enacted, raise community expectations of compliance with them even where, in the interests of flexibility, States are permitted to contract out. It follows that if States wish to participate in and benefit from that particular activity, they ought to recognize and observe these norms as the price of their participation.[19] This involves the "sanction of reciprocity".[20] Non-compliance with the norm entails a disentitlement to enjoyment of the activity in the company of other States belonging to the norm-establishing organization.

---

[16] Fawcett, J. E. S., "The International Monetary Fund and International Law", (1964) 40 *B.Y.I.L.* 34. Failure of a State to comply with an undertaking under the constituent instrument of an international organization will not necessarily lead to the automatic application of sanctions by other member States. Indeed, the organization may take steps to ensure that, for the greater good of the community, sanctions not be applied. For an example of this, see Gold, Joseph, "The Duty to Collaborate with the International Monetary Fund and the Development of Monetary Law", Reprinted from *Law, Justice and Equity*, London, 1963 at p. 144: "It did not follow from the adoption by France of its new exchange system that other members [of the IMF] were released from all exchange rate obligations and that they were therefore entitled to retaliate by establishing rates of exchange for their currencies and the French franc as they saw fit." Article IV, Section 4 (a) of the Fund Agreement was an important element on which the Fund relied "to prevent a retaliatory scramble on a breach of obligation". (*Ibid.*, p. 151).

[17] Lande, *op cit.*, note 2 *supra*, 164; also in FM-3. See also Fisher, Roger, "Bringing Law to Bear on Governments", (1961) 74 *Harv. L.R.* 1134-1135; also in Falk and Mendlovitz, *The Strategy of World Order*, Vol. 2, *International Law* 75-85.

[18] Extracts from an address of the Hon. Ernest A. Gross taken from the Verbatim Record of the Public Sitting of the ICJ in the South West Africa Cases, May 19, 1965, reproduced in FM-3, 82.

[19] FM-3, 88.

[20] See note 13 *supra*.

ICAO exercises an extensive normative function and adopts much technical regulatory [21] material in the form of standards and recommended practices and procedures as well as regional plans for equipment and services. But ICAO's legislative function is limited and States are free to contract out of most ICAO decisions concerning the material in question. The contracting-out process involves the notification of differences to the regulatory material. This notification is formally desirable since what is involved in the non-compliance of a State with regulatory material is a lessening of community expectations. The notification is also substantively desirable in order that those engaged in international air navigation may know the technical conditions under which the flight of an aircraft is going to be performed at any particular point in the ICAO constituency.

Before this discussion on sanctions is closed, it will be appropriate to give the following examples of sanctions in the Chicago Convention that would serve to bring about compliance with decisions of the Assembly and Council.

(1) Failure to pay, within a reasonable period, contributions to the regular budget voted by the Assembly may lead to suspension of voting power in the Assembly and in the Council.[22]

(2) A Contracting State will not recognize as valid certificates of airworthiness and certificates of competency and licenses of personnel issued or rendered valid by another Contracting State in which the aircraft is registered unless the requirements under which such certificates or licenses were issued or rendered valid are equal to or above the minimum standards which may be established from time to time pursuant to the Convention.[23] The standards in question would be those adopted by the Council and found in Annexes 1 (Personnel Licensing) and 8 (Airworthiness) to the Chicago Convention. Non-compliance of a State with the standards adopted by the Council for the certificates and licenses concerned would lead to the non-recognition of these documents for the purposes

---

[21] For convenience, the word "regulatory" will be used in this paper as referring, in particular, to ICAO standards, practices and procedures and, by extension, to regional plans for equipment and services. These items, normative in character, are adopted with varying degrees of formality and create community expectations of compliance which also vary in degree. They all require implementation action on the national level, the exception being the case of the rules of the air applicable over the high seas (See note 42 *infra*).

[22] Chicago Convention, Article 62. In the earlier sessions of the Assembly there was a tendency to suspend the voting power of defaulting States. Thus, at various times, the voting power of the following States was suspended: Bolivia, Czechoslovakia, El Salvador, Guatemala, Jordan, Nicaragua, Paraguay, Peru and Poland. But the Assembly later adopted a more flexible policy in regard to arrears of payments and the sanction of suspension of voting power has not been applied for many years. For further details, see C-WP/3924 28/1/64, pp. 17-27. See, in Doc 8770, Resolution A16-56—Action to be taken in the case of Contracting States failing to discharge their financial obligations to the Organization.

[23] Chicago Convention, Article 33.

of international air navigation. The Convention provides for endorsement of certificates and licenses, which fail to satisfy the international standards [24] and prohibits the aircraft or personnel concerned from participating in international air navigation, except with the permission of the State or States whose territory is entered.[25]

(3) Depending on circumstances, under Chapter XVIII of the Convention, a final and binding decision on a disagreement concerning the interpretation or application of the Convention and its Annexes may be rendered by the Council, the International Court of Justice or an arbitral tribunal.[26] The Convention provides for compliance with this decision and stipulates the following penalties: (a) If the Council has decided that an airline of a Contracting State is not conforming to the decision, each Contracting State undertakes not to allow the operation of the airline through the airspace above its territory.[27] (b) The Assembly shall suspend the voting power in the Assembly and in the Council of any Contracting State that is found in default under the provisions of Chapter XVIII.[28]

The fact that a disagreement concerning the interpretation or application of the Convention or of an Annex (which is, through a Council decision, merely *adopted* and only subsequently becomes *effective* and *applicable*) can be brought before the Council could be an incentive for a State to comply with the provisions of the Convention and, in the case of an Annex, not only with the provisions of the Annex, but also with Council decisions relating to it. Nevertheless, in the case of an Annex, due allowance would have to be made for the contracting-out concept mentioned above.

One may now turn to a detailed consideration of the pursuance of the objective of the practical effectiveness of decisions under various headings.

4. *Pursuance of objective through various forms of action*

(1) *New treaty*

Inter-governmental conventions and agreements have been adopted by an ICAO body or by conferences held under the auspices of ICAO. All of these documents have been subject to ratification, adherence, acceptance or some form of consent of the States concerned. Examples of such documents are: Convention on the International Recognition of Rights in Aircraft, adopted by the Assembly at its second session at Geneva in 1948;[29]

---

[24] *Ibid.*, Article 39.
[25] *Ibid.*, Article 40.
[26] *Ibid.*, Articles 84-85.
[27] *Ibid.*, Article 87.
[28] *Ibid.*, Article 88.
[29] The only convention adopted by the Assembly to date has been the Convention on

Convention on Damage Caused by Foreign Aircraft to Third Parties on the Surface, adopted at an International Conference on Private Air Law, held under the auspices of ICAO at Rome in 1952; [30] Agreement on North Atlantic Ocean Stations adopted at an International Conference held under the auspices of ICAO at Paris in 1954.[31]

(2) *Organizational decision*

An example of an organizational decision in ICAO is the action taken by the Assembly or Council in adopting rules of procedure which are binding on States participating in meetings of those bodies (Chicago Convention, Articles 49 (d) and 54 (c)).

(3) *Resolution*

In ICAO, there are resolutions of the Assembly, Council and various subsidiary bodies (e.g., Air Navigation Commission, divisional meetings, regional meetings, meetings of the Legal Committee, conferences). None of the resolutions of bodies below the level of the Council would have binding force, though the Air Navigation Commission adopts some technical regulatory material to which the contracting-out principle applies.

(4) *Recommendation*

Recommendations may be adopted by various ICAO bodies. By definition, they are not binding.

(5) *Consensus*

The use of the consensus [32] process (i.e., decision-making without the taking of formal votes) is increasing in ICAO as elsewhere in the UN family,[33]

---

the International Recognition of Rights in Aircraft (Geneva, 1948); Doc 7620; 310 U.N.T.S. 151 (1958).

[30] For example, the Convention on Damage Caused by Foreign Aircraft to Third Parties on the Surface (Rome, 1952); Doc 7364; 310 U.N.T.S. 181 (1958).

[31] Doc 8080-JS/579. Acts on the Joint Financing of the North Atlantic Ocean Stations. Contains the Agreement on North Atlantic Ocean Stations, signed at Paris on 25 February 1954; 215 U.N.T.S. 249 (1955). This agreement has been subsequently amended.

[32] This is the "consensus of the whole" as distinct from the "majority consensus". For a discussion of the latter, see Lande, *op. cit.*, note 2 *supra*, 165; also FM-3, 230.

[33] For example, in the United Nations Committee on the Peaceful Uses of Outer Space and the Special Committee on Principles of International Law concerning Friendly Relations and Co-operation among States. One writer has sounded the wise warning that "consensus" without state practice is not productive of a rule of law. See Gross, Leo, "The United Nations and the Role of Law", (1965) 19 *International*

though the decisions reached through this process are no more or no less binding than decisions reached through other processes.

5. *Encouragement of governments*

(1) *Co-ordination of policies*

A good example of a resolution encouraging governments to co-ordinate policies is the Assembly resolution containing the consolidated statement of continuing ICAO policies relating specifically to air navigation.[34] Many provisions of this resolution in effect urge governments to adopt the same policy in regard to specified matters.

(2) *Enactment of consistent municipal legislation*

The very purpose of the adoption by ICAO of Standards, Recommended Practices and Procedures (SARPS), and other regulatory material is to encourage governments to enact consistent municipal legislation which will include this material. Thus, the forewords to ICAO Annexes contain the following note:

"Use of the text of the Annex in national regulations:
   The Council, on 13 April 1948, adopted a resolution inviting the attention of Contracting States to the desirability of using in their own national regulations, as far as practicable, the precise language of those ICAO Standards that are of a regulatory character and also of indicating departures from the Standards, including any additional national regulations that were important for the safety or regularity of air navigation."

Obviously, much of the material in the Annexes cannot be incorporated textually into national regulations and some of the provisions will require amplification, e.g., certain provisions of Annexes 6 (Operation of Aircraft) and 8 (Airworthiness of Aircraft). But a number of the Annex provisions, especially those in Annex 2 (Rules of the Air), can be found, without textual change, in national regulations.[35]
   Conventions on air law adopted by ICAO-sponsored conferences can

---

Organization 557. For the distinction between "parliamentary consensus" and "political consensus" see Falk, Richard A. "On the Quasi-legislative Competence of the General Assembly", (1966) 60 *A.J.I.L.* 788. See also, on this, notes 99 and 100 *infra*.
[34] Resolution A16-19. A lengthy resolution on this subject is adopted at the triennial sessions of the Assembly and lays down the policy for the future development and implementation of technical norms in the field of international air navigation.
[35] There are fifteen Annexes to the Chicago Convention. Annex 9 is concerned with the facilitation of international air transport. The remaining fourteen Annexes, which are concerned with technical matters, are as follows: 1—Personnel Licensing; 2—Rules of the Air; 3—Meteorology; 4—Aeronautical Charts; 5—Units of Measurement to be used in Air-Ground Communications; 6—Operation of Aircraft; 7—Aircraft Nationality and Registration Marks; 8—Airworthiness of Aircraft; 10—Aero-

lead to consistent municipal legislation.[36] Countries of the British Commonwealth tend to append the text of a convention as a schedule to enabling legislation.[37] In the United States, however, ratification of, or adherence to, a convention makes it the law of the land without the necessity of enabling legislation.[38]

Certain decisions of the Council not concerned with International Standards and Recommended Practices (SARPS) can produce consistent municipal legislation. For example, the definition of "scheduled international air service" adopted by the Council in 1952 [39] has been incorporated into the national laws of some Contracting States or used in practice by other Contracting States.[40]

6. *Inducement of governments to undertake formal obligations to act*

The various ways in which governments are induced by ICAO to undertake formal obligations to act will become apparent from what is stated in the discussion on implementation below.

7. *Circumstances in which the "binding" decision (whether cast as a treaty or an action formally approved by prescribed voting procedures in the international organization) becomes directly effective upon the nationals of Member States without the requirement of further government action*

The Council resolved, in adopting Annex 2 (Rules of the Air) in April 1948 and Amendment No. 1 to that Annex in November 1951,[41] that the Annex

---

nautical Telecommunications; 11—Air Traffic Services; 12—Search and Rescue; 13—Aircraft Accident Inquiry; 14—Aerodromes, and 15—Aeronautical Information Services. A number of Annex provisions would be meaningless unless supplemented by appropriate provisions in national laws and regulations. In other cases, the wording of Annex provisions has to be adapted before the substance can be included in national provisions.

[36] See, for example, Article 28 of the Rome Convention on Damage Caused by Foreign Aircraft to Third Parties on the Surface (1952) which provides that: "If legislative measures are necessary in any Contracting State to give effect to this Convention, the Secretary-General of the International Civil Aviation Organization shall be informed forthwith of the measures so taken."

[37] See, for example, the text of the Rome Convention (note 30 *supra*) which is set forth in a schedule to the Foreign Aircraft Third Party Damage Act, 3 & 4 Eliz. II (Can. 1955), c. 15.

[38] This is so in the case of the Convention for the Unification of Certain Rules relating to International Carriage by Air, Warsaw, 12 October 1929 in respect of which the United States of America deposited an instrument of adherence on 31 May 1934.

[39] Doc 7238-C/842 Action of the Council, 15th Session (1952), 14; Doc 7278-C/841.

[40] For reports on the extent to which States were able to implement this definition by early 1954, see AT-WP/356, 361 and 362.

[41] See Foreword to Annex 2 (Rules of the Air), 5th edition, March 1966, 6.

constituted "Rules relating to the flight and manoeuvre of aircraft" within the meaning of Article 12 of the Convention. Over the high seas these rules apply without exception since Article 12 provides, *inter alia,* that

"Over the high seas, the rules [meaning the rules of the air] shall be those established [by the Council] under this Convention."

Therefore, when the Council adopts rules of the air and declares that they are applicable over the high seas, they apply to aircraft of ICAO Contracting States and the air crew on board without any further implementing action being required on the part of those States other than to take steps to ensure compliance by their aircraft and crew members with the rules so applicable.[42]

A Council decision which adopts, and provides for the eventual coming into effect and applicability of, international standards on personnel licensing (Annex 1) can, through the operation of Articles 39 and 40 of the Convention, bind persons to comply with that decision provided that the State issuing or validating the license has not filed with ICAO differences relating to the standards which the Council decision makes otherwise applicable to the class of license or certificate concerned. Thus, according to Article 39, any person holding a license who does not satisfy in full the conditions laid down in the international standards relating to the class of license or certificate which he holds shall have endorsed on or attached to his license a complete enumeration of the particulars in which he does not satisfy such conditions. Admittedly, the State has to intervene in order to make the endorsement on the license. But once the endorsement exists, the Convention applies directly to the holder of the endorsed license and stipulates, in Article 40, that no personnel having such a license "shall participate in international [air] navigation, except with the permission of the State or States whose territory is entered".

Another example of a binding decision that is directly applicable to a national of a Contracting State would be the imposition of a penalty (namely, denial of permission to fly internationally) on an airline of a Contracting State where the airline does not conform to a decision rendered by the Council in the case of a dispute concerning the interpretation or application of the Convention or its Annexes.[43] Such a case of non-compliance has not yet arisen.

---

[42] For further information concerning Article 12 and the application over the high seas of rules of the air adopted by the Council, see Carroz, J. E., "International Legislation in Air Navigation over the High Seas", (1959) 26 *J.A.L.C.* 158-172; for the German version of this note, see (1959) 8 *Zeitschrift für Luftrecht* 3-24. See also Buergenthal, Thomas, *Law-making in the International Civil Aviation Organization* (Syracuse University Press, 1969), 80-85.

[43] Chapter XVIII, Articles 84-88.

II. TECHNIQUES AVAILABLE IN ICAO TO ENCOURAGE COMPLIANCE WITH DECISIONS

1. *General*

Routine decisions of the Assembly and Council on various subjects request States to take appropriate action and to advise the Secretariat of the action taken. Similarly, certified copies of conventions adopted at meetings held under the auspices of ICAO are sent to States with the request that they become parties to these documents.[44] Requests in regard to matters such as the foregoing may also be made orally through contact of Secretariat officials with national officials. These are all relatively routine techniques.

But it is in the area of implementation of the ICAO regulatory material (standards, practices, procedures and air navigation plans for facilities and services) that ICAO has developed detailed techniques for implementation. Because ICAO experience in this kind of implementation has been so vast, the relevant techniques will now be described in detail. Before this description is given it will be necessary to examine the method of adoption and approval of ICAO regulatory material and air navigation plans.

2. *ICAO regulatory material and air navigation plans*

With a view to securing the highest practicable degree of uniformity in relation to aircraft, personnel, airways and auxiliary services in all matters in which such uniformity will facilitate and improve air navigation, ICAO adopts international standards, recommended practices and procedures dealing with a wide range of subjects.[45] It also approves regional plans covering facilities and services required for air navigation.[46] The various types of the foregoing material will now be discussed.

---

[44] In 1952, the Council decided that the approved minutes of the relevant meetings of the Council would be an adequate record on which the Secretary General would make and retain an adequate copy of each Annex or amendment thereto. See Doc. 7283-C/842 Action of the Council, 15th Session (1952), 9 and C-WP/1060. But while certified true copies of conventions adopted at meetings held under ICAO auspices are sent to States, certified true copies of Annexes or amendments thereto are not. Nevertheless after adoption by the Council, the so-called "green" edition of the Annex or amendment is sent to States and they are invited to take with respect to that copy the actions indicated in the resolution of adoption.

[45] Chicago Convention, Articles 37, 54 (1) and 90.

[46] *Ibid.*, Article 28.

(1) *International Standards and Recommended Practices (SARPS)*

These are adopted by the Council in accordance with Articles 54 (1), 37 and 90 of the Convention on International Civil Aviation and are designated, for convenience, as Annexes to the Convention. A two-thirds vote of the Council is required for adoption of an Annex. The uniform application by Contracting States of the specifications compromised in the International Standards is recognized as necessary for the safety or regularity of international air navigation, while the uniform application of the specifications in the Recommended Practices is regarded as desirable in the interest of safety, regularity or efficiency of international air navigation. Knowledge of any differences between the national regulations or practices of a State and those established by an International Standard is essential to the safety or regularity of international air navigation. In the event of non-compliance with an International Standard, a State has, in fact, an obligation, under Article 38 of the Convention, to notify the Council of any differences. Knowledge of differences from Recommended Practices may also be important for the safety of air navigation and, although the Convention does not impose any obligation with regard thereto, the Council has invited Contracting States to notify such differences in addition to those relating to International Standards.

(2) *Procedures for Air Navigation Services (PANS)*

These are approved [47] by the Council for worldwide application. They comprise, for the most part, operating procedures regarded as not yet having attained a sufficient degree of maturity for adoption as International Standards and Recommended Practices, as well as material of a more permanent character which is considered too detailed for incorporation in an Annex, or is susceptible to frequent amendment, for which the processes of the Convention would be too cumbersome. As in the case of Recommended Practices, the Council has invited Contracting States to notify any differences between their national practices and the PANS when the knowledge of such differences is important for the safety of air navigation.

(3) *Regional Supplementary Procedures (SUPPS)*

These have a status similar to that of PANS in that they are approved by the Council, but only for respective application in the nine geographical regions [48] established by ICAO both to cater for different types of flying op-

---

[47] By a simple majority and not a qualified majority of two-thirds as required by Article 90 (a) of the Chicago Convention for the adoption of the Annexes.
[48] Until 1967, there were only eight regions and these did not cover the polar areas

erations and to facilitate detailed planning of needed facilities and services to support these operations. They are prepared in consolidated form, since certain of the procedures apply to overlapping regions or are common to two or more regions. More often than not the SUPPS are approved by the President of the Council under delegated authority. If States have differences in respect of SUPPS, they are encouraged to notify them to ICAO.

(4) *Regional Plans*

Plans for the nine ICAO regions include the enumeration of many tens of thousands of facilities to be established and operated or services to be rendered, at points that ICAO regional meetings have defined and that the Council has approved, after review of the reports of these meetings by the Air Navigation Commission. Under the Convention each State is individually responsible for providing the recommended facilities and services within its territory, albeit "so far as it may find practicable" (Article 28). But financial and technical resources vary widely between States in a region and this poses a problem in implementation of regional plans.

(5) *Development of SARPS, PANS and SUPPS*

The story of the development of SARPS and PANS will serve to indicate the great extent to which States are consulted in advance of their becoming applicable and this consultation is in itself a step towards implementation.

(a) Divisional-type meetings (open to all Contracting States), panels of limited membership and other bodies prepare recommendations for SARPS and PANS, or for amendments thereto. The steps in this operation are broadly as follows:

(i) The Air Navigation Commission decides that such a meeting should be held and a final decision thereon is taken by the Council.

(ii) States are consulted on the agenda and comment on advance documentation.

(iii) Documentation from the Secretariat, Contracting States and international organizations is placed before the meeting.

(iv) The report of the meeting is reviewed by the Air Navigation Commission in the light of comments received from States, international organizations and the Secretariat.

---

and large portions of Canada and the United States. On 16 June 1967, the Council increased the regions to nine and included the corresponding polar areas. See C-WP/ 4594, 3/5/67 and Doc 8678-13 C/972-13, 1/8/67, Council, 61st Session, 13th Meeting, 198-199, 201-211. For a history and description of the ICAO Air Navigation Regions, see Doc 8144-AN/874/2 Directives to Regional Air Navigation Meetings and Rules of Procedure for Their Conduct, pp. 24-25.

(v) The SARPS and PANS in final form are submitted to the Council for adoption or approval as the case may be.[49]

(b) The Council *adopts* the SARPS in a formal manner and the resolution of adoption stipulates, *inter alia:*

(i) *Effective date:* This is the date by which the Annex becomes effective unless in the meantime the majority of the Contracting States have indicated their disapproval.[50] To date, there has been no such indication of disapproval.

(ii) *Data of applicability:* This is the date by which Contracting States are to be ready to implement and, if unable to do so, are obliged to notify ICAO of differences between their own national practice and that established by the International Standards contained in the Annex.[51] This gives the other Contracting States notice of the inability of the notifying State to satisfy community expectations arising out of the adoption of Annexes and amendments thereto. In practice, States are requested to notify differences with regard to Recommended Practices since, as stated above, knowledge of these differences may be important for the safety of air navigation.

(c) PANS and SUPPS being concerned with the detailed application of SARPS, need not originate as recommendations of meetings; they are *approved* (not *adopted*) by the Council, there being no two-thirds majority vote required for approval of this material as in the case of the adoption of SARPS.[52]

Since the approval of the PANS and SUPPS leads to community expectations in regard to the way in which air navigation will be carried on, here also there is a functional need for the notification of differences that may exist. Therefore, States are requested to notify differences to PANS and SUPPS, even though not obliged to do so under the Convention.

(6) *Development of Regional Air Navigation Plans*

The plans for air navigation facilities and services needed in a region and for regional procedures to be applied are developed at Regional Meetings as recommendations to the Council[53] and, after review by the Air Navigation Commission, are approved by the Council.

---

[49] Doc 8143-AN/873 Rules of Procedure for the Conduct of Air Navigation Meetings and Directives to Divisional-type Air Navigation Meetings, 27 March 1961. For discussions on ICAO SARPS, see Buergenthal, *op. cit.,* note 42 *supra,* 57-122 and Yemin, Edward, *Legislative Powers in the United Nations and Specialized Agencies* (Leyden, 1969), 114-151.
[50] Chicago Convention, Article 90.
[51] *Ibid.,* Article 38.
[52] *Ibid.,* Article 52 which provides in part that: "Decisions of the Council shall require approval by a majority of its members."
[53] Doc 8144-AN/874 Rules of Procedure for the Conduct of Air Navigation Meetings and Directives to Regional Air Navigation Meetings, 27 March 1961.

(7) *Regulatory material on facilitation of international air transport*

The ICAO regulatory material on facilitation of international air transport is developed and adopted in a manner similar to that applicable to technical items. Annex 9 to the Convention contains Standards and Recommended Practices on facilitation of international air transport. These provisions aim at (i) eliminating all unessential documentary requirements, (ii) simplifying and standardizing the remaining forms, (iii) providing certain minimum facilities at international airports and (iv) simplifying handling and clearance procedures.[54] Obligations in regard to the notification of differences are the same as in the case of the technical regulatory material.

3. *Implementation of ICAO regulatory material*

(1) *Introduction*

From its very inception, ICAO has been preoccupied with the necessity for effective implementation of its regulatory material in the technical field and Regional Plans. This preoccupation is reflected in policy resolutions on implementation adopted at the major sessions of the ICAO Assembly and in the constant effort by the subsidiary organs and the Secretariat to translate policy into action.

The process of implementation begins before the decision adopting or approving the material to be implemented becomes applicable and, indeed, even before the decision is taken. Thus, in the case of amendments to an Annex, States will be consulted on the agenda for the meetings (whether of a division open to all Contracting States or a panel of limited membership) at which the draft amendments will be prepared. The States are asked to send comments on the working papers, are free to participate in divisional-type meetings, are consulted by the Secretariat on all reports emanating from these and other similar meetings and have their comments considered by the Air Navigation Commission which approves draft amendments for submission to the Council.[55] States are also given an op-

---

[54] For a more detailed description of the aims of ICAO in the field of facilitation, see Doc 7891-C/906/2 Aims of ICAO in the Field of Facilitation, 2nd edition, 1965. The IMCO has paid ICAO the compliment of modelling a Convention and an Annex thereto on Annex 9 to the Chicago Convention and relevant provisions of the Chicago Convention. See Erler, Jochen, "The New Convention on Facilitation of International Maritime Traffic", (1967) 13 *McGill L. J.* 323-328 and Alexandrowicz, C. H., "The Convention on Facilitation of International Maritime Traffic and International Technical Regulations: A Comparative Study", (1966) 15 *I.C.L.Q.* 621-659. For the text of the Convention, see IMCO publication entitled "International Conference on Facilitation of Maritime Travel and Transport, 1965" (London, 1965).
[55] Doc 8144-AN/874, note 53 *supra*, 2-6.

portunity to disapprove material adopted by the Council[56] and will, in any event, be given many months' warning before an amendment becomes applicable. In addition, prior to the Council's decision adopting the material there will be a careful evaluation of its necessity and the cost of implementation.

The basic steps in the implementation process will emerge from the ensuing discussion. The steps may vary in detail depending on whether SARPS, PANS, SUPPS or Regional Plans are involved.

In the case of SARPS, PANS and SUPPS, the Council and the Air Navigation Commission keep the progress in implementation under constant review and file reports with the Assembly [57] which, in turn, adopts related up-to-date policy statements on implementation.[58] An outline of some of the problems encountered in the implementation process and some of the solutions suggested from time to time will be found below.

As to Regional Plans, there is a constant attempt to remedy deficiencies in the plans for facilities and services required for international air navigation in the nine ICAO regions. The Assembly receives reports on this subject and also adopts up-to-date policy statements. A Special Implementation Panel was established by the Assembly in 1965 [59] as a temporary body to examine the adequacy of Regional Plans and to make appropriate recommendations. As this was a thorough-going examination, the problems uncovered by it and the suggested solutions found in its report will be given below. This group was succeeded by a Standing Group of the Council on Implementation established in 1960 to keep the question of implementation of Regional Plans under review.[60]

(2) *Implementation of SARPS and PANS: problems and solutions*

The difficulties for States to keep their regulations and operating instructions amended to conform to the current provisions of ICAO Annexes (SARPS) and PANS are not inconsiderable. The problems arising in the implementation process and the solutions therefor can vary depending on whether or not the SARPS are associated with Regional Plans [61] which involve the cost of furnishing facilities and services. Nevertheless, in the interest of developing a composite statement of these problems and solutions,

---

[56] Chicago Convention, Article 90.

[57] For examples, see A15-WP/28 TE/5 31/5/65 and A15-WP/40 TE/9 22/4/65.

[58] Resolutions A15-8 and A16-19: Consolidated Statement of Continuing ICAO Policies related Specifically to Air Navigation.

[59] Resolution A10-7: ICAO Policy and Programme for the Provision of Air Navigation Facilities and Services.

[60] Doc 8097-C/926 Action of the Council, 40th Session (1960), 26-27.

[61] Material contained in the ensuing discussion is taken from statements presented to the 15th Session of the Assembly. See A15-WP/28 TE/5 31/3/65 and A15-WP/40 TE/9 22/4/65.

no attempt will be made to draw this distinction.

After the SARPS and PANS have been adopted or approved by the Council the following sequence of actions is required:

(a) Proper changes made by States and in good time in their regulations and instructions. This involves: (i) The embodiment of SARPS and PANS in the national legislation or regulations; (ii) The preparation of manuals or operating instructions under enabling legislation; (iii) Distribution of ICAO texts for use at installations.

(b) The practical application by States of the changes. This entails instructing personnel and, perhaps, obtaining or modifying equipment.

Problems

Problems arising in the implementation of SARPS and PANS include:

(a) Difficulties in establishing national aviation legislation due to lack of personnel skilled in the preparation thereof.

(b) Difficulties in the administration of national air navigation regulations. Here arises a need for consistent administrative decisions based upon expert knowledge of what is required, the exercise of considerable executive power, and the support of properly drawn detailed aviation legislation. In addition, there must be a constant enforcement of national aviation legislation by highly qualified persons and many such persons.

(c) The inability of States to cope with frequent amendments to ICAO regulatory documents due to the frequency and sophisticated nature of the amendments and the voluminous and scattered ICAO documentation resulting therefrom. This results in a considerable backlog of unimplemented material.

(d) The many cases where procedures (e.g., for air traffic services, communications and meteorology) on the national level are many years out of date both at air navigation installations and the headquarters of the national civil aviation department. In 1965, it was estimated in ICAO that perhaps 25 per cent of ICAO Contracting States had been able to maintain the operating instructions at their installations essentially in step with ICAO, another 25 per cent were using instructions that were one to three years out of date and the remaining 50 per cent were even further out of date.

(e) The lack of complete co-ordination among SARPS and PANS.

(f) The lack of funds in certain States for providing trained personnel, services and equipment.

(g) Particular national, regional and environmental conditions which can affect implementation.

(h) The necessity of translating the highly technical language of the regulatory material from the ICAO texts (in English, French or Spanish) into the local language or languages of the implementing State.

174

Possible solutions

Possible solutions for solving the problems just mentioned include the following:

(a) *Increase the national administration's capability of taking necessary action on all amendments to SARPS and PANS.* This can be done through such varied means as: ICAO Secretariat missions to States; United Nations Development Programme projects; the preparation of guidance documents (manuals, circulars, etc.) that would assist States in the organization of departments concerned with such activities as airworthiness, operations and personnel licensing and in the drafting of specific national regulations; bilateral arrangements of developed States with developing States; regional and inter-regional projects; regional civil aviation training centres; informal implementation meetings on certain subjects (e.g., aeronautical maps); development of common services to serve two or more States and special regional teams on implementation.

(b) *Decrease the frequency and number of amendments.* The advantage of slowing the pace of amendments would be that it would assist the administrative handling of amendments on the national level and the institution of amended practices at operating installations. Although this solution has been discussed in ICAO circles, it has been rejected because basic ICAO documents must keep up with the most advanced developments and techniques. ICAO specifications should not be allowed to become obsolescent in a dynamic industry. Otherwise, difficulties could arise in areas of high density traffic and complex traffic. Indeed, in those areas States introduce new practices and procedures long before equivalent provisions are included in ICAO documents.

(c) *Reduce the content of Annexes to broad basic material.* Although the transfer of the more detailed material to PANS would simplify the administrative processing of amendments in many States, the problem of bringing the amended practices into actual use would not be greatly reduced.

(d) *Consider the possibility of having two sets of specifications: one simplified and stable, the other complex and flexible.* Requirements for stability and flexibility could be reconciled. But the argument against this is that it would constitute a retrograde step. The objective should be to attain universal implementation of a single comprehensive set of specifications. Any downgrading of the specifications in respect of less demanding areas would penalize operators.

The essential elements to be borne in mind in considering any change in policy would be: (i) The highest level of stability for areas of low traffic density; (ii) A high degree of flexibility for areas of high traffic density; (iii) Compatibility between the practices in high density and low density areas to ensure satisfactory services to aircraft traversing more than one area and to permit a satisfactory inter-working of the ground services network.

175

But if points (i) and (ii) are valid, the present concept of a basic document for worldwide application in all its detail, kept up to date by amendments of the same character, will not survive. True, a change so as to bring about more stability would put implementation within the capability of the administrations in areas of low density traffic; but the documents would not continually reflect the most advanced practice. Unfortunately, the latter is what happens in practice in many administrations in areas of low density traffic.[62]

The advantages of flexibility are that of the quick amendment of the basic documents in application to areas of high density traffic, since they could be designed for those areas alone. In theory, the practice in the two types of areas would be different, although compatible.

The Assembly, in 1965, introduced a form of flexibility into the implementation process. It requested the Council to seek measures that will facilitate the task of States in instituting current ICAO practices and procedures at their operating installations. The Assembly further stated that, in developing such measures the Council, after considering the possible impact upon Contracting States, may deviate from present policies and practices relative to the content, applicability and amendment of the Annexes and PANS, other than the provisions of the Convention, if it found such deviation unavoidable in order to accomplish the objective. After ascertaining that the action would be acceptable to States, the Council was to give effect to any such measures, to the extent practicable, without further action of the Assembly.[63]

(3) Reporting of differences or intent to comply

A prime difficulty faced by States in notifying ICAO of the extent to which they comply or do not comply with regulatory material is that of the yardstick against which to measure non-compliance which leads to the filing of differences. The Secretariat gives advice to States, as appropriate, on whether or not their practices constitute differences from ICAO, SARPS and PANS. Nevertheless the view has been expressed that there is a need to develop detailed guidance material on the reporting of differences, preferably in the form of clear criteria enabling States to determine readily whether or not their individual practices constitute differences. This would be particularly useful to new Contracting States. An early step in this direction was taken as long ago as 1950, when the Council adopted a set of principles governing the reporting of differences from ICAO Standards, Practices and Procedures. (See Appendix "A" hereto) [64]

---

[62] For a discussion of the question of flexibility, see Doc 8542 A15-TE/52 Report of the Technical Commission, 15th Session of the Assembly (1965), 36-37.
[63] Resolution A15-12: Measures to facilitate implementation of SARPS and PANS.
[64] See also AN-WP/3309 15/5/67 which is a Secretariat note concerning the publication of differences in Aeronautical Information Publications.

(4) *Assembly policy statements on the implementation of SARPS and PANS*

The process of implementation of SARPS and PANS is the object of careful study by the Assembly at its triennial sessions. The Assembly policy statement, adopted in 1968, concerning the formulation of SARPS and PANS, contains much material on their eventual implementation. Thus, after defining the expressions "Standard" and "Recommended Practice",[65] the resolution contemplates a high degree of stability in SARPS so as to achieve necessary stability in national air navigation regulations; a limitation of amendments; a special effort to ensure complete co-ordination among SARPS and PANS as well as freedom of the Annexes from errors or defects of language; consideration by States of recommendations for new SARPS and PANS or amendments to SARPS and PANS for a period of three months before the Council acts on these recommendations; detailed comments of the States on these recommendations; the establishment of the date for disapproval by States so as to allow study by them during the full period of three months provided in Article 90 of the Convention and the fixing of dates of applicability of SARPS in such a way that sufficient time will be allowed to enable States to complete their arrangements for implementation thereof. The resolution also provides that such steps as may be feasible should be taken to ensure that standards involving the provision and operation of facilities and equipment, whilst ensuring safety and regularity, take into account the importance of securing the correct balance between the economic aspects of, and the operational requirements for, such standards. It is further provided that a programme for the application of amendments to SARPS and PANS should be followed so that the relevant national regulations of Contracting States will not be required to be amended more frequently than at intervals of one year,[66] departures from this policy taking place only in exceptional circumstances.

Having thus established a policy concerning the development of the SARPS and PANS which paves the way for their eventual implementation, the Assembly then proceeds to adopt a policy statement specifically concerned with their implementation. The Council is instructed to encourage and foster the implementation of SARPS and PANS and to assist States in such implementation, using all available means, including the United Nations Programme of Technical Assistance,[67] technical advice

---

[65] Resolution A16-19, Appendix D.
[66] The Council also establishes a common date of applicability for all amendments to SARPS and PANS. For example, for the year 1969, the date chosen was 18 September. See Doc 8808-C/985 Action of the Council, 65th Session (1968), 10.
[67] This now comes under the United Nations Development Programme with which ICAO is associated.

and expert assistance from the Regional Offices, and the training activities of the Air Navigation Bureau.[68]

The resolution indicates that emphasis is to be placed on the application of SARPS and PANS in specified fields. In the case of the implementation of the programme relating to aeronautical information services and aeronautical maps and charts, attention is drawn to use to be made of formal and informal regional meetings, experts' assistance to States and the common use by States of facilities on the basis of bilateral or multilateral agreements.

States are to continue and, where necessary, intensify their efforts to apply, at their operating installations, practices and procedures that are in accordance with the current SARPS and PANS.

States are to consider the practicability of modifying the internal processes by which they give effect to the provisions of SARPS and PANS, if such modification would expedite or simplify the processes or make them more effective.

States are urged to report to ICAO in respect of their territories all cases of non-compliance with, or incomplete implementation of, SARPS and PANS and, at suitable intervals, to provide the Organization with reports on the progress made in implementing SARPS and PANS or on the reasons for non-implementation. The notifications by Contracting States of their intent to comply with or differ from the SARPS and PANS are to be made as fully effective as possible and Contracting States are to be kept currently informed of such notification by: (a) requests by ICAO for reports from States that have not fully reported or have never reported; (b) prompt issuance of notifications as supplements to the relevant documents. The differences are to be monitored by the Organization with the object of encouraging the elimination of those differences that are important for the safety of air navigation or are inconsistent with the objectives of the international standards.[69]

Closely linked to the foregoing policy statement is an Assembly Resolution [70] which permits the Council to deviate from present policies and practices relative to the content, applicability and amendment of the Annexes and PANS, other than the provisions of the Convention, if it finds such deviation unavoidable in order to facilitate the task of States in instituting current ICAO practices and procedures at their operating installations.

---

[68] Resolution A16-19, Appendix F.
[69] *Idem.*
[70] Resolution A15-12.

(5) *Publications used by ICAO as an aid in the implementation of SARPS and PANS*

ICAO prepares various publications as an aid in the implementation process. These publications include the items described below.

Supplementary material published with Annexes
The Annexes contain attachments which, in some instances, include material as a guide to the application of the Annexes.

ICAO Field Manuals
Field manuals published by ICAO are also an aid in implementation. These derive their status from SARPS and PANS from which they are compiled. They are prepared primarily for the use of personnel engaged in operations in the field, as a service to those Contracting States that do not find it practicable, for various reasons, to prepare them for their own use.

Technical manuals
ICAO-prepared technical manuals provide guidance and information in amplification of the SARPS and PANS, the implementation of which they are designed to facilitate. For example, Doc 7192-AN/857 Part GEN-1 Training Manual Part GEN-1—*Licensing Practices and Procedures* (1963) contains detailed information for guidance in the implementation of personnel licensing specifications found in Annex 1 (PEL). Illustrative of the details involved in the implementation process are some of the main chapter headings, thus: the role of the personnel licensing section (PEL) in a civil aviation administration; laws and regulations governing licensing; elements of a license; technical training in relation to licensing; technical examinations and their relation to licensing; the action of licensing and licensing staff. The publication contains no less than twenty detailed appendices.

ICAO Circulars
ICAO Circulars make available specialized information of interest to Contracting States and some of them are of direct use in the implementation process. For example, CIRCULAR 53-AN/47/3 *Flight Crew Fatigue and Flight Time Limitations,* 3rd ed., 1964, pp. 155, contains detailed material on the implementation of paragraph 4.2.7.4. (Flight time and flight duty periods of crew members) of Annex 6 (Operation of Aircraft—International Commercial Air Transport).

(6) Development and Implementation of regulatory material on Facilitation

The development of regulatory material on facilitation is achieved through means similar to those used in the development of technical regulatory material. Periodic meetings on facilitation put forward recommendations for standards and recommended practices which, after review by States and the Air Transport Committee of the Council, are adopted by the Council as amendments to Annex 9 (Facilitation) to the Chicago Convention.[71]

The process of implementation, predictably enough, consists in assistance given by ICAO to States in implementing the facilitation programme. The means used include co-operation with other international organizations and with appropriate regional meetings of other bodies dealing with facilitation matters, participation in regional studies when these have facilitation aspects and the arranging of visits to States by facilitation experts of the Secretariat.

Here, too, the Assembly adopts resolutions exhorting States to implement Annex 9, to report differences from the provisions of Annex 9, to continue in their efforts to eliminate those differences and to liberalize the formalities imposed on international tourist traffic carried by commercial and non-commercial aviation.[72]

In 1958, the Council issued a document stating ICAO's aims in the field of facilitation. In the view of the Council, this document sets forth the needs of international civil aviation in such a way as to provide a guide to Contracting States for future planning in this field and to inform and assist other organizations interested in the promotion of facilitation. A second edition (Doc 7891-C/906/2) was issued in 1965. This publication contains a lengthy section devoted to the means of attaining the aims of ICAO in the field of facilitation.

Many of the Contracting States have established national facilitation Committees, including representatives from the aviation, customs, immigration, public health and tourist departments as well as airline operators to take all the necessary steps for the application of the provisions of Annex 9 in their respective territories. In a number of cases, close co-operation has been achieved between States, either by way of regional meet-

---

[71] The SARPS on Facilitation inevitably take two forms: (1) A *negative* form, e.g., that States shall not impose more than certain maximum requirements in the way of paper work, restrictions on freedom of movement. (2) A *positive* form, e.g., that States shall provide certain minimum facilities for passenger convenience for traffic which is merely passing through. Whenever a question arises under a *negative* provision, it is assumed that States will, wherever possible, relax their requirements below the maximum set forth in the SARPS. Whenever there is a *positive* provision, it is assumed that States will, wherever possible, furnish more than the minimum set forth in the SARPS.
[72] Resolutions A16-27 and A16-28.

180

ings or otherwise, resulting in a considerable simplification of border-crossing formalities on flights between their territories.

4. Implementation of Regional Plans

(1) General

Regional Plans provide for the supply of thousands of items of services and facilities and involve substantial expenditures for personnel and equipment. Their implementation poses special problems since financial and technical resources vary widely between States in a region.

(2) Special Implementation Panel (1956-1959)

The problems involved in the implementation of Regional Plans and the solutions therefor were stated in detail in a report of the Special Implementation Panel recommended by the Assembly in 1956,[73] and appointed by the Council almost immediately after the Assembly.[74] This Panel was composed of the President of the ICAO Council and six high aviation officials respectively from Brazil, France, Netherlands, Spain, United Kingdom and United States of America. In view of the high-level calibre of the members of the Panel and the exhaustive nature of its lengthy worldwide study, its statement on the above-mentioned problems and solutions is of permanent interest. A summary of this statement follows. In reading this summary, it should be noted that the Panel, by implication, assumes the existence of a civil aviation organizational structure in each country and also of a national aviation legislation. That these may not exist on anything like an adequate scale is obvious from the difficulties described earlier in connection with the implementation of SARPS and PANS. The Panel Report contains, so to speak, an inventory of problems on the operating level where services, equipment and skilled technical personnel are required.

Problems
   The problems covered by the Panel's report[75] include the following: (a) There is a limit to what can be asked from, or recommended to, a sovereign State in terms of taking exceptional measures to remedy a deficiency. (II-4)

---

[73] Resolution A10-7.
[74] Doc 7763-C/896 Action of the Council, 29th Session (1956), 37-42.
[75] Doc 7966 A12-EX/1. For convenience, references to the source of the material given below will be incorporated in the text of this paper in parentheses. The Roman numerals will refer to Parts of the Panel's report and Arabic figures to paragraphs of the report.

(b) The time required to obtain implementation is relatively longer than desirable. (II-4)

(c) In some cases operational, rather than political considerations should govern implementation so that it should take place in the territory of more than one State (e.g., Flight Information Regions) or on a regional basis (e.g., air traffic control services). (II-10.3.1 and 10.3.3)

(d) The need for highly skilled personnel. (II-10.3.3)

(e) The need for fewer and larger centres (air traffic control). (*Idem*)

(f) The need for States to develop and improve techniques and practices to meet new requirements and to train personnel to carry out these techniques and practices. (II-10.4.2)

(g) The need for fixed and expendable equipment, new organizations, operating and maintenance personnel educated in new techniques and for communications to be provided or improved to permit rapid and reliable exchange of data. (*Idem.*)

(h) The pattern of operations may not be an ideal or efficient one. (II-10.5.3)

(i) The regional plan must reflect valid requirements. Best results will be obtained if the entire area can be brought to an adequate level of performance. (II-10.5.3)

(j) The financial difficulties of the government as a whole. (II-10.5.7.)

(k) The structure of civil aviation machinery, or its position in the overall government organization, is such that its effectiveness is diminished. (II-10.5.8)

(l) International political complications. (II-10.5.9)

(m) The ever-present prospect of changes in regional plans is detrimental to implementation. (II-10.5.10)

The Panel noted a number of special difficulties which it encountered in its own work in the implementation process: The poor response to correspondence with States, subsequent to a visit, containing questions or suggestions for remedial action; the reluctance of some States to use foreign personnel at least as a remedial measure, even when funds are available; the unwillingness of States to ask for loans, or to explore how loans might be obtained using the good offices of the Panel, even when the Panel had suggested such a step; the disappointment on the part of some States that the Panel had not been able to offer or give assurances of more concrete help, such as gifts of money, equipment or personnel, or immediate joint financing or technical assistance; and, lastly, the reluctance of airlines to participate in schemes which might assist to solve some of the major deficiencies but where charges for improved services would result. (Part III-2)

Solutions

The Panel suggested the following solutions for the above-mentioned problems:

182

(a) Visits to States by experts (e.g., in case of communications). (II-10.2.2)

(b) Co-operative measures among States (e.g., in the flight checking of navigational aids). (II-10.2.6)

(c) Remedy the lack of spare parts (e.g., in case of communications equipment). (II-10.2.7)

(d) Better salaries and working conditions for personnel so as to retain them in Government service. (II-16)

(e) Insistence on the importance of international civil aviation to the State's economy. (II-17)

(f) Technical solutions

    (i) ICAO Technical Assistance Programme

    —Better share of technical assistance funds.

    —Difficulties in regard to technical assistance include: time required to build up a complete technical organization and poor salaries for personnel who are given training. (II-20.1.5)

    (ii) Bilateral technical assistance

    —Need to avoid duplication of effort or conflicting advice among those States furnishing technical assistance on a bilateral basis.

    (iii) Assistance by ICAO Secretariat. (II-20.3)

(g) Financial solutions (II-21)

    (i) Governments themselves could supply funds, although there are needs other than those of aviation to be met. (II-21.1)

    (ii) Loans from international lending institutions. (II-21.4)

    (iii) Purchase of equipment by instalments. (II-21.5)

    (iv) Bilateral financial assistance between States. (II-21.6)

    (v) Joint financing under the Convention. (II-21.7)

    (vi) User charges. (II-21.8)

(h) Operating agencies of the Government have the advantage of being autonomous and better prospects for recruiting personnel. (II-22)

Desirable characteristics of an instrument of ICAO to assist in implementation

(a) Implementation problems should be tackled on a statewide or system (i.e. COM, MET, ATS etc.) basis. (III-6)

(b) Consideration of the economic aspects of non-implementation of facilities and services, as well as the purely technical aspects. (III-7)

(c) High level consultation with States which may be more productive of results in procuring implementation. (III-8)

(d) Freedom of discussion with States by those authorized to encourage implementation. (III-9)

(e) Briefing for visits to States. The political, social and economic situation of State visited should be known by those authorized to encourage implementation. (III-10)

(f) Requests for Council action on problems hindering implementation should be dealth with expeditiously. (III-II)

(3) *Standing Group on Implementation of the Council*

The Special Implementation Panel (1956-1959) is not to be confused with the Standing Group on Implementation of the Council. In 1959, the Assembly called for an effort to ascertain major deficiencies in air navigation services on the main international air routes.[76] Secretariat surveys were made of three regions. On considering these reports, the Council decided that the machinery for promoting the implementation of regional plans should take the form of a standing group with a permanent membership of five (the President of the Council—Chairman, the President of the Air Navigation Commission and the Chairmen of the Air Transport, Joint Support and Finance Committees) and a "floating" membership to be selected by the President of the Council on an *ad hoc* basis and to be made up of representatives on Council and members of the Air Navigation Commission, Air Transport Committee and Joint Support Committee familiar with a particular problem or geographical area, and of such persons outside the Organization as the President might wish to call upon.[77] The Group is still in existence and meets regularly to consider problems of implementation.

(4) *Assembly policy statement on implementation of Regional Plans*

As in the case of SARPS and PANS, the Assembly adopts policy statements concerning the implementation of Regional Plans. The preoccupation with implementation is evident even in the Resolution concerned with the formulation of Regional Plans and Regional Supplementary Procedures and SUPPS. Thus, in 1968, the Assembly instructed the Council to

"ensure that implementation dates in Regional Plans involving the procurement of new types of equipment be realistically related to the ready availability of suitable equipment, preferably from more than one source." [78]

The detailed Resolution [79] on the implementation of Regional Plans and SUPPS provides for prompt information to each Contracting State of the

---

[76] Resolution A12-5.
[77] *Op. cit.,* note 60 *supra,* 26-27.
[78] Resolution A16-19, Appendix E, clause (5).
[79] Resolution A16-19, Appendix G. In Resolution A15-10, the Assembly directed the Council "to revise and improve the guidance provided for regional air navigation meetings in respect of: (a) the relationship between planning and implementation; and (b) the establishment of an order of priority for implementation of air navigation facilities and services required by regional plans; and (c) the importance of adequate maintenance and efficient operation of facilities and services that have been or will be provided."

recommendations applicable to it for the provision of air navigation facilities and services under an approved Regional Plan and of the associated implementation dates approved by the Council; the preparation by Contracting States and the keeping up-to-date of suitable manning plans for the orderly implementation of Regional Plans; the giving of priority by Contracting States to these items which are of such a nature that lack of implementation is likely to result in serious deficiencies; periodical progress reports on implementation; criteria for the reporting of deficiencies (by users to States and by States to ICAO where there has been no remedial action by the State concerned); improvement of effectiveness of methods by which deficiencies are isolated and eliminated, and reduction to a minimum of the time taken for investigation of reported deficiencies and action on them by the Organization.

There are various ways and means whereby the Organization fosters and assists in the implementation of Regional Plans, thus: request of a State for assistance from ICAO after exploring all methods and means for implementation of Regional Plans with which that State is concerned; the holding of informal meetings of States whether initiated by States or convened by the Secretary General; assistance by the Council to States; assistance through the Expanded Programme of Technical Assistance, technical advice and assistance from the Secretariat and the training resources of the Secretariat; assistance of States by ICAO Regional Offices, and co-ordination, in particular at the regional level, of all activities of ICAO that can contribute to the implementation of Regional Plans.

As to the economic and financial aspects of the implementation of Regional Plans, the Assembly, in 1965, indicated that, before applying to ICAO for joint financing under Chapter XV of the Convention, States would be expected to obtain implementation by means of loans for capital expenditures, operating agencies, technical assistance or other means compatible with the Convention. The Assembly also insisted on the need for user and provider States to give serious consideration, in particular at regional meetings, to the economic justification of projected air navigation facilities and services; requested the Council to assist States, as far as feasible, in their consideration and evaluation of the economic and financial aspects of the Regional Plans; invited States to examine with other States in the region whether the implementation of the particular Regional Plan could be carried out through bilateral or multilateral arrangements and issued a directive to the Council to follow closely and analyse pertinent developments in the areas of operational research, systems analysis, and cost/benefit methodology for the information of and possible application by Contracting States to planning in connection with air navigation facilities and services. This lengthy policy statement was reduced by the Assembly in 1968 to include only this directive to the Council.[80]

[80] Resolution A15-5: Economic and Financial Aspects of the Implementation of Re-

(5) *Proposal for the establishment of an Aviation Development Fund*

The establishment of an Aviation Development Fund was proposed at the Fifteenth Session of the Assembly (1965). The proposal envisaged a fund to finance projects or activities designed to implement or assist in the implementation of regional and national programmes related to overall plans of ICAO for the development of civil aviation. The fund would primarily provide capital and goods (e.g., telecommunications and navigational aid equipment), but would also cover recurring expenses for maintenance and operation on a diminishing basis. It would be administered by an ICAO Executive Committee which would approve individual projects of up to five years' duration. The proposed fund would not compete with or replace existing sources of air programmes but would be regarded as supplementary to them.[81] The Council and its Standing Group on Implementation having examined this proposal, had doubts as to its practicability, effectiveness and feasibility, but at the same time pointed out alternative methods of financing (e.g., bilateral aid, loans from lending institutions).[82]

III. TOPICS AND QUESTIONS

1. *The choice of techniques to carry out an agreed course of action*

(1) *Undertakings of member States in presumably binding form (Desirability)*

The extent to which it will be possible to have member States of an international organization undertake in binding form to carry out a policy or action will depend on many factors. A prime factor will be whether the constituent instrument of the organization contains provisions whereby the member States agree to be bound by certain decisions of the organization. In the absence of such provisions, the decisions of the organization will, for the most part, be implemented to the extent that compliance with them is to the mutual advantage of the member States. This is particularly true of functional organizations where compliance with technical regulatory material adopted or approved by these organizations gives member States the advantage of an ordered participation in a technical activity. For example, in the Convention on International Civil Aviation, compliance

---

gional Plans. See, for shorter version of Resolution A15-5 as amended by the Assembly in 1968, Doc 8770, pp. 84-85.

[81] Doc 8522 A15-EX43, 21-22.

[82] Doc 8665-C/970, Action of the Council, 59th Session (1966), 27.

with technical regulatory material prepared by ICAO will promote, as contemplated by the Chicago Convention, the "safety, efficiency and regularity" of international civil aviation.

(2) *Varying degrees of legal obligation implied by various forms of expressing approval by member States*

(a) *Ratification of the terms of a treaty*
A State that ratifies a protocol of amendment to the Chicago Convention,[83] ratifies or adheres to a convention on air law adopted by the ICAO Assembly[84] or a diplomatic conference convened under the auspices of ICAO,[85] ratifies or adheres to an agreement adopted by the European Civil Aviation Conference for which ICAO supplies Secretariat services,[86] accepts or accedes to an agreement on the joint financing of air navigation facilities and services adopted by a conference held under the auspices of ICAO[87] is legally bound to implement the protocol, convention or agreement as the case may be. The joint financing agreements provide for certain modifications subject to the consent of the Contracting States and once this consent is given, the States are legally bound to honour their commitments.[88]

---

[83] As at June 1st, 1970, five protocols of amendment to the Chicago Convention had been drawn up as a result of Assembly action. Such amendments come into force when ratified by the number of Contracting States specified by the Assembly. The number so specified must be not less than two-thirds of the total number of Contracting States. (Article 94 (a)). The Chicago Convention provides that the Assembly, in its resolution recommending adoption of an amendment, may provide that any State which has not ratified within a specified period after the amendment has come into force shall thereupon cease to be a member of ICAO and a party to the Convention. The Assembly has not yet made such a recommendation. On the other hand, the IMCO Assembly, when adopting, in 1964, the amendment which increased the membership of the Maritime Safety Committee, invoked Article 52 of the constituent instrument of the IMCO and provided for loss of membership of a State which did not ratify the amendment within a specified period. See IMCO Resolution A.70 (IV) in IMCO Assembly, 2nd Extraordinary Session (1964), Resolutions and Other Decisions, 6 and United Nations Juridical Yearbook, 1964, 202-203.
In the Protocol on the Authentic Trilingual Text of the Convention on International Civil Aviation (Chicago, 1944) opened for signature at Buenos Aires on 4 September 1968, it is provided that States may become parties to the Protocol either by: (a) signature without reservation as to acceptance, or (b) signature with reservation as to acceptance followed by acceptance, or (c) acceptance.
[84] See note 29 *supra*.
[85] See note 30 *supra*.
[86] Multilateral Agreement on Commercial Rights of Non-Scheduled Air Services in Europe. Doc 7695; 310 U.N.T.S. 229 (1958).
[87] For example, the Agreement on the Joint Financing of Certain Air Navigation Services in Iceland (Geneva, 1956). Doc 7725-JS/562; 334 U.N.T.S. 13 (1959).
[88] *Ibid.*, Articles V and VI.

(b) *Failure to make timely objection*

If the majority of the ICAO Contracting States do not, within a specified time, register their disapproval with the Council, of an Annex (or amendment thereto) to the Chicago Convention, the Annex and amendment thereto become effective.[89] As has been seen from the description of the process of making Annexes applicable, the Annex is not absolutely binding on States even at the date of coming into effect (except in the case of Annex 2 (Rules of the Air) in so far as it applies over the high seas). But at least at this date, the Annex has a certain form for the purposes of the next phase of its life.[90]

It is recalled that Article 38 of the Convention provides for the obligatory notification of differences to Annex material and amendments thereto. If, by the date on which the Annex becomes applicable, a State has not notified ICAO of differences between the standards in the Annex material and its national practice, there is a presumption that it has complied with the standards in all respects and it is therefore bound to comply with them, for so long thereafter as it does not notify differences. But, as has been seen in the discussion on implementation, ICAO experience shows that a State which has notified no differences is not necessarily complying in all respects with standards in the Annexes. Non-notification in many instances may imply quite the contrary position.

The President of the Council has delegated authority to approve Regional Supplementary Procedures (SUPPS). Proposals for amendments are requested by a State or group of States and are circulated by the Secretary General to all States considered to be affected. If there is no objection, the Secretary General circulates the proposal to members of the Air Navigation Commission and the representatives on the Council with a request that he be notified within a certain delay (seven days to three weeks) whether formal discussion is desired. If there is no request for formal discussion, the proposal is approved by the President of the Council. If, on the basis of the original inquiry of the Secretary General, a State objects, and consultation does not remove the objection, the matter will be considered by the Air Navigation Commission and, if amendment is necessary, by the Council. There is a similar procedure for consequential amendments drafted by the Secretary General, although the Air Navigation Commission can ultimately approve such amendments under delegated authority. While failure to make the above-mentioned objections will not make the SUPPS binding, the technique of absence-of-objection has an important role to play in the process of consultation which leads to the es-

---

[89] Article 90 (a). It has not yet happened that the majority of States have registered their disapproval of an Annex or of an amendment thereto.

[90] A few months after the Annex (or the amendment thereto) becomes effective, it becomes applicable, the date of applicability being specified by the Council in the resolution of adoption.

tablishment of a text that raises community expectations. Again, as in the case of the Procedures for Air Navigation Services (PANS), while the notification of differences to SUPPS is not obligatory, it is encouraged if there are differences to notify.

(c) *Modification of treaty by qualified majority*

The amendments to the Chicago Convention bind only those States that have ratified the respective protocols of amendment. The amendments come into force only in respect of States which have ratified them when ratified by the number of States specified by the Assembly. (Art. 94 (a)) In practice, States have acted so as to comply with constitutional and housekeeping amendments even though they have not ratified them.[91] Thus, no States have objected to the convening of the Assembly less often than annually or to the holding of elections to a 27-member Council instead of a 21-member Council. This does not mean that the non-ratifying States are not free to object. On the other hand, if an issue were to arise under the amendment which introduced Article 93 bis into the Convention, this amendment being concerned with a political matter (e.g., cessation of membership) difficulties might conceivably be raised by those States which have not ratified it.[92]

The Danish-Icelandic agreements on joint financing provide for their amendment in regard to finances, equipment and services provided the consent of States responsible for 90 per cent of the contributions is obtained;[93] and some very substantial amendments have been made to the agreements in this regard. States not consenting are not bound to contribute to the financing of the cost of new equipment and services.

A striking example of international legislation is that of the adoption by a two-thirds majority (18 out of 27 members) of the ICAO Council of the rules of the air which are applicable without deviation over the high seas.[94] The affirmative vote of 18 ICAO member States can thus bind the remainder of the 119 member States.[95]

(d) *Voting for a decision*

There are certain decisions which bind a State whether or not it votes for them. For example, when the Assembly adopts the scale of assess-

---

[91] None of the amendments to the Chicago Convention has yet been ratified by the total membership of ICAO. In fact, only four of the five protocols of amendment which exist have come into force.

[92] This article is concerned with the cessation of membership in ICAO of a State whose government the United Nations General Assembly has recommended be debarred from membership in international agencies established by or brought into relationship with the United Nations.

[93] Note 88 *supra*.

[94] This flows from the provisions of Article 12 of the Chicago Convention. See also Note 42 *supra*.

[95] As at May 1, 1970.

189

ments by a majority vote, States in the minority, or not voting at all, are bound to pay their contributions to the ICAO budget.

Obviously, in the case of the adoption of the rules of the air applicable over the high seas, and as set forth in Annex 2 to the Chicago Convention, only the 27 Council member States, out of the 119 ICAO member States would have an opportunity to vote,[96] and the rules might be adopted by a vote of only 18 Council member States. Nevertheless all 119 ICAO member States are bound by the decision of the Council.

(e) *Voting for a recommendation*

It is very doubtful that a State which votes for an ICAO recommendation has a strict legal obligation to comply with it. Much would depend on the nature and content of the recommendation and each case would have to be examined in the light of the surrounding circumstances. The most that can be said is that an affirmative vote of a State for a recommendation could raise an expectation of compliance by that State with the recommendation.

In the somewhat special case of a Recommended Practice included in an Annex, in respect of which Recommended Practice only a Council member State is entitled to vote, a certain expectation of compliance could arise not only in relation to that State, but also in relation to a non-Council State that had no opportunity to vote. The expectation would arise in the latter case from the fact that the Council, in adopting a Recommended Practice included in an Annex, acts on behalf of all ICAO member States and, in practice, States are encouraged to comply with Recommended Practices and to notify ICAO if they do not comply with them. A similar situation exists in the case of the approval of PANS and SUPPS. Their approval by ICAO raises expectations of compliance in the absence of notification of differences by the States.

(f) *Other expressions of consensus*

Sometimes a consensus will become manifest through a decision taken in the absence of objection. Thus, at the 14th session of the Assembly in 1962, it was agreed, in the Executive Committee and the Plenary Meeting of the Assembly itself, that, in the absence of objection, States that had not ratified the amendment to the Chicago Convention increasing the number of Council seats from 21 to 27 could both vote in the election for all 27 Council members and stand for election.[97]

An important decision was taken at the 15th session of the Assembly in 1965 when the Delegation of Romania was seated in the absence of ob-

---

[96] Article 90 (a) of the Chicago Convention provides that Annexes require for their adoption the vote of two-thirds of the Council (i.e., 14 out of 27 Council Member States), at a meeting called for that purpose.
[97] Doc 8270 A14-EX/31, para. 8.

jection. Romania had previously deposited an instrument of adherence to the Convention with the Government of the United States of America under Article 92 of the Convention [98] instead of seeking admission under Article 93 as a State not contemplated in the categories of States described in Articles 91 and 92 (a).

2. Legal effects of member States' approval of decisions

(1) *The practical significance and the assumed legal effect of a State's support and formal vote for a recommendation, resolution, interpretation and formal decision through its representative in an international organization*

(a) *Practical significance*

In the case of a housekeeping decision (e.g., assessments for the budget) a State would be bound even if it had not voted in favour of the decision. A State voting for a recommendation would not be bound to implement it, although, on the basis of its affirmative vote, there might be an expectation that it might implement the recommendation. In the case of a consensus, representatives may make it clear that they participate in the consensus formation without binding their governments. This happened in the Subcommittee on Article 77 of the Chicago Convention which reached a consensus on the possibility of the registration of aircraft of international operating agencies on other than a national basis.[99] At the same time, within the organ concerned, there may be a strong feeling of loyalty to the consensus on the part of the members once it has been achieved.[100]

---

[98] A15-WP/112 EX 18; Doc 8522 A15-EX/43, 2-3.

[99] The consensus process is, of course, well established in the United Nations as witness the use of it in such bodies as the Committee on the Peaceful Uses of Outer Space and the Special Committee on Principles of International Law concerning Friendly Relations and Co-operation among States.

[100] This was particularly evident in the session of the ICAO Subcommittee on Nationality and Registration of Aircraft Operated by International Operating Agencies (known as the "Subcommittee on Article 77" [of the Chicago Convention]) held in January 1967 (LC/SC Article/Report 7/2/67). Once the consensus had been reached on the main topic under discussion, there was strong opposition within the Subcommittee to any attempt to break it, although the members of the Subcommittee at the same time reserved the positions of their governments. At the 16th session of the ICAO Legal Committee, held in September 1967, the discussions on Article 77 of the Chicago Convention led to a weakening of the consensus and, indeed, to a threat on the part of the representative of a major State to abandon it because a change had been made in the language of the consensus. (Doc 8787-LC/156-1, p. 161) The consensus survived the Legal Committee discussions and the Council, on 14 December 1967, adopted a resolution on nationality and registration of aircraft operated by international operating agencies. (Doc 8722-C/976). Through the operation of Article 77, that resolution is binding on all ICAO Member States.

(b) *Assumed legal obligation*

In many cases, a State's support and vote for a decision will lead to the assumption that it is legally bound by the decision. Other decisions are binding in view of the binding nature of certain provisions of the Chicago Convention to which the decisions relate and any State, irrespectively of whether or how it votes at the meeting at which the decision is taken, is bound, for example, to pay assessments once the scale therefor is adopted by the Assembly;[101] to recognize election of the Council once it has taken place;[102] to recognize the election of the President of the Council once he has been elected by the Council[103] and to acknowledge a Council decision under Article 87 of the Convention as binding.[104] The contracting-out principle would not apply to these decisions. States will, on occasion, act as though bound by decisions that they have not ratified. For example, they so act in relation to amendments to the Convention concerning the holding of sessions of the Assembly less often than annually and the election of a Council of twenty-seven members instead of twenty-one.[105]

(2) *Instances in which national authorities have acted to carry out decisions of an international organization even though their representatives have not voted for them, or have actively opposed them in the international organization*

The International Conference on Private Air Law, held in 1952, adopted and opened for signature the Convention on Damage Caused by Foreign Aircraft to Third Parties in the Surface.[106] One of the most debated questions at that Conference was whether the Convention should provide that suits could be brought only in the courts of the State where the damage was caused (single-forum solution) or in a number of courts of different States (multiple-fora solution). Australia and Canada both voted for the second solution; but the Convention, as adopted, included the first.[107] Nevertheless, both Australia and Canada later ratified the Convention.

A State whose representatives at a session of the Assembly are opposed

---

[101] If it does not pay the assessments, it may have its vote in the Assembly and Council suspended in pursuance of Article 62 of the Chicago Convention. See note 22 *supra*.

[102] The Council is elected at the triennial sessions of the Assembly. See Article 50 of the Chicago Convention.

[103] Article 51 of the Chicago Convention provides for the election of the President who is an international official and represents no State.

[104] Article 87 of the Chicago Convention provides for the imposition of a very severe penalty for non-compliance: "Each Contracting State undertakes not to allow the operation of an airline of a Contracting State through the airspace above its territory if the Council has decided that the airline concerned is not conforming to a final decision rendered in accordance with the previous Article."

[105] For the case of the Council election, see under item (f) of III 1 (2) above.

[106] Note 30 *supra*.

[107] Rome Convention, Article 20.

to certain budget estimates, which are nevertheless adopted, in practice pays the whole of its assessed contribution, presumably because it considers itself to be bound by the relevant Assembly resolution.

It sometimes happens that, in the ICAO Council, there is a split vote as to the agenda or the site of a meeting. States on the minority side of the vote do not for that reason refuse to be represented at the meeting.

(3) *Whether concepts of legal obligation are invoked in such instances*

In the case of assessments for the regular budget of ICAO a concept of legal obligation could be invoked and ultimately non-payment could lead to the imposition of the suspension of voting power and services.[108]

(4) *The obligation, if any, to carry out, through national measures, decisions of an international organization voted for by the representative of a State*

Normally, the legal obligation to implement a decision through national measures would flow not from the casting of an affirmative vote, but from the provisions of the Organization's constitution. Thus, irrespectively of whether a State's representative on the ICAO Council has voted for or against the decision or abstained from voting, the State is bound to comply with the rules of the air adopted by the Council for inclusion in Annex 2 to the Chicago Convention and declared by it as being applicable over the high seas. This is an exceptional case since the ICAO Standards included in an Annex are normally based on a "contracting-out" concept. According to this concept, a State voting for a Standard in the Council can later file differences to it. Article 12 of the Convention provides that the rules of the air in force over the high seas are those established from time to time under the Convention and States are bound to ensure their observance.[109]

(5) *Use made of approval ad referendum*

Due to the relatively few cases of binding decisions in ICAO, approval of decisions *ad referendum* (the expression being here used in a flexible and non-technical sense) would be the rule. In this sense it would apply to Assembly resolutions and decisions except those concerned with such items as the establishment of the scale of assessments, the budget, the suspension of voting power of States in arrears in their contributions and the election of the Council. In the non-technical sense the expression *ad referendum* could also apply to most Council decisions except those

---

[108] Chicago Convention, Article 62.
[109] *Ibid.*, Article 12; note 42 *supra*.

dealing with the adoption of rules of the air for application over the high seas, the power delegated to the Council to make assessments applicable to new States joining ICAO (this exercise of the Council's delegated authority being subject to approval by the Assembly,[110] but not by the new State concerned) and a decision of the Council under Article 87 of the Convention.

A special case is that of the Final Act of the North Atlantic Ocean Stations Conference of 1960 which included amendments that modified extensively the financial arrangements contained in the Agreement on North Atlantic Ocean Stations of 1954. The Conference contemplated the preparation of a Protocol of amendment only if the Council considered this to be necessary. The Council later decided that the recommendations of the Conference could be implemented without modification of the 1954 Agreement and therefore did not prepare a protocol of amendment.[111] This line of action was not surprising since so many of the arrangements in the field of joint financing of air navigation services are subject to modification by consent of participating States. Flexibility of amendment of the arrangements makes it easier to keep the subject-matter of the arrangements up to date with technological requirements. In addition, the co-ordinating role played by the ICAO Council and Secretariat ensures that the consents of States will be elicited in regard to financial changes in the agreements and thus the requirements for more formal procedures of ratification and acceptance of changes are obviated.

The *ad referendum* concept taken in the technical sense applies to conventions adopted by the Assembly or conventions and agreements adopted by ICAO-sponsored meetings. These documents provide variously for States to become parties to them by actions which include the deposit of an instrument of ratification or acceptance following signature by representatives of the States concerned.

3. *Internal legal effects of decisions of international organizations*

(1) *Extent to which the various modes described in 1 and 2 above are regarded as being obligations upon governments to adopt consistent policies, legislation and administrative regulations*

There are certain provisions of the Chicago Convention which require that legal effect be given, on the national level, to certain decisions of ICAO:

---

[110] For a typical resolution, see A15-32: Confirmation of Council Action with respect to the assessments of Trinidad and Tobago, Jamaica, Algeria, Rwanda, Somalia, Yemen, Kenya, Malawi, Zambia, Mali and Togo. See, also, A16-50.
[111] Doc 8080-JS/579 Acts on the Joint Financing of the North Atlantic Ocean Stations 1954 and 1960. See, also, Doc 8845-JS/628 Acts on the Joint Financing of the North Atlantic Ocean Stations 1954 and 1968.

—Rules of the air: Each Contracting State undertakes to keep its own regulations in respect of the rules of the air uniform, to the greatest possible extent, with those established from time to time under the Convention. (See Article 12, second sentence) [112]

—Recognition of certificates and licenses: "Certificates of airworthiness and certificates of competency and licenses issued or rendered valid by the Contracting State in which the aircraft is registered, shall be recognized as valid by the other Contracting States, provided that the requirements under which such certificates or licenses were issued or rendered valid are equal to or above the minimum standards which may be established from time to time pursuant to this Convention." (Article 33) The effect of Article 33 is that the policy, legislation or administrative regulations, as the case may be, of a particular State, in so far as concerns the issuing or validation of certificates of airworthiness or personnel licenses, must be equal to or better than the minimum standards adopted by a Council decision.

(2) *Extent to which the various modes described in 1 and 2 above are regarded as directly creating rights and obligations in the nationals of governments giving their approval*

Provided States comply with the internationally accepted minima for personnel licensing and airworthiness certification, there is a reciprocal recognition of certificates of airworthiness and personnel licenses. The beneficiaries of this recognition are the individuals (whether or not nationals of the State that has issued or validated the certificates or licenses) who hold the licenses or the individuals or airlines whose aircraft have the certificates of airworthiness. Other things being equal (e.g., subject to the obtaining of permits for commercial services), those individuals who hold proper papers have the right to participate in international air navigation.

In the case of the Convention on the International Recognition of Rights in Aircraft (Geneva, 1948),[113] which was adopted by the ICAO Assembly, property rights of individuals in aircraft are affected, in the sense of being recognized internationally, provided the rights have been constituted in accordance with the law of the Contracting State in which the aircraft was registered at the time of their constitution and are regularly recorded in a public record of the Contracting State in which the aircraft is registered as to nationality. The individual's nationality would be irrelevant provided the property rights were registered and recorded as stipulated by the Convention.

The contract of carriage by air, which is entered into by private persons and airlines, is affected when a State becomes a party to certain doc-

---

112 Note 42 *supra.*
113 Note 29 *supra.*

uments adopted by ICAO-sponsored conferences. The two documents concerned are the Protocol to Amend the Convention for the Unification of Certain Rules Relating to International Carriage by Air Signed at Warsaw on 12 October 1929 (The Hague, 1955) [114] and the Convention, Supplementary to the Warsaw Convention, for the Unification of Certain Rules relating to International Carriage by Air Performed by a Person Other than the Contracting Carrier (Guadalajara, 1961).[115]

The Convention on Offences and Certain Other Acts Committed on Board Aircraft (Tokyo, 1963), [116] which was also adopted by an ICAO-sponsored conference, affects individuals engaged in flights specified in the Convention.

(3) *Illustrative examples of variations in law and practice among Member States of particular organizations in giving effect to treaties or decisions of international organizations as directly applicable to municipal law, and of the legal reasoning invoked to support such applications*

The question of differences filed in respect of ICAO regulatory material has been discussed earlier in this paper. The basic reasons for the filing of differences are (i) inability of the State concerned to comply with the minima specified in the material or (ii) the ability of the State to do better than those minima. These are not so much legal reasons as technical reasons due to the lack of equipment or trained personnel in the case of (i), or superior technology in terms of equipment and personnel in the case of (ii). Here it should be recalled that a standard in an ICAO Annex is an international minimum (except in Annex 9—Facilitation—where minima and maxima are specified). More details concerning this question of differences need not be given here. It may, however, be observed that the legal foundation for the filing of differences in the case of ICAO standards in Annexes is the contracting-out concept found in Article 38 of the Chicago Convention.

(4) *The extent to which the growth of international organization activity has an impact on the traditional theories of incorporation of treaty obligations, and now of international organization decisions, into municipal law*

In the technological field where financial outlay and trained personnel are required in order to implement technical regulatory material, the contracting-out principle, which permits of flexibility in implementation, is favoured over the requirement of paper compliance which may be valueless.

---

[114] Doc 7632; 478 U.N.T.S. 371 (1963).
[115] Doc 8181; 500 U.N.T.S. 31 (1964).
[116] Doc 8364.

The technical material adopted by ICAO is implemented on the national level partly by provisions in statutes, but, for the most part, in subsidiary legislation (decrees, orders-in-council, notices to airmen, aeronautical information publications (AIPS)) and even in operating manuals.

Similar flexibility is found in the Danish/Icelandic Joint Financing Agreements (1956) under which certain air navigation services are provided in the North Atlantic Area.[117] The agreements are couched in terms that enable changes to be made in services, equipment, capital, expenditures and operating costs—which changes are reflected in the annual budgets of the participating States—without the necessity of using protocols of amendment. The consent of States to changes is transmitted to ICAO and the agreements are under constant adjustment with the ICAO Council and Secretariat playing an important co-ordinating role. The Danish-Icelandic Agreements prior to 1956 did not contain the same flexibility and were subject to a more formal process of amendment.

(5) *Illustrations of practical problems that have arisen in the experience of international organizations*

These illustrations are given under the heading entitled "II. Techniques available in ICAO to encourage compliance with decisions".

(6) *Examples of conflicts between "organization law" and municipal law of member States*

National boundaries and air traffic services areas
Strict adherence to national boundaries could hinder meeting the operational needs of international air traffic. Therefore, ICAO encourages States not to insist on observance of sovereignty and to review their air traffic service areas on the basis of technical and operational considerations rather than on the basis of national boundaries. States are also encouraged, when so required to meet the operational needs of international air traffic, to negotiate with other States with a view to reaching agreement on the delineation of flight information regions (FIRs), control areas (CTs) and control zones (CTRs), extending across national boundaries.[118] In addition, while the ICAO Rules of the Air over the high seas are to be applied without deviation, States which furnish Air Traffic Control services over the high seas falling within their control areas are allowed to apply their national Air Traffic Control services over the high seas with the differences filed by them pursuant to Article 38 of the Convention.[119]

---

[117] For Icelandic Agreement, see note 87 supra; for Danish Agreement, see Doc 7726-JS/563; 334 U.N.T.S. 89 (1959).
[118] Resolution A16-19; Appendix R.
[119] Foreword to Annex 11, 5th ed., March 1966, 6.

Regional Plans-Equipment for Prague Airport

In 1956 the Czech Government complained to the ICAO Assembly that it was unable to procure certain equipment required in order to implement an ICAO Regional Plan at Prague Airport. It could not get the equipment since export permits were refused by supplier contries.[120] The matter was referred to the ICAO Council which found no solution for it.[121]

Double taxation

There can be a conflict between "organization law" applied internally to an organization's employees, but not applicable externally to a member State and the municipal law of that State which is also applicable to those employees. The danger of such a conflict arose when ICAO was contemplating the introduction of a staff assessment plan applicable to all staff at a time when there was no provision in the Federal Income Tax Act (Canada) which would permit ICAO employees, who were Canadian nationals, a set-off for an internal levy paid by them to ICAO on their ICAO salary and emoluments. Although, in this case, the Canadian Government was not bound to do so, it avoided the conflict by amending the Income Tax Act in advance of the introduction of the ICAO Assessment with the result that an ICAO Canadian employee who pays an assessment to the Organization pays little, if any, tax under the Income Tax Act.[122]

When the Province of Quebec, the political subdivision of Canada in ICAO has its headquarters, introduced income tax in 1954, no similar provision was included in its Act. An arrangement was, however, made with the Province whereby non-Canadians would not have to file tax returns. The Canadian staff members have to pay income tax to the Province, but are reimbursed by ICAO mostly through funds received from the Federal Government.[123]

4. Compliance: Measures to help assure that Member States committments or obligations are carried out

(1) Reporting procedures

States are obliged under the Chicago Convention to notify differences between their national regulations and the ICAO Standards contained in An-

---

[120] Resolution A10-12: Elimination of Deficiencies at Prague Airport.

[121] Doc 7763-C/896 Action of the Council, 29th Session (1956), 15.

[122] *Income Tax Act*, R.S.C. 1952, c. 148, s. 41 (4). See, on arrangements with Canadian Government concerning privileges and immunities, Dai, Poeliu, "The Headquarters Agreement between Canada and the International Civil Aviation Organization", (1964) 2 *The Canadian Yearbook of International Law* 205-214.

[123] Doc 7763-C/896 Action of the Council, 29th Session (1956), 6. See Dai, *op. cit.*, note 122 *supra*, 212-213.

nexes and are encouraged to notify differences in respect of Recommended Practices, Procedures for Air Navigation Services (PANS) and Regional Supplementary Procedures (SUPPS). These differences are published by ICAO. The implementation process in regard to this regulatory material as well as the implementation procedures followed for Regional Plans is discussed above.

Assembly resolutions remind States of the importance of ratifying or adhering to ICAO-sponsored conventions on air law.[124]

That an amendment to the Chicago Convention can be quickly brought into force was demonstrated when, as a result of an intensive campaign for ratification,[125] the amendment increasing the size of the ICAO Council entered into force in July 1962 only thirteen months after its adoption at an extraordinary session of the Assembly.

(2) *Formal inspections*

There is no provision under the Chicago Convention for formal inspections concerning compliance with ICAO decisions. But, as seen earlier in this paper, inspections are made by Regional Office staffs who are sometimes given temporary help in order to follow up difficult questions of implementation.

(3) *Judicial proceedings*

If any disagreement arises between two or more Contracting States of ICAO relating to the interpretation or application of the Chicago Convention and its Annexes and cannot be settled by negotiation, it must, on application of any State concerned in the disagreement, be decided by the ICAO Council. The disagreements contemplated could include questions of implementation of ICAO decisions and the Council's role under the Convention is a judicial one. Provision is made for appeals from the Council decisions on disagreements to the International Court of Justice or, under appropriate circumstances, to an *ad hoc* arbitral tribunal.[126] Penalties for non-conformity with a final and binding decision in regard to a disagreement are very severe including suspension of the operations of airlines of a defaulting State in the territory of other Contracting States[127] and the suspension of voting power in the Assembly and Council of a defaulting State.[128]

---

[124] E.g., Resolutions A10-39 and A12-23.
[125] The year 1962 was an election year for the Council which is elected for a three-year term. There was a successful attempt to have the amendment come into force before the 1962 session of the Assembly at which the election was to take place.
[126] Chicago Convention, Articles 84 and 85.
[127] *Ibid.*, Article 87.
[128] *Ibid.*, Article 88.

5. Special problems of federated States

ICAO has encountered this problem to some extent in connection with privileges and immunities to be granted by Canadian and Quebec authorities to the organization, national representatives and the staff located at the headquarters in Montreal.[129]

At the International Conference on Private Air Law, held under ICAO auspices at Rome, in 1952, Australia and Canada intimated that they would have difficulty in accepting a clause in the Convention on Damage Caused by Foreign Aircraft to Third Parties on the Surface.[130] This clause provided for the bringing of suits under the Convention in a single forum. Nevertheless these two States were among the first to ratify the Convention.

6. Amendment of constituent instruments through methods other than explicit approval by all members

(1) Provision concerning amendments

Amendments to the Chicago Convention come into force when ratified by the number of States specified by the Assembly. The number so specified must be not less than two-thirds of the total number of Contracting States.[131] In practice, the Assembly specifies the number as being two-thirds of the membership at the time it adopts the amendment.[132] The amendment comes into force only in respect of States which have ratified it.[133]

(2) ICAO experience with specific amendments

In practice, States that have not ratified certain amendments have not objected to their application to them. For example, States comply with the amendments to Articles 48 (a), 49 (e) and 60 which permit the convening of the Assembly once every three years instead of annually as specified in the orginal text of the Chicago Convention.[134] Indeed, States have enjoyed quite important privileges under an amendment which they did not ratify. In 1961, the Assembly adopted an amendment which was to have the effect of increasing the number of Council seats from 21 to 27.[135] The amendment entered into force on 17 July 1962. At

---

[129] Dai, op. cit., note 122 supra, 205-214.
[130] Note 30 supra.
[131] Chicago Convention, Article 94.
[132] Resolutions A1-4, A8-1, A8-4, A13-1 and A14-5.
[133] Chicago Convention, Article 94. See Buergenthal, op. cit., note 12 supra, 199-228; Zacklin, Ralph, The Amendment of the Constitutive Instruments of the United Nations and Specialized Agencies (Leyden, 1968).
[134] Resolution A8-1.
[135] Resolution A13-1.

the 14th session of the Assembly, held in August-September 1962, it was agreed that States that had not yet ratified the amendment could both stand for election to the augmented Council and could vote in the election.[136]

(3) *Avoidance of an amendment*

In 1956, at the 10th session of the Assembly, it was decided not to amend the Chicago Convention (as had been proposed) so as to delete item (e) of Article 29 (Requirement that an aircraft carry a journey log book) and Article 34 (Journey log book). Instead, the Assembly adopted Resolution A10-36 (Journey log book) which, for those States that chose to follow it constituted, in effect, an amendment to the Chicago Convention. The operative part of the resolution reads as follows:

"The *Assembly Resolves* that the General Declaration, when prepared so as to contain all the information required by Article 34 with respect to the journey log book, may be considered by Contracting States to be an acceptable form of journey log book; and the carriage and maintenance of the General Declaration under such circumstances may be considered to fulfill the purposes of Articles 29 and 34 with respect to the journey log book."

Curiously enough, the Council later failed to adopt a United Kingdom proposal to delete from Annex 6 to the Chicago Convention the provisions concerning the journey log book. The affirmative vote of 13 was one short of the two-thirds majority of 14 required by the Convention, at that time, for the adoption of an amendment to an Annex.[137]

IV. CONCLUSION

It is seen from the foregoing that ICAO decisions are of a wide variety and that the problems of implementation are closely related to the types of decisions and even more so to their subject-matter. The bulk of ICAO's substantive decisions is concerned with technical regulatory material and most of this is adopted on a "contracting-out" basis. Implementation of these decisions depends not so much on legal rules as on the good-will of Contracting States and their need to comply with the technological laws of air navigation if they are to participate in it effectively. In this respect, ICAO is hardly different from any other functional international organization engaged in normative activities. Nor does the fact that many of the sanctions attaching to non-implementation of ICAO decisions are of a para-legal nature deprive them of significance in discussing the question of implementation. Whether compliance with an ICAO-adopted

---

[136] Doc 8270 A14-EX/31, para. 8.
[137] Doc 7763-C/986 Action of the Council, 29th Session (1956), 17.

norm is induced by the threat of a legal sanction or a natural sanction flowing from non-compliance with technological norms will not make much difference provided compliance is achieved.

The difficulties in procuring implementation of the ICAO technical regulatory material are, to a great extent, a result of the technological gap between the developed and developing countries. A basic factor hindering implementation is the lack of *men, matériel* and the *money* to pay for the training and retention of men and the acquisition and maintenance of matériel. This is what might be called the "3-M" gap.

Possibly radical solutions are needed. One solution suggested for some of the difficulties of implementation in respect of the supply of facilities and services for air navigation might, if it proved to be practicable, simplify difficulties or even eliminate them in advance. It has been suggested that systems planning be applied to the introduction of new aircraft types. In future, steps would be taken to harmonize the aircraft and infrastructure. The implications of these measures for both providers of facilities and services, on the one hand, and the operators, on the other, would have to be determined and analyzed before the characteristics of the aircraft were frozen and before the airlines were committed to its operation. The hope has been expressed that this approach would narrow the gap between infrastructure and aircraft with a consequent saving in money and men.[138] Only the future will tell whether and to what extent this will produce useful results.

The pragmatic activities of ICAO as a functional international organization are not productive of much "law", if the expression is used in terms of a rule the non observance of which involves the application of a sanction by the law-giver. Nevertheless inherent in ICAO decisions in the normative field may often be severe natural sanctions which deprive those who do not comply with the decisions of the benefit of safe and fruitful participation in international civil aviation. On the other hand, decisions of a constitutional and housekeeping nature involve sanctions which tend to be legal since they are based expressly, or by necessary implication, on the provisions of ICAO's constituent instrument, the Chicago Convention.

The law of international organization is at a very primitive stage and provisions for the application of legal sanctions in the functional field tend to be somewhat rare. However, man must needs work with the tools at hand. Therefore, at least in the case of functional international organizations, he must not ignore the importance of *natural* sanctions as an aid to securing compliance with certain decisions. At the same time, he will also make use of the few *legal* sanctions available. Ideally, the increase in the implementation of international norms due to the pressure of technological requirements would obviate the need for sanctions of any kind. Unfortunately, the world is far from this ideal state. But nothing less than a

---

[138] C-WP/4595. See Assembly Resolution A16-5.

perfect world community should be the goal of man. An ordered regime of international civil aviation brought about by a full implementation of multilateral decisions in the aviation field is an instrument *par excellence* for use in achieving that community.

Appendix A[1]

PRINCIPLES GOVERNING THE REPORTING OF "DIFFERENCES"

At its 11th Session (1950), the Council adopted a set of principles to govern the reporting of differences from International Standards contained in Annexes to the Convention, Recommended Practices, Specifications, Procedures and Supplementary Procedures. These principles are set forth below.

Subject No. 14.14: Effect of Deviation by Contracting States from International Standards and Reservations to Regional Air Navigation Plans

Principles Governing the Reporting of "Differences" from ICAO Standards, Practices and Procedures [1]

At its meetings on 29 September, 3 and 10 October and 12 November, the Council considered the 79th Report of the Air Navigation Commission (C-WP/650), containing the Commission's recommendations concerning the notification by States and the dissemination by ICAO of "differences" from ICAO Standards, Practices and Procedures, and related papers by the Representative of Canada (C-WP/720), the Representative of the United Kingdom (C-WP/722) and the Secretary General (C-WP/749). At the last of these meetings it approved the following principles to govern the reporting of differences:

"1) *Differences from International Standards contained in Annexes to the Convention*
  A) That Contracting States, when notifying ICAO of the differences between their national regulations and practices and the international Standards contained in Annexes in compliance with Article 38 of the Convention, be requested to give particular attention to those differences knowledge of which is essential to the safety or regularity of international air navigation;
  B) That the following criteria, or such of them as are appropriate to a particular Annex, be brought to the attention of Contracting States to be used as a guide in determining reportable differences:
i) When the national regulations of a Contracting State affect the operation of aircraft of other Contracting States in and above its territory
a) by imposing an obligation within the scope of an Annex which is not covered by an ICAO Standard;
b) by imposing an obligation different in character * from that of the corresponding ICAO Standard;

---

[1] The material herein is extracted from Doc 7188-C/828, Proceedings of the Council, 11th Session, Part II, 32-35.
* The expression "different in character" in (i) (b) and (ii) (a) would be applied to a national regulation which achieves by other means the same objective as that of the

c) by being more exacting than the corresponding ICAO Standard;

d) by being less protective than the corresponding ICAO Standard.

ii) When the national regulations of a Contracting State applicable to its aircraft and their maintenance, as well as to aircrew personnel, engaged in international air operations over the territory of another Contracting State.

a) are different in character * from that of the corresponding ICAO Standard;

b) are less protective than the corresponding ICAO Standard;

iii) When the facilities or services provided by a Contracting State for international air navigation

a) impose an obligation or requirement for safety additional to any that may be imposed by the corresponding ICAO Standard;

b) while not imposing an additional obligation differ in principle, type or system from the corresponding ICAO Standard;

c) are less protective than the corresponding ICAO Standard.

2) *Differences from Recommended Practices*

A) That, although differences from Recommended Practices are not notifiable under Article 38 of the Convention, Contracting States be invited to notify the Organization of the differences between their national regulations and practices and any corresponding Recommended Practices contained in an Annex when the knowledge of such differences is important for the safety of air navigation;

B) That, as a guide to determining the differences to be notified, States be invited to use the criteria in (1) (B) above, in so far as they are applicable.

3) *Differences from Specifications, Procedures and Supplementary Procedures*

A) That Contracting States be invited also to notify the Organization of the differences between their national regulations and practices and any corresponding procedures contained in Procedures for Air Navigation Services (PANS), Supplementary Procedures (SUPPS) and Specifications ** approved by the Council for application by Contracting States on a world-wide or regional basis, when the knowledge of such differences is important for the safety of air navigation;

B) That, in inviting Contracting States to notify differences from Procedures for Air Navigation Services, it be pointed out that a difference arising from compliance with a Supplementary Procedure would not be regarded as a reportable difference;

C) That, in determining the differences to be reported, States be invited to use the criteria in (1) (B) above, in so far as they are applicable."

The Council also approved the recommendation of the Air Navigation Commission that

"The final edition of an Annex issued by the Organization should include a loose-leaf Supplement, indicating in an index table, by States, the notification of significant differences in respect of the various paragraphs of the Annex, the table to be followed by a list, by paragraphs of the Annex, of the actual differences reported"

—and the revised draft resolution for the adoption of an Annex set out in Appendix B to C-WP-749. The determination of the form of State Letter on the adoption of an Annex and of the machinery for notifying differences from PANS, SUPPS and Specifications was left to the Secretariat.

---

corresponding ICAO Standard and so cannot be classified under (i) (c) or (d) or (ii) (b)

** To date the only "Specifications" issued by ICAO are the Specifications for Meteorological Services to International Air Navigation (Doc 5714-MET/511), which were approved by the Council for world-wide use on 17 September 1948 and came into force on 1 January 1949. [Note: This footnote is, of course, out of date in 1970.]

The Secretariat was asked to prepare, for separate consideration at an appropriate time, an interpretation of the word "procedures" as used in Article 38, and recommendations as to the principles which should govern the reporting of differences from Annexes not relating to air navigation, such as Annex 9 (Facilitation of International Air Transport).

SELECT BIBLIOGRAPHY ON THE DEVELOPMENT OF ICAO TECHNICAL REGULATORY MATERIAL

Buergenthal, Thomas, *Law-making in the International Civil Aviation Organization* (Syracuse University Press, 1969).

Cheng, B., *The Law of International Air Transport,* (London, 1962), 63-71.

Codding, George A., Jr., "Contributions of the World Health Organization and the International Civil Aviation Organization to the Development of International Law", (1965) *Proceedings of A.S.I.L.* 147-153.

Drion, H., "The Council of ICAO as International Legislator over the High Seas", *Studi* Ambrosini. (Milan, 1957).

Erler, Jochen, *Rechtsfragen der ICAO: Die Internationale Zivulluftfahrtorganisation und Ihre Mitgliedstaaten* (Cologne, Berlin, Munich, 1967).

Fuller, W. E., "ICAO International Standards in the Technical Annexes—Their Effect within the United States and Validity under the Constitution", (1952) 21 *Geo Wash. L.R.* 86-103.

Jones, H. H., "Amending the Chicago Convention and its Technical Standards Can Consent of all Member States be Eliminated", (1949) 16 *J.A.L.C.* 185-213.

Le Goff, M., "Les Annexes techniques à la Convention de Chicago", (1956) 19 *R.G.A.* 146-156.

Le Goff, M., "L'activité des divisions techniques au sein de l'OACI", (1951) 14 *R.G.A.* 419-432.

Lemoine, M., *Traité de Droit aérien* (Paris, 1947), 58.

Malintoppi, A., "La fonction 'normative' de l'OACI", (1950) 13 *R.G.A.* 1050-1053.

Mankiewicz, R. H., "L'adoption des Annexes à la Convention de Chicago par le Conseil de l'Organisation de l'Aviation civile internationale", *Meyer Festschrift,* Düsseldorf, 1954.

Pépin, E., "Le Droit Aérien", (1947) 71 *Recueil des Cours de La Haye* 503.

Pépin, E., "ICAO and Other Agencies Dealing with Air Regulation", (1952), 19 *J.A.L.C.* 152.

Riese, O., *Luftrecht* (Stuttgart, 1949), 126.

Ros, E. J., "Le pouvoir législatif international de l'OACI et ses modalités", (1953) 16 *R.G.A.* 25-35.

Saba, H., "L'activité quasi-législative des institutions spécialisées des Nations Unies", (1964) 111 *Recueil des Cours de La Haye* 603-690.

Shawcross and Beaumont on Air Law, 3rd Ed., (London, 1966), Vol. I, 58, 213-216.

Sheffy, M., "The Air Navigation Commission of the ICAO", (1958) 25 *J.A.L.C.* 281, 428.

Yemin, Edward, *Legislative Powers in the United Nations and Specialized Agencies* (Leyden, 1969).

Zacklin, Ralph, *The Amendment of the Constitutive Instruments of the United Nations and Specialized Agencies* (Leyden, 1968).

DECISIONS OF INTERNATIONAL ORGANIZATIONS—
EFFECTIVENESS IN MEMBER STATES
SOME ASPECTS OF THE LAW AND PRACTICE OF FAO

by *Jean Pierre Dobbert* *
Office of the Legal Counsel, Food and Agriculture Organization of the United Nations

A. SCOPE AND METHOD OF INQUIRY

The present paper is primarily intended as a "law and practice" report, showing the methods and procedures which have developed within the constitutional framework of FAO to elaborate and formulate decisions susceptible of finding a large measure of support among the Organization's Member Nations and to ascertain the effectiveness of such decisions, particularly where effectiveness depends on active participation of individual governments. It is neither meant to be exhaustive nor to give a perfectly balanced picture of the legal problems which the Organization is facing in this field. In fact, while the vast majority of legally binding provisions is to be found in the Constitution and in treaties concluded by, or within the framework of, FAO, particular attention will be given to certain procedures and instruments whose legal nature is still in the midst of a process of evolution.[1]

In examining the general theme "Decisions of International Organizations—Effectiveness in Member States", it may be appropriate to attempt a definition of the principal terms used and thereby to limit the scope of the inquiry. Perhaps, since no general validity is claimed for such definitions,[2] it would be preferable to refer to methodological assumptions.

First, the term "International Organizations" (IO's) is to be understood as "Intergovernmental Organizations" (IGO's). While the value and influence of Non-Governmental Organizations (NGO's) must be recognized, the problem of effectiveness of decisions in *Member States* can normally arise only in relation to IGO's.[3] On the other hand, a number

---

* The opinions expressed in this article are strictly those of the author and do not necessarily reflect the views and policies of FAO.

[1] See example given on pp. 238 ff. below.

[2] Being essentially a "case study", this paper is not intended as a contribution to the *doctrine* of international organizations; accordingly, no attempt is made to discuss legal theory, and references to legal literature have been deliberately kept to a minimum.

[3] This assumption may be too restrictive with respect to certain organizations—such as the ILO in whose constitutional structure, functions, and processes of making or implementing decisions NGO's play an essential part. It is considered valid, however, for most organizations, including FAO, although—as will be shown later—NGO's may initiate, and substantially contribute to, the formulation of normative decisions of IGO's.

of agencies and programs—particularly in the UN System—enjoying considerable autonomy (both internally and in their relations with governments) may, in many respects, share with IGO's the problems relating to the effectiveness of decisions made within their sphere of competence. This would apply, *inter alia,* to such agencies and programs as UNDP (Special Fund and EPTA Sectors), UNCTAD, UNIDO, UNICEF, UNITAR, UNHCR and the Joint UN/FAO World Program (WFP). They are not infrequently referred to, with the Specialized Agencies, as "functional organizations" or "functional agencies".

Secondly, the term "Decision" might be limited to official (formal or informal) statements by the constitutionally competent organ of an IGO declaring, interpreting or intending to modify a given factual or legal situation, and affecting the Organization as such, or any organs thereof, or any or all of its Member States or—in exceptional cases—other Organizations or Non-Member States.

Thirdly, while any decisions of IGO's are susceptible, in certain circumstances, of affecting some or all Member States, even though they may not be specifically addressed to such States, it would seem logical to place the main emphasis on decisions the effectiveness of which depends, to some extent at least, on the active participation of Member States in their implementation.

Fourthly, the concept of effectiveness is largely, but not entirely, coterminous with the concept of compliance; in view of the complexity of some decisions (or of the situation which they are intended to meet), their objectives may not always be attained even in the event of full compliance while, in exceptional cases, decisions may prove relatively effective even in the absence of compliance.

Finally, political, economic or psychological factors may determine the degree of effectiveness or compliance; accordingly, they have to be taken into account in the process of decision making and in the evaluation of the results of decisions. The assessment of these factors and of the effect on individual and collective behaviour of States is primarily within the province of political science. These factors do not appear to be germane to the essentially legal problem as to whether, to what extent, and under what conditions decisions are binding on Member States.[4] The present paper is intended to examine various questions related to this legal problem, the examples being mainly drawn from, and the conclusions—perhaps inevitably—influenced by, the law and practice of FAO.

---

[4] This delineation does not imply that the processes of decision making and implementation are entirely within the ambit of political science; the procedure by which decisions are reached, the form in which they are adopted, and the methods by which they are implemented nearly always involve legal problems.

B. GENERAL OBSERVATIONS

1. *Sources*

The principal sources to which the lawyer normally turns for ascertaining the legal nature and scope of a decision are (i) the constituent instrument of the Organization and (ii) the "secondary" rules adopted by its governing bodies; he will also have to take into account the ever growing volume of constitutional practice as developed by the Organization and the instruments produced in accordance with such practice.

The form of decisions, the method of adoption, their scope *ratione materiae* or *loci* (and, in some cases, *personae* or—perhaps more appropriately—*nationis*) and the extent to which they are to be considered binding depends in the first place on the constituent instrument (Constitution, Convention, Articles of Agreement) of each Organization. The relevant provisions of that instrument will vary according to whether the drafters intended to give to the Organization primarily the character of a research institution or of a forum for discussion and exchange of information or whether they intended to endow it with regulatory or operational functions, it being understood that many Organizations which originally belonged to the former category have gradually assumed more comprehensive responsibilities, by way of constitutional amendments and—not infrequently—a liberal interpretation of existing constitutional provisions. The questions concerning the effectiveness of decisions would, at least theoretically, appear to be confined to Organizations exercising operational or regulatory functions.

In the second place, all Organizations have adopted one or several sets of rules interpreting, spelling out and, in some cases, supplementing their constituent instruments. These rules—covering a wide field and known under widely different names, such as regulations, standing orders, general rules, financial regulations—are usually adopted by, or on the authority of, the supreme governing body and as such are binding on all organs of the Organization and on Member States. On the one hand, they are more detailed and thus in a sense less flexible than the constituent instrument; on the other hand, they are more flexible in the sense that the procedure for amending individual provisions is usually simpler, and the body which has jurisdiction to amend such rules is often authorized to suspend a given rule or grant exceptions therefrom in individual cases, either by virtue of a specific provision or according to the doctrine of implied powers. At any rate, the detailed provisions relating to the procedure for the adoption of decisions, to their form, scope and legal effect and to methods of ascertaining their effectiveness are more likely to appear in this "secondary legislation", than in the constituent instrument.

Thirdly, some Organizations have established special procedures for developing and adopting standards, either by treaty or by some less formal methods. While the basic provisions concerning such procedures are normally contained in the constituent instruments and the rules referred to above, the scope and legal effects of such standards and the methods of ascertaining—or perhaps ensuring—their application by Member States are often determined by provisions embodied in the instrument which lays down the standards. Again, either a governing body of the Organization or a special body established by virtue of the treaty or other instrument laying down the standards, or created by decision of a governing body, may be authorized to exercise certain normative, fact-finding or supervisory functions.

Fourthly, each Organization has developed—and continues to develop—its own constitutional practice, with a view to resolving the new or changing policy, technical, and practical problems confronting it. The provisions reflecting this practice are often scattered in resolutions, recommendations, and reports of governing bodies. They are not always easy to trace and even when they are identified, it is often difficult to determine whether they were intended to introduce a new method, thus setting a precedent for similar situations arising in the future, or whether they should be regarded as reflecting an *ad hoc* decision limited to a particular situation.

Finally, since international organizations are often faced with similar or related problems, there is an increasing tendency—at any rate within the UN family—for mutual consultation with a view to reaching analogous solutions. In view of the differences between the functions, structure and constitutional provisions and practices of the various Organizations, it may not always be possible to achieve identical solutions, but the fact remains that a coordinated approach tends to result in reliance by one Organization on methods applied or precedents set by another Organization. Proposals elaborated and decisions reached in this way would also seem to be more susceptible of finding favour with governments of Member Nations than proposals or decisions, however desirable and adequate, which would be unprecedented and based on the sole initiative of a single Organization.

2. *Principal Forms of Decisions*

While the formal acceptance of the constituent instrument—as an indispensable condition for membership—makes it mandatory for the accepting State to carry out the obligations laid down in that instrument, these obligations are, with some notable exceptions, in such broad, sometimes even abstract, terms that concrete problems concerning compliance are less likely to arise as long as the instrument is considered in isolation. Decisions of the Organization, which represent one of its most dynamic elements may, however, give concrete form and specific contents to such obligations. Here, it may be possible to distinguish between three broad categories of decisions, depending on the form in which they are adopted.

(a) *Treaties*

A considerable number of multilateral conventions have been concluded under the auspices of—or "within"[5]—an international organization which is, however, usually not a signatory or contracting party. These conventions may be open to all or a predefined group of Member States and—in certain cases—also to Non-Member States.

Although, for some Organizations, conventions may play an important part or even be the principal method for achieving the objectives laid down in the constituent instrument, the question as to whether and to what extent these conventions must be considered "decisions" of the Organization is not easy to answer. Even the choice of criteria may present certain difficulties, but it would seem that the degree of the Organization's participation in the operation of the conventions constitutes a relevant factor.

Formal agreements are often concluded between an organization and one or more Member States. These agreements are normally subject to approval by a governing body, but even where the power to enter into such agreements has been conferred upon the Secretariat, they undoubtedly constitute decisions of the Organization in the full sense, and for some Organizations—particularly the financial institutions—they play a prominent part in the implementation of programs and policies of the Organization.

(b) *Adoption of Norms not Incorporated in Treaties*

Some international organizations have found it necessary or desirable to elaborate rules, principles, or standards, mainly of a technical nature, without recourse to formal treaty procedures. The elaboration, in which groups of experts play an important part but which as a rule also involves consultations with Member Governments— both individually and by the convening of meetings—is not necessarily simpler or more expeditious than the drawing up of a convention, but the adaptation of norms within this category to developments in science and technology (or possibly economic conditions, including terms of trade and balance of payments situa-

---

[5] This distinction, explained in the commentary of the International Law Commission regarding Art. 4 of the Draft Articles on the Law of Treaties—now Art. 5 of the Vienna Convention on the Law of Treaties—may pose some problems with respect to the role of certain organizations in the drawing up and implementation of regulatory treaties. Cf. ILC Report, 18th Session, Doc. A/6309/Rev. 1; 61 A.J.I.L. 296 (1967).

tions) can be effected more rapidly than in the case of a treaty revision. On the other hand, the legal effect of such rules, principles or standards are not always easy to determine. While the normative intent and character constitutes an essential element, it is necessary to examine separately for each norm or set of norms, whether, to what extent and under what conditions they are binding on Member States. If any generalizations are possible, one might say that these norms are usually not considered legally binding on Member States unless they have been expressly accepted as such,[6] that they are hardly ever self-executory[7] and that no provision is normally made for the adoption of sanctions by the Organization in the event of noncompliance by a Member State.[8]

(c) *Other Decisions*

The bulk of decisions of international organizations belong to neither of the two categories discussed under (a) and (b) above. They are usually incorporated in resolutions or recommendations or simply included in the narrative part of session reports; sometimes they purport to establish rules or guidelines of a substantive or procedural nature, but more frequently they deal with individual or limited collective problems or situations. It seems virtually impossible to establish generally valid criteria for determining the legal effect of such decisions.[9] The extent to which they may be considered legally binding must be examined, on a case-by-case basis, in the light of the constitutional provisions and practices of each organization.[10]

---

[6] In some cases—e.g. WHO Sanitary Regulations—States may be bound unless they "contract out" by rejecting the norm or by formulating reservations; however, some formal obligations, such as submission of reports on law and practice in the field covered by the decision, may be incumbent on all Member States.

[7] They usually include provisions enjoining governments to take appropriate legislative and administrative measures.

[8] This does not exclude "natural sanctions" or the creation of an indirect reciprocity relation, in the sense that governments having accepted the norm may accord less favourable treatment to countries that have not accepted it or that are not complying with its terms.

[9] Even the most painstaking exegetic efforts may be defeated by the almost infinitely varied terminology adopted for formulating decisions of this kind. The verbs most frequently used to solicit government action are *urge, request, recommend, invite,* but the body taking a decision may also just *express the hope* or simply *feel* that governments *should take* or *should consider taking* the action contemplated. The action itself may be described in more or less precise terms, but more often it is couched in generic terms which can be fully understood only in the light of information contained in the preambular or narrative part of the document incorporating the decision—or perhaps other documents expressly or implicitly referred to therein; thus governments are often invited to take *appropriate action,* or to *consider the adoption of such measures as they may deem appropriate.*

[10] As far as FAO is concerned, it would seem that the only decisions within this category involving legal obligations of Member Nations are amendments to the Consti-

1. *Formal Instruments*

(a) *Constitution, General Rules of the Organization and Financial Regulations* [11]

The FAO Constitution, which entered into force in October 1945 and has been amended a number of times in subsequent years, contains only few provisions which constitute direct and precisely formulated legal obligations for Member Nations.[12] The Constitution lays down three specific obligations:

(i) it enjoins Member Nations to grant certain privileges and immunities to the Organization and its staff;

(ii) it requires Member Nations to transmit to the Organization periodical reports on food and agriculture and, upon request, additional information;

(iii) each Member Nation undertakes to contribute annually to the Organization its share of the Budget, as apportioned by the Conference.

In addition to these specific obligations, which will be examined in some detail below, the Constitution lays down, in its Preamble and Article I, certain obligations of a general nature; these provisions, while not susceptible of direct application *stricto sensu*, do in effect open the way for the adoption of decisions of a regulatory or operational character which might be potentially or effectively binding upon Member Nations.

According to the Preamble, Member Nations agree to promote separate and collective action, *inter alia,* for raising levels of nutrition and standards of living of the peoples under their respective jurisdiction; Article I-2 provides that:

"The Organization shall promote and, where appropriate, shall *recommend national* and international *action* with respect to

(a) ...

(b) the *improvement* of education and *administration* relating to nutrition, food and agriculture ...;

---

tution, the General Rules or the Financial Regulations and decisions relating to the level of the Budget and of the Scale of Contributions. Accordingly, this category of decisions will not be considered in the main part of this paper, subject to the aforementioned exceptions.

[11] The Staff Regulations, which have been adopted—and may be amended—by the FAO Council, need hardly be mentioned as they do not contain any direct obligations for Member Nations.

[12] Unless otherwise stated, the term "Member Nations" should be understood, in this paper, to comprise Associate Members, i.e. any territory in respect of which the Conference has approved an application for Associate Membership submitted by the State having the responsibility for the international relations of the territory concerned.

(c) the *conservation* of natural *resources* and the *adoption of improved methods* of agricultural production;

(d) the *improvement* of processing, marketing and distribution of food and agricultural products;

(c) the *adoption of policies* for the provision of adequate *agricultural credit,* national and international;

(f) the *adoption of international policies* with respect to agricultural *commodity arrangements."*

(Italics added)

Pursuant to Article I-3, "it shall also be the function of the Organization... to furnish such *technical assistance* as Governments may request... and... generally to take *all necessary and appropriate action* to implement the purposes of the Organization set forth in the Preamble." (Italics added).

It is in fact within the framework set up by the above provisions that the Organization has been able to develop its constantly expanding activities which in turn entail a complex system of rights and obligations.

A few observations may be indicated with respect to the fulfilment by Member Nations of the specific constitutional obligations referred to above and to the measures taken by the Organization to ensure such fulfilment.

As regards the granting of privileges and immunities in accordance with Articles VIII-4 and XVI-2 of the Constitution,[13] it must be borne in mind that these provisions pre-date the adoption of the Convention on the Privileges and Immunities of the Specialized Agencies, which contains much more specific and detailed provisions. Moreover, that Convention is binding not only on States that have become parties thereto; pursuant to certain provisions included in practically all Standard EPTA Agreements[14] and Basic Agreements of the UN Special Fund,[15] governments of countries receiving assistance under these Programs are required to apply the provisions of the Convention to the Specialized Agencies providing such assistance. Even more detailed provisions may be found in the Headquarters Agreement and certain Host Agreements concluded with countries in which FAO maintains Regional Offices. Generally speaking, therefore, the scope of the above-mentioned constitutional provisions is now limited to the Organization's regular program activities in countries that are not parties to the Specialized Agencies' Convention. These provisions nevertheless retain a certain value, inasmuch as they cover "facilities" (which may partly

---

[13] Pursuant to these provisions, the Organization is assimilated to diplomatic missions, the senior FAO staff to diplomatic personnel and the other FAO staff to non-diplomatic personnel attached to diplomatic missions. However, a Member Nation is only required to fulfill the obligations deriving therefrom "insofar as it may be possible under its constitutional procedure."

[14] Art. V-1 (b).

[15] Art. VIII-2. These provisions have not been modified in the revised version of the Agreement drawn up as a result of the establishment of UNDP (EPTA and SF Sectors).

overlap with the concept of "privileges" in the Specialized Agencies' Convention); moreover, Article VIII-4 also provides—as an alternative— that FAO staff should not be treated less favourably than staff of other public international organizations.[16] The scope of this provision may have been widened, at any rate potentially, as a result of the adoption of the Vienna Convention on Diplomatic Relations and it remains a basis for negotiations with governments where FAO staff is accorded a treatment less favourable than that of other organizations.

Beyond this, however, if a government which has expressed its willingness to act as host for a meeting to be convened by FAO fails to assume a formal undertaking that it will grant admission and functional immunities and facilities to participants, the meeting is cancelled or the venue changed.

Article XI of the Constitution requires Member Nations to communicate periodically to the Organization reports on progress made toward achieving the purpose of the Organization as set forth in the Preamble to the Constitution and on the action taken on the basis of recommendations adopted and conventions submitted by the Conference, the form and frequency of such reports being determined by the Conference. The Director-General is to prepare analyses of such reports and submit both reports and analyses to the Conference for consideration. He may also request Member Nations to submit additional or special information or documentation pertaining to the purposes of the Organization.

In view of the somewhat less than satisfactory response of governments, the Conference has repeatedly changed the periodicity (between 1 and 3 years) and the form (on one occasion even leaving the choice of the form entirely to Member Nations); and the Council and the Programme Committee have repeatedly considered the problems connected with these Reports. The results achieved by these reviews have not been convincing. Only on one occasion (1948) did more than 60 percent of the Members submit reports; in 1964, the percentage had dropped to 20. The majority of the reports arrived after the dateline and the form was often not adhered to; as a result, the Secretariat was not always in a position to prepare an analysis for submission to the Conference.[17] New proposals, submitted by the Council [18] to the Fourteenth Session of the Conference provided for reports to be presented every two years (covering the second year of the preceding biennium and the first year of the current one), according to a detailed guideline which included "any actions taken on

---

[16] ". . . to accord to such other members of the staff the immunities and facilities which may hereafter be accorded to equivalent members of the staffs of other public international organizations."

[17] Cf. Doc. C 65/21; Report of the FAO Conference (hereafter referred to as "Conf. Rep."), 13th Session (1965), paras. 138-144.

[18] Report of the FAO Council (hereafter referred to as "CL. Rep."), 47th Session (1966), paras. 56-62; Doc. C 67/24.

the basis of recommendation made by the Conference" with respect to (i) securing increases in production of crops, livestock, forests and fish; (ii) raising nutrition levels and living standards (including family planning) and, more particularly (iii) improvement of the condition of rural populations. Moreover, information would be requested on specific subjects, to be treated in the Organization's Report on the State of Food and Agriculture. The Article XI Reports were to be submitted by 31 March and reminders were to be sent to governments that failed to meet the dateline. These proposals have been approved by the Conference in November 1967.[19]

The Conference, at its Fifteenth Session, noted that only six Reports had been received by 30 June 1969, the dateline fixed by the Director-General, that a total of twenty-eight reports (or 23 per cent) had been received by the opening of the Conference, and that only a few reports had followed the guideline attached to the Director-General's letter. In these circumstances, the Conference "felt that the requirements of Article XI had lost much of their meaning since the adoption of the Constitution, were difficult to comply with, especially by developing countries, which had other responsibilities of a higher priority, and that, in any case, the reports were of little practical value since other more rapid and effective means were now available to obtain needed information." [19a] Accordingly, the Conference decided that no reports should be required for 1969-70, and "that the matter should be further considered by the Council, the Programme Committee and the Committee on Constitutional and Legal Matters with a view to proposing to the Sixteenth Session of the Conference an appropriate amendment to Article XI to bring it up-to-date." [19b]

Some of the reasons for the situation described above are stated in the Report of the Fifteenth Session of the Conference; others may be more difficult to identify with any degree of certainty. What appears to be lacking, at least to some extent, is a *communis opinio necessitatis;* this, in turn, may be due, at least in part, to the fact that a considerable amount of detailed statistical and other information is requested from some or all Member Nations at more or less frequent intervals, particularly when a Secretariat study is being prepared on a specific subject. Moreover, the Organization disposes of a number of informal fact-finding methods, *inter alia,* through technical assistance programs and various regional bodies established under Articles VI or XIV of the Constitution.[20] The in-

---

[19] Conf. Rep. 14th Session (1967), paras. 208-213. The Council had recommended that the new procedure be followed on an experimental basis for two biennia, but the Conference decided to review at its next session (1969) the results of this procedure in relation to the 1967/68 biennium.

[19a] Conf. Rep., 15th Session (1969), paras. 193, 195.

[19b] *Ibid.,* para. 196.

[20] The six regional bodies established by virtue of Agreements concluded under Article XIV and approximately 20 regional commissions established by resolutions of

crease in membership, mainly due to the accession to independence of a number of developing countries, may have played a certain part, as probably did the expansion of the Organization's program activities.[21]

One cannot exclude the possibility that the number, quality and usefulness of the Article XI Reports might be increased by the creation of some institutional machinery—similar to that established by other Organizations (e.g. a committee of experts or an intergovernmental body) charged with a critical evaluation of the Reports. It is difficult to tell, however, whether FAO's governing bodies will give favourable consideration to a solution which would require supplementary machinery and might place an additional burden on Member Nations.

As regards the financial obligations of Member Nations towards the Organization, the legal position is basically simple and straight forward. At each of its Regular Sessions, the Conference determines, by two separate resolutions, the level of the Budget and the Scale of Contributions; pursuant to Article XVIII-5 of the Constitution, a two-thirds majority of the votes cast is required for the approval of the budget level. The obligation of each Member Nation "to contribute annually to the Organization its share of the Budget" is laid down in Article XVIII-2 of the Constitution, and the two aforementioned resolutions merely give concrete shape to this obligation. Accordingly, the obligation of a Member Nation is not affected in any way by the positive or negative vote which it may have cast on the Budget or the scale of contributions. The same applies, *mutatis mutandis,* to any vote on the level of the Working Capital Fund.[22]

The sanctions to be applied to defaulting States are clearly stated in the Constitution and the General Rules. Any Member Nation whose arrears in contributions reach the equivalent of the amount due for the two preceding calendar years loses its voting rights at the Conference, unless the Conference grants a specific exception.[23] A Member Nation in this position

---

the Conference or Council under Article VI-1 meet at regular (mostly 2-year) intervals; they are serviced by the FAO Secretariat which also acts as focal point between sessions, not only for collecting, analyzing and disseminating information which is likely to facilitate the deliberations of these bodies, but also for providing guidance, as appropriate, during sessions and for assisting Members in implementing the decisions or recommendations of these bodies.

[21] When the Constitution—including Article XI—was drawn up, the activities of FAO were practically limited to the "Regular" Program, and the Article XI Reports were in effect centered on subject-matters directly or indirectly connected with that Program. In 1967, the funds allocated for the Regular Program amounted to approximately $25 million, while those made available for technical assistance and related field programs (mainly UNDP and Freedom-From-Hunger Campaign) exceeded $60 million. Special reports are prepared for each of the projects carried out under these field programs. Cf. Doc. C 67/26 "Review of FAO's Field Activities", *passim,* especially pp. 123-130.

[22] Cf. Financial Regulation 6.2.

[23] Pursuant to Art. III-4 of the Constitution, the Conference may grant such exception "if it is satisfied that the failure to pay is due to conditions beyond the control of the

is not eligible for membership in the Council and if it is already a Member of the Council, it is considered as having resigned.[24] Finally, former Members of the Organization that left arrears may not be invited to attend any meetings of FAO in an observer capacity unless the Council, in special circumstances, decides otherwise.[25]

(b) *Conventions and Agreements under Article XIV of the Constitution*[26]

Pursuant to Article XIV of the Constitution, as supplemented by Rule XXI of the General Rules, the Conference may approve and submit to Member Nations general multilateral conventions or multilateral agreements limited to a specific geographic area; the latter may also be approved by the Council.[27] Detailed provisions, contained in Article XIV and in Rule XXI GRO, deal with the preparatory steps, enumerate certain essential provisions to be included in conventions and agreements and establish the procedure for signature, ratification, accession and acceptance. These provisions are further amplified by the "Principles and Procedures which should govern Conventions and Agreements", which were adopted by the Conference in 1957 and cover such subjects as participation, territorial application, entry into force, reservations, amendments, supplementary agreements, interpretation and settlement of disputes, with-

---

Member Nation". Voting rights have been suspended on several occasions and in some cases the above provision has been applied to restore voting rights either without any conditions attached (cf. Conf. Rep., 15th Session (1969), paras. 29-30) or after the Member Nation concerned had undertaken to settle its arrears according to an installment plan approved by the Conference (cf. Conf. Res. No. 33/65).

[24] Rule XXII, paragraphs 5 and 7 of the General Rules of the Organization (hereafter referred to as "GRO").

[25] Statement of Principles Relating to the Granting of Observer Status to Nations, Appendix C to Conference Report, Ninth Session (1957). FAO Basic Texts, Vol. II, Section I, Appendix, Part B, paragraph 4.

[26] There are three Conventions—International Plant Protection Convention (UNTS No. 1963, Vol. 150, p. 67) International Poplar Convention (UNTS No. 5902, Vol. 410, p. 155) and the Constitution of the International Rice Commission (UNTS No. 1613, Vol. 120, p. 13) and six Agreements—Plant Protection Agreement for South East Asia and Pacific Region (UNTS No. 1963 (a), Vol. 247, p. 400) the Agreements establishing the General Fisheries Council for the Mediterranean (UNTS No. 1691, Vol. 226, p. 237) and the Indo-Pacific Fisheries Council (UNTS No. 1615, Vol. 120, p. 59) respectively, the Constitution of the European Commission for the Control of Foot-and-Mouth Disease (UNTS No. 2588, Vol. 191, p. 285) and two Agreements Establishing Commissions for Desert Locust Control in South West Asia (UNTS No. 7663, Vol. 529, p. 217) and in the Near East (UNTS No. 8575). These instruments are published (as separate fascicles) in volume III of the FAO Basic Texts and their status is shown in the Statutory Reports submitted to each Session of the Conference. Cf. C 67/45 and Sup. 1., C 69/40 and Sup. 1., Conf. Rep. 15th Session (1969), paras. 601-604.

[27] The majority prescribed for approval by the Conference is two-thirds of the votes cast; in the case of Council approval, it is two-thirds of the membership of the Council.

drawal and denunciation, and depositary functions.[28] While the application of these normative texts—or of provisions incorporated in conventions or agreements in accordance with such texts—may in some ways affect Member Nations, very few concrete problems have arisen in FAO practice, and it may therefore be unnecessary to examine these provisions in the present context.

As conventions and agreements are treaties between States, they are only binding on the parties. However, the decision of the Conference or Council approving the instrument not only establishes the finality of the text but also confirms, albeit implicitly, that it is in conformity—with respect to both form and substance—with the constitutional principles and basic policies of the Organization. Moreover, as all of these instruments place certain responsibilities on the Organization—particularly when they provide for the establishment of a new body—the approval also comprises the acceptance of such responsibilities, including the program and financial implications. In this connection, it may be noted that the operation of the majority of existing conventions and agreements is financed exclusively out of the Regular Budget;[29] where provision is made for an autonomous budget, the cash contributions made by contracting parties are paid into a Trust Fund administered by FAO in accordance with the Financial Regulations.[30]

While thus the legal framework defining the Organization's role in the elaboration, adoption and implementation of conventions and agreements is clearly laid out in the Basic Texts, the question of effectiveness is more difficult to answer. It would go beyond the scope of the present inquiry to investigate whether these treaties are effective instruments for attaining the Organization's policy objectives and—conversely—in what way the treaties, and particularly the bodies created thereunder, are susceptible of exercising an influence on the Organization's programs and policies. This interaction no doubt exists but its finer ramifications are sometimes difficult to trace; suffice it to say that reports and recommen-

---

[28] Conf. Res. No. 46/57; Conf. Rep. Ninth Session (1957), Appendix B; FAO Basic Texts, Vol. II, Section VII.

[29] Article XIV-3 (c) of the Constitution provides that a Convention or Agreement shall "not entail any financial obligations for Member Nations not parties to it other than their contributions to the Organization provided for in Article XVIII, paragraph 2 of this Constitution"—i.e. the Regular Budget, which normally covers the administrative and servicing costs.

[30] Autonomous budgets operating on funds contributed by contracting parties have been created for the European Commission for the Control of Foot-and-Mouth Disease and the two Desert Locust Control Commissions. The adoption of emergency measures to combat animal diseases and locust infestations at a regional level is thus facilitated, both financially and administratively. In addition, some Agreements (e.g. those establishing the Indo-Pacific and the Mediterranean Fisheries Councils) provide for the possibility of undertaking research and development projects, jointly financed on an *ad hoc* basis by some or all contracting parties.

218

dations and less formal information and advice flow in both directions. Sessions held by bodies established under these treaties (so-called Article XIV Bodies) provide opportunities for conveying and explaining to government representatives, at the technical level, decisions and recommendations of the Organization's governing bodies, for devising concerted measures towards their implementation, and for ascertaining the effect which has been given by individual countries to earlier decisions and recommendations; practical results, difficulties and shortcomings are often described and analysed in written or verbal reports presented by individual delegations or communicated to the Secretary of the Body—invariably an official of FAO.[31] The conclusions reached at such sessions are normally incorporated in a report and often take the form of recommendations which may be addressed to Members of the Body (i.e. participating governments) or to the Director-General of FAO, who is required, under specific provisions contained in the relevant conventions and agreements, to bring to the attention of the governing bodies any recommendations having policy, program, or financial implications.[32] Recommendations aiming at technical assistance not infrequently result in regional projects under the UN Development Program (UNDP)—sometimes supported by food aid from the World Food Program (WFP)— and even capital investment projects developed jointly by FAO and IBRD; many of these subsequent measures are thus directly or indirectly generated by the mechanism of conventions and agreements under Article XIV of the Constitution.

While the *effectiveness* of these international instruments with all its facets permeates many activities of FAO and poses a number of (predominantly non-legal) problems, the question of *compliance* or non-compliance has hardly ever arisen. This may largely be due to the fact that the majority of these instruments contain only few provisions imposing direct obligations on contracting parties, and most of these obligations are not particularly burdensome.

Certain conventions and agreements contain provisions requiring the contracting parties to establish national institutions or authorities for dealing with matters covered by the convention or agreement, or to designate existing national institutions or authorities for the purpose. As examples, one might mention the national plant protection authorities created pursuant to Article IV of the International Plant Protection Convention and the national poplar commissions established under Article IV of the International Poplar Convention.[33] In each of these cases, the name and de-

---

[31] Cf. FAO Basic Texts, Vol. II, Section VII, para. 32 (iii).
[32] *Ibidem*, para. 30. The Director-General is also required to take these recommendations into account when preparing the Organization's Program of Work and Budget.
[33] Under an amendment recently adopted by the International Poplar Commission and subsequently approved by the Conference at its Fourteenth Session in November 1967,

scription of the scope and competencies of the national authority or commission has to be transmitted to the Director-General of FAO who in turn circulates this information to all other contracting parties. As direct communications are frequently exchanged with and between these national authorities or commissions without recourse to diplomatic channels, it is easy for the FAO Secretariat and each contracting party to ascertain the fulfilment of this treaty obligation by the other parties.

Certain agreements provide for the adoption of emergency measures in the event of outbreaks of animal diseases or plant pests, or in case of a desert locust infestation. Obviously, to be effective, such measures must be taken rapidly and by concerted action; this presupposes the existence of an administrative and technical machinery and of efficient channels of communication, the absence of which may be no less prejudicial than non-compliance with specific treaty obligations. It is therefore no pure coincidence that more specific obligations are laid down in the agreements with respect to emergency measures and that they make provision for common resources and autonomous budgets.[34] It may be assumed that compliance is encouraged by a distinct interest of self-protection, but it is equally facilitated by the ready availability of common resources, particularly where the countries primarily responsible for the adoption of emergency measures are not the same as those deriving the principal benefits from such measures.[35]

Provisions of a directly regulatory nature are contained in only three Conventions and Agreements. Under Article V of the International Plant Protection Convention, each party is required to issue phytosanitary certificates stating all relevant data on plants sent across international borders and to maintain certain prescribed import controls. The Convention contains no specific safeguards;[36] reliance may be placed on the fact

---

contracting parties may, instead of appointing a national poplar commission, entrust some other suitable body with the functions normally incumbent on such commissions. Cf. Doc. C 67/45 Sup. 1, Conf. Res. No. 18/67.

[34] It may be noted that, in view of the limits—both *ratione materiae* and *ratione loci*—inherent in existing Agreements, some provision had to be made to enable FAO to cope with emergencies of this kind which were outside the scope of these Agreements. This has been done, as regards livestock diseases by way of granting to the Director-General, in consultation with an advisory expert committee and the FAO Finance Committee, authority to withdraw up to $500,000 from the Working Capital Fund. Cf. Conf. Rep. 13th Session (1965), para. 506; Conf. Res. No. 35/65. This authority has recently been extended to desert locust emergency control measures, and the aggregate amount was increased from $500,000 to $750,000. Cf. CL. Rep. 51st Session (1968), paras. 304-308; Doc. C 69/50; Conf. Rep. 15th Session (1969), paras. 619-622 and Conf. Res. No. 17/69, superseding Conf. Res. No 35/65.

[35] This applies particularly to locust control measures, which must be taken in breeding areas—often hundreds of miles away from infestation areas.

[36] Indeed, some provisions are clearly intended to limit import control and inspection measures to the minimum necessary for achieving the purposes of the Convention and to avoid undue interference with international trade.

that States Parties will find it difficult to participate in any trade or non-commercial exchange of plants unless they observe the regulatory provisions of the Convention. As a result of this "natural" sanction, the provisions of the Convention are widely applied also by States that are not Parties thereto.

The Plant Protection Agreement for South East Asia and the Pacific Region (which, by virtue of its Preamble, is considered a "Supplementary Agreement" under Article III of the International Plant Protection Convention), not only specifies measures for the exclusion of the South American leafblight of Hevea from the Region but also authorizes the Plant Protection Committee, established under Article II of the Agreement to adopt stricter standards than those set by the general Convention for the importation of plants from outside the Region; the Committee has repeatedly availed itself of this authority. While the methods for ascertaining compliance with the regulatory provisions contained in the Agreement or adopted by the Committee are similar to those described with reference to the general Convention, the existence of a body composed of representatives of the Parties provides certain additional opportunities for both FAO and Member Governments to observe the implementation of the Agreement and, if necessary, to ensure compliance.[37]

The Constitution of the European Commission for the Control of Foot and Mouth Disease imposes on the Members of the Commission the duty to take specific measures (slaughtering, immunization, vaccination, or a combination thereof), to make arrangements for the typing of virus as required by the Commission and to communicate to the Commission immediately the results of such typing and any other information it may require to carry out its functions. Obviously, the control measures as contemplated in the Constitution of the Commission cannot become really effective without appropriate legislative and administrative measures at the national level. Pertinent data and documentary evidence relating to such measures are communicated to the Secretariat of the Commission, circulated to Members, and evaluated by both FAO and the Commission itself. While this evaluation may occasionally lead to certain observations during sessions of the Commission, it would seem that a *communis opinio necessitatis* of the Parties has been instrumental in avoiding any clear cases of non-compliance.

---

[37] In the event of a dispute that cannot be settled by the Committee, the government or governments concerned may, under Art. VII of the Agreement, request the Director-General to appoint a committee of experts to consider the dispute. The findings and determination of that committee would however not appear to be binding on the parties to the dispute. The more explicit and detailed provision of Article IX of the Plant Protection Convention would presumably be applied, *mutatis mutandis*, at any rate to disputes between countries that have also adhered to that Convention.

(c) *Agreements under Article XV of the Constitution*

Article XV of the Constitution [38] provides that the Conference may authorize the Director-General to enter into agreements with Member Nations for the establishment of institutions dealing with questions relating to food and agriculture; the Conference may in a particular case or cases delegate the power of approval of such agreements.[39] As in the case of Conventions and Agreements under Article XIV, detailed "Guiding Principles" have been laid down for the conclusion of Article XV Agreements, both with regard to form and procedure and concerning the provisions to be included in each Agreement.[40] Only two Agreements have so far been concluded, both dealing with the establishment of regional forestry institutes.[41] One of these Agreements, concerning the Establishment of a Near East Forest Rangers' School,[42] is bilateral, while the other, relating to the Latin American Forest Research and Training Institute,[43] is plurilateral, with a bilateral element in the sense that any Member Nations having territories in Latin America may adhere and withdraw, but that the denunciation by the host government or FAO would automatically result in the termination of the Agreement.[44] Both Agreements show certain characteristics of charters of incorporation; the institutions created thereby have their own organs,[45] are endowed with legal personality, enjoy certain privileges and immunities *vis-à-vis* the host government; [46] they have fi-

---

[38] This provision was inserted in the Constitution in 1957. See Conf. Rep. 9th Session (1957), Appendix I, page 263.

[39] A special delegation of authority is required in each case, while the Council has general authority to approve Article XIV Agreements.

[40] These Guiding Principles, which were laid down by the Council in response to a request of the 9th Session of the Conference (Conf. Res. No. 48/57) concern Article XV Agreements generally; in addition, the Council established certain guidelines with respect to "FAO Policy Regarding Assistance in Establishing Regional Research and Training Institutes" (See CL. Rep. 29th Session (1958), paras. 71-78 and Appendix B). The two sets of rules which are practically interlocking have been reproduced in Section VIII of Volume II of the Basic Texts.

[41] FAO has assisted in the establishment and operation of a number of other institutes, chiefly on the basis of UNDP (Special Fund) projects; in these cases, the Plan of Operation fulfils a role similar to that of an Article XV Agreement. This may also account for the fact that no further Agreements have come into force since 1959.

[42] Conf. Rep. 9th Session (1957), App. E, Basic Texts, Vol. III, fascicle 9. In fact, this Agreement has recently been terminated by way of denunciation by the Syrian Government, and the Institute is now operated by the Syrian Government in conjunction with the League of Arab States (Cf. Doc. CL51/35; CL. Rep. 51st Session (1968), paras. 262-263). Although the Agreement is no longer in force, a brief comparison between the essential provisions of the two instruments may nevertheless be of legal interest.

[43] Conf. Rep. 10th Session (1959), App. E, Basic Texts, Vol. III, fascicle 8.

[44] Art. XXI 1 (a). It is also terminated if the number of parties drops below four (*ibid.*, para. 1 (b)).

[45] Near East Forest Rangers' School: Governing Body and Director; Latin American Institute: Governing Council, Executive Committee, President, and Director.

[46] Functional immunities and facilities in the case of the Latin American Institute;

nancial resources of their own and an autonomous administration.[47] Yet, while FAO is not concerned with day-to-day administration, it exercises certain control functions; the Director and the President[48] are appointed in consultation with the Director-General of FAO, who is also represented in an advisory capacity on the governing bodies of the institutes; FAO may provide or assist in procuring technical and/or financial assistance; it receives annual reports; its principles regarding observer status of nations and international organizations are to be applied *mutatis mutandis*. Some additional functions were conferred on the Director-General by the Rules of Procedure adopted by the governing bodies of these institutions. Both institutions have received financial and technical aid from, or through, FAO during an initial period, with the concomitant guidance and control regarding operations and administration. The Latin-American Institute has been self-supporting for many years, but throughout the ten years of its existence the Near East Forest Rangers' School was headed by an interim Director appointed by the Director-General of FAO and paid from EPTA funds and its finances were a administered as an FAO Trust Fund; this interim arrangement was covered by the Protocol to the Agreement, which was terminated at the same time as the Agreement.

(d) *Host Agreements*

Like most of its Sister Agencies, FAO has concluded a Headquarters Agreement, as well as a number of Regional (and Sub-Regional) Office Agreements.[49] This type of agreement, the subject matters covered by them and the problems they may pose have received ample coverage in legal literature,[50] and it would therefore seem unnecessary to analyse them in the present context with reference to effectiveness or compliance.

---

application, *mutatis mutandis*, of specific provisions of the Convention on the Privileges and Immunities of the Specialized Agencies with respect to the Near East Forest Rangers' School.

[47] The method of financing is somewhat different: while the operations of the Latin-American Institute are primarily financed by Parties to the Agreement on the basis of a scale of contributions attached to the Agreement (which may be modified by a two-thirds majority), the revenue of the Near East Forest Rangers' School was derived mainly from fees payable by Governments sending students to the School.

[48] Only for the Latin-American Institute.

[49] Regional Office Agreements have been concluded with Chile, Ghana, Thailand and the United Arab Republic (Egypt); Sub-Regional Office Agreements with Brazil and Kenya. The latter Agreements were denounced in the course of 1969 and partly replaced by agreements for the establishment of FAO country representatives' offices.

[50] Cf. *inter alia*, Ph. Cahier: *"Etude des accords de siège conclus entre les Organisations internationales et les Etats où elles résident"* (Milano, 1959) and sources cited in that monograph.

(e) Technical Cooperation Agreements

FAO has participated in the Extended Technical Assistance Program (ETAP, later renamed EPTA) since its inception in 1949 [51] and has since become a party to EPTA "Standard" Agreements concluded with approximately 85 countries.[52] Likewise, FAO has had a major share in the United Nations Special Fund (UNSF) since its establishment; the Basic Agreements are, however, bilateral instruments between the Special Fund and recipient countries, while plans of operation concluded with one or several countries thereunder for the execution of individual projects are signed by both the Special Fund and FAO as Executing Agency. The decisions of principle regarding participation of FAO in these programs (now merged in the United Nations Development Program—UNDP) have been taken by the FAO Conference,[53] and both Conference and Council devote continuing attention to the field programs and, in particular, their effectiveness and their impact on the Organization's Regular Program activities.[54]

However, despite the increasingly important role played by the governing bodies of FAO, many policy decisions on the orientation of these programs and on the functions, rights and duties of UNDP, Executing Agency and recipient countries are taken by other intergovernmental bodies

---

[51] ECOSOC Resolution 222 (IX) and General Assembly Resolution 304 (IV). A comprehensive analysis of FAO's participation in the initial period is given in Conf. Rep. 8th Session (1955), paras. 115-128 and Conf. Res. No. 16/55.

[52] These Agreements have been concluded by (or on behalf of) all Agencies that are Members of the Technical Assistance Board (TAB) with recipient countries.

[53] General Assembly Resolution 1240 (XIII). Arrangements for FAO participation were outlined in Council Resolution No. 5/29 and subsequently endorsed and amplified by the Conference. See Conf. Rep. 10th Session (1959) paras. 479-489 and Conf. Res. No. 44/59. FAO has, ab initio, had a major share in UNDP Project activities. Annual FAO/UNSF expenditure gradually rose from $460,800 in 1960 to nearly $53 million in 1969. By the end of 1969, FAO had been entrusted with 443 prejects out of a total of 1.182 for all UN Agencies. This proportion is reflected in current earmarkings by the UNDP Governing Council: FAO's share was 36.9%, followed by that of UN (18.8%) and UNESCO (15.7%). See Docs. C 67/26, p. 7; C 69/18, pp. 20f.; DP/SF/Reports, Series B, no. 9 (January 1970).

[54] The numerous and close links between Regular Program activities and field programs—mainly under UNDP—as well as the constantly growing importance of the latter have induced the governing bodies of FAO to assume more extensive control functions to be exercised with particular regard to the harmonious integration of these activities in the overall policies of the Organization, an aspect which could perhaps not be adequately covered by intergovernmental bodies in the United Nations i.e. UNDP Governing Council, ECOSOC and General Assembly. Cf. Conf. Rep. 13th Session (1965) and Conf. Res. No, 8/65 "Future Conference Review of Development Programs". The objectives, methods and operating procedures were examined in considerable detail by the last two Sessions of the Conference (cf. Conf. Rep. 14th Session (1967), paras. 453-471; 15th Session (1969), paras. 197-253; but only a passing reference is made in the Report of the 14th Session (para. 455) to shortfalls in counterpart contributions as a factor hampering the successful implementation of projects.

within the UN System. The task of drawing up the legal instruments (mainly plans of operation) and of deciding any questions that may arise in the course of implementation are generally incumbent on the Secretariat of the Executing Agency, acting in consultation with the UNDP Secretariat or Resident Representatives.[55] This concerns in particular the execution by recipient governments of the obligations they have assumed under the instruments referred to above.

In this connection, it might be noted that, generally speaking, the provisions placing obligations on recipient countries have been laid down in the basic resolutions or have subsequently received, at least in substance, the approval of a governing body before they are actually incorporated into specific bilateral (or plurilateral) instruments; it would appear that the requirement for such approval serves a double purpose: on the one hand, it protects the recipient governments against the mere possibility of arbitrarily stringent obligations, and, on the other hand, strengthens the position of the Secretariat in negotiating such agreements and in endeavouring to ensure proper implementation.

Obviously, the Executing Agency and the UNDP Secretariat will often concentrate their efforts on finding practical solutions even where problems may have arisen from the failure of a recipient country to meet its obligations, but fundamentally the Secretariats are responsible vis-à-vis their respective governing bodies for ensuring that the policy guidelines laid down by these bodies are adhered to. On the other hand, it may occur that there is a high incidence of non-compliance with a particular obligation, in which case it is for the Secretariat to bring the matter to the attention of the competent governing bodies and possibly to recommend alternative solutions. However, in spite of those elements of flexibility and despite the absence of means of enforcement *stricto sensu,* it may be assumed that the possibility of a suspension or cancellation of the project concerned on the ground of non-compliance by the recipient government with its contractual obligations, and the concomitant risk of rejection of future project applications submitted by that government, are likely to act as incentives for compliance.

It is interesting to note that the terms of agreements concluded between the Joint UN/FAO World Food Program (WFP) [56] and recipient gov-

---

[55] We touch here on an interesting fundamental problem, which cannot be discussed in the present context: the extremely complex nature often inherent in what appears in the form of a decision by an international organization but really represents the result of inter-agency consultations at various levels and may call for continuous consultations in the course of implementation.

[56] This Program was established by UN General Assembly Resolution 1714 (XVI) and FAO Conf. Res. 1/61 for an experimental period of three years to provide food aid in emergencies and in support of development projects. It was extended on an open-ended basis by General Assembly Resolution 2095 (XX) and FAO Conf. Res. No. 4/65. Cf. *World Food Programme Basic Documents,* Third Edition, 1966.

ernments are even more stringent than the corresponding instruments of UNDP. Paragraph 18 (a) (i) of the General Regulations of WFP, as adopted by ECOSOC and the FAO Council, specifies *inter alia* that:

"Such agreement shall provide to the Program the right to observe all phases of project operation from the receipt of commodities in the country to final utilization, to receive audited accounts at agreed intervals, and to suspend or withdraw assistance in case of *serious* non-compliance."
(Emphasis added)

The Pro-Forma Basic Agreement of WFP in fact provides for the possibility of suspension or withdrawal [57] of assistance

"in the event of failure on the part of the Government to fulfil *any of its obligations* assumed under the present Agreement or any agreement concluded by virtue thereof."
(Emphasis added)

This provision would appear to suggest that the decision as to whether, in a particular case, non-compliance is to be considered "serious" lies solely or at any rate primarily with WFP.[58]

2. *Quasi-legislative Instruments*

The traditional technique of securing acceptance and application of standards and principles by way of incorporation in formal treaties which States may then adhere to by a voluntary but formal act is probably still prevailing in international practice. However, two other techniques have been increasingly applied in recent years.

The first instance concerns the adoption by an international organization of standard setting instruments which are directly binding on Member States, although they may not always be self-executing and in some cases States may be given an opportunity to "contract out".[59] Generally speaking, these instruments either emanate from supranational organizations or constitute "secondary legislation" in the sense that they spell out substantive provisions of a Convention or establish procedures and modalities for its implementation.[60]

---

[57] It should be borne in mind that title to commodities supplied by WFP passes to the government upon delivery in the recipient country, whereas UNDP retains title to equipment and material at least until completion of the project. Accordingly, WFP agreements stipulate that if assistance is withdrawn and the Project Agreement terminated, WFP may also request that commodities supplied but not yet distributed be returned to WFP.

[58] Whether sanctions could be taken by the Executive Director of WFP or would require a decision by the Intergovernmental Committee (IGC) would depend, *inter alia*, on the question whether the project concerned was approved by the IGC or by the Executive Director by virtue of a delegation of authority under paragraph 9 of the General Regulations.

[59] Cf. Footnotes (6) and (7) above.

[60] The adoption of rules of procedure, financial regulations and similar rules does not

The second instance concerns the adoption by an international organization of standards, codes of principles or schemes, without recourse to formal treaty procedure; some may be more in the nature of detailed recommendations, while others are potentially binding in the sense that Member Governments may be invited to declare their acceptance and, upon acceptance, to present law and practice reports or avail themselves of some joint machinery.

Since FAO is not a supranational organization and has adopted very few conventions of a normative character requiring or allowing for "secondary legislation", the first category of instruments need not be considered here.[61] On the other hand, some examples belonging to the second category may well be worth examining, especially as they do not appear to have received to date the coverage in legal literature which they deserve.

(a) *Code of Principles concerning Milk and Milk Products*

The initiative for establishing internationally acceptable practices designed to protect both consumers and producers of milk and milk products was taken in 1954 by the International Dairy Federation (IDF).[62] It was recognized that to achieve this purpose it would be necessary to (i) apply a uniform terminology, thus avoiding misleading designations, particularly in international trade, (ii) define standards of composition of individual products, and (iii) establish rules on methods of sampling and analysis. After having undertaken some preparatory work in consultation with other international bodies, such as the International Standards Organization (ISO), the IDF requested the assistance of FAO for the development and use of definitions and standards on an international basis and proposed the

---

—indeed should not—modify the substantive obligations of contracting parties, but it may give more concrete form to such obligations. The situation is slightly different as regards the amendment of Annexes or Schedules of Treaties by a (qualified) majority decision of contracting parties.

[61] The list of plant diseases set out in Annex A to the Plant Protection Agreement for South East Asia and the Pacific Region may be modified, pursuant to Article III of the Agreement, by the Regional Plant Protection Committee. Similarly, the scale of contributions set out in Appendix I to the Constitution of the European Commission for the Control of Foot-and-Mouth Disease may be modified by a two-thirds majority of the Commission Members (Art. XIII-1). However, while such amendments are likely to affect the obligations of contracting parties, they can hardly be regarded as "standard-setting" in the full sense of the term.

[62] The principal international NGO in the fields of manufacture and trade of dairy products. The initiative of IDF and its continuing close association with the elaboration of standards illustrates the essential role which may be incumbent on NGO's in the "normative" work of IGO's. Numerous other examples could be cited in connection with the Codex Alimentarius standards as well as commodity trade arrangements, international regulation of fisheries, etc.

establishment of a committee of government experts for this purpose. The FAO Conference at its Ninth Session (1957) unanimously endorsed the proposal submitted [63] and adopted Resolution No. 16/57 whereby it requested the Director-General to establish a committee.

"to formulate recommendations concerning the use of descriptions, definitions, minimum standards of composition, marking and labelling and standard methods of analysis"

and recommended to the committee

"that it set out its recommendations ... in such a manner ... as will enable Governments so wishing to accept them without having recourse to treaty procedure, and that it advise on the formulation of procedures under which national governments might provide for effective application and reporting."

The Code of Principles was adopted by the Committee of Government Experts at its Second Session in 1959, and Governments were invited to inform the Director-General whether they would apply the Code and what measures they intended to take to achieve its application.[64] In the course of its twelve sessions held to date, the Committee has adopted seven "composition" standards for milk products, including a general standard on cheese,[65] as well as sixteen individual cheese standards [66] and eight standards relating to methods of sampling and analysis,[67] and also a number of "Explanatory Notes" relating to the Code or the standards which may be regarded as authentic interpretations of the provisions to which they refer.[68]

With the establishment of the general Food Standards Program and the Codex Alimentarius Commission under the joint auspices of FAO and WHO,[69] the question arose how the work on milk standards could be integrated in the larger framework of the Codex Alimentarius, without risking adverse effects on the methods and progress of codifying milk standards.[70] For the time being, this was resolved, on the one hand by trans-

---

[63] Doc. C 57/58 (and Sup. 1); Conf. Rep. 9th Session (1957), paras. 202-206.

[64] *Code of Principles concerning Milk and Milk Products and Associated Standards*, Sixth Edition, Rome, 1968 (hereafter referred to as "Milk Code 1968"), 146 pp.

[65] They cover Butter and Whey Butter (A-1), Butterfat and Butteroil (A-2), Evaporated Milk (A-3), Condensed Milk (A-4), Milk Powder (A-5), Cheese in general (A-6), and Whey Cheese (A-7); draft Standards on Processed Cheese (A-8), Cream (A-9), and Cream Powder (A-10) are in an advanced stage of elaboration.

[66] i.e. Cheddar, Danablu, Danbo, Edam, Gouda, Havarti, Samsoe, Cheshire, Emmental, Gruyère, Tilsiter, Limburger, Saint-Paulin, Svecia, Provolone, Cottage Cheese. Suggestions for some 50 additional cheese standards are under consideration.

[67] They cover sampling of milk and milk products (B.1), determination of fat content of milk powder (B.2) and of cheese (B.3), of acidity in butterfat (B.4), of the refractive index of butterfat (B.5), of fat content of milk (B.6) and evaporated and sweetened milk (B.7) and of salt content of butter (B.8).

[68] Cf. Milk Code 1968, pp. 7, 21.

[69] See pages 238-256 below.

[70] Conf. Rep. 11th Session (1961), para. 262; Conf. Res. no. 12/61.

forming the Committee of Government Experts into a subsidiary body *sui generis*—practically a "committee of the whole"—of the Codex Alimentarius Commission [71] and, on the other, by exempting standards prepared by that Committee from the application of the more elaborate procedure established for preparation of other food standards.[72]

The Code of Principles is a very concise instrument consisting of an introductory paragraph, a Preamble, which describes the purpose of the Code,[73] and six Articles, defining milk, milk products and composite products (Articles 1-3) establishing general rules on the designation of "other" products (Article 4), on labelling, presentation and publicity (Article 5) and determining the "extent of application" (Article 6).

The very conciseness of the Articles of the Code, while highly commendable—in fact, the Articles may in some respects be considered a masterpiece of legal drafting—poses a number of problems of interpretation, which are only partly solved by the Explanatory Notes and by the provisions of composition standards adopted pursuant to the Code. It is not possible to examine these problems in the present context,[74] but the scope of the Code, as defined in Article 6 deserves particular attention, inasmuch as it has an important bearing on the obligations of States accepting the Code and the standards adopted thereunder.

Paragraph 1 stipulates that the provisions of the Code "shall apply to all products therein considered whether imported, exported or produced

---

[71] Rule IX of the Commission's Rules of Procedure provides for the establishment of various types of subsidiary bodies; para. 1 (a), which was drafted especially to meet the particular requirements of this Committee, refers to "subsidiary bodies which it [the Commission] deems necessary for the accomplishment of its work in the finalization of draft standards."

[72] As against the ten steps for Codex standards in general, between six and eight steps are prescribed for the elaboration of standards under the Milk Code, depending on the type of standard; the procedure varies from one category to another: regarding procedure for elaboration of standard methods of sampling and analysis, see Report of Tenth Session of the Committee of Government Experts, Appendix III; for individual cheese standards, *idem*, Ninth Session, Appendix III (a); for milk product standards, *idem*, Eleventh Session, Appendix X.

[73] I.e. "to protect the consumer . . . and to assist the dairy industry on both the national and the international levels by:
Ensuring the precise use of the term "milk" and the terms used for the different milk products;
Avoiding confusion arising from the mixing of milk and/or milk products with non-milk fats and/or non-milk proteins;
Prohibiting the use of misleading names and information for products which are not milk of milk products and which might thereby be confused with milk or milk products; and
Establishing (a) definitions and designations; (b) minimum standards of composition, and (c) standard methods of sampling and analysis of milk and milk products."

[74] Many of these problems, which usually involve technical and commercial as well as legal aspects, are reflected in the Session Reports of the Committee of Government Experts and might well warrant a separate investigation.

and offered for sale upon the home market". This provision has been slightly qualified in the Explanatory Note,[75] to the effect that "as an interim measure ... a country applying the Code would not be restricted by its provisions when exporting to a country which did not apply the Code." Although the Note goes on to state that since the effectiveness of the Code depends largely on a number of countries applying it, speedy and wide acceptance would hasten the achievement of its objectives, the fact remains that it makes allowance for "double" standards, the first being applicable to the home market and to the export to countries that have accepted the Code, and the second being allowed for export to other countries.[76]

This regulation resembles the reciprocity relation established between parties to multilateral conventions. However, the reciprocity is restricted by the fact that composition standards are considered minimum standards. Thus, Article 6.4 of the Code provides that they are "not intended to affect the adoption and use of more rigorous requirements or standards under domestic legislation." As a result of this provision, acceptance of, and compliance with, the Code and a given composition standard does not necessarily enable a country to export its products to other countries on a basis of reciprocity. A similar reservation in favour of domestic law is made in respect of "standard methods of sampling milk and milk products." [77]

No specific form is prescribed for the communication by which a government notifies its acceptance. Notifications have been received in the form of letters or notes verbales from Ministries of Foreign Affairs, Agriculture, Economic Planning, Health, or from Embassies in Rome; even affirmative replies from the above authorities to a questionnaire circulated by the Secretariat have been considered valid acceptances.[78] It would seem difficult to apply stricter formal requirements to notifications of acceptance of individual standards than to those relating to the Code of Principles.

Article 6.3 of the Code of Principles provides that, in "adapting their

---

[75] Milk Code 1968, p. 8.

[76] It is not quite clear whether the same flexibility extends to composition standards, i.e. whether a country having accepted both the Code and a given Composition Standard—e.g. on milk powder—may export products not meeting the standard requirements—e.g. sub-standard milk powder—to a country that has accepted the Code but not the Composition Standard.

[77] Standard No. B-1. The substantive provisions are preceded by the following statement under the heading "Foreword": "These instructions (sic) are intended to provide basic rules for commercial transactions in international trade. They are not intended to replace official methods of sampling and analysis prescribed by national Food Legislation for the purpose of internal control". No such "Foreword" appears in any of the other sampling and analysis standards.

[78] Cf. Synoptic Table of Government Replies, in Milk Code 1968, pp. 82-88.

practices to this Code, governments undertake to give earnest and sympathetic consideration... to the individual standards established in association with the Code..." This provision would seem to confirm a certain hierarchy of norms in the sense that the Code of Principles is the basic instrument and individual standards may be regarded as secondary legislation. Translated into treaty language, the Code would be the Convention and the individual standards could be assimilated to additional Protocols. Under this construction, acceptance of an individual standard would seem to be conditional upon prior acceptance of the Code. A number of countries have, however, accepted composition standards without accepting the Code as such. Similarly, some countries have accepted individual cheese standards, but not the General Standard (A-6) for Cheese. Nevertheless, even in the absence of express acceptance of the "higher" set of norms, a country accepting a specific standard would presumably be expected to apply those norms which are implied in, or spelled out by, the individual standard concerned. Thus, in a "Note Applicable to All Standards of Composition," it is stated that "these Standards are understood to be governed by the provisions of the Code of Principles." [79] The relation between the General Standard for Cheese and individual cheese standards is alluded to in connection with the procedure for the elaboration of individual cheese standards; by a footnote, governments are enjoined to accept the General Standard (A-6) before presenting a request for the elaboration of an individual cheese standard.

Some problems have arisen in connection with the adoption of individual cheese standards, on account of a pre-existing multilateral treaty covering in part the same subject matter. The Stresa Convention of 1 June 1951, concerning the Use of *Appellations d'Origine* and Denominations of Cheese,[80] establishes certain principles and procedures designed to protect producers and consumers against false or misleading designations and other unfair trade practices and, to that effect, defines the terms "cheese" (Article 2) and "processed cheese" (Article 7) and sets up minimum standards for labelling, weight and date indications (Articles 6, 8). Its principal objective is, however, to protect specific brands or varieties of cheese which are enumerated in two Annexes set forth in the Protocol to the Convention. Annex A lists *appellations d'origine* which "are the object of internal legislation reserving their use ... to cheese manufactured... in traditional regions by virtue of local, loyal and uninterrupted usage" (Article 3). Annex B lists denominations of cheeses protected by the legislation of one or more countries; in contradistinction to the va-

---

[79] Milk Code 1968, p. 11.
[80] Convention, Protocol and Protocol of Signature of 1 June 1951 and supplementary Protocol, done at the Hague on 15 July 1951. The Convention came into force on 1 September 1953; the following countries are parties thereto: Austria, Denmark, France, Italy, Netherlands, Norway, Sweden and Switzerland.

rieties listed in Annex A, the varieties listed in Annex B may however be produced, and the denominations used, by other Contracting Parties, on condition that they have the characteristics as defined in Annex B (Article 4).[81] The Convention establishes a detailed procedure for adding other varieties to each of the Annexes and leaves the final decision regarding both the definition of characteristics and the inclusion itself to a Permanent Council consisting of one representative of each of the Contracting Parties.[82] Within two years from the date of ratification or of inclusion of a given cheese variety in one of the Annexes, as the case may be, Contracting Parties are required to bring their legislation into conformity with the Convention.[83] Article 9 of the Convention provides for the settlement of disputes by the Permanent Council, by way of conciliation proceedings and, in the last resort, by recourse to the International Court of Justice. The Convention may be denounced, subject to one year's notice [84] but no provision is made for reservations.[85]

While it would go beyond the scope of this paper to give a detailed comparative analysis of the Stresa Convention and of the cheese standards adopted by the FAO/WHO Committee of Government Experts, the existence, side by side, of two different methods of international standard setting, covering the same subject matter and pursuing similar objectives calls for certain observations, particularly as it has given rise to some problems in recent years.

The most obvious difference lies in the number of participating countries; while the Stresa Convention has been concluded between eight countries in Western Europe,[86] all States Members of WHO or FAO may participate in the elaboration and adoption of standards [87] and —once adopted—may

---

[81] The Stresa Protocol, as amended by the Hague Protocol, lists four varieties in Annex A and 30 varieties in Annex B.

[82] Art. 5. New varieties may be added to Annex B by a simple majority of the Permanent Council members, while additions to Annex A require a majority of three-quarters.

[83] Arts. 2.2, 5.8. This period has been extended, in respect of certain countries, to 3 years by the Hague Protocol.

[84] Art. 11.

[85] At the time of signing the Convention, all three Scandinavian countries formulated two identical reservations, which the other signatories did not accept; the Protocol of Signature gave these countries three months to withdraw their reservations and stipulated that "the status of Contracting Party shall be accorded only to those of the three States having formulated reservations, which shall have revoked both of the reservations". According to the Hague Protocol, certain concessions were made to these States, and the reservations were withdrawn.

[86] Although, pursuant to Art. 10.3, the Convention "after it has come into force, ... shall be open to adhesion by any state", no adhesions have taken place to date; two countries which participated in the drawing up of the Convention at the Stresa Conference (Belgium, U.K.) did not sign it.

[87] Draft standards are circulated for comment to Members of the Committee of Government Experts and to other Member Nations of FAO or WHO. Recent sessions

232

accept them.[88] On the other hand, the Stresa Convention establishes a number of precise rights and duties binding on all Contracting Parties alike, while the system established (and still being developed) for Codex standards allows for considerable flexibility.

Once the Permanent Council has determined the characteristics of a given cheese variety and decided (by the majority required for the pertinent Annex) to include it in one of the Annexes, those characteristics constitute an "absolute" standard, and all Contracting Parties become automatically bound by the standard and the duties deriving from the inclusion in the Annex; they have to adapt their legislation within two years to conform to the international standard; if a variety has been included in Annex A, all Contracting Parties, except the State to which the *appellation d'origine* has been accorded must discontinue the production of that variety,[89] and if the designation of a variety is included in Annex B, all cheese produced or offered for sale under that designation must conform to the characteristics determined by the Permanent Council.[90]

As against this, a standard adopted by the Committee of Government Experts is in no way binding on Member States, even if they have voted in favour of the standard, unless they have submitted a written declaration of acceptance. As has been noted above, the acceptance of composition standards does not preclude a country from adopting or using more rigorous requirements under domestic legislation; this applies to both the General Standard for Cheese and to individual cheese standards. It would seem, however, that some countries in accepting a standard have declared that they apply *less* rigorous requirements,[91] and there is no evidence of any objections having been made to such declarations.

As regards the translation of international standards into national legislation, the introductory paragraph to the Code of Principles (which presumably applies, *mutatis mutandis,* to composition standards) states that "Governments which... declare their willingness to apply the Code are... requested to state whether they can indicate the date by which they will be able to bring their national requirements into conformity with its provisions..."[92] Accordingly, declarations of acceptance have been subdivided into three groups, viz.:

---

of the Committee of Government Experts have been attended by representatives of more than thirty countries from all regions.

[88] The Code of Principles has been accepted by 71 Governments, the General Standard for Cheese by 36; the number of acceptances for individual cheese standards generally varies between 9 and 16.

[89] In view of the comparatively small number of Contracting Parties, the "monopoly" of the country benefiting from the *appellation d'origine* under the Convention is a relative one.

[90] Certain derogations are permitted for cheese designed for export to countries other than Contracting Parties (cf. Stresa Protocol, Arts. II.3, IV.1).

[91] Cf. Status of Acceptances of Standard A-6—Notes on National Requirements, in Milk Code 1968, pp. 94-95.

[92] Milk Code 1968, p. 3.

(i) Countries whose position has been adapted to conform to the Code;
(ii) Countries which have undertaken to adapt their position to the Code and have indicated a specific target date for this purpose;
(iii) Countries which have either declared their agreement in principle with the Code or stated their intention to adapt their position to it when legislative changes are envisaged.

In 1968, the number of countries in groups (i) and (iii) was 32 and 35 respectively, while only 4 countries were listed in group (ii).[93] As regards the latter, it may be noted that the determination of the target date for the adoption of legislative or administrative measures is left to the discretion of the individual governments. With respect to the countries in group (iii), their status may have to be reviewed in the light of the General Principles of the Codex Alimentarius, once they will be extended to milk standards generally, inasmuch as declarations of "agreement in principle" or vague declarations of intention to adapt their legislation to the Code may then no longer be recognized as acceptances.[94] It may be significant in this connection that the FAO Conference at its Fourteenth Session (November 1967) specifically recommended that steps should be taken towards full integration of the work of the Committee of Government Experts in the procedural framework established by the Codex Alimentarius Commission.[95]

---

[93] *Ibid.* p. 81.

[94] See below, pp. 250-53. The Committee of Government Experts, when discussing, at its Tenth Session (August 1967), the acceptance of standards within the framework of the proposed General Principles, expressed the opinion that "unlike standards elaborated under the Code of Principles, the Code ... itself could not be regarded as a Standard, in the context of acceptance."

[95] Conf. Rep. 14th Session (1967), para. 523. Both the Committee of Government Experts and the Commission devoted considerable time and effort in order to arrive at a satisfactory solution of the various problems involved; Governments have repeatedly been consulted and a number of proposals and counterproposals have been put forward by the Commission, its Executive Committee and the Committee of Government Experts, but certain questions still remain in suspense: although the "governing paragraph" concerning the relations and respective competencies of the two bodies (originally laid down as para. 10 of the CAC Rep., 1st Session) has been the subject of several redrafts, final decisions still have to be taken on the following questions: (1) should the Committee have full competence for all questions concerning milk and milk products or should decisions of the Committee be subject to review by the Commission, and if so, what kind of decisions? (2) should draft standards on milk products have to be submitted to the general subject Codex Committees (labelling, hygiene, additives, pesticide residues, etc.)? (3) Should the Committee or the Commission (or both) deal with acceptances of standards? (4) Should acceptances be made in accordance with the provisions of the Milk Code or should they follow the rules laid down in the General Principles of the Codex Alimentarius? (5) Would, in the latter case, the validity of past acceptances be affected? Nevertheless, considerable progress has been made, and solutions for most of these problems are in sight. Cf. Reports of Committee of Government Experts, 11th Session (1968), paras. 11-15; 12th Session (1969), paras. 22-28; Reports of the Codex Alimentarius Commission, 6th Session (1969), paras. 121-124; 7th Session (1970)—Provisional Report—paras. 27-33.

In the event of a dispute concerning the interpretation or application of the Stresa Convention, provision is made for a settlement procedure.[96] No such procedure is provided for under the Code of Principles. Nevertheless, the Committee of Government Experts acting, as it were, in a quasi-judicial capacity has examined a number of questions arising from declarations of acceptance and, at least in one case, decided that the designation of a given product "did not correspond with the requirements of the Code" and therefore recommended that the government "give its active attention to the possibility of bringing its federal and state legislation into line with the requirements of the Code." [97]

The reference to "federal and state legislation" calls for a brief observation. The Constitution and General Rules of FAO refer to obligations of, and relations with, Member Nations and Associate Members, and where the term "government" is used, it is manifestly intended to apply to the central or—in the case of federal states—the federal government.[98] None of the Conventions and Agreements concluded under Article XIV of the Constitution contain a federal clause or any provisions implying the possibility of state (provincial, cantonal) jurisdiction in the field covered by the instrument.[99] In this situation, the introduction of a federal clause in Article 6 of the Code of Principles appears as a remarkable novelty in FAO constitutional practice. The relevant provision reads as follows:

"6.2. In view of the relationship between a Federal Government and its constituent States or Provincial Governments, wherever some or all of the provisions of this Code are not regarded as appropriate for Federal action, Federal Governments undertake to make effective arrangements for the reference of such provisions to the appropriate authorities with the request that they give active consideration to the amendment of their State or Provincial requirements in conformity therewith."[100]

Mention has been made above of certain problems which have arisen

---

[96] Art. 9; see above, p. 232.

[97] Milk Code 1968, p. 9 (Decision No. 4).

[98] The establishment by a Member Nation of a National FAO Committee which, under General Rule XXXV.2, "may be utilized as a suitable instrument for coordinating the participation of the said Member Nation ... in the activities of the Organization", might in certain cases prove useful for promoting coordination of Federal and State policies, but there is no indication that the enabling provision quoted above was specially intended to meet this situation.

[99] The provision on "territorial application" included in Conventions and Agreements is principally designed for application to "non-metropolitan" territories and does not lend itself to limiting the territorial scope of a given instrument to specific subdivisions within the "metropolitan" territory of a federal state.

[100] Milk Code 1968, p. 6. There are strong indications that this provision may have been inspired by Art. 19, para. 7 (b) of the ILO Constitution; the phrases "... [provisions] ... not regarded as appropriate for federal action" and "... make effective arrangements for the reference of such [provisions] to the appropriate authorities ..." are practically identical with those used in the ILO Constitution.

out of the parallel existence of two standard setting methods within the same field.

The first problem arose from the fact that the characteristics as determined by the Permanent Council in respect of a cheese variety included in an Annex to the Stresa Convention constituted an "absolute norm" while composition standards adopted by the Committee of Government Experts under the Code of Principles were generally considered to be minimum standards. Some governments felt that a uniform standard should apply to any one variety known by a specific designation, while others maintained that Article 6.4 of the Code of Principles, which allows for the use of more rigorous requirements under domestic legislation, was applicable to all composition standards, including individual cheese standards. The Committee eventually decided to maintain the concept of the minimum standard, but emphasized that international standards would have to be relatively strict and precise in order to ensure an accurate and effective use of the designation of individual cheese varieties.[101] While a high degree of uniformity was considered desirable, the Committee felt that some latitude might be built into the standard, but that if such important matters as fat content were involved, the label bearing the designation would have to give a clear indication as to the quality standard (e.g. percentage of fat content).[102]

Two closely connected, yet distinct problems have arisen in connection with requests for the elaboration of standards for cheese varieties which have been included, or might be eligible for inclusion, in either Annex A or Annex B of the Stresa Convention.

With respect to the latter category (Annex B), some governments maintained that only the country which had to be regarded as the original producer of the cheese variety concerned—often referred to as country of origin[103]—is entitled to request the elaboration of an individual cheese standard; alternatively, if several countries submitted proposals for a standard, the characteristics of the cheese variety set out in the proposal of the country of origin should prevail in all cases. Other governments found it difficult to consent to a rule which would grant to the country of origin a quasi-monopolistic position. At its Ninth Session (1966), the Committee reached a compromise solution to the effect that, as far as possible, the initiative for the elaboration of a standard should come from the country (or countries) of origin, which should, however, endeavour to reach an agreement on the proposed standard with other interested countries. If a country other than a country of origin should wish to pro-

---

[101] Cf. Report of Eighth Session of Committee of Government Experts, para. 30.
[102] *Idem*, Ninth Session, paras. 12-13.
[103] This designation has sometimes led to confusion as it was erroneously construed to imply that the cheese variety is protected by an *appellation d'origine*.

236

pose a standard, it would have to endeavour, before officially filing a request, to reach agreement on the proposed standard with the country (or countries) of origin and other interested countries, with a view to presenting a joint proposal. The Committee recognized that the adoption of a standard might be impossible if the country of origin—being also a major producer—found the terms of the proposed standard unacceptable; it felt, however, that difficulties of this kind could presumably be avoided if the above procedure for preliminary negotiations were followed.[104]

The problem of the elaboration of standards for cheese varieties to which an *appellation d'origine* had been granted, either by national legislation or under the Stresa Convention (Annex A), has given rise to extensive debates over the last years and has not yet been resolved. Some countries have taken the line that the Committee of Government Experts should refuse to consider any request for the elaboration of a standard for a cheese variety with an *appellation d'origine* if the country under whose legislation that *appellation* has been granted objects to such elaboration.[105] Other countries felt that such an unconditional right of veto could not be recognized in favour of a single country of origin; they held that if a country which had accorded an *appellation d'origine* to a cheese did not wish it to be the subject of an international cheese standard, it should be required to prove the existence of differences between the variety thus protected and "similar" varieties produced in countries which were in favour of elaboration of a standard. According to a further view, the elaboration of an international standard should not be ruled out, but the burden of proof should lie with the countries which claimed that the cheese variety produced by them was identical with that protected by an *appellation d'origine*. To the extent that the distinction was based on organoleptic properties, it might be necessary to establish that the variety having an *appellation d'origine* could not be produced with the same characteristics outside the region of origin. Neither the establishment of an *ad hoc* tripartite Committee of Experts (France, Italy, Switzerland) by decision of the Committee at its Tenth Session, nor subsequent bipartite negotiations between Italy and the United States led to any tangible results.[106]

A similar problem, though not related to *appellation d'origine* under the Stresa Convention, has arisen in connection with the elaboration of a standard for Blue Stilton, a cheese protected by a "certification trade mark" under British law and therefore—at least potentially—within the

---

[104] Cf. Report of the Ninth Session of the Committee of Government Experts, paras. 9-10.
[105] See, in particular, Declaration by the Italian Delegation, *ibidem*, Section IV, pp. 27-28.
[106] See Report of Tenth Session, para. 12 (establishment or tripartite Committee); *idem,* Eleventh Session, paras. 16-19 (report of tripartite Committee); *idem* Twelfth Session, para. 39 (outcome of bilateral negotiations).

purview of the Paris and Madrid Conventions of the protection of industrial property rights.[106a]

(b) *Codex Alimentarius*

(i) *Origin and Basic Structure*

The origin of the Joint FAO/WHO Food Standards Program can be traced to three principal sources, viz. (1) the work carried out under the auspices of the Committee of Government Experts on Milk and Milk Products described above; (2) the extensive preparatory work undertaken jointly by FAO and WHO in the fields of food additives [107] and pesticide residues; [108] and (3) the initiative taken by a number of European countries for the establishment of a *Codex Alimentarius Europaeus* under the direction of the European Council for the Codex Alimentarius.[109]

Following recommendations of the FAO Conference at its Eleventh Session and of the WHO Executive Board at its Twenty-Ninth Session, a Joint FAO/WHO Conference on Food Standards held in Geneva in October 1962 formulated a number of recommendations regarding the program,

---

[106a] Convention for the Protection of Industrial Property, concluded at Paris on 20 March 1883 and revised at Brussels (1900), Washington (1911), The Hague (1925), London (1934), Lisbon (1958), and Stockholm (1967); Convention on the International Registration of Marks, concluded at Madrid on 14 April 1891 and last revised at Nice (1957) and Stockholm (1967). See Reports of Committee of Government Experts, Eleventh Session (1968), paras. 20-22; *idem,* Twelfth Session (1969), paras. 33-36, and the study prepared by the Secretariat for the Committee's Thirteenth Session, Doc. MDS 70/8 (b), April 1970.

[107] Following a WHO/FAO Conference on food additives held in 1955, the two Organizations established a joint expert committee, which proposed certain specifications for identity and purity of selected antimicrobials, antioxidants and colouring substances; it had been intended at one time to publish these in book form, "comparable to the *International Pharmacopeia*": C. Conf. Rep., 10th Session (1959), para. 338. The Committee has not been absorbed by the Food Standards Program but acts in an advisory capacity on scientific problems, while the Codex Committee on Food Additives established under that Program elaborates criteria and tolerances in relation to specific food standards.

[108] Apart from convening an intergovernmental conference on pesticides and establishing an Expert Committee on Pesticides in Agriculture, FAO also set up, jointly with WHO, a Committee on Pesticides Residues, which acts, *inter alia,* as an advisory body to the Codex Alimentarius Commission and more particularly to the Codex Committee on Pesticide Residues whose role is similar to that of the Codex Committee on Food Additives. Cf. FAO Conf. Res. 8/61 "The Use of Pesticides in Agriculture."

[109] This Council, after having carried out valuable work, both on individual draft standards and on general principles, was absorbed by the Codex Alimentarius Commission, as "Coordinating Committee for Europe", after agreement had been reached that a Coordinating Committee for Europe would be established within the framework of the Commission and that the Food Standards Program would offer opportunities for the elaboration of regional standards as well as worldwide standards. Cf. Report of the Codex Alimentarius Commission, (hereinafter referred to as "CAC Rep."), Second Session, pp. 20-22, 69-71.

policies and procedures of the Commission, which held its first Session in June 1963.[110]

The institutional framework within which this codification of food standards was to proceed, was clearly set out by the FAO Conference at its Eleventh Session [111] and subsequently endorsed by the World Health Assembly.[112] The work was entrusted to a Joint Commission consisting of all Member Nations and Associate Members of FAO and WHO which "have notified the Director-General of FAO or WHO of their desire to be considered as Members." [113] States eligible for membership (but not desiring to become full members) and—subject to certain conditions—other States (not so eligible) may be invited at their request to attend meetings of the Commission and its subsidiary bodies in an observer capacity.[114] The Commission was authorized to establish subsidiary bodies, subject to the availability of the necessary funds, and to adopt and amend its own rules of procedure subject to approval by the appropriate organs of FAO and WHO.[115] The operating expenses of the Commission and of the joint secretariat were to be defrayed by a special Trust Fund administered by FAO and maintained from voluntary contributions "accepted... through or with the approval of participating governments;" [116] however, "expenses involved in preparatory work on draft standards undertaken by participating governments" were, as a rule, to be "defrayed by the Government concerned." [117] Although the Food Standards Program gained considerable impetus during the initial period (1963-1965), it was recognized that the method of voluntary contributions provided a somewhat precarious financial basis and might have discouraged some countries from becoming members of the Commission. Accordingly, the Program was absorbed, as from 1966, by the regular Programs and Budgets of its parent Organizations.[118] However,

---

110 The Second Session took place in September 1964, the Third in October 1965, the Fourth in November 1966; the Fifth in February 1968, the Sixth in March 1969, and the Seventh in April 1970.
111 Conf. Rep., 11th Session (1961), paras. 258-263; Conf. Res. No. 12/61 and Appendix D (Statutes of the Codex Alimentarius Commission).
112 Resolution WHA 16.42, adopted by the Assembly at its 16th Session, May 1963.
113 Statutes of the Commission, Art. 2.
114 Ibid. Arts. 3, 4. States that are not members of either FAO or WHO but are members of the UN may be invited in accordance with the constitutional provisions of FAO and WHO relating to the granting of observer status to nations.
115 Ibid. Arts. 6, 7.
116 Ibid. Art. 8.
117 Ibid. Art. 9. Under an amendment, adopted by the FAO Conference in 1963 and by the World Health Assembly in 1964, the Commission was authorized to recognize "as its operating expenses" (and thus chargeable to the Trust Fund) certain costs incurred by Governments in undertaking work on behalf of the Commission. Conf. Rep. 12th Session (1963) paras. 506-507 Doc. CL 43/31. However, this enabling provision has always been used very sparingly, and practically all costs are borne by Governments which assumed responsibilities for the preparatory work.
118 Conf. Rep. 13th Session (1965), paras. 314, 341-343. As a consequence of this

this decision, while giving increased stability to the Program, did not affect its basic structure and methods of operation as reflected in the Statutes and the Rules of Procedure of the Commission.[119]

Pursuant to Rule X, inserted into the Rules of Procedure at the Second Session of the Commission, two detailed methods were established for the elaboration and acceptance of worldwide and of regional standards, respectively. The ten steps or *gradus ad parnassum* which a proposed standard has to climb include, at different stages of the elaboration, two consultations with governments individually (Steps 3, 6), three "readings" by the appropriate expert body (Steps 2, 4, 7) and two "readings" by the Commission (Steps 5, 8).[120] The procedure is virtually the same for worldwide standards and for standards elaborated upon request of the countries belonging to a region or group, except for the first and the decisive stages, where these countries have a preponderant voice.[121] Regional or "group" standards are also open for acceptance by countries not belonging to the region or group, and if "the Commission determines that a sufficient number of Members have formally accepted it" a regional standard may be published as a worldwide standard.[122]

While the responsibility for deciding on the elaboration of standards, for allocating preparatory work and for finalizing and adopting draft standards is, in principle, reserved to the Commission, the bulk of the preparatory work is carried out by its subsidiary bodies established under Rule IX of its Rules of Procedure. Of the three categories of subsidiary bodies provided for in Rule IX.1, two are represented only by one body

decision, the Statutes were further amended; see CL Rep. 47th Session (1966), para. 218 and Appendix B, and World Health Assembly Resolution WHA 20.27 (May 1967).

[119] Reproduced in *Codex Alimentarius Commission Procedural Manual*, 2nd edition, Rome (FAO) 1969 (hereafter referred to as "Procedural Manual"). Since the functional mechanism of the Commission and the methods for the elaboration of standards are largely determined by, or on the basis of, the Rules of Procedure, it is hardly surprising that the formulation and recurrent revisions of these Rules have played an important part in the deliberations of the Commission and its Executive Committee. Cf. CAC Reps. 1st Session (1963), Appendix B, (pp. 36-45); 2nd Session (1964), paras. 4-10, Appendix A, (pp. 48-55), Appendix B (pp. 72-81); 3rd Session (1965), para. 11, Appendix II (pp. 57-66); 4th Session (1966), paras. 6, 13, Appendix II (pp. 95-104); 5th session (1968), paras. 65-72; 6th session (1969), paras. 28-42; Seventh session (1970), prov. Report, paras. 15-19. Certain of these problems have also been considered by the FAO Committee on Constitutional and Legal Matters: cf. Doc. CL 43/42, paras. 5-12.

[120] Cf. Procedural Manual, pp. 25-31. In the course of this elaboration, the standard gradually evolves from a "proposed draft standard" to a "Codex standard".

[121] The term "decisive" relates to Steps 5 and 8 where the Commission is called upon to adopt or amend a (draft) provisional standard. Where a regional Coordinating Committee has been established and/or a Coordinator appointed, the countries of the region concerned have further opportunities of exercising their influence on the formulation of the proposed standard.

[122] This extension constitutes the "eleventh Step" in the procedure applicable to regional standards.

each,[123] while the Codex Committees, representing the third category, have become quite numerous, covering a wide field of activities.

The method by which they are set up and operate appears simple enough, although it is without precise precedent in FAO history and poses certain problems of coordination, which have, however, been largely resolved.[124] A government accepts responsibility for assuming the chairmanship of a Codex Committee to which the Commission has decided to entrust preparatory work.[125] While sessions are convened by the Secretariat,[126] in consultation with the Chairman of the Committee and—in the case of proposed regional standards—the Coordinator for the Region, the host government is responsible for making the necessary arrangements and for bearing the costs other than those connected with the attendance of representatives of governments, secretariat staff or observers of international organizations.[127] In order to facilitate advance planning and budgeting, both by the Commission's parent Organizations and the participating governments, the Commission usually adopts, at each of its regular sessions, a "Recommended Timetable of Meetings" for the following year, as part of its proposed Program of Work.[128]

The above sketchy outline of the institutional framework within which

---

[123] They are the two bodies which were brought within the framework of the Codex Alimentarius Commission, i.e. the Committee of Government Experts for Milk and Milk Products, the only body having authority, under Rule IX.1 (a) to finalize standards, and the Coordinating Committee for Europe (see Note 109 above), now established under Rule IX.1 (b) (2). A proposal for the establishment of a coordinating committee for Africa, made in 1965, is still under consideration (cf. CAC Rep., 3rd Session, para. 8; *idem*, 4th Session, para. 11; *idem*, 6th Session, paras. 74-75).

[124] Apart from the coordination of the work of the individual Committees the distribution of responsibilities between the Secretariat and Governments in charge of preparatory work has also presented some problems. See Note 126 below.

[125] The establishment, terms of reference and reporting procedures of subsidiary bodies are decided upon by the Commission, in exceptional cases by the Executive Committee (Rules IX.5 and III.2 of the Rules of Procedure). The designation of the country responsible for appointing the chairman is made by the Commission at each Regular Session (*Ibid.* Rule IX.10). It should be noted, however, that certain preparatory tasks may also be—and are in fact being—entrusted to specialized industrial and trade organizations.

[126] Initially, the convening and conducting of sessions was left almost exclusively to the host government or chairman, but the Commission recognized that a certain uniformity was desirable and therefore at its Fourth Session adopted detailed "Guidelines for Codex Committee", covering both procedural and substantive aspects. See CAC Rep., 4th Session, pp. 42-48; Procedural Manual, pp. 47-58.

[127] Rule XI.3, 4 of the Rules of Procedure. Cf. also Note 117 above. In view of the increasingly large attendance (in some cases exceeding 100 participants), the number of working papers and reports and the interpretation and translation requirements resulting from the use of several working languages, the costs to be borne by host governments are by no means negligible.

[128] Art. 9 of the Statutes and Rule XI.1 of the Rules of Procedure. Cf. CAC Rep. 5th Sessions, paras. 184-185; *idem*, 6th Session, para. 196; Docs. Alinorm 69/32 and 70/27.

the elaboration of standards takes place seems necessary as a background to facilitate the appreciation of the legal problems which may arise in connection with the Codex Alimentarius. But before turning to some of these problems, the outline should be supplemented by a brief survey of the Codex Committees, to illustrate, *inter alia,* the broad scope, *ratione materiae,* of the Food Standards Program. The diagram appearing on pages 248-9 below not only shows the wide coverage, as well as the various types of subsidiary bodies; it also obviates the need for even a selective enumeration of individual committees. Among the Codex Committees, there are two main categories, viz. General Subject Committees and Commodity Committees, which again may be "worldwide" or "regional". Each of these Committees elaborates a number of standards,[129] but the General Subject Committees are also called upon, at an early stage (Step 3), to review and comment on such sections of proposed commodity standards as may deal with the subject (e.g. hygiene, additives) within their respective terms of reference. On the extreme left of the diagram, there are four joint FAO/WHO groups of experts which do not form an integral part of the Food Standards Program but often act in an advisory capacity to the individual Codex Committees.[130] On the extreme right of the diagram, there are two joint ECE/Codex groups of experts which likewise have existed for many years, previously as joint FAO/ECE groups; although they have not been fully absorbed by the FAO/WHO Food Standards Program, they are following the same procedures for the elaboration of standards as Codex Committees.[131]

(ii) *Nature and Scope of Codex Standards*

The General Principles of the Codex Alimentarius in their present form [132] recapitulate the purpose of the Codex (para. 1),[133] then define the

---

[129] The number varies between one single standard (Food Labelling) and 25 standards (Processed Fruits and Vegatables). Cf. complete list of standards in the course of elaboration in Doc. ALINORM 69/36. Without taking into account the standards adopted (or in course of preparation) under the Code of Principles for Milk and Milk Products, approximately 200 Codex Standards are in various stages of elaboration. In the course of its last three Sessions (fifth to seventh), the Commission has adopted standards for some 40 commodities, as well as a general standard on labelling of prepackaged foods.

[130] These groups were established before the Codex Alimentarius Commission (cf. Note 108 above) and their terms of reference are generally not limited to food standards.

[131] In addition, ECE has established, many years ago, a Working Party on standardization of Perishable Foodstuffs, which cooperates with the Codex Alimentarius Commission and its subsidiary bodies (see Note 138 below).

[132] CAC Rep., 6th Session, Appendix IV; Procedural Manual, pp. 19-24. Much more detailed general principles, including a considerable number of definitions, had been included in the drafts of the Codex Alimentarius Europaeus and of the Latin-American Food Code (see CAC Rep., 1st Session, Appendices E.1 and E.2). These provisions have now been largely incorporated in the draft "General Subject" standards and

242

scope of the Codex as a whole (para 2) [134] and the *nature* of individual Codex standards (para 3).[135] The scope of the Codex is very wide, indeed, since it embraces "all the principal foods", although the main emphasis is clearly placed on foods "for distribution to the consumer." Similarly, the criteria to be included in any Codex standards, in accordance with the specifications set out in para. 3 of the General Principles, are quite comprehensive. However, after comparing the relatively straightforward purposes of the Food Standards Program, the scope of the Codex and the nature of standards, as defined in the General Principles, with the rather complex structure and procedure outlined in a rather fragmentary way in the preceding section, one might be inclined to suspect a concerted effort, on the part of the national and international bureaucracies to follow Parkinson's Law to the letter. A brief description of the complex infrastructure on which the Codex is being developed may serve to show that this suspicion is hardly warranted. With current technolo-

---

analysed in the "General Principles of Food Legislation", a Secretariat study established on the basis of replies to a detailed questionnaire and further government comments (Doc. SP 10/30—GPFL—Revised Ed. July 1967), which may well be conducive to a certain harmonization of domestic legislation and thus facilitate implementation of Codex standards.

[133] The purposes of the Food Standards Program, as laid down in Art. 1 of the Commission's Statutes, have been reformulated in narrative form in para. 1 of the General Principles, as follows:

"1. The Codex Alimentarius is a collection of internationally adopted food standards presented in a uniform manner. These food standards aim at protecting consumers' health and ensuring fair practices in the food trade. The Codex Alimentarius also includes provisions of an advisory nature in the form of codes of practice, guidelines and other recommended measures intended to assist in achieving the purposes of the Codex Alimentarius. The publication of the Codex Alimentarius is intended to guide and promote the elaboration and establishment of definitions and requirements for foods to assist in their harmonization and in doing so to facilitate international trade."

[134] "The Codex Alimentarius includes standards for all the principal foods, whether processed, semi-processed or raw, for distribution to the consumer. Materials for further processing into foods should be included to the extent necessary to achieve the purposes of the Codex Alimentarius as defined. The Codex Alimentarius includes provisions in respect of food hygiene, food additives, pesticide residues, contaminants, labelling and presentation, methods of analysis and sampling. It also includes provisions of an advisory nature in the form of codes of practice, guidelines and other recommended measures." The last sentence was added by the Commission—together with the penultimate sentence of paragraph 1 (note 133)—at its Sixth Session, in the light of the Opinion of the Legal Counsels of FAO and WHO, concerning the Commission's authority, under its Statutes, to adopt Codes of Practice: CAC Rep., 6th Session, Appendix III.

[135] "Codex standards contain requirements for food aimed at ensuring for the consumer a sound, wholesome food product free from adulteration, correctly labelled and presented. A Codex standard for any food or foods should be drawn up in accordance with the Format for Codex Commodity Standards and contain, as appropriate, the criteria listed therein."

gical progress and the important development in food production, processing and trade, the many interests and moving forces have assumed certain aspects of a complex electromagnetic field, in which positively or negatively charged power nuclei are moving swiftly in varying directions, receiving and giving impulses of attraction or repulsion, temporarily converging or colliding and then resuming a fresh course of their own. Without characterizing these interests and their dynamic interplay, it may be useful to enumerate some of them. On the production side, there are the primary producers of tropical and temperate zone agricultural products, of dairy and animal products, not to forget fishermen; then we find enterprises, small or large, preparing semi-processed foods and the food processing and ancillary industries, including cold chains, canning and food packing plants; in the food trade, most countries have their own wholesale and retail organizations, usually subdivided by categories of foodstuffs, including import and export agencies with varying degrees of State participation, as well as supermarket chains; on the government side, certain authorities are in charge of public health, others of promoting agriculture or food production, still others foreign trade; on the international market, food exporting and food importing countries are facing each other, and so are developed and developing countries, with common and/or competing interests, depending on the products considered; the international organizations participating in the food standards work may place particular emphasis on different aspects, such as food hygiene, or increased production and distribution, or facilitation of international trade. It is against this somewhat bewildering background that the Food Standards Program in endeavouring to elaborate standards, which may not be common denominators of all possible interests, but represent a solution which is in conformity with the aims of the Program, takes into account up-to-date scientific and technological methods and data and is, on the one hand sufficiently clear and precise and, on the other, sufficiently simple and flexible to find a large measure of consensus among those who will eventually be responsible for ensuring its effectiveness. To attain this objective, it is indispensable to associate with the elaboration of standards not only governments but a representative cross-section of those bodies—governmental or non-governmental, worldwide or regional—having special knowledge of and/or special interests in the subject matter of the proposed standards.[136] Technically satisfactory work of this type can

---

[136] A detailed survey of these organizations, divided by fields of activity and listing standards developed or under preparation at the time, may be found in the Appendix to the Report of the Joint FAO/WHO Conference on Food Standards (Geneva, 1962), which immediately preceded the formal establishment of the Codex Alimentarius Commission. More recently, this "vast capillary network of international bodies of all sorts" has been described in an interesting and challenging monograph by F. Townsend: "Food Standards—Their Importance, Limitations, and Problems with Special Refer-

best be performed in *specialized* groups consisting of government experts who are not only conversant with the legislation and objectives of their governments but are also assisted, and perhaps sometimes guided, by experts from industrial or trade organizations: hence the relatively large number of Codex Committees whose composition reflects the expertise and interests just described. In addition, a standard cannot be formulated in a manner acceptable to a large preportion of those who will be called upon to accept and apply it, unless several opportunities are offered to them for holding consultations at various levels, for suggesting changes and considering those suggested by others: hence the elaborate 10-Steps procedure.

To revert to the scope and, more particularly, the form and contents of Codex standards, a certain diversity in the presentation of standards may be necessary on account of differences existing between the subject matters to be regulated, but apart from these objectively justified differences, it seems to be not only conducive to efficient working methods, but also in the interest of acceptability and effectiveness of standards, that they should follow, as far as possible, a uniform pattern. Before it was possible to work out this pattern or layout—which has become known as "format"—it was necessary to agree on the scope of Codex standards. Should such a standard be a complete, immutable standard—sometimes referred to as "recipe standard"—or a minimum, adaptable standard? In the former case, few countries might be able to accept it without reservations, and changes in food technology or habits might require frequent amendments; in the latter case, many countries could only accept a standard if they were enabled to impose more or less numerous stricter requirements—as they could not be expected to "lower" national standards already in force in their territories—which again might hamper rather than facilitate international trade, particularly if the minimum was set at the lowest possible level compatible with public health requirements. Or should there be a dual standard for one and the same product, i.e. a minimum standard acceptable as such to many countries, and a trading standard more adapted to the requirements of developed countries with more sophisticated food laws and regulations and possibly including detailed quality and grading criteria? These and a number of other possibilities have been examined and weighed by governments and the Codex Alimentarius Commission in the course of the past few years,[137] *pari passu* with the concrete elaboration of individual standards in the Codex

ence to International Work", published in Vol. I of *Quality Control in the Food Industry* (Academic Press, London and New York, 1967) pp. 285-365.

[137] Cf. Report of FAO-WHO Conference on Food Standards (Geneva 1962), paras. 7-13 and CAC Reps., 1st Session, para. 13; 4th Session, para. 18, as well as the various reports of the Executive Committee and the Committee on General Principles, where this has been a recurrent theme.

Committees and the study of general principles of food legislation.[138] The formula now used by the Codex Committee is that of a single Codex standard—thus avoiding the possibility of confusion which might arise from the existence of dual standards—which is not "complete" but contains all essential elements (including, where necessary, certain quality criteria), not only regarding composition proper but also comprising, where appropriate, provisions on hygiene, contaminants, sampling and analysis, weights and measures, packing and labelling. The single standard thus evolving would not be a minimum standard in the sense that any foods failing to meet its requirements would have to be considered virtually unfit for human consumption, nor would it be so elaborate as to be acceptable only to countries with highly sophisticated domestic standards. Obviously, national differences in levels of development, food production and consumption habits are not likely to disappear and the elimination, by way of international legislation, of differences between national food laws and regulations is undoubtedly a long and gradual process. Accordingly, if it is decided that a single standard should be adopted for each commodity, the variables have to be accommodated by way of different types or degrees of acceptances; these will be dealt with under (iii) below.

The format of Codex commodity standards, after having gone through several metamorphoses is now available in what might be regarded as its "final" *form*.[139] The headings are as follows: Name—Scope—Description —Essential Composition and Quality Factors—Food Additives—Contaminants—Hygiene—Weights and Measures—Labelling—Methods of Analysis and Sampling. It will be noted that *essential quality factors* are maintained; according to the relevant Explanatory Note they "should also include the quality of the raw material, with the object of protecting the health of the consumer", as well as organoleptic properties; they may specify "basic quality criteria for the finished products, with the object of preventing fraud", and tolerances for defects, but should not include

---

[138] Cf. Note 132 above and CAC Rep., 4th Session, para. 20. As evidenced by the passages cited, delimitation between national and international standard principles is still in a state of flux; this also applies to the question of definition of terms: thus, in accepting a number of definitions in connection with the Codex General Principles, the Commission "emphasized that they were not intended for governments to use in their national food legislation" (CAC Rep., 4th Session, para. 18).

[139] The *format,* as reproduced in the Procedural Manual (pp. 39-41), lists the individual headings and contains a number of explanatory notes—following to some extent the precedent set by the Code of Principles for Milk and Milk Products. The format is not a legally binding instrument but—as stated in the introduction—"intended for use as a guide by the subsidiary bodies of the . . . Commission in presenting their standards, with the object of achieving, as far as possible, a uniform presentation of commodity standards." However, the "Notes on the Headings" are legally relevant for interpretation purposes, particularly where individual standards deviate from the format or make use of optional provisions mentioned therein.

"at this stage" grades or quality classes.[140] *Food Additives* and *Contaminants* are expressed in terms of maximum tolerances of specified substances, subject to review and approval by the Codex Committees on Additives and Pesticide Residues, respectively. The Note on *Hygiene* distinguishes between "specific mandatory hygiene provisions" to be included in the standard and references "to applicable Codes of Practice" which need not set out *verbatim,* unless they are to be considered mandatory. It may be noted in this connection that the Commission, while recognizing the usefulness of Codes of Practice in appropriate cases, has declined to follow the example set by the Committee of Government Experts on Milk and Milk Products of opening such codes for formal acceptance by Governments.[141] Hygiene factors are obviously of crucial importance for the wholesomeness of food, but while unhygienic practices in handling, processing, transport or storage may be traceable in the finished product, the legal norms governing these subject matters may go somewhat beyond the scope of food standards proper.[142] In a different sense, this also

---

[140] A large number of quality and grading standards have been established by certain NGO's with a wide range of interests, such as the International Organization for Standardization (ISO), and others specializing in particular types of commodities. Perhaps even more important are the trading standards elaborated by the various Commodity Councils (wheat, sugar, coffee, etc.) and by intergovernmental organizations and agencies with wider terms of reference, such as ECE, OECD and the European Economic Community. To cite but two examples from the standardization work carried out under the aegis of the FAO Committee on Commodity Problems (CCP), the Cocoa Study Group has prepared a model ordinance and Code of Practice on cocoa beans, which is also being used as a basis for the proposed Codex Standard on cocoa beans under consideration by the Codex Committee on Cocoa Products and Chocolate; the Study Group on Citrus Fruit has made an important contribution to the European Standard for Citrus Fruit, adopted in 1963 by the ECE Working Party on Standardization of Perishable Foodstuffs. For further examples, cf. CAC Rep., 1st Session, Appendices K. 1-18 and FAO Doc. CCP 66/13, Section V. The importance of taking into account existing quality grades for primary commodities in connection with the elaboration of Codex standards was stressed at a recent session of the Executive Committee by the representative for Africa, with particular reference to developing countries exporting primary products; cf. Doc. ALINORM 68/4, para. 3.

[141] See note 134 *supra.* The Codes of Hygienic Practice, elaborated and adopted according to the same procedure as standards, have also been published as "recommended" codes and sent to governments, though *not* for acceptance. They could, in principle, also be printed in the Codex Alimentarius, but the criterion could obviously not be the same as for standards (i.e. acceptances received).

[142] Two examples gleaned from FAO activities related to the development of international trade may serve as an illustration. A study by D. D. Tapiador and J. E. Carroz on "Standards and Requirements for Fish Handling, Processing, Distribution and Quality Control" (FAO Fisheries Report No. 9, Rome 1963, 252 p.) is not only a preliminary step towards the preparation of a Code of Practice for the manufacture, distribution and marketing of fish and fishery products, but also a guide for the Codex Committee on Fish and Fishery Products in the elaboration of individual standards. FAO and various other organizations (e.g. WHO, OECD, EEC and OIE) have done a considerable amount of research concerning sanitary regulations applied to animals

247

JOINT FAO/WHO FOOD STANDARDS PROGRAM *

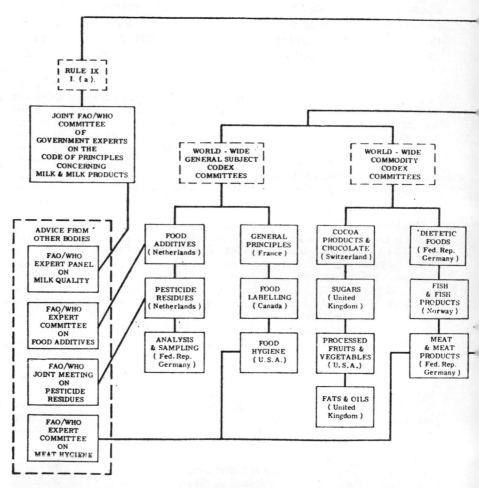

* Reproduced from the Procedural Manual, by courtesy of the FAO/WHO Food Standards Branch.

248

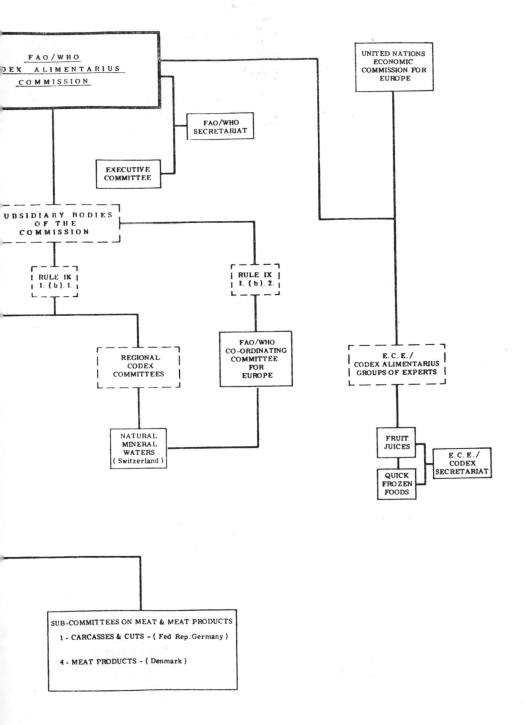

FAO/WHO
DEX ALIMENTARIUS
COMMISSION

UNITED NATIONS
ECONOMIC
COMMISSION FOR
EUROPE

FAO/WHO
SECRETARIAT

EXECUTIVE
COMMITTEE

UBSIDIARY BODIES
OF THE
COMMISSION

RULE IX
1. (b). 1.

RULE IX
1. (b). 2.

REGIONAL
CODEX
COMMITTEES

FAO/WHO
CO-ORDINATING
COMMITTEE
FOR
EUROPE

E.C.E./
CODEX ALIMENTARIUS
GROUPS OF EXPERTS

NATURAL
MINERAL
WATERS
(Switzerland)

FRUIT
JUICES

QUICK
FROZEN
FOODS

E.C.E./
CODEX
SECRETARIAT

SUB-COMMITTEES ON MEAT & MEAT PRODUCTS

1 - CARCASSES & CUTS - (Fed Rep. Germany)

4 - MEAT PRODUCTS - (Denmark)

applies to weights and measures and especially to labelling, which is often governed by national legislation to prevent fraudulent or misleading designations and unfair competition covering food as well as non-food products.

These considerations concerning the nature and scope of standards are not, as they might at first appear, only vaguely related to the question of effectiveness: on the one hand, international food standards have to be grafted on to the most diverse national—even provincial or local—laws, regulations, customs and practices, and their acceptability and impact will depend on the right blend of precision and flexibility, mandatory and permissive elements; on the other hand, the extent and type of acceptance which each standard will receive, the qualifying declarations that accepting States are likely to make and the degree of compliance and enforcement are in many ways pre-conditioned by the formulation of the standard.

(iii) *Acceptance of Codex Standards*

The questions discussed above are of considerable importance at the present juncture as the first series of draft standards have been adopted by the Commission at Step 8 and sent to governments for acceptance at Step 9.[143] Procedural requirements are hardly touched upon: a country may accept a Codex standard "in accordance with its established legal and administrative procedures"; no provision has been made regarding the form in which acceptances or declarations are to be communicated.[144]

The provisions of the General Principles concerning acceptance have undergone many changes before reaching their present form. Following the example of the Milk Code, the Commission originally envisaged three forms, i.e. full acceptance, acceptance with a declaration of more rigorous requirements, and acceptance with a proviso that acceptance would become effective after a stated number of years.[145] The Codex Committee

---

and animal products. The data obtained should also be of assistance to the Codex Committee on Meat and Meat Products in the elaboration of Codex standards, under various aspects, including hygiene criteria.

[143] Initially, the procedure for the elaboration of standards provided for acceptance by Members of the Commission only, but the pertinent provisions (Steps 9 and 10) were amended by the Commission at its 5th Session to extend the possibility of acceptance to all Member Nations of FAO and WHO. A slight difference still remains insofar as Commission Members "notify the Secretariat of their acceptance" while other Member Nations "are invited to notify the Secretariat if they wish to accept the recommended standard".

[144] Acceptance will undoubtedly have to be in writing. While it may not be feasible to insist on formal instruments of acceptance, all declarations should presumably express clearly and unambiguously the government's intent to accept the standard according to one of the modalities set forth in the General Principles and should be signed by an authority competent to assume, on behalf of the government, the obligations connected with acceptance.

[145] CAC Rep., 4th Session, Appendix III.

on General Principles proposed the introduction of "partial acceptance", on the ground that this would enable certain governments to accept a standard in a way which would take into account the particular conditions prevailing in their country and still contribute towards achieving the aims of the Codex Alimentarius; however, when the Commission considered this suggestion, a number of delegations felt that the very concept of acceptance might become illusory if any government could freely and unilaterally modify a standard, and the Commission therefore gave preference to a form of acceptance which would permit "minor deviations" only.[146]

In the light of the views expressed in the Commission and the comments submitted by governments individually in writing, the Committee on General Principles proposed, and the Commission adopted, what might be regarded the final version of the provisions on acceptance, eliminating "partial acceptance" and acceptance with a declaration of more rigorous requirements but maintaining the other three forms; at the same time, the legal implications of acceptance were redefined, and since it was found that they would have to be different for commodity standards and for general subject standards, respectively, the latter were made the subject of a separate paragraph.[147] The brief analysis of the acceptance procedure given below will be based on the paragraph concerning commodity standards (4), with appropriate references to the corresponding provisions in the paragraph on general subject standards (5).

Both paragraphs 4 and 5 consist of three sections, dealing with the different ways of acceptance and the legal implications of acceptance (A), the obligations of Member Nations unable to accept a standard (B), and additional implications contingent upon acceptance (C).

The *chapeau* covering all types of acceptance specified in paragraph 4A provides that the codex standard accepted by a country is to apply to "distribution of the product concerned, whether imported or home produced, within its territorial jurisdiction." The emphasis having been placed on distribution within the territory of the accepting country, it would seem permissible to produce commodities falling short of the requirements of the Codex standard if they are intended for export to countries that

---

[146] Doc. ALINORM 68/9, paras. 5-6. The various opinions expressed in the Commission are reflected in CAC Rep., 5th Session, paras. 14-20.

[147] Doc. ALINORM 69/9, paras. 6-14, Appendix II; CAC Rep., 6th Session, paras. 12, 13, 16, Appendix IV. It should be noted, however, that some delegations expressed certain reservations with respect to the implications of the acceptance procedure and supported the view of the Committee on General Principles "that the acceptance procedure was provisional in nature and could be re-examined if necessary in the light of experience". (CAC Rep., 6th Session, para. 13). Although the Commission therefore adopted this procedure "on a provisional basis", substantive changes will hardly be made for some time to come, but procedural provisions may well be added in due course.

have not accepted the standard. This implication has not escaped the Commission's attention, but it was felt that the mandatory extension of the standard to such commodities would place accepting States in a disadvantageous position vis à vis non-accepting States in competing for export markets and might therefore also discourage acceptance of Codex standards.[148]

Full acceptance is characterized as follows:

"(i) *Full Acceptance*
(a) Full acceptance means that the country concerned will ensure that a product to which the standard applies will be permitted to be distributed freely, in accordance with (c) below, within its territorial jurisdiction under the name and description laid down in the standard, provided that it complies with all the relevant requirements of the standard.
(b) The country will also ensure that products not complying with the standard will not be permitted to be distributed under the name and description laid down in the standard.
(c) The distribution of any sound products conforming with the standard will not be hindered by any legal or administrative provisions in the country concerned relating to the health of the consumer or to other food standard matters except for considerations of human, plant or animal health which are not specifically dealt with in the standard." [148a]

Sub-paragraph (a) stipulates a "positive" obligation on the part of an accepting government, i.e. to ensure free distribution of products conforming to the standard, while sub-paragraph (b) involves a negative obligation, i.e. to prohibit distribution within its territory of products at variance with the standard. Sub-paragraph (c) reinforces [148b] and at the same time qualifies the "positive" obligation: obviously, acceptance of a standard cannot imply the obligation not to prevent free distribution in the sense that the accepting country would have to abolish all restrictions, such as import quotas and customs duties; the reference to "considerations of human, plant or animal health" provides an additional safeguard which may be desirable because the Codex standards are not intended as "complete" standards, and may prove useful particularly with respect to raw or semi-processed foods exported from areas infested by epidemics or plant pests and to perishable foodstuffs generally.

---

[148] Cf. CAC Rep., 6th Session, para. 14—The solution is similar to that adopted for the Milk Code: see note 76 *supra*.—The *chapeau* for paragraph 5 A is almost identical, the only difference consisting of the expression "distribution of the products to which the general standard applies" instead of "distribution of the product concerned."
[148a] The corresponding provisions regarding general subject standards (para. 5 A (i)) are similar, except that they are condensed in a single paragraph comprising the substance of sub-paragraphs (a) and (c), but omitting sub-paragraph (b).
[148b] The double negative formulation in this sentence (no hindrance) may be due to the fact that the provision was originally intended only for the distribution of *imported* products (cf. CAC Rep., 3rd Session, Appendix III: ". . . acceptance would imply an undertaking by the importing country not to hinder . . . distribution . . .").

The second type of acceptance (paragraph 4A(ii)) is defined as follows:

"(ii) *Target Acceptance*
Target acceptance means that the country concerned indicates its intention to accept the standard after a stated number of years and will meanwhile not hinder within its territorial jurisdiction the distribution of any sound products conforming with the standard by any legal or administrative provisions relating to the health of the consumer or to other food standard matters except for considerations of human, plant or animal health which are not specifically dealt with in the standard." [149]

Target acceptance is primarily, but by no means exclusively, intended for developing countries, which may be expected to raise the level of their food legislation so as to be able to apply the Codex standard fully within a number of years which they are free to determine when they declare their target acceptance; in view of the definition of target acceptance as a declaration of intention, it may be assumed that the period stated in the declaration may also be extended by a unilateral decision. On the other hand, the obligation to permit *ex nunc* the distribution of products that are in conformity with the standard would seem, *prima facie,* to preclude a combination of target acceptance and acceptance with minor deviations.

The third type of acceptance is defined as follows:

"(iii) *Acceptance with Minor Deviations*
Acceptance with minor deviations means that the country concerned gives full acceptance as defined in paragraph 4A(i) to the standard with the exception of minor deviations which are recognized as such by the Codex Alimentarius Commission; it being understood that a product complying with the standard as qualified by such minor deviations will be permitted to be distributed freely within the territorial jurisdiction of the country concerned. The country concerned will further include in its declaration of acceptance a statement of such deviations, the reasons for them, and also indicate:
(a) whether products fully conforming to the standard may be distributed freely within its territorial jurisdiction in accordance with paragraph 4A(i);
(b) whether it expects to be able to give full acceptance to the standard and, if so, when." [150]

This form of acceptance departs in three important respects from the "acceptance with a declaration of more rigorous requirements" under the Code of Principles concerning Milk and Milk Products. First, the deviations envisaged may imply less rigorous or more rigorous requirements, or possibly both. Secondly, the deviations must be minor and it is for the Commission to determine whether they can be recognized as such; in the event of a negative determination, the acceptance as such

---

[149] Target acceptance of general subject standards is also provided for, but para. 5 A (ii) does not stipulate any obligation regarding distribution of sound products meeting the standard.
[150] The parallel provision on general subject standards (para. 5 A (iii)) does not include the second clause of the first sentence ("it being understood . . ."), nor sub-paragraph (a).

253

is not valid. Thirdly, the accepting government is required to specify the reasons for the proposed deviation and to indicate whether products conforming to the standard may be distributed within the territory and whether (and when) it intends to give full acceptance to the standard.

It will be interesting to see what interpretation the Commission will give to the term "minor deviation" and what procedure it will apply to examine declarations involving deviations. As regards the substantive aspects, it could establish a set of criteria, perhaps on a tentative basis, for determining whether a given deviation is minor or not, or else proceed empirically and gradually evolve certain criteria in the light of experience. As regards procedure, it may be assumed that a preliminary examination of declarations will be made by the Secretariat, which might in some cases suggest to the government concerned to provide such additional explanations as may facilitate the Commission's determination as to the nature of the deviation. The declarations (and possible additional explanations) would presumably be circulated to the Members of the Commission, which would have to decide on the nature of the proposed deviation; it may, however, refer individual declarations to a subsidiary body (Codex Committee) for advice or require the Executive Committee to carry out a preliminary screening of declarations.[151]

Paragraph 4B, which concerns non-acceptance, reads as follows:
"A country which considers that it cannot accept the standard in any of the ways mentioned above should indicate:
(i) whether products conforming to the standard may be distributed freely within its territorial jurisdiction;
(ii) in what ways its present or proposed requirements differ from the standard, and, if possible, the reasons for these differences."[152]

The provisions of paragraph 4B (as well as 5B) contain the verb "should" (in French: *est invité à préciser*) in regard to the indication which non-accepting countries are to furnish. The Commission in fact "emphasized" that these provisions "were a request or exhortation to governments and did not imply any binding obligation on governments".[152a] It is nevertheless worth noting that governments unable to accept a standard are expected to submit a report, while no provision is made for governments accepting a standard to report on legislative or administrative measures taken or envisaged to give effect to the Codex standard within their territory. This does not mean that the questions relating to possible methods of facilitating the application of standards have been overlooked.

---

[151] The Committee on General Principles at its Third Session expressed the opinion that, for the time being, the Secretariat should submit to the Executive Committee, in appropriate cases, declarations of acceptance, and that the Executive Committee would present recommendations to the Commission which would have to examine the situation and decide on controversial questions. See Doc. ALINORM 69/9, para. 15.
[152] The corresponding provision on general subject standards (para. 5 B) omits subparagraph (i), but is otherwise identical in substance with para. 4 B.
[152a] CAC Rep., 6th Session, para. 15.

The need for adopting domestic legislative and administrative measures to adjust national laws and regulations to Codex standards, as well as enforcement measures for giving effect to such standards has been repeatedly mentioned in discussions of the Commission and its subsidiary bodies.[153] The Codex Committee on General Principles has suggested, and the Commission adopted, a text, as para. 4C (i) of the General Principles, which makes no specific reference to legislation nor to enforcement but contains some original and constructive ideas:

"A country which accepts a Codex Standard according to one of the provisions of 4A is responsible for the uniform and impartial application of the provisions of the Standard as they apply to all home-produced and imported products distributed within its territorial jurisdiction. In addition, the country should be prepared to offer advice and guidance to exporters and processors of products for export and promote understanding of and compliance with the requirements of importing countries which have accepted a Codex Standard according to one of the provisions of 4A." [153a]

While the "uniform and impartial application" undoubtedly represents an obligation with which the accepting country has to comply, the remaining provisions—as well as those of paragraph 4C (ii) quoted below—are in the nature of advice or exhortations.[153b]

As regards the question of ascertaining or ensuring compliance at the international level, no provision has so far been included in the General Principles with respect to domestically produced foods intended for distribution on the home market. Products exported are covered by para. 4C(ii) of the General Principles:

"Where, in an importing country, a product claimed to be in compliance with a Codex Standard is found not to be in compliance with that standard, whether in respect of the label accompanying the product or otherwise, the importing country should inform the competent authorities in the exporting country of all the relevant facts and in particular the details of the origin of the product in question (name and address of the exporter), if it is thought that a person in the exporting country is responsible for such non-compliance."

As may be seen from this paragraph, no sanctions in the proper sense are provided for; they may in fact not be necessary. In the sphere of domestic production and trade, enforcement might safely be left to the proper national, provincial and municipal authorities, while in international trade, the combination of the principle of *caveat emptor* and appropriately functioning food inspection services at customs clearance stations and ports may provide adequate safeguards. The Committee on General Prin-

---

[153] CAC Rep., 4th Session, para. 14; Docs. ALINORM 68/4, para. 11, PG/67/1, pp. 2-4; PG/68/4, *passim*; ALINORM 68/9, para. 10 and ALINORM 69/9, paras. 9, 11-13.

[153a] Paragraph 5 C, concerning general subject standards is practically identical with paragraph 4 C.

[153b] The reference cited in note 152 a *supra* is also applicable to paragraphs 4 C and 5 C.

ciples, in considering ways of dealing with sub-standard products, held *inter alia* that "an imported food below the standard can be returned to its country of origin, which can dispose of it in a way which suits it".[154]

Among the remedial measures that could be considered, mention was made of replacement of wrong or misleading labels, change in composition, and reconditioning; destruction or conversion into products for animal feeding have only been envisaged in respect of food which is found to be unfit for human consumption.[154a] While the General Principles are thus pointing to the methods of disposing of commodities that are not in conformity with Codex standards and leave the question of imposing sanctions entirely to national authorities, it may be noted that the recommended standard on labelling of prepackaged food contains a provision which is likely to help in identifying the responsible persons or entities and to facilitate civil, administrative or penal action.[154b]

After some hesitations, the Committee on General Principles recommended the addition of a provision on the withdrawal or amendment of acceptances, which was finally adopted by the Commission, as paragraph 6 of the General Principles:

"6. The withdrawal or amendment of acceptance of a Codex standard by a country shall be notified in writing to the Codex Alimentarius Commission's Secretariat who will inform all Member States and Associate Members of FAO and WHO of the notification and its date of receipt. The country concerned should provide the information required under paragraphs 4A(iii), 5A(iii), 4B or 5B above, whichever is appropriate. It should also give as long a notice of the withdrawal or amendment as is practicable.[155]

According to this provision, a State may not only withdraw the acceptance of a standard, but also deposit a declaration modifying the original declaration of acceptance and thus specify more (or less) stringent requirements, provided, of course, that these modifications are recognized by the Commission as "minor deviations". The last sentence of the paragraph represents a compromise between those delegations which favoured a fixed period of notice and those which felt that a notification should become effective immediately upon receipt by the Secretariat; the present version is intended to protect the interests of producers and exporters and, at the same time, to enable governments to take immediate measures when necessary in the interests of public health or for other cogent reasons.[155a]

---

[154] Doc. ALINORM 68/9, para. 9 (iv).
[154a] Doc. ALINORM 68/9, para. 9; CAC Rep., 5th Session, paras. 28-29.
[154b] Paragraph 3.4 prescribes that "the name and address of the manufacturer, packer, distributor, importer, exporter or vendor of the food shall be declared".
[155] Cf. Docs. PG/68/6; ALINORM 69/9, paras. 18-19; CAC Rep. 6th Session, para. 17.
[155a] For a more detailed study of various aspects of constitutional law and of public and private international law, cf. J. P. Dobbert: *"Le Codex Alimentarius—Vers une nouvelle méthode de réglementation internationale"* in *Annuaire Français de Droit International*, Vol. XV (1969), pp. 677-717.

256

(c) *Principles and Guidelines for the Disposal of Agricultural Surpluses*

The Codex Alimentarius has been examined in detail because, apart from its growing practical impact on food production and trade, it is largely virgin land for the international lawyer and will undoubtedly pose new legal problems even when those related to its formative stages which have been discussed above will have been resolved. Before concluding this paper, it may be desirable to describe the operation of a set of standards, which may serve to illustrate a different aspect of international "legislation" that is less evident in the Food Standards Program: the creation of a negotiation machinery to interpret and apply international standards which by themselves may be less strictly binding on accepting States than Codex standards.

(i) *Food Surplus and Shortages: Attempted Solutions*
Food shortages due to crop failures have been recurrent events in the history of mankind and famines had been accepted in many parts of the world, like plagues and wars, as one of those inevitable scourges threatening the community at certain intervals. Food surpluses in quantities creating serious economic problems were virtually unknown until large-scale, intensive and export-oriented production was developed in the twentieth century. Generally speaking, neither famine relief nor measures for surplus disposal were considered to be responsibilities of the international community, and only during and after World War II did food aid become an integral part of schemes developed either on a bilateral basis— mainly by the United States—such as Lend-Lease, European Recovery Program and the Agricultural Trade Development and Assistance Act of 1954, more commonly known as Public Law (P.L.) 480,[156] or according to a plurilatoral concept, such as the Colombo Plan [157] and the EEC scheme,[158] and—finally—multilateral programs carried out under UN auspices, in particular UNRRA,[159] UNICEF,[160] UNKRA [161] and the joint

---

[156] Among the numerous publications, including several country monographs, concerning the operation of the programs launched under this Law, particular reference should be made to the U.S. Government's *Semi-Annual Reports on Activities Carried out under Public Law 480*, published regularly since 1954. Cf. brief summary in Note 192 below.

[157] The Colombo Plan for Cooperative Economic Development in South and South East Asia provides for various types of assistance—including food aid—of a predominantly bilateral character within a multilaterally coordinated framework, Cf. *Annual Reports of the Colombo Plan Consultative Committee.*

[158] EEC: *L'aide alimentaire de la CEE aux pays en voie de développement—Problèmes posés et possibilités réelles.* Bruxelles, 1965.

[159] UNRRA: *The History of the United Natons Relief and Rehabilitation Administration* 3 vol. New York (Col. Univ. Press) 1950.

[160] UNICEF generally obtains its supplies on the open market. While UNICEF also accepts appropriate contributions in kind, including both food and non-food com-

UN/FAO World Food Program (WFP).[162] Leaving aside any political motivations which may have played a part in the launching of some of these programs, it is beyond doubt that they represent the first large-scale attempt to bridge the gap between food deficient and surplus producing countries in areas where this could not be achieved by normal trade.

It has been recognized for a long time that the existence, and methods of disposal, of agricultural surpluses are liable to have adverse effects on normal patterns of production and international trade. Short of such drastic measures as destruction of surplus stocks and strict limitation of quantities that may be produced (or acreage put under cultivation),[163] surpluses may be poured into commercial channels, with the attendant risk of market prices falling below remunerative production levels, or disposed of by way of grants or under concessional terms, which might, however, cause harmful interference with normal patterns of production and trade. None of the proposals formulated during the immediate post-war period for international action to resolve, among other international commodity problems, the questions concerning surplus disposal were accepted:[164] neither the World Food Board, proposed to the FAO Conference in 1946, nor the International Commodity Clearing House, considered by the FAO Conference in 1949, nor the International Trade Organization provided for in the Havana Charter ever saw the light of day. It may be noted in passing

---

modities, most projects involving the use of surplus commodities appear to be implemented in conjunction with other agencies disposing of surpluses, such as the World Food Program. Cf. *Reports of the UNICEF Executive Board*, June 1965 (doc. E/4083, Rev. 1), paras. 21, 189-192, and May 1966) (doc. E/4220, Rev. 1), para. 29.

[161] Cf. *Rehabilitation and Development of Agriculture, Forestry and Fisheries in South Korea.* FAO Mission Report for UNRRA (New York, 1954), p. 243.

[162] A comprehensive survey of literature on food aid generally and multilateral aid in particular may be found in *Food Aid: Selective Annotated Bibliography on Surplus Utilization for Economic Development* prepared by Elizabeth Henderson, Rome, 1965. Cf. also J. E. Carroz and J. P. Dobbert: *Le Programme Alimentaire Mondial*, in Annuaire français de droit international, 1966, pp. 336-376.

[163] Such measures would be inconsistent with the basic aims of FAO as laid down in the Preamble and Art. I of its Constitution (cf. pp. 212-213 above). It is significant that the Conference, in commending the problem of prevention of surpluses to the "serious attention of governments", mentioned the following possible measures: selective expansion of production, increased consumption, more efficient distribution, higher nutritional levels, coordinated development of agriculture, and the lessening of obstacles to trade" (Conf. Rep., 8th Session (1955), para. 48). In the Guiding Lines for Dealing with Agricultural Surpluses (discussed in Section (iii) below), it is stipulated that ". . . the adjustment of supply and demand should be sought in the expansion of consumption . . . rather than in the reduction of production" and that unavoidable output reductions ". . . should be brought about . . . through economic disincentives rather than through physical restrictions."

[164] For a detailed account of international initiatives during the first post war decade, see *Functions of a World Food Reserve—Scope and Limitations* (published in 1955 as FAO Commodity Policy Study No. 10, in response to UN General Assembly Resolution 827 (IX)), pp. 43-61.

that in spite of the apparent lack of success of these proposals, each of them has yielded certain "by-products" of a lasting nature.[165]

(ii) *The establishment of international norms*

In view of the unprecedented accumulation of surplus stocks in the years following the Korean war, the FAO Conference at its Seventh Session considered the difficulties encountered by world trade in absorbing supplies of certain commodities. The Conference stressed that current distribution difficulties should not be allowed to interfere with the pursuit of long-term agricultural development programs and that, in accordance with FAO's basic aims, courageous policies for increasing consumption—particularly in countries with consumption levels—should be regarded as the principal remedy for the absorption of excess supplies. In its Resolution No. 14/53, "Disposal of Agricultural Surpluses" the Conference noted however "the fears of many Member Nations that the disposal of surpluses might have harmful effects on the economies of many countries" and therefore recommended that excess stocks should be disposed of "in an orderly manner so as to avoid any undue pressure resulting in sharp falls of prices on world markets" and that in the case of disposal under special terms, "there should be an undertaking from both importing and exporting countries that such arrangements will be made without harmful interference with normal patterns of production and international trade". By the same Resolution, the Committee on Commodity Problems (CCP) was requested to formulate "the principles which should be observed by Member Governments" and to consider "the most suitable means of disposing of surpluses, including proposals for setting up consultative machinery through which the disposal of agricultural surpluses can be facilitated".

Pursuant to this Resolution, a Working Party on Surplus Disposal elaborated a series of nine Principles and of seven Guiding Lines [166] which

---

[165] As a result of a recommendation by the Preparatory Commission on World Food Board Problems, calling for the creation of a World Food Council, the FAO Council was established in 1947 to act as the main organ on world food questions between Conference sessions. In the absence of a sufficient number of ratifications, the Havana Charter never entered into force; however, a number of its provisions were incorporated in the General Agreement on Tariffs and Trade (GATT) and Chapter VI, containing a set of rules and procedures for the conclusion and operation of commodity agreements has not only been applied in connection with such agreements, but also left its mark on the terms of reference of the FAO Council (cf. GRO XXIV.1 (e)), in conjunction with ECOSOC Resolution 30 (IV) of 28 March 1947) of the Interim Coordinating Committee on Commodity Problems (ICCICA) and, many years later, the United Nations Conference on Trade and Development (UNCTAD). While the FAO Conference, at its Fifth Session (1949) rejected the proposals for an International Commodity Clearing House, it did establish a Committee on Commodity Problems, whose range of influence has grown over the years, *inter alia*, through the establishment of various Commodity Study Groups and other subsidiary bodies, such as the CSD.

[166] This report (doc. CCP 54/2) analyzes in considerable detail the numerous economic

were recommended to Governments by the CCP[167] and endorsed by the Council in Resolution No. 2/20; the CCP further requested the Director-General "to transmit to Member Governments... the... statement of "Principles of Surplus Disposal Recommended by FAO", asking [them] to inform him... whether they are prepared to adhere to these Principles" ... and drew "the attention of Member Governments to the ... Guiding Lines formulated by the CCP..."[168] The distinction between these two instruments as regards binding effect is brought out even more clearly by Conference Resolution No. 11/59, which, after "concluding that the FAO Principles and Guiding Lines are as adequate today as they were when first developed", requested the Director-General "to invite Member Nations which have not already done so to signify their *agreement to adhere to the FAO Principles* and to *take the Guiding Lines into account*". (emphasis added)

No special form is prescribed for notification of adherence, nor is provision made for dealing with reservations. To date, some 50 countries, including all major exporters and importers of agricultural commodities,[169] have notified their adherence, mostly in the form of Notes Verbales or letters from the Ministry of Foreign Affairs, the Ministry responsible for agriculture or trade, or the permanent representative accredited to FAO; none of these notifications have been accompanied by any reservations.

(iii) *Structure and Scope*

The *Principles* are subdivided into three main sections, i.e. General Principles (1-3), Principles Governing Sales on Concessional Terms (4-7), and Principles Governing Sales of Government Stocks in Exceptional Volume, or at an Exceptionally Rapid Rate (8-9).

The General Principles insist on the need, already stressed in Conference Resolution No. 14/53, to raise levels of consumption, to dispose of surplus stocks in an orderly manner so as to avoid sharp falls in prices,[170]

---

and social problems connected with surpluses and possible disposal measures and safeguards.

[167] Doc. CL 20/17, paras. 12-21. The CCP stressed the importance of surplus utilization for the acceleration of development programs (Res. No. 2 (23)) and the desirability of close cooperation with IBRD (Res. No. 3 (23)); these views were subsequently endorsed by the Conference in Conf. Res. No. 7/55.

[168] *Ibid.* CCP Res. No. 1 (23). The Principles and Guiding Lines, together with the texts of the principal resolutions and an "Explanatory Note by the Director-General" have been issued in a small FAO publication: *Disposal of Agricultural Surpluses— Principles recommended by FAO*, 2nd edition, Rome 1963.

[169] The include, *inter alia*, Argentina, Brazil, Canada, Denmark, France, Federal Republic of Germany, India, Japan, Netherlands, New Zealand, Pakistan, United Kingdom, United States.

[170] The objective of a stabilization of prices in international trade cannot, of course, be attained by a control of surplus disposal measures alone. Thus, the various commodity agreements and arrangements have created a complex system of import and export

and to avoid harmful interference with normal patterns of production and trade in connection with transactions under special terms.[171]

The central section, which lays down the Principles governing transactions on concessional terms, first reiterates the concept of "additionality" and defines the criteria to be taken into account in ascertaining whether a proposed transaction may constitute some danger of displacement of commercial sales of identical or related commodities;[172] it then spells out the manner in which these criteria are to be applied to the most important categories of transactions on concessional terms, i.e. for development aid, for special welfare distribution programs, and for emergency relief.[173] In view of the relative rigidity of the criteria and in recognition of the need for—and beneficial effect of—food aid, implicit allowance has been made for the possibility of disregarding them in cases where the "advantages to countries benefiting from special disposal measures" are found to outweigh "the possible harm done to other countries". Finally, this section of the Principles lays down certain provisions regarding assurances against resales or trans-shipments to other countries and against exports by the beneficiary country of supplies of identical or related commodities.[174]

---

quotas, minimum and maximum prices and stocks, trade terms and price support policies.

[171] While the main emphasis had initially no doubt been placed on the protection of international trade, the need for avoiding adverse effects on the price structure of agricultural products in countries receiving surplus commodities has been increasingly recognized. The establishment of national buffer stocks in recipient countries by means of surplus commodities had been a recurrent theme both in the United Nations and in FAO. Cf. UN General Assembly Res. 827 (IX), 1025 (XI), 1496 (XV) and the comprehensive report on *National Food Reserve Policies in Underdeveloped Countries* (FAO Commodity Policy Studies No. 11), Rome 1958. Although it was recognized that such reserves would be useful for stabilizing supply and demand, for relieving foreign exchange difficulties of food deficient developing countries and for meeting emergency situations, studies and experimental projects undertaken in various countries have shown that the existing technical, economic and administrative infrastructure is generally not adapted for an efficient operation of large-scale food reserves.

[172] These criteria include, *inter alia*, the exporter's normal share in the region's imports of the commodity concerned, the share of the exports on special terms in relation to the total imports of the same commodity in the region concerned, the degree of importance of trade in the commodity to the economy of the exporter and to the economies of competing exporters, the character and extent of concessions offered, possible adverse effects on commercial market prices and on the stability or desirable expansion of production and trade in the importing and exporting countries. All these aspects were re-examined in detail in connection with the recent review of the terms of reference of the CSD, where the definition of the so-called "usual market requirements" (UMR) caused considerable difficulties. Cf. Note 217 *infra*.

[173] It should be noted that the above categories are based on the purpose of the end-use of the commodities (rather than on the legal or economic character of the transaction). Cf. Note 185 *infra*.

[174] Agreements concluded by the US Government under P.L. 480 contain a standard clause prohibiting resale and trans-shipments. Pursuant to Article 40 (3) of the International Coffee Agreement, 1968, deliveries to certain scheduled countries with a low

261

The last two Principles deal with large-scale releases on foreign markets of commodities held in government stockpiles; governments proposing to undertake such releases "should, whenever practicable, consult with other countries interested in the possible effects of such transactions."[175]

Four of the seven *Guiding Lines* are concerned with measures to prevent the accumulation of cumbersome surpluses, while the remaining three deal with additional factors to be taken into account in considering surplus disposal measures; these include policies of full employment and economic development,[176] the needs of economies of less developed countries largely dependent on export receipts for a limited number of primary products,[177] and problems concerning the balance of payments.[178] In weighing the advantages against possible harmful effects of individual transactions under concessional terms, these factors, while only included in the Guiding Lines, may be just as relevant as those specified in the Principles, either generally,[179] or in relation to specific types of transactions, i.e.

---

consumption level are not chargeable to the export quota, subject to the provision of appropriate guarantees against re-export to a third country not so scheduled; sanctions are provided for in the event of a breach of such guarantees.

[175] These Principles have been reiterated, in substance, in a decision adopted by the Contracting Parties of GATT in March 1955 (cf. GATT, *Basic Instruments and Selected Documents*, 3rd Supplement, Geneva, 1955); even in a time of diminishing surplus stocks of important commodities (e.g. grains), they remain entirely valid: it appears that complaints in recent years have been directed less against transactions on concessional terms (i.e. food aid) than against the adverse effects of excess stocks and forms of trading that are regarded as harmful to the interests of countries heavily dependent on agricultural exports. Cf. *Food Aid and Other Forms of Utilization of Agricultural Surpluses* (FAO Commodity Studies No. 15, Rome 1964), Summary and Conclusions, paras. (vii), (xiii).

[176] This aspect has gained particular importance under Title II ("Food for Wages") of P.L. 480, and, most prominently, in the implementation of WFP projects.

[177] The use of the productive potential of food exporting developing countries under an expended multilateral food aid program has been advocated by UNCTAD (Recommendation A.II.6 of Final Act of the first Conference, Geneva 1964) and has been examined under a study program on multilateral food aid, called for by General Assembly Resolution 2096 (XX). Cf. also subsequent Resolutions and documents, in particular G.A. Res. 2462 (XXIII), docs. E/4538 and C 69/55, submitted to ECOSOC and FAO Conference, respectively.

[178] In food deficient countries, the provision of food aid (e.g. in the form of sales for local currency or of outright grants) may, at least temporarily, have a beneficial effect on the recipient country's balance of payments to the extent that it replaces commercial imports. The need to allow for a reduction of such imports in order to avoid an excessive drain on scarce foreign currency reserves has also been recognized by certain commodity agreements (Sugar Agreement, 1958, Art. 26; Wheat Trade Convention, 1967, Art. 12), which provide for the possibility of adjusting import obligations, subject to consultation with the International Monetary Fund.

[179] Principle 5 stipulates that "In weighing advantages . . . against the possible harm . . . account must be taken of the relationship of possible sacrifices to the economic capacity of the countries concerned, and in particular of the effects of such sacrifices on their rates of development."

development aid,[180] welfare program,[181] and emergency relief.[182]

There can be no doubt that these Principles and Guiding Lines, and the related studies which preceded and followed their adoption have had effects going well beyond the limits of surplus disposal: they have not only been invoked in bilateral and multilateral consultations between governments in relation to commodity agreements and arrangements, but have paved the way for the development of both bilateral and multilateral food aid programs, in particular the World Food Program in whose General Regulations the Surplus Disposal Principles have been incorporated by reference;[183] they are also reflected in commodity agreements, perhaps most significantly in the International Grains Arrangement, 1967, which has been adopted in August 1967 and came into force on 1 July 1968. In fact, Art. 24 of the Wheat Trade Convention[184] not only requires the contracting parties (referred to as "Member Countries") "to conduct any concessional transactions on grains in such a way as to avoid harmful interference with normal patterns of production and international commercial trade" and to "undertake appropriate measures to ensure that concessional transactions are additional to commercial sales which could reasonably be anticipated in the absence of such transactions;" it specifically provides that "such measures shall be consistent with the Principles

---

[180] According to Principle 6 (1) (b), possible dangers of displacement of commercial sales (by programs for development aid) "will have to be weighed against the advantages resulting from such programs to the receiving country and to the world at large".

[181] Under Principle 6 (2) (b), the danger of displacement is to be weighed against "the character and extent of the benefits resulting from the contribution to the welfare program".

[182] In relation to emergency relief, the relevant factors are, according to Principle 6 (3) (c), "the volume of relief and the character and extent of the concessions offered, and their probable effect on the total commercial imports of the stricken country and on the trade of competing exporters."

[183] WFP General Regulations—as revised pursuant to General Assembly Resolution 2095 (XX) and FAO Conf. Res. No. 4/65—paras. 13, 19-21. *World Food Programme Basic Documents*, Third Edition revised March 1966, pp. 20, 27. Cf. also D. A. Fitzgerald: *Operational and Administrative Problems of Food Aid* (WFP Studies No. 4, Rome 1965), pp. 19-22, and J. E. Carroz and J. P. Dobbert: *op. cit.*, pp. 359-361.

[184] The International Grains Arrangement 1967 (Doc. TD/WHEAT.4/1; UN Sales No. E. 68.II.D.5), negotiated under the joint auspices of the International Wheat Council and UNCTAD, consists of a Wheat Trade Convention and a Food Aid Convention. The latter would seem to constitute a novelty both in the field of international conventions and as a method of "surplus" disposal. It lists 11 countries and the European Economic Community, which are required to supply specified quantities of grains—or the equivalent thereof in cash—amounting to a total of 4.5 million tons annually; in principle, 25% of cash contributions are to be used for the purchase of grains from developing countries. A Food Aid Committee, established by Article VI and consisting of the Contracting Parties, is required to supervise the implementation of the Convention.

of Surplus Disposal and Guiding Lines recommended by the Food and Agriculture Organization of the United Nations." [185]

(iv) *The Consultative Machinery*

The Principles and Guiding Lines are primarily intended for application by governments disposing of, or receiving, surplus supplies, but to facilitate their application, the CCP Working Party which drew them up proposed, and the CCP and the Council approved, the establishment of consultative machinery in the form of a standing Consultative Sub-Committee on Surplus Disposal, generally referred to as "CSD". Membership was to be open "to all FAO Member Nations who wish to contribute actively, and on a regular basis, to the carrying out of the Sub-Committee's mandate". Moreover, "other FAO Member Nations could attend meetings of the Sub-Committee as observers, with the right to participate fully in... discussions on any subject in which they are particularly interested."[186]

The terms of reference of the CSD were originally defined as follows: [186a]

(1) to keep under review developments in the disposal of agricultural surpluses, and to assist FAO Member Nations in developing suitable means of surplus disposal;
(2) to provide a forum for the discussion of proposals, programs, policies or transactions of Member Governments for the disposal of agricultural surpluses in the light of the principles recommended by the Seventh Conference Session and in the Report

---

[185] The Contracting Parties are thus legally bound to apply these Principles, even if they have not adhered to them by means of a notification to the Director-General of FAO. It may be noted that special transactions" (i e, all transactions other than commercial purchases) are defined, both generally and by categories of transactions, in Art. 3 (2) of the Convention. These categories include sales on concessional credit terms or on the basis of a tied loan, sales for (non-transferrable) currency of the importing country, sales under trade agreements with special payment or clearing arrangements, barter transactions and gifts. Some of these transactions which are basically commercial purchase but comprise certain concessional elements have been characterized as "grey area" transactions and carefully studied by the CSD in recent years.

[186] CCP Rep., 23rd Session (1954), para. 34. The CCP did not follow the Working Party's proposal for membership of selected Member Nations (Doc. CCP 54/2).

[186a] In the course of a recent review of the terms of reference and procedures of CSD, paragraph (1) remained unchanged but paragraphs (2) and (3) were extensively revised and supplemented by detailed provisions on consultation and notification procedure and by a catalogue of transactions to which these procedures should apply. On the other hand, national "proposals, policies and programs" were removed from paragraph (2), as experience has shown that there is considerable reluctance on the part of governments to bring before an international forum proposals intended for national action, and—as the CSD formulated it—"it would be unrealistic to suppose that prospective legislation could be the subject of open debate and criticism by an international consultative body" (cf. doc. cited in Note 197 *infra*). Nevertheless, since policies and programs are frequently reflected in individual transactions which are the subject of consultations, the application and interpretation of policies and programs will undoubtedly continue to be discussed in the CSD.

of the CCP Working Party on Surplus Disposal, and to promote the observance of these principles;

(3) to report periodically to the CCP, it being understood that copies of its reports and summary records of its proceedings, including any conclusions, should be circulated to FAO Member Nations as soon as possible.

The CSD, which has been meeting in Washington regularly, at monthly intervals, ever since its establishment in 1954, has often had to interpret not only the Principles and Guiding Lines, but also its own terms of reference and the procedures which might be conducive to rendering its deliberations more effective.

When the CSD, following a request by the CCP, endorsed by the Conference,[187] reviewed its terms of reference and procedures in 1958, it first endeavoured to clarify and define some of the terms used in the Principles and Guiding Lines and its own terms of reference. It found that it was not possible to arrive at a generally acceptable and precise definition of "surplus" but also reached the conclusion that for the purpose of its work such a definition was unnecessary; however, it did define the term "surplus disposal" [188] and gave interpretations of a number of other terms relevant for determining the scope of its functions; from there, it proceeded to an examination of the consultative machinery and of the "obstacles and deficiencies which arise in carrying out... [its] terms of reference" [189] and eventually drew up a number of recommendations for "strengthening the foundations for consultation",[190] which were subsequently endorsed, subject to certain qualifications, by the Committee on Commodity Problems.[191]

With respect to the first task in para. 1 of its terms of reference, viz. "to keep under review developments in the disposal of agricultural surpluses", the CSD has for many years been concerned principally with the surplus disposal program of the United States, administered under P.L.480, not only because it represented by far the largest single and probably the most differentiated program,[192] but also because the United States was one

---

[187] Conf. Rep., 9th Session (1957), paras. 26-32; Conf. Res. No. 6/57.

[188] "Surplus disposal of an agricultural commodity in international trade is an export operation (other than a sale covered by an international commodity agreement) arising from the existence or expectation of abnormal stocks, and made possible by the grant of special or concessional terms through government intervention" (Doc. CCP 58/7, para. 18).

[189] *Ibid.*, paras. 4-16.

[190] *Ibid.*, paras. 17-28, 40-42.

[191] CCP Rep., 30th Session (1958), paras. 61-69.

[192] Supplies made available under P.L. 480 represent roughly 30 per cent of total U.S. agricultural commodity exports. The Act originally contained three titles. Title I authorized the sale of surplus agricultural commodities against payment in the currency of the recipient country. Funds accruing from such sales are partly used for financing common defence programs, for local expenditures of the U.S. Government, and for loans to private enterprise, but the main share has consistently been ear-

265

of the few countries to declare "official" surpluses in the sense that sales, gifts and barter transactions made under P.L.480 were restricted to those commodities declared by the Secretary of Agriculture to be in surplus. The situation has changed, to some extent, in recent years, as the emphasis gradually shifted from the search for constructive uses for "burdensome surpluses" towards international action designed to relieve hunger and malnutrition and to use food aid as capital input in development projects or support of longer term development plans; this might require the spreading of the cost of food aid programs among exporting and importing developed countries,[193] the better utilization of the productive capacity of food-exporting developing countries [194] and eventually even the deliberate utilization of excess agricultural production capacity in industrialized countries.[195] While these problems and the major policy issues go well beyond the terms of reference of the CSD,[196] the evolution of intergovernmental attitudes was clearly highlighted—not to say revealed—by a CSD study in 1963,[197] prepared as part of its function "to keep under review developments in the disposal of agricultural surpluses."

Apart from the trend just described, there were two further developments affecting trade in agricultural and related commodities in a manner which had a bearing on the functions exercised by the CSD: first, the extension

marked for grants or loans to recipient governments, principally for economic development purposes. Title II provided for grants of surplus commodities from stocks held by the Commodity Credit Corporation (CCC) for famine relief and other emergencies and —since 1960—also for economic development; contributions to WFP are likewise financed under this title. CCC-held commodities may be used, under Title III, (a) for grants to voluntary agencies carrying our welfare activities (including school feeding programs) both in the United States and overseas, and (b) for bartering certain categories of materials and equipment, mostly by means of contracts with private U S firms. Title IV, which was added in 1959, provides for long-term credit sales (up to 20 years) of surplus commodities by the U.S. Government and—under an amendment of 1962—also by private firms. For more details, cf. D. A. Fitzgerald, op. cit. (Note 183 above) pp. 1-15 and FAO Commodity Studies No. 15 (cited in Note 175 above), pp. 9-11, and sources indicated there.

[193] The first important steps in this direction have already been taken, in the form of the World Food Program and—on an even larger scale, though limited to grains— the Food Aid Convention; contributions under these schemes are, however, not made exclusively by developed countries.

[194] Cf. S. R. Sen: Implications of the UNCTAD and Argentine Proposals for the Modification of the World Food Programme, doc. WFP/IGC: 8/15 (August 1965).

[195] This trend is reflected, inter alia, in the "Food for Peace Act" of 1966, amending P.L. 480 (cf. declaration of U.S. representative in the FAO Council, CL 47/P.V.7, paras. 13-17) and in General Assembly Resolutions 2096 (XX) and 2155 (XXI).

[196] Apart from the UN itself and its "total facilities . . . including UNCTAD, UNDP and WFP", the Resolution for the Program of Studies on Multilateral Food Aid (A/Res. 2096 (XX)) specifically enumerates FAO, IBRD, IMF and GATT among the agencies that are to participate in the Study Program.

[197] Doc. CCP 63/20: "Changing Attitudes Toward Agricultural Surpluses." The Conference appears to have recognized the significance of the findings and conclusions set out in the Study (Conf. Rep., 12th Session (1963), paras. 63, 64).

266

in scope and diversification of the so-called "grey area" transactions, which comprise both commercial and concessional features; secondly, the establishment of machinery within the framework of other intergovernmental bodies, with the task of keeping under review surplus situations and food aid programs. In the light of these developments, it became increasingly difficult to ascertain (1) the extent to which Member Nations that had accepted the Principles were in fact observing them; (2) the scope to be attributed to the obligations concerning notification and consultation with regard to the various types of concessional transactions; (3) the extent of duplication or overlapping as between the intergovernmental bodies dealing with surplus disposal and/or food aid.

In January 1968, the CSD set up a Working Group, consisting of 8 Members (governments) and the Chairman and Vice-Chairman of the CSD, to carry out a reappraisal of the CSD functions. The report produced by the Working Group [198] not only contains a wealth of information but a searching analysis of the problems of definitions and procedures and of various questions regarding the authority and functions of CSD in relation to its parent body, Member Governments, and other organizations. While it did not offer any definite solutions, it identified the policy, economic and legal issues which would require consideration by CCP and possibly by FAO's Governing Bodies, as it "must be clearly recognized that... its [the CSD's] effectiveness is in danger of withering away unless certain critical issues are resolved." [199]

The CCP, after a preliminary discussion,[200] established a Working Group, which drew up at its first session, a catalogue of 19 transactions with concessional features [201] and, at its second session, examined all issues exhaustively, reached agreement on nearly all of them, and submitted a detailed report and recommendations to the CCP.[202] From a methodological point of view, the Working Group followed an inductive rather than deductive approach: instead of trying to redefine the somewhat elusive concept of "surplus disposal" and "food aid", it specified the types of transactions to which the notification and consultation procedures should apply, irrespective of whether the commodities concerned might be considered "surplus" or not. This has been characterized as "a major step

---

[198] Doc. CCP/CSD/68/44—CCP 68/7/2: "Role of Sub-Committee (CSD) in light of Current and Prospective Developments in Agricultural Surpluses and Food Aid." As stated in the transmittal letter written by its Chairman, the CSD, in "accepting this Report for transmission to the CCP ... noted that this did not commit Governments represented on it to agreement with any specific recommendations of the Report..."
[199] *Ibid.*, para. 98.
[200] Doc. CCP 68 : 43/PV-1, p. 5; PV-6, pp. 3-14; PV-7, pp. 1-17. The preliminary conclusions of the CCP were submitted to the FAO Council in Doc. CL 51/4 and generally endorsed by the Council. Cf. Docs. CL 51/PV-6, pp. 30-33; PV-7, pp. 1-26; CL. Rep., 51st Session, para. 39.
[201] Doc. CCP : FU/CSD 69/8.
[202] Doc. CCP : 69/13/1.

forward in this area." [203] Of the 19 categories of "near commercial and extra-commercial transactions" listed by the Working Group, 13 were selected as falling within the scope of CSD consultations. They include donations of commodities for free distribution or sale to consumers in the recipient country (1, 2); monetary grants by an exporting country to an importing or supplying country or to an intergovernmental organization for the procurement of commodities (in the exporting or supplying country or on the open market) to be delivered to the recipient country (3-5); commodities transferred through WFP (6); sales for non-convertible or partly convertible currency (or goods or services) placed at the disposal of the contributing country (7-8); loans of commodities repayable in kind (9); sales based on long or medium term and/or concessional interest rate credits or loans (10, 11), gifts and sales with provisions tying imports under special terms with commercial imports from the contributing country (12, 13). As regards sales at reduced prices (14) and subsidized exports and imports (15), the Working Group found that the notification and consultation procedures carried out under Article XVI, in conjunction with Articles XXII and XXIII, of the General Agreement on Tariffs and Trade, while perhaps not fully satisfactory in all respects, should not be unnecessarily duplicated.[204] Various views were expressed as to the commercial or concessional nature of barter transactions (16, 17) and non-convertible currency clearing transactions (18) and to the need for subjecting them to reporting and consultation procedures under GATT or CSD; the fact that they were not included in the "catalogue", would seem to indicate preference for consultations on concessional features of this type within GATT, without necessarily precluding consideration within the ambit of CSD.[205] Finally, in considering other government sponsored transactions interfering with normal commercial trade (19), the Working Group generally agreed that the catalogue of transactions it had drawn up was not exclusive and that the CSD should be enabled to propose to the CCP the addition of new categories falling within the scope of the Principles on Surplus Disposal to which reporting and consultation procedures might be extended.[206]

After extensive deliberations, both the CCP and the Council endorsed the catalogue drawn up by the Working Group, listing the categories of transactions to which the notification and consultation procedure is to apply;[207] it was included, in the form of an annex, in the Resolutions adopt-

---

[203] Doc. C 69/I/PV-3, p. 3 (Statement by Director of Commodities and Trade Division).
[204] Doc. CCP: 69/13/1, paras. 42-46, Annex I ("GATT Obligations and Procedures for Notification and Consultation").
[205] Ibid., paras. 47-49.
[206] Ibid., para. 50.
[207] Cf. Docs. CL 53/PV-1, pp. 3-25; PV-4, pp. 3-6; PV-6, pp. 5-10. With respect to

ed by the two bodies;[208] both Resolutions also endorsed the proposal that the catalogue might be subsequently modified by decision of the CCP.

The machinery for consultation and notification operated under CSD auspices during the first 15 years has undoubtedly produced remarkable results, but while substantive criteria had been covered in the Principles and Guidelines, the procedure had a somewhat tenuous basis. No specific provision was made for advance notification of proposed concessional transactions; the CSD had only recommended that "whenever possible, Member Governments should inform the Sub-Committee in advance of proposed changes in policy on surplus disposal."[209] With respect to prior consultations, the recommendation had been of a distinctly hortatory nature:

"There should be agreement in principle for consultation on a bilateral basis between countries exporting surpluses and interested third-party countries before arrangements are concluded with recipient countries and also during the currency of a program. Importing countries would be expected to consult with interested exporting countries if requested to do so." [210]

The new procedure as approved by the CCP and slightly amended by the Council is couched in more definite terms:

"Before carrying out any transaction in agricultural commodities* of a type mentioned in the Catalogue of Transactions, and taking into account the special situations covered in paras. (3), (4) and (5), below, the supplying country shall:
(a) undertake bilateral consultations with countries substantially interested by reason of their exports of the commodity concerned to the recipient country;
(b) notify the CSD of the main features of the proposed transaction in order to

---

some transactions, certain governments reserved their position: see Doc. CCP 69/28; CL 53/4, pp. 24-25.

[208] CCP Resolution No. 2/44; Council Resolution 1/53.

[209] This recommendation and other recommendations concerning procedures were laid down in para. 40 of the "Report on Consultative Machinery and Consultation" (doc. CCP 58/7 Add. 1); they were subsequently included in the "Report on the Operation and Adequacy of the FAO Principles of Surplus Disposal and Guiding Lines" (doc. C 59/10) and endorsed, in substance, by the Conference (Conf. Rep., 10th Session (1959), paras. 93-96).

[210] With reference to the first clause, the CCP interpreted the term *agreement in principle* as indicating the desirability of prior consultations, it being understood that when this should not be feasible, "countries should take the earliest steps to discuss the arrangements with third-party countries" (CCP Rep., 30th Session (1958), para. 66). As regards the second clause, the Council held "that the Governments of countries importing surplus goods on concessional terms were not under any obligation to take steps for prior consultations on such contracts with third countries" (CL Rep., 29th Session (1958), para. 32). It is interesting to note that the CSD recommendation and— at least implicitly—the above two qualifications have found their way into the Wheat Trade Convention 1967, Art. 24 (3) of which reads as follows:
"Member countries when engaging in concessional export transactions shall consult with exporting member countries whose commercial sales may be affected by such transactions, to a maximum possible extent before such arrangements are concluded with recipient countries."
* Excluding transactions involving small quantities of seed and planting material supplied to developing countries.

provide other countries directly interested in exports of the commodity an opportunity for bilateral consultations, it being understood that this would not result in any lengthening of the total period of consultation." [211]

The "special situations" referred to in the introductory phrase concern in the first place transactions effected through intergovernmental organizations that are already subject to special consultative rules (e.g. WFP) or whose operations are unlikely to interfere with normal production and trade patterns (e.g. UNICEF, UNRWA); here, no obligations are incumbent on donor countries. *Ex post facto* notification only is required in the case of emergency transactions and government to government transactions of relatively small size and not involving sales in local markets of recipient countries. Periodical notifications with a view to possible bilateral consultations are required in respect of programs and projects carried out through private charitable organizations.

The idea of reciprocity has in a sense always been implied in the consultation and notification procedures: a country which made regular use of the CSD machinery for its surplus or food aid transactions and took into account objections or suggestions presented by other governments could reasonably expect that its own objections or suggestions would be taken into consideration, whilst a country which failed to do either of these things could not rely on such expectations. In the new procedure, the concept of reciprocity has been explicitly laid down, preceding all other provisions:

"All reporting and consultative obligations and procedures shall be based on the principle of reciprocity among Member Nations and Associate Members."

The principle of reciprocity would, however, appear to apply mainly to relations between donor countries; the position of developing countries has been safeguarded under the new procedure, in the sense that, in their capacity as recipient countries, they are not required to take any steps for prior consultation and reporting and should not be denied, on account of the application of that procedure, food aid that may be urgently needed by them.[212]

In addition, special consideration is to be given to interests of developing countries in local production, marketing, and export.[213]

---

[211] CL Rep., 53rd Session, pp. 4-5.

[212] "The Committee reaffirmed that, as agreed by the Council at its Twenty-Ninth Session, the governments of recipient countries continued to be under no obligation to take steps for prior consultation or reporting. The Committee agreed that, in keeping with the spirit of the FAO Principles of Surplus Disposal and Guiding Lines, the recommended procedures for consultations and reporting should not constitute an obstacle to, or cause undue delay in, the provision of food aid which was urgently required by a developing deficit country."

[213] "The Committee agreed that special consideration should be given to the interests of developing exporting countries which depended heavily on export earnings from agricultural commodities. It also agreed that special consideration should be given to the safeguarding of local production and markets of developing countries."

270

With respect to possible overlapping or competition between the CSD procedures and those instituted by other Organizations or under international conventions, mention has been made of GATT, in connection with the catalogue of transactions; a delineation of responsibilities should not present particular difficulties but since a given transaction may include some features of interest to GATT and others falling within the terms of reference of CSD, one cannot exclude the possibility of consultations taking place—successively or even simultaneously— in both fora. Similar situations may arise under Article 43 of the Sugar Agreement, 1968, which enables the Sugar Council to determine the conditions governing donations of sugar by exporting members which "shall provide, *inter alia,* for prior consultations and adequate safeguards to normal patterns of trade;" members are required to notify the Council of donations, and other members whose interests may be affected thereby may request consideration of the matter by the Council. Special or concessional transactions under Articles 3 or 24 of the Wheat Trade Agreement, 1967, are subject to reporting and consultations within the framework of the International Wheat Council, in accordance with he provisions of Article 16 of that Agreement and Rules issued thereunder, while donations under the Food Aid Convention have to be reported to the Food Aid Committee; it is interesting to note that some countries report their donations—if handled on a bilateral basis— to both the Food Aid Committee and the CSD, while others take the view that where consultation machinery has been established under a commodity agreement, transactions in the commodities concerned should remain outside the ambit of the CSD.[214] In the field of dairy products, where important initiatives have recently been taken by various organizations, including GATT, FAO, and EEC, developments appear to be in a state of flux.

In view of the rather complex situation just described, it was obviously not easy to find a common denominator for the various currents and cross-currents, and the paragraph included in the new CSD procedures has some features of a Salomonic sentence:

"The Committee recognized that in relation to the transactions it had identified, member Nations may also have incurred obligations in other organizations and under international agreements, and that nothing recommended above in any way diminished these obligations or commitments. Likewise, nothing recommended above detracted from the generality of the FAO Principles of Surplus Disposal."

One issue on which it has not been possible to reach agreement in the Working Group or the CCP is the procedure for establishing the usual marketing requirements in transactions subject to prior consultations. The term "usual marketing requirements" (UMR) has been defined as a requirement that the normal level of commercial imports be maintained by a recipient country, in addition to any concessional imports of the same

---

[214] Cf. CCP 68 : 43/PV-7, pp. 13, 8.

or a related commodity. This concept appears to be generally in keeping with the principle of "additionality" discussed above. Difficulties arise where the UMR is to be tied to commercial imports from the donor country ("tied UMR"); the same applies where provision is made for additional commercial imports from the donor country in the event of exports by the recipient country of the same or related commodities ("tied offsets"). Tied sales have for many years been an established practice of the United States Government in the implementation of P.L.480, although similar methods of protecting commercial exports have undoubtedly also been applied by other countries. Apart from the question of principle, the questions relating to the most appropriate and fairest methods of calculating and negotiating the UMR have given rise to a number of discussions and studies [215] which have contributed to a clarification of some important points. With a view to resolving the questions still in suspense, the CCP decided to ask the Director-General to invite further government comments and to reconvene the Working Party prior to the next session of the CCP (scheduled for Autumn 1970) and charged the Chairman of the Working Party (acting as Rapporteur) with the task of conducting informal consultations in the intervening period.[216] The Council accordingly requested the CCP "to finalize this part of its recommendations at its Forty-Fifth Session." [217]

Having examined the consultation and notification procedure, we may now return to the terms of reference of the CSD, the revision of which was part and parcel of the review of the negotiating machinery operating under CSD auspices. As was stated above,[218] the general review and advisory function described in the first paragraph of the terms of reference has not been modified. Paragraph 2, however, has been brought into line with the new procedures approved by the CCP; it now reads as follows:

"(b) to provide a forum for *consultations and notifications,* including *usual marketing requirements,* of transactions of Member Nations and Associate Members of the Organization of the *types in the attached catalogue* and any *other types of transactions* as may subsequently *agreed by CCP,* in the light of the Guiding Lines and Principles of Surplus Disposal endorsed by the Conference;" (emphasis added).

This paragraph contains four distinctly new elements: First, it specifically mentions "consultations and notifications," in line with the terminology used for describing the duties to be assumed by Member Nations in re-

---

[215] Cf. Report on "Tried Sales", doc. CCP 69/13/3, and CCP Rep., 44th Session (1969); doc. CL 53/4, paras. 153-162.

[216] Doc. CL 53/4 Add. 1, paras. 7-9.

[217] CL Rep., 53rd Session, para. 13. While recognizing that the CCP resolution setting forth the new procedure could not be fully operative until the UMR issue had been resolved, the Council noted that transactions involving UMR provisions were currently being notified to the CSD, which "had a continuing responsibility to review certain questions relating to [UMR], in particular transactions involving 'tied sales'." *Ibid.,* para. 14.

[218] See Note 186 a *supra.*

spect of surplus disposal and food aid transactions; these terms are much more precise than the term "discussion" hitherto used. Secondly, the inclusion of the UMR, while still provisional, pending a final clarification of the issues discussed above, tends to indicate a more or less general acceptance of the fundamental concept of maintaining a certain stability in the commercial trade patterns established, as far as possible, on objective and ascertainable criteria. Thirdly, the functions of the CSD in this field are tied to a catalogue of 13 types of transactions approved by the CCP. Finally, the possibility of modifying the catalogue, without any change in the terms of reference as such has been envisaged.

For the third paragraph of the terms of reference, the Working Party presented three alternative versions,[219] two of which still maintained the concept of a "forum for discussion of proposals, programmes, policies" of Member Nations; the CCP gave preference to the third alternative, which is both shorter and more generic:

"(c) and more generally to provide a forum for the examination of any difficulty that may arise in the light of the Guiding Lines and Principles of Surplus Disposal endorsed by the Conference, and to promote observance of the Principles, it being understood that these Principles and Guiding Lines should not be interpreted as applying only to surplus disposal in the narrow sense;"

Three essential elements of the CSD's mandate are laid down in this short paragraph: (i) promotion of observance of the FAO Principles (which was already contained in para. (2) of the previous text), (ii) discussion of any difficulties in their application, and (iii) a confirmation of the practice already followed by the CSD, whereby it does not have to confine itself to surplus disposal in the strict sense but can also deal with food aid, grey area transactions and commercial transactions resulting from the liquidation or reduction of strategic stockpiles or the operation of buffer stocks. This trend of broadening the terms of reference is further enhanced by the flexibility granted to the CSD in the interpretation of its mandate.[220] Moreover, by means of a last clause (para. 1(d)), added by the CCP, the CSD has been authorized "to consider any other matters arising from the recommendations of the CCP at its Forty-Fourth Session on procedures for consultation and notification."

The recognition of functions exercised by other organizations and of the need for co-operation with such organizations is reflected in the revised text

---

[219] Cf. Doc. CCP : 69/13/1, para. 67, at p. 16, and Annex II.

[220] Paragraph 2 of the terms of reference of the CSD reads as follows:
"In carrying out its mandate, the Sub-Committee shall bear in mind the continuing need for steps to raise consumption levels, particularly in areas in need of development and among vulnerable and low-income groups, taking fully into account the special considerations embodied in the Guiding Lines affecting this aim; and shall also take into account policies of selective expansion of agricultural production and trade. The Sub-Committee shall interpret its mandate in a flexible way."

of para. 6 of the terms of reference of the CSD.[221] It may be noted in this connection that the EEC, which disposes of certain surplus stocks and is empowered to exercise control functions in the field of external trade of its Member States, pursuant to Articles 43, 113 and 116 of the Rome Treaty, has agreed, within its sphere of competence, not only to observe the FAO Principles of Surplus Disposal, but also to participate in the consultation and notification procedures as adopted by the CCP and endorsed by the Council.

The broadening of the terms of reference of the CSD did not affect its consultative character: its function has never been, and is not now, to take decisions that would be binding on Member Nations. As is clearly evident from paragraph 4 of the terms of reference, Member Nations should give consideration to, but need not accept, conclusions reached by the CSD.[222]

The question as to whether the CSD could adopt any recommendations and, if so, to whom they should be addressed, has been considered when the CSD's terms were first reviewed in 1958. It was determined at that time that the CSD had authority to make recommendations to the CCP, but not to individual governments. This limitation might well have defeated the effectiveness of recommendations—particularly those relating to individual transactions—inasmuch as governments could hardly be expected to delay their decisions until the CCP had an opportunity to consider and endorse the recommendations and to transmit them (with or without change) to interested governments.[223] However, the CSD found that:

"In practice, this does not have much significance. Discussions on particular transactions between representatives of member countries, whether carried out bilaterally or in the full Sub-Committee, and indeed conclusions on courses of action which require the agreement of individual governments, clearly involve recommendations to governments. Such recommendations have the same effect as a report by the Sub-Committee." [224]

It would not seem that these findings of the CSD have been contested or

---

[221] "Bearing in mind that Member Nations and Associate Members may have incurred obligations in other organizations and under international agreements, international organizations who are entitled to send observers to the CCP shall also be entitled to send observers to the Sub-Committee. On matters of primary concern to other intergovernmental bodies, the Sub-Committee should request the Director-General to invite the assistance of these bodies, and shall cooperate with them in avoiding the overlapping of functions."

[222] "Since governments remain free as to whether or not they accept any conclusions reached by the Sub-Committee in its reviews of proposed or adopted measures, the main value of the work of the Sub-Committee lies in the opportunity offered for the exchange of information and for consultations. The value and effectiveness of this consultative machinery will depend primarily on the cooperation given to it by Member Nations and Associate Members of the Organization, in respect to both the communication of information and the consideration of the Sub-Committee's conclusions."

[223] While the CSD meets at monthly intervals, the CCP normally holds only one or two sessions per year.

[224] Doc. CCP 58/7 Add. 1, para. 13.

274

that the *modus procedendi* implied therein created any difficulties: otherwise, the Working Group which reviewed the CSD functions in 1969 would undoubtedly have covered this aspect in its report to the CCP.

While the need for effective machinery for consultation and notification has been widely recognized, there is no evidence that machinery for the settlement of disputes has ever been advocated.

Since the CSD is regarded as a forum for consultations, divergent views may well be expressed by its members on specific transactions or more general issues. Divergencies or complaints could arise mainly in connection with issues such as non-observance of the Principles or Guiding Lines, failure to comply with consultation and notification duties, or interference with normal trade patterns by transactions that are not subject to advance notification.

The CSD, in its report to the CCP just cited, reached the following conclusion:

"The Sub-Committee should act as a forum to which third-party countries might subsequently refer specific complaints if they did not consider that their views had received sufficient consideration, or if there had been no bilateral consultation."

The CSD may thus examine complaints and incorporate its finding and conclusions in its reports, but it would be difficult to maintain that it acts in a quasi-judicial capacity. Its effectiveness is not based on any powers to enforce the Principles of Surplus Disposal—powers which not even the governing bodies of FAO possess—but on its "role of a standing committee," which provides "that relatively rare opportunity for continuing consultations and deliberations..."[225] and also on the flexibility of its consultative procedures. However, beyond playing its role as a forum for consultations on surplus disposal transactions, the CSD has acted—perhaps unwittingly—as a catalyser in the progressive recognition, among governments and intergovernmental organizations, of the intricate pattern but largely complementary nature of trade and aid and has made a tangible contribution towards the development of norms and procedures for reconciling divergent interests and meeting vital needs of an expanding world community.

D. CONCLUSIONS

The principal purpose of the present paper, as outlined in the introduction, is to describe the methods and procedures which have been developed within the constitutional framework of FAO for formulating decisions and rendering them effective.

The first conclusion might be that a decision, however defined or characterized, cannot be considered in isolation. Even more than the

---

[225] Doc. CCP 58/7 Add. 1, para. 14.

travaux préparatoires in the case of international conventions, the reports, recommendations and other preliminary steps leading to the formulation of decisions need to be taken into account if an attempt is made to evaluate the scope and effectiveness of such decisions. Moreover, a decision usually cannot become effective in the absence of what is colloquially called "follow-up"; in other words some procedural, and possibly institutional, arrangements are often indispensable to ascertain the effects of decisions and to amplify or modify them as the need arises: this often leads to new decisions.

The second conclusion that suggests itself is that the interaction between international organizations, both at the secretariat and intergovernmental levels, has become so manifold that it is sometimes difficult to identify a decision as being attributable to a single organization; the procedures developed show significant differences from one organization to the other but similar legal techniques, methods and formulations can sometimes be found in relation to organizations or subject matters which otherwise seem quite unrelated.

The third conclusion that seems to emerge is that the process is very complex and that the determining factors in its evolution are to be found in the need to respond to factual situations and practical needs, rather than in the deliberate development of a coherent doctrine and its systematic application to given situations and problems. International organizations are living organisms in a constantly changing political, economic, social and technical setting and the empirical method almost inevitably prevails in devising ways and means of resolving legal problems for which traditional concepts and techniques do not provide a ready answer.

It is perhaps one of the most challenging tasks of the legal staff of international organizations to recognize these problems, to place them in the proper perspective, to assist in evolving solutions which are both legally sound and practically effective, and thereby to make a contribution, however modest, to the development of international law.

NOTES ON DECISIONS OF THE WORLD HEALTH ORGANIZATION

by *F. Gutteridge*
Director, Legal Office, World Health Organization

This note outlines the constitutional background and the manner in which legislative or quasi-legislative decisions have been taken by the World Health Organization, through its Governing Bodies. For this purpose, the treatment excludes WHO's constitutional arrangements for the adoption of Conventions and Agreements which follow on more or less traditional lines those of the other organizations in the United Nations system. A relative innovation in the WHO Constitution is the authority given to the World Health Assembly to adopt international regulations. This authority is contained in Article 21 which provides that such regulations may concern:

(a) sanitary and quarantine requirements and other procedures designed to prevent the international spread of disease;
(b) nomenclatures with respect to diseases, causes of death and public health practices;
(c) standards with respect to diagnostic procedures for international use;
(d) standards with respect to the safety, purity and potency of biological, pharmaceutical and similar products moving in international commerce;
(e) advertising and labelling of biological, pharmaceutical and similar products moving in international commerce.

Article 22 of the same Constitution goes on to provide that regulations adopted pursuant to Article 21 shall come into force for all Members of the Organization after due notice has been given of their adoption by the Health Assembly, except for such Members as may notify the Director-General of rejection or reservations within the period stated in the notice.

These provisions were inserted in the WHO Constitution on the proposal of Surgeon-General T. Parran, Chief Delegate of the United States of America at the Technical Preparatory Committee convened by the Economic and Social Council which met in Paris from 18 March to 5 April 1946.[1]

The conception behind them was not entirely novel in that they were based on certain provisions of the Convention on International Civil Aviation [2] as well as of the International Sanitary Convention for Aerial Navigation of 1933.[3]

At the International Health Conference which met in New York from 19 June to 22 July 1946 these provisions were formally adopted by the

---

[1] Off. Rec. Wld Hlth Org., No. 1, Annex 7, p. 46.
[2] Articles 37, 38, 54 and 90.
[3] Article 61.

participating delegates. The report of the Conference declared that probably the most significant contribution to international legislative technique in the health field made by the WHO Constitution lay in the power it conferred upon the Health Assembly to adopt regulations on a broad range of technical matters.[4] Nevertheless, in the course of the Conference certain delegations considered that the "contracting out" provisions incorporated in the Constitution constituted an infringement of national sovereignty. Various alternative proposals were suggested including:

(a) the compulsory inclusion in all international health regulations of a denunciation clause whereby any Member bound by such regulations could denounce them within three years after their entry into force upon six months' notice;
(b) a provision whereby Members would acknowledge receipt or regulations notified by the Director-General, the period for rejection or reservation then running from the date of such acknowledgement;
(c) an arrangement whereby only temporary regulations applying new knowledge and techniques to the control of the international spread of disease would enter into force automatically for all members, such temporary regulations being binding upon members for one year only. Other regulations would require formal acceptance by governments.

It is interesting to note that the Committee on Administration and Finance of the International Health Conference, responsible for discussing the provisions relating to international regulations, suggested to the Conference that the subject matter of regulations should extend to the prevention of the importation by States of biological, pharmaceutical and similar products which did not conform to standards adopted by the Health Assembly. This provision was objected to by a number of delegations, in particular, those from Latin America on the grounds that it dealt with questions of commercial policy which did not properly fall within the jurisdiction of the Health Organization.[5]

Little more than fifteen years after the entry into force of the Constitution and based upon complaints by the developing countries that they were being flooded with sub-standard drugs, the sixteenth World Health Assembly adopted a resolution requesting the Executive Board to examine ways and means of ensuring that drugs exported from a producing country should comply with the drug control requirements applicable in that country for domestic use. This resolution led to an extended study on the problem of the quality control of pharmaceutical preparations moving in international commerce.

At the International Health Conference the Belgian delegation had proposed the incorporation into the Constitution of a procedure which would have permitted the Health Assembly to make formal recommendations to Members based upon the practice of the International Labour Organization. This procedure would have pledged Member States within

---

[4] Off. Rec. Wld Hlth Org., No. 2, p. 20.
[5] *Ibid.*, p. 21.

eighteen months to bring each recommendation before the authority or authorities competent to enact legislation or to take other appropriate action. In view of the authority conferred upon the Organization with regard to conventions and regulations the Conference adopted a modified form of this proposal which gives to the Health Assembly authority to make recommendations to Members but which requires them merely to submit annual reports on the action taken with respect thereto. Thus, the Health Assembly is empowered under Article 23 of the Constitution to make recommendations to Members with respect to any matter within the competence of the Organization.

In order to understand the manner in which the Organization has given effect to these constitutional provisions it must be recalled that, while the WHO Constitution followed at the time of its adoption the traditional lines for the constituent instruments of other specialized agencies, WHO was nevertheless the successor Organization to the United Nations Relief and Rehabilitation Organization (UNRRA). UNRRA, it is recalled, had been extremely active in the health field and had spent very considerable sums of money for this purpose during the period of its activity.[6]

The Interim Commission of WHO and subsequently the first World Health Assembly accepted the obligations and assets of UNRRA and undertook to perform and continue the activities transferred by that Organization to the extent possible with the remainder of the funds made available. Moreover, a number of staff who had been serving with UNRRA joined the staff of the World Health Organization early in the life of the Organization. As a result of this, the work of the Organization from the beginning tended to be concentrated upon direct action in the territories of its Member States rather than on the so-called central technical services.

In collaboration with UNICEF, WHO was instrumental in developing some of the legal techniques later used by the United Nations Development Programme for concluding arrangements in countries where projects are carried out. The World Health Assembly, at its second session in 1949, adopted a "Supplemental Operating Programme" which was to be financed by voluntary contributions by the Members of WHO. This arrangement was however superseded by the Technical Assistance Programme.[7]

Nevertheless, at an early stage in the life of the Organization, preliminary studies were undertaken on the possibility of drawing up a single set of regulations to replace the Sanitary Conventions which had been concluded over a number of years, each with a specific objective in view. In 1950 a draft of the International Sanitary Regulations, prepared by an Expert Committee on International Epidemiology and Quarantine, was sent to all Member States for comment. The draft was revised and then

---

[6] In 1946, UNRRA expended 82 million dollars on health, although its activities did not cover so large an area as those of WHO.
[7] Off. Rec. Wld Hlth Org. No. 21, Annex 22.

considered by a Special Committee, established by the third World Health Assembly, which met in April and May 1951 before the fourth World Health Assembly. That Assembly continued the Committee as its Committee on International Sanitary Regulations, the Regulations were further considered and the final text was adopted by the fourth World Health Assembly on 25 May 1951.[8] Of particular interest to the lawyer are certain of the final provisions of these Regulations, giving to the Health Assembly control over the acceptance of reservations to the Regulations in order to ensure, as far as possible, that reservations which a State might consider necessary in its special circumstances are accepted as reasonable by other Members. A reservation, therefore, is valid under the Regulations only if it is accepted by the Health Assembly. The Health Assembly does not withhold its acceptance without solid grounds but it has the duty to object to a reservation when it considers that it would substantially detract from the purpose of the Regulations. If a reservation is not accepted by the Health Assembly the regulations do not come into force for the State concerned until the reservation is withdrawn and the State remains bound by the previous sanitary convention to which it has acceded.

The World Health Assembly has also taken advantage of the regulatory provisions of the Constitution in the field of health statistics. International co-operation in health statistics has a history as long and as eventful as that of the sanitary conventions. The first international statistical congress was held in Brussels in 1853. A second international congress was held in 1855, at which a compromise list adopted by the congress served as the basis for the international list of causes of death, the preparation of which was entrusted to the International Statistical Institute in 1891. The idea of decennial revisions came from the American Public Health Association in 1898 and such revisions were subsequently made in Paris in 1900, 1910 and 1920. When the League of Nations came into being it co-operated with the International Statistical Institute in the further development of the International lists. This led to the third and fourth revisions in 1929 and 1938.

The World Health Organization Interim Commission continued this work and an International Conference for the sixth revision of the International List of Diseases and Causes of Death was convened in Paris in April 1948. The International Statistical Classification of Diseases, Injuries and Causes of Death, drawn up by that Conference, was formally adopted by the first World Health Assembly in July 1948, together with WHO Regulations No. 1, the Nomenclature Regulations.[9]

Both the International Sanitary Regulations and the Nomenclature Regulations have been revised and added to in the period which has elapsed

---

[8] Resolution WHA 4.75. Handbook of Resolutions and Decisions of the World Health Assembly and Executive Board, p. 61.
[9] Resolution WHA 1.36, *op. cit.*, p. 12.

since their adoption. At the present time, both sets of Regulations are under review. In the case of the International Sanitary Regulations, it is proposed to institute a complete review, bearing in mind that, on many occasions where epidemics have taken place, it has been evident that there is a tendency on the part of governments to disregard the regulations and to apply *ad hoc* sanitary measures, occasionally of an extremely restrictive nature, as, for example, in the case of the recent cholera epidemics in the Eastern Mediterranean area. In the case of the Nomenclature Regulations, the Regulations are to be considerably simplified, the bulk of their clauses being re-issued in the form of a recommendation, the actual lists being removed from the Regulations so that they may be adopted from time to time by the World Health Assembly without having to go through the normal regulatory processes. The reason for this is that a number of governments consider that the regulatory procedure is too rigid and renders it impossible for a government having become bound by the Regulations to make small adaptations at a later stage.

The Nomenclature Regulations adopted in 1948 and the International Sanitary Regulations adopted in 1951 represent legislative action taken at a relatively early period in the history of WHO, before the membership had grown through the admission of a large number of African and Asian States, most of them developing countries. Since 1951 the Health Assembly has not adopted any further regulations.

Nevertheless, it has been necessary for the Organization, in order to carry out its constitutional functions, to make arrangements to regulate a number of activities in the public health sphere, which can only be determined at the international level. We refer here to such matters as biological standardization,[10] the development of an international pharmacopoeia,[11] the development of international nonproprietary names for drugs,[12] the establishment of drug safety standards,[13] the establishment of a drug early warning scheme [14] and other related matters of a similar nature.

The reader will note that many of these activities could be the subject of international regulations under the provisions of Articles 21 and 22 of the WHO Constitution. Nevertheless, the Assembly has been content to deal with these matters by means of simple recommendations or resolutions rather than by the adoption of formal regulations. Since the idea behind the incorporation into the Constitution of the provision relating to international regulations was to simplify treaty making in this sphere of activities one may ask why the Organization has apparently not taken advantage of these provisions and has preferred to adopt measures of an even more flexible nature.

---

[10] Resolutions WHA 3.8 and 18.7.
[11] Resolution WHA 3.10.
[12] Resolution WHA 3.11.
[13] Resolutions WHA 13.41, 16.36, 17.39 and 19.47.
[14] Resolutions WHA 18.42 and 19.35.

The reasons appear to be both organizational and technical. On the organizational side, as pointed out above, the Organization began its life with a tendency to direct its major efforts towards direct action in the field, due in part to its inheritance from UNRRA. This tendency became enhanced at a later stage through the admission of a considerable number of developing countries, more inclined to support field work than technical activities which may not have appeared to them to be of much direct interest. On the technical side, historically, standards and norms have been drawn up initially by committees of experts specially designated for the purpose. It has appeared to international health workers from the inception of the work of international organizations in the public health field that it would hardly be proper for a health organization to adopt "official science"; therefore the reports of expert committees are not adopted as such, but are merely communicated to Member States as representing the collective views of the experts and not the official views of the Organization, although since the experts are men of the highest renown in their fields, their reports have considerable persuasive authority. Moreover, in the last years the progress in the medical sciences has been so rapid that even the relatively simplified procedure for the adoption of international regulations has not been sufficiently flexible to take account of these rapid changes. For example, in the case of the programme for the proposal and recommendation of international non-proprietary names for drugs, many of the non-proprietary names proposed at the commencement of the programme are no longer in use simply because the pharmaceutical preparations to which they refer have themselves become obsolete. The simple procedure for the proposal and recommendation of these names adopted by the Executive Board and by the World Health Assembly in the form of a resolution makes it possible, for example, to substitute one name for another in cases where a dispute exists, a procedure which would be extremely difficult if the names had been the subject of the regulatory procedure provided for in Article 21 of the Constitution, in view of the possibility of States making reservations.

An additional factor is that certain of the activities which have been proposed for international action are not fully regulated at the national level, for example the problem of the purity and potency of pharmaceutical preparations destined for export.

In this same sphere, the Organization has actually abrogated existing legislation in favour of the procedure of recommendation. In 1952, at a conference which took place during the World Health Assembly, the Brussels Agreements of 1906 and 1929 on the Unification of Pharmacopoeial Formulas for Potent Drugs were abrogated and no legislative provisions which might otherwise have been made under Article 21 of the WHO Constitution were adopted in their place, since the Executive Board considered that the termination of these agreements would suffice for the time being, the International Pharmacopoeia, which embodies revised formulas for these drugs, retaining its status as a recommendation of the World Health Assembly.

In view of the large measure of acceptance of simple decisions of the Executive Board and of the Health Assembly in the technical field, it is questionable to what extent in the future, the World Health Organization will adopt further international regulations. In his article on the effect of resolutions of the General Assembly of the United Nations[15] Johnson states that the value of resolutions "depends upon the degree of objectivity surrounding the circumstances in which they were adopted." In the highly technical spheres which have been referred to above, it would seem that Member States are content to rely on the skill and objectivity of the experts which have drawn up the proposals which have been subsequently communicated to members under resolutions and decisions of the World Health Assembly and the Executive Board. This process, bordering on the legislative, has the advantage of great simplicity and flexibility and permits changes to be made and notified without undue difficulty.

In those areas where scientific or technical considerations are predominant, it can be said that virtually no problems have ever arisen over compliance with commitments or obligations. If one is to take an example such as the international standards and units for biological substances adopted by the World Health Assembly and submitted to Members in the form of a recommendation,[16] its is hardly likely that "rival" international standards would be used in any country, though local standards may in certain cases be used.[17] The same may be said for such similar matters as statistical definitions, approved laboratories and institutes for yellow fever vaccine production.[18] Problems of compliance begin to arise when other factors, commercial, industrial, administrative, etc., have to be taken into consideration. Thus the WHO programme for designating international non-proprietary names (generic names) for pharmaceutical preparations [19] has not been universally accepted, since it has not yet been possible to devise a practical procedure for resolving cases where a proposed international name conflicts or is alleged to conflict with an existing trade name.

In practice, compliance has been sought through persuasion rather than by the introduction of any direct procedures. Much of this work is done through the Expert Committees and Expert Advisory Panels that have been established to deal with the different branches of knowledge in the subjects for which the Organization has responsibility. The recommendations of these Committees, while not being binding on the Organization, nevertheless can not easily be ignored or disregarded.[20]

---

[15] BYIL, XXXII, p. 97.
[16] Resolution WHA 18.7.
[17] Resolution EB 13.11.
[18] Resolution [EB 2.R 5] and EB 13.R 52.
[19] Resolution WHA 3.11.
[20] Ante, p. 7.

An important factor where relationships between governments is concerned is an organizational one. WHO has a highly developed regional structure, based on express constitutional provisions to that end.[21] The Organization's technical assistance programme is carried out through its Regional Offices and since it was envisaged from the inception of the Organization that the Regional Offices would have as one of their roles the collection and dissemination of epidemiological intelligence, they have proved to be effective in handling problems which have arisen in the administration of sanitary and quarantine procedures.

Thus, the sheer difficulty inherent in the treaty-making process when dealing with a large number of States, as at present constituting the membership of the World Health Organization, the technical considerations involved in the international health field, the advantages resulting from reciprocal acceptance of standards and norms drawn up by a body which has the confidence of States, the background of the general policy of the Organization have tended to result in the World Health Organization turning away from the traditional treaty-making process towards a more direct procedure in those areas in which it is competent and where international action is necessary to lay down international standards and to co-ordinate the activities of governments.[22]

---

[21] WHO Constitution, Chapter XI—Regional Arrangements.
[22] Cf. Bowett, *The Law of International Institutions* (1963). Higgins, *The Development of International Law through the Political Organs of the United Nations* (1963). *Legal Advisers and Foreign Affairs* (1964). Parry, "Sources and Evidences of International Law (1965). The binding force of League Resolutions." *BYIL*, 1935, XVI, pp. 157-160. Sloan, "The Binding Force of a Recommendation of the General Assembly of the United Nations", *BYIL*, 1948, XXXII, p. 97. Gross, "The United Nations and the Role of Law, International Organization", XIX, p. 556. The Shimoda Case, *Japanese Annual of International Law*, 1964, No. 8, p. 216. Friedmann, *The Relevance of International Law to the Processes of Economic and Social Development, Proceedings of the American Society of International Law*, Washington, D.C., 28-30 April 1966, p. 12. Falk, "On the quasi-legislative Competence of the General Assembly", 60 *AJIL*, p. 782.

DECISIONS AND OTHER MEASURES TAKEN BY THE INTERNATIONAL ATOMIC ENERGY AGENCY

by *Werner Boulanger*
Director, Legal Division International Atomic Energy Agency

The ability of the International Atomic Energy Agency (IAEA) by decision or other suitable means to effect action or omission by one of its Member States or their nationals is determined legally by the Agency's Statute and other legal instruments based thereon, and factually by its special field of work. Under its Statute (Article III.A), the Agency has two main functions:

(a) To *promote* research on, and development and practical application of, atomic energy for peaceful uses throughout the world,
(b) To *protect* humanity against the dangers emanating from the radioactive properties of nuclear materials on the one hand and against the possibility of their use for military purposes on the other.

With regard to the "promoting" activities of the Agency, no problems will normally arise from decisions, proposals, or advice. These measures will, as a rule, be in the interest of Member States or their nationals; they would therefore have little reason not to accept them.

The same is true of the Agency's activities in the field of protection of health and safety. There, the standards and regulations are developed by the Agency in close cooperation with Member States. The practice in formulating safety standards is to organize meetings of experts to consider drafts prepared by the Secretariat. The panel members are specialists from Member States and other interested international organizations. The draft regulations elaborated by the panel are communicated to the Member States for comment. The standards and regulations are then submitted to the Agency's Board of Governors for approval. They are published with the Board's authorization and constitute international standards designed to serve as a basis for national legislation and regulations. In regard to Member States these standards and regulations are only recommendations; they are, however, under the Agency's Statute, binding with regard to its own operations and may, by agreement, become binding with regard to projects undertaken with the Agency's assistance (Article XI). In this latter case the Agency can satisfy itself about the observance of any health and safety measures prescribed either through an expert, who frequently assists in the project on the spot, or through its inspectors mentioned below.

A similar procedure was used when the need arose to facilitate the international transport of radioactive substances by establishing uniform safety regulations. Following a 1959 resolution of the Economic and Social Council of the United Nations, the Agency convened two panels to formulate regulations dealing with the transport of radioisotopes, radioactive ores and residues of low specific activity on the one hand and with the transport of large radioactive sources and fissile materials on the other. Again experts from member countries and representatives of various international organizations participated in this work. The international standards for the transport of radioactive materials were approved by the Board of Governors in September 1960 for application to the operations of the Agency and to those undertaken with its assistance; the Board also invited Member States to use these regulations as the basis for developing their own national regulations and the organizations concerned to apply them to the international transport of radioactive materials. The Transport Regulations were reviewed, from 1962 to 1964, in a number of meetings organized by the Agency of experts from Member States and representatives of a large number of interested organizations. The Revised Regulations were approved by the Board of Governors in 1964 and published in May 1965. They now provide a lasting framework of principles and rules, supplemented by appropriate technical data, for the safe transport of radioactive materials by land, water and air. In order to keep the technical aspects up-to-date in the light of new knowledge and experience gained, the Director General of the Agency was authorized by the Board of Governors to make the changes of detail which would prove necessary from the technical viewpoint, without infringing the principles and rules approved by the Board. Proposed changes must be brought to the notice of Member States 90 days in advance, and the Agency will take due note of the observations or information communicated to it.

The Agency's Transport Regulations are also used as the basis for transport regulations issued by international organizations competent for transport by rail, road, inland waterways, sea and air. Thus the International Regulations Concerning Carriage of Dangerous Goods by Rail (RID) established by the Central Office for International Railway Transports in Berne, which apply in 24 countries in Europe and the Near East, were revised on the basis of the IAEA's Regulations. The Maritime Safety Committee of IMCO approved in February 1966 Provisions Relating to the Transport of Radioactive Substances by Sea conforming to the revised IAEA Regulations. The Committee recommended that the Member States of IMCO and the Governments which had participated in the 1960 Conference on Safety of Life at Sea should adopt these draft provisions as the basis for their national regulations. The IATA Regulations Relating to the Carriage of Restricted Articles by Air have also been revised to take into account the fact that several countries among the principal producers of radioisotopes are in the process of adopting the IAEA Regulations for their national airline networks.

The examples given above show how, by close cooperation between the IAEA and experts from member countries and from other organizations and with member governments, IAEA standards for the protection of health and safety and for the transport of radioactive substances become international as well as national standards. This means that the problem of putting into effect a decision of the IAEA in a Member State will scarcely arise.

The real problems may, theoretically, be assumed to present themselves mainly in connection with the application of the Agency's safeguards system. Under this technical term we understand the activities

"designed to ensure that special fissionable and other materials, services, equipment, facilities, and information made available by the Agency or at its request or under its supervision or control are not used in such a way as to further any military purpose; and to apply safeguards, at the request of the parties, to any bilateral or multilateral arrangement, or at the request of a State, to any of that State's activities in the field of atomic energy" (Art. III. A.5).

This provision of the Statute clearly indicates that the "controls" by the Agency are applicable only with the prior consent of a Member State given in the form of an agreement with the Agency. Such an agreement can be:

(a) A *Project Agreement* under Article XI of the Statute, by which a Member or group of Members requests "the assistance of the Agency in securing special fissionable or other materials, services, equipment and facilities necessary for research on, or development or practical application of, atomic energy for peaceful purposes." Such an agreement must include "undertakings by the Member or group of Members submitting the project: (i) that the assistance provided shall not be used in such a way as to further any military purpose; and (ii) that the project shall be subject to the safeguards provided for in Article XII, the relevant safeguards being specified in the agreement" (Art. XI.F.4);

(b) A *Safeguards Transfer Agreement,* whereby at the request of two or more Member States the safeguards functions envisaged in a bilateral or multilateral agreement for cooperation between them are transferred to the Agency. Such agreements were concluded with the USA and 19 of its partners, the United Kingdom and Denmark, and Canada and Japan;

(c) A *Unilateral Safeguards Submission Agreement* by which the Member State submits all or part of its nuclear activities to Agency safeguards. Such agreements were concluded with the USA for four reactors and the United Kingdom for the Bradwell nuclear installation.

The details for Agency controls are contained in the safequards agreements or in supplementary agreements thereto. They consist of a *bookkeeping* system for source material (natural uranium and thorium) and special fissionable material (Pu-239, U-233, U-235) and *periodical reports.* Their main and generally best known feature is, however, the *inspections* on the spot carried out by Agency inspectors appointed with the concurrence of the Member State. The rights and obligations of such inspectors as well as of Member States are spelled out in detail both in the Statute and in the documents approved by the Board of Governors (The Agency's Safeguards System—1965—(INFCIRC/66) and its extension to reprocessing plants (CC(X)/INF/86) and the Inspectors Document (GC-(V)/INF/39).

While it can be assumed that a Member State, when concluding a safeguards agreement, has every intention not to violate it, this may, for one reason or another, change later on. Due to a change of policy a State may wish to escape from its obligations under the safeguards agreement. The violations of the agreement may take the following form:

(1) Use of safeguarded items to further any military purpose—commonly referred to as a "diversion";
(2) An interference with the control system in order to conceal a diversion;

287

(3) An interference with the control system for some other reason, which may range from convenience (avoiding the burden of making reports), to embarrassment (at an unexplained loss), to nationalistic pride (objecting to outside checks). Of course what appears to be a violation based on one of these grounds could really be one based on a desire to conceal an actual diversion and therefore the control authority might have to treat it as such;

(4) Some other violation of any provision of the safeguards agreement—e.g. the violation of the patent clause of a Project Agreement.

Both the sanctions to be used by the Agency in case of non-compliance as well as the procedures for them are regulated in Article XII.C of the Statute. If an inspector finds any "non-compliance" with the terms of a safeguards agreement, he must report to the Director General of IAEA who "shall thereupon transmit the report to the Board of Governors." The Board must then determine whether or not it finds any non-compliance to have occurred. If its finding is positive it must call on the Member State to remedy forthwith such non-compliance. The Board must also report its findings to all Member States as well as to the Security Council and General Assembly of the United Nations. If the State does not comply within a reasonable time, the Board may take the following measures:

(a) Direct that all assistance being provided by the Agency or by its Member States be curtailed or suspended;

(b) It may call for the return of materials and equipment made available to the State;

(c) It may also suspend the Member from the exercise of the privileges and immunities of membership, in accordance with Article XIX.B.

The measures envisaged under (a) and (b) will of course be effective only if and to the extent that the Member State is receiving assistance by or through the Agency and if it does not refuse to return material and equipment already received. The only real sanctions may be those taken by the Security Council or the General Assembly of the United Nations pursuant to the Board's report.

It seems too early to speculate on what powers of decision the Agency will have once a non-proliferation treaty has entered into force. The safeguards agreements which, under the Treaty for the Prohibition of Nuclear Weapons in Latin America, will have to be concluded between Latin American States and the Agency may give some indication of future developments. They will very probably follow to a large extent the existing system which, while using the Agency's technical expertise for the control mechanism, leaves the final political decisions to the proper political bodies of the United Nations.

SELECT BIBLIOGRAPHY

Mason Willrich, "The Development of International Law by the International Atomic Energy Egency", 1965 *Proceedings of the American Society of International Law.*

Mason Willrich, "Safeguarding Atoms for Peace", 60 *American Journal of International Law* (1966).

Paul C. Szasz, "The Law of International Atomic Energy Safeguards", 1967 *Revue Belge de Droit International.*

Ha Vinh Phuong, *International Aspects of Regulatory Work in Radiation Protection,* Paper submitted to the 7th Japan Conference on Radioisotopes, Tokyo, May, 1966.

N.B. This was written in 1967, prior to extension of IAEA safeguards to conversion and fabrication plants and prior to the Non-Proliferation Treaty.

DECISIONS OF THE UNIVERSAL POSTAL UNION

by *Dr. Z. Caha*
Assistant Director-General of the International Bureau of the Universal Postal Union

I. INTRODUCTION

1. Within the field of activity[1] of the Universal Postal Union (UPU), a distinction can be made between decisions:

(a) as regards the body: decisions of Congress, of the Executive Council (EC), of the Management Council of the Consultative Committee for Postal Studies (MC/CCPS), of the Training Committee (TC) and the "decisions" of the International Bureau (IB);

(b) as regards the form and legal quality of the decision: clauses of international treaties concluded by member countries[2] (Acts of the UPU), interpretation of Acts of the UPU, resolutions and recommendations (*voeux,* i.e. formal opinions).

2. The various UPU bodies use different kinds of decisions according to the powers conferred upon them. Thus Congress, which is primarily the legislative body, is alone competent to conclude treaties governing various postal services.[3] In administrative matters, both Congress and the other bodies use resolutions and recommendations. For interpretation, see paragraph 33.

3. As regards the main criterion of the subject-matter of this study, namely "The Legal Scope of Decisions within the Member States of an International Organization," this paper deals firstly with the international postal treaties concluded within the framework of the UPU (the Acts of the

---

[1] The UPU's basic fields of activity are the following:
(a) normal activity, i.e. the regulation of the international postal service, which is operated by the Postal Administrations of the member countries;
(b) activity carried out by the UPU bodies with the cooperation of the member countries and relating to the improvement of the postal service (studies on various technical postal problems, the organization of the training of officials of Postal Administrations and UPU technical assistance);
(c) activity assigned to the UPU by the UN as a mandate and carried out by UPU bodies (UNDP technical assistance).

[2] The term "countries" of "member countries" is the official title in the UPU.

[3] The basic Act of the Union provides for the possibility of convening administrative conferences to deal with questions of an administrative character (Constitution, Article 16). It has been suggested that administrative conferences could be entrusted, *inter alia,* with the revision of purely technical Acts, such as the Agreements, which would considerably facilitate the work of Congress. However, this idea, which was considered by the UPU Executive Council in connection with the simplification and acceleration of the work of Congress, was not adopted. It is true to say that there are no administrative conferences in the UPU (CE 1966, Doc 7, p. 2 (English text)).

Union), because these are the only decisions directly binding upon the member countries. The other kinds of decision of the UPU bodies will then be discussed, especially in so far as they relate to the members of the UPU.

II. THE ACTS OF THE UNION

(1) *General*

4. The position of the postal service in most member countries (as a monopoly and a State prerogative) has, from the foundation of the UPU, made it necessary for its members to conclude agreements at intergovernmental level. All postal activity, which includes in the first place the transport of postal items from one country to another, if necessary through the instrumentality of third party member countries, has the following characteristic features:

(i) Interdependence of Postal Administrations and reciprocity in their mutual relations.

(ii) Uniformity of transport conditions, especially as regards rates and responsibility. This uniformity is expressed in technical language in Article 1 of the UPU Constitution:

"The countries adopting this Constitution comprise, under the title of the Universal Postal Union, a single postal territory for the reciprocal exchange of letter-post items."

However, this uniformity is flexible enough to enable the Administrations to adapt their services to the conditions of the international service (e.g., they have adequate latitude for fixing the international basic rates, and various ancillary services are only optional).

(iii) Freedom of transit, which is guaranteed throughout the entire territory of the Union, is only the logical consequence of the first two characteristics. It is the keystone of the entire operation of the international service (see Constitution, Article 1(1) *ad fin.*: "Freedom of transit is guaranteed throughout the entire territory of the Union").

5. The legal consequences of the special character of postal activity governed at international level are summarized in the postulate of the single legal basis for relations between all Postal Administrations—in other words, by the simultaneous entry into force of the Acts of the Union enacted by a Congress and the parallel abrogation of the corresponding Acts of the previous Congress (Article 31(2) of the Constitution). This concept to some extent ignores the legal documents which create the member countries' formal commitments as regards the Acts of the UPU. As legal status is sometimes lacking, it is the *de facto* situation which is the determining factor for the countries' relations with the UPU. This *de facto* situation is the basis of a concept generally recognized by the UPU,

namely the "tacit ratification" of the Acts of the Union: implementation by a UPU member country of the Acts of the Union is sufficient for it to be considered a member of the Union with full rights. This "tacit ratification" is all the more important because never in the history of the Universal Postal Union have all the member countries ratified the Acts of the Union that have been enacted by a Congress.

6. The Acts of the Union are as follows:

(a) Constitution of the Universal Postal Union and its Final Protocol

(b) General Regulations of the Universal Postal Union and their Final Protocol

(c) Universal Postal Convention, Final Protocol and Detailed Regulations

(d) Agreement Concerning Insured Letters and Boxes, Final Protocol and Detailed Regulations

(e) Agreement Concerning Postal Parcels, Final Protocol, Detailed Regulations, Final Protocol

(f) Agreement Concerning Postal Money Orders and Postal Travellers' Cheques, Detailed Regulations

(g) Agreement Concerning the Giro Service, Detailed Regulations

(h) Agreement Concerning Cash-on-Delivery Items, Detailed Regulations

(i) Agreement Concerning the Collection of Bills, Detailed Regulations

(j) Agreement Concerning the International Savings Bank Service, Detailed Regulations

(k) Agreement Concerning Subscriptions to Newspapers and Periodicals, Detailed Regulations

7. Before the 1964 Vienna Congress, the Acts referred to under 6(a), (b) and (c) constituted the "Universal Postal Convention," which, like all the other Acts, was renewed by each Congress. As the Convention was the organic document of the UPU (it is in fact the Charter of that international organization, i.e. the existing Constitution), the legal question arose whether the UPU itself is legally reborn at every Congress. This view, though logical, created certain legal difficulties which have been overcome in practice by the concept of "tacit ratification" to maintain the continuity of the Union. As stated in paragraph 5, there have been, in the history of the UPU, countries which, during a number of regimes inaugurated by the various Congresses, have performed no legal action (signature, accession or ratification) signifying a legal relationship with the UPU. On the other hand, they have admittedly always implemented the Acts of the Union, and have never been regarded as having left it.

(2) *Structure of the Acts and Their Approval at International Level*

8. As regards the structure of the Acts and their approval at international level, the following points should be mentioned:

(a) The main Acts (Constitution, Convention, General Regulations and

292

Agreements) are always concluded on behalf of the Governments of the member countries, whereas the Acts containing executory provisions of a technical nature (the Detailed Regulations of the Convention and Agreements) are concluded on behalf of their Postal Administrations. This distinction, which goes back to the origins of the Union (Treaty of Bern, 1874, Article 13), was intended to avoid burdening Congress unnecessarily with purely technical and minor questions, and to leave it entirely to postal experts to revise these provisions at administrative conferences. However, Congress acquired the habit, from the very foundation of the Union, of revising the Regulations itself and submitting them for signature at the same time as the other UPU Acts. This difference in the legal nature of the UPU Acts had the result that the UPU does not require confirmation in a specific form of the signatures appended by the representatives of the Administrations when the Regulations are revised. Accordingly, in many countries the signatures of persons who signed as representatives of the Administration are not confirmed, and the Acts in question are not included in the ratification procedure to which the other Acts are subject.[4]

(b) As regards their structure and the obligations imposed, the Acts of the Union deal with the relations between Postal Administrations.[5] Quite exceptionally, individuals are only referred to in provisions dealing with the responsibility of the sender of a postal parcel. This structure of the Acts of the Union makes it necessary for their provisions to be repeated in various national regulations governing the postal service, the "legal status" of which (in virtue of postal laws and orders issued by the Government, or postal regulations issued by the Postal Administration) depends upon each country's constitutional regulations.[6]

(c) Lastly, a distinction must be made between the compulsory and the optional international postal service. Each member country of the UPU has to implement the Universal Postal Convention (and its Detailed Regulations). Before the 1964 Vienna Congress, both the organic provisions (the present Constitution) and the letter-post provisions (the present Convention) formed a single treaty (the Universal Postal Convention). The division effected at Vienna raised some extremely complex legal problems, which have been solved in two different ways, one at international level

---

[4] Cf. note 3 to paragraph 2, on administrative conferences.

[5] The Convention and Agreements contain the basic rules applicable to the various postal services. All operational provisions liable to vary and therefore of a purely administrative nature are confined to the Detailed Regulations.

[6] A Postal Administration proposed at the 1952 Brussels Congress that the structure of the Acts of the Union should be adapted to that of national legislation, the criterion of which is the postal customer (this would mean transferring all the compulsory provisions for users to the Convention and Agreements, and retaining the provisions concerning Postal Administrations only in the Detailed Regulations). Although the Brussels Congress decided to proceed with the rearrangement of the Acts on that basis, it has never been possible to distribute their contents on those lines (1952 Brussels Documents, I, p. 68; II, pp. 311 and 312).

and the other at national. The simultaneous existence of an organic Charter, on the one hand, and a treaty governing the compulsory activity of the UPU member countries, on the other, and the need, at national level, to submit for constitutional approval a treaty declared compulsory at international level, raised problems the solution of which, on the practical plane, can be regarded as a happy compromise.

The General Regulations, the Convention and its Regulations were declared "compulsory Acts" in order to maintain the situation which existed before the 1964 Vienna Congress. All the member countries were then obliged to accept not only the whole of the provisions governing the organization and operation of the Union, but also the general provisions of the international postal service and those relating to the letter-post service. This makes for a clearer distinction between this Act and the Agreements, which are optional.

The fact that the General Regulations, the Convention and its Detailed Regulations are compulsory at international level does not exempt member countries from having the Acts approved at national level in accordance with their constitutional rules, in conformity with Article 25(3). Also, the principal of "tacit approval" applies in the case of a member country which has not formally approved the said Acts but nevertheless applies them. However, this is only additional to the obligation which already exists in the Constitution.

The optional service is governed by various Agreements. Once member countries have acceded to an Agreement, they are obliged to implement it. It seems unnecessary to go into details in this connection.

(d) In view of what is said at (a) and (c) above, it can be stated that the Constitution which was concluded at Vienna in 1964 at the Fifteenth Congress, and came into force on 1 January 1966,[7] creates the permanent legal basis of the UPU. The question of "legal renewal" no longer arises.[8]

---

[7] For the full text, see *UN Juridical Yearbook 1964*, pp. 195-202.

[8] *Constitution, Article 22:* Acts of the Union

"1. The Constitution is the basic Act of the Union. It contains the organic rules of the Union.

2. The General Regulations embody those provisions which ensure the application of the Constitution and the working of the Union. They shall be binding on all member countries.

3. The Universal Postal Convention and its Detailed Regulations embody the rules applicable throughout the international postal service and the provisions concerning the letter-post services. These Acts shall be binding on all member countries.

4. The Agreements of the Union, and their Detailed Regulations, regulate the services other than those of the letter post between those member countries which are parties to them. They shall be binding on those countries only.

5. The Detailed Regulations, which contain the rules of application necessary for the implementation of the Convention and of the Agreements, shall be drawn up by the Postal Administrations of the member countries concerned.

6. The Final Protocols annexed to the Acts of the Union referred to in paras. 3, 4 and 5 contain the reservations to those Acts."

Such a situation makes superfluous the concept of tacit ratification (approval) of the Convention and General Regulations. The member countries, by implementing these Acts, are merely applying the provisions of Article 22(2) and (3) of the Constitution.

(3) *Approval of the Acts of the Union at National Level*

9. As regards the necessity for the Acts of the Union to be approved at national level, it is worth while mentioning below the changes made in the draft Constitution before it was submitted to the Vienna Congress. The following are the comments of the Expanded Executive and Liaison Committee ("Documents de la CEL élargie 1959", p. 413):

10. "Although in principle we are in favour of abolishing the notion of 'ratification' in the Acts of the Union, we considered it preferable to retain this method of approval for the Constitution, because the decision to cooperate within the framework of the UPU raises fundamental questions which depend upon national sovereignty. We also wanted to respect tradition and take into account the directives of the Ottawa Congress, according to which ratification would be retained for the implementation of the organic provisions of the Union.

11. "For the approval of the other Acts, finding a sound solution was a more complicated matter. The resolution of the Ottawa Congress provided that the Expanded ELC was to devise a method of putting the technical measures into force that should be simpler and more rapid than ratification as provided for in the Ottawa Convention. However, as the choice of procedure for approving international treaties depends essentially upon the constitutional laws of the member countries, efforts to find a satisfactory solution encountered almost insuperable obstacles:

"(a) When preparing its first preliminary draft, the Subcommittee for the General Review of the Convention did not deal with the question of approval so far as the Convention and the General Regulations were concerned; it merely considered the implementation of these two Acts as sufficient proof of approval by the appropriate national authorities. It should be noted that there seemed to be no reason why this implementation should cause legal or practical difficulties, inasmuch as the Convention and General Regulations were declared 'compulsory Acts' by Article 19 of the Constitution.

"(b) This basic solution was not approved by the Expanded Committee. A number of delegations considered that it was impossible not to provide expressly for the approval of the Convention and the General Regulations. It was argued that an express provision was necessary to protect the interests of member countries of the Union whose constitutional law required the approval of international treaties.

"(c) For that reason, the text finally adopted was that which appears in

295

Article 23(3) of the Constitution, which refers, not to 'ratification', but simply to 'approval' of the Acts of the Union other than the Constitution. This provision enables countries whose constitutional laws so permit to consider themselves bound simply by their plenipotentiaries' signature at Congress, or to approve Acts other than the Constitution by a simpler system than ratification as at present provided for.

11. "Lastly, it should be mentioned that some countries saw in the existence of the binding clause in Article 19 of the Constitution an incompatibility with countries' untrammelled right to approve or not to approve a treaty. This objection was overruled by the Committee, which refused to admit the existence of such incompatibility for a number of reasons, including the existence of a similar provision in the ITU Convention, which makes the Administrative Regulations compulsory while also submitting them for the approval of the appropriate national authorities (see ITU Convention, Montreux 1959, Article 15)."

(4) *Reservations*

12. The technical character of the Acts of the Union, on the one hand, and the fact that Congress decisions are taken by majority vote—a majority which depends upon the Act in question—on the other, determine the method of settling the admissibility of reservations. In the Report on the Work of the Union, 1963, the International Bureau of the UPU published some comments on reservations to the UPU's Acts. These comments are also given in the United Nations Juridical Yearbook 1964.[9] The gist of them is given below.

13. "Doctrine, which defines a reservation as a unilateral act by a State at the time of signature, ratification or adherence to a treaty with a view to excluding or altering the effect of certain provisions of this treaty in regard to the said State, is divided on the question of the legal significance of reservations, and more especially on their acceptance by the other States which are parties to a treaty, *in cases where the treaty itself is silent on the matter*.

14. "These theories are not of great interest to the UPU, precisely because the Vienna Constitution settles the problem by providing, in Article 22(6), that any Final Protocols annexed to the Acts of the Union shall contain the reservations to these Acts.

15. "This provision will make it necessary for countries that wish to avail themselves of a reservation to submit it in the form of a proposal and have it confirmed by Congress for insertion in the Final Protocol of the Act to which it relates. The Constitution thus officially confirms the practice that has been in force since the London Congress in 1929 and

---

[9] At pp. 269-270.

arose out of a resolution of that Congress (Documents of the London Congress, Vol. II, p. 155).

16. "This being so, it must be admitted that it is not possible for a member country to make new reservations after signature of the Acts of Congress, unless it subjects the reservation to the procedure for amendment of the Acts in the interval between Congresses, to complement the Final Protocol of the Act concerned.

17. "We are inclined to believe, however, that at the time of admission of a new member country, or of adherence to an unsigned Act, the member country concerned may avail itself of an existing reservation. It would, in fact, be an arbitrary act to refuse a country the benefit of a reservation enjoyed by some other member country, although the grounds may be different. Let us say rather that the approval of a reservation by Congress is more a matter of the admissibility of the text of the reservation than of the beneficiary country."

18. As the reservations take into account the particular situation of the Administration of each member country which has made them, a situation recognized by the other parties in the form of a Final Protocol as mentioned under 14 above, there is no provision expressly authorizing the other member countries which are parties to an Act of the UPU to apply the Act in question as regards the Administration of the reserving country with the same reservation. There is, of course, nothing to prevent a member country from making a counter-reservation, but this has never occurred.

19. The waiving of a reservation existing in favour of a member country does not need to be submitted for approval. In this case, a communication made through the International Bureau for the benefit of the Administrations of member countries is enough. However, if it is desired, between Congresses, to alter the reservations appearing in the Final Protocol, unanimity is necessary, assuming that the alteration is admissible (see e.g., Article 69 of the Convention).

20. "With regard to the unilateral declarations by which member countries react to a given political situation or handle their relations with some other State, they are not, properly speaking, reservations. Consequently, they are not subject to any particular procedure, and may be submitted at any time.

21. "In Vienna, in 1964, several countries submitted declarations of a political nature at the time of signature of the Acts. Congress decided that these would be published at the same time as the Acts of the Vienna Congress and, in accordance with Article 101(5) of the General Regulations of the UPU, notified to the member countries of the Union through diplomatic channels, together with the decisions taken by Congress (i.e., Acts of the Union and other decisions)."

(5) *Amendments to Acts of the Union*

22. The Acts of the Union can be amended either in Congress or between Congresses when only the technical Acts are concerned (excluding the Constitution and General Regulations). The amendments are made on the basis of formal proposals, which can only be submitted by the Postal Administrations of member countries, the Executive Council or, as regards proposals submitted in Congress, by the CCPS Management Council [10] in accordance with the procedure described in the General Regulations. As to amendments to Acts of Congress, they must be adopted by the requisite majority, which is laid down in each of the Acts which it is proposed to amend. As stated above, because the amendments to the technical Acts of the Union are very numerous,[11] all the Acts, except the Constitution, are totally renewed at every Congress; they are treated in the normal way for the conclusion of treaties, i.e., they are signed and then ratified or approved according to each member country's constitutional rules. They go into force simultaneously after a fairly long period, generally twelve to eighteen months after Congress.

23. The General Regulations of the UPU authorize Postal Administrations to amend the Acts of the Union between Congresses. Each Act lays down the majority necessary for a proposal to become executory; generally speaking, the majority required for the adoption of an amendment between Congresses is higher than that required for meetings of Congress. Thus substantive amendments require in principle unanimity of the votes cast.[12] Less important provisions can be amended by two-thirds of the votes cast, and a simple majority is required for drafting amendments and for an authentic interpretation.

24. Amendments adopted by a referendum among Postal Administrations take effect as regards all member countries three months after notification; they require no further act of approval.

25. The procedure for amending Acts between Congresses, laid down in Articles 119-122 of the General Regulations, is at present very little used. It may be pointed out that, out of ninety-one amendments adopted since the creation of the UPU, fifty-nine were accepted during the first twenty-five years of its existence. Since 1947 there have only been six minor amendments; this can be explained by the virtual perfection of the technical Acts, which no longer need urgent amendments, and by the legis-

---

[10] The Management Council's capacity to make proposals is doubly restricted: firstly, the proposals must arise directly out of opinions expressed by the Council or out of the conclusions of studies it has carried out, and secondly, the proposals must be approved by the Consultative Committee for Postal Studies, a body consisting of all the member countries and subordinated to the Management Council.

[11] Recent Congresses have had to consider as many as 1,500 proposals.

[12] The proposal submitted at the 1964 Vienna Congress, in favour of the abolition of the unanimity rule, was rejected (Vienna Documents, I, p. 348; II, pp. 980 and 981).

lative role of the Executive Council. The latter body is instructed by Congress to carry out various studies, most of them of a legislative nature.[13] Amendments to the Constitution, in particular, can only be made in Congress.

26. In addition to the ordinary procedure described above, there exists in practice a short-term extraordinary consultation in which Administrations are sometimes informed that those which do not reply within the time-limit laid down will be considered to have accepted the suggestion. However, this procedure cannot be applied to any amendment of the texts of the Convention or Agreements (including their Regulations). It is prescribed for urgent cases when, for instance, temporary exceptions or derogations are proposed (e.g., a consultation about compiling land and sea transit rate statistics). Very recently, there were consultations about some most important questions (such as exceeding the ceiling of the Union's ordinary annual expenditure). This procedure has been criticized by some members of the UPU, on the ground that it was a derogation from the provisions of the Ottawa Convention, which fixed the annual ceiling for the period during which the Ottawa Acts would be in force.

Alteration of the Constitution

27. The sponsors of the creation of a UPU Constitution, while considering that it would have a certain stability and would remain unaltered, provided a number of variations in the article dealing with amendments.

28. It is interesting to note that after lengthy discussion by the body responsible for preparing a draft Constitution, and also at the Vienna Congress, the latter adopted the same solution as that adopted for the other Acts renewed at Congress.

29. Article 30 of the Constitution reads as follows:

Amendment of the Constitution
1. To be adopted, proposals submitted to Congress and relating to this Constitution must be approved by at least two-thirds of the member countries of the Union.
2. Amendments adopted by a Congress shall from the subject of an additional protocol and, unless that Congress decides otherwise, shall enter into force at the same time as the Acts renewed in the course of the same Congress. They shall be ratified as soon as possible by member countries and the instruments of such ratification shall be dealt with in accordance with the procedure laid down in Article 26.

30. The alternative texts which were not adopted by Congress were as follows:
Alternative 1: "Amendments adopted[1] shall come into force as regards all member countries when they have been accepted by two-thirds of the member countries in accordance with their constitutional rules."

---

[13] For example, the Vienna Congress instructed the EC to make some forty studies, most of which will have to be terminated by formal proposals to Congress.

Alternative 2: "Amendments adopted by the procedure laid down in paragraph 1 [14] shall come into force as regards all member countries when they have been accepted by two-thirds of the member countries in accordance with their constitutional rules, within a period fixed by Congress; this period must not be less than six months from the date on which Congress closed. Member countries which have not notified their acceptance within this period shall be considered as abstaining." [15]

31. Thus the classical rules for the creation of commitments arising out of international treaties were not applied.

III. OTHER DECISIONS

32. Decisions other than the legislative Acts of the Union developed considerably after the Union was given, firstly, new bodies, and secondly new activities.[16] In this paper we shall be concerned only with the most important bodies of the Union, omitting those whose activity is limited to a well-defined field and whose decisions are only optional as regards the member countries, namely the opinions of the CCPS Management Committee and the recommendations of the Training Committee.

Authentic Interpretation of the Acts

33. The authentic interpretation of the Acts between Congress is expressly entrusted to the Postal Administrations of the member countries, and is effected by referendum (see, e.g., the Vienna Convention, Article 69(2)(c)(II)). After an interpretation by the Executive Council had been challenged, the Union decided in 1953 that only interpretations approved by referendum are binding. However, duly adopted interpretations by Congress—a prerogative inherent in legislative bodies—are also binding.[17]

---

[14] Approval in Congress by two-thirds of the member countries represented at it.

[15] For the discussion about amendments to the Constitution, see "Documents de la Commission exécutive et de liaison (élargie) 1959", pp. 414-416, and the 1964 Vienna Congress documents, Vol. II, pp. 1002 and 1003.

[16] At the outset (1874) there were only the Universal Postal Congress and the International Bureau; in 1947 (Paris Congress), the Executive and Liaison Committee (the present Executive Council) as an administrative body representing the Union between Congresses; then, in 1957 (Ottawa Congress), the Consultative Committee for Postal Studies, an advisory body responsible for technical, economic and operational studies, together with its executive body, the Management Council, were set up (see now Articles 17 and 18 of the Constitution and 102, 104 and 105 of the General Regulations); lastly, in 1964 (Vienna Congress), a Training Committee composed of four members of the EC and four members of the CCPS Management Council, under the chairman of the Executive Council, was set up (1964 Vienna Congress, Resolution C12).

[17] Interpretations have not been much favoured by the UPU. The only authentic

34. All other interpretations which any UPU body may have to give—especially the Executive Council or the International Bureau (which gives its opinion on a question, whether in dispute or not, at the request of the parties concerned: see Article 112(2) of the General Regulations) are not binding.

35. Some comments on other decisions of Congress, the Executive Council and the International Bureau are given below:

(1) Congress

36. Originally, Postal Congresses had a purely legislative function; now that their activity covers, *inter alia,* the administrative field of the UPU, decisions in that field generally take the form of resolutions, which are binding upon the bodies to which they relate.[18] Among the resolutions which are binding upon member countries should be mentioned those adopted by virtue of an express provision in the Acts (e.g., the Resolution of the Vienna Congress voted in accordance with Article 21(4) of the Constitution and dealing with the assignment of member countries to a number of contribution classes to defray the expenses of the Union).

37. Congress recommendations and formal opinions are in no way binding upon the Administrations with which they are mainly concerned. They are sometimes the outcome of a proposed amendment to the Acts which was not adopted, but the object of which deserves the attention of Postal Administrations.

38. It should be noted that, for the first time in the history of the Union, member countries received from the Austrian Government notification of all the decisions taken by the Vienna Congress.[19] All the decisions of that Congress have also been published together with the respective Acts.[20]

---

interpretation between Congresses since the Second World War was in 1954, and related to air-mail correspondence. Congresses do not use this type of decision.

[18] See, e.g., Resolution C22, on the immediate implementation of the provisions adopted by the Vienna Congress in connection with the Executive Council and the CCPS Management Council; Resolution C18, containing the approval of the CCPS studies programme and its implementation; Resolution C12, on the organization of vocational training; Resolution C14, on the organization of the work of the International Bureau, etc.

[19] Hitherto, only Acts drawn up by Congress were notified through diplomatic channels.

[20] At the same Vienna Congress, political declarations made unilaterally by various delegations during Congress or on signing the Acts were for the first time grouped together under the title "Declarations Made on Signature of he Acts". These are not strictly "decisions", since Congress did not have to state its views about them.

(2) *Executive Council*

39. The powers of the Council are laid down restrictively in the Acts (see, e.g. Article 102 of the General Regulations). The Council has a certain power of decision, but this is limited to clearly defined fields relating mainly to the internal operation of the Union and its bodies (considering the Union's budget in accordance with the General Regulations, Article 102(5)(j)(i), etc.).

40. In the postal field, the Council is empowered to prepare studies on questions assigned to it by Congress or adopted on its own initiative. However, in principle it is not authorized to take decisions on the basis of the results of such studies if the decisions would commit UPU members. At the most, the Council can draft proposed amendments to the Acts for submission to Congress or submit them to a referendum of member countries between Congresses.[21]

41. The Council can also make recommendations of an optional nature to the Administrations of member countries.[22]

(3) *International Bureau*

42. The International Bureau, a permanent body serving as a liaison, information and consultation body for Postal Administrations (Article 20 of the Constitution), is not empowered either to take decisions regarding the postal service or even to make proposals for the amendment of the Acts. As part of its activity, it can be instructed to make studies or to state its views on simple questions, but these views are purely advisory; similarly, the views expressed by the Bureau at the request of Administrations are purely for information and, as such, in no way binding.

43. A UPU member country and its Postal Administration may be bound:

(a) directly by a Resolution which is simply the implementation of the provisions of the Acts (e.g., of Article 21(4) of the Constitution). Such cases are very rare, and they have the character of an administrative act. It can be said that, in principle, the Acts of the UPU give the bodies of

---

[21] The Vienna Congress entrusted the Council with some forty legislative and administrative studies. The same Congress also had to consider a large number of proposals by the EC for the amendment of the Acts. At the moment, the Council has just submitted to the Administrations of member countries a proposed amendment to an article in the Detailed Regulations of the Convention, the amendment of which is necessary owing to the measures taken in virtue of Article 108 of the General Regulations, which deals with the languages used for publishing the Union's documents.

[22] See, e.g., the recommendation on the use of a new postal form—IB circular 155/1966.

the Union no power to draw up clauses which would be binding upon member countries or their Postal Administrations:

(b) by an interpretation of the Acts adopted by the Administrations between Congresses;

(c) indirectly, as members of a collective body, by decisions affecting that body or adopted by it.

NOTE ON THE EFFECTIVENESS OF DECISIONS ADOPTED BY THE CONTRACTING PARTIES TO THE GENERAL AGREEMENT ON TARIFFS AND TRADE

by *Eric Wyndham White*

1. The General Agreement on Tariffs and Trade (GATT) is a multilateral treaty embodying rules for the conduct of trade among its "members", called contracting parties. In addition, contracting parties accept supplementary obligations (concessions) agreed upon in negotiations; these are generally in the form of maximum rates of customs duty, leviable on goods imported from the territories of other contracting parties, and are inscribed in schedules annexed to the GATT.

2. A contracting party is fully obligated to observe certain provisions of the GATT. Other provisions are obligatory only to the fullest extent not inconsistent with existing legislation (i.e. legislation existing on the date of the protocol under which the contracting party has accepted the GATT), provided that the legislation on which a measure is based is by its terms or expressed intent of a mandatory character—that is, it imposes on the executive authority requirements which cannot be modified by executive action.

3. The obligations assumed by contracting parties relate to matters within the jurisdiction of their national governments and, generally, they have also undertaken to make the GATT effective in the separate customs territories for which they have international responsibility. In addition, contracting parties have undertaken to take such reasonable measures as may be available to them to ensure observance of the provisions of the Agreement by the regional and local governments and authorities within their territories.

4. The General Agreement contains provisions intended to ensure its good administration. Article XXV requires representatives of the contracting parties to meet from time to time for the purpose of giving effect to those provisions which involve joint action and with a view to facilitating the operation and furthering the objectives of the Agreement. The contracting parties acting in this context are designated "the *Contracting Parties*". Thus the *Contracting Parties* serve as a governing body and their annual meetings assume the functions of a conference or an assembly.

5. The provisions of the General Agreement have been amended by numerous protocols drawn up by the *Contracting Parties*. An amendment of certain basic provisions (in particular, the most-favoured-nation clause) cannot enter into force until it has been accepted by all contracting parties. Amendments to other provisions enter into force for contracting parties which have accepted them when they have been accepted by two-

thirds of the contracting parties. Certain amendments drawn up in 1955 entered into force in 1957, but have not yet been accepted by one of the contracting parties which, therefore, is committed only to the previous text. Further amendments—inserting three additional articles—entered into force in 1966; these have not yet been accepted by several contracting parties which, however, have been invited to implement the amendments "on a *de facto* basis to the extent allowed by existing constitutional and legal possibilities".

6. The *Contracting Parties* have also drawn up agreements and declarations which contain supplementary obligations, or interpretations and rules for the implementation of GATT obligations, but these are binding only on contracting parties which accept them. A non-signatory is not debarred from bringing a complaint that, as a result of a supplementary agreement, benefits which should accrue to it under the GATT are being nullified or impaired (see paragraph 13 below). The *Contracting Parties* also draw up protocols containing terms for the accession of non-contracting parties to the GATT; if accession follows, all contracting parties are bound to accord GATT treatment to their trade with the acceding countries (even though they may have voted against the approval of the terms) unless they invoke the provisions of Article XXXV in order to withhold such treatment.

7. Protocols of amendment, supplementary agreements, and declarations are open to acceptance by signature or by letter addressed to the Director-General by the Head of State or Head of Government. An acceptance qualified by the words "subject to ratification", "subject to approval" or "ad referendum" is regarded merely as an expression of the intentions of the government; it is not considered as fully binding until the qualification has been withdrawn. An acceptance accompanied by a reservation would be referred to the other governments to ascertain whether they had objections.

8. Rulings on questions concerning interpretation of provisions of the Agreement have been given by the Chairman of the *Contracting Parties* and by the *Contracting Parties* themselves. In one instance a ruling by the Chairman was challenged but was then upheld by a formal vote. On another occasion the Chairman ruled that the *Contracting Parties* were competent to interpret the Agreement and that "it was open for any government disagreeing with an interpretation to take the dispute which had given rise to such an interpretation to the International Court, although neither a government nor the *Contracting Parties* acting jointly could take a ruling of the *Contracting Parties* to the Court". However, most of the rulings on points of interpretation derive from opinions formulated by working parties or panels and set out in reports submitted to and adopted by the *Contracting Parties*. Precedent is an important element in the rulings and decisions of the *Contracting Parties* and in the twenty years since the GATT entered into force a substantial body of "case law" has devel-

oped. In a number of instances some contracting parties have reserved their position or have placed on record their disagreement.

9. Many provisions of the General Agreement require or authorize the *Contracting Parties* to take decisions on matters affecting the operation of the GATT, for example:

—to request information or reports on action taken by contracting parties,

—to concur in or give consent to certain action by contracting parties,

—to formulate rules governing certain action by contracting parties,

—to request contracting parties to review action taken by them in certain matters,

—to call upon contracting parties to engage in discussions or consultations,

— to determine whether action taken or measures imposed by contracting parties are consistent with the rules of GATT, and if not to make recommendations to the contracting parties concerned,

—to determine whether action by a contracting party is likely to be damaging to the trade of other contracting parties and, if so, to release injured parties from appropriate obligations towards the party taking the action,

—to authorize contracting parties to enter into negotiations for the modification or withdrawal of concessions,

—to determine which contracting parties have a substantial interest in concessions to be modified or withdrawn,

—to determine whether adequate compensation has been offered by contracting parties engaged in such negotiations,

—to agree on joint action to promote the objectives of the Agreement.

10. Generally, such decisions (in appropriate cases—especially when presented in formal language—called "recommendations", "resolutions" or "declarations") are adopted without voting, the Chairman merely taking the consensus of the meeting. If a formal vote is considered desirable, or if it is requested by a contracting party, such a decision can be adopted by a simply majority of the contracting parties present and voting, although on certain matters a majority of two-thirds of the contracting parties, or of the votes cast, is required. It not infrequently happens that a representative will reserve the position of his government, either because he has been instructed to do so or because he has not received instructions. In some cases it is laid down in the GATT (or it may be established in the decision itself) that contracting parties are required to accept or to comply, e.g. to participate in consultations, but in most cases there is only a moral obligation. Some contracting parties have failed to comply with decisions, e.g. to provide full information about measures which are inconsistent with the GATT, and the *Contracting Parties* have no means other than persuasion to bring about compliance.

11. However, most of the important desicions have been taken under para-

graph 5 of Article XXV which permits the *Contracting Parties* to waive an obligation of a contracting party. If the *Contracting Parties* are not in session, voting is by postal ballot and is closed after thirty days. The *Contracting Parties* have agreed that when examining an application for a waiver from an important obligation of the GATT they will satisfy themselves "that the legitimate interests of other contracting parties are adequately safeguarded". Usually governments to which waivers are granted are required to submit annual reports on action taken and on the development of trade in products affected and these are examined by the *Contracting Parties*. Some waivers are of limited duration or are subject to review periodically. Under certain other provisions the *Contracting Parties* may authorize a contracting party to depart from the strict observance of its obligations. Since waivers and other authorized derogations constitute a relaxation of obligations no question of enforcement or effectiveness arises. But a contracting party would not be precluded from bringing a complaint subsequently on the grounds that benefits accruing to it under the agreement were being nullified or impaired in a manner which could not have been foreseen when it acceded to the GATT.

12. A dispute between contracting parties, in respect of any matter affecting the operation of the Agreement, which cannot be settled in consultation among them, may be referred to the *Contracting Parties*. Having examined the matter, the *Contracting Parties* may make recommendations to the parties concerned, but can only urge them to comply. In most cases the contracting parties concerned have taken action in accordance with the recommendations addressed to them, but if the action recommended is not taken the matter remains on the agenda of the annual sessions of the *Contracting Parties*. One case, in which it was recommended to a government to amend certain laws so as to bring them into conformity with the General Agreement, came up for consideration at nine successive sessions before the government concerned finally complied with the recommendation. In another case it was brought to the notice of the *Contracting Parties* in 1952 that a number of contracting parties were maintaining measures which were contrary to the rules of GATT; the *Contracting Parties* recommended to the governments concerned that the measures be removed, but the item is still on the agenda for the annual sessions—some governments having complied with the recommendation while others still maintain the measures in question.

13. A formal complaint that benefits accruing under the Agreement are being nullified or impaired or that the attainment of an objective of the Agreement is being impeded, as the result of action by a contracting party, of its failure to carry out its obligations or of any other situation, may be brought before the *Contracting Parties* under Article XXIII. Having examined the case, the *Contracting Parties* may make recommendations or give rulings. A recommendation is made when it is considered that it would lead to a satisfactory adjustment of the matter and a ruling is given

when there is a point of contention on fact or law. Further, the *Contracting Parties,* if they consider the circumstances are serious enough, may authorize a contracting party to suspend the application to any other contracting party of such concessions or other obligations under the Agreement as they determine to be appropriate.

14. Finally, it should be noted that a contracting party, because it is dissatisfied with a decision of the *Contracting Parties* or for other reason, may withdraw from the GATT by giving 60 days notice.

THE EUROPEAN COMMUNITIES

by *Michel Gaudet*

Director-General, Legal Service of the Commission of the European Communities

I. THE CHOICE OF TECHNIQUES TO CARRY OUT AN AGREED COURSE OF ACTION

To achieve its aims the EEC has at its disposal a number of very diversified legal instruments, from the classical techniques used by international meetings to the specific instruments provided by the EEC Treaty.

A. *Specific measures*

The Community institutions may issue a variety of specific measures of the types defined in Article 189 of the EEC Treaty, which vary in their binding force both as regards their components (objectives and means) and their addressees.

1. "Regulations shall have a general application. They shall be binding in every respect and directly applicable in each Member State." The three characteristics of regulations are then their general field of application, their binding force and the directness of their applicability.
    (i) "...the regulation, being of an essentially normative character, is applied not to a limited, designated, or identifiable group of persons, but to essentially abstract categories envisaged as a whole." [1]
It is an act applicable to objectively determined situations.
    (ii) Regulations are binding in every respect. They are complete legal acts with all that is required for them to take effect without further normative intervention. [2]
    (iii) They are immediately applicable in all member States. They have force of law throughout the Community without requiring any national formula of incorporation or execution. "The regulations shall be published in the official gazette of the European Communities. They shall enter into force on the date fixed in them or, failing this, on the twentieth day following their publication" (Article 191, first paragraph).
    Regulations confer rights or impose obligations on individuals, and these rights or obligations can be invoked in the courts.

---

[1] Court of Justice of the European Communities, Cases 16 and 17/62 *Recueil, Vol.* VIII, p. 918.
[2] Regulation may, however, specify precise and limited action by the States.

2. "*Directives* shall be binding, as to the result to be achieved, on each member State to which they are addressed, while leaving to national authorities the choice of form and means."

(i) Unlike regulations, directives are binding only on the member State or States to which they are addressed.

(ii) Their effectiveness depends on the action taken by the State, which is left with a margin of discretion as to methods of implementation. Directives are binding only as to the result to be achieved.[3]

(iii) As directives can concern one or more member States, they must be "notified to those to whom they are addressed" (Article 191, second paragraph).

3. "*Decisions* shall be binding in every respect on those to whom they are addressed."

(i) Like directives, decisions concern addressees who are referred to by name.

"Directives and decisions shall be notified to their addressees and shall take effect upon such notification" (Article 191, second paragraph). This characteristic distinguishes them from regulations which are of universal application.

(ii) Directives and decisions differ, however, as to the status of addressee and the margin of discretion allowed.

Decisions may be addressed to individuals as well as to member States.

(a) *Decisions addressed to individuals,* which are binding in every respect, are directly applicable to the addressee after notification.

In this respect, their effects are similar to those of regulations.

(b) *Decisions addressed to member States* bind those member States.

4. "*Recommendations and opinions* shall have no binding force." These acts are akin to traditional instruments.

5. Lastly, reference can be made to the various measures which are not mentioned in Article 189, but which are taken by the Community institutions in the course of their duties; these include decisions on budgetary matters and the general programmes for the removal of restrictions on freedom of establishment and freedom to supply services. It must also be pointed out that the Community is authorized to conclude agreements with non-member countries and international organizations (Articles 111, 113, 114, 228, 231, 238).

---

[3] It must be noted however that in practice the content of directives tend to be more and more precise and detailed.

The four kinds of measure described in Article 189 are adopted by the Council and Commission "in the discharge of their duties and in accordance with the provisions of this Treaty", that is, as part of the responsibilities falling upon them, according to the ways and means laid down in, and in the circumstances specified by the Treaty

Their originality consists in the process by which they take shape in common institutions, i.e. by a vote subject to certain conditions and not by diplomatic commitment.

These decisions are taken by the institution as a body; they can bind States and even individuals. The binding character of the measure depends on its nature and not on the form of approval (majority or unanimity), which has no influence on its binding power.

The choice between these different types of measure may be laid down in the Treaty or it may be left to the initiative of the institutions, either by means of an alternative expressly offered by the Treaty or because of the very general terms used therein.

If the institutions are given the choice of form for an act, they take various considerations into account, in particular the objective aimed at by the Treaty and the legal means of protection conferred upon individuals.

These considerations derive from the points raised in the above examination of the various types of measure. Regulations are more suitable than directives when the steps to be taken must be uniform, precise and detailed, with no latitude as regards method of execution. Directives allow the States greater scope for adjustment to their legal systems and make it easier to take into account different national situations.

When common organizations had to be set up for the different agricultural markets (cereals,[4] pigmeat,[5] eggs,[6] poultry,[7] fruit and vegetables,[8] milk and milk products;[9] beef and veal,[10] and rice,[11]) the regulation was the form adopted for the basic and for certain implementing measures, as it was indispensable to set up a uniform body of rules, providing a complete and detailed machinery, to be equally effective everywhere and giving individuals the right of appeal. On the other hand, when it was necessary to provide measures to facilitate the transition from the national market systems to the common organization, a directive was drawn

---

[4] Regulation No. 19, *Official Gazette of the European Communities,* 20 April 1962, p. 933.
[5] Regulation No. 20, *ibid.,* p. 945.
[6] Regulation No. 21, *ibid.,* p. 953.
[7] Regulation No. 22, *ibid.,* p. 959.
[8] Regulation No. 23, *ibid.,* p. 965.
[9] Regulation No. 13/64, *ibid.,* 27 February 1964, p. 549.
[10] Regulation No. 14/64, *Official Gazette of the European Communities,* 27 February 1964, p. 562.
[11] Regulation No. 16/64, *ibid.,* p. 574.

up allowing member States considerable freedom of choice.[12]

Likewise Regulation No. 17 [13] was adopted to implement the principles set out in Articles 85 and 86. The choice was dictated by the result to be attained: rules which create identical conditions of competition, which can bind individuals and which are accompanied by sanctions. Article 85, moreover, had already been found to be directly applicable.[14]

A further example of making the form selected fit the aim is provided in the agricultural sphere by the shift from a transitional system involving execution through the member States to a system which is applied directly. In the first stage of progressively organizing the markets, the Commission fixed the free-at-frontier prices of cereals between the member States and the c.i.f. prices of cereals from non-member countries. It addressed a decision to each member State, to which the task was left of calculating the levies and imposing them by a domestic measure.[15]

At the single market stage for cereals, which came into force, on 1 July 1967, the Commission established itself by regulation the uniform levy on imports from third countries, which is directly applicable in the member States.[16]

B. *The classical methods*

1. Resolutions and records in the minutes express agreement reached at a meeting.

(a) *A resolution* is a declaration of intent, political in character but without legally binding force, which states formally that it has been decided to act in a specified manner.

The Community institutions have adopted several resolutions on agriculture, among which may be quoted the resolutions [17] in which the Council agreed to take the decisions enabling market organization for milk products, beef and veal, and sugar to be implemented on given dates and also invited the Commission to submit the requisite proposals by given dates.

(b) *Inclusion of an item in the minutes* is also political in its import.

---

[12] Commision directive on certain transitional arrangements in the cereals sector, *ibid.*, 9 June 1962, p. 1367.

[13] Regulation No. 17, *ibid.*, 21 February 1962, p. 204.

[14] Court of Justice of the European Communities, Case 13/61, *Recueil*, Vol. VIII, p. 89.

[15] Regulation No. 19, *Official Gazette of the European Communities*, 20 April 1962, p. 933.

[16] Regulation No. 120/67/CEE, *Official Gazette of the European Communities*, 19 June 1967, p. 2269.

[17] *Official Gazette of the European Communities*, 20 April 1962, p. 1006.

2. The *international convention* of classical type is also used. It may be provided for in the Treaty, as in the case of Article 20, which deals with determination of the duties on the products in List G annexed to the Treaty, and of Article 220, which has been the basis for various drafts or preliminary drafts of Conventions, such as the draft conventions concerning jurisdiction and the execution of judgments in civil and commercial matters and concerning the reciprocal recognition of companies and legal persons, the preliminary draft of a convention on bankruptcy and related procedures.

Such conventions have a supplementary character in the case of the draft European patent convention and the draft articles of a European-type company.

3. A class of decision midway between the traditional and specific instruments has made its appearance in the practice of the European Communities. *The decisions of the Representatives of the Governments of the member States meeting in the Council* cover an area exceeding the competence expressly attributed to the Community institutions, but the purpose they serve is analogous to the aims specified in the Treaty. These decisions [18] deal with a variety of subjects. The most characteristic example is that of the decisions of 12 May 1960 and 15 May 1962 [19] on speeding up achievement of the aims of the EEC Treaty.

The nature of the decisions of the Representatives of the Governments meeting in the Council is difficult to define.

(i) They have the character of international commitments and also certain Community aspects, the importance of the latter varying from one case to another. As a rule they have been looked upon as simplified agreements which are not submitted to national parliaments for approval. These decisions generally contain a final provision worded as follows: "The Governments of the member States shall within one month notify the Secretary-General of the Council whether under their domestic law any action is required to implement the present decision; if so, they shall immediately notify the Secretary-General when this action has been completed."

(ii) The decisions of the Representatives of the Governments meeting in the Council also have certain features which distinguish them from traditional international agreements, because the member States use the institutional framework provided by the Treaties, in particular the procedures and certain forms. The Commission, for instance, submitted to the

---

[18] They number about 60 so far—Professor Schermers, Besluiten van de Vertegenwoordigers der Lid-Staten; Gemeenschapsrecht? (*Sociaal Economische Wetgeving*—October/November 1966, No. 10/11).

[19] *Official Gazette of the European Communities*, 12 September 1960, p. 1217 and 28 May 1962, p. 1284.

Council its proposals for the speed-up in the form of recommendations and the Representatives of the Governments adopted, with some amendments, the recommendations in the form of a decision taken in the Council.

The decisions were signed by the President of the Council and published in the official gazette of the European Communities.

They provided a basis for certain acts of the Community institutions and national authorities. The EEC Commission took several further decisions on the strength of these acceleration decisions.

The internal implementing conventions accompanying the Association Conventions of the Community and which are also concluded by the Representatives of the governments meeting in the Council, rather belong to the group of traditional international commitments. Indeed they are signed by the plenipotentiaries of the member States and contain a formula according to which they shall be approved by each member State in accordance with its constitutional rules.[20]

II. LEGAL EFFECTS OF MEMBER STATES' APPROVAL OF DECISIONS

Because of the structure of the Communities and the particular ways in which their decisions are reached (these are described in Section I above) this point does not call for many remarks.

In the case of measures adopted by the Commission (regulations, directives, decisions), the question of how the member States vote does not arise; they are bound by the measures taken by the Commission, an independent body which acts on the principle of joint responsibility and on which the States as such are not represented.

In the case of measures taken by the Council, to which each Government delegates one of its members, it must be recalled that a favourable or unfavourable vote by a State in no way affects the binding force of the collective decision. All that must be considered is whether the substantive and procedural rules have been observed—a matter over which the Court of Justice of the European Communities exercises control; any State which considers that a decision is not in accordance with these rules may appeal against it.

The EEC Treaty provides for the following types of vote: by simple majority, by qualified majority, and unanimous.

[20] Two conventions accompanying the Association Convention with Greece, *Official Gazette of the European Communities*, 18 February 1963, p. 350 and 352; two conventions accompanying the Association Convention with Turkey, *ibid.*, 29 December 1964, p. 3703 and 3705; and two conventions accompanying the Association Convention with the African and Malagasy States associated with the Community, *ibid.*, 11 June 1964, p. 1490 and 1493.

Voting by simple majority is the general rule (Article 148(1)): "Except where otherwise provided in this Treaty, the conclusions of the Council shall be reached by a majority vote of its members". However, a large number of particular measures require either unanimity or a qualified majority, so that in practice this general rule is rather the exception.

The EEC Treaty also provides for a gradual change-over from unanimity to a qualified majority as the transitional period advances.

The method of calculating the qualified majority is set out in Article 148(2), which establishes a weighting system: "Where the conclusions of the Council require a qualified majority, the votes of its members shall be weighted as follows:

Belgium	2
Germany	4
France	4
Italy	4
Luxembourg	1
Netherlands	2

Majorities shall be required for the adoption of any conclusions as follows:

Twelve votes in favour where this Treaty requires that they be reached on a proposal of the Commission, or
Twelve votes including a favourable vote by at least four members in all other cases."

Article 149 says moreover that, "When by virtue of this Treaty the Council is acting on a proposal of the Commission, it may amend the proposal only if it is unanimous."

Here the purpose of unanimity is to strengthen the role of the Commission in preparing decisions.

On unanimity, Article 148(3) states: "Abstentions by members either present or represented shall not prevent the adoption of Council conclusions requiring unanimity." It could be deduced that a qualified majority is sometimes more difficult to achieve than unanimity in case of abstention. In reality, the practical interest of Article 148(3) is to allow a member of the Council to express displeasure (which may seem called for on the national plane) without however blocking the decision.

There are several examples where decisions have been adopted by a majority vote, for instance in the budgets and in tariff matters. These decisions have been simply accepted and implemented by the States in the minority. That States have on occasion voted against the budget, has not prevented them from making their contribution towards the expenditure decided upon.

Furthermore, a State which had voted against the adoption of a regulation [21] and had expressed legal reservations, attacked the regulation before

---

[21] Regulation No. 19/65 conferring on the Commission the power to grant exemp-

the Court of Justice,[22] thereby showing that it did not intend to refrain unilaterally from implementing the decision and that it contested its legality by process of law.

Insistence on unanimity, even when only a simple or qualified majority is required, may prove desirable without the Community character of the decision being jeopardized. For example, for the adoption of the first regulation on restrictive agreements, although since the end of 1960 the Treaty no longer required more than a qualified majority, the Council and the Commission deemed it preferable that this regulation, giving the Commission very wide powers, especially to carry out its investigations, should be adopted unanimously.

Lastly decisions may be adopted unanimously without a particular effort having been made to achieve this.

The Luxembourg agreements brought about certain adjustments of an interpretative nature to the strict application of the majority principle. The right to decide by majority vote does not mean that unanimity must not be sought, especially when it is a matter of vital interest to one of the member States. Any divergence of views, however, cannot block the working of the Community:

"I. Where, in the case of decisions which may be taken by majority vote on a proposal of the Commission, very important interests of one or more partners are at stake, the members of the Council will endeavour, within a reasonable time, to reach solutions which can be adopted by all the members of the Council while respecting their mutual interests and those of the Community, in accordance with Article 2 of the Treaty.

II. With regard to the preceding paragraph, the French delegation considers that where very important interests are at stake the discussion must be continued until unanimous agreement is reached.

III. The six delegations note that there is a divergence of views on what should be done in the event of a failure to reach complete agreement.

IV. The six delegations nevertheless consider that this divergence does not prevent the Community's work being resumed in accordance with the normal procedure." [23]

III. INTERNAL LEGAL EFFECTS OF DECISIONS OF INTERNATIONAL ORGANIZATIONS

A. The measures (as defined in Article 189 of the Treaty) that can be taken by the Community Institutions fall into two classes which vary in the ef-

tions, by regulations, under Article 85(3) to certain classes of agreements, *Official Gazette of the European Communities*, 6 March 1965, p. 533.
[22] Court of Justice of the European Communities, case 32/65 (Italian Republic v. EEC Council and Commission) *Recueil*, Vol. XII-4, p. 564
[23] Extract from the minutes of the Council meeting of 29 January 1966.

fect they have in the member States: there are measures which are binding only on the States themselves and require action by them, and there are those which affect individuals directly, conferring rights or imposing obligations (cf. Section I). This raises the problem of the direct applicability of acts of the Community, a problem which also arises in connection with the provisions of the Treaty itself.

1. The domestic courts and the Court of Justice of the European Communities have had to pronounce on the point whether certain rules established by the European treaties could be invoked directly by individuals, and they have evolved interpretative criteria based mainly on the nature and subject of the measure in question.

Article 31 of the EEC Treaty has been recognized as directly applicable by the Italian Council of State [24] and Article 70 of the ECSC Treaty by the French Council of State.[25] Numerous decisions of the Tariefcommissie in the Netherlands have dealt with the legality of charge in the light of Articles 12 and 16 of the Treaty. The direct applicability of Article 85 has been very much contested by judges in various countries. While certain courts in Germany and the Netherlands have accepted that it was directly applicable,[26] others have not.[27]

The Court of Justice of the European Communities, whose task (cf. below) is to give a uniform interpretation of the Treaty, has established certain criteria enabling the self-executing character of its provisions to be recognized, for example in the well-known Van Gend and Loos judgment: "To know whether the provisions of an international treaty have such an effect it is necessary to look at its spirit, its content and the terms used.

... Community law, therefore, apart from legislation by the Member States, not only imposes obligations on individuals but also confers on them legal rights... The latter arise not only when an explicit grant is made by the Treaty, but also through obligations imposed, in a clearly defined manner, by the Treaty on individuals as well as on Member States and the Community Institutions." [28]

The Court has thus recognized direct applicability of Articles 12,[28] 37 (2) [29] and 53 [29] of the EEC Treaty, which clearly impose a prohibition in

---

[24] 7 November 1962, *Foro Padano* 1963, V, p. 34.

[25] 22 December 1961, S.N.C.F., *Gazette du Palais*, 25 May 1962.

[26] Landgericht Düsseldorf, 6 December 1960, *Wirtschaft und Wettbewerb* 1960, p. 805; Oberlandgericht Frankfurt, 19 January 1962, *Der Betriebsberater* 1962, p. 735; Court of Appeal of Arnhem, 28 June 1961, *Nederlandse Jurisprudentie* 1962, p. 438.

[27] Zutphen Court, 11 July 1958, *Wirtschaft und Wettbewerb* 1958, p. 779; Amsterdam Court, 3 March 1960, *ibid.*, 1960, p. 773.

[28] Court of Justice of the European Communities (C.J.E.C.), case 26/62, *Recueil*, Vol. IX, p. 6.

[29] C.J.E.C., case 6/64, *Recueil*, Vol. X, p. 1141.

binding terms. It also recognized direct applicability of Article 95 which imposes a precisely defined obligation.[30]

Besides the provisions of the Treaty recognized as self-executing, Community regulations and decisions addressed to private individuals are measures that are directly applicable.

(a) *Regulations*

Besides its general field of application, the essential characteristic of a regulation lies in its direct applicability (cf. Sec. I). For the Community a regulation is the normative act par excellence: "... the Community legislates directly and exclusively in all matters that need to be regulated uniformly and in detail in pursuit of the objectives laid down in the Treaty."[31]

The direct applicability of regulations does not raise problems for the national courts; it is a principle which they have accepted on many occasions. Divergences arise only through the interpretation of these regulations in the national or the Community context. These divergences are of particular value in bringing out the importance of the role played by the Court of Justice of the Communities in obtaining a uniform interpretation of Community acts (cf. B 3 below).

(b) *Decisions addressed to individuals belong to the directly applicable acts of the Community.*

According to Article 192 of the EEC Treaty, "decisions of the Council or of the Commission which include a pecuniary obligation on persons other than States shall be enforceable (forment *titre exécutoire*)." This enforceability gives them a character and value similar to decisions taken in individual countries by their own authorities.

An example that can be quoted is that of fines inflicted under Article 92 of the ECSC Treaty (which is analogous to EEC Article 192), which have been enforced by domestic courts.[32]

---

[30] C.J.E.C., case 57/65, *Recueil*, Vol. XII, p. 293.
[31] Hallstein, "The European Community: a new legal order", address given on 19 November 1964 at the Faculty of Law and Economics in Paris.
[32] All these cases have arisen in Italy:
Pretura di Roma, 11 March 1964, *Foro Italiano* 1964, I, p. 866;
Tribunale di Napoli, 22 April 1964, *Foro Italiano* 1964, I, p. 1253;
Tribunale di Mondovi, 24 July 1964, *Foro Padano* 1965, IV, p. 17;
Tribunale di Roma, 22 September 1964, *Common Market Law Reports* 1966, p. 20;
Tribunale di Milano, 24 June 1964, *Common Market Law Reports* 1965, p. 1.
It was on the occasion of an enforcement case that the Italian Constitutional Court affirmed the constitutionality of the ECSC Treaty (27 December, 1965, Acciaierie San Michele, *Common Market Law Review* 1966, p. 81).

2. The other measures available to the Community Institutions, i.e. directives, decisions addressed to the member States, opinions and recommendations, are generally considered not to be directly applicable, for the Treaty does not attribute this characteristic to them. It must be noted, however, that for directives, and even more for decisions, this distinction is tending to become blurred.

(a) As regards decisions addressed to the member States, while certain courts have affirmed that they bind only the member State addressed and do not have a binding effect on nationals of a Member State,[33] the Finanzgericht of Hamburg [34] has recognized that "customs authorities are not authorized to disregard the decision, which is for them of a binding nature."

As decisions are binding in every respect and do not allow a discretionary margin of implementation, they therefore have, in practice, effects comparable to those of regulations.

In giving a verdict on the admissibility of an appeal, the Court of Justice of the Communities recognized that a Commission decision amending or abolishing national safeguard measures is directly applicable and concerns the individuals affected as directly as the measures it replaces.[35]

(b) Directives often concern matters calling for very elaborate rules. They also often are the result of a compromise worked out in great detail. So their provisions tend to become more and more precise and detailed, leaving very little freedom to the States in the means to use for implementing them.

In any case, directives constitute one of the elements for judging objective legality, for the national authorities find that they have to be taken into account when national rules are being implemented or interpreted.[36]

It also may in certain cases seem arbitrary to deny the direct effect of certain provisions of a directive which, in their content, do not differ from treaty provisions recognized by the Court of Justice as having a direct effect, particularly when the directives impose an unconditional obligation to abolish a national measure or to refrain from doing something.

B. The growing activity of international organizations and specifically of the European Communities has had a very distinct influence on traditional concepts regarding the incorporation in domestic law of obligations deriv-

---

[33] Finanzgericht Rheinland Pfalz, 27 March 1963, *Entscheidungen der Finanzgerichte* 1963, p. 444 and 25 March 1965, not published;
Finanzgericht Bremen, 3 September 1963, *Common Market Law Reports* 1964, p. 295.
[34] 19 November 1964, *Common Market Law Reports* 1965, p. 268.
[35] C.J.E.C., cases 106 and 107/63, *Recueil*, Vol. XI, p. 533.
[36] This is what the Berlin Administrative Court did in its judgment of 26 October 1962 (*Common Market Law Reports* 1964, p. 5).

ing from treaties and acts of international organizations. This influence has shown itself in the constitutional, legislative and judicial approach to problems raised by the international organizations, and specifically the European Communities.

1. The constitutions of most member States now contain provisions authorizing delegation of powers to international organizations: for example, Article 24 [37] of the German Basic Law; Article 11 [38] of the Italian Constitution; the preamble to the present French Constitution, in the form of a reference to the 1946 Constitution; [39] Article 67(1) of the Netherlands Constitution as revised in 1953 and 1956, [40] Article 49(bis) [41] of the Luxemburg Constitution.

For the Netherlands and Luxemburg, it is their participation in the European Institutions which has entailed these changes in their constitutions; draft amendments are being studied in Belgium for the same reason, but these have not yet been completed.

Moreover, certain constitutions clearly state the primacy of international law over domestic law as, for example, does the French Constitution of 1958 in its article 55. [42]

The Netherlands Constitution, which in this respect is the most advanced, has systematically regulated relations between domestic law and international law by confirming the supremacy, not only of the provisions of treaties, but also of the decisions taken by international organizations. [43]

---

[37] "The Federation may, by legislation, transfer sovereign powers to international institutions."

[38] "Italy . . . , on conditions of equality with the other states, agrees to the limitations of her sovereignty necessary to an organization which will assure peace and justice among nations, and promotes and encourages international organizations constituted for this purpose."

[39] "On condition of reciprocity, France accepts the limitations of sovereignty necessary to the organization and defence of peace."

[40] "Subject where necessary to the provisions of Article 63 (procedure for approving derogations from the Constitution), powers in the fields of legislation, administration and jurisdiction may be delegated by a convention or by virtue of a convention to organizations founded upon the law of nations."

[41] "The exercise of powers reserved by the Constitution to the legislature, the executive or the judiciary may be temporarily delegated by treaty to institutions founded upon the law of nations."

[42] "Treaties or agreements duly ratified or approved shall, upon their publication, have an authority superior to that of laws, subject, for each agreement or treaty, to its application by the other party."

[43] Articles 66 and 67(2), as revised in 1953 and 1956:
(a) Article 66: "Legislative provisions in force within the Kingdom shall not be applied in cases in which such an application would be incompatible with clauses by which everyone is bound, contained in agreements which have been concluded either before or after the entry into force of such provisions."
(b) Article 67(2): "Articles 65 and 66 shall apply by analogy to the acts of international organizations."

In the countries where this possibility exists, the constitutionality of the European Treaties has been referred to the courts.

The Italian Constitutional Court, twice called on to make a pronouncement, has in the Costa/Enel [44] and Acciaierie San Michele [45] judgments recognized that the Treaties are in conformity with the Constitution.

In Germany the Finanzgericht of the Rhineland-Palatinate has questioned the constitutionality of the EEC Treaty and of an agricultural regulation.[46] The Federal Constitutional Court (Bundesverfassungsgericht) refused to rule on the constitutionality of the law ratifying the EEC Treaty because the provision of the agricultural regulation was in the given instance, not applicable and therefore the question was not pertinent for the pending litigation.[47]

Various courts [48] have admitted that the transfer of responsibilities to the EEC institutions was in conformity with the Basic Law by virtue of its Article 24 and did not conflict with the principle of separation of powers. So the Bundesfinanzhof refused to submit the matter of the constitutionality of the agricultural regulations to the Bundesverfassungsgericht or to await its decision in the case submitted to it by the Finanzgericht of the Rhineland-Palatinate, considering that there were no legitimate grounds for doubt.[49]

2. The increase in the normative activities of the European institutions has led in the member States to a tendency to modify the traditional division of powers between legislature and executive. The reasons underlying this development are as follows: [50]

(i) Parliamentary procedure is slow and complex;
(ii) The sovereign character of the legislature seems incompatible with the function of executing Community law;

---

[44] 7 March 1964, *Foro Italiano* 1964, I, p. 465. The Court affirmed the regularity of the procedure adopted to conclude the Treaty: "This rule (Article 11 of the Italian Constitution) means that when certain conditions are complied with, it is possible to conclude treaties involving limitations of sovereignty and to make them enforceable by an ordinary law."

[45] 27 December 1965, *Common Market Law Review* 1966, p. 81. The Court recognized the compatibility of the ECSC Treaty with certain provisions of the Constitution concerning the judicial protection of individuals (Articles 102 and 113).

[46] 14 November 1963, *Common Market Law Reports* 1964, p. 130. The Court deems contrary to the principles contained in Articles 20, 79(3) and 80 of the Basic Law the power attributed by the EEC Treaty to the Council of Ministers to issue regulations in matters reserved to the legislature.

[47] 5 July 1967, *Neue Juristische Wochenschrift* 1967, p. 1707.

[48] Verwaltungsgericht Frankfurt am Main, 17 December 1963, *AWD des BB* 1964, p. 60, and 7 July 1965, *id.* 1965, p. 299; Finanzgericht Bremen, 3 September 1963, *Common Market Law Reports* 1964, p. 295.

[49] 25 April 1967, not published.

[50] Sohier-Mégret report on "Le rôle de l'exécutif national et du législateur national dans la mise en oeuvre du droit communautaire", *Bruges Week* 1965.

321

(iii) Legislative procedure re-opens political debate on the substance of Community measures already adopted;

(iv) There is no adequate sanction when Parliament refuses to comply with the Community measures;

(v) Executive procedure, on the contrary, is far better adapted to the function of implementing Community law in the domestic context and here its use is not disturbing because it does not deprive the parliaments of a substantive power.

The use of executive procedure to implement the Treaty is illustrated by the following examples.

Sometimes governments use the power they have to make orders implementing domestic laws to implement provisions of the Treaties and of Community acts, considering those as part of their domestic law.[51] Furthermore power is delegated by the legislature to the executive, even in countries like Germany, where such transfer of power is subject under article 80 of the Basic Law to very strict conditions.

The German law ratifying the EEC Treaty[52] had already conferred on the Government power to implement by order (Rechtsverordnung) certain articles of the Treaty in customs matters. Article 77 of the law of 14 June 1961 widened the powers given to the Government and replaced the need for the Bundestag's prior agreement by approval subsequent to publication of the order, which is deemed to have been given if the order is not annulled within three months.[53]

In Italy the ratification law, in its Article 4,[54] and subsequent laws[55] have delegated considerable power to the Government in the conditions stipulated by Article 76 of the Constitution. The executive has also used the special procedure provided by Article 77 of the Constitution (decree-laws made without delegation, to be converted into ordinary law by a given date, failing which their validity lapses), e.g. to implement the common agricultural policy.[56]

In France the Government already has since the passing of the 1958

---

[51] Measures necessary to implement Article 13 of EEC Regulation No. 17 were taken by the Italian Government in the form of a presidential decree of 22 September 1963 (*Gazetta Ufficiale*, 11 January 1964) as if a national law were being implemented. Since 1964, EEC decisions on customs matters have been executed in France by presidential decree as if they were domestic laws.

[52] Law of 27 July 1957, *Bundesgesetzblatt* II, p. 753.

[53] *Bundesgesetzblatt* 1961, I, p. 758. Article 77 of this law has been amended by the laws of 18 August 1962, 4 September 1962, 25 March 1964 and 9 September 1964 which grant the Government further powers in customs matters.

[54] Law of 14 October 1957 (*Gazetta Ufficiale*, Supplemento ordinario, 23 December 1957).

[55] See e.g. Law of 20 December 1960 (*Gazetta Ufficiale*, 22 December 1960), Law of 26 January 1962 (*ibid.*, 5 February 1962) and Law of 1 February 1965 (*ibid.*, 15 February 1965).

[56] See e.g. Decree-Law of 30 July 1962 (*Gazetta Ufficiale*, 30 July 1962) which became the Law of 28 September 1962 (*ibid.*, 12 October 1962); Decree-Law of 11 September 1963 (*ibid.*, 12 September 1963) which became the Law of 3 November 1963 (*ibid.*, 11 November 1963).

322

Constitution autonomous power under Article 34 to issue rules and regulations in all matters not expressly reserved to the legislature. Furthermore Parliament empowered the Government, on the basis of Article 38 of the Constitution, to issue orders to implement the EEC common agricultural policy [57] and the EEC directives on freedom of establishment and freedom to supply services.[58]

3. Lastly, the domestic courts have felt the need for closer collaboration with the Court of Justice of the European Communities because of the innumerable problems arising from the application of Community law.

Numerous divergencies have indeed been observed within one and the same State or between one State and another in decisions made by courts called on to pronounce on the application of Community measures.

In Germany, for instance, the Bremen Financial Court [59] considered that the countervailing charge placed on imports of agricultural products from non-member countries in addition to the Community levy was incompatible with Article 20 of Regulation No. 19 on the gradual establishment of a common organization of the market in cereals, because it constituted in fact a charge having equivalent effect to a customs duty, while the Nuremberg Financial Court, in two judgments,[60] attributed to it the character of a fiscal charge compatible with Community rules.

The Berlin Administrative Court in a judgment of 26 October 1962 [61] held that any national of a member State is entitled to a residence permit if he complies with the conditions of Regulation No. 15 concerning the free movement of workers in the EEC, while for the Munster Oberverwaltungsgericht [62] Regulation No. 15 does not conflict with the maintenance in force, in conformity with articles 48(3) and 56(1) of the EEC Treaty, of rules governing the residence of foreigners which are justified by reasons of public policy *(ordre public)* and public security.

In similar cases the Munich Court of Appeal [63] held that vertical agreements prohibiting exports, if notified to the Commission, were provisionally valid according to Article 4(2) of Regulation No. 17, as the Amiens Court of Appeal [64] held that, as long as the Commission had not embarked upon the necessary procedure, the national authorities remained competent to judge those agreements which, applying only to the home territory, do not

---

[57] Law of 8 August 1962, *Journal officiel de la République française,* 10 August 1962.
[58] Law of 14 December 1964 *(Journal officiel de la République française,* 15 December 1964) renewed by the Law of 6 July 1966 *(ibid.,* 7 July 1966).
[59] 9 April 1963, *Common Market Law Reports* 1964, p. 304.
[60] 23 April 1963, *ibid.,* p. 96 and 23 March 1964, *ibid.,* p. 310.
[61] *Ibid.,* 1964, p. 5.
[62] 10 September 1963, *ibid.,* 1965, p. 53.
[63] Oberlandesgericht München, 30 May 1963, *ibid.,* 1964, p. 87.
[64] 9 May 1963, *JCP* 1963, No. 13222, confirmed by the Cour de Cassation, 23 October 1964, Dalloz 1964, p. 753.

fall under Article 85(1) of the EEC Treaty and cannot be exempted by notification from the prohibition provided by this article; it refused to apply to the Court of Justice for an interpretation of the Community provision in question.

These examples illustrate clearly the difficulties that may arise from differences in interpretation of Community law by domestic Courts. Consequently these courts are using more and more frequently the machinery provided by Article 177 of the EEC Treaty.

Article 177 states that: "The Court of Justice shall be competent to give preliminary rulings concerning:

(a) The interpretation of this Treaty;
(b) The validity and interpretation of acts of institutions of the Community;
(c) The interpretation of the statutes of any bodies set up by an act of the Council, where the said statutes so provide.

Where any such question is raised before any court of one of the member States, the said court may, if it considers that a decision on the question is essential to enable it to render judgment, request the Court of Justice to give a ruling thereon.

Where any such question is raised in a case pending before a domestic court of a member State, from whose decisions there is no possibility of appeal under domestic law, the said court is bound to refer the matter to the Court of Justice."

The Court of Justice is thus called upon to assume a supervisory role which ensures unity of case law in the Community and prevents the disequilibrium which could result from divergent interpretations.

The procedure under Article 177 having made it possible (see part A of this Section) to define a common notion of direct applicability, it also contributes considerably to the judicial protection of individuals.

A widespread readiness to apply for interpretations will furthermore make it possible to settle the conflicts that inevitably arise between Community and domestic law, the member States not yet having uniform rules for dealing with such conflicts.

While there are certain countries where the constitution (France, Netherlands) or case law (Luxemburg) recognize the primacy of international law over domestic law, there are others where a dualist conception of the manner in which international law is received (Germany and Italy) leads, by the principle of assimilation, to a subsequent law being given preference over a Community act (lex posterior derogat priori).

Often case law has attempted to ensure the primacy of international law by a conciliatory interpretation or by denying that a conflict exists.[65] But the clearly expressed intention of the legislator may make such attempt impossible.

---

[65] Invoked mainly in Italy (Corte di Cassazione 12 July 1957, *Foro Italiano* 1958, I, p. 1294).

The Costa/Enel case brought up the problem in acute form in Italy. The Italian Constitutional Court recognized the primacy of the subsequently enacted law, treating the conflict between the Treaty and domestic law as a conflict between norms of equal rank.[66]

The Court of Justice of the European Communities had affirmed the primacy of Community law. This primacy is an evident corollary of the Community law being law common to six member States and the indispensable condition of its effectiveness which depends essentially on its consistent and uniform application:

"Whereas the reception into the law of each member country of provisions which are of Community origin and, more generally, the letter and spirit of the Treaty are such that it is impossible for the States to assert the supremacy over a legal system accepted by them on a basis of reciprocity of a subsequent unilateral measure: such a measure therefore cannot be invoked against the common legal system;

"Whereas the executive force of Community law cannot vary from one State to another in favour of subsequent domestic law without jeopardizing the achievement of the aims of the Treaty referred to in article 5(2), nor cause discrimination, forbidden by Article 7;"

"Flowing as it does from an autonomous source, law born of the Treaty cannot therefore, given its original specific nature, be opposed in the courts by a national law, whatever it may be, without losing its Community character and without the legal basis of the Community being jeopardized;" [67]

Article 177 offers, therefore, the means of ensuring, in any case, the primacy of Community law thanks to the authority of the interpretation of the Community provision given by the Court of Justice.

The preceding may have illustrated the importance of the machinery provided by Article 177; it is the requests for preliminary rulings that allow the problem submitted to the domestic court to be placed in its true Community context, and assure in this way an uniform application of the Community law in all member countries.

Experience shows that the domestic courts are becoming more and more aware of the significance of this provision. More and more applications for interpretation are being made to the Court of Justice by Courts and Tribunals of different nature of all the member States.[68] Close and enlightened co-operation is developing between the Court of Justice and the domestic courts.

---

[66] 7 March 1964, *Foro Italiano* 1964, I, p. 465. The German Constitutional Court, in a noted judgment (concordat case) came to the same conclusion, refusing to recognize the primacy of a treaty over domestic law (26 March 1957, BVerfGe Vol. 6, p. 362).

[67] CJEC, case 6/64, *Recueil*, Vol. X, p. 1159.

[68] From the beginning of this year, 18 applications have been made.

IV. COMPLIANCE—MEASURES TO HELP ENSURE THAT MEMBER STATES' COMMITMENTS OR OBLIGATIONS ARE CARRIED OUT

The EEC Treaty, subsequent measures and the practices adopted have established a body of institutions and measures which make it possible to ensure that the Community's decisions are carried out by member States.

Here again we find the traditional techniques used in the classical international organizations and judicial procedures peculiar to the European institutions.

Article 155 of the EEC Treaty instructs the Commission to "ensure that the provisions of this Treaty and the measures pursuant to it taken by the institutions are carried out".

Article 5 lays down a general line of conduct for member States: "Member States shall take all appropriate measures, whether general or particular, to ensure the carrying out of the obligations arising out of this Treaty or resulting from measures taken by the institutions of the Community. They shall facilitate the execution of the Community's tasks."

A. *Traditional techniques*

The member States and Community institutions co-operate constantly by exchanging information, by consultation, by regular reviews and by confrontation.

1. The Commission has extensive means of obtaining information:

(i) Its staff systematically scrutinizes the official publications of the member States to ensure that the measures being taken conform to the Treaty. They are in close contact with government departments in the various countries which, in accordance with Article 5, must facilitate the tasks of the Community and make available all necessary information and facilities.

(ii) Article 213 of the EEC Treaty allows the Commission to be given very wide powers defined in general terms: "For the execution of the tasks entrusted to it the Commission may, within the limits and under the conditions laid down by the Council in accordance with the provisions of this Treaty, collect any information and carry out any checks that may be needed."

Community acts, such as Regulation No. 17 on restrictive agreements (Article 14) [69] have given the Commission vast powers of supervision and inquiry. By other acts surveys of wages and investments have been organized. [70]

---

[69] *Official Gazette of the European Communities*, 21 February, 1962, p. 204.

(iii) Other Treaty provisions require the member States to inform or consult the Commission in certain specific cases. For instance, Article 93 on aids says: "1. The Commission shall in conjunction with member States keep all systems of aids existing in those States under constant review. It shall propose to the latter any appropriate measures required by the progressive development or by the functioning of the common market." ... "3. The Commission shall be informed, in sufficient time to enable it to submit its comments, of any plans to grant or alter aids."

Article 102 (approximation of laws) reads: "1. When there is reason to fear that the introduction or amendment of a provision imposed by law, regulation or administrative action may cause distortion within the meaning of Article 101 above, the member State desiring to introduce or amend such provision shall consult the Commission. After consulting the member States the Commission shall recommend to the States concerned such measures as may be appropriate to avoid the distortion in question."

Co-operation and reciprocal provision of information between the Commission and member States are, moreover, called for again and again in the Treaty (Articles 43, 49, 54(3b), 103, 105, 118, etc.).

Also Community acts specify expressly that the member States must inform the Commission of the measures taken to implement them.

2. Advisory bodies have been set up in accordance with the Treaty or with subsequent decisions with the aim of working out, under the auspices of the Commission, a common line of action.

Various advisory committees undertake studies at regular intervals and render opinions with a view to promoting co-ordination of the member States' policies.

For example, the Monetary Committee's task according to Article 105 is:
(i) To keep under review the monetary and financial situation of member States and of the Community and also the general system of payments in member States, and to report regularly thereon to the Council and to the Commission;
(ii) To deliver opinions at the request of the Council or of the Commission or on its own initiative, for submission to these institutions.

The Short-term Economic Policy Committee, set up by a Council decision of 9 March 1960 [71] "co-operates in the process of consultation between mem-

---

[70] For wages:
Regulation No. 10, *Official Gazette of the European Communities*, 31 August 1960, p. 1199;
Regulation No. 14, *ibid.*, 16 August 1961, p. 1054;
Regulation No. 28, *ibid.*, 28 May 1962, p. 1277;
Regulation No. 151, *ibid.*, 13 December 1962, p. 2841;
Regulation No. 188/64, *ibid.*, 24 December 1964, p. 3634.
For investments: Directive 64/475/CEE, *ibid.*, 13 August 1964, p. 2193.
[71] *Official Gazette of the European Communities*, 9 May 1960, p. 764.

ber States and the Commission provided for in Article 103 of the Treaty."

The task of the Medium-term Economic Policy Committee, set up by a Council decision of 15 April 1964,[72] is to use "all available information and especially the studies of economic prospects made by a group of experts attached to the Commission, to draft a medium-term economic programme..."

The Budget Policy Committee [73] has to "study and collate the main lines of the budgetary policies of the member States."

The Committee of Governors of Central Banks in the EEC [74] is responsible "for conducting consultations relating to the general rules and the main lines of policy of the central banks, in particular as regards credit, the money market and the exchange market."

The system of "Management Committees," provided for by all the basic agricultural regulations,[75] provides a characteristic example of the permanent contacts between the representatives of the member States and of the Community.

Each Management Committee is responsible for a group of agricultural products and is composed of representatives of the member States and the Commission. The Committees have to assist the Commission in the task of adopting the necessary measures to implement the basic regulations. This leads in practice to regular exchanges of views and common studies.

3. In general there is constant co-operation at all levels between the member States and the Community institutions through official bodies, some of which have been described, as well as at meetings of experts and working parties.

The extent of this co-operation is shown by the variety of possibilities and methods of action provided by innumerable Community acts. The Commission may act:

(i) In contact with the government departments in the member States;
(ii) In collaboration with the member States or their government departments;
(iii) After reference to the member States (outside the Committees);

---

[72] *Official Gazette of the European Communities*, 22 April 1964, p. 1031.
[73] Council decision, *ibid.*, 21 May 1964, p. 1205.
[74] Council decision, *ibid.*, 21 May 1964, p. 1206.
[75] Regulation No. 19, *ibid.*, 20 April 1962, p. 933 replaced by Regulation No. 120, *ibid.*, 19 June 1967, p. 2269 (cereals); Regulation No. 20, *ibid.*, 20 April 1962, p. 945 replaced by Regulation No. 121, *ibid.*, 19 June 1967, p. 2283 (pigmeat); Regulation No. 21, *ibid.*, 20 April 1962, p. 953 replaced by Regulation No. 122, *ibid.*, 19 June 1967, p. 2293 (eggs); Regulation No. 22, *ibid.*, 20 April 1962, p. 959 replaced by Regulation No. 123, *ibid.*, 19 June 1967, p. 2301 (poultry); Regulation No. 23, *ibid.*, 20 April 1962, p. 965; Regulation No. 13/64, *ibid.*, 27 February 1964, p. 549 milk and milk products; Regulation No. 14/64, *ibid.*, 27 February 1964, p. 562 beef and veal; Regulation No. 16/64, *ibid.*, 27 February 1964, p. 574 rice.

(iv) After compulsory reference to a Committee or to the member States through a Committee or on the proposal of a Committee;

(v) After reference to the Council;

(vi) After reference to a Management Committee and subject to a decision by the Council if the Committee has disagreed;

(vii) After reference to the member States through a Management Committee and subject to amendment by the Council (agricultural safeguard clause formula);

(viii) In agreement with the member States.

B. *Judicial procedures*

The EEC Treaty provides judicial procedures to ensure that the States respect their obligations. For this purpose cases can be brought before the Court of Justice of the European Communities either by the Commission (Article 169) or by a member State (Article 170).

Application of Article 169 is one means the Commission has of carrying out its task as defined in Article 155.

The conditions and pattern of the procedure are very similar in the two cases.

The aim is not so much to penalize past action as to induce an offending State to adopt a certain line of behaviour.[76] This explains the division of the procedure into two stages: pre-trial proceedings, when conciliation is attempted, and the proceedings proper, which are opened only if the former fail.

1. *Procedure under Article 169*

(a) *Pre-trial proceedings*

The stage prior to the litigation before the Court consists mainly in a warning in the form of a reasoned opinion.

The Commission has exclusive power of initiative: "If the Commission considers that a member State has failed to fulfil any of its obligations under this Treaty, it shall issue a reasoned opinion on the matter after giving the State concerned the opportunity to submit its comments."[77]

So far three-quarters of the cases have been concluded at the first stage of the proceedings, generally with the State in question taking measures to put matters right.

Otherwise the Commission issues a reasoned opinion setting out the Commission's position on the alleged non-compliance and inviting the State to take measures to put an end to it. According to the Court "the

---

[76] Submissions Roemer, Court of Justice of the European Communities (CJEC), Case 20/59, *Recueil*, Vol. VI, p. 709.

[77] In certain urgent cases covered by Articles 93(2) and 225 of the EEC Treaty the Commission may bring the matter directly before the Court of Justice without issuing an opinion.

opinion must be considered sufficiently reasoned for legal purposes when it contains a coherent account of the reasons which convinced the Commission that the State in question has failed to comply with one of its obligations.[78]

A lack or insufficiency of reasons would render the procedure irregular and the suit, consequently, would not be admissible; for the reasons submitted form a substantive element in this preliminary stage. The member State requested to conform to the opinion within the time-limit allowed must be clearly informed of the reasons why the Commission deems its conduct contrary to the Treaty.

(b) *Litigation*

"If the State concerned does not comply with the terms of such opinion within the period laid down by the Commission, the latter may bring the matter before the Court of Justice" (Article 169, second paragraph). The expiry of the period is followed by the proceedings proper which are governed by stricter rules.

To date, the Commission has used its power, under Article 169, second paragraph, to file a suit in only ten cases.

Admissibility of a suit is subject to the condition that the State has not conformed to the reasoned opinion in the period allowed, that is to say that it has not taken the measures recommended. Even if the State conforms to the opinion after the expiry of the period, the suit is admissible, the Commission still having "an interest in having the question decided at law whether there has been non-compliance." [79]

The States cannot block the application of Article 169 by submitting to the Commission requests for exemption or safeguard measures. The procedures for derogating from the general rules of the Treaty, "distinct by their nature and their effects from the comminatory procedure at the disposal of the Commission by virtue of Article 169, can in no way render the latter ineffective." [80]

Furthermore, the failure of a State or the Community to carry out its obligations cannot dispense the other member States from fulfilling their obligations for, "apart from the cases expressly provided for, the terms of the Treaty forbid the member States to take the law into their own hands." [81]

No time-limit is fixed for the Commission to bring the case before the Court.

The proceedings before the Court of Justice follow the rules established by the Statute of the Court and its rules of procedure. The Court has, in

---

[78] CJEC, Case 7/61, *Recueil*, Vol. VII, p. 654.
[79] CJEC, Case 7/61, *Recueil*, Vol. VII, p. 653.
[80] CJEC, Cases 2 and 3/62, *Recueil*, Vol. VIII, p. 825.
[81] CJEC, Cases 90 and 91/63, *Recueil*, Vol. X, p. 1232.

particular, the power to order an investigation (rules of procedure, Article 45). The other member States may intervene, but only to make submissions tending to support or oppose the case of one of the original parties to the suit (Statute, Article 37 and rules of procedure, Article 93). The Court of Justice may, in any cases before it, prescribe any necessary interim (EEC Treaty, Article 186).

The Court has the widest powers of investigation in seeking out and judging the facts. It must consider as a whole the actual behaviour of the State, without being bound by the account given in the reasoned opinion.

2. *Procedure under Article 170*

This procedure, by which a member State seeks a finding against another member State for failure to fulfil its obligations, is very similar. "Any member State which considers that another member State has failed to fulfil any of its obligations under this Treaty may bring the matter before the Court of Justice."

(a) *Pre-trial proceedings*

Article 170, however, calls for the prior intervention of the Commission: "Before a member State institutes, against another member State, proceedings relating to an alleged infringement of its obligations under this Treaty, it shall bring the matter before the Commission" (Article 170, second paragraph). [82] Once the matter has been referred to the Commission by the State, which must indicate clearly its intention to call for an investigation into the non-compliance, the Commission instigates a written and oral discussion: "The Commission shall deliver a reasoned opinion after the States concerned have been given the opportunity both to submit their own cases and to reply to each other's case both orally and in writing" (Article 170, third paragraph). A three-sided debate begins in which not only the alleged offending State and the Commission take part, as in the case of Article 169, but also the State that has raised the matter.

The role and scope of the reasoned opinion are different in the two procedures. The main purpose of the opinion, which can be negative (inconceivable where Article 169 is concerned), is to give information to the States and the Court. The reasoning must be detailed, but any irregularity in the reasoned opinion will not have the same effect on the admissibility of the suit as in the case of Article 169. It will simply have the effect of invalidating the reasoned opinion, but will not deprive the requesting State of its right to institute proceedings. That State will be in the same situation as if the Commission had not issued an opinion within three months, for "if the Commission has not given an opinion within a period of three months from the date on which the matter was brought before it, the ab-

---

[82] Articles 93(2) and 225 of the EEC Treaty dispense the State from this condition.

sence of such opinion shall not preclude the bringing of the matter before the Court of Justice" (Article 170, fourth paragraph).

(b) *Litigation*

At the proceedings stage the suit goes ahead quite independently of the results of the reasoned opinion.

In the circumstances referred to in Article 170, fourth paragraph, that is if the Commission has not given an opinion, it is not the Commission's silence but the alleged non-compliance of the State which is attacked. If the reasoned opinion does not recognize the failure to fulfil an obligation, this does not prevent the requesting State from filing a suit immediately.

If the Commission does recognize such failure, the requesting State will probably wait for the other State to conform to the reasoned opinion, but nothing in the text of Article 170, as against that of Article 169, obliges it to do so.

Subject to these observations, the procedure under Article 170 follows the same rules as that under Article 169. So far the procedure has not been applied in practice as no suit has been filed in Court under Article 170.

The Court decision closing the proceedings proper instituted under Article 169 or 170 may either reject the suit as inadmissible or dismiss the case or recognize the failure to fulfill the obligation.

The judgment is of a declaratory nature, as the Court does not have the power to quash the legislative or administrative acts of member States. It confines itself to recognizing the failure, without indicating how it is to be remedied.

Article 171 states: "If the Court of Justice finds that a member State has failed to fulfil any of its obligations under this Treaty, such State is bound to take the measures required to comply with the judgment of the Court." While the judgment is not enforceable of itself in the member State, it has all the authority that attaches to court decisions, and experience has shown that this has always been sufficient. Would it be otherwise, or would the measures taken not prove to be sufficient the Commission or the other member States would have to institute further proceedings that would lead to a finding of failure to comply with Article 171. The case has never arisen and in practice there are no examples of States refusing to comply with the Court's judgment.

As has been seen, moreover, these procedures are not often carried through to the end of the proceedings in Court. No proceedings have been instituted in Court on the basis of Article 170. Out of ten suits filed by the Commission under Article 169, only seven have resulted in judgments. The other three cases (18/61, 22/63 and 38/65) were concluded without the Court having to make a pronouncement.

Of the six member States, the German Federal Republic alone is a true federal State.

In Italy the existence of regions with a special statute raises some problems analogous to those that can occur in a truly federal State.

A. In Germany the execution of the obligations deriving from the EEC Treaty has not so far led to controversy, the powers of the Länder being fairly limited in those fields which concern the EEC, but problems could arise in connection with the execution of directives on the right of establishment or on vocational training, since cultural matters come under the Länder authorities.

1. Certain arrangements have been made to safeguard the rights of the Länder, which are represented in the Bundesrat or Federal Council.

The question was raised during the debates which preceded ratification of the Treaties, and Article 2 of the Ratification Law provides an answer. "The Federal Government shall keep the Bundestag and the Bundesrat constantly informed on developments in the Council of the European Economic Community and the Council of the European Atomic Energy Community. Where a Council decision will require German domestic legislation or when it creates law that will be directly applicable in the Federal Republic of Germany, the Bundestag and the Bundesrat shall be informed before the decision is taken."

In practice the Federal Government keeps the Bundesrat regularly and rapidly informed of all Community measures, in particular of all the proposals which the Commission submits to the Council. This gives the relevant Bundesrat committees an opportunity to examine the texts and to submit to the Government views which often influence the latter's attitude when the subject is being discussed in the Council of the Communities.

2. Like the Federal authorities, the Community Institutions consider that care should be taken to ensure that Community decisions do not upset, even unintentionally, the constitutional division of powers between Federal authorities and Länder, as could happen if, for instance, power to take certain actions were given to specific bodies or if the Länder were required to set up new organs for the implementation of Community law.

3. The essential problem is that of ensuring that commitments undertaken by the Federal Government are executed by the Länder. So far there have been no actual cases which have led to a dispute, and the question of principle has been avoided. If it should be raised, there are two theories which could be advanced in order to ensure the execution of the Commitments accepted by the Federal Government.

333

(i) If as most writers agree, and as has apparently been confirmed by actual experience, it is up to the Länder to execute the Community measures in fields where the Länder are competent, they are responsible to the Federal Government for taking the necessary action. The Federal Government can demand that any necessary measures be adopted by virtue of the principle of "Bundestreue", or federal loyalty; there have been many cases where the Constitutional Court has been called upon to ensure that the principle of "Bundestreue" is observed.

(ii) The second theory (defended by von Mangoldt and Klein) is that Article 24 of the Basic Law, which authorizes the transfer of powers to international organizations, can be said to involve a change in the division of powers between the Federal Government and the Länder as far as the application of Community measures is concerned.

B. In Italy the regions are required to exercise their powers with due respect for the international commitments undertaken by the State. This principle is implicit in article 117 of the Constitution,[83] which delimits the powers of the regional bodies, and it has been accepted by the Constitutional Court.[84]

When the Constitutional Court was called upon to deal with a concrete case, it annulled a law for aid to shipbuilding which had been passed by the regional Parliament in Sicily without the Italian Republic having had the possibility to respect the requirement, contained in Articles 92 and 93 of the EEC Treaty, that there should be prior consultation within the Commission. The Court pointed out that "it would be wrong to attach importance to the fact that the Regional Statute for Sicily does not expressly include "respect for international commitments" among the limitations on the legislative powers of the region, as has been done in other statutes which were approved subsequently (Article 3 of the Special Statute for Sardinia; Article 2 of the Special Statute for the Val d'Aosta; Article 4 of the Special Statute for the Trentino-Alto Adige). Even when there is no specific stipulation, it cannot be supposed that autonomous regions have been given sovereign powers." [85]

It appears then that if any measure taken by the regional authorities conflicts with the commitments of the State under the European Treaties, that measure will be unconstitutional.

---

[83] Art. 117 runs: "Subject to the limits imposed by the fundamental principles laid down by State legislation, and provided there is no conflict with the national interest and the interest of other regions, regions shall enact legislation in the following fields..."

[84] See Perassi, la Costituzione e l'ordinamento internazionale, p. 36.

[85] 9 April 1963, *Foro Italiano* 1963, I, p. 860.

VI. AMENDMENT OF CONSTITUTIVE INSTRUMENTS THROUGH METHODS OTHER THAN THE EXPLICIT APPROVAL OF ALL MEMBERS

Next to procedures for amending the treaty by agreement between member States requiring ratification in accordance with their respective constitutional rules, the EEC Treaty, in Article 235, contains a special clause allowing the Community Institutions to deal with unforeseen situations. So does the Euratom Treaty in Article 203.

Article 95 of the ECSC Treaty even provides for two special forms of amendment, one of which requires the consultation of the Court of Justice. Therefore particular attention is first given to this article.

A. *The ECSC Treaty*

Article 95 provides for two forms of procedure, one known as "small revision" (third and fourth paragraphs), the other to cover cases not expressly provided for (first and second paragraphs).[86]

The procedure under the third and fourth paragraphs is examined first because it is closest to amendment proper.

1. Under the procedure for "small revision", the rules of the Treaty governing the powers of the High Authority can be adjusted where the appearance of unforeseen difficulties or a profound change in market conditions make such adjustment necessary.

Article 95, third paragraph, says: "If, after the period of transition provided for in the Convention containing the transitional provisions, unforeseen difficulties revealed by experience in the methods of executing this Treaty, or a profound change in the economic or technical conditions directly affecting the common market for coal and steel should require an amendment of the rules for the exercise by the High Authority of the powers conferred upon it, appropriate amendments may be made provided that they do not modify the provisions of Articles 2, 3 and 4, or the relationship between the powers of the High Authority and those of the other institutions of the Community."

The procedure described in the fourth paragraph involves the successive intervention of all the Community Institutions.

"These amendments shall be proposed jointly by the High Authority and the Council acting by a five-sixths majority. They shall then be submitted to the opinion of the Court. In its examination, the Court shall be fully competent to review any matters of law and fact. If the Court should find that the amendments conform to the provisions of the preceding paragraph,

---

[86] G. Olivier, "Aspects juridiques de l'adaption du traité CECA à la crise charbonnière", *Cahiers de Droit Europeen*, No. 1, p. 1 & No. 2, p. 163.

they shall be forwarded to the Assembly. They will come into force if they are approved by the Assembly acting by a majority of three-quarters of the votes cast representing a two-thirds majority of the total membership."

Regarding the respective roles of the various Institutions, it must be noted that the Assembly intervenes only in the last resort after approval by the Court and that it does not have the power of initiative nor the practical possibility of introducing amendments; the Court's opinion is decisive since it cannot be disregarded; a unanimous vote in the Council is not required, but there must be a five-sixths majority.

Cases of application

(i) The small revision procedure has been used to remedy social consequences of the coal crisis due to increased competition from fuel oil and imported coal. The field of application of Article 56 regarding resettlement measures has been extended to cover the possibility of "profound changes in the marketing conditions of the coalmining or of the iron and steel industry, not directly connected with the introduction of the common market. . ."

The Court recognized that there had been a profound change in the marketing conditions of the coalmining industry and that the widening of the conditions in which Article 56 could be applied did not exceed the limits fixed in the third paragraph of Article 95.[87]

(ii) The second attempt at a small revision concerned article 65 regarding agreements between enterprises. This attempt failed because it was rejected by the Court.[88] The Court admitted the possibility of amending Article 65(2) of the Treaty in order to enable the High Authority to authorize types of agreement other than those specified in the text. But it deemed too vague a "proposal that would merely provide for the authorization" of agreements concerning adjustment to new marketing conditions and above all considered that it was impossible to set aside the limits placed by Article 65(2)(c) on the size of cartels without infringing the stipulations of Article 95, third paragraph.

In these cases the Court which, according to Article 95, fourth paragraph, is "fully competent to review any matters of law and fact" showed great prudence in the judgments which this provision enables it to make. It did consider that "the introduction of new conditions permitting the exercise by the High Authority of a power in circumstances other than those specified by the Treaty does not constitute introduction of a new power." The Court therefore accepts that a small revision may lead to the widening of the powers of the High Authority but within the fields transferred to the Community. It has in fact been cautious on how far-reaching the small revision may go; in its view the possibility of authorizing restrictive agreements exceeding the size fixed by Article 65(2)(c) ran counter to Article 4(d) of the Treaty and the transformation of a "prior examination system" into a "review of the facts and later direct inter-

---

[87] Court of Justice of the European Communities, Opinion 1-60 of 4 March 1960, *Recueil*, Vol VI, p. 93.
[88] CJEC Opinion 1-61 of 13 December 1961, *Recueil*, Vol. VII.

vention" amounted to the "attribution of a new power."

The Court pointed out furthermore that "there could be no derogation from the normal procedure of review except in cases where neither the general structure of the Treaty nor the relations between the Community and the member States will suffer." That is why the Court, faced with a proposal that would not just have extended the benefits provided by social provisions but would have modified the essential elements of competition, showed great prudence, which may be explained by the fact that Article 95, fourth paragraph, allows the Treaty to be revised against the will or without the co-operation of one of the member States.

2. Procedure under article 95, first and second paragraphs

This procedure has, according to the Court, the sole object "of instituting a system of derogation peculiar to the Treaty in order to enable the High Authority to face an unforeseen situation." [89]

Article 95, first paragraph, stipulates: "In all cases not expressly provided for in this Treaty in which a decision or a recommendation of the High Authority appears necessary to fulfil, in the operation of the common market for coal and steel and in accordance with the provisions of Article 5 above, one of the objectives of the Community as defined in Articles 2, 3 and 4, such a decision or recommendation may be taken with the unanimous agreement of the Council and after consulting the Consultative Committee."

Unlike the small revision, Article 95, first and second paragraphs, can be applied from the beginning of the transitional period. The procedure applicable, which requires the unanimous agreement of the Council of Ministers, is to be found in other articles of the Treaty (53(b), 54, 81), while Article 95, fourth paragraph, discussed above, provides for a most unusual procedure involving all the Institutions of the Community.

Application of Article 95, first paragraph, is subject to the presence of two essential elements, the existence of a case "not expressly provided for" and the need to attain one of the objectives defined in Articles 2, 3 and 4.

Cases of application

Decisions on what constitutes a case "not expressly provided for" has not failed to raise difficulties, as the application of the clause shows. Are these only cases omitted unintentionally by the authors of the Treaty but similar to those that have been provided for, or on the contrary are they situations justifying the use of methods which are totally different or even run counter to those laid down in the Treaty?

The High Authority has taken the middle road, considering that it is pos-

---

[89] CJEC, case 9/61, *Recueil*, Vol. VIII, p. 449.

sible on the basis of Article 95, first paragraph to use the funds from levies for needs other than those stipulated in Article 50 but rejecting recourse to this provision, to settle the problem of Ruhr coal sales agencies, though it accepted this as a basis for authorizing the establishment of a Community system of aid to the coalmining industry.[90]

In certain respects, then, it seems that the first and second paragraphs of Article 95 go beyond the "small revision", for the latter concerns modification of the rules for the exercise of the powers of the High Authority and must necessarily be based closely on the text of the Treaty, while the main purpose of Article 95, first and second paragraphs, is to fill the gaps in the High Authority's means of action while complying with the stipulations of Article 5 (i.e. ways and means of intervention and relations between the institutions and enterprises).

Lastly it must be noted that Article 95, first and second paragraphs, may serve as a basis for a decision whose scope and duration must be adapted to the situation justifying its adoption.

B. *The EEC Treaty*

Article 235 of the EEC Treaty specifies how the Community institutions may take decisions in cases not provided for by the Treaty but falling within the powers of the Community.

"If it becomes apparent that action by the Community is necessary to achieve, within the framework of the common market, one of the aims of the Community, and this Treaty has not provided the powers needed for such action, the Council, acting by means of a unanimous vote on a proposal of the Commission and after the Assembly has been consulted, shall enact the requisite provisions."[91]

As results from its terms, the situation referred to in this provision is quite similar to the one referred to in Article 95, first and second paragraphs of the ECSC Treaty.

The meaning and scope of Article 235 have been defined in the Commission's reply to written question No. 20 submitted by M. Vredeling:[92]

"Article 235 covers the case where the Treaty, while assigning to the Community a specific aim, has not provided the means of action to achieve this aim. In such a case the Council, acting on a proposal of the Commission and after consulting the European Parliament, is called upon in its capacity as a Community Institution to take the necessary steps in the

---

[90] Decision 3-65, *Official Gazette of the European Communities*, 25 February 1965, p. 180.
[91] Article 203 of the Euratom Treaty is identical in its terms to article 235 of the EEC Treaty. Up to now, it has not yet been applied.
[92] *Official Gazette of the European Communities*, 7 June 1967, p. 2151.

forms set out in Article 189 of the Treaty. Article 235, therefore, does not provide for the conclusion of supplementary agreements between the member States but the adoption of a Community act."

Cases of application

Article 235 has been used in the first place to provide special rules for processed agricultural products not listed in Annex II to the Treaty. As the rules of the Treaty and subsequent Community acts concerning abolition of national protection measures are quite different for agricultural products and the other ones, difficult problems arose for processed products, to which legally the less strict rules for agricultural products could not be applied. Therefore a system has been created on the basis of Article 235 tending to harmonize the rules to be applied to those products with the rules applicable to agricultural products.[93]

Article 235 also constitutes the legal basis for the third acceleration of the time-table for setting up he custom union. As has been discussed in Section I, the first two accelerations had been decided by the Representatives of the Governments of the member States, meeting in the Council. For the definite implementing of the customs unions it has been considered preferable to adopt an act of the Council based on the Treaty. As the Treaty does not provide for all the necessary powers to that effect, Article 235 has been referred to.[94]

Finally, in the social field, Article 235 served as the basis for the Decision of 22 December 1966 on a Community grant to Italy for the purpose of aid to redundant sulphur-mine workers and scholarships for their children.[95]

These precedents may indicate that Article 235 will probably play an important role in the further development of the EEC, as more occasions may occur which the authors of the Treaty have not foreseen. Up to now, none of the acts, taken on the basis of Article 235, has been challenged before the Court of Justice.[96]

---

[93] See e.g. *Official Gazette of the European Communities*, 20 April 1962, p. 999, and 28 October 1966, p. 3361.
[94] *Ibid.*, 21 September 1966, p. 2971.
[95] *Ibid.*, 31 December 1966, p. 4168.
[96] This paper describes the situation as of 1967, and does not deal with subsequent evolution.

THE COUNCIL OF EUROPE

by *Dr. H. Golsong*
Director of Legal Affairs of the Council of Europe

I. TYPE OF "DECISIONS"

1. The aim of the Council of Europe, according to its Statute [Article 1(a)], is

"... to achieve a greater unity between its Members ..."

The Statute provides [Article 1(b)] that

"this aim shall be pursued through the organs of the Council by discussion of questions of common concern and by agreements ("conclusion d'accords") and common action in economic, social, cultural, scientific, legal and administrative matters and in the maintenance and further realisation of human rights and fundamental freedoms."

In its Article 15, the Statute stipulates furthermore that the Committee of Ministers, the organ which acts on behalf of the Council,

"shall consider the action required to further the aim of the Council of Europe, including the conclusion of conventions or agreements and the adoption by Governments of a common policy with regard to particular matters. Its conclusions shall be communicated to Members by the Secretary-General. In appropriate cases, the conclusions of the Committee may take the form of recommendations to the Governments of Members, and the Committee may request the Governments of Member States to inform it of the action taken by them with regard to such recommendations."

2. The Statute thus envisages two main types of "decisions", namely,

(i) *Recommendations* addressed to Governments of member States, and

(ii) the *conclusion of Conventions or Agreements*.

II. RECOMMENDATIONS TO GOVERNMENTS

3. Recommendations are addressed to Governments by way of Resolutions of the Committee of Ministers. These Recommendations generally contain guiding principles for action to be taken by member States in the field considered by the Resolution.[1]

4. Recommendations to Governments adopted by way of Resolutions are, in principle, addressed to the Governments of all member States. They therefore require for their adoption

---

[1] Recent examples: legislation concerning detention pending trial; training of prison staff; doping of athletes; regulations concerning frontier formalities.

"the unanimous vote of the representatives (of Member States) casting a vote, and of a majority of the representatives entitled to sit on the Committee (of Ministers)" [Article 20(a) of the Statute].

The Rules of Procedure of the Committee of Ministers (Deputies) provide furthermore [Article 8, para. 1(e)], that a representative may approve the adoption of a Recommendation but reserve the right of his Government not to act thereon.

5. The "binding" nature of a Recommendation is, of course, open to discussion. In principle, Governments are expected to act in accordance with the principles laid down by the Recommendation. The choice of means of implementation is, however, a matter of national concern. In any case, Recommendations to Governments of member States have no immediate legal effect within member States, even in those States in which a "self-executing" international treaty provision results in the treaty being considered part of the law of the land upon ratification.

This state of affairs has not prevented national Parliaments or even Courts of law from referring to a Recommendation in order to justify or to explain action (or decisions) within municipal law, for example: a recent judgment by the German Federal Constitutional Court on detention pending trial.

III. CONVENTIONS OR AGREEMENTS

6. The wording of the above-mentioned statutory provisions with regard to Conventions or Agreements is not very precise.

Conventions or Agreements are not, as one might deduce from Article 1 of the Statute, concluded by the Council of Europe. Although elaborated within the Council, Conventions or Agreements listed on the table of the "European Treaty Series" are not legal instruments of the Council. They are agreements between States, members of the Council of Europe,[2] and therefore require signature by each individual Government and subsequent ratification (provided that the treaty was not signed without reservation as to ratification) by each signatory State.

No member State is obliged to sign and ratify a Convention elaborated within the Council of Europe. On the other hand, some of the Conventions at present in force are open to ratification only by States members of the Council.

Finally, there are a number of important links, obviously differing in nature according to the contents of the treaty, between those Conventions and the Council. Thus, in the large majority of cases, the Secretary General acts as depositary of the treaty. The power to make decisions about

---

[2] The Preamble begins generally with the following sentence: "The member States of the Council of Europe, signatory hereto . . . Have agreed as follows . . ."

requests by a non-member State to accede to a given Convention is given to the Committee of Ministers. In other cases, the election of members to bodies set up under the terms of a Convention is entrusted to an organ of the Council (Committee of Ministers and/or the Consultative Assembly). The control over the implementation of a Convention also belongs in many cases to a body of the Council of Europe. Furthermore, the expenses relating to the functioning of special bodies set up under the terms of a Convention are in principle covered by the Council of Europe. The only exception are costs involved in the implementation of "partial agreements" (see para. 10 below).

7. A Convention or Agreement is submitted to signature by member States only after the Committee of Ministers has proceeded to a vote on the subject, that is: has decided to open the Convention or Agreement to signature.

What is the significance of this vote and what is the majority required in such a case?

8. Such a vote has never been considered and has never had the form of a Recommendation to Governments.

Furthermore, as we have seen, Conventions or Agreements are not proclaimed as such by the Committee of Ministers and are not legal instruments of the Council as such; the vote means in the first place an agreement as to the final text of the Convention, a *ne varietur* decision.

Secondly, as all the Conventions concluded within the Council refer in one way or another to the Council and its statutory aim, the vote means also a *nihil obstat* of all member States on the subject. It is therefore important that *none* of the member States vote against the opening of a Convention to signature.

Thirdly, whatever the majority in favour of the decision might be and provided that no opposition has been expressed, the vote further means in all those cases (90% of the treaties so far concluded) in which the Convention refers to organs of the Council for its implementation (the Committee of Ministers for the purpose of electing members of special supervisory bodies set up under the terms of the Convention, the role of the Secretary General as depositary of the treaty, etc.), an undertaking by the Committee of Ministers to accept the fulfilment of those functions by bodies or organs of the Council of Europe. It also implies an undertaking by the Council to cover the costs of functioning of those bodies whenever they act under the terms of the Convention.

9. This vote is not a Recommendation to Governments, nor another form of collective action of the Council envisaged by the Statute. On the other hand, it has certain consequences for the Organization as such (see para. 8 above).

The voting is therefore governed by the following conditions:
—no specific majority is required;
—a minumum of three States (the minimum for the conclusion of a

342

multilateral treaty) should express their willingness to sign the Convention;

—there should be no opposition by any other member State of the Council.

10. Special conditions are laid down under the terms of a statutory Resolution of 1951 for the vote on *"partial agreements"*.

"Partial agreements", as opposed to Conventions within the meaning described above, are prepared for only a certain number of member States previously fixed, and are therefore not open to signature or ratification by other member States. Furthermore, if special bodies are set up under the terms of the Agreement, the costs involved are not covered by the general budget of the Council, but only by its Contracting Parties.

It is important to note that a "partial agreement" can only be concluded within the Council of Europe if none of the member States has opposed against the vote on the opening of the agreement to signature.

IV. MEASURES OF IMPLEMENTATION

11. With regard to *Recommendations,* the Statute provides in its Article 15(b) that the Committee of Ministers

"may request the Governments of Members to inform it of the action taken by them with regard to ... recommendations."

In application of this provision, the Committee of Ministers agreed in 1958 to examine, in principle, once a year the information received from member States on the implementation of Recommendations. Periodical (2, 3 or 5 years) furnishing of information is provided for in some Recommendations.

12. So far as Conventions are concerned, there are a great variety of mechanisms. The most advanced system of control of implementation is, of course, provided for by the European Convention on Human Rights.

The European Social Charter also provides for a special reporting system with examination of the reports received by special bodies [a body of independent experts (Article 25) and a committee of governmental representatives (Article 27)] and final opinion, eventually accompanied by appropriate Recommendations, expressed by the Committee of Ministers, after having heard the views of the Consultative Assembly (Articles 28 and 29).

Other Conventions with special machinery for supervision of implementation are the following:

—The European Convention on Establishment (special body: the Permanent Committee of Representatives of Contracting States—Article 24);

—the European Convention on the Establishment of Companies (special body: Permanent Committee—Article 11);

—the European Convention on the Punishment of Road Traffic Offences (special body: the European Committee for Crime Problems—Article 28);

—The European Cultural Convention (special body: the Committee of Experts in Cultural Matters, now the European Council for Cultural Co-operation—Article 6);

—the European Convention on the International Classification of Patents for Invention (special body: Committee of Experts on Patents—Article 2; it is to be noted that this Committee is empowered to elaborate further or to modify the International Classification of Patents. Any elaboration or modification approved by that Committee of Experts shall enter into force six months after all Contracting Parties have been notified of such decision, unless, however, at least two of the Contracting Parties have raised an objection to the proposed elaboration or modification not less than one month before the expiry of the said period of six months).

13. Furthermore, pursuant to a Resolution voted in 1961[3] the Committee of Ministers examines annually reports from each member State indicating:

—which Conventions, Agreements or Protocols concluded within the framework of the Council of Europe it has ratified;

—the steps it has taken towards the ratification of other Conventions, Agreements or Protocols;

—where considered possible and appropriate, the reasons why any Conventions, Agreements or Protocols have not been submitted for ratification within a period of eighteen months after signature.

The European Committee on Legal Co-operation, a subsidiary body of the Committee of Ministers, also examines regularly the state of ratifications by member States of Conventions coming within the competence of that Committee.

14. With regard to the implementation of both Recommendations and Conventions, the *role of the Consultative Assembly* of the Council of Europe is of decisive importance.

Not only the Assembly discusses in open session the reports of the Committee of Ministers on the state of ratifications of Conventions, etc., or votes "recommendations" to the Committee of Ministers requesting the ratification of instruments opened to signature, but very often the members of the Assembly intervene in their national Parliaments in order to recommend the signature and ratification of Council of Europe Conventions by their authorities. This has proved to be a most efficient means of implementation. The efficiency of this practice has been considerably increased since the setting up, by the Assembly, of a Working Party on relations with National Parliaments. It is very often this Working Party which selects items on which action is recommended to be taken by members of the Assembly within their national Parliaments, especially with a

---

[3] Resolution 61(1).

view to encouraging ratification of Conventions. Thus a real parliamentary pressure group is acting within the member States in favour of the signature or ratification of Conventions. It is this latter aspect which is not only special to the Council of Europe, but has also led to most satisfactory results.

APPLYING, AND EFFECTING COMPLIANCE WITH, DECISIONS (WITH REFERENCE TO THE EUROPEAN CONVENTION ON HUMAN RIGHTS)

by *A. H. Robertson*
Head, Directorate of Human Rights, Council of Europe

A. STATUTORY TEXTS

Article 32 of the Convention

(1) If the question is not referred to the Court in accordance with Article 48 of this Convention within a period of three months from the date of the transmission of the Report to the Committee of Ministers, the Committee of Ministers shall decide by a majority of two-thirds of the members entitled to sit on the Committee whether there has been a violation of the Convention.

(2) In the affirmative case the Committee of Ministers shall prescribe a period during which the High Contracting Party concerned must take the measures required by the decision of the Committee of Ministers.

(3) If the High Contracting Party concerned has not taken satisfactory measures within the prescribed period, the Committee of Ministers shall decide by the majority provided for in paragraph (1) above what effect shall be given to its original decision and shall publish the Report.

(4) The High Contracting Parties undertake to regard as binding on them any decision which the Committee of Ministers may take in application of the preceding paragraphs.

Article 50

If the Court finds that a decision or a measure taken by a legal authority or any other authority of a High Contracting Party is completely or partially in conflict with the obligations arising from the present Convention, and if the internal law of the said Party allows only partial reparation to be made for the consequences of this decision or measure, the decision of the Court shall, if necessary, afford just satisfaction to the injured party.

Article 53

The High Contracting Parties undertake to abide by the decision of the Court in any case to which they are parties.

Article 54

The judgment of the Court shall be transmitted to the Committee of Ministers which shall supervise its execution.

Article 3 of the Statute

Every Member of the Council of Europe must accept the principles of the rule of law and of the enjoyment by all persons within its jurisdiction of human rights and fundamental freedoms, and collaborate sincerely and effectively in the realisation of the aim of the Council as specified in Chapter I.

Article 8 of the Statute

Any Member of the Council of Europe which has seriously violated Article 3 may be suspended from its rights of representation and requested by the Committee of Ministers to withdraw under Article 7. If such Member does not comply with this request, the Committee may decide that it has ceased to be a Member of the Council as from such date as the Committee may determine.

B. THE DE BECKER CASE

A journalist of Belgian nationality, Raymond De Becker, was, during the occupation of Belgium by the Nazis, the editor-in-chief of the well-known Brussels daily, "Le Soir". After the liberation, De Becker was sentenced in 1947, on a charge of collaboration with the enemy, to lifelong imprisonment, which was reduced by a measure of clemency in 1950 to 17 years' imprisonment. In 1951 he was granted a conditional release. Nevertheless, one of the results of his conviction was forfeiture of the rights listed in Article 123 *sexies* of the Belgian Penal Code, including:

(e) the right to have a proprietary interest in or to take part in any capacity whatsoever in the administration, editing, printing, or distribution of a newspaper or any other publication;

(f) the right to take part in organizing or managing any cultural, philanthropic or sporting activity or any public entertainment;

(g) the right to have a proprietary interest in or to be associated with the administration or any other aspect of the activity of any undertaking concerned with theatrical production, films or broadcasting.

The application lodged by De Becker in September 1956 having been declared admissible,[1] the Commission, after the failure of an attempt to reach a friendly settlement, drew up a report in which, by 11 votes to 1, it expressed the opinion

"that paragraphs (e), (f) and (g) of Article 123 *sexies,* insofar as they affect freedom of expression, are not fully justifiable under the Convention whether they be regarded as providing for penal sanctions or for preventive measures in the interests of public security. They are not justifiable insofar as the deprivation of freedom of expression in regard to non-political matters, which they contain, is imposed inflexibly for life without any provision for its relaxation when with the passage of

---

[1] See the text of the Decision in *Yearbook of the Convention* II, p. 214.

time public morale and public order have been re-established and the continued imposition of that particular incapacity has ceased to be a measure 'necessary in a democratic society' within the meaning of Article 10, paragraph 2, of the Convention." [2]

The De Becker case was brought before the Court by the Commission in April 1960. Two days before the first hearing—set for 3rd July 1961—there was published in Belgium the Civic Black Lists Act ("Loi relative à l'épuration civique") of June 30th 1961, which, *inter alia,* amended paragraphs (e), (f) and (g) of Article 123 *sexies* in such a way as to limit the forfeiture of the rights listed therein to activities of a political nature. It also provided an opportunity for De Becker to seek a remedy, through the Courts, even for this last remaining ban.

Thus amended, Article 123 *sexies* was judged by the Commission to be compatible with the Convention. In its submissions at the hearing of 5th October 1961, the Commission requested the Court

"to note that the limitations maintained by the Act of 30th June 1961 as regards freedom of expression, insofar as these apply to Mr. De Becker, do not go beyond the 'formalities, conditions, restrictions, or penalties' authorised in Article 10, paragraph 2 of the Convention." [3]

However, the Court was not required to pass judgment. At the conclusion of the hearing on 5th October 1961, De Becker sent a letter to the Commission stating that his claim had been met by the law of 30th June 1961 and that he was withdrawing his Application.[4] Noting that on the day when the hearings terminated the Commission and the Belgian Government had made concordant submissions asking that the case should be struck off its list, the Court decided, on 27th March 1962, by six votes to one, that there was no reason to continue its examination of the case *ex officio* [5]

The De Becker case was, in fact, only a test case, since other Belgian citizens, as a result of their attitude during the occupation of Belgium, had forfeited the same rights as the Applicant. The importance attached to the De Becker case by the Belgian Government is thus understandable. The law of 30th June 1961 was voted by the Belgian Parliament at the Government's request, with reference to the very procedure then taking place in the De Becker case before the organs set up under the Convention.

---

[2] The Commission's Report will be found in the publication of the European Court of Human Rights entitled "De Becker Case", Series B: Pleadings, Oral Arguments, Documents, 1962, pp. 11-153.

[3] *Ibid.,* p. 216.

[4] *Ibid.,* p. 254.

[5] The Judgment appears in Series A of the publications of the European Court of Human Rights.

C. THE APPLICATIONS BY OFNER, HOPFINGER, PATAKI AND DUNSHIRN AGAINST AUSTRIA

The decisions whereby the European Commission of Human Rights declared these four Applications admissible[6] have led to a revolution in Austrian penal procedure. Those decisions cast doubts upon the conformity with the Convention of the provisions in the Code of Penal Procedure of 1873 under which appeal proceedings and the hearing of a plea of nullity usually take place at non-public hearings, in the absence of the accused and his counsel, but in the presence of the Public Prosecutor or his representative, who is heard by the Court.

Immediately after the Commission's decisions were delivered, the Austrian Minister of Justice, as a first step, sent a circular to councel in the Public Prosecutor's department requesting them to cease attending non-public hearings of the Court of Appeal and the Supreme Court. This action was designed to prevent future or current trials from giving rise to fresh admissible applications.

As a second step the Minister of Justice tabled a Bill in Parliament amending the Code of Penal Procedure by introducing rules requiring oral proceedings in the presence of both parties and reestablishing the principle of "equality of arms" between the accused and the Public Prosecutor. The Bill, adopted on 18th July 1962, became law on 1st September of that year.[7]

The problem was still not solved, however, if the Austrian Government desired to prevent an unfavourable opinion by the Commission in two of the four cases, namely those of Pataki and Dunshirn. The other two cases, those of Ofner and Hopfinger, had meantime resulted in the opinion of the Commission that there had been no violation of the Convention, an opinion confirmed by the Committee of Ministers.[8] Clearly, however, this was an opinion which related only to these particular cases. In addition, some 20 similar cases were still pending before the Commission.

Consequently, on 26th March 1963 the Austrian Parliament felt it advisable to adopt a new law, which came into force on 5th April 1963, under the terms of which all those whose Applications concerning the appeals procedure have been declared admissible by the Commission are entitled to request the opening of new appeal proceedings before the Court—though not before the same judges—which examined the original appeal.[9]

In its report, the Commission, while considering that the earlier procedure was not compatible with the Convention, asked the Committee of

---

[6] See text of decisions in *Yearbook of the Convention* III, p. 323 (Ofner Application), p. 357 (Pataki Application), p. 371 (Hopfinger) and in *Yearbook* IV, p. 187 (Dunshirn).
[7] See extracts from the law in *Yearbook of the Convention* V, p. 344.
[8] *Yearbook of the Convention* VI, p. 708.
[9] *Yearbook of the Convention* VI, p. 804.

Ministers not to take action on the cases outstanding, since the new legislation was calculated to give satisfaction to the Applicants. The Committee of Ministers adopted the Commission's proposal.[10]

---

[10] Resolution (63) DH 2 of 16th September 1963, *Yearbook of the Convention* VI, p. 736.
N.B. This note was written in 1965. It does not relate later decisions of the Court of Human Rights or of the Committee of Ministers of the Council of Europe.

BINDING DECISIONS IN THE INTER-AMERICAN SYSTEM AND THE CENTRAL AMERICAN COMMON MARKET

by *F. V. Garcia-Amador*
Director, Department of Legal Affairs, Organization of American States

The present paper is based upon the essential premise that "bindingness" depends primarily on the competence attributed, explicitly or implicitly, to the international organ concerned. Accordingly, within the framework of the OAS, strictly speaking, there is only one competence of this kind: the one provided for in Article 20 of the Inter-American Treaty of Reciprocal Assistance (Rio Treaty), according to which "decisions which require the application of the measures specified in Article 8 shall be binding upon all the Signatory States which have ratified this Treaty, with the sole exception that no State shall be required to use armed force without its consent". The competence attributed to the Organ of Consultation in this Article is an "explicit" one and is equivalent to that of the Security Council of the United Nations under Article 25 of the San Francisco Charter. Furthermore, in accordance with Article 17 of the Rio Treaty, decisions are taken by the Organ of Consultation by a two-thirds majority vote. On the other hand, Article 20 stipulates only one exception, namely, the case of the adoption of a measure constituting the use of armed force. Finally, these decisions may be taken in connection with cases either of armed attack or of any other act of "aggression which is not an armed attack", as well as of "any other fact or situation that might endanger the peace of America" (Articles 6 and 9).

Decisions involving the application of the measures contemplated in Article 8 or, more specifically, the breaking of diplomatic and consular relations and the interruption of economic relations, have been applied to two countries: the Dominican Republic in 1960 and Cuba in 1964. It is of interest to note in this context that in 1962 the Organ of Consultation, acting in application of the Rio Treaty, took a measure not expressly provided for in Article 8 of the Treaty—that of excluding the "present Government" of Cuba (not Cuba as a member State) from its participation in the inter-American system. This seems to be an example of the exercise of the so-called "inherent" competence, or at least "implied" competence of international organs.

The Central American Common Market, one of the two Latin American integration processes, despite its apparent disarticulation reveals a notable degree of maturity and effectiveness in its institutional framework and legal regimen. Therefore, if what interests us is not this rather formal aspect, but legal and institutional reality, the image that we obtain from the study of the "living law" in this process of economic integration is completely different. As a matter of fact, one of the main factors contributing to the functioning of the Central American Common Market is the institutional structure of this integration process, established in the treaties, particularly in the General Treaty of Central American Economic Integration (1960), and developed and strengthened through the practice of the organs and institutions of the Common Market. This constructive practice and the instruments themselves have also generated an aggregate of principles and rules that reveal the existence of a true "community law" in full force and evolution.

To illustrate, two of the organs—the Central American Economic Council and the Executive Council, both intergovernmental and the second authorized to adopt its decisions by a majority—have been given law-making powers similar to those of the institutions of the European Communities. These are, naturally, the organs which the General Treaty has made responsible for the direction of integration and the coordination of the economic policy of the five countries, through the application and administration of the Treaty, and the adoption of the measures necessary to achieve the fulfillment of the commitments of the Treaty and other agreements and to resolve the problems that arise in the interpretation or the application of its provisions (Articles XX, XXI and XXII).

The regulatory powers are expressly established in the General Treaty and in other instruments of the Common Market. Thus, under Article V of the Treaty, "The Executive Council shall establish, by regulation, the procedure to be followed in order to determine the origin of the goods"; and it is the Council itself that is to prepare the uniform regulations for the Central American Agreement on Fiscal Incentives to Industrial Development (Article 47). Likewise, the Protocol to the General Treaty that contains the Uniform Central American Customs Code (CAUCA) provides in Article 182 that "The Executive Power or Branch of each state shall issue regulations to this Code, as multilaterally agreed at a meeting of the Central American Economic Council. Changes in these regulations shall be made through the same procedure." Although it is up to each state to put the regulations to these instruments into effect, according to their respective domestic procedures, their preparation and their actual adoption is reserved to the competent organs of the Common Market, in order that their contents shall not vary from one state to another.

In a way, the general law-making power that is exercised by the organs of integration, in spite of the fact that this is not explicitly attributed to any one, is most important and, potentially, it offers unsuspected possibilities. One example will suffice to demonstrate how far the exercise of this "implicit" power has gone up to now: Resolution No. 71 of the Executive Council complemented the General Treaty, in the sense that it established rules applicable to situations not provided for in Article VI thereof. Decisions or resolutions of this organ come into effect in each country by mere notification. At this time it should be observed that this no longer deals with the mere "regulation" of an international treaty, but with "complementing" it; that is, with establishing and putting into effect new rules concerning matters governed by it.

The executive powers given to the organs of integration by the General Treaty and other Central American instruments, which are, besides, quite numerous and specific, are also very significant. To illustrate the principal ones in accordance with the already cited Article VI of the General Treaty, the imposition of domestic taxes on consumption depends, in specific circumstances that are indicated in the article itself, on a favorable decision of the Executive Council. And by virtue of Article V, this Council not only is competent to regulate the procedure to be followed to determine the origin of goods, but also to verify this whenever a state requests its intervention for that purpose. The instruments that establish the regime of integrated industries contemplate various powers of this kind. Thus, for example, in the basic instrument itself, the Agreement on the System of Central American Integrated Industries (1958), the determination of "Central American Industries" is entrusted, in each concrete case, to the Central American Commission on Industrial Integration (Article II) whose functions were subsequently assigned to the Executive Council by virtue of Article XXII of the General Treaty.

Certain of these powers contemplate the adoption of decisions and measures directly applicable to private persons. Perhaps the most outstanding example is Article XIV of the San José Protocol to the Agreement on Equalization of Import Charges, relative to unfair trade practices (that is, practices "which cause or threaten to cause damage to Central American production, especially when it is a case of importing commodities at prices below their normal value or of export subsidies" as stated in Article XII). To confirm the existence of such practices, reads Article XIV, "there shall be applied, through a decision of the Executive Council, to the consignees of the respective commodities or shipments, a sanction of one hundred dollars per gross kilo and one hundred percent *ad valorem,* without prejudice to any other measure which the Council may decide upon. The decision of the Council will have validity for the five member countries. The sanction will continue to be applied as long as the situation or practice which gave rise to it continues to exist, and will be suspended by decision of the Executive Council."

Reference should be made to one of the cases which clearly reveals the powers that the organs of the Common Market exercise directly over individuals. Resolution 36 of the Executive Council constitutes an application, in particular, of Article 25 of the Protocol to the Agreement on the System of Central American Integrated Industries (1963). Pursuant to it, the said Council "shall in due course fix the selling prices for tires and tubes produced in the plant, on the basis of a report prepared by the Permanent Secretariat concerning the actual prices quoted in the Central American countries for similar products on the aforementioned date," that is, December 1, 1962. The aforementioned Resolution 36 reads as follows:

1. To approve, for the purposes of Article 25 of the Protocol to the Agreement on the System of Central American Integrated Industries, the list of maximum prices to consumer credit purchasers for the tires and tubes that are being produced by the integration plant GINSA, S.A., and that are listed in Appendix 2 to the present minutes. In this case, the credits shall be for a period of at least 90 days and not more than 120 days.

2. The distributor shall grant a discount of at least 15 per cent for cash sales.

3. The producer, in turn, shall grant a discount of at least 22 per cent in credit sales to the distributors, with a term of at least 90 days.

It can be seen that Resolution 36 not only established an obligation for the company or producer but also imposes another, also directly, on the distributor. It should be noted that the former obligation is expressly provided for in Article 25 (paragraph 1), but not the latter. In other words, in the exercise of an apparently implicit, or in any event, inherent power, the Executive Council established an obligatory rule of conduct for another category of individuals.

PROCEEDINGS

edited by *Stephen M. Schwebel*

PARTICIPANTS

Elting Arnold, General Counsel, Inter-American Development Bank

Sir Kenneth Bailey, Special Advisor on International Affairs, Department of External Affairs, Canberra, Australia

Werner Boulanger, Director, Legal Division, International Atomic Energy Agency

Z. Caha, Assistant Director-General, International Bureau, Universal Postal Union

J. P. Dobbert, Office of the Legal Counsel, Food and Agriculture Organization

Alexander Elkin, formerly Legal Adviser, Organization for European Economic Co-operation

Gerald F. FitzGerald, Senior Legal Officer, International Civil Aviation Organization

F. V. Garcia-Amador, Director, Department of Legal Affairs, Organization of American States

Joseph Gold, General Counsel and Director of Legal Department, International Monetary Fund

H. Golsong, Director of Legal Affairs, Council of Europe

Rosalyn Higgins, The Royal Institute of International Affairs

Elihu Lauterpacht, Q. C., Cambridge University

E. J. Mestmäcker, Director, Institute for Foreign and International Commercial and Economic Law, University of Münster

Lester Nurick, Deputy General Counsel, International Bank for Reconstruction and Development

Oscar Schachter, Deputy Executive Director and Director of Research, United Nations Institute for Training and Research

Stephen M. Schwebel, Executive Vice President, American Society of International Law

Louis B. Sohn, Harvard Law School

Eric Stein, University of Michigan Law School

John R. Stevenson, President, American Society of International Law

N. Valticos, Chief, International Labor Standards Department, International Labor Office

C. H. Vignes, Legal Officer, World Health Organization

Miss Editha Fuchs, Reporter

THE THEME OF THE MEETING: BY WHAT MEASURES MAY
THE DECISIONS OF INTERNATIONAL ORGANIZATIONS (IN
THEIR VARIOUS POSSIBLE FORMS, RANGING FROM
RECOMMENDATIONS FOR ACTION BY MEMBER STATES TO
DECISIONS THAT ARE LEGALLY BINDING) BE MADE
EFFECTIVE?

I. THE CHOICE OF TECHNIQUES TO CARRY OUT AN AGREED COURSE
OF ACTION

The techniques of making decisions legally binding and practically effective. Should an agreed objective be pursued through the adoption of a new
treaty, or an organizational "decision" (and what forms do "decisions"
take?), or a recommendation, a resolution, or some other device? Is the
desired end best achieved by encouraging governments to coordinate
policies and enact consistent domestic legislation, or by inducing them to
undertake formal, international obligations to act? In what circumstances
may the "binding" decision (whether cast as a treaty or an action formally approved by prescribed voting procedures of the international organization) become directly effective upon nationals of member states
without the requirement of further governmental actions? Are varying
degrees of legal obligation implied by various forms of expressing approval by member states: ratification of a treaty, failure to make timely
objection when, as provided by the terms of a treaty, modification of its
terms is authorized in the absence of such objection; modification of a
treaty not specifically accepted by a state when the terms of the treaty
authorize such modification by a qualified majority of parties; voting for
the decision of an international organization; voting for a recommendation, or other expression of consensus?

II. LEGAL EFFECTS OF APPROVAL OF DECISIONS BY MEMBER STATES

What is the practical significance, and the assumed legal effect, of a
state's support and formal vote for a recommendation, resolution, interpretation, formal decision, etc., through its representatives in an international organization? Are there instances in which national authorities have
acted to carry out decisions of international organizations even though
their representatives have not voted for them, or actively opposed them?
Are concepts of legal obligation invoked in such instances? Conversely,
what, if any, obligation is implied to carry out, through national measures,
decisions of international organizations that a state's representative has
voted for? What use is made of approval *ad referendum?*

III. INTERNAL LEGAL EFFECTS OF DECISIONS OF INTERNATIONAL ORGANIZATIONS

To what extent are the various modes described in I and II regarded as being obligations upon governments to adopt consistent policies, legislation, administrative regulations and the like, and to what extent are they regarded as directly creating rights and obligations in the nationals of governments giving their approval? Illustrative examples of variations in law and practice among member states of particular organizations in giving effect to treaties or decisions of international organizations as directly applicable domestic law, and of the legal reasoning invoked to support such applications. Is the growth of activity of international organizations having any impact on the traditional theories of incorporation of treaty obligations, and now decisions of international organizations, into domestic law? Illustrations of practical problems that have arisen in the experience of international organizations and examples of conflicts between "organization law" and domestic law of member states. How have differences been resolved in practice?

IV. COMPLIANCE: MEASURES TO HELP ASSURE THAT THE COMMITMENTS AND OBLIGATIONS OF MEMBER STATES ARE CARRIED OUT

An exploration of the techniques for checking upon and encouraging compliance by member states with decisions of international organizations, for example, the reporting procedures of the ILO, multilateral economic reviews, such as those in the IMF and OECD, assisted by the secretariat; formal inspections, and judicial proceedings.

V. THE SPECIAL PROBLEMS OF FEDERAL STATES

The problem of making international obligations or commitments binding upon the constituent units of a federal state, when the subject matter is within the constitutionally assigned legislative competence of the constituent units, is perhaps most familiar with reference to the United States. What techniques have been used by international organizations to deal with the "federal problem"?

360

VI. AMENDMENT OF CONSTITUENT INSTRUMENTS OF INTERNATIONAL ORGANIZATIONS THROUGH METHODS OTHER THAN EXPLICIT APPROVAL BY ALL MEMBERS

This general problem in the law of treaties is of particular importance with regard to the constituent instrument of international organizations. What has been the experience of specific organizations with techniques such as that used in the International Coffee Agreement?

FUNCTIONAL ORGANIZATIONS, POLITICAL ORGANIZATIONS AND IMPLIED POWERS

Mr. Stevenson (Chairman):

The conference is open. May I invite general comments upon the agenda. In particular, I should appreciate the authors of papers pointing out what they regard as important issues specially suitable for discussion.

If I might make a preliminary comment, it seems to me that there is a wide similarity in one respect of papers presented by conference participants from the functional international organizations: they have all found that the most effective means of implementing decisions are informal means which had not originally been contemplated when the constitutions of their respective organizations were drafted. The standby arrangements of the International Monetary Fund are a case in point. Mr. Lester Nurick's paper (International Bank for Reconstruction and Development) demonstrates clearly the effectiveness of influences brought to bear in the negotiation of bilateral loan agreements as contrasted with technical enforcement procedures.

The conference might examine whether this experience, most pronounced in the technical organizations, is equally relevant for the international organizations of a more political character.

Mr. Schachter:

The discussion should consider the use of informal arrangements as well as obligatory instruments. It should not concern itself with details of procedures of implementing decisions in particular organizations, but rather with "what direction to push in"—with the general lines of desirable future development in rendering the decisions of international organizations effective.

Mr. Stevenson:

I propose to follow the headings of the agenda. I suggest that we begin with topic I ("The choice of techniques to carry out an agreed course of action"). It would be helpful if Professor Stein and Professor Mestmäcker could comment upon Mr. Gaudet's paper (as he has been unable to attend).

Professor Mestmäcker:

I would like to point out one issue that appears to be relevant: that is the relation of functionalism and implied powers of international organizations. How far do the functions of an organization force certain powers upon it—even if they are not provided for? I think that we have this issue very clearly with respect to the International Monetary Fund, the World Bank and ICAO and it certainly is most relevant for understanding the EEC as a legal and economic enterprise.

Professor Stein:

This raises a very interesting analogy in the national context. I have in mind the relationship between the executive and the parliament. If you look at the United States Senate resolution of advice and consent to the U.S. ratification of OEEC, it contains an "understanding" which on the face of it is complete gibberish, but what it says is we, the Senate, want to make absolutely sure that this treaty will not be interpreted so as to increase the power of the President to the prejudice of the Congress.

The implied power issue in international organizations is very closely linked to the domestic distribution of power issue, particularly in a highly structured set-up like the U.S., and perhaps even more in Germany than in the U.S.

Mr. Stevenson:

One question that struck me on reading Mr. Gaudet's paper is whether it was really necessary for national constitutions to have been changed so explicitly to make it clear that the EEC could do various things. Constitutional amendment in the United States is no easy process.

Professor Sohn:

I would like to say a word or two about the relationship between what we are doing now and future problems: the U.N. has finally adopted the Covenants on Human Rights and the slow process of ratification has started. Once they become the law—and I think they will become law, even though some experts are pessimistic about it—many experiences of the ILO, the European experience and others are going to become very relevant. It is really important to see the effectiveness of the various procedures that have been adopted by other organizations before embarking on the new U.N. venture. I hope that we will not only discuss the past but also the future and see what we might suggest for future developments in the U.N. Assuming, for example, that a non-proliferation treaty is adopted, it is going to create various problems of inspection, enforcement and so on. It is easy to say: we shall give some powers to the IAEA to do something about these problems, but no work has been done in order to see *how* it could be done, how effective it could be.

I would like to make also a general observation: when I was reading all these papers, it impressed me greatly that all the techniques which we have developed in international law with respect to treaties, their interpretation, application, etc., have really very little meaning when you apply them to this constitutional type of instrument. This experience is really similar to that of domestic law in the field of constitutional law. Consequently, domestic law, especially in countries with federal or other complicated structures of government, might be more relevant.

Mr. Valticos:

Our discussion should be in the light of the adoption last December of the Covenants on Human Rights, which may have important and far-reaching effects. It gives us a great opportunity and we should make the most of it. We could also discuss the legal character of the Declaration on Human Rights; but we now have the Covenants in the form of treaties which will —once ratified by a sufficient number of states—be considered as universal law in this field. Compliance will then become one of the greatest problems. It may also have great influence on all the treaty systems of the U.N. and the Specialized Agencies.

Mr. FitzGerald:

I read the various papers with great interest and was greatly enlightened as to what the various organizations are doing in practice. But I found myself confused because I was unable to make a complete synthesis of these activities in my own mind. The problem here may be that of the political versus the functional, the integrated versus the non-integrated. (Some organizations—usually the Specialized Agencies—have a much lower degree of integration than others. Among the regional organizations, the OAS has a lower degree of integration than the EEC.) You also have the question of universal organizations versus the regional ones, and, the academicians will find this very difficult to accept, the extremely high degree of the para-legal or meta-legal content in some organizations.

Then there is the question of the application of constitutions. The functional international organizations are very often prisoners of their secretariats and of their national representatives; but nevertheless they are flexible enough to follow para-legal or meta-legal practices in applying their constitutions.

How are we going to extract from among all the ideas in the papers before us what is available for common use? One of our prime functions would be to see what is common and could be further developed. It may then be found that what is left is something so related to specific organizations that there is no use trying to make it common. In that respect I was particularly impressed by the papers from the representatives of the financial organizations.

Mr. Stevenson:

Would you like to say a few words here, Mrs. Higgins, since you are in a sense the person who has prepared a paper which deals most directly with the political agencies? I think the question which has just been raised is one of the recurring questions which we are going to have, namely, whether the lessons that we get from the functional agencies can be applied to the political agencies and whether we should be dealing with these as completely separate questions or whether there is a certain degree of transferability.

Mrs. Higgins:

In my paper, I pointed to what I feel is the ever present difficulty to try and find a constant for one political organization. The major problem in the U.N. on compliance techniques for one political organization is difficult enough; whether one can standardize through the functional organizations to a greater degree is something I would be very much interested to see. It may be that the variables in the functional organizations are considerably less because they deal with much more technical problems.

WHAT IS A "DECISION" OF AN INTERNATIONAL ORGANIZATION?

Mr. Lauterpacht:

One of the problems about which I was left in doubt after I had read these most interesting papers is: what is a decision? We are really considering what are the various forms of a decision, always assuming that a decision has been taken, or that there is an agreed course of action. I have the feeling that some of these techniques about which I have read in the papers reflect the fact that the states concerned cannot all agree on a course of action—and therefore these techniques are adopted for the purpose of avoiding defeat and the crystallization of the disaccord.

Mr. Golsong:

May I come back to the very interesting problem of compliance and implementation of treaties, such as the Covenants? My first question is: is a treaty adopted by an international organization a decision of the organization? In the ILO probably, yes, but what is their nature in the U.N. or other organizations? Are they adopted in the form of a recommendation or not? If we take the Covenants, it was simply decided to open them for signature, and the Secretary General expressed the hope that states sign and ratify them. Nevertheless there are a number of links between the treaty—which has perhaps a different legal instrument in its source from the organization as such—and the organization.

Mr. Nurick:

One thing that struck me is that there may be a very great difference among the organizations represented here. On the one end you have the Fund, the World Bank and the IDB. Most of the work they do is reflected in agreements which the organization makes with the outside: a borrower or a guarantor, or whatever is the case. That, in a sense, represents the major part of the work of those organizations. The decisions which are inherent in those agreements are the decisions which the organization takes possibly without any kind of formal action at all: it is simply a decision that the organization takes—to make a loan, or not to engage in an operation, to say that this particular course of conduct is one which the organization favors or does not favor, and the result may be that you will have or will not have a bi-lateral agreement, a contract. And that I think is quite different from the cases of many of these other organizations, where the action they take is represented by formal decisions of the organization which are binding on all members. The Fund I suppose is in a special position, as it represents both these types of organizations. On the one hand the Fund makes standby arrangements. On the other hand, it endeavors to enforce a kind of code of conduct which is binding on all members. As far as the standby arrangements are concerned, it is pretty hard to see exactly what they are, legally speaking. Although the standby arrangements are not regarded as legal instruments their effect may well be somewhat the same as what the World Bank does and the IDB does, in much more formal kind of agreements. As Mr. Lauterpacht has inquired, what is a decision? I think the most important of the actions taken by some of the international organizations are not reflected in formal decisions as such.

Mr. Schachter:

I think that this point is a very interesting one, but I would be inclined to draw a somewhat different conclusion. I am not at all sure whether a fruitful approach would not be to view the relationships in terms which are not too different from contractual relationship. In fact a bargaining model may be a more useful way of looking at the Rhodesian problem than a legislative model. The line drawn so sharply between the financial group of international organizations and others is not as firm as it seems. I think, however, that Mr. Nurick's suggestion is a very fruitful one because it shows a way to approach these compliance problems even in more general terms—through looking at the bargaining relationships that are created. Of course, I am not using "bargaining" solely in the commercial sense, but in the wider aspect to cover pressures, inducements and incentives used by the parties to achieve their aims in situations in which authority alone is not sufficient for a settlement. This would be true in cases like Rhodesia, South Africa, the Middle East, Article 19 of the U.N. Charter, or in the aviation field, where legislation is not necessarily the best way of approaching the precise problem. I think Mrs. Higgins touches on this when she talks about controlling a specific situation, in contrast with the objective of setting standards.

Professor Sohn:

Let me just say a word on the bargaining or bilateral model. This is becoming more and more important in many international organizations, not only in the Bank and Fund. This is due to the existence of a variety of technical assistance programs, operated by many agencies and constantly multiplying. If you look at the volumes of the U.N. Treaty Series, you discover that they contain a great many agreements between international organizations and states.

Coming back to Mr. Schachter's related problem, I think one of the papers mentioned the fact that compliance problems are of two types: one is when you try to force something on somebody, objecting to a violation and doing something about it in a negative sense; the other possibility is to do something positive or helpful about it, trying to help someone to comply rather than punish him for non-compliance. And here again the family of international organizations taken together has much more value and power in that respect than the U.N. alone.

Professor Stein:

This relation between international organization law and general international law is something extremely troublesome. I have an uneasy feeling that we are all wrong if we insist on fitting the law-making activities of modern international organizations into the strait jacket of Article 38 of the Statute of the International Court of Justice which lists the traditional sources of international law. Yet, I suppose, this may be necessary from the *de lege lata* viewpoint.

Mr. Elkin:

I would like to pick up a few questions which arose earlier. There was one question put by Mr. Lauterpacht: what is a *decision?* When we try to answer that question, let us forget about the constitutions of international organizations which give the word "decision" a very specific meaning: in the EEC, for instance, "decision" means something very specific; in other organizations it may mean something more general. The French, of course, have a very good word for this: "acte d'une organisation". The English equivalent would be "measures" or "formal measures", and yet, often it is not a "measure". I think what we ought to call it for the purpose of our discussion here is a "formal act". I use the word "formal" advisedly because what happens in practice very often is that the technicians work out a scheme, pass it on to a political level, or straight to the legal advisor, and say: now you draft the "act". Consensus may be there, but there is no *outward* act yet by the organization or a decision of the organization. It seems that we should be concerned with the latter, with the "formal act". We may discuss also the problem of how consensus comes about.

Mr. Nurick thought that there was a very special position as regards the World Bank and the IMF. I am not quite sure. The World Bank enters into contractual relationships which are expressed in legally binding loan agreements. Mr. Gold says that standby arrangements, which have an immense significance, are deliberately not framed as legal obligations. Deliberately they are not framed as legal obligations. But they are bilateral. Do you think that is what makes the difference; does it really? In the Code of Liberalisation of the OECD, which was a general act applying to all member states, there were a number of provisions dealing with two specific states which could not carry the general burden of obligations. There was a specific regime for them. That established a bi-lateral relationship between the organization and those two states.

Another point that interests me was Mr. Golsong's query: what are treaties which emanate from organizations? What is the relationship between that treaty and the organization? We had quite an interesting experience in the OECD in this respect. It shows that the question is technical and practical, not just one of general jurisprudence. In the past, we very often *recommended* to our members to sign very important financial agreements; and then we realized that if one of the members would not sign, the recommendation would fall to the ground because the *whole mechanism* of the treaty depended on the cooperation of *every* member. Well, we changed our practice and began to adopt formal acts containing a *binding* obligation for all members to sign the treaty and to ratify it. Why did we do that? We could have set out all the substantive obligations in a formally binding decision of the organization right from the beginning and have no treaty. But that is where Parliaments come in. The national delegations said: you cannot do that, this matter has to go before our Parliament. Therefore it has to be in a form of a treaty, it cannot be a "decision". But the treaty had to be signed by *every* member. So we had to have a formal decision binding the members to sign and ratify it. On the value of treaties generally: are they important? When you analyze it, provisions of treaties with which we are concerned in the economic organizations vary a good deal. Very often many of them are purely programmatic; some others contain specific obligations which have to be carried out; others are in-between—advising or obliging to pursue a certain *policy*—and a policy which can only be formulated in a general way.

In a homogeneous, small European organization, where Parliaments are very close or where even one of its institutions, the Assembly, is manned by national parliamentarians, the problem is very different from worldwide organizations. In the former case, there is bound to be a change of power distribution under the national constitutions as the result of the permanent activities of an international organization. The very fact that there is a permanent delegation which obtains its instructions from the executive gives the executive a certain power which has to be made compatible with the original distribution of powers under the national constitution.

That is why Mr. Gaudet pays such attention to the problem of what national constitutions of EEC member states say. You could not do without this, because parliamentarians are too near and because the whole machinery there is so closely knit that it would be impossible to have undertakings accepted without close consultation between the executive and parliament.

369

Professor Schwebel:

On this question of what is a "decision", and its nomenclature, I wonder whether an alternative way of wording things might not be a "purpose-ful act". It seems "formal act" could be a bit restrictive—particularly in the context of an organization such as the International Bank. Are we not really concerned with giving effect to an international organization's wish to do things and wish not to do things, whether expressed in a formal decision or not?

Mr. Stevenson:

There were actually two points that Mr. Elkin made. I agree with one to a certain extent—maybe there is a difference for analytical purposes between "formal acts" and other acts. But his second statement was that we, as lawyers, should not be concerned with anything but formal acts. I disagree strongly with that.

In the case of the World Bank, for example, some of the most effective results have been achieved in connection with its economic reports: re-commendations which were kept confidential. The Bank's loan agree-ment, the "formal act", had nothing to do with the fundamental changes in the economies of countries that were carried out as a result of the Bank's informal recommendations. I certainly agree that there was a "purposeful act" to prepare this economic report. It seems to me it is very much a concern of ours to consider other than only formal acts, be-cause frequently it is through informal means that international organi-zations actually achieve their objectives.

Mr. Schachter:

I agree, we are not primarily concerned with formal acts. We are prima-rily concerned with behavior, practice and with what happens when a decision calls for action. Now, this again raises the basic issue of our whole conception of what constitutes law in this context. This is a practical, as well as a theoretical, problem. In international organizations, there are im-portant areas of practice and of informal types of consensus (which in many important cases tend to be implicit rather than explicit) that have normative effects but do not quite fit into the "sources" of law as they are generally accepted.

We might consider this question—namely: in what way should we broad-en our conception of law so as to give the authority of law to the implicit rules of the game and to practice which is accepted as obligatory in interna-tional organizations. This is not an easy question to answer. On the one hand, when I write about this as a scholar, I use a broad conception, very close to that of McDougal: law depends on the attitudes of the community as to what is required. This does not depend necessarily on whether a requirement has a particularly formal authentication or authorization. A designated requirement becomes law when it is regarded as emanating

370

from legitimate authority and is likely to be complied with. In that sense, practice develops into law, or gentlemen's agreements may be viewed as legal obligations. The difficulty in practice, however, is to say: we now have law, even though the governments seem to characterize practice as something less than law. Therefore we are in a sense operating on a double standard, and part of the practical technique is to utilize terminology such as "practice accepted as law" to make the point that rules develop without formal enactment.

When viewed from the outside it seems to me obvious that much of the law, as I have defined it, really *must* be found in practice and consensus. I do not want to use the word practice alone because that is not necessarily the crucial aspect. The crucial point is the expectation about what is required so that in some cases you may have a single expression of a consensus in a resolution which will be accepted for a long time as a statement of obligatory requirements. If we place our sole emphasis on U.N. practice as customary law, it does not quite cover those situations which did not involve repetition and continued usage but nonetheless involved an understanding that a specific obligation resulted from a resolution or an informal agreement or simply the tacit rules of the game. One may say that one would dilute the concept of law too much by taking all expectations of what is required as expressions of law. I am sure that a number of you, particularly those among you from this side of the Atlantic, probably believe that we should somehow reserve the sanctity of law for a more limited category of acts, performed with appropriate formality or sanctioned as "custom". I would question that myself—I would think that it may be stultifying and also unrealistic to exclude from the category of legal requirements those norms which have developed through or have been manifested in informal patterns of behavior whether manifest in usage or informal consensus. In short, the terms of Article 38 of the Statute of the International Court of Justice may not adequately account for the law of international organizations.

Professor Sohn:

I would like to give a concrete example of that statement with which we are all familiar: a few years ago the U.N., after some negotiations and discussions, adopted a declaration on the rights and duties of states in outer space. It was said that this action created binding obligations, because (a) it was unanimous and (b) the states concerned have expressly accepted it as being binding. For a few years, we were proceeding on this assumption. We had done everything that was necessary to codify the rules of law relating to outer space. A few years later, the United States and the Soviet Union came to the U.N. and said, we would like to have a treaty on this subject which will be subject to ratification and so on. After some efforts, the treaty was drafted, not much more explicit than the declaration—it does not have many more details—but it was accepted and now has been ratified by a few states. But it is certainly far from having as much support as the declaration has had. Now, what is the effect of those two documents: which of them has created new law, which of them is important? Was the request for the treaty based on the assumption that something was wrong or insufficient about the declaration?

Mr. Lauterpacht:

If I may go back for a minute to Mr. Schachter's statement, my own thinking becomes clarified if I draw a distinction in terms of the basis of obligation. It seems to me that we are dealing with three categories of situations:

(1) where a legal obligation comes into existence by reason of the operation of the constitution, for example when a decision has been taken by an organ which has a decision-taking power.

(2) a legal obligation arises out of some separate legal act, as when the organization adopts a treaty which is then open for signature or accession and the legal obligation flows from the treaty itself.

(3) then there is a quite distinct, third situation: where you do not have a formal source of legal obligation, but where such obligation as can be described in legal terms is almost extra-contractual.

COMMUNITY EXPECTATIONS OF COMPLIANCE

Mr. Schachter:

Isn't it true in each case that you are really faced with making a prediction about how states are going to regard that act in the future? This is the crucial point. We may have a formal decision by a legally competent authority which will be ignored. We may have a treaty which is a dead letter treaty. But we may have an unstated, unwritten, type of consensus which is a "Rock of Gibraltar", as far as practice goes. This is the heart of our problem. As I see it, the crucial factor is whether the decision or rule— however it has been articulated— is regarded as likely to be complied with and has issued from an entity or group regarded as possessing legitimate authority and competence to adopt such requirements.

Mr. Valticos:

Although one might agree from a political science point of view with what Mr. Schachter has just said, I still think that some sort of distinction on the lines suggested by Mr. Lauterpacht would be quite useful because it would have a bearing on what we will have to consider at a later stage, the methods of possible implementation. Of course, we can think of various measures of supervision designed to help states to comply, but the measures can certainly not be the same—according to whether they were based on formal undertakings on a basis of a treaty or on such general consensus which may create "Gibraltar Rocks" but around which it would be more difficult to establish a supervisory "Home Fleet", to guard this "Gibraltar Rock".

Sir Kenneth Bailey:

Just one point: neither of the two great states which proposed the Outer Space Treaty in 1966 did so for legal reasons, or for any final belief in the insufficiency of the declaration of 1963. They carefully avoided any pronouncement on that issue. The Soviet Union had of course as early as 1962 urged that the obligation should be put into treaty form. And the very first document in the Outer Space Committee was a document proposing a declaration to be adopted and ratified by states. It was at a much later stage, about two years later, that the U.S. said they would rather have a resolution because a resolution would come into effect more quickly. So, the declaration was adopted in 1963 and it was for quite political reasons that the U.S. proposed a treaty. But nobody will expect that the treaty was necessary because of the insufficiency of the resolution of 1963. The United States went further than most of the rest of the states in 1963 in declaring that they accepted the resolution not because the adoption of the resolution by the General Assembly made it international law, but because its terms were declaratory of what *they* understood to be the customary law of states binding upon them as such. The Soviet Union stated substantially the same thing. The two space powers both accepted it not because they accepted the resolution as binding but because they accepted it as declaratory of practice, in that case practice being very short.

One more observation: Mr. Schachter spoke about the difference between a formally obligatory legal act or decision which may not be complied with and a more informal undertaking or understanding which *is* complied with. On the political side the obligations that are universally complied with are gentlemen's agreements. There are very few of them because of the insufficient area of agreement. But the gentlemen's agreements in the U.N. are universally accepted and complied with.

Mr. Elkin:

I only wish to say that I would like to get on the bus with Mr. Lauterpacht, but get off a bit earlier than where Mr. Schachter is travelling. I am quite happy about Mr. Lauterpacht's catalogue, but I think it is not complete. I think Mr. Schachter's ideas about expectations being at the basis of the act are absolutely correct. That is really what one has to *deal* with as a legal advisor.

But I am looking for some *expression* of the act. Perhaps unfortunately, I used the word "formal"—I did not mean "formal" in the sense of a catalogue of *legally binding* decisions at all. All I meant to convey was that a decision may come into existence in the council chamber or it may be contrived and expressed in one of those notes occasionally drafted at the luncheon table of the Secretary General. But one must look for a *permanent* expression of it and it is in that sense that I used the word "formal", which I think ought to be acceptable.

Professor Mestmäcker:

I wonder whether we do not want to distinguish between the possible effects that may flow from legal acts and the legal acts themselves. As a minimum requirement of a legal act we must have a willful act on the basis of something legal. In our context I would suggest that this might be "an act in exercise of the organizational functions". It has to have a relationship to the purpose and task of the organization and it must be recognizable as an act, not as a formal act, but as a willful act, a purposeful act.

The acts of international organizations and the social effects flowing from them should be differentiated on the basis of expectations of third persons who consider the act to be legally relevant and the social effects as a whole that flow from international organizations. This distinction is indispensable in the context of the EEC because the economic effects of the EEC are so widespread that it would be impossible to qualify these effects in all respects as legal effects. Again it is necessary to distinguish individual acts which are taken in exercise of the legal function of that organization, which does not mean that the overall effects of the organization are legally irrelevant. The compliance with the Treaty goes probably far beyond those individual acts that we are prepared to qualify as legal.

The effects may give an indication—in the long run or in the short run —how far people complying with certain standards do so because this is the law, or because they do it as a matter of economic necessity. The qualification of an act as a legal act serves certain purposes: to find out whether the act has any relation to the organization, whether the organization is bound by it, whether there may be judicial review and so forth. It is just a summary of probable legal relevance that we want to articulate in finding an act to be a legal act. It is probably not too restrictive to adopt as a guideline "an act in exercise of the organizational functions".

Mrs. Higgins:

I had in fact slightly reworded Professor Schwebel's original suggestion from a "purposeful act" to a "purposeful act of an authorized organ" but I gladly now enlarge this to a "purposeful act of an authorized organ for an organizational function". Perhaps we can all reach agreement on that; there seems to be merit in doing so. I think that purposeful as opposed to formal acts *is* important, because the relevant thing here is not always having a record of it, as Mr. Elkin suggested.

Mr. Gold's paper points very well to the importance of silence on occasions in the legal decision-making process of the IMF. And yet, we would surely all agree that this is a purposeful act of the appropriate organ, which is authorized and for an organizational function. It seems to me that we have really been talking about two problems: we have been talking simultaneously about the nature of the form and about the legal results flowing from the form.

So far as the nature of the form is concerned, the very narrow traditional definition of decision would, I imagine, be an "act from which a legal obligation flows", that is to say that if a state does not comply, there is perhaps the possibility of a sanction but certainly the knowledge of breach of obligation. I think there is something to be said for not defining decisions of international organizations this narrowly for a variety of reasons. Firstly one can imagine a whole range of "purposeful acts", etc. to which this does not apply. And specifically because one can imagine acts which are in this narrow, traditional sense decisions for the organization but merely recommendations for the members. One runs immediately into the problem of the organization acting *qua* organization and *qua* the community of members.

For example, the recent draft Covenants on Human Rights: it is perhaps arguable that these are recommendations to members to accede to the conventions. And yet—so far as any obligation between members is concerned —the source would be the acceptance of the treaty by those members. But an obligation *already* exists between the organization and members insofar as the clauses contained ask the Secretary General to do certain things, namely to try and urge nations to become members, to report on how successful it has been. This presumably gives rise to small costs on the budget. A nation is going to be required to contribute to those costs. It seems to me that at this point we move from discussion of obligation as it relates to our definition of decisions on to a discussion of obligation in general in the legal process. I very much agree with the remark that this *is* a relevant distinction because we may find different compliance techniques in these two sets of obligations. I agree with Mr. Schachter in the view that it is repeated practice together with a general consensus continuing to be applicable through time which is a relevant criterion; in other words, the criteria of community expectations in the future on future situations.

I would very much like Mr. Schachter to spell out the point he made on having occasionally to operate on a dual standard.

GENTLEMEN'S AGREEMENTS AND THE LAW

Mr. Schachter:
The dilemma of the legal advisor dealing, for example, with the case of an established practice about distribution of seats in a U.N. organ is whether he can characterize that practice as "law", that is, as binding (not

simply lawful). I have been called upon to answer the question, for example, whether it is now the rule that Western Europe must get 7 seats and Africa 5 seats in the distribution of seats for the UNCTAD Committee on Preferences or whatever it is. In point of fact agreements of this kind are complied with but there are dissidents at each point who raise the question of its binding effect. Now, in a scholarly context, I would say the practice followed is as clear an indication of a rule as you could find in U.N. custom. And yet, I would hesitate to say to a committee that this is law. The reason is that there is a gap between the accepted, conventional thinking of what is law and the more realistic approach which an outside observer can take. Governments are prepared to recognize and follow precedent or informal agreements but in the absence of formal criteria, a Secretariat legal advisor will have to avoid saying that they are now legally bound to do so. Nonetheless, we must recognize that in this context as in constitutional law it may be the precedent or gentlemen's agreements that create the most binding and firmest rule. Thus, there is something wrong in excluding them from the category of law.

Professor Sohn:

Does it make a difference to you that the original agreement on the Security Council seats was a so-called gentlemen's agreement, not written down in a U.N. document? On the other hand, two years ago after an increase of seats, a General Assembly resolution was adopted which said: from now on the seats will be distributed in such and such a way. Is the General Assembly resolution more of a law for you than the other agreement, or is it not law either?

Mr. Schachter:

One difficulty is that the original Security Council agreement did not include many members and therefore you have a separate issue in that case. Perhaps it is not the best case for testing this point. I am really talking about the other type of case where the evidence is quite clear as to general acceptance. Where the evidence is clear, where you have had a long practice, or firm expectations (where there is no long practice) and where there is no formal recording of agreement. You may be pressed to say whether it is law. The point is a practical one and cannot be disregarded, for the characterization of practice as law has significance. To say it is "binding but not law" will only create more confusion. You may try to get around the point by saying you take it that there is an agreement, but then of course people would say: we can challenge an agreement of others, we are not bound by an agreement to which we were not parties. Now are we bound by practice which has not been formally reduced to law? These are substantial arguments in the international organ and they cannot easily be answered by an international legal official who is expected to be restrained and circumspect in his pronouncements. However,

376

an objective observer may well conclude that there is a rule that the parties concerned expect to follow in the future. How do we know that? I would take the view that we look at all the evidence and all the facts. We look at all the facts to see what predictions we can make about how states will look upon the supposed rule in the future. We do not limit the inquiry to formal points and I would be very much surprised if we could end up with *any* points which are considered absolutely decisive for a determination of what is likely to be done in the future. When I say we must look at all the facts, that includes for example, judgments that a rule may not outlive a particular configuration of political circumstances.

Professor Sohn:

I understood what you said with respect to a gentlemen's agreement, but I still have difficulties in understanding what you mean by the necessity of evidence and so on. We have a clear resolution of the General Assembly saying we adopt this amendment to the Charter with the understanding that the new way in which the seats should be divided is such and such. Suppose that five years later the General Assembly says, we prefer to do it some other way. What would be your legal advice? That the General Assembly can do what it pleases the second time or that there has been a legal commitment on the part of the General Assembly to maintain the distribution?

A SUPPLEMENTARY AGENDA

Mr. Stevenson:
Permit me to draw your attention to the following supplemental agenda:

AGENDA ITEMS I AND IV

(1) In what different ways and for what analytical purpose may the various actions of international organizations be usefully characterized as:
(i) Formal or recorded acts
(ii) Legally binding acts
(iii) Purposeful acts
(iv) Acts in exercise of the functions of an organization and to effect its purpose
(v) Acts creating community expectations.

(2) Relevance of experience of functional international organizations for general international organizations:
(i) Does their relatively greater independence from national governments, frequent bi-lateral character of their relations with members and frequent ability to confer economic benefits as well as to regulate, make their experience of limited applicability to the implementation and compliance of general or political international organizations?

(3) To what extent is success of functional international organizations in affecting policy by making use of informal, frequently non-explicit techniques, not purporting to create binding obligations, applicable to general international organizations and organizations concerned with political questions?

ADDITIONAL QUESTIONS

(1) Specific cases of implementation techniques and compliance to be considered:
(i) Rhodesia
(ii) South Africa
(iii) U.N. financial assessment and Article 19

(2) Future problems:
(i) Ratification and implementation of U.N. Human Rights Covenants
(ii) Implementation of a Non-Proliferation Treaty
(iii) The financial integrity of international organizations

(3) Relationship of international organization law to international law:
(i) Is international organization law more analogous to constitutional law than international law?
(ii) To what extent is international law applicable to the acts of international organizations?
(iii) Do international agreements prepared by or under the auspices of international organizations differ in kind from other international agreements?

Mr. Stevenson:

I might draw your attention to the first item on our supplementary agenda which is an attempt to summarize part of the discussion which we have had, namely how we can best describe, and for what purposes, the different types of actions which international organizations have taken.

There also is the type of action that the World Bank and to a lesser extent the IMF are concerned with—I should of course also include the Inter-American Bank—in determining that a particular country's economic or fiscal policy should be changed in specific respects. Now, frequently this is not recorded in any way; it is often just a suggestion from the staff of the World Bank or the mission that has gone to a particular country, yet, it is a very important aspect of the legal acts which were taken later in drawing up the agreement. I am not sure as to the extent to which this falls in any of these categories. This is something I would like to revert to when discussing Mr. Nurick's paper.

VARYING KINDS OF "DECISIONS"

Mr. FitzGerald:

The first thing that I should like to revert to is the question of what are decisions.

I suppose, when dealing with the ILO type of treaty where you have the ILO constitutional instrument itself providing for the adoption of conventions, you are dealing with a decision of an international organization in the classical sense. On the other hand, if you are dealing with a convention adopted at a conference which was convened under the auspices of an international organization to which even non-member states of the organization are invited, as happens in the so-called diplomatic conferences, it is hard to say that you are dealing with a decision of the organization. Here you are dealing with a decision of a conference which has a separate existence. So in the first case, i.e., that of the ILO, the answer to Mr. Lauterpacht's question would be "yes" and in the second probably "no".

Our discussion progressed into the work of the Bank and the Fund, much of which is reflected in bi-lateral agreements or arrangements concluded between these bodies and states that are receiving loans or some kind of financial assistance. Here you are getting into difficult area of implementation. There are organizations in which a huge area of work is covered by bi-lateral agreements. The same comment could be made with regard to bi-lateral technical assistance arrangements.

The community expectations element exists in this case in that the members of the organization other than the member directly involved in a bilateral agreement with the organization will expect the organization itself, and the state concerned, to comply with the provisions of the agreement. On the other hand, there *is* a multi-lateral element in these agreements in the sense that you have *international standards* that are, in effect, incorporated by reference into the agreements and which one would expect the state party to the bi-lateral agreement to comply with. So, to that extent, the community of states in a particular organization would expect the assisted state to comply with these standards established multilaterally and also, depending on the international organization concerned, established with varying degrees of formality. We have something similar in the ICAO regional agreements for financing air navigation facilities in the North Atlantic area. The universal and multilateral element of normative material is written into these agreements. The same element can also be included in bi-lateral agreements.

There is also the question of the *"non-decision"* which nevertheless confers a benefit on the organization. For example, ICAO negotiated a headquarters agreement with the Government of Canada which covered material within the constitutional ambit of the federal government. But there was a gap in that there were certain things that only the Quebec Government could give the organization in the way of privileges and one of these concerned income tax exemption. There was also the question of exemption from succession duties. Representations were made to the Quebec Government over a period of years and nothing much happened. Finally some kind of informal exchange of letters took place and privileges were granted by the Quebec Government. Later on, the Quebec Government adopted an Order-in-Council. Now, to my knowledge, ICAO deliberative bodies and representatives of states did nothing whatsoever about this Order-in-Council, except that they took the benefits that were accorded under it. There is still no formal agreement between the ICAO and the Quebec Government.

So, by a unilateral act of the Quebec government, the Organization secures quite marked benefits from that Government. This is what I call a *non-decision* on the part of the Organization.

There is also the question of the forms of decisions. This leads one to wonder whether we should try to define "decision". Sometimes it is more helpful to leave things somewhat obscure until it is seen more clearly where we are going.

If we try to define the term "decision" with too much precision we may find that we are excluding a large area of the work of international organ-

380

izations in which there is a relatively large degree of informality, for instance, acts of the secretariat which possibly raise community expectations. The secretariat could be considered as a kind of organ which could, at a low level, take decisions which it may be permitted to take under the constitution without reference to the deliberative bodies. This may happen in questions of internal housekeeping, in the application in detail of certain broad decisions of deliberative bodies and without any decision whatsoever having been taken by a deliberative body. There are so many informal arrangements between secretariats and governments that they cannot be left out of our study. This is a very important element of the work of the international organization; it is what you may call an interstitial element, that is, the secretariat work of filling in the cracks.

One may be accused of loose thinking in this regard and one may be told that legislatures on a national level do not legislate by way of non-action, nor do they legislate by inadvertence. But we are not dealing with law on the national level; we are dealing with a lex that is very *imperfecta* and we must fill in these gaps as best we can, given the present stage of development, or non-development, of this law which we are attempting to create on a very pragmatic basis.

If we must formulate some sort of definition of "decision" for the purpose of discussions here, my own interpretation would take a combination of Mrs. Higgins' item (1) (iv) (Supplemental Agenda) "Acts in exercise of the functions of an organization and to effect its purposes" and Mr. Schachter's item (1) (v) "Acts creating community expectations". The incorporation of the idea of "community expectations" can certainly help in regard to the acts of the secretariat, since there may be acts of the secretariat which may or do create community expectations.

My last point is the question of the extent to which the traditional concepts of international law apply to international organizations. This is really the nub of our discussion. The traditional sources of international law as contemplated in Article 38 of the Statute certainly *do* apply to many activities of international organizations.

But there are some cases that are not covered by Article 38. We are developing a new kind of law. What we are dealing with to a great extent is a kind of "constitutional law in action". This is an ongoing process. We are not looking at international constitutional law as a language that is frozen and not to be changed. We are, so to speak, dealing with a living tree, whereby one accommodates the concept of the language of the constitution to present needs. At least in the technical organizations, the language of constitutions has been stretched to accommodate certain things which would not have been done 20 years ago, under the same language. You may have one word in, let us say, the ICAO constitution, for example, "airworthiness", which is the top of a pyramid grown from regulatory material, practice and so on. These constitutions can be considered as living trees and I do not think that we must look at them only in the light of traditional concepts. That would hinder the development of international law.

The next question is whether there can be a law without sanctions. Of course, there are sanctions which are built into the activities of functional organizations, for example the reciprocity doctrine. If one does not comply with the rules of the game, one cannot participate in it. Or if one does participate, the participation will not be beneficial. There are built-in sanctions. We are dealing with this *lex imperfecta* which is in the developing stage. Therefore, can we not be somewhat daring and say: let us take what elements of traditional law we can find—even without the legal sanctions of fine and imprisonment—and couple these elements of hard law in the traditional sense with national sanctions or the doctrine of reciprocity? This will give us, at least on the functional level, some sort of international organization law. This law would afford a certain degree of predictability as to what may happen tomorrow.

Professor Schwebel:

Just a word on gentlemen's agreements that struck me when we were discussing it: to some extent, the gentlemen's agreement cited then, the allocation of seats in the Security Council, lent a degree of support to Mr. Elkin's point about the usefulness of recorded agreements. If you recall, there was grave dispute, until the time a resolution of the General Assembly was adopted, about defining the nature of the gentlemen's agreement. The U.S. maintained that Eastern Europe was not entitled to a seat after the first election, and other states, particularly the Soviet Union, maintained the contrary. So can there be question both on the contents of the agreement and whether it was really maintained quite as faithfully as some suggest?

On the question of definition of the contents of decisions, perhaps we might think of item (1) (iii), "purposeful acts", as embracing omissions as well. I meant it in that sense.

As to the decision-making capacity of the Secretariat—to which Mr. Fitz-Gerald alluded—of course, it is most significant and has been so dramatically illustrated in recent months in the U.N. We have had the Secretary General of the U.N. taking the decision to withdraw the U.N. Emergency Force—something which certainly had an effect on international organizations and affairs. Under the Charter, the Secretary General unquestionably has substantial decision-making capacity, in the sphere of Article 97—in respect of administrative matters, being chief administrative officer of the Secretariat—and of course this is reflected in other agencies by comparable clauses; under Article 98, in respect of those powers that can be delegated to him by U.N. organs; under Article 99 insofar as he exercises the discretion to bring something to the Security Council's attention, and the various implied powers that may be said to flow from that article.

Mr. Arnold:

I would like to make a few observations about international banks. The exposition in Mr. Nurick's paper largely applies in substance to the situation in the IDB. Also there are some differences, which I would like to refer to, but I read the paper with care and noted only half a dozen points which I thought were sufficiently different of which to take note. This is mainly true of details of procedure. Our Bank's Charter was deliberately patterned to a large degree on that of the World Bank, although there were some important differences. I think as regional banks have been developed the small differences have become more numerous but you can still see similarity with the World Bank in the Charters of the African and Asian Banks. I cannot speak for the European Bank. It differs from all the rest, as I understand it, as it does not have any users among its members. It is a consortium of lenders rather than users. And this is important, because, in principle, the motivation of the Latin Americans in setting up our Bank was to have to a degree an organization of users. However, the presence of the United States in the Bank as a major stockholder does produce a considerable effect of having a principal lender present. This would not be true at all in the African Bank, but it is probably at least equally true in the case of the Asian Bank, where some of the regional members are in fact lenders.

I think it is only fair to say that the disciplinary effect of an institution like ours as to international law is less. I do not mean to imply by this that the difference is disastrous by any means, but there is a tendency undoubtedly toward understanding the problems of the borrowers. In our work, I do not know that we think a great deal of formulating "mutual standards." We do of course have standards but the focus of our activity is based on producing loans. We do pay a great deal of attention to the improvement of particular borrowers and we include numerous clauses in our contracts to further such improvement. We offer very substantial amounts of technical assistance and grants, some paid for out of loans.

I would also like to comment on two or three more points, one about headquarters matters. We have our headquarters in a federal government and we have no headquarters agreement. None of the three financial institutions in Washington has. We can live happily without one, partly because after all the United States is highly developed in this respect. In the United States, federal law is binding on the states and whenever one of the states wants to tax one of our people, we have been able to correct it. The exemptions of our Charter apply because they have been established as the law of the land by the legislation authorizing United States membership. I do not hesitate to say that so far we have been quite successful in this approach.

In our Bank, the acts of the "general secretariat", which we call the management, are extremely important. There is a very close relationship between our governing board and our management. Our immediate governing board consists of the Executive Directors, seven in number, elected by the 20 member countries. Our Board of Governors is a very formal body which deals only with high policy questions. In practical terms, important matters are dealt with by the Executive Directors. We do a good deal on the basis of statements of internal policy adopted by the Executive Directors which are not very formal documents but always useful for the operations of the Bank.

Finally, on the question of the traditional concept of international law and the concept of the charter interpretation, it may be of interest to say that we pay practically no attention to formal international law in our Bank. We just go ahead interpreting our charter very liberally. For example, we received 500 million dollars from the United States Government in the form of a trust fund, when the charter says absolutely nothing specific about such funds. We have received trust funds from non-member countries, when the charter says nothing about receiving funds from non-member countries in this way. These are only two of the broadest examples of our liberal interpretation.

We have been very much indebted to the World Bank for guiding practical operations in our Bank and we have modeled our contracts quite closely to theirs. One of the things we have borrowed is their statement that the contracts are not governed by the law of any particular country. This is an interesting point, because the World Bank does take this position on the basis that all of its agreements are international agreements and therefore international law applies. We cannot take that position in all cases because many of our agreements are with private borrowers and they frequently are not guaranteed by the central government so there is no good basis on which to hang the idea of international agreements. On the other hand, we do not wish to be bound by local law; contracts will be interpreted and executed in "good faith". It is sometimes difficult to apply, but we did have an arbitration once in which the umpire, a Swiss, had no difficulties with this concept. He proceeded in equity in a broad sense and this was the basis on which the arbitration was conducted. Naturally, we do have to apply local law when we have a mortgage.

A word on sanctions: our important sanction is that we could stop making loans to a country.

We do have the rule that we will not make loans to a country which is delinquent over payments to the Bank. Except for a couple of private borrowers, there has never been a case where a loan was truly in default, but occasionally there are minor delays in payment. If a loan is pending before the Executive Directors and the management finds that a country is behind in its payments, the Directors do not consider the loan.

Mr. Schachter:

One problem in relation to effectiveness (in the sense of compliance) is to consider in particular contexts what types of decision would be likely to be effective. I would even be prepared to abandon the word "decision" and bring in the word "communication". I would use the broadest term to describe the activity that emanates from an international organization which has effects or in which effects are sought—and this would certainly also embrace non-action, tolerances, a great many things which do not approach the usual meaning of decision.

I would not even interpose the notion of "purposeful" as a significant point because a great deal of international law has developed (as have common law and constitutional law) through tolerances which are not purposeful in the sense of trying to achieve a particular end. I can think of a number of cases where unintended effects resulted from such tolerances or acquiescence.

One significant aspect is the fact that much of the effectiveness of international organizations is found in behavior that does not involve explicit decisions or clear obligation. This experience is probably shared by all of the international organizations.

Mr. Elkin:

I would like to support the notion of a "recorded act", as distinct from "formal act", to define actions of international organizations. You, Mr. Chairman, seem to question the words "recorded act" because the World Bank influences member states to change their laws by means of a mere suggestion. I think that there is each time a question of *evidence*. If the word "recorded" means "evidenced", then I am perfectly satisfied. At some stage or other there may be a discussion with a particular member state why it did not change the law or why it changed the law the way it did. There must be some kind of evidence as to what was originally intended.

I do not attach too much importance to the distinction between bi-lateral and multi-lateral acts for two reasons: first of all, in my OECD experience, we very often put bi-lateral provisions into a multi-lateral act. I think that if you deal with an economic "measure" concerning say Luxembourg and the United States at the same time, you will have to do this; otherwise the "measure" will not be effective—it becomes a meaningless "act". Secondly, because you may have a number of bi-lateral acts, you do in fact use the same standards. Beyond that, if you have a group of homogeneous economic states and you have bi-lateral operations with some of them, the operations react on each other. There is therefore a close functional relationship. This may perhaps not apply in the case of the IBRD when it deals with, say, two underdeveloped countries far away

385

from each other. But within the EEC or similar communities there is that effect.

As to the requirements of "purposeful", I cannot make up my mind; as a legal advisor I must be able to interpret a specific case in the light of a specific purpose. Therefore I am rather reluctant to abandon the requirement of "purposeful". However, I do not take this as broadly as Mrs. Higgins does when she speaks of the effectiveness of a decision.

I was a little worried, although I agree in general with Mr. FitzGerald, when he gave an example of a non-decision. I always considered the kind of operation he mentioned not as "decisions" of the international organizations, because they do not serve *directly* their purpose or their functions. They are just like buying notepaper for the organization—the kind of bi-lateral transactions which enable the organization to carry out its operations in a physical sense.

The significant word Mr. FitzGerald brought up is "airworthiness". It might bring us to the next subject of this discussion. What we want to overcome is what we may call a conceptual type of international law—but we do not want to stay without any concepts at all. What we really want to proceed to is the formation of many new concepts. As regard the "variables" Mrs. Higgins referred to earlier, when one tries to analyze the concept of these variables, they look pretty thin and empty. In fact, however, these new concepts are full of meaning: take "balance of payment difficulties" or "export subsidies" or a number of other economic terms.

They were originally words on which you could not get economists to agree, but gradually, in a number of treaties and decisions, these economic terms acquired the quality of semi-legal or legal concepts. This is really where we have to proceed to. Perhaps Mrs. Higgins will reveal to us the meaning of some concepts in the political field—words like "aggression," there must be many others. "Reciprocity" is another notion that should be analyzed. There are two kinds of reciprocity; the reciprocity as regards rights and obligations in a specific transaction and the *real* reciprocity under which a legal advisor of an economic organization —which is fairly tightly knit—lives permanently: the hard bargaining which precedes the decision. It is the real *quid pro quo,* not in a specific decision, but based on the knowledge of each nation's delegate that if he does not give in a little bit today he will be faced with a very stiff position tomorrow on something entirely different. This is a type of reciprocity which is immensely effective for promoting consensus within economic organization procedures.

Mr. Stevenson:

The definition of the various types of acts of international organizations is really part and parcel of dealing with the question of what type of acts should be selected in order to achieve effectiveness.

Mrs. Higgins:

I had some difficulty in understanding Mr. Elkin's dismay at my distinction between effectiveness and compliance. I thought what I said was rather a commonplace, namely that there are two separate ideas (1) whether the measure that you chose even if carried out is going to achieve the end, which I term "effectiveness" and (2) whether you can get the addressees to carry out the directive or the decision which I termed "compliance".

I believe Mr. Elkin said that we should not deal with the former; the legal advisor is only concerned with compliance. I believe the legal advisor has necessarily to be concerned with both compliance and effectiveness. What I understand of the office of the legal advisors in the U.N. is, that it is essential that advice should be given on questions of effectiveness as well as compliance if one does not wish to be in the situation of resolutions being passed which really are not suitable for carrying out the purposes of the organization.

Mr. Elkin urged that although we might move away from conceptual jurisprudence we should not want to throw out *all* legal concepts. I certainly agree with him. I was merely suggesting that in the functional agencies there is a much higher, broader degree of both effectiveness and compliance than in the U.N. So far as the U.N. is concerned it seems to be absolutely essential that we must go behind the label, behind concepts, and actually look at the variables. Until we do this we are not harnessing all the techniques available to us to secure both compliance and effectiveness.

For example, to define aggression, we have to look at *all* of the variables and *all* of the circumstances, what McDougal would term as the multi-factoral analysis. One cannot just seek "the correct legal concept."

It is on a state-to-state level that one sees the working of reciprocity. I am unhappy about our viewing it on the organization-state level. Normally one thinks of reciprocity on the organization-state level as the ability of the organization to withdraw—in case of non-compliance—the benefits of participation or, more specifically, actually resources at its disposal. And, of course, the U.N. when operating in the peace and security area does not have physical resources at its disposal, the way the economic agencies do—therefore there is no directly related sort of reciprocity available to the international organization and I tried in my paper to indicate also that there are strong political reasons for not exercising the possibility of the withdrawal of benefits of participation. Moreover, because of the plenary structure of the Assembly, frequently the potential withdrawers of benefits are the same as the addressees. This comes about because of the different structural situation from the executive organs, for example, of the Bank and the Fund. The addressees of potential sanctions may be either few and important (which operates against the sanction being em-

387

ployed) or many (in which case one gets very near the situation where there is a low continuing community expectation of the proper course of action to follow). It therefore seems to me, given the efficacy that Mr. Schachter talked about, of the nuance, the implicit, we really ought to look at the question of how this can be harnessed to effectiveness and compliance.

We have to consider all the appropriate forms of techniques, the methods at hand to secure compliance. Isn't the present U.N. instrument rather blunt—I do not just mean the Charter but the way decisions are made on particular problems? And it is because of these reasons that I wish to look behind the concepts even if it means surrounding myself with some variables.

Sir Kenneth Bailey:

Referring to Mr. Arnold's statement that his organization did not follow much international law, that very international law supplied him with a justification for the kind of activity he describes in its presumption that: "what the charter does not forbid, it permits".

I do not want to delve further into the concept of "decision". I am content with any of the substitute alternative phrases. I would like to say something about the considerations that go to the effectiveness of decisions, in a broad sense, of an organization in member states. I would like to give a view that recognition of (a) the distinction between decisions in respect of which there is a legal duty applied by a member state; (b) decisions in respect of which there is a political or moral duty applied; and (c) decisions in respect of which there is no duty applied, is both relevant and important.

The difficulty and the imprecision of definition and of assigning a particular decision or act of communication to one category or the other is important but for our purpose it can probably be set aside altogether.

I would like to make a footnote on gentlemen's agreements. I do not think gentlemen's agreements are a difficult case: if parties make an agreement which they intend to be carried out strictly but which they do not want to be regarded as entering the sphere of legal relations or sanctions, they make a gentlemen's agreement. It is a concept in the common law system and flows from that system into international law.

No legal duty can exist to comply with a recommendation. Freedom to reject seems to be inherent in the nature of the recommending process —what distinguishes a recommendation from an order, a direction or directive, a regulation, a command. If the addressee is not free to reject a recommendation, it is misnamed a recommendation. I am strongly disposed to think that a member state is under no political or moral duty to accept a recommendation of an international organization either. I would think it is under a duty—probably a legal duty—to consider a recommendation in good faith—but having done that, in principle, the duty

388

stops. I think that this position is not even really altered in the case where the representative of a member state has supported the recommendation in the international organization concerned. The analogy is so close with the position of a member state in relating their acceptance or otherwise, the ratification or otherwise, of a treaty which had been signed by the plenipotentiary of the member state concerned.

I admit, I have probably not given full weight to the possibility of distinctions being drawn between international organizations of a functional character and those of a political character and between technical organization recommendations of a political character.

It is quite otherwise of course where the treaty itself requires nothing in the way of ratification—where the treaty can operate on signature without further act. In my own thinking, a recommendation is inherent in a process of *ad referendum* and that is in the nature of the recommending process. I recognize that on this last point, perhaps on the last two points, I have rejected the view expressed by Mrs. Higgins in her own paper and am open to hear some further exposition on this point.

I have probably been thinking too exclusively of the position of a member state in relation to the recommendations of the General Assembly. There it seems to me the discretion allowed to a member state is *a fortiori* to the treaty case. Having regard to the circumstances in which resolutions of the General Assembly are so frequently reached and decided, the most controversial case in recent times was the U.N. Declaration on Non-Intervention in 1965, which was adopted by 109 votes for, one abstention and none against. My own government voted in support, saying at the same time that, although it accepted the resolution as a declaration of intention, it could not accept it as a legal obligation—as a satisfactory legal text. That resolution was a compromise in which it was impossible for any nonsponsor to secure any alteration because it emerged from a political package deal between the Eastern European group, the Latin American group and the non-aligned group. I think that the political circumstances in which General Assembly resolutions are so often taken nowadays emphasize the desirability for lawyers to recognize that the government has at least the same freedom from the duty to comply with a recommendation as it has to ratify a treaty signed by its representative.

Professor Schwebel:

A word about Sir Kenneth Bailey's reference to the "Non-Intervention Resolution" and the inference that might be supposed to flow from saying in certain cases only that a recommendation is not binding. In that case, Australia and the United States *did* say that they regarded the "Non-Intervention Resolution" not so much as not binding—though clearly they so regard it—as not being an authoritative statement of the law. This is the principal point which I believe they had in mind, and non-binding character is a corollary of that point. Normally of course a re-commendation of the General Assembly does not give rise to an obligation binding in international law, nor does it enunciate, nor is it expressive of, the state of international law; it is simply a recommendation of policy on a particular point. Now, in this case, certain states, indeed the majority of the Assembly, believe that the "Non-Intervention Resolution" is an authoritative expression of what international law is, and not what international law came to be by reason of the resolution. The point of the United States and Australia was that, while the resolution *did* well state certain political desiderata, it was not an actual or altogether accurate statement of the law and, therefore, those states voted for it as an expression of their desire that intervention not occur, but did not treat it as an authoritative statement of the law.

Sir Kenneth Bailey:

There are just three sentences I would like to say in clarification of my statement on the Non-Intervention Resolution:

1. In giving its reservation statement, the delegation of Australia did not in any sense have in mind reserving to itself a right to intervene in the affairs of other governments or not to comply with the general intent of the resolution.

2. The language of the resolution was so loose and so wide that, in its ordinary meaning, the resolution would prohibit not only all normal practice of diplomacy but every type of endeavor to influence other governments by negotiations and that we thought to be dangerous as well as silly.

3. The only purpose that I had in mind in mentioning this particular resolution was the unsatisfactory manner in which resolutions may come up for consideration in the General Assembly, leading to the possibility of decisions being made on political principles. Therefore they should not be taken as formal, legal, or moral commitments.

HIERARCHY OF DECISIONS

Professor Sohn:

One thing we have not focused enough upon is the hierarchy of decisions of international organizations, the fact that certain decisions are of higher effectiveness than others. Various acts and instruments of international organizations have now a recognized value. Let us start with the U.N. Charter. I do not think that anybody would at this point try to argue that any member nation can say that it is not bound by the Charter and we have even seen attempts to say that non-members are bound by it to some extent. Of course that does not help much to answer: what does a particular obligation in the Charter mean? You remember one of the first cases we had in the U.N. was the case relating to the Indians in South Africa. General Smuts argued that, while he agreed that fundamental human rights should be protected, this could not be done until an agreement were reached on another international instrument that defined those fundamental freedoms and human rights. The U.N. then proceeded to do this very thing; it adopted a Declaration on Human Rights and said that this document constituted at least a catalogue of the fundamental human rights, that those were the rights we meant to protect when we adopted the Charter. Some people think therefore that that Declaration is not merely a recommendation but has a different value from other, ordinary resolutions, firstly because it interprets what was meant in the Charter and secondly because it was adopted almost unanimously. Just as with Mr. FitzGerald's example of "airworthiness", here we have the phrase "human rights and fundamental freedoms", and the Declaration helps in interpreting it. Of course, other people say that it is not enough because when we have the next concrete case we do not know whether it falls under the Declaration or some other international provision or a Charter provision unless there is an authoritative decision. We have to have, for example, a body authorized to take a decision under Chapter VII of the Charter, and dispel the remainder of the doubt. The United Kingdom in the Rhodesia case said that, after the Security Council has adopted a binding decision on the Charter, everybody is obliged to follow it. The British were thus permitted to stop somebody else's ship on the high seas because the Security Council said they could do it. So, there is no doubt; we have now a binding provision of the Charter, a declaration of general scope interpreting the Charter, and a particular decision by the Security Council under Chapter VII.

To turn to the General Assembly, the Charter arrangement seems to have been that it can just make recommendations which are simply recommendations and therefore not binding, though given by a very important body. It is not a decision; at least that is what we thought in 1945. But during the last 20 years we seem to have developed a hierarchy of Assembly decisions. The Secretary General in an almost unnoticed statement said in the Suez case in the beginning of 1957 that the General Assembly's decisions which simply applied the Charter—which merely stated that in this particular case the Charter had been violated—were binding as applications of the Charter, not as Assembly recommendations. According to this view, the General Assembly's decision is merely a mechanism by which the binding character of the Charter is applied to a concrete case. Then you have the resolution of the General Assembly entitled "Uniting for Peace" where, as many people said, the General Assembly filled the vacuum caused by the veto in the Security Council. Under that resolution, the General Assembly made certain assertions as to its powers, and later it started exercising these powers. It adopts accordingly peacekeeping recommendations which are considered to be almost as binding as if they were decisions under Chapter VII. On the other hand, we have recommendations of the General Assembly that seem to be written almost in the same language as if they had been adopted under the "Uniting for Peace" Resolution—for instance, in the South African case—but are *not* under "Uniting for Peace".

Each of these decisions is slightly different. We cannot say simply that a recommendation is recommendatory; there are at least three or four or five different categories of recommendations which have different effect. In each case, it also matters whether the nations adopting a recommendation say that they are willing to be bound by it. By these various acts a nexus of obligations is established, from which they cannot get away, except under conditions that they themselves have made.

On the other hand, when it is a pure and simple recommendation, it is just that. Then it does not have that special, hierarchical status which can be gained by being an interpretation of something higher. It may be a difficult question for lawyers to decide whether this particular resolution belongs to category A or B. In the declaration on "Racial Discrimination", which the Assembly adopted by a unanimous vote, the Assembly also said that all states "shall fully and faithfully observe" that declaration, thus implying that the countries agreed to be bound thereby. They also put a provision into this declaration expressing the view that they considered two earlier declarations similarly binding. The power of states to bind themselves is unlimited; they can always accept additional obligations through the medium of a decision of an international organization.

This is true not only with respect to the United Nations but other organizations. We find in the ILO a classical example of those non-decisions which are decisions. In his article in 1939 on the interpretation of the ILO Constitution, Jenks pointed out that there are many decisions of the International Labor Office which say that the Office does not have any authority under the Constitution to interpret provisions of ILO conventions, and that the only binding interpretation can be given by the Court. Nevertheless, as a particular country has asked the Office for an opinion, they proceeded to give it. In some cases this went even a step further, and the Office said: we have given an opinion. This opinion has been properly published in the Official Bulletin and nobody has protested against it. Therefore, from now on our interpretation of convention A is embodied automatically in conventions B and C which were adopted later and they should be interpreted in accordance with our interpretation.

In ICAO, various difficult problems arose with respect to international traffic: which air operation should be classified as a scheduled airline and which not? This was not even an interpretative decision. The ICAO Council somehow made a decision on this issue, and somehow it became accepted by everybody as an interpretation although it was not done on the occasion of a dispute, under a special clause in this Organization's Convention relating to the Council's power to decide disputes.

So you have this hierarchy of decisions, under the guise of interpretation

392

and rooted in the binding character of the original document. There is the additional fact, in a case such as that of ICAO, that this seems to be the only body available for making a decision on the particular point. Such a decision seems binding, especially if there is no protest. If something is adopted and nobody seems to be protesting, this decision of an international organization becomes automatically part of what is customary international law.

Moreover, some decisions of international organizations, while they do not create law directly, become nevertheless part of the evidence from which law is derived, and if an international court is trying to look for principles and finds a General Assembly decision saying that "genocide is a crime under international law", this is going to be pretty good evidence, especially if nobody has objected to the statement.

INTERNATIONAL LAW AND THE LAW OF INTERNATIONAL ORGANIZATIONS

Mr. Lauterpacht:

I noted with a certain anxiety the suggestion that when dealing with the law of international organizations we are somehow not dealing with international law. What is happening when one gets the development of concepts, such as "airworthiness" or "balance of payments", is that we are getting to developments or glosses upon particular treaty provisions, which may or may not come to have a wider significance outside the limits of a particular treaty.

One of the interesting innovations in International Law Reports is the introduction of a table of treaties which has as its primary purpose the reflection of the growing significance in international case law of the interpretation of treaties. One can look into this table of treaties and see the wide range of words and phrases which have been technically construed.

Professor Sohn is right to emphasize the significance of practice coupled with the lack of protest as a source of international organization law. If it is right to say within a single given organization that an interpretation pursued without protest is the correct interpretation, can one then go on and say that this is, so to speak, a general law of international organizations? Can one say that there is a carry-over of interpretation from one constitution to another with the consequence that the development of a particular constitution may also create in the absence of protest a presumption perhaps that *that* interpretation is the correct one to be applied in *another* constitution?

If the answer is in the affirmative then of course the problem of protest is enormously enlarged because every time a situation occurs, let us say, in the most remote of organizations and there is an absence of protest, then perhaps states have to worry about the significance of that vote in relation to comparable situations in other organizations. I believe that there is some justification for the proposition that where one treaty is interpreted in a particular way, comparable clauses in other treaties can bear the same interpretation. Out of this we could achieve a situation in which we have a general law of international organizations.

I was struck with the understandable tendency for us not to become too concerned with the definition of what is legally binding and what is not legally binding. In view of the fact that international organizations exist for the purpose of *doing* things, it is the function of the legal advisor to see that things get done, without worrying whether the instrumentality of the operation is technically binding or not. At the same time, while we have on the one hand this blurring of the lines between obligation and non-obligation it is interesting that, on the other hand, we have reference to such practice as gentlemen's agreements. I was struck particularly by the way Sir Kenneth Bailey defined gentlemen's agreements, as being a situation in which the bodies intend to adhere strictly to an arrangement which is not legally binding. If you have a situation in which parties are prepared to define precisely their relation and yet do not want to call it a legal relationship, we must ask ourselves the question, why don't they want to call it a legal relationship? What is the significance of not calling it a legal relationship? Is there something more in legal relationship? It brings us back to the fact that to qualify a situation as legally binding must have some political purpose.

CHARACTERIZATION OF THE ACTS OF INTERNATIONAL ORGANIZATIONS: A SUMMARY

Mr. Stevenson:

Different characterizations of acts of international organizations may be useful for different purposes:

(1) As international lawyers, we are interested in the means of achieving compliance with or effectiveness of any request by an international organization for action or non-action, providing this has been communicated to the states in question... In a very broad sense international lawyers are interested in "communications" between international organizations or, more narrowly, in "purposeful acts" of international organizations.

(2) In a somewhat lower order of generality, participants were stated to be concerned with "acts in the exercise of international organizations functions and creating community expectations." It may be useful to establish what acts are normative in the sense of providing a basis for predictability within international organizations' respective areas of interests.

(3) A narrower definition—and a more traditional one—is "those acts which are considered legally binding." A number of participants thought that this distinction was without meaning for our purpose but others felt

that it was very important because of the central importance that many states attribute to whether or not a particular act is legally binding.

(4) It was felt useful by some to distinguish between formal or recorded acts of international organizations and ones that are not so recorded. The point was made that a recorded act had greater precedential effect than the informal, unrecorded act.

We also discussed at some length: when is a state obliged?

(1) Some were of the view that, by definition, a recommendation does not imply a legal obligation even where a representative of a state votes in favor of a recommendation.

(2) Others suggested that the case was not quite so clear and that if states at the time when they adopted a recommendation said certain things or if a recommendation was in essence an interpretation of a charter or a treaty obligation, a legal obligation may very well be involved.

(3) It was also suggested (at least in some of the papers) that a considerable number of states considered themselves morally bound to implement the resolution which they voted for.

Finally, we discussed the question of whether international organization law was part of international law. There were different points of view but there was general agreement that, as international lawyers, the participants should be concerned with international organization law. Some were of the view that international organization law was basically treaty law and as such international law. Other participants stressed that certain aspects were somewhat different from international law—perhaps, in some respects more akin to constitutional law. On the other hand, sharp exception was taken to the point of view that the interpretation of the articles of an agreement of an international organization was not governed by international law.

Another subject to be considered is, what techniques are most effective? Apparently a number of the functional organizations are resorting more and more to informal as opposed to formal means of achieving their objectives, relying particularly on bi-lateral bargaining techniques and the bestowing or withholding of benefits. Is this because of structural inadequacies of these international organizations? Is it because of the lack of adequate formal implementation means, such as exist in the EEC, that the functional agencies find it more effective to use these less formal means? Should more elaborate enforcement machinery and structure be provided?

ARE TREATIES DECISIONS OF INTERNATIONAL ORGANIZATIONS?

Mr. Golsong:

I am not so much concerned with the academic problem of defining acts of international organizations as with evidence to create precedent.

I would not even introduce into the discussion the concept of non-decisions. I must say that I disagree with the example given by Mr. FitzGerald concerning the Province of Quebec; I feel that this was really not a decision of an international organization but a unilateral action of a member state.

I would like to refer back to our discussion as to whether treaties are to be considered as decisions of international organizations. Mr. FitzGerald suggested only to consider as decisions of international organizations treaties concluded within organizations such as the ILO. This might be right from a very formalistic point of view, but I think that treaties concluded outside the ILO experience—concluded under the auspices of international organizations—have the character of decisions, even though they are not subject to strict voting rules as, for example, recommendations may be. You have, for example, in the Charter of the U.N., no reference to conventions concluded among states. So the first result is a discussion about the requirements for voting or authorizing a group of states to conclude a treaty within the organization, referring to its political authority, making use of its institutional framework, and so on. This is an open question. Furthermore, treaties concluded under the auspices of international organizations have to be interpreted in a different way in the case of dispute. Probably the *will* of the contracting parties as one of the basic elements of interpretation in traditional international law is much more difficult to apply, especially if you have a treaty which was elaborated among a smaller group of states than the group of states which finally has adhered to it. And how far do you have to refer to the preliminary work of the organization?

According to the traditional view, a treaty is the higher form of international law, at least placed on a higher stage than a recommendation. On the other hand, we are faced with the problem whether a binding recommendation (the question is only interesting insofar as it is a recommendation which is more than the reflection of what the states consider already customary law) commits the state to follow the guidance and direction indicated by the recommendation. Maybe this is so, and perhaps the United States and Australia (in the case of the Resolution on Non-Intervention) thought it necessary to state that they are not considering this recommendation legally binding. One might conclude that in all cases where no reservation is stated the recommendation becomes binding. In our smaller organization, we have the provision, which is expressly set forth in the regulations, that a state is authorized to vote in favor of a recommendation but also authorized to state at the same time that it is not prepared to act thereon. Is there not otherwise a presumption that the state *is* subject to the guidance of such a recommendation even if its terms are vague?

Paradoxically, a recommendation needs in a great number of cases a larger number of votes than the opening of a covenant. Even if you can

396

adopt a recommendation with a simple majority of votes in the U.N., I think the feeling is that only those recommendations which are supported by a large majority, or unanimously, have a somewhat binding character for those who support the idea of being bound by it. But then you have the situation that a binding recommendation needs a larger support than a decision for opening a convention for signature and ratification and, furthermore, the recommendation appears to be much more strict in its presentation. We heard here that there are situations where states, even if they want to produce and submit amendments to the original text, are not in a position to do so, and that therefore a recommendation is sometimes so strict that there are no possibilities for expressing reservations on specific points. But this is often possible in the case of treaties; treaties are much more flexible if you compare them with recommendations in this sense and, nevertheless, we say that treaties are on a higher level of the hierarchy.

Professor Sohn:

One point about the relationship between the Declaration and the Covenants that bothers me, is, to what extent the Covenants have some kind of a force with respect to the states which have not ratified them, i.e., to what extent are the U.N. Covenants also recommendations, or as good as recommendations?

Mr. Boulanger:

My main difficulty with the question of the substance of the point Mr. Golsong made, is this: it is not enough to concentrate on the words "recommendation", "treaty", "covenant" and so on. We must widen considerably our frame of reference to cover a number of factors. Intent, and more important, behavior, predictable behavior, is much more significant than the words themselves. The use of a recommendation may be totally misleading in the complicated world of international organizations. There are an infinite number of different types of language, of formulae used, but beyond that—and much more important—there is a great deal of variety in terms of intent, of interest, of power, of all the factors which we evaluate when advising our clients. There is no reason why the legal profession should close its eyes and play with words alone and exclude these other factors. I do agree that hierarchy of norms plays a role, characterization of what is binding plays a role, constitutional authority plays a role, but there are far more important elements which may affect compliance. There are many resolutions which in explicit terms state obligations or declarations of what is law, but still, we would not predict that they will in fact be followed. We know that they have a great deal of rhetoric—of lip service—and they would be discounted as guides to future behavior. This would even be true of a domestic statute in some circumstances; after all, we have dead-letter laws. The heart of our problem is

397

that we do not have one or two or three identifying tags that we can play with in determining the effect of resolutions that may or may not be regarded as statements of legal obligations. The other point that we must take into account is this: Mrs. Higgins has given us her set of variables. I think she has not given us enough of them. But, I think, that is the way the problem has to be dealt with.

Mr. Golsong:

I agree that we need variables within the framework of what is called a recommendation. There is a wide range of possibilities. But as soon as we use the word of a more classical concept, a treaty, I think we cannot completely distinguish the treaty from a recommendation.

I wonder, if you take the Declaration on Human Rights that is, in 1967, considered declaratory of legal norms, and if you also take a particular law of the Declaration that is also formulated in one of the Human Rights Covenants and this Covenant is ratified, let's say by a large majority of U.N. member states, but on the particular point of law there are about 50 reservations expressed, what is then the position of the same principle as expressed without reservation in the Declaration?

Mr. Schachter:

You have already given the answer: you have yourself indicated that the evidence of reservations that has now contemporaneously appeared weakens the effect of what was previously a general statement.

THE EFFECT OF A FAVORABLE VOTE FOR A RECOMMENDATION

Mrs. Higgins:

It does seem to me that there is a genuine ambiguity in this problem of interpretation of whether a state, when it votes in favor of a recommendation, is bound to comply with it. This is genuinely open to debate.

On the other hand there are really three options available to a state: it can vote against, it can abstain, or vote for, making a collateral statement indicating that it does not believe the statement to be a correct enunciation of the law or one that requires action from it. So that if it declines to exercise any of these three options and votes for, with adequate time for consultation at home, having gone through the *ad referendum* process, it is then arguable that it is bound. The consequence that flows from putting this argument is that you do not promote a greater than necessary disparity between actions of organizations and the consequences which flow from them. And as international lawyers we should be concerned in not opening up this disparity.

But I appreciate also that there is an argument on the other side: namely, that if states are to be bound by recommendations, even those for

which they vote, it is arguable that you are impeding the normal transactions of communications of an international organization, because states
that believe that this was so would be reluctant to vote for resolutions.
However, there are arguments on either side but what is relevant is: to
see the *consequences* that flow from adopting acts.

Mr. FitzGerald:

What happens if you have a body, something like a governing body of
limited membership or the ICAO Council which, in adopting a recommendation, is really acting for the membership at large? What is the effect for
states voting for a recommendation in those circumstances? Here you
would have 80 odd states that have not participated in the development
of the recommendation at all, with the exception of a few preliminary
talks.

Mrs. Higgins:

This is a different point. My point went to the acceptance really by vote
of states of a recommendation, an acceptance that arguably changed the
nature of the recommendation. It is not the recommendation that binds,
but the acceptance of the states through the vote. The example you offer
is something quite different and goes to the question of whether in a particular organization any community expectation as to whether the non-
voting state is being bound has been built up.

Mr. FitzGerald:

The reason why I raised this point was because in functional organizations a vast amount of the decisions are made by these governing bodies
of limited membership.

THE BINDING CHARACTER OF AN ACT

Mr. Lauterpacht:

I am led to believe that the complication is really about the word "binding." Our difficulty stems from trying to determine whether something
does bind or does not bind and the answer is that there are some things that
bind to the first degree, some to the second, and others to the third. I was
particularly struck when reading the paper where Mr. Gold talks about
the standby arrangements. The reason why the Fund was so careful not
to contribute to the legal status of standby arrangements is, as Mr. Gold
states, that they do not want to put a country in the position of having broken the law. What we find all the time is that it becomes more and more
difficult to say that something is really law and all we are concerned with
is a situation in which a prescription is needed. The problem is to determine just how compelling the prescription is, how much weight it carries.

Professor Mestmäcker:

I would like to pursue a little bit further the problem of the binding quality of recommendations. The different degrees of binding character certainly do not exhaust the possible legal relevance of recommendations if you look at the EEC treaty, where recommendations are defined as being not binding.

The use the treaty makes of recommendations in giving the Commission authority to issue recommendations is such that the legal relevance of recommendations may be more considerable than that of a decision. For example, under Article 37, the Commission may issue recommendations in order to prepare state trading monopolies for the general application of the treaty rules. During the transitional period these monopolies are supposed to be "adjusted" so as to eliminate all discrimination. In issuing these recommendations, the Commission had to interpret the treaty and these interpretations underlying the recommendations have been referred to by the Luxembourg Court of Justice as legal authority. The most important indications how certain parts of the treaty are to be interpreted thus flow from recommendations that are not binding.

Another important aspect of these recommendations is that, although they are supposed to prepare the member states for the application of the general rules of the treaty, as a matter of economics it would be very difficult to comply with these rules at the end of the transitional period without having complied with the recommendations of the Commission. This is the reason why those recommendations are almost universally followed. In issuing the last recommendation for "adjustment" the Commission had, in effect, to decide the legal position of the state trading monopolies as such.

Another point I want to refer to is the importance treaties or conventions have in implementing the EEC treaty. In numerous instances, the treaty provides that the member states shall enter into conventions. Insofar as these conventions are entered into there is no doubt that the rules of these conventions are community law and participate in the special legal character of the community. Consider, however, those treaties where the member countries have to come to the conclusion that the instruments of the EEC treaty do not suffice to reach the goals of the Common Market, e.g., the European Patent Convention, Trade Mark Convention or the draft of the European Companies Convention. Here, the harmonization of national laws does not suffice because it is the nationality of the traditional regulation that interferes with the goals of the EEC. Are treaties like these part of the community law as well? Are the rules of interpretation adopted by the Court for the EEC treaty applicable? There are opposing views. Some stress the traditional character of those treaties as instruments of international law. There are others who insist that those treaties are as much community law as the treaty itself; the implication for the interpretation and application of those rules within the community and in member countries are far reaching indeed.

I would like to point out the importance which the difference between compliance and effectiveness has in the EEC context. In general there is, of course, a very close relation between the appropriate technique for reaching a certain result in accordance with the goals of the treaty. In interpreting individual provisions, the basic purposes of the treaty have to be taken into account. This is one of the most important rules of interpretation stressed again and again by the Luxembourg Court. Nevertheless, there is a considerable practical, economic and legal difference between compliance and effectiveness. I would like to illustrate that point by referring to the *Grundig/Consten case* decided by the Commission and confirmed by the Luxembourg Court.

The Commission prohibited contractual export prohibitions imposed by one firm exporting from Germany to France. Compliance in this case simply means that the firms concerned must not effect prevention of exports or imports. But the effects of the decision are something quite different. The effect sought by the Commission, the immediate effect was, to make possible the free flow of goods within the Common Market. The possibility of reaching this effect depended upon a series of secondary considerations. I am singling out but one: the contractual export prohibitions are mostly applied to trademarked and pricemaintained goods. In Germany, resale price maintenance is legal. In France, resale price maintenance is prohibited. The business reason for export prohibitions is to maintain different levels of prices for the same goods in member countries. Once the export prohibitions are eliminated, the goods from the low price country may flow into the high price country and prices level out. In Germany, the civil law validity of resale price maintenance depends upon proof that the producer is in a position to effect resale price maintenance for all his goods completely. He must guarantee that the price-maintained goods cannot be obtained without the restrictive covenant. A comparable problem arises in the United States with respect to "non-signer clauses". In Germany, the requirement of effective completeness of price maintenance cannot be satisfied as soon as export prohibitions are illegal. A producer who does export his goods to France cannot guarantee that these goods will not flow back to Germany, and in France price maintenance is illegal so that restrictive covenants are impossible. Consequently the producer's resale price maintenance contracts in Germany may become unenforceable. A case like this came up recently. A German court held that the resale price maintenance contracts for color TV sets by a subsidiary of General Electric were unenforceable because the export restrictions necessary for the completeness of the system were unenforceable. General Electric then announced that they were not going to impose further resale price maintenance contracts. This was a district court decision; if it is upheld by the Bundesgerichtshof, the Commission has in effect made impossible resale price maintenance which is explicitly permitted under the German law. Although this effect was known by the Commission and taken into account it is not dealt with in the decision. We find a chain effect of a decision by the Commission on the basis of community law. Before the Luxembourg Court, the German Government intervened arguing that the Commission had no authority to make this ruling because of its effects upon a legal institution in Germany.

The simple answer to this is that the consequences of community law in the domestic law of all six countries may be quite different. But the equal enforcement of community law in all countries makes it impossible to take into account the individual legal consequences in the member countries.

The last point I want to make is that no German administrative body or court could have made such a ruling because the German court would have been bound by the German statute permitting resale price maintenance. In enforcing Community law, the Commission effected a partial breakdown of resale price maintenance in Germany. This effect is something quite different from compliance.

The implications of the decision go beyond resale price maintenance and touch upon trade marks as well. Once you have a registered trade mark in France and in Germany you can theoretically—by using the trade marks—effect the same restrictions as by contractual restraints. In this respect, the court held that trade marks may not be used in contravention of the goals of the treaty. The implications of this ruling for national trade mark law are potentially far-reaching.

Professor Stein:

To put it in a more simplified form, the proposition that the Commission urged upon the Court and on which it won was that, after all the customs barriers have been removed, private enterprises could replace the customs barriers by private restrictive practices, in this case contractual prohibitions of parallel exports from one Member State to another; unless this power of private enterprises is stricken down, there just will not be any Common Market.

MORE ON THE DEFINITION OF A DECISION AND ITS EFFECTIVENESS

Mr. Dobbert:

I would merely like to make a few points arising out of the discussion on the types of international agencies. I must admit that I have been slightly disturbed by the widening of the scope of the concept of "decisions" which has been attempted. Those among us who are either university teachers or have been imbued by the political atmosphere of the General Assembly tend to give considerable weight to a number of factors which undoubtedly are very important for the purpose of *decision-making*. The process of working out a text which involves finding sufficient authoritative support is, I think, a relevant aspect, and the material relating to this process may be used later on as evidence for interpreting final decisions. But the decision itself should be regarded as the *tangible, precise* result on which we have to rely. We in the Specialized Agencies are very often in a position of being surrounded by technicians who ask: can we do that, or can we not do that? Is this legal or not? Can you show us a way in which it can be done? In this particular context, we have to have a solid basis on which we can proceed to advise our colleagues from the technical, administrative and economic departments on the one hand and government delegations and intergovernmental bodies on the other hand. I would, therefore, like to propose an outline of decisions as I understand them.

A decision for the purpose of our present discussion might be considered: a pronouncement by the constitutionally competent organs of an international organization, creating, declaring, interpreting or proposing to change a given factual or legal situation, and affecting the organization as such or any organs thereof or any or all of the member states or, in exceptional cases, other organizations or non-member states.

This is merely a tentative definition which leaves aside deliberately what have been referred to as non-decisions, except of course, that a non-decision may also be considered a decision to postpone action or not to take action at this time, or to refer the matter back to another organ. That is a decision but not a substantive one, since it is designed to defer final action on a particular issue.

I think the term "communications" used by Mr. Schachter puts us too far away from anything sufficiently precise as a basis for determining its legal scope and intent, for instance, whether it is a statement purporting to interpret, or attempting to change, a situation. But I think the term "pronouncement" is rather more suitable from our point of view.

One further assumption I would like to make, though this may narrow the scope of our discussion: while any decisions of international organizations are liable—in given circumstances—to affect certain or all member states, the emphasis could perhaps be placed on decisions, the effectiveness of which depends to some extent at least on the active participation of member states in their implementation. In the light of what Professor Mestmäcker said, I have myself become a little doubtful because obviously it can work round various corners. States are caught almost unawares by a decision becoming effective and thus, in extreme cases, almost undermine their own domestic legal systems. All of a sudden they may find themselves in a position where a decision has become effective and legally binding in a certain aspect without their active participation. But perhaps these cases are rather the exception than the rule.

Mr. Elkin:

I am really concerned with the general line of our discussion. Some people think they have made things quite clear by saying we are concerned with the international law. Of course we are. But what we are concerned with is the new type of international law. We are navigating—and the art of navigation requires a good deal of caution, a certain amount of conservatism. In many ways our methods of work are methods of constitutional law. That is one of the characteristics of the new type of international law, of the new method of interpreting constitutional instruments that makes them grow like a "living tree." We are no longer ruled by the liberalistic 19th century concept that would make us adopt methods of interpretation of private contracts in respect of treaties and decisions.

That is why I was so concerned about the term "effectiveness". Now, Mrs. Higgins said herself that so far as "effectiveness" is concerned, i.e. whether a given decision that is carried out will achieve a particular aim, it may well be that the legal advisor's role is more limited than that of his colleagues in the political and economic departments. This is the point. If you include an element of purpose—I use the *legal* concept of "purpose"—into your notion of decision, if you judge "effectiveness" in the light of the "purpose", I agree. But what worries me is what "effectiveness" really means. I was concerned about the example quoted by Mrs. Higgins—whether goods could be imported or not into Rhodesia—because it seemed to me that the purpose of that decision was just that—and no *more*.

Let us take two examples. The first concerns a multilateral system of payments within a group of states. The system provides a periodic setting off of balances. There is a net surplus or deficit of each member state each month which has to be settled promptly either by granting credit or by payment of gold. We must make that decision "effective". Here, as a lawyer, you can help your colleagues in the economic department with a number of suggestions as to how to do this. But then there is the other type of decision which is meant to be binding on the members. They want, for example, to create a modicum of unemployment. (This is occasionally disguised by the phrase *"maintenance* of full employment".) You have to draft a decision providing for a number of measures which should lead to a certain amount of unemployment, not too much and not too little, in order to "deflate." You draft that decision—it is awfully difficult for you yourself to see where the "effectiveness" lies—where does it end and where does it not end? What may happen with that type of exercise is that the operation may be successful but the patient may die, or the operation may be unsuccessful but the "deflation" may come about for some other reason. That is what happens in practice. What I wanted was to advocate extreme caution in this art of navigation when you discuss "effectiveness". "Effectiveness" must be strictly related to "purpose" and

404

the "purpose" must be a legal purpose which can be interpreted from evidence, not a general aim of economic policy.

Then we come to the problem of hierarchy. Now I have an idea which is rather vague and may be wrong, but it may be of use for this discussion. In any legal system you have substantive law and you have law of evidence, or the law of procedure. I always thought that, in a way, substantive rights are all the time accompanied by procedural rights, expressly or by implication. Everybody knows what prescription means: the procedural rights die, yet the binding contract subsists. But you cannot enforce it. However, what we are concerned with is not purely a question of enforceability. Mr. Lauterpacht put his finger on it when he said that the problem is really one of the binding nature of decisions.

May I now speak of "recommendations" using that expression in the sense in which a constituent instrument uses this term or the terms "decision" or "directive"—in the same formal sense as the terms are used in Article 189 of the EEC Treaty. These terms are very useful. Delegations are happy if you can bring the proposed act within a particular term used in the constituent instrument. They know where they are. But occasionally they come to you and say: we cannot go before Parliament if we do that. We are, however, in agreement that the proposed action should be taken. Now, Sir Kenneth Bailey said that you then arrive at a "gentlemen's agreement". I think a "gentlemen's agreement" becomes a kind of tag in the type of international law with which we are concerned. I agree absolutely with what Sir Kenneth said yesterday about recommendations to member states. I am afraid I cannot go further than say that the states have a duty to examine a "recommendation". But, of course, in any "recommendation" which you draft you can add a paragraph saying that by such and such a date each government should report on its implementation. This is the sort of ILO constitutional procedure where each government must report on the reasons why it carried out or did not carry out a "recommendation". I do not think we can go beyond this.

THE CHOICE OF LEGAL TECHNIQUES

Mr. Elkin:

A point on legal techniques: they depend upon the subject with which you are dealing. It seems to me a tremendous achievement—in view of the good it has done—that the stand-by arrangements of the IMF were developed. There is one significant element in this development. Constituent instruments of some organizations have been drafted a long time ago. They were drafted with a specific aim in mind. This aim can become out-of-date. New problems come within the purview of the organization, and you have to bring them within the constitutional instrument and develop appropriate techniques. Occasionally they are the kind of problems which did not exist when the constituent instrument was drafted. Purely for political reasons it also happens that the drafters of the instrument focused their attention on something which afterwards proves completely irrelevant. Something which they did not consider at the time as important becomes all-important.

Mr. Boulanger:

We have discussed at great length the question of the definition of decisions and their effectiveness, but the question of choice of techniques which is on our agenda has been mentioned only occasionally. I think I should remind those among us who are not "practitioners" of international law that the choice of techniques is not always in the hands of the legal advisors of the organization. He, of course, would prefer to select that technique which is most effective, but many times the choice has already been made for him by the constituent instrument or by the statute. Sometimes the choice is made on purely budgetary reasons. He would believe a convention adopted by an international conference would be most effective and the best means to employ, but he would find that this is a very tedious procedure which requires much money and much work. So he must take another approach which might be the adoption by the governing body of a recommendation or an agreement which is then opened for acceptance by member states. I am referring to the agreement of the privileges and immunities of the Specialized Agencies. He might also use the technique which I described in my paper of calling panels of experts and then giving their proposals to the governments for comments, and then, after these comments, preparing a final text which is then approved by the governing body and sent to the governments for acceptance. There are also occasional cases where representatives of member governments approach the legal advisor with a proposal for a resolution or recommendation. You might tell them that this is not the right way to achieve their aim, but they will insist. They may even be doubtful about the effectiveness, but they need a recommendation for internal purposes, for their parliament or something.

So even if he advises to the contrary, the member governments might insist on a resolution or a recommendation. There might also be—and there frequently is—a change in the choice of technique. You may start out by proposing a decision of one kind or another—and now I am referring to my experience with one of the European Communities, where I sat on the government side of the table—you may find that suddenly it turns out that, politically, this kind of decision is not acceptable, that the permanent representatives, maybe all the members of the Council, meet in the office of the Secretary General of the Council and then come up with a decision which then raises for international lawyers the question of "what is it?"

In this connection I may be permitted one remark—I am glad Sir Kenneth Bailey has already introduced the phrase "gentlemen's agreements". Referring to the Luxembourg agreements, I think they can be—if they must be classified—considered as European "gentlemen's agreements". I am adding "European" because in my experience there *is* such a European sense in the government delegations, not only on the staff of the European Community. They really work in a European spirit, in the spirit that this work of the European Community must go on; it must succeed. I can assure you that some of them have real difficulties with the instructions they get from their governments sometimes. But still, they work on and they eventually find a solution, such as a gentlemen's agreement. For them, since they represent their governments, such a decision is binding. And they would rather resign than lose face with their colleagues there. I think that this is a very important aspect of international law in operation.

To sum up, I think the choice of technique depends very much on the individual case and on the individual circumstances and one cannot say in advance that this or that technique will be more effective. In regard to effectiveness I would like to associate myself with Mr. Elkin. For the legal advisor the main point is compliance because, there may be differences of opinion about effectiveness. You may have experiences where a great number of important member countries consider the result as effective if there is no actual result despite compliance by members.

Mr. Caha:

I find the discussion of the definition of decision useful but I suppose it will be rather difficult to find one. It would not cover all the practices of all Specialized Agencies, not to mention all international organizations.

In the UPU, the question seems to be clear because we have 800 pages of agreements; all exchanges of postal letters are implemented in the form of intergovernmental treaties. In these treaties there are some optional clauses which are equal to recommendations. The UPU has difficulty in making these recommendations obligatory. It had to settle questions which were not laid out in its acts. We had to pass the ceiling of our expenditure, which was a very difficult question because our Congress was postponed. I mention this problem because we might connect it with the agenda point on the financial integrity of international organizations. In the UPU, the general concept is that all decisions or acts are decisions. It is a more general term and, generally speaking, acts, agreements and treaties are legally binding in principle.

Mr. FitzGerald:

In the United Nations, where all the states have representatives on the spot, states have a duty and even the capacity to examine recommendations. This examination may be carried out by clusters of states or individual states. But in the functional agencies, you will possibly find that, while states have a duty to examine recommendations, they have a total incapacity to do so. This distinction must be made.

Mr. Elkin mentioned that many organizations are working under constitutions that were drawn up long ago, in some cases two decades ago. Some of them, including my own organization, have had no difficulty in bringing new problems under the rules of the constitution. In fact, except in the case of housekeeping, there is an extreme reluctance to amend the constitution.

On the question of the choice of techniques mentioned by Mr. Boulanger, there are many techniques chosen and decisions made which have never even seen the office of the legal advisor. In fact the techniques or discussion of them will be carefully kept away from the legal advisor for fear that he might put too much embalming fluid around the decision which it is desired to keep as flexible as possible. Indeed, I derive a considerable degree of amusement in reading text books on air law in which I find discussed, on a legal basis, items which have never even seen the Legal Bureau of ICAO or any legal body within ICAO. When we are discussing the choice of techniques, let us not assume that the legal advisor had a great opportunity to give his advice.

THE EXPERIENCE OF THE EUROPEAN ECONOMIC COMMUNITY

Mr. Stevenson:

I think we should go on now to the discussion of the various papers and I would suggest that we begin with the paper prepared by Mr. Gaudet. I think Professor Mestmäcker and Professor Stein can probably answer any questions on this paper. (In this way we shall take the discussion of organizations dealing with regional problems first, since Professor Mestmäcker has to leave us today unfortunately.) Are there any general questions?

Mr. Elkin:

I would like to refer to the Directives mentioned at the outset of Mr. Gaudet's paper: "Directives tend to become more and more precise." I would like to hear a little bit more about this subject. In other words, there seems to be a decrease in importance of the Directive provided for in Article 189. Do Directives in fact take more and more the form of Regulations? Is the technique of Directives still an important medium? Apart from the catalogue in Article 189, the Treaty itself mentions decisions on budgetary matters, general programs and agreements. I would like to know a little more about the legal characteristics of the general programs. I think they are provided particularly during the transitional period.

Being a classical jurist, Mr. Gaudet speaks of resolutions and entries in the minutes as acts of a "political character". In the OECD,

408

the Resolutions and Regulations are all, or most of them, published, but really only for government use. Acts of the EEC which come under Article 189 of the treaty are published in the Official Journal. I take it that acts of a political character are not published in that Journal. Am I right? What are their legal consequences?

Professor Mestmäcker:

Directives are still very important instruments, particularly in the field of assimilation of legislation. The degree of preciseness depends upon the subject matter. Where highly technical matters are to be coordinated, the distinction of Article 189 between binding goals and freedom in the technique of effecting these goals blurs as a matter of fact. In other fields, such as company law, the distinction has substantive meaning. I do, however, not think that the preciseness of a directive as such is incompatible with the treaty.

The general programs are rather close to recommendations; their function is to announce a plan of action and to accommodate the gradual implementation of the goals of the treaty.

Mr. Elkin:

What are the legal consequences of a resolution?

Professor Mestmäcker:

It is just a technique applied by the Council of Ministers to force its own path.

Mr. Nurick:

But is not a resolution normally a legally binding decision?

Professor Mestmäcker:

The legally binding techniques are specified by the treaty. A resolution to act in a certain way is not binding; those resolutions never settle problems of substance, rather they have been directed to procedure.

Mr. Lauterpacht:

What happens if the scheduled timetable is not fulfilled?

Professor Mestmäcker:

Whenever the timetable had not been fulfilled, the Council simply stopped the clock. Usually they went on negotiating until they reached agreement.

Professor Stein:

The exception to this was the June 1965 meeting of the Council that started the crisis. In that case, the French delegate was in the chair and he refused to "stop the clock" and adjourned the meeting because the Council had not met the timetable and he held this was a violation of prior agreement. The French then withdrew their delegates from most of the Community organs. This "empty chair" policy was pursued by the French until a new agreement was reached in Luxembourg early in 1966.

Mr. Elkin:

Another question comes up in section 3 of Mr. Gaudet's paper: "The decisions of the representatives of the governments of member states meeting in council cover an area exceeding the competence express-ly attributed to the Community institutions, but the purpose they serve is indistinguishable from the aims specified in the treaty." What does Mr. Gaudet mean by this sentence?

Professor Stein:

Mr. Boulanger mentioned the permanent representatives of the member states to the Communities. These representatives backstop the Council of Ministers and "prepare" its decisions. Their influence has been growing. Their principal function has been to represent national interest *vis-à-vis* the Commission but as things have turned out, in addition to watching over national interests they now often explain and defend the Commission's views and the Community interest as formulated by the Commission *vis-à-vis* their respective governments.

Professor Sohn:

Could you give me some clarification on how the changing of dates of the timetable was done? Does the advancing of the dates for the removal of customs duties represent an actual change in the treaty?

Professor Stein:

When the governments decided to speed up the removal of the customs duties and establishment of the common external tariff, they could not find any express authorization for this in the treaty. So they chose a com-promise between those who were willing to do it by an act of the Council of Ministers and those who were worried that making this a Community Act would give the Community too much power. Therefore they invented a new form, an agreement "taken by the six governments in the forum of the Council of Ministers" and this new thing is neither a Community Act nor an ordinary international agreement.

Mr. Schachter:

We have been talking about reasons: what about the consequences— are there indications of achieving different results?

Professor Stein:

We have to consider the consequences in terms of judicial review.

Professor Sohn:

Are these decisions subject to judicial review?

Professor Mestmäcker:

No, while the decisions taken as provided for by the treaty *are* subject to judicial review.

Professor Stein:

In other words, if it had been done by a decision of the Council of Ministers, any member could go to the Luxembourg Court and attack it.

Mr. Schachter:

Is it in consequence of that more effective?

Professor Mestmäcker:

No, it is simply that they are actions not provided for in the treaty. They are not more effective.

Another interesting point is that in the treaty the end of the transitional period is very often referred to as the coming into force of certain rules and regulations or provisions of the treaty. The end of the transitional period is the coming into force of the customs union. But the customs union will be effective before the time provided for by the treaty; this does not mean that with respect to all the other provisions referring to the end of the transitional period, the end of the transitional period changes.

Mr. Elkin:

This comment is not really so shattering as it may sound, because there are provisions in the EEC treaty which include an acceleration clause.

I refer to Mr. Gaudet's section on Judicial Procedures. That section deals with Articles 169 and 170 of the treaty. Mr. Gaudet says that the procedure is divided into two stages. He refers to the first stage as the "pre-trial proceedings". This pre-trial procedure is in the hands of the Commission and one of the media most important in it is what the treaty calls the "reasoned opinion". This has something to do with the problem of *administrative* interpretation, and I would be very grateful for some enlightenment on this point—whether the reasoned opinions have become instruments of interpretation or represent settlements of problems of a very individual character.

Professor Mestmäcker:

Generally, whenever the Commission addresses a member state wanting

411

the member state to do something, it starts by spelling out the context of the treaty, interpreting the treaty and deriving therefrom the obligation of the member state. The reference to the authority of the Commission under Article 169 and the requesting of governments to do what is provided for in the treaty are always interpretative statements at the same time.

FORMALITY IN THE EEC AND INFORMALITY ELSEWHERE

Mr. Stevenson:

I take it from Mr. Gaudet's paper that there has been an increase in the executive as opposed to the legislative activities of the Common Market institutions. He states that there has been increasing reliance on executive procedures because this has been a much more effective way in obtaining compliance.

In the case of the functional agencies, a number of them, particularly WHO and to a certain extent ICAO have indicated that better results were achieved through means that were not really contemplated under the original agreement. This is certainly true for the financial agencies. Further reliance on the various compliance and enforcement techniques contemplated in the constituent document has generally not been the most efficient means of getting things done.

The reverse seems to be true in the case of the Common Market. There, reliance has been placed primarily on the *formal* enforcement techniques which have been incorporated in the constituent document. The question I want to raise is: whether perhaps the reason that the other agencies have not been able to use the specified techniques is that they do not have as complete a judicial and other enforcement machinery behind them; and that, therefore, they have resorted more to the informal techniques. Now, perhaps this paper does not take into account enough of the informal techniques that have been used in the Common Market. But it certainly seems clear that they are utilizing even down to judicial enforcement the machinery which the other agencies seem reluctant to use.

Mr. Vignes:

As far as the sanitary regulations are concerned, they are maintained; the non-obligatory standards are used for other technical matters such as biological standardization, quality control of drugs, etc.

Professor Stein:

I have a feeling that there is a development in the direction suggested: increasing reliance on consultation; voluntary, recommended standards. But the Gaudet paper certainly leaves the impression that in the Community there is a great reliance on legal powers to make law and to enforce law. I think it is probably accurate as applied to compliance and enforcement of decisions. But the 1965 crisis and the Luxembourg experience which we discussed warned the Commission that if it sticks its head out too far, it may have it cut off. The Commission's consultation prior to adoption of a formal proposal is as a rule extensive and increasingly so, and this, I think, does not appear in this excellent paper. It could not appear there because the paper does not deal with the lawmaking process. I wonder whether it would be accurate to say that we are faced with a development where the worldwide groupings like WHO and ICAO do not rely on formal lawmaking powers whereas the regional organizations go to the limits of their powers.

Mr. Stevenson:

But you do agree that in fact in the Community the reliance on the legal powers is very great?

Professor Stein:

It is certainly greater than in other organizations but the exact pattern may be changing. There are very fine nuances. I would say that in the Community the most important power of the Commission in the lawmaking process is the power of initiative. It is the power to submit—it is an obligation under the treaty to submit—proposals of new laws and policies to the Council which the Council then enacts. Now you can spot instances in the past where important proposals were submitted by the Commission without consultation with the national governments. The radical Europeans hold that if the Commission consults the national governments before it submits its proposal to the Council it really defeats, at least in part, the original idea of the treaty that the Commission ought to be detached from national interests and should formulate its proposal in the light of the community interest using its own judgment, taking into account, of course, the national differences, but being itself detached.

After the 1965 crisis, which stopped the whole Common Market for six months, the Commission is likely to be much more careful in using its initiative and making proposals without very detailed consultations with the governments. I would go as far, but not further than that.

Professor Mestmäcker:

I would like to point out that there are in the everyday business of the Commission numerous techniques not provided for in the treaty, even techniques that are used rather formally. When the Commission was faced with the necessity of giving guidance to industry on the interpretation of Articles 85 and 86, it was obviously impossible in a short time to issue a sufficient number of formal decisions which would make clear the Commission's interpretation. The Commission then decided to publish an interpretative note in the Official Gazette spelling out how it would probably interpret the treaty. This, of course, is without prejudice to a later ruling by the European Court. This has been done repeatedly. The statement of intent by the Commission takes various forms such as declarations of a member of the Commission before the European Parliament. This too is a very important process by which the Commission makes known its approach to immediate and important problems in applying the treaty. The consultation process within the Commission is so varied that it is almost impossible to enumerate the different techniques. Possible participants of consultative groups are: officials of the Commission, officials of member governments, scholars of the member countries, representatives of interest groups, such as agriculture or industry. Within the Commission there are close to 100 of those panels that do work on different phases of community policy. Very often their function is to prepare public opinion in the member states for future actions of the Commission and to inform the Commission what the prevailing opinion among scholars or representatives of government or of industry is.

From my own experience, I can relate that there are at times rather strong pressures not to adhere to the formal process provided for by the treaty but simply to resort to negotiations with the potential addressee of a decision in order to avoid a formal commitment or a formal obligation. I should say that in the field of individual decisions where the Commission has an authority of its own, the Commission has been extremely reluctant to deviate from the formal process. Mr. Gaudet's paper certainly is correct and he, of course, has been very influential in that adherence to the treaty. The reason behind this approach which is sometimes called "legalistic" is this: the institutional structure of the Community implies that there is something like a community interest in the long run, which in individual cases makes it necessary to neglect the short-run interests of member countries.

Actually the EEC is a legal institution that develops its own law and is regulated to a certain extent by majority decisions. The Commission feels very strongly that the form of action should indicate that this community interest is paramount and is being realized in individual decisions.

In the field of competition policy, I know of no instance where the Commission has acceded to a request to proceed informally. This definitely has not been changed by the Luxembourg agreement. What has been changed by the Luxembourg agreement is this: in the relation of the Commission to the Council the emphasis is more on the Council; and the function of permanent representatives has become much more important. Nevertheless, the Commission in quite a number of cases submits formal proposals to the Council of Ministers although there were reservations on the part of member governments. This exercise of the functions ascribed to the Commission by the treaty is an indispensable part of the institutional framework of the community. However, the Commission has become more cautious and the function of the permanent representatives has grown to such an extent that they at times have created bottlenecks in the conduct of community policy.

Mr. Elkin:

I think it may be of some help if I asked you to remind us of all of the provisions of the treaty. What happens to the proposal of the Commission which goes before the Council if the Council wishes to amend it?

Professor Mestmäcker:

The Commission's proposal may be changed by the Council of Ministers only unanimously or it may reject it by majority—but it cannot adopt it in its amended form unless it has been approved by the Commission.

Mr. Arnold:

Referring to your question, Mr. Chairman, I see it from the point of view of a regional organization. I think there is a reasonable answer to the question in seeing the difference between the character of the EEC and various other organizations.

In the first place I did want to say that our discussion of how to define various acts was of great interest. From a practical point of view it is very important for a given organization to know what to do and in the most effective and appropriate way, to carry out its business, regardless of what its charter may say about formal sanctions or procedures. Those of the banks provide for expulsion of recalcitrant members and give the boards of governors or directors extensive powers to interpret the charter. But certainly in my institution it would be most ill-advised to proceed in a highly formal manner.

In an organization like the Inter-American Development Bank, the members are certainly not prepared to accept strong action from the Bank. Therefore we have to operate in other ways. I did point out in my paper how this operation was achieved with reasonably satisfactory practical results. As a given type of case it is of some importance. This procedure was based on the fact that there is a specific provision in the charter dealing with the problem of exchange rates and the procedure which we used is founded on that provision but without direct use of the strong authority it appears to confer. In other words, formal procedures can probably be most effective when they are used to carry out an obligation clearly stated in the charter; but it may be much better to carry out that obligation by means other than those apparently specified. I think what Mr. FitzGerald was saying is very much the same. I believe therefore it is almost impossible to make the comparison which Mr. Stevenson's question implies. You have to think strictly in terms of what are the circumstances of a particular organization, what means are most appropriate. I do not think that our Bank should be criticized for not being formal and I do not think from our point of view, we should criticize the EEC for adopting rather

415

formal means. It seems to me that by and large, each is using the method which is appropriate for its own circumstances.

Mr. Stevenson:

I think that the issue is perhaps presented more squarely in the case of some other organizations, where in the papers it has been indicated that the reason that conventions were no longer being promoted was because of the delays inherent in the convention-making process. The only question is, assuming that the members were willing in a technical area, such as health or postal service, to give the organization more decision-making legal power, would the organization utilize that power rather than informal measures?

Mr. Arnold:

I very thoroughly agree as a lawyer that important decisions are much better carried out with a reasonable degree of formality.

Mr. Dobbert:

A first point in connection with the EEC: the constituent instrument was conceived on entirely different lines than in the case of most other organizations. It was probably intended to create the first supranational organization. This in a way has connotations of a built-in institutional system, much more closely related to the constitutional systems of the member states.

The second point that the members of the Community consist not only of a small number of nations but also of nations with reasonably homogeneous economic, social and legal systems and concepts, so that the institutional systems and procedures which were devised for the Community had a common ground in all member states. Now, these aspects are certainly not present in the case of the U.N. and Specialized Agencies. You have a very diversified membership; you have a very large membership; there is no claim to supranationality. The sovereignty of member states is embodied, in the case of the U.N., in the Charter and emphasized all the time, and therefore I think it would be inconceivable—even if the aims were the same as the EEC, which I do not think they are—to have the same institutional system.

Mr. FitzGerald:

First of all, Mr. Chairman, you had suggested that ICAO was possibly producing better results by not following the procedures that were laid down in the Chicago Convention. On the contrary, ICAO is certainly following the provisions laid down in respect of the adoption and implementation of this quasi-regulatory material discussed in my paper. If ICAO appears to act otherwise it does so only in terms of the practical application of what is spelled out in rather broad language in the Chicago Con-

416

vention. Insofar as concerns the possible non-application of sanctions, found in the Chicago Convention, this is common to many organizations. There is an extreme reluctance to apply sanctions, except as a last resort.

As to the question of judicial control, of course we have in the Chicago Convention a chapter dealing with what would appear to be judicial control. On examination one will find that this again would be a kind of extreme sanction, namely, to bring a recalcitrant state before the ICAO Council. That, of course, is a rather curious body to which to give judicial functions.

Mr. Stevenson:

Another question I have is whether it would not be more efficient if you could get the member states to agree to give the governing body in a limited technical area the legally binding means of doing directly what it now has to do by means of convention.

Mr. Gold:

I would like to make just one point in connection with your question, Mr. Chairman, and that is to warn against the dangers of generalization. It does seem that one relevant difference is that in the case of the EEC, although there is of course a difference in the voting strength of the members, it is on the whole rather balanced and not enormously varied as among the countries. In the Fund, the weighted voting results in an enormous difference in voting strength, ranging all the way from almost 25% for the United States to infinitesimally small percentages for some members. One result of this is that we avoid voting. We have found that the voting strength is so disproportionate that this in itself produces resistance to voting, although it is not the only reason for that attitude. I would say, therefore, that one has to look very closely at the institution to see what produces the greater addiction to formality or informality. Certainly, I would say for the Fund, weighted voting has itself led to the disappearance of voting and to a preference for informal procedures.

Professor Sohn:

I would like to suggest that we differentiate between three different kind of acts:
(1) Acts of a legislative or quasi-legislative character, whether they are called "conventions" (as in ILO) or "regulations" (as in WHO).
(2) Acts of an interpretative character or decisions in disputes between either the organization and members or among members.
(3) Acts of a bi-lateral character (which are especially important in the Fund and the Bank).

One cannot apply the same kind of procedure to these three different kinds of acts. It might be better to try to divide those acts in distinct categories and we might try to concentrate first on the legislative development in the Community. To what extent have the Communities really developed the legislative power which was conferred upon them, and to what extent is this power exercised by formal or informal means? The same differentiation should be applied to the interpretative and dispute-deciding decisions, and also to the bi-lateral relations between the Bank and the Fund, on the one hand, and their members, on the other hand.

Mr. Nurick:

One point as to the formal way in which the Community acts as compared with other organizations which may act differently: I would like to amplify somewhat on what Mr. Gold said. I would think that one of the reasons the Community acts as it does is because it is very difficult for it to distinguish between one country and another. It would be very hard for it to treat one of its members differently from another. That is not true in our case certainly. In some respects we treat all countries alike, for example, the Bank charges all borrowers the same interest rate. In other respects, we do take into account differences among countries depending on the differing problems of the countries.

But I do not think it is only a question of different voting power. I can see why in the Community there would be a strong tendency to act formally —so that it makes sure that what it does for one it does for all.

Professor Mestmäcker:

This is of course one reason. The treaty expressly prohibits any discrimination between member states and between nationals of member states. The Luxembourg Court invoked this rule in finding that community law takes precedence over municipal law because this was the only way of ensuring equal validity and effect of community law in all member states. The one thing I wanted to add which I probably should have done much earlier is this: very early in the history of the European Coal and Steel Treaty, the High Authority tried to issue a decision which was against a specific provision of the treaty but arguing that this particular action would more effectively further the general aims of the treaty. Here the Court held that whenever the treaty provides specific rules, they have to be observed and that there was no power to disregard special rules because of the general aims of the treaty. The legal obligation to adhere to the specific provisions of the treaty has been spelled out by the Court repeatedly and this rule has been often referred to as a basis of the Commission's practice. Again the Court was very conscious of preserving the constitutional structure of the treaty as it was envisaged originally.

Professor Stein:

Considering that we spent so much time on the nature of formal acts, I want to go back for a second to the treaty and enumeration of the various acts. We talked about regulations which are directly applicable law in national legal orders and about directives and decisions and we also mentioned recommendations. There is a very interesting form which we did not mention and that is the "opinion".

What is an opinion? It was put into the treaty to allow the Commission to say certain things, perhaps for the purpose of experimentation, and not be held to it in terms of being responsible for it before the Court of Justice. The treaty makes it quite clear that the classification of the forms in which the Community organs act is very closely related to the legal protection before the Court.

For example, according tot the Coal and Steel Treaty, a firm that wants to build another furnace and finance it from its own surplus must nevertheless tell the High Authority that this is what it proposes to do and the Authority issues an opinion on the proposal. Now, you have a situation where someone wanted to build a new installation. He wanted to use not only his own money but outside money. He was obliged to seek an opinion from the High Authority and the High Authority's opinion was negative.

You cannot keep that sort of thing secret, even though the High Authority does not publish it. The bank heard about it and told the man, look, if the High Authority says this is not a good project, then we will not give you any money. Now, this man goes before the Court and says, I was obviously damaged by this opinion which I think is completely wrong, therefore, I need a remedy—I want you to say that this opinion is wrong. The Court says—no! The treaty says that an opinion is an opinion and cannot be attacked and it does not really change your legal position—therefore we cannot do this.

The last point I want to make is the procedure whereby a national court has to stop a case before it between private parties whenever a question of Community treaty interpretation is raised. It must stop the proceedings and ask the Community Court in Luxembourg to give a preliminary ruling. And that proceeding ought to be kept in mind when we talk about other ways of compulsory and non-compulsory interpretations, such as the IMF and the Bank's power to interpret with binding effect the meaning of their Charters. In other words, we ought to keep in mind the various devices built into these international organizations to ensure a degree of uniformity in the interpretation of the constituent instruments. The interesting thing is that the most important constitutional type rulings of the Luxembourg Court were not made in the course of regular treaty enforcement where the Commission goes before the Court and says Germany or Italy etc. violates the treaty or a regulation. Most important constitutional statements relating to the character of the Community as a new legal order and the relationship of Community law and national law were made in the course of proceedings for a preliminary ruling under Article 177. That has proved perhaps even more important, both in terms of defining the constitutional nature of that treaty, but also in terms of assuming a degree of uniformity of application of the treaty and of the acts of the Community institutions.

Mr. Stevenson:

There is one point this suggests. We have talked about how strong the powers of the Community are, but, as pointed out in this paper, the Court of Justice's judgments are strictly of a declaratory nature. They could not themselves quash legislation or administrative acts. Do you think that has been in any way a limitation on its effectiveness?

Professor Mestmäcker:

It is important to differentiate. The Court has authority to declare acts of the Community invalid. All acts of the Commission are subject to judicial review in the general sense and this of course is a very important function too.

Mr. Stevenson:

I quote from Mr. Gaudet's paper: "The judgment is of a declaratory nature, as the Court does not have the power to quash the legislative or administrative acts of member states."

Professor Mestmäcker:

Article 177 makes clear that the European Court does not have authority to pass upon the validity of acts of member states. Otherwise, the Court would be in a position to apply the law of all member states. The only way to ensure a uniform interpretation of the treaty was to set apart for this particular purpose national law and community law, the Community Court restricting itself to passing upon the interpretative problems of community law. So far there is probably no case where national courts have not followed the interpretative ruling of the European Court. I should add that the weakness of this procedure is in the practice of the Court not to pass upon the merits of the individual case, but to limit itself strenuously to the interpretative ruling. In doing so, the Court in quite a few cases has been rather abstract in saying, for example, a matter like this may be held to be a discrimination without spelling out what the criteria of a discrimination are. Thus the discretion left to the national court in applying such a ruling in an individual case is rather broad. The Court obviously wants to leave as much power to the national courts as possible. Once experience shows that this is not sufficient to ensure compliance, the Court will probably be more specific in its interpretative rulings. This is a matter of development of the Court's practice.

Mr. Stevenson:

I follow that, except for one point: it seems to me all Mr. Gaudet is saying here is that, in the case of legislative or administrative acts of a member state, the Court of the Community can say that they are invalid as conflicting with the Community law, but it cannot effectively say they are ineffectual.

Professor Mestmäcker:

No. I said the Community Court determines only what Community law should be. To give you an example: if you have a regulation by a Dutch or German authority, there are different procedures under national law by which you may invalidate such a regulation. Consequently, if the Court had the task of passing upon the validity of such an act—which it has not—it would have to apply national law because the community law is but one legal aspect of the case. And it is this aspect only that may be referred to the Court for an interpretative ruling.

THE EXPERIENCE OF THE COUNCIL OF EUROPE

Mr. Golsong:

I would like to follow very briefly the agenda of our meeting and in passing through make a few observations relating to the Council of Europe as one of the smaller organizations with a body of membership to which common legal concepts are more or less familiar. This makes perhaps part of our task much easier but, on the other hand, we have to deal with states to which the form of a legal act is important. What kind of decisions does the Council of Europe use within the organization? For the time being and for the purpose of our discussion, I would like to leave aside the recommendations of one of the organs, namely, the Consultative Assembly. The Assembly adopts recommendations, but these are more or less of no binding effect. But they may contribute to policy-making and, by that, later on, to lawmaking.

If we stick to the acts of the ministerial body, I would like to make a preliminary remark, particularly in regard to what we have heard from the representatives of the financial and banking institutions. We have also a very small institution operating within the Council of Europe: The Resettlement Fund for Refugees and Over-population. Decisions of the Fund are resolutions adopted by the governing body. Those resolutions are of course binding on governments: for example, a resolution adopting the general loan regulations. This is binding without reference to national parliaments and is not subject to ratification.

If we come to the normal decisions, and to evidence or pronouncements of the Committee of Ministers, I have to say, first of all, that most of these decisions are taken by the Committee of Deputies and not by the Ministers themselves. (A committee which is, by the way, not mentioned in the statutes and is composed of the same persons as those who have the quality of permanent representatives.) I would like to add, however, that I make a sharp distinction between permanent representatives of governments to the organization on the one hand, and, on the other hand, the same persons when they meet in the Ministerial Council as deputies of their foreign ministers. We have instances where the permanent representatives meet outside the machinery of the Council to discuss arrangements of interest to a group of states, for example, questions of privileges and immunities and so on. But that is *not* done within the Ministerial Council where they act as representatives of their foreign ministers.

The recommendations are not considered to be strictly legally binding. We have the other particular feature, however, that states cannot only abstain when a vote is taken on a recommendation but can also vote in favor and at the same time say that it is not in a position to act on the recommendation. Most of these recommendations urge governments to introduce special legislation within their national legal order and stick to general principles.

We have furthermore records of the minutes. Perhaps I can give an example. When preparing an agreement on privileges and immunities of the judges of the European Court on Human Rights, the point was raised of exemption from taxation of allowances paid to judges. To meet this point, we made a record of the minutes of the meeting saying that there was general agreement that these allowances had the character of subsistence allowances. We accordingly informed the judges by letter that this was decided by the Committee of Ministers without a formal vote. The national tax administrations have in all cases respected this sort of pronouncement or evidence of an informal nature.

The most concrete form of action are the conventions and agreements concluded within the Council of Europe. They are not really decisions of the organization. In effect they are agreements and conventions among states and there is no obligation to ratify, or to sign and subsequently to ratify these instruments. In fact, however, that they have been prepared within the Council of Europe—that the ministerial body has decided to open them for signature—has a certain number of legal effects which I tried to mention in my paper. According to our practice, opening these conventions for signature is not subject to formal voting requirements under the statutes or the rules of procedure of the Committee of Ministers. At the same time, this instrument is a purposeful act for the achievement of the aims of the Council of Europe. Furthermore, such conventions accept certain functions or duties for organs or bodies of the Council of Europe, and not only ministerial functions.

Now, as to the choice between various instruments.

I have alluded to a case where it was preferred not to have a given rule in a treaty because the treaty is normally and regularly subject to approval by national parliaments. In fact we prefer to deal by way of treaty if there is a substantive change of national law envisaged either by way of uniform legal regulations, or by regulations as in the case of the Human Rights Convention and similar treaties, with immediate effectiveness in some of our member states, according, of course, to their national constitutional requirements.

Here I come to the legal effects of decisions in member states or with regard to member states: as I said in my paper, whenever a vote is taken on a recommendation, the state has the possibility of putting on record its disagreement or abstention; if it has not done so then of course one expects that it has to act and also to comply with the future supervising procedure.

The next item on the agenda is the internal legal effect of a treaty or decision. With regard to recommendations, I said before that there is no immediate legal effect within a state. Sometimes we had cases in which national courts have referred to recommendations just to interpret a given rule of law, either a statute or a treaty provision. For example, we had a recommendation on the conditions under which a person could be detained pending trial. This of course was complementary to the Human Rights Convention and was used in some cases by national courts in order to illustrate the effects of the basic rule of the Human Rights Convention.

With regard to internal legal effects, perhaps I may refer to one of the recent cases in the human rights machinery against Belgium on the linguistic legislation.

In that case, the Belgian government raised an exception, protesting the jurisdiction of the Court, among other reasons because it said the question was one of domestic jurisdiction. It is true that we have a pertinent treaty, but, Belgium argued, it is up to us to see how we should implement the Convention. That contention was rejected.

The internal legal effects of our conventions have in some of our member states, particularly in Austria, particular consequences. Under the formal constitutional arrangements, an international treaty provision could have been implemented by the courts of law in Austria. Now, especially because of the impact of the Human Rights Convention on Austrian law, the Austrians changed their constitution in 1964 and provided a new machinery which of course is also applicable with regard to non-Council of Europe treaty provisions: a special machinery of general transformation and special transformation—as they call it—of treaty provisions within general law. The whole object of the revision was to safeguard the role and the intervention of parliament before accepting an international treaty provision as internal law—eventually with the application by the national judge.

Among our member states with a constitution receptive to international treaty provisions we have also the Netherlands. The Netherlands have at present under consideration a change of the constitution somewhat to the same effect, to prevent application of international treaty provisions of a self-executing character within internal law; they would require, under a draft now before a special committee, that parliament should in each case give its approval with a qualified majority vote.

Now as to compliance: there are numerous reporting systems mainly inspired by the ILO experience. What we have seen in the efficiency of this reporting system is that without some degree of publicity the reporting system cannot work. The notable example is Article 57 of the Human Rights Convention. Under Article 57, the Secretary General is entitled to request member states to inform him about the way in which they have implemented the requirements of the convention in their internal law. That was never used until two or three years ago, when a request was sent to all governments to give this sort of information. Publicity is provided under that rule. But there is no follow-up machinery—with the effect, of course, that the information received is very irregular and not equivalent from one state to another. Some states have given very substantive information, others have confined themselves to a very short statement that "everything is all right at home".

IMPLEMENTATION MACHINERY OF THE COUNCIL OF EUROPE

Mr. Schachter:

I am not clear about publicity in the Council of Europe. There are two aspects—one is the need for an expert committee to examine the material and make observations and the other, I take it, is the need for publishing or disseminating the material and perhaps comments made by such a committee. If proposals were made for wider publication (perhaps with some kind of committee procedure) and these were not adopted, so that it was construed to mean that nothing could be done and the reports therefore remained in the files of the organization, is it felt that the secretariat could do nothing beyond this? Is that the case?

Mr. Golsong:

Yes. But, nevertheless, we hope to make appropriate use of these reports in the Secretary General's general report to the Assembly about the stage of implementation of human rights requirements within the organization. Then he can indirectly refer to information received. It would be difficult to quote the information received directly to the Assembly, the latter being a public body.

Mr. Schachter:

The information comes from governments, I take it, and therefore the publishing of the information presumably is not likely to cast any reflection on the government, judging from the normal flow of government responses to this sort of thing. An evaluation of the reports, at least observations on them, is required, and therefore it falls upon the secretariat or upon some independent, non-governmental body, to do this. Is that the way it stands?

424

Mr. Golsong:

For the time being, there is no such evaluation. But we hope to open the way to independent evaluation through the Secretary General's annual statement to the Assembly about the application and implementation of the various human rights instruments. Then it will be up to the Assembly, a body of parliamentarians, to consider this statement and perhaps put additional questions to the Secretary General and to make subsequently some sort of evaluation which would have some influence on governments.

Mr. Valticos:

There are two distinct devices in existence for the supervision of the implementation of human rights. On the one hand, we have the complaints device of the European Convention on Human Rights. On the other hand, we have the European Social Charter which provides for a reporting system.

The ILO system makes use of both these complementary devices, and we have been able to see how these two systems complement one another. The advantage of the complaints procedure is that it permits a much more detailed and thorough examination. The primary disadvantage is that it depends on a complaint being made and this often depends on the political background. We know that in both the ILO and the Council of Europe the right to lodge complaints is not limited to governments but where, in the Council of Europe, it is so limited because a state has not accepted the right of individual petition, governments may hesitate to file a complaint as it would be considered an unfriendly act. Interstate cases have arisen in circumstances like those which prevailed in Cyprus and between Italy and Austria. The position is that some serious situations existing in Europe at the present time cannot be submitted to the Court's examination if no government takes the initiative of bringing them before the Court.

On the other hand, we have the system of regular reports with which the ILO has had much experience. The ILO Constitution provided for reports by governments on the application of conventions and for a summary of these reports to be laid before the Conference. For the first seven years, this was the full extent of the ILO system and, even with the publication of the governments' reports, the experience was very disappointing. You cannot expect big assemblies or meetings to make a thorough evaluation of reports, including critical comment, questions, observations, etc. if a summary of the governments' reports is just laid before them. They might put some questions in some exceptional cases but there would not be the sort of thorough, objective and recurring examination which would also have the advantage of avoiding the psychological effect of litigation, and of making reporting and the examination and evaluation of reports a routine procedure applied impartially to all governments. Thus nothing happened until after seven years a body of independent experts was appointed to make this sort of evaluation. (This type of body is also provided for under the European Social Charter.) It was established for a trial period in 1926 and it is still in existence. It has no constitutional existence but is based on a resolution of the Conference and on a decision of the Governing Body; it has progressively assumed the greatest moral authority and its pronouncements are very rarely challenged. I believe there is always room for the combination of the two systems. There is room for the system of judicial complaint in bigger cases and with the knowledge that this will not be used as a general system but only in exceptional cases of a certain gravity. And there is need for a regular, routine reporting, although reporting is not enough; what finally matters is the use made of it, the examination, the evaluation of the reports by independent persons, if possible, outside the government, by a body which would carry out its functions in a quasi-judicial manner.

If therefore it were possible to conceive of the creation of additional machinery for examination of reports on the European Convention, that might fill the gap which would exist if a serious case arose and no complaint were filed.

Mr. Golsong:

Conditions may now be quite positive to move into this direction, keeping in mind the ILO experience. Such a development would complement the machinery at present available, which is still lacking the "droit d'evocation". There is no possibility that a body in Strasbourg at present—without having been asked either by a state or by an individual applicant—can deal with a violation of human rights, so that we would then have the third possibility of dramatic action by a collective body within the Council of Europe.

Mr. Lauterpacht:

There are two questions which I would like to ask.

The first is whether, within the terms of the present structure of the constitution of the Council of Europe and of the Human Rights Convention, it is possible for the Assembly unilaterally to require of the Secretariat the examination of reports which the parties to the Convention have sent in?

Mr. Golsong:

Yes, it is perfectly possible.

Mr. Lauterpacht:

The second question is: emphasis was put (a) on publicity and (b) on the possibility of third-party examination. Both of these call, presumably, in the Council of Europe context, for a measure of amendment to existing instruments; does there remain a third possibility for which there is also a precedent in the ILO practice, that is, that the Secretariat should suggest to governments that the form of the reports should be changed to contain particulars, so that comparison is easier and omission more relevant?

Mr. Golsong:

There is a coincidence of development. The Secretariat had prepared a first draft and this draft formula was not under Article 57 of the Human Rights Convention. At present, we have elaborated something under the terms of the Social Charter. That is approved before we send it out by the committee of independent specialists sitting in that committee. So, if we want to do the same for the Human Rights Convention we probably have to look for some backing of another body within the Council of Europe. You see, the difference between the Secretary General in our organization and the Secretary General of the United Nations is that he has no statutory qualification in our organization. The Secretary General of the Council of Europe is not a statutory body or organ under the present constitution. He is there, with the sole function of assisting the other bodies, the two statutory organs, namely the Committee of Ministers and the Consultative Assembly.

Professor Sohn:

In addition to the Human Rights Convention and the Social Charter, the Council of Europe has adopted some 30 or 40 other conventions. I wonder whether some of these other conventions have provided for some implementation machinery or follow-up machinery?

Mr. Golsong:

At present this *is* the tendency in the most recent treaties, and also for some treaties concluded previously.

That trend is manifested either by way of reporting or by way of providing in the treaty for a special body operating within the Council of Europe which is entrusted with the task of following up the implementation of the treaty. This latter course was chosen, for example, in a very technical treaty, dealing with road traffic offences. This is in turn of great interest to those who deal in penal law, because the terms of this convention provide for the first time for the possibility of transferring penal proceedings from one state to another, namely the first state being the state where the offence has been committed and the second, the state in which the offender is a permanent resident, disregarding his nationality.

The second innovation of this treaty is to arrange for the execution of penal judgments in another state—the state of residence of the person. The permanent committee of experts on penal law, specifically mentioned in the treaty, is entrusted with the task of following up the implementation of the treaty and will help in cases of dispute among states on the treaty's interpretation. Reporting systems are provided for under the cultural Convention, under the Social Charter and other more technical conventions. They have provided for information about national legislation, all the treaties dealing with uniform laws, arbitration and so on. And finally there is a type of treaty where there is a constant process of modification required because of the subject matter dealt with, for example, the classification of patents. The system has been elaborated and is entering into force on the 1st of January 1968. Subsequently, there will be a committee of experts, which is operating already in the Council of Europe for patents, and is referred to in that treaty with the task of proposing amendments. These amendments are enforced within six months after notification of the governments unless at least two of the contracting parties have objected to them.

So there is a variety of implementing machinery. What is most important for its efficiency are reports to the Consultative Assembly and the possibility of parliamentarians of the Assembly acting at home in order to favor either, first of all, the ratification of a treaty, or, secondly, to help with compliance in a given case.

Professor Sohn:

Have questions actually been asked in parliaments about the conventions?

Mr. Golsong:

Yes, very often. It is perhaps worthwhile mentioning that there is a special group of parliamentarians in which delegates of each national delegation sit. This group meets regularly in order to consider and examine, first of all, recommendations of the Assembly recently passed, as well as action taken by the ministers and the state of signature and ratification of conventions. They pick out the more important among the actions of our member states and prepare collectively parliamentary questions which are then tabled in member parliaments in more or less the same terms. Once they have worked out these questions they are even translated, in Strasbourg, into the working languages of all of our parliaments, including Turkish and Icelandic. This of course is a sort of pressure group, and it has had tangible, beneficial effects.

Mr. Elkin:

Mr. Golsong told us that there is a provision that a country may vote in favor of a recommendation but at the same time state that it does not intend to comply with it. What use has been made of that rule?

Mr. Golsong:

I know of no instance where it has been used.

Mr. Garcia-Amador:

I want to confine my remarks to Inter-American bodies. I start from the basic premise that the binding character of an act or decision depends on the competence conferred upon the organization. The only organ which has such power is the Organ of Consultation of the Rio Treaty.

The first situation in which this competence was exercised was in the Dominican Case in 1960 during the Trujillo regime. This was a case of aggression, constituted by an attempt on the part of the Trujillo regime on the life of a head of state, the president of Venezuela. The Organ of Consultation, after an exhaustive investigation of the facts, came to the conclusion that the attempt constituted an act of intervention and aggression on the part of one state against another and that therefore the measures provided in the Rio Treaty were applicable.

Accordingly the Organ of Consultation resolved to apply diplomatic and economic sanctions to the Dominican regime. The decision of the Organ was promptly complied with; the American Republics one after another severed diplomatic and consular relations with that regime as well as all trade relations with it.

The Cuban situation has required several applications of the Rio Treaty. The first one was in February 1962 when the Government of Cuba, not Cuba as a member state, was excluded from its participation in the organs of the Inter-American system. It is interesting to note that this measure of exclusion is not specifically contemplated in Article 8 of the Rio Treaty; therefore it could only be explained and justified on the basis of an exercise of an implied competence on the part of the Organ of Consultation, particularly if we take into consideration that the primary reason leading to exclusion was based on the fact of the adherence of the Cuban Government to Marxism/Leninism and its close association with the Sino-Soviet bloc, which was considered as incompatible with the principles and purposes of the Inter-American System.

The second application of the Rio Treaty to the Cuban situation was in connection with the missile crisis.

It is worthwhile noting, on the one hand, that the resolution urging dismantling of the missile establishment was addressed to two governments: the Cuban Government and the Soviet Government. In this respect a decision, if it was a "decision," was taken vis-à-vis not only a member state but also a non-member state.

On the other hand, it is interesting that the other decision was to recommend to member states to exercise the right of self-defense both individually and collectively.

The third application of the Rio Treaty was in connection with the introduction of weapons on the part of the Cuban Government into Venezuelan territory for the purpose of helping the guerrilla warfare that was taking place there. After a thorough investigation, the Organ of Consultation decided, as in the Dominican case, to apply diplomatic and economic sanctions against Cuba. In this particular case, it is worth noting that sanctions were applied to a country whose government had been deprived of its representation in the Inter-American Organs, including the Organ of Consultation. This decision, which was very strongly opposed by 4 of the 20 Latin American countries, was complied with by 3 of the 4 opponents, Uruguay, Bolivia and Chile.

There are two alternatives in addition to condemning the policy of Cuba: (1) to apply again to the countries of the Free World to collaborate with members of the Inter-American System in their effort to stop the continuing aggressive policy of Cuba or

(2) to apply to the United Nations for action on the part of the world organization against the Cuban Government more effective than those that have been taken in the past by the Organs of Consultation with limited or no practical or effective results.

THE EXPERIENCE OF FUNCTIONAL INTERNATIONAL ORGANIZATIONS

Mr. Stevenson:

I think it would be advantageous for our discussion if we treat first the agenda questions as they relate to the functional agencies. In that connection, I would like to refer to one point I personally was interested in and which I think flows logically from our discussion. When we were discussing the European Communities and the extent to which the Communities relied on formal acts and the relatively greater enforcement procedure to ensure the compliance they enjoy, the point was made that the Communities are quite different in that they involve countries which are relatively homogeneous, have relatively the same conditions and aspirations and are all animated by a considerable interest in the success of basic Community objectives. On the other hand, we also learned that some of the acts that the Communities are taking are very far-reaching for the internal economies of the member states. The Communities are apparently legislating in areas which had traditionally been considered exclusively within the domain of the national parliaments.

It seems to me that, in the case of the functional agencies, where the area is much narrower and much more technical, it might not be so necessary to have such a homogeneous group of countries, and yet, it might still be possible to have more legislative power. So the question I would like to ask, taking the example of WHO, although it would also be applicable to some of the other agencies, is: is the traditional treaty-making process too slow or for other reasons is it not suitable for keeping up with technical progress? Would it not be possible to have somewhat more legislative power vested in the agency or the parliamentary congress or

430

council of the agency? I note that this was considered in connection with the UPU for its administrative matters although administrative conferences have not been held. I also note that in the case of ICAO with respect to the rules of the air over the high seas there is a legislative power vested in ICAO. I just wonder, thinking in terms of compliance and effectiveness, whether it would or would not be helpful if additional legislative power in these technical areas were given to these agencies? Or from the standpoint of effectiveness and compliance is more to be achieved by not attempting to legislate but simply by attempting to seek voluntary compliance?

THE EXPERIENCE OF THE INTERNATIONAL CIVIL AVIATION ORGANIZATION

Professor Stein:

I just have one question in connection with ICAO: why is it that the rather extraordinary power under Article 12 was used only in one instance, with respect to the rules of overflight of the high seas, and in no other case and that very early in the life of the organization and not at all later on?

Mr. FitzGerald:

This is a very penetrating question. But the point is, that a very narrow interpretation is given to this expression "rules of the air". It concerned the rules governing flight and manoeuvre of aircraft; they are relatively few and are contained in Annex 2 to the Chicago Convention. This Annex has not been amended very frequently. It was one of the first Annexes adopted by ICAO and the occasion for adopting any other rule applicable over the high seas on a legislative basis really has not arisen since that time, except insofar as Annex 2 has occasionally been amended. Now it can be submitted that the air traffic control rules found in Annex 11 are also rules of the air. This is a debatable point. The ICAO Council has never gone so far as to say that the air traffic control rules to be found in Annex 11 of the Convention *are* rules of the air within the meaning of Article 12 of the Convention. Even though the point was debated early in the ICAO history, there was a great reluctance to say that. When you get into air traffic control, you are getting away from pure rules of the air in the sense that most technical people understand the term.

Only recently, Professor John Cooper died at the age of almost 80. I had often congratulated him on having probably reached the high water mark in terms of international legislation. He was a member of the drafting committee of the Chicago Conference when it prepared Article 12 which includes the particular sentence stipulating, in effect, that the rules of the air adopted by ICAO are binding over the high seas. It is most remarkable that the ICAO Council can adopt this legislative material by a statu-

431

tory two-thirds vote of its members. When Annex 2 was adopted the Council had 21 members, and it was legislating for some 130 million square miles of the high seas. Article 12 is certainly a remarkable legislative provision to have in a convention.

The rules of the air over the high seas must apply without any deviation, because otherwise there could be chaos. If you dig into the legal basis of what goes on in terms of control of aircraft over the high seas—as distinct from rules of the air in Annex 2—you find many gentlemen's agreements. There is really no sound legislative basis for the provision of air traffic services over the high seas. These will be in the form of regional plans and so on, aircraft will go from one country to another, one control to another, as they follow along their flight path over the high seas.

Professor Stein:

Isn't there any suggestion to expand to other areas the legislative power embodied in Article 12?

Mr. FitzGerald:

I would say, no. The reason for this is the very basis for the adoption of the regulatory material in the Chicago Convention. It is a very flexible instrument, it is a very realistic one, too.

It is not just enough to get paper compliance, it is not just enough to adopt 15 Annexes and other technical materials and then consider that a legislative action has taken place. Some states require technical assistance in order to implement the law.

ARE OPERATIONAL REPLACING LEGISLATIVE TECHNIQUES?

Mr. Schachter:

I would like to follow up on this and put a question to all of the functional agency people. It seems to me that what Mr. FitzGerald has just told us is one strand in what is a fairly common pattern, as true in the United Nations as it is in most of the functional agencies. Namely, that, in contrast to what happened during the League of Nations period, the use of the treaty for regulation or for achieving whatever objectives were in mind, has been heavily discounted in the U.N. and Specialized Agencies. It would take no great trouble for us to work out the reasons for that; some have just been mentioned. A great deal has to do with the rapidity of change, its complexity as well as with the lack of compliance. And it is not dissimilar from developments in national governments where administrative techniques, administrative agencies have become much more common in comparison with legislative regulation. I would suggest that we do not spend time going through the reasons or the advantages of the legislative technique. I think what we ought to focus on is the kind of supplementary action, measures and acts that ought to be adopted (and I would put it more in terms of what ought to be in the future than in terms of what has been adopted in the past). What ought to be done in order to give effectiveness to basic decisions or basic purposes? A good example of a general category which would be relevant to this is technical assistance. In the ILO, as in many of the U.N.'s economic and social activities in respect of which treaties were the characteristic League of Nations' technique, now technical assistance is the characteristic U.N. method. There must be a great deal more to the story than that and I would put this as a general inquiry: Let us look to that aspect rather than going into explanations as to why your agency no longer uses treaties.

Mr. Stevenson:

I would agree to that, subject to one qualification: it seems to me that the paper on WHO stressed not so much the effectiveness and compliance points but rather the fact that the legislative process itself, insofar as it involved the traditional treaty-making procedures, took too long. It does not seem to me that this necessarily excludes using a more expeditious legislative process. Now, if Mr. Schachter is correct, no matter how you improve and speed up the legislative process, this is still not the way to do it. What I would like to know from WHO and perhaps from UPU representatives is whether it is the deficiencies in the legislative process itself or whether this is not a proper area in which to legislate.

Professor Sohn:

I think it would help us if we could have the people of the various agencies confirm or deny Mr. Schachter's statement that the legislative process by way of treaties has by now been abandoned or put in second place. The Director General of the ILO has said many times that ILO has to shift from legislative process to operational; what Mr. Schachter was saying is operational, because technical assistance is part of the operational aspects of the ILO and other agencies. It might be useful if we go systematically through the three processes:

(1) to what extent is the treaty method still being used?
(2) to what extent has the administrative regulation process been improved and how further can it be improved?
(3) to what extent is it possible to replace legislative activity by operational activity?

THE EXPERIENCE OF THE INTERNATIONAL LABOR ORGANIZATION

Mr. Valticos:

Mr. Schachter has provided quite a provocative basis for the discussion. Of course, we cannot generalize even among the functional organizations.

433

Legislative techniques very often depend firstly, on the constitutional framework within which the various agencies function, secondly on subject matter, and thirdly, on timing. We should take these three considerations into account. In the ILO we are not at all under the impression that the legislative techniques have been abandoned. They are and still remain the backbone of our activities. If technical cooperation has expanded it does not mean that we have abandoned legislative activity, but that our means of action have been supplemented by new techniques. We now have two very different types of activities, the legislative on the one hand and the operational on the other hand, which we try to coordinate.

Now, of course, the situation may greatly depend, as I said, on the constitutional framework of the organization. The ILO Constitution provided, from the beginning, for the adoption of conventions which would create international obligations as one of its essential means of action.

The situation also depends on the subject matter. For the ILO dealt with labor and social conditions and this is a matter for which you can perhaps more readily envisage the adoption of conventions designed to set standards to be introduced in individual countries than is the case in some more technical or financial fields. This being so, we have always felt that the conventions system, apart from its historical value, has the advantage of creating the sort of international obligations on which the Organization can more firmly base its action, and the pursuit of its effort to promote their application when they are formally accepted. Even when they were not formally accepted by a State, conventions constitute a form of guidelines for it. It is however essential to have a sufficiently sound system for supervising compliance in order not to make a mockery of these instruments. In this effort to seek compliance, we have developed various means covering the various situations which arise.

In this field, it is true that the most formal compliance techniques provided for in our Constitution, the techniques based on formal complaints and commissions of enquiry, are very seldom used. The less formal techniques, which involve the examination, on a routine basis, of the reports submitted by the governments, observations made on them and of discussion became the rule.

However, even this examination on the basis of the some 3,000 reports received every year, has a certain formal character, in the sense that it is conducted in a quasi-judicial manner. It is entrusted to a body of independent persons who consider that they are appointed on their personal capacity, and not as representatives of governments, to express their views without any sort of prejudice and on an equal footing for all states concerned. But they are not afraid of identifying cases of violation and making use of the *mobilization of shame*. They have gone even further. A few years ago our Conference Committee on the Application of Conventions adopted and published in its report what they called the "special list" and which is usually considered as the "black list" of states which

434

for a number of years have failed persistently to apply some important provisions of conventions they have ratified. At the same time, it has a "white list": the list of the cases of progress achieved during that year.

This might seem at first sight a pedagogic approach, but states are very sensitive when it comes to their international reputation and image. The first time this list appeared, one state was on it because it had not—as it should have done under the convention it had ratified—raised the minimum age of employment in industry from 14 to 15 years. That government did not like that at all. The government representative went to the plenary conference and asked that the state's name be deleted from the list. There was a long discussion and the plenary session of the conference did not accede to this request. Shortly afterwards, the law was changed. This does not happen every year, of course. We have had violations, sometimes serious violations. The reasons are sometimes that the country finds that its own vital or national interests are at stake or sometimes that it ratified a convention too lightly and the economic and social conditions do not allow implementation. Sometimes, and more frequently I think, it is just a case of bad administration.

But the position would be much worse if we had no binding instruments, if we had no system of supervision and did not try by this process year after year to impress upon governments the need to live up to the convention. The one thing which is essential is, to give the governments concerned the feeling that they are fairly treated, that the work of examination has been thoroughly done. This needs a highly experienced, trained and loyal staff. It also means that the bodies which pass judgment on implementation are not political bodies, that they must not be made up of government representatives who, whatever they may say, will be influenced consciously or unconsciously by the political position of their government. When we had, three years ago, a commission of enquiry to look into the conditions of alleged forced labor in Angola and Mozambique, had it not been composed of members such as former judges rather than government representatives, it would not have been given the same facilities in the country and the governments concerned, in the midst of difficult political tension, would not have accepted its recommendations as readily as they did, nor would they have acted upon them in the same way.

My belief is that this is not at all as yet the twilight of legislative action in the field of international organizations. I even think that if circumstances had been different, the action of the U.N. in the field of human rights might have been much stronger had the Covenants been adopted some 20 years earlier, at the time of the Universal Declaration, and some strong procedure of implementation established. Of course it is easy to speak in terms of "ifs"—but personally I think this is a very effective means of implementation. It does not follow of course that one does not use informal actions to supplement these formal procedures.

On the contrary, and technical assistance is one such method—states very often ask us for advice on establishing a system of social security or changing their labor legislation. But one should ask on what basis—on what principles—will the technical assistance experts work? You need a code of good practice and our conventions and recommendations are aimed at providing this. The danger is that if you choose an English expert he will apply English traditions; if you choose a French one he will apply French traditions and so on. At least the ILO expert will take with him a valuable set of guidelines which has gradually been recognized, on a universal basis, as being good practice and the standards of which he will try progressively to implement, so that a country may one day can reach the objective which they represent.

VARIOUS MODES OF INTERNATIONAL LEGISLATION

Mr. Arnold:

I think one could assume from some of the observations that there is only one method of legislating. Perhaps I misunderstood, but it seems to be thought that treaties are the only method of international legislation. At least in the practice of the United States, a legislative effect can equally well result from what is called a regulation. And I believe that is what is being done in the European Community.

I took Mr. Stevenson's question to cover legislation under a broad definition and I took it that he was enquiring whether the legislative function could not today be fulfilled by decisions of the governing body rather than necessarily by a treaty.

Mr. Stevenson:

That was my question.

I think your point about the subject matter of different agencies influencing this of course is very important. I can see in the area of the ILO it would be much more difficult to act by a majority vote. But the question I would like to come to and I would like to direct it to Mr. Vignes (WHO) and Mr. Caha (UPU) is whether it might not be a good thing—where you are dealing with something that is much more technical in nature—to vest power to legislate in the agency or some parliamentary body of the agency to make decisions by majority vote? Is not the reluctance to use formal procedures not accounted for in part by a deficiency in the present legislative process and not necessarily and solely because these matters are better handled in an informal manner?

Mr. Vignes:

I would like to underscore Mr. Valticos' statement. The World Health Assembly has not renounced its legislative function. It frequently uses its legislative power. The simpler procedure adopted now falls within the legislative power of the Assembly. For instance, if we take the Regulations, we normally have a strong legislative power with a very strong degree of effectiveness. But in fact, in WHO, by adopting an easier procedure, a recommendation for instance, we achieve more or less the same effect.

I would like to refer to Professor Stein's remark when he said that WHO had abandoned the Regulations. This is not the case, although part of the Regulations are now expressed in recommendations. The Regulations will always remain the structure and contents of our basic approach.

Professor Stein:

But in legal terms: what used to be in a regulation is now in a recommendation?

Mr. Vignes:

Only for some technical aspects.

Mr. Stevenson:

Suppose that what is now in a recommendation were legally binding. Suppose the Executive Board or the Assembly of WHO had the authority by majority vote to adopt legally binding regulations. Do you think this would have any effect, as far as compliance and effectiveness is concerned —would it help or hurt?

Mr. Vignes:

We have the same procedure for adopting regulations as we have for adopting recommendations—they require the same majority. But the difference is that the regulation enters into force after a certain delay, usually after nine months. The recommendation enters into force immediately. If you adopt a regulation like the International Sanitary Regulations you have an instrument which binds states, and if you adopt a recommendation, strictly speaking, you have no legally binding act. In fact, there is a substantial difference.

Mr. Stevenson:

So it would probably hurt, if you were to provide that you could adopt something that would become effective immediately and was legally binding?

Mr. Vignes:

I cannot see that this would result in any difference. Mr. Gutteridge explained the situation in his paper. When we wish to apply something very rapidly we prefer to use the simpler procedure of a recommendation, as it has a more immediate effect. This procedure permits more flexible modification in the future according to change of circumstance.

Mr. Stevenson:

In a footnote of your paper, Mr. Caha, you indicated that consideration had been given to holding administrative conferences that could deal with the revision of purely technical matters and that could act by majority vote rather than through postal conventions: was this approved?

Mr. Caha:

This procedure was considered by the UPU Executive Council, but it was not adopted.

All member countries or at least the majority regulate their postal activities by a monopoly. And this situation has obliged the UPU from the beginning to create itself as an intergovernmental body.

I must confirm what Mr. Valticos said about the ILO. On the international level, and as concerns the classical activities of the UPU, we have never abandoned the formal legislative functions; we have always had intergovernmental treaties.

Mr. Elkin:

There is one interesting problem which is almost of a philosophical nature: where does the process of regulation begin to set *standards*? This is a dialectical concept. Normally, standards require legislation, and regulation requires ordinary, binding decisions by an organization. But gradually general standards are established by individual acts of regulation.

Mr. Boulanger:

I think I should mention the fact that the IAEA has never had any legislative power for very obvious economic and political reasons. The power of making decisions was kept to a minimum or should I say to nothing at all. So for us, one method of legislation would be by convention, but this is very tedious and takes time. Then also in this very fast developing field it would not be a very good method. So we have adopted a system, described in my paper, of calling in experts, having panels develop "standards" which are then accepted by the member states and introduced into their own legislation. Especially in the field of health protection and transport, the same method is used by Euratom and the European Nuclear Energy Agency of OECD. They use the technical data provided by the International Commission on Radiological Protection; from there they go on to give the material to member countries who are only too glad to receive it and to enact it as law or as regulation if they feel the necessity.

Professor Stein:

Do you not have a fairly important power to impose standards in negotiated project agreements?

Mr. Boulanger:

This is true of course. All the project instruments are bi-lateral agreements and if you want to have our assistance you must apply these standards.

Mr. Vignes:

In WHO we also have a traditional practice whereby conventions and agreements come into force when accepted by states, provided for under Article 19 of the Constitution, but up to now we have never applied this Article. The normal practice of the organization is to use the contracting-out system rather than the contracting-in, and the regulations adopted by the Health Assembly constitute an example of this practice.

LEGISLATION OF THE FOOD AND AGRICULTURE ORGANIZATION

Mr. Dobbert:

To start on the general question of the replacement of more formal procedures by less formal and perhaps more effective ones, I think that the trend in FAO is rather significant. We have had more conventions and agreements under Article XIV in the early history of FAO than there have been lately. But this, I think, is due to various factors. One of them is that once you have dealt with most essential subject matters which states feel should be dealt with by formal instruments that are binding on those who adhere to them, then the need becomes reduced. The second reason is that many of our conventions and agreements are not of a regulatory nature although some of them are operational, particularly to the exent that they are on a self-financing basis (in other words, the implementation and operation of the agreement is not or not entirely financed by the regular budget, but on the basis of a scale of contributions of parties or out of voluntary contributions).

There is one other important aspect which perhaps we have not yet mentioned and which derives, on the one hand, from accelerated scientific and technological development and, on the other hand, from the time usually required, not so much for the conclusion of agreements as for amending or revising them. I think that if texts in the technological field are to remain in keeping with developments, a rather flexible and swift amendment procedure may be required.

This is perhaps one of the reasons why another system—namely that of creation of norms by less formal procedures, which, however, are also subject to individual consent, and become binding only if accepted in a way similar to treaty ratification—has gained ground, probably at the expense of formal treaty procedure. It would seem that the time element as far as the *elaboration* of standards is concerned is not decisive for the choice of the instrument; to judge from FAO experience, the elaboration of standards may take five to eight years until a standard is ready for adoption. In the field of joint FAO/WHO work on food standards, a very detailed and often time-consuming procedure has been set up, consisting of ten different steps in the course of which individual governments and expert committees are given several opportunities to propose amendments to provisional draft standards. But the *acceptance* of these standards is generally simpler; although their acceptance may entail some domestic legislation, they do not require ratification which frequently delays the coming into force of conventions or agreements.

Technical assistance has been mentioned earlier, and I think we also have to take into account that bi-lateral agreements are based on objective standards and not invented by the Secretariat. As many of us know, the Standard Agreements for technical assistance, the Basic Agreements of the U.N. Special Fund and in the same way the agreements of the World Food Program are mainly governed by general regulations adopted by the competent intergovernmental bodies; the standards set by such regulations and other decisions of these bodies are then transplanted into specific agreements. Thus, even bi-lateral agreements, which have gained momentum in the activities of the international organization, are partly the result of a quasi-legislative process.

MORE ON ILO CONVENTIONS

Professor Schwebel:
Having watched the difficulties from the executive end of the United States Government in getting things through the U.S. Congress, I must say that I have a certain sympathy for approaches other than the traditional legislative one. Take for example the ILO sphere—I think we adhere only to about seven ILO conventions, largely concerning seamen's conditions. More generally, in the social/human rights sphere, the attitude in Congress is that it is fine for the other fellow but we do not need it, we have our standards, but as for doing something about international standards, that is a rather impertinent suggestion and causes all sorts of constitutional problems. This is the situation with which the Executive is confronted in the Senate. This may not be as acute in more technical areas. Especially in those areas, contracting out has a great deal of appeal. There it seems to be easier, and the Congress may be willing to accord international organizations a certain amount of authority, particularly if it is recommendatory and not obligatory. But it is very cautious.

Mr. Valticos:
It is true that the United States for constitutional reasons have only ratified seven international labor conventions. But we do not look at the chart of ratifications as a yardstick for the state of progress in member

states. Moreover there is some prospect of having some more substantive conventions ratified by the United States.

Professor Sohn:

I think the ILO shows something interesting in this report. As Mr. Valticos pointed out, they do not only have a chart of ratifications but also a system of reporting which extends even to non-ratified conventions and this provides the ILO with the opportunity of saying that the United States and other countries meet the standards of a convention, even though they have not ratified it.

Mr. Valticos:

I must say that the reports from the United States on the unratified conventions are extraordinary, because they describe the position in 50 states in a very detailed way. On the basis of these reports we reached some very interesting conclusions. So that if the United States has not ratified many conventions it does not mean that there is no means of evaluating the degree of implementation.

Mr. Golsong:

We have heard that the choice between the traditional treaty approach and the more flexible systems of legislation is partly determined by the subject matter. In the case of the ILO—if you change the minimum industry employment age from 14 to 15 it is something of a permanent character and not subject to changing living conditions; but if you deal with world health regulations, that is quite a different subject.

Here I wanted to make an observation about Mr. Vignes' statement. He said that regulations and recommendations are the same because they require the same majority. Now, the difference to me is that the regulation is much more weighty, it is an instrument much nearer to the treaty. You can only denounce it after three years with a previous notice of six months and so on, whereas a recommendation is more flexible. As the latter is not legally binding, and if a state finds it is impossible to comply, it can easily make the point at the next conference and either ask for an amendment or make a statement that according to this and that situation it is not possible to act upon the recommendation. Whereas for a regulation it is a very difficult procedure to get rid of—quite apart from the internal parliamentary need for ratification on implementation of a regulation as for a treaty.

THE INFLUENCE OF NON-GOVERNMENTAL ELEMENTS

Mr. Golsong:

The second observation concerns Mr. Valticos' statement about the implementation machinery within ILO, particularly the very effective functioning of the reporting system. He said that the basic philosophy behind it is the mobilization of shame. But I wonder whether we have the same possibility in other functional organizations. Is it not because in ILO you have in addition to governmental representatives also non-governmental representatives, which is a very important factor in your machinery and gives you wider possibilities for that mobilization of shame?

Mr. Valticos:

The tri-partite structure of our organization gives us of course, an element of additional strength. But this would not disappear in other organizations because the mobilization of shame also depends on a certain amount of publicity. Then action is more likely to be taken than if it remains in the records of the organization.

Mr. FitzGerald:

I should like to supplement this: considerable stress has been placed on the tri-partite nature of the ILO and on the fact that the representatives can exercise certain pressures. In respect of international organizations other than the ILO, a similar effect can be produced by observers. For example, in the case of ICAO, the International Air Transport Association, composed of about 100 of the world's scheduled airlines, and which is one of the prime consumers of ICAO activities, plays a non-constitutional role in policing what the ICAO does. IATA's opinions are not lightly cast aside. IATA comes forward with the most helpful documentation at the ICAO meetings, and especially at the technical meetings. The same would be true for the International Federation of Airline Pilot's Associations which would represent the workers. So you do have in a way the industry and the workers in ICAO with observer status.

STANDARD SETTING AND PRACTICAL ASSISTANCE

Mr. Schachter:

As lawyers, we have to be concerned with norm creation, legislation and the application of conventions—most of my own writings have essentially pressed for this by urging the expansion of the legislative role as much as possible. I would like to point out, however, that the greater part of activity in the economic and social field—if you take international officialdom—is not concerned with this aspect. The areas of concern in the world today—leaving out the political side—the world trade problems, industrial development, the whole economic development effort, are generally approached in terms which are substantially different from the traditional approaches. We should take this into account and then try to relate it to our problem. I am not talking now about simplifying the process of norm creation—I am talking about the problem of trying to control a situation or to improve things. One question is: in what circumstances do we gain by standard setting and enunciating principles. This was certainly a major effort in UNCTAD. Some of the developed countries objected to this process, particularly the U.S., but developing countries often espouse "obligations" as a pressure device. Of course they also are concerned with other types of action. They want a transfer of resources, they want money, putting it simply. And then they also want other things, which are related to making their objectives effective. Perhaps we ought to try in terms of each agency's experience to give some thought to the more positive or constructive areas of work rather than the policing of rules. There is both a need for norms and a need for means to bring about conditions of encouraging compliance. Examples of the latter include fact finding, and watchdog, supervisory action in certain areas. Perhaps more important is improving the so-called practical means, such as public administration and legal techniques within the countries.

Mr. Nurick:

You said it would be desirable to set standards; what do you mean by standards, can you give us some examples?

Mr. Schachter:

In each field, for example in your field, the Bank has required from time to time in concrete cases a certain conduct of behavior on the part of governments. This can sometimes be generalized as standards of conduct.

Professor Sohn:

In the OAS Charter, you have a beautiful example of standard setting in the economic field in the constitutional document.

Mr. Schachter:

And in the U.N. resolutions in the field of trade, the objectives expressed may in some cases be called standards.

Professor Stein:

Maintenance of basic community price levels, that sort of thing.

Mr. Nurick:

I was trying to think of what you meant in terms of a particular kind of operation, of the application of standards to a particular project that somebody wants to do. This is where I get into trouble, because the standards you mentioned are so general that they would not answer this type of problem.

Mr. Schachter:

There are cases where it is not appropriate or useful to try to introduce abstract formulations into the particular projects. The problem is to determine just when and in what respect guidelines of a general character will be helpful in influencing conduct.

Professor Sohn:

The following example relates to Mr. Nurick's question: when we were working on the Special Fund a few years ago, one of the big problems was how do you establish standards by which an organization having only a limited amount of money available could decide who or what activities should have priority. Attempts which were then made to develop such standards were unsuccessful, but at least they indicated the scope of the problem. It is very often easier to establish an organization and provide it with sufficient money to do what it wants than to agree on standards for its guidelines. If people had clearer ideas what standards an organization such as the Bank should apply, they could have arranged for spending the money in some intelligent, logical way instead of leaving it purely to somebody's administrative discretion. But they just could not agree on some reasonable standards and had to delegate the power of decision to the organization.

Mr. Schachter:

I meant mainly standards of conduct as, for example, with regard to domestic saving within underdeveloped countries and control over the flight of capital. There are constant repetitions of standards of behavior for developing countries, just as on the other side there are standards for mulated for the advanced countries as, for example, for tariff preferences and commodity prices. There is a great deal of material that constitutes standards of conduct for states in the economic field. The equivalent in the political field may be found in the various declarations on "Essentials of Peace" or "Non-Intervention" and so on.

Professor Sohn:

We are really concerned with two kinds of standards: standards which the organization itself should observe and standards which the states should observe. We should concentrate on the second category but let us not forget about the former.

Mr. Lauterpacht:

I do not know whether anybody here enjoys as I do to talk about the great meals one has had. In a sense we are rather like a group of chefs sitting around discussing recipes. And some of us are meat cooks, some are sauce cooks, others are pastry cooks and others are vegetable cooks. We are talking about different things!

There are of course certain fundamental principles, such as, without heat you cannot cook, but ultimately the question of whether a particular technique of making a sauce is applicable to the cooking of vegetables is in a sense an inappropriate or an impossible subject for discussion. It seems to me that when we are talking about techniques that are applicable in the context of banks or financial matters, we are talking about something that is not applicable to non-financial organizations such as the ILO or WHO. So, all we are doing is sitting around talking about recipes and wondering what to do with them. There is something to be said though for making a cookbook. Then anybody who would like to find out how to make a particular kind of concoction will see that the experience of that particular category of cook has been, let us say, that a strictly legislative technique will not work, and that recommendations are not bad and that (on the whole) customers would like nothing more than a simple establishment of standards. And therefore I am just wondering whether—in order to see the thing actually focused in a precise way—the trend of the discussion could be towards the establishment in a logical form of the various diverse elements which we have been passing round the table. I wonder whether one could try and systematize one's list of techniques and relate the *success* of these techniques to a particular context. This is really asking for synthesis as opposed to analysis.

Mr. Stevenson:

I am not sure whether I follow you completely. You said that you would like to have the specific techniques described. Do you mean by the various agencies or an attempt to discuss in a general way the various techniques that are available?

Mr. Lauterpacht:

What I was looking for was perhaps less discussion now but an attempt to enumerate, to synthesize, the discussion in an orderly manner. All we are doing at the moment is to add to what we have already discussed and what we have in writing. My specific suggestion at this point is that we should probably try to list the various techniques.

Mr. Stevenson:

As you have more specifically in mind what you want, I suggest that *you* do it.

Mr. Lauterpacht:

If everyone here were to draw up such a list, one would come up with something which I think would be really quite valuable.

Mr. Stevenson:

I really think what we were trying to do was to find areas in which the experience of different agencies was similar. It is one thing to say that ILO which deals with social and political questions cannot necessarily rely on the same techniques as WHO or ICAO. But I think there is a great similarity between what WHO is doing and ICAO, just as I think that there is a great deal of similarity between ILO and what the Council of Europe is doing. So, I do not think it is a question of everyone coming up with their pet remedies. Have not, for example, Mr. Golsong and Mr. Valticos very definitely agreed as to the techniques?

Mr. Elkin:

Just to go on from Mr. Lauterpacht's statement: there is the restaurateur and the consumer. We have two legal or objectively limiting elements in international organizations, of varying quality. On the one hand, there is the constituent instrument under which you operate, and in it you have, for each organization, a statement of aims. On the other side, there is national legislation, or the national constitution. These two elements narrow down the possibility of a synthesis, but the synthesis is still possible.

To return to the proceedings which in a sense illustrated what you said, namely, the dialogue between Mr. Schachter and Mr. Nurick. Here is a situation to which I referred earlier. I spoke about "effectiveness" and gave an example. When we deal with payments arrangements, we have to be extremely precise in drafting the instrument. However, whether they should take the form of a multi-lateral payments "decision" or a multi-lateral payments "agreement" is a question for the delegations to decide in the light of their constitutional requirements.

We were asked that question: whether the European Payments Union or the European Monetary Agreement could take the form of a "decision" of the OEEC. We replied "yes" but most national delegations said, please make it a "treaty" because in our national constitution we have to submit it to parliament, and it looks much better if it is a "treaty" which will be "ratified" by which, of course, they meant parliamentary "approval".

Now, the other example I gave was when I spoke of "deflation" through deliberate increase in unemployment. There the situation was very difficult from the point of view of "effectiveness".

"Effectiveness" in the field of economic relations alone is achieved in different ways; some of them are complicated. So it is a very complex process. That is why in a sense it cannot be identified in all fields. But, after all, national administration is a very complicated business too. In an international community it is a pluralistic process, and the standards have to be worked out very gradually.

Mr. Stevenson:

I think that there is a basic difference between the financial institution and the other functional agencies. I think Mr. Schachter raised the question of other techniques that the functional agencies could use. Before we turn to the banks and in order to prepare the basis for this synthesis, I would like to hear about some of the other aspects of the operations of the non-financial functional agencies.

Mr. Schachter:
As concerns the compliance techniques and effectiveness, I would like to hear a bit more from Mrs. Higgins.

THE MOBILIZATION OF SHAME

Mrs. Higgins:
I have a question first on the "mobilization of shame." I wonder whether we could try and explore this on a broader footing. We talked a little about the ILO experience and I would be extremely interested in knowing what general lessons we could draw from this. Within ILO we have learned that the system works as well as it does largely for two reasons: one, because the shame is mobilized by individual experts and not by political government appointees, and this is extremely important. Secondly, because it is largely home-directed, through the tripartite system. It is very significant that shame is mobilized within the country which is found lacking rather than in a state-to-state confrontation, and of course this point does link up very directly with the inadequacy which we have all commented on, on a state-to-state procedure as an effective way of securing compliance. We have these two factors within the ILO system: the experts plus the home direction of the shame.

I wonder how those relate to the problem of getting your "carrots" and "sticks" operating together. In the ILO, the mobilization of shame of course is very closely linked with the helping hand to rectify the situation. And I believe I understood there that this is largely done not publicly but privately, in a detailed questionnaire, for example, which goes out to states to find out what the real problem is about compliance. This questionnaire sent out by the experts is not published in the annual report and I wonder here if there are lessons to be learnt generally.

My other query is the question of the role of the Secretariat, as opposed to experts in this mobilization of shame on the one hand and the holding out of the "carrots" of inducement on the other. That is to say, does the operation of this dual system *necessarily* require individual experts? The reason I ask this is because one sees very rapidly the difficulty of using that system in a multi-purpose agency such as the U.N. There you look for compliance over a vast range of issues; to have a standing body of experts who over a course of years build up a reputation of great impartiality would be an exceedingly hard thing to do. How far could these roles therefore be subsumed by an integral part of the organization, such as the Secretariat itself?

Mr. Schachter:

Do we not always have the "carrot" and the "stick"? This is my earlier point about the bargaining model. Every agency is concerned simultaneously with the "carrot" and "stick" operation in the compliance field.

Mr. Valticos:

To answer Mrs. Higgins' questions: first, as regards the informal sort of procedure, at the beginning all comments and observations of the Committee of Experts were public. It started as completely open, the only change that was made in the first report of the Committee of Experts in 1927 was that the governing body objected to the word "criticism". They asked that it be replaced by the word "observation". But that was the only alteration and all the observations were published. It was only some ten years ago that this was changed—the main reason being a practical one: the report of the Committee of Experts is designed to constitute a basis at the conference for discussion by the government, employers' and workers' representatives. The Committee of Experts is a body of highly qualified legal, or administrative, persons who sit *in camera*, examine the reports received from the governments and reach some conclusion as to whether a convention is completely applied by the reporting government. Then at the conference stage, three months later, a Conference Committee meets and calls the government representatives to discuss these points with them. The Conference is in session for three weeks, but the number of observations increased along with the number of reports. Finally, they became so unmanageable that it was decided to place only the most important cases before the Conference and the rest sent to the governments directly. This helped in a way, because with informal direct requests, as they are called, the Committee of Experts could more easily explain the position, and even indicate the various possibilities of correcting the situation. Some sort of assistance is thus given before the matter becomes public. There may be a period of several years before the government decides to rectify the position. If there is no improvement, the matter becomes public.

I would like to add something which is not in my paper: last March or April, the Committee f Experts celebrated its 40th anniversary. And, as on the occassion of all anniversaries, it looked less to the past than towards the future. It found the situation in no way discouraging, but still examined how it could be further improved. One of the suggestions concerned the problem of how to proceed in a number of hardcore cases where for various reasons there was no progress. So the Committee of Experts suggested that in some cases it might appear that the purely formal character of this exchange—and even discussion—might be supplemented by some form of direct contacts between the government on the one hand and the Committee or a representative of the Director General of the ILO on the other, so that, over the years, and even sometimes before the case reached the stage of public observation, a sort of informal discussion could take place; it might be either with an official or an independent personality or a member of the Committee. This was one of the suggestions that was made in order to introduce some informal elements in the formal procedure, while it was understood that the formal procedure would of course have the final word. This is something which is intended to supplement formal procedures now in operation and in which the Secretariat of course plays a role—it is not very public—but it helps in the process.

Professor Sohn:

It might be useful if we could discuss the reporting system or equivalent procedures of the other agencies, and if we could find out why in a sense it has not been as successful in them as in the ILO and of only *minor* importance in their work.

Mr. Stevenson:

I would like to defer the discussion of the banks until later.

Mr. Gold:

I must really claim membership of the two groups, the financial and the regulatory agencies. We are in fact a regulatory agency dealing with currencies, and I would like to mention some points in connection with Mrs. Higgins' questions concerning the mobilization of shame.

This is very much available to us and is being used. And I wish to make clear that our use of it is not wholly associated and in some respects not even associated at all with the use of our resources. The Fund Articles contain a code of conduct, a set of precise, although rather few, obligations directing the countries how they must behave in connection with the value of their currency and so on, and for deviations from that code they must secure the approval of the Fund, so that the deviation can be regarded as consistent with the Articles and carry the stamp of legality.

This is a very important fact because of the reaction of countries to the failure to get the Fund stamp of approval on these practices that are deviations. It is an important fact that countries are very sensitive about getting the Fund's stamp of approval. But this is not sensitivity produced by the prospect that the country will not be able to get access to the Fund's resources. In fact, they may get access to the Fund's resources even if they continue some of these practices. But I repeat that there is a great desire to ensure that they will be able to get the Fund's approval for practices they feel they must resort to even if they do not contemplate use of the Fund's resources.

449

Incidentally, a general lesson of the Fund's experience which I would like to stress is the importance of the possibility for giving approval to practices of deviation. Flexibility in the application of standards of obligations is very important. I feel one must look at the field in which one is operating to see to what extent one should be able to depart from basic obligations and have escape clauses because of the great variety of problems that have to be faced.

The short point that I have tried to make is that, even without the fear of financial loss, because a country does not seek resources, it is nevertheless important for it to be able to say that its practices are consistent with international obligations. The best explanation I can think of for this in the case of the Fund is that our field is specialized and well defined. The members feel that they belong to a club of a homogeneous character, so that departure from the rules of the club is regarded by all as unworthy conduct. This may not be true in other organizations but it has been a feature of Fund experience.

THE MOBILIZATION OF SHAME (CONTINUED)

Mr. FitzGerald:

In the ICAO, you have a terribly heavy natural sanction in case of non-compliance with the ICAO material, namely that of death. You do not really need a mobilization of shame. In the ICAO, we are doing something which is measurable. If you do not comply with a particular way of flying you will not fly—or if you try to, you will not fly for very long. It is as simple as that!

That is not to say that we do not have sanctions which have the connotation of mobilization of shame. For example, in the Chicago Convention, we have a provision whereby the Council can report to the Assembly any infraction of the Convention.

We also have a provision whereby, if a state feels that another is not complying with Annexes, it can take the matter to the Council. The sword of Damocles is always standing over the heads of states. But these are ultimate remedies. We have the best one in natural sanctions. You have these natural sanctions also in other Organizations. If you do not follow the FAO Codex Alimentarius, your nationals are going to die of food poisoning; you are going to poison people in other countries with faulty exports, or people will not accept the food you are exporting if it does not meet the standards. If you do not follow the WHO Health Regulations people will die of all sorts of diseases.

I have tried to prepare this rather horrendous paper of mine to set down once and for all what I thought was the sum total of the experience in implementation. I tried to put together what has been developed by the ICAO technical people. I have set down a very lengthy check-list and

many of the items on the check-list apply with equal validity to the impl
mentation process in the other technical agencies. I am sure that peop
from the other functional agencies who have read that part of my paper
had some responsive chord struck in their breasts. My conclusion is that
the implementation process comes down to what I call the 3-M formula:
Men—Material—Money. The most important thing of these three is money. The nature of the subject matter is controlling the type of instrument to
be used, for example, convention, resolution, or recommendation. The nature of the subject matter also determines the type of people who handle
the material on an international deliberative level and also in the national
governments.

This can very seriously affect implementation on the national level. For
example, the Director of Civil Aviation in some countries may be a colo-
nel in the Air Force who is buried under a heap of people in the defense department. He may be the head of a small sector of a Department of Transport, Communications and Power. How can such people get parliamentary
time or even time in the local cabinet? These are real problems. How can
they compete for their share of the appropriations from the national budget or get budgetary appropriations passed? So if you are going to apply
a technique of mobilization of shame, what you are really saying to some
people in some countries is, "Shame on you for being poor". You cannot
do that sort of thing. This is particularly true of the developing countries
and, to some extent, it is even true in the more developed countries. If
you have a budget of two billion dollars a year, you may be sure that civil
aviation is going to get a relatively small part after you have taken out
the material for defense, and health purposes, and trade purposes and so
on. There is not very much left over for civil aviation, which is only part of
the whole complex of transportation. These are only a few, almost non-
legal points that I wanted to make, and I believe that they are realistic
points.

Mr. Stevenson:

Would you like to reply to Professor Sohn's statement, Mr. Dobbert,
that your compliance system has not worked so well?

Mr. Dobbert:

I think Professor Sohn has seen the early proceedings of FAO and he
knows of course Article XI, which requires submission of regular reports
by the member nations, and which indeed has not become, as the corresponding constitutional provisions in certain other organizations, the basis
for an effective measure of fact-finding on the implementation of decisions
of the organization.

The reasons are briefly explained in the Annex to my paper (extract
from U.N. document A/6228). The reasons are not so much those Professor Sohn mentioned, when he said, "although members have complied with

451

the obligation to submit reports, the Secretariat of the organization had not succeeded in analyzing those in an effective manner." I think the reasons are rather deeper.

Before you have reports as an effective means of checking compliance, you have to know what you have to comply with. Now, the Constitution itself has very few binding provisions on which reports could usefully be made. As regards the instruments which contain regulatory provisions, they usually have their own built-in system of reporting. Most of these conventions provide for the establishment of a body; that body meets at regular intervals and prepares its report, reflecting any reports that it may get from the participating countries. These reports are sometimes submitted *in toto* to the governing bodies but it is the obligation of the Director General to put before the governing bodies of the FAO any parts of the reports that have policy or financial implications. This in a way takes care of at least part of the contents which one might normally expect to find in Article XI reports. Moreover, under Article XI, the Director General or the governing bodies may request countries to submit reports on specific items. Now, this power has been used very extensively and governments have sometimes complained—rightly or wrongly—that they were getting too many requests for reports on statistics, animal or plant diseases, cooperatives, and on various other subjects; so, this has been another cause of draining these regular reports of their content.

It may well be that in future—although this might be a bit speculative—the regular reports are going to be geared to the subject which the Conference or the Council decided should be highlighted in the Director General's Annual Report on the State of Food and Agriculture, where he also gives a general review of the activities of the Organization. With respect to the methods for analyzing and evaluating those reports, and possibly submitting them to the quasi-judicial enquiries of the ILO type, I should say that while some of us might at times cast an envious eye on the Committee of Experts of the ILO these methods are probably less suitable for FAO than for the ILO where the regulatory functions have a much greater importance.

Mr. Vignes:

I quite agree with Mr. Dobbert. The WHO Constitution provides for annual reports from the countries stating the health situation in their country. These reports are submitted to the Annual Assembly.

Mr. Valticos:

I do not want to give the impression that everything is perfect in the ILO. Some of the methods we are thinking about, while keeping the procedures which we have now and which we believe are quite effective, are the following:

(1) development of more direct contacts with governments, discussions and so on;

(2) coordination, as closely as possible, of our technical operation with standard-setting procedures.

There is already an elaborate system according to which, when the ILO sends an expert in the field to advise on a matter on which standards exist, irrespective of whether the country has or has not ratified the convention concerned, the expert is briefed on difficulties encountered in the application of these standards, as they appear from the normal procedure of supervision. He has this as a sort of reference in his work and is able to see to what extent, in his field, he can give advice and seek remedies to the existing problems, taking into account the economic, social, and political conditions of the country.

Mr. Schachter:

This is a sort of fact-finding function.

Mr. Valticos:

A sort of technical assistance function, for it helps the government to overcome these problems. We are very careful not to give the impression that we are sending people to try to investigate the situation. It is kept separate from the formal procedure but it sometimes helps. Also what happens quite often is that we are consulted by countries wishing to revise their labor code, or change their labor legislation, or draft labor legislation. The amendments that we propose as a technical organization assisting governments aim at achieving compatibility with international standards or the possible progressive change of the legislation to meet those standards.

(3) A third direction in which we are trying now to improve the situation is public administration. I said earlier that public administration is one of the weaknesses in many countries, especially as labor ministries are not among the priority ministries in various countries, and this is the reason for some of the difficulties we have encountered. We have therefore been quietly organizing for the last three years a very useful system of seminars for labor officers in the various regions. We started it in East Africa for the English-speaking countries, in Nairobi; the following year in Cameroon for the French-speaking countries. We did it last year for Latin American countries in Lima; we are intending to do it this year in Asia. And this informal method, where we send two officials to sit with senior officers of the ministries concerned to discuss with them the question of international and national standards, helps them, first, to understand their obligations and the meaning of the standards, what is to be done, what remains to be done. Second, it helps us to understand their problems, the difficulties they have encountered. This sort of informal discussion has proved to be effective in all the areas concerned. We have noted an imme-

453

diate improvement of the situation in the action taken, in the reports, and so on.

So these are three directions in which we have been trying to strengthen the formal legal procedures, which remain the backbone, by: (1) direct diplomatic action, (2) technical cooperation in general and (3) more particularly assistance given to civil servants.

Professor Sohn:

Do you have resident representatives?

Mr. Valticos:

In the field of technical assistance, there are U.N. resident representatives who work closely with representatives of other agencies; and we have now a number of regional officers in various parts of the world, who may also take some part in these discussions on standards. But sometimes the matter is highly technical and specialized: social security and so on, which you cannot expect an expert on manpower to know in detail, but as far as possible we make use of our regional set-up.

Mr. Gold:

On this last point, Fund experience has been very similar. We find that the field of technical assistance is a very useful new field, and a way in which it can be made easier for members to comply with the general objectives of the Fund. We have done three things in the recent past, and all of them indicate possibilities for the future:

(1) the Fund posts resident representatives, who remain Fund staff, to various countries where they give very wide economic advice.

(2) We recently established two new facilities. One is a central banking service in the Fund which sends out experts to give advice on the drafting of central bank legislation and the administration of central banks. In connection with the latter, we have set up a panel of experts made available to us by central banks throughout the world. They are not detached from their own service and they do not become Fund staff personnel. They go into the field for a year or two to give advice on central banking.

(3) Part of the advice we have given countries on occasion is that they should do something about fiscal administration or fiscal legislation. This led us finally to establish a second new facility in the form of a fiscal affairs department. It is giving advice on legislation and on administration. It enables us to be more practical in urging countries to take action in those matters.

I feel certain that in the future we will find new fields in the economic sphere where we can give advice and to something practical about putting it to work.

Mr. Caha:

In connection with the mobilization of shame, it may be remembered that, in the UPU, there is a lack of shame. More and more countries and regional organizations insert reservations to our acts. They do not agree to the general regulations adopted at our Congress, and they insist on applying their regional or local dispositions. As you know, the main term of the UPU is a "single postal territory". The same conditions are applied in a single postal territory. Before the Second World War, there were only 20 to 30 member countries. At the Ottawa Congress, the main objective was to have more member countries, so the possibility of reservations was adopted. First the Anglo-Saxon countries filed reservations. But, and I express my personal opinion: if the Union accepts any more reservations we shall soon no longer have a common system. There is really a lack of shame, countries are not ashamed at all to adopt reservations. The only article under which we cannot accept any reservation is the article dealing with the "reacheminement".

Mr. Elkin:

I would like to make some remarks about the mobilization of shame. Mrs. Higgins spoke of its counter effects in terms of recalcitrant positions and counter charges. There is a much more dangerous result of the mobilization of shame, namely the consolidation of support for the government at home. From the Spanish Civil War through to South Africa, and possibly in the case of Israel over Jerusalem, the dangerous effect of mobilization of shame is the consolidation of home opinion. This is a limitation of the mobilization of shame technique in the political field. And Mr. Gold has spoken against mobilization of shame in his organization. I was delighted with what he said because the OECD doctrine was against mobilization of shame in the regional field. He has shown us that it is exactly the same on a world scale. The reason for it is the snowball effect of any action indicating that shame ought to be mobilized. This is dangerous in the financial and economic field. The reason is that, in an economic organization, member countries deal with each other in good days as well as in bad and are continuously "in session"—in a different sense from the Security Council which deals with crisis only. So there is a continuity of consideration of the problems of each country. And that is why I was also so pleased when Mr. Schachter spoke of "moving a situation along" rather than changing it. If in the political field there were the same sort of continuous review of external political problems, I think mobilization of shame would disappear, but more effective means would be found to cope with situations. There are similar indications of this in a smaller field, in the activities of the Commission established under the European Human Rights Convention which, I am certain, would not subscribe to the doctrine of mobilization of shame. They can settle many problems by not making them public, by not mobilizing shame. In some cases governments have

455

changed their final legislation before any formal action by the Commission was taken, or they have taken administrative action.

INTER-AGENCY COOPERATION IN SETTING STANDARDS AND ENSURING THEIR OBSERVANCE

Mr. Dobbert:

I would like to come back to Mr. Lauterpacht's metaphor: he has spoken about recipes. If you want to devise your recipes, one way of doing it is to see what is going on in your next door neighbor's kitchen, even in his innermost kitchen. Our meeting here is perhaps not the most effective means of devising within our own sphere of activities better methods—always keeping in mind the constitutional limitations of the organization in which each of us is working. But the inspiration we gain here may well be one of the media through which improved or combined methods of establishing rules and of seeing that they are carried out can be devised.

I was going to make the same three points that Mr. Valticos has made; they are also valid as far as FAO is concerned, with very minor variations. I would just like to mention two points which we have not touched upon so far. First, the translation into binding instruments of principles or standards that in themselves are not binding, or only to a very limited degree; the second point is the increasingly important role of inter-agency cooperation. I would like to illustrate these two points with one particular example.

The essential provisions of the World Food Program Project Agreements and Basic Agreements are laid down in the General Regulations of the World Food Program, not in the form in which they could be inserted into the bi-lateral agreements but at any rate in substance. These provisions do have some teeth. Paragraph 18(a) (i) of the General Regulations of the WFP stipulates that such agreements "shall provide to the program the right to observe all phases of project operations from the receipt of commodities in the country to final utilization, to receive audited accounts at agreed intervals, and to suspend or withdraw assistance in case of serious non-compliance."

Now, this has been translated into a clause in the WFP Agreement. The *pro forma* Agreement in fact provides for the possibility of suspension, withdrawal of assistance, and here I quote again: "in the event of failure on the part of the government to fulfill any of its obligations assumed under the present agreement or any agreement concluded by virtue thereof." This provision, which does not mention *serious* non-compliance, might suggest that the decision as to whether non-compliance is considered serious lies solely, or primarily, with WFP.

In this connection, we should note that the provisions placing obligations on the recipient countries have generally received, at least in substance,

456

the approval of the governing body. That protects, on the one hand, the recipient countries from even the possibility—however remote—of any arbitrary line of action on the part of the Secretariat in negotiating agreements. But it also strengthens the back of the Secretariat in negotiating an agreement; it can point out that these obligations are laid down in the General Regulations and that any government requesting assistance has to accept and comply with these obligations.

The second problem of inter-agency cooperation can also be illustrated on the basis of the Agreement, not only on account of the structure of WFP which is a joint UN/FAO enterprise, but also because at the time of decision-making or when a project is devised, various agencies are consulted to make sure that it is not contrary to their policies. But there is more than that. Before a project is approved, it is sent to the ILO, which checks it very carefully. Some of the foodstuffs used by WFP in certain projects are distributed in part payment of wages. There are ILO conventions on that particular aspect and WFP wants to be sure that in implementing these projects it does not run counter to the standards established by ILO. The same is true incidentally, but to a more limited extent, with WHO. A small number of regular staff of ILO, WHO and UNESCO are employed full time on WFP business, scrutinizing projects, watching their implementation and assisting in the evaluation of results.

The WHO liaison officer makes sure that the project is in conformity with the health standards established by WHO. The same applies, *mutatis mutandis*, to UNESCO. If there is a school feeding project, UNESCO may say that a given school is not really worth supporting or that another school, which follows UNESCO Standards, deserves to be supported. So, indirectly, we have in one project and one project agreement a machinery for ensuring compliance with standards established in other organizations.

As far as FAO is concerned, FAO has established Principles on the Disposal of Agricultural Surpluses. Adherence to these Principles is considered extremely important because of the possible interference of surplus disposal transactions with normal or developing trade in agricultural products. A special negotiating machinery has been established in the form of a Sub-Committee on Surplus Disposal which holds very frequent sessions in Washington and which gets not only bi-lateral but also multi-lateral food assistance.

The General Regulations of WFP contain strict provisions, mainly in paragraphs 13 and 20. The latter reads as follows:

"Adequate consideration shall also be given to safeguarding commercial markets and the normal and developing trade of exporting countries in accordance with the FAO Principles of Surplus Disposal."

In fact, all WFP projects are submitted in draft form to the Washington Sub-Committee for examination as to conformity with FAO Surplus Disposal Principles.

What I have said may show that one single instrument can serve to combine the whole gamut of international standards established not only within the organization from which it emanates but also in other organizations.

THE FINANCIAL INSTITUTIONS

Mr. Stevenson:

I would suggest that we now move on in our discussion to the financial institutions. I think we were all struck in reading the papers by the great amount that has been achieved in terms of regulation by both the World Bank and the IMF through means that were not contemplated when the constituent instruments were prepared. It seems to me that the economic consultations in which the Bank is engaged in are very far-reaching. In the case of these two institutions is it because of the possibility of using the "carrot" as well as the "stick" or for other reasons that we had such a unique development?

I was interested in Mr. Gold's statement earlier that it is not purely the fact that the financial benefits were available but I wonder, if they were completely absent, whether you would have the same situation, or whether it is not a combination of both the financial benefit and the great benefit that accrues from the technical assistance rendered that makes the difference?

The other aspect of what has happened here and which is very interesting is the emphasis on the confidential nature of the various suggestions provided.

I would like to throw open the meeting to any general question directed to the financial agencies.

Mr. FitzGerald:

Various agreements include certain standards; in other words, recipients of technical assistance would be expected to comply with ICAO standards. Assuming that the Fund, or the Bank, would ask the people to comply with their own standards, governing whatever financial activities were involved, would they also write into the loan agreement standards established by any of the Specialized Agencies? This is another method of implementation rather like the one that Mr. Dobbert mentioned.

Mr. Gold:

The Fund does not make its resources available for particular projects, for particular enterprises; the resources are made available for *general* balance of payments purposes.

458

Mr. Nurick:

To answer Mr. FitzGerald's question, I have to ask him first what he means by international standards. Strictly speaking, without knowing more about what he means, the answer I would have to give is no. We write many different types of agreements and whatever we regard as proper standards will be reflected either in these agreements or in decisions of various kinds that were taken leading up to the making of the agreement or later on in supervision of those agreements. Therefore I think to talk about borrowing international standards from others is probably misleading.

Professor Sohn:

For instance if you lend money for the purpose of building an airport, are your own people not going to consult the ICAO standard specifying how an airport with a specific amount of traffic should be built?

Mr. Nurick:

We would certainly consult all relevant standards.

Mr. FitzGerald:

Let me give an example: the ILO has conventions on the hours of work and non-discrimination. Suppose the Bank loaned money for construction of a steel mill. Would the Bank put into the loan agreement a fair-labor practice clause modeled on relevant ILO material, even in a country where the ILO conventions had previously not been applied?

Mr. Nurick:

The answer is no. We look at the steel mill. We look at what problems there may be in building and operating that steel mill. If there are legal problems which may arise because of a treaty we will want to know about them, and we will have to take them into account. But we are not likely to incorporate fair labor standards as such into our agreements. I can give you another example: there was an effort made at one time, early in the history of the Bank, to have us incorporate a kind of an international anti-trust clause in our agreements. There too we said no, that this was none of our business.

Mr. Stevenson:

It seems to me that which is significant is not so much the specific provisions that you put in with respect to a particular project but rather the informal understanding about the country's entire economic policy which occasionally is reflected in a letter of representation. It seems to me that this is the most pervasive regulation. You are directing yourself to a country's entire economic position. How are these policies derived, where

459

there is just an informal understanding; are they reflected in any place other than the staff's economic report?

Mr. Boulanger:

My question is: in giving a loan for the construction of a nuclear power plant would you not think of inserting in the agreements some provision that the technical standards such as those developed by the IAEA, among them also safety standards, are observed; because observance of the technical standards will diminish the risk.

Mr. Nurick:

As you know, we are studying this problem right now. We have a group in the Bank working on it. We have never made that kind of a loan but I am sure we will some day and I cannot say exactly what we will do. But it may well be that we will do as you say.

Mr. Schachter:

Essentially you do not regard yourself as an organization to bring about compliance with decisions of other international organizations?

Mr. Nurick:

It is not a matter of bringing about compliance, it is a matter of seeing that if we finance a project it is a sound project. I can give you another example. We cooperate very closely with UNESCO on education projects and with FAO on agricultural projects. That does not mean that we incorporate the FAO standards or the UNESCO standards in our agreement, but when we are finished with a project in those fields presumably both FAO and UNESCO are satisfied that their own standards have been adequately taken into account.

Let me say very briefly what we do, and in this respect I would like to distinguish the Bank from the Fund. The Charter of the Bank does not provide for our being a regulatory agency. We are supposed to make loans for productive purposes and there are certain Charter injunctions: for example, we cannot tie our money to be spent in a particular country. But aside from these very broad expressions of policy, most of the policies of the Bank are decided by what the Bank itself regards as the proper way of running the institution. I should mention that, at Bretton Woods, one of the difficult problems as far as the Bank was concerned was what to call the institution. There was considerable feeling that the word bank was not a good one as not being properly descriptive, and I have some sympathy for that. It is certainly not a bank in the normal sense—it is not a commercial bank, not a central bank; it is more like an investment bank but it is much more than an investment bank. Another interesting aspect of this is the fact the Bank has operated in a way completely different than was envisaged at Bretton Woods. There the whole emphasis was on the guaranty power of the Bank, in other words, it was felt that the Bank would guarantee loans made by private persons and that is what the Federal Housing Administration does in the U.S. It was felt that this was how the Bank would operate; in fact the Bank has never done it, not once.

There are other examples of how the Bank has, like other Specialized Agencies, evolved from the conception of its founders. The Charter of the Bank, unlike those of most of the international organizations, is not particularly restrictive, it provides the way in which the Bank gets its money, gives the Bank certain powers and provides that the Bank can do or cannot do certain things. From there we take it on ourselves. The first inquiry that the Bank makes before it grants a loan is what you might call the "country inquiry". Before we make any loan we will take a look at the economic situation of the country, to see what its resources are, what its priorities are, how much debt it has, how it has responded to obligations in the past, what it is capable of doing and what its problems are. That kind of a study is largely carried out by economists on our own staff or other whom we recruit especially for that purpose. They will spend some time in the country and then they will write a report; that report will be a general economic report about the country, a survey of the country, it will lay down certain guidelines as to where they think development is required and where not and will indicate priorities. For example, the report may say that more emphasis should be put on agriculture and transportation rather than on industry and communications. After that research, the next process is investigation of a particular project. Let us assume that the general economic report is finished, and the country says to the Bank, fine, you are saying we need a railroad or we need a utility, we now want to submit an application for a loan for that project.

Mr. Stevenson:

This economic report is prepared by the staff. But in essence it is a suggestion of economic policy to the country. Is the report adopted by the Executive Directors before it goes to the country?

Mr. Nurick:

No, but I should add that the whole question of the relationship of the Bank's staff, of the Bank's management or the Secretariat, and the Executive Directors is a very complicated question, as I am sure it is in all international organizations. The point is that the proposals for a loan come from the President to the Directors. The Directors can approve or disapprove it. The Directors are responsible for the policy of the Bank. But the President is responsible for submitting proposals to the Directors. It is of course more complicated than that. The reports are circulated to the Directors for their information, and the Directors make comments on them.

461

Professor Stein:

Can the Board overrule the President on the question of submission of projects?

Mr. Nurick:

Well, here is an example. Suppose a country comes to the Bank and says we want to build a railroad, we regard this railroad as very important to our economy. The President looks at it and says, no, we think it is not important for one reason or another and we do not want to finance it. Normally that is the end of the matter.

Mr. Stevenson:

Suppose the economic report says you have to make these changes in your fiscal policy and you have to make these changes in your liquidity policy, and suppose these changes are not made?

Mr. Nurick:

I was coming to that, first of all the report does not usually say: you have to do this or that. The question Mr. Stevenson raises will only come up at the time that the Bank considers whether to embark on a lending program in that country. You may have a country that for one reason or another is so badly run that the Bank may feel that it cannot give a loan to that country at all.

Early in its history, the Bank adopted a policy of not making loans to a country which had defaulted on its external obligations or which had expropriated property without making compensation, unless it was taking adequate steps to take care of the matter. This long preceded what in the United States is called the Hickenlooper amendment, although it is similar. As a corollary, the Bank would say, if you do pay those debts then we will consider putting your country back on the list of countries to whom we consider granting loans.

The Bank—and this is more like the Fund—when it finishes this general economic survey will try to draw up a set of principles which it would like the country to follow. However, in some cases, it may not do this at all. It may simply say that we made this survey, there are many things wrong with this country, nevertheless we are willing to make a loan for a particular project in a particular industry. In that case our attention will not be directed to the country as a whole but to that particular sector. Suppose we have made this general survey, and we find that the country needs more electric power, we therefore want to consider making a loan for a hydro-electric facility in a country. At that point, we look at that project and we see whether it meets certain standards but here I use the word standards in a rather different way from the way it was mentioned before. Over the years we have established certain standards to guide ourselves in determining whether a utility project is a viable one

462

or not, for example, whether or not a project will earn a certain rate of return on invested capital. And if it does not, we say this is an uneconomic use of a country's resources and they should spend their money doing something else. That happens rather frequently.

Then we have a different group of technicians go and take a look at that electric project and they will write a report on it. That report will say: for us now to make a loan you must agree to raise your rates or you must agree to hire a competent manager or you must agree not to incur a certain amount of debt in relation to assets and so forth. As you see, it is a combination of the sort of thing that you might find in a trust indenture plus things that we put in for purely developmental purposes, like the rate of return.

The way that the Bank takes care of a particular problem depends a great deal on the country itself. Now we have countries that have become too rich for us. We are practically out of business in Europe; Australia and Japan are infrequent borrowers. Once you leave these and a few other countries, the administration in many other countries is such that our problems become more difficult. We have to use more technical assistance facilities in less developed countries than we would otherwise.

Mr. Stevenson:

With respect to general economic policy, do you normally go ahead simply on the basis of an understanding that certain changes will be made? Or do you wait until the government has in fact taken certain measures which indicate that the program will be carried out?

Mr. Nurick:

In most cases we will, as far as general economic questions are concerned, go ahead without any formal understanding. We don't often get a formal understanding on general economic questions. We do get letters of representation from them and we will agree with them that there are certain steps they should take and we also agree with them as to the timing. But these are not generally formal legal undertakings, but we do expect compliance. I think as far as general economic questions are concerned, we are less formal than the Fund. On the other hand, we are far more formal and far more legal when start writing agreements about particular projects.

SANCTIONS OF THE WORLD BANK

Mr. Stevenson:

But if in fact they do not comply with their representations when they come for a loan for the second time do you hesitate?

463

Mr. Nurick:

Well, then of course you get to the question of sanctions. There has been much talk during the last few days about the way in which international organizations prefer not to use their heavy weapons to secure compliance. This is certainly true with us too. We have very heavy weapons in our agreements; one of them is a clause that we call the prematurity clause. If there is a default in an agreement, we have the right to premature a loan, which means that the entire principal amount of the loan becomes due. We have never done that. And I think that it is unlikely that we will, except to protect ourselves in case of bankruptcy of a private corporation or reorganization of a public company. But we do have other weapons, and one of them is a very important one: we have the right to suspend further payments on a loan. This is a way in which we do use sanctions. We do cancel portions of loans, or suspend payments on loans; not very often, but on occasion.

Professor Sohn:

Are sanctions limited to the project itself? If the country does not comply with your suggestions about the direction of its general economic development, for instance, with respect to building something in addition to what you gave them money for, would you not apply sanctions for such a reason?

Mr. Nurick:

The Bank is changing its policies in some respects now. Let us suppose we were to finance a road: in financing it, we say that the road must meet certain standards in order to accommodate the traffic. Now, our road people say, what is the point of requiring that road to be maintained properly, if all the other roads in the country are not maintained properly? So the road people in the Bank will try to write into the agreement provisions which will require the country to maintain all the roads. Now there you get to the question of how far you can go and write an agreement which says in effect that you have to maintain every road in your country according to certain standards in order to get a loan from the Bank.

Here again it depends on the relation of what we are doing to the situation of the country in general. If the road is just a small segment of a country's road system, we are not likely to require such an arrangement. If it is a large loan for a large highway and if we expect to make more of those loans, we may well put in a provision to say that all the roads will have to be maintained properly. If that covenant were violated, then there could be a sanction but it would only apply to that particular loan, although we could always refuse to make additional loans—a powerful sanction in itself.

There is also an ultimate sanction: a provision in the Charter which says that, if a country violates its obligations to the Bank, the Bank can expel the country from membership. This is not written into our agreements but I think that if a country did violate its obligations to the Bank, the Bank could expel a country from membership. The only time we have expelled a member was in the case of Czechoslovakia. This was not because of a violation of a payment or other obligation due under a loan but because Czechoslovakia failed to pay the Bank a subscription payment on account of her membership. We expelled her and so did the Fund.

Mr. Lauterpacht:

You did say that it is very rare to get a formal understanding on general economic questions, that is, implying that occasionally you have. Has anybody ever fallen down on one of those formal understandings on general economic questions?

Mr. Nurick:

I can't be very specific as to that. I should point out, however, that the lawyers in the Bank try to handle these problems and write agreements in such a way that both we and our borrowers know when there is a legal obligation involved. If there is a violation of a legal obligation, then under our agreements we can suspend disbursements or cancel the undisbursed balance of the loan. On the other hand, it may be that we have a general understanding on economic policy without there being a legal obligation.

Let me give you an example. When we made a loan for the Volta project in Ghana, we assumed that the Ghanaian economic policies would follow a certain course. In fact the policies turned out to be different from what we had anticipated. I refer in particular to the incurring of foreign debt in amounts which have proved to be too heavy a burden for the country to sustain. Yet I would not say that this involved a violation of any legal obligation to the Bank.

Professor Sohn:

You continued to pay the loan?

Mr. Nurick:

Yes, and, as a matter of fact, and this is interesting, the Volta project went along without any difficulty at all. I know of no big project in the Bank which had fewer problems once we reached agreement.

Mr. Stevenson:

As far as general economic policy is concerned then, the real sanction is the continuing accessibility of the Bank for further financing. You have never used one of these clauses whereby you can suspend payments because circumstances make it unlikely that the loan will be paid in order to suspend payment on the basis of failure to follow a general economic policy. Does it have to be because of a more specific covenant?

465

Mr. Nurick:

The language you cite is a clause common to all the international banks and national ones too, probably. But I can't recall any case where we have ever used that clause to suspend a loan because of failure to live up to an agreement relating to general economic policies; it has always been, as far as I remember, in relation to action or non-action on a specific project, although of course that situation might change.

Mr. Golsong:

I see in Mr. Nurick's paper and it is quite obvious that the Bank is an intergovernmental institution; yet it must conduct its business in a business-like way in order to get money for its loans. Now, I wonder whether Mr. Nurick can tell us whether these two different basic principles have ever led to difficulties of interpretation of the Articles of Agreement? Furthermore, what is the policy of the Bank concerning disposition of the profits?

Mr. Nurick:

On the first question, the answer is yes; questions like that have not arisen lately but they came up particularly when the Bank borrowed money for the first time. The bankers wanted us to interpret our Articles of Agreement to take care of certain problems. The way in which we could borrow, at least the only way we could borrow 20 years ago, was to use as backing for the bonds, not our loans because we had not made any loans yet, but the unpaid portions of our subscriptions of our member countries. When a country joins the Bank, it pays in a relatively small part of this subscription; the rest of it is not called, and can only be called in order to pay our own debts. Now the bankers wanted to be sure that that uncalled subscription money would be available to pay the debts if it was necessary to call on it. In those days, we were particularly interested in the U.S. portion of the subscription because Europe had not yet recovered from the war. Our Charter is silent as to the way in which the Bank can call these unpaid subscriptions, if it has to make a call to meet its debts. The bankers and their lawyers asked, first, whether or not the Bank had an obligation to make a call on an unpaid portion; secondly, what would happen if on the call one country defaulted, would that in any way affect the obligation of the other countries? There was a series of questions like that, and what we did was to submit certain questions of interpretation to our directors under our interpretation powers. There were certain questions and certain answers. The answers were, yes, that we did have an obligation to make a call if we needed money to pay our debts; and that if a member defaulted on a call, that would not excuse another member from paying the amount of its subscription.

Let me give an example. Suppose we owe a 100 million dollars. We make a call—we have to make it in proportion to the capital stock of sub-

466

scriptions of member countries—and the response is 50 million dollars. We are then obligated to make another call for 50 until we get all of the 100. In making the second call all countries including the countries that have responded to the first call must again respond on the second call, and so on.

On the question of the use of our profits: we have large profits, I think this year our profits were about 175 million dollars, and our reserves total about a billion dollars. But again these figures are misleading. It is not money that we give back to member shareholders as dividends; we have never paid dividends. What we have done is to pay a portion of our profits during the last three years to the International Development Association, which is our "soft-loan" affiliate. That is the organization which has been set up to make loans to countries which cannot afford bankable loans.

Mr. Golsong:
But the IDA has not the same membership?

Mr. Nurick:
No, not exactly the same membership but almost the same. During the last three years we have paid 75 million dollars each year to the IDA. Most of the rest of the reserves is purely a bookkeeping item in a sense, since it is money that we use in our business; we keep on lending it.

Until the last few years, the Bank had all the money it needed simply because it could borrow all it needed. But we cannot borrow unless the country we borrow from gives us permission to do so and that means that if we want to borrow in the United States, we have to get the permission of the Secretary of the Treasury. He has problems of his own—balance of payments problems—and we cannot get the permission as easily now as we could. Secondly, we borrow from any place where we can lay our hands on money at a reasonable price. We would like to borrow in Europe but in Europe too the interest rates are high and again we get into the question of permission. We cannot assume, as we used to assume, that we have unlimited sources of funds.

PRACTICE OF THE INTERNATIONAL MONETARY FUND

Mr. Gold:
I should like to make a number of points as a result of the discussion so far. They will refer to aspects of the Fund's practice. First, I need only repeat that the financial assistance of the Fund is for general balance of payments purposes and therefore resources are put up for the support of general policies and not for particular projects.

My second point is this—and this does flow from the fact that the Fund is a regulatory agency as well as a financial institution. Mr. Nurick made

467

the point that the IBRD tends to report on countries only or mainly on occasions when a loan is imminent or envisaged. Now, in the Fund this is not true. In fact the reverse may be true, that is to say on the occasion of financial operations there may be no report other than a very brief paper recommending the approval of the proposed transaction. The reason is that, as a regulatory agency, we have periodic reports whether or not any financial operations are in view. These annual reports are, as I said in my paper, made under certain provisions but the jurisdictional foundation supports an enormous weight. Each year every country is the subject of a very far-ranging discussion and assessment of its general economic position, and a final judgment of the country is made under Article XIV. This report may of course be the background paper during the course of the year if a financial operation is entered into. In that case the paper will be brought up-to-date.

I would like to say a little bit more about the subject of financial reports, the examination of them, and judgments based on them. These become more and more a feature of the financial world. It has become a pat expression to describe the process as multi-lateral surveillance. Countries either in the large context of the Fund or in smaller groups regard it as a very important privilege to be able to comment on each other's economic affairs. The Fund was a pioneer in this field because it had explicit jurisdiction and authority to conduct these examinations, but they now proliferate in other institutions and other groupings. Let me give you a few examples. Working Party Number 3 of the OECD conducts this same sort of examination in a smaller conclave of industrialized countries. The General Arrangements to Borrow is a giant stand-by under which the ten richest members of the Fund have promised to lend resources to supplement the Fund's own resources to conduct operations with these ten members. The ten countries wanted an opportunity to discuss the policies of the country for which the money would be lent to the Fund before finally agreeing to meet a call under the General Arrangements. They have therefore established special procedures for consultation among themselves and with Fund representatives on these occasions.

Then there are consortia which are springing up on all sides in the financial world. The Fund and IBRD have understandings under which consortia are conducted, sometimes for the purpose of rescheduling debts and sometimes for general financing purposes. The Fund or the Bank act as the sponsor or the chairman of these consortia, and lenders will join with the international institutions in order to decide what would be a rational financial arrangement for the country.

All of these procedures tend to produce what has been called common standards of financial and economic behavior. Obviously, with the inter-relationship of international organizations and informal groups, there will be progress toward generally accepted principles of sound economic and financial behavior.

468

Let me pass to another point which again relates to the generalization of standards. I would like to say something about the original intention of the Bretton Woods Conference for the economic organization of the world. The original purpose was of course that there would be a trinity of organizations: the Bank to take care of the capital needs and development, the Fund to take care of currencies and the balance of payments, and a trade organization. The intention to have a trade organization alongside the balance of payments and currency institution resulted from the fact that countries can usually conduct the very same economic policies both by the trade route or by the currency route. For example, what a country can do by tariffs it can do by multiple currency practices. The choice will often depend on the capacity of the national administration to employ one technique rather than the other. It was necessary to have two organizations with complementary jurisdiction. But of course the world trade organization did not come into being, and therefore less ambitious arrangements were made. There remained, however, the question of similar standards for GATT and the Fund in their respective spheres. Naturally arrangements were made between the Contracting Parties and the Fund that were intended to ensure that similar standards would be applied and that financial and economic judgments in the two fields would be the same. This, of course, is valid only for the common members of the Fund and GATT and raises the really fascinating legal problem of non-members of the Fund that are members of GATT. I hope to be writing something about the interesting techniques that are written into GATT on the obligations of non-members of the Fund to sign a special exchange agreement by which they agree to abide by the standards of the Fund without actually being a member of the Fund or enjoying its privileges.

I would like next to comment on a question and the reply by Mr. Nurick on one of the Bank's practices under its loan agreements. I have tried to show how extremely cautious we are that stand-by arrangements should be very precise and objective about the circumstances in which a member can itself recognize that resources will no longer be available so that it will never be taken by surprise. But this was not always so. There was a time when the protection of the Fund's resources was given too great a weight in the balance sought between assurance to the Fund of the proper use of its resources and assurance to members that resources were available so that they were able to pursue their policies with that assumption. It became the practice to write into all stand-by arrangements what was called a "prior notice clause" which said that, if at any time the Fund gave notice, the member could no longer utilize its privilege under the stand-by arrangements. After a while they provoked resistance, with the result that the clause was abandoned, and never used again. It has enhanced the caution with which the objective criteria that I have mentioned, as conditions of the use of resources, are drafted. They are carefully scrutinized to see that they are truly objective and do not involve the kind of subjective judgment on the part of the Fund that was involved in the prior notice clause.

I want now to say something about the use of Fund income. The Fund has large reserves although not as large as the IBRD's, but they are sizeable and growing. The Fund has the power to make a preferential distribution of net income to those countries whose currency subscriptions are used on a net basis to provide financial assistance to other countries; let us call them "creditor countries". The Fund could make a preferential distribution to them of up to 2 per cent from the net income of each year, but has not done so. We have retained our net income, so that in fact it enhances our resources; they supplement the currency and gold we hold for our operations. The Fund has induced countries to believe that their privileges to use the Fund up to the amount by which they are creditors is a secure and virtually automatic right. The Fund has convinced members that these privileges are an asset that can be included in their balance sheet of national reserves. This asset is referred to as gold tranche rights, the rights to draw on a virtually automatic basis an amount equivalent to the gold subscription and amount of credit members have given through the Fund. There is no need to go into details now, but during the last five years the question of the creation of a further new asset which can be distributed to member countries has arisen. The size of gold tranches depends on the existence of deficits on the part of member countries. A member country that has a deficit comes to the Fund, which will sell it the currency of another member. The currency of A is sold to B and A gets an asset position in the Fund. Since the creation of that asset depends on the existence of deficits, its addition to world reserves is fortuitous. For a number of reasons, the world has come to the conclusion that it is a good thing to organize the volume of international reserves rationally, to do so by a deliberative act of creation. Accordingly, the ten major financial member countries have decided on the outline of an agreement under which a facility would be established in the Fund by which the world could in future create and distribute reserve assets. The new asset could well carry interest, and it seems almost certain therefore as a result that the other Fund asset, the gold tranche, will also have to carry interest. The Executive Directors will probably recommend that hereafter interest be paid, probably at the same rate on the gold tranche as on the future new asset.

In the past, the question of the distribution of the Fund's net income has resulted in great differences of opinion between the creditor and the debtor countries. Now, even the debtor countries recognize the inevitability of this and the logic of not creating arbitrary distinctions among reserve assets in the Fund. I must also add that many of the former debtor countries have become creditor countries. The Fund has generalized the use of its currencies and instead of dealing largely in U.S. dollars, it deals in about 20 currencies and the list is growing.

FINANCIAL CONSORTIA

Mr. Elkin:

You threw the meeting open to the discussion of the question as to whether the Bank through its loan transactions can produce any common standards. We know now what happens in the individual loan transaction and in relation to the economic policy of the borrower. Perhaps what has not been quite fully explained is the role of consortia which Mr. Gold has mentioned. If I remember rightly, the IMF is a member of the Turkish and the Greek consortia which bodies representing Governments and intergovernmental organizations try to help a country along specific lines, taking into account certain economic policies which they discuss with Turkey and Greece. I would be very grateful for an elucidation of the question whether the fact that the IMF is a member of the consortium in any way expands that notion of continuity of availability of loans to which you, Mr. Chairman, referred—whether the real sanction is that the country concerned will not obtain any more loans because of her economic policy.

The other point concerned reporting. I am sure that Mr. Gold, when he said that the IMF was a pioneer as regards these economic policy reports, meant on a world scale. The original, of course, is the Marshall Plan. Originally they were reports of the recipient countries on use of Marshall aid to the OEEC. This is the sort of technique which I think is not necessarily limited to financial or economic policy. It can be used in many other organizations—in particular, as the examination or the "cross-examination" technique. What happens is that the OECD Secretariat prepares a draft report for the annual review of a specific country, taking into account also the recommendations of the OECD or the IMF. Another country not a party is appointed as an "examiner." The reports are then discussed in a committee, and the examining country asks questions. The "examinee" has the right to refuse to reply, but in fact, in my experience, that right is exercised in a few cases for security reasons; normally speaking, countries reply. You would expect the reports to be rather colorless as a result of that kind of procedure. In fact they are not, judging by the comments in the financial and economic press. The significance of these multi-lateral exercises lies also partly in the process of the discussion of the draft report in the committee by government representatives. So there is an element of "surveillance" in it. It is interesting to contrast this procedure with another report which economists and financial people find useful. It is the report of the Executive Secretary of the United Nations Economic Commission for Europe. He, too, produces an annual report partly on the same countries, and he does this entirely on his own responsibility. But he has often got into hot water for doing so because his reports are more controversial.

I hope that Mr. Nurick will say a word about Turkey and Greece and also in this connection tell us about differences that he sees between his organization and the European Investment Bank, which, on a smaller scale, is there to help the less developed regions within the member countries.

Mr. Nurick:

About Mr. Elkin's question on consortia, the word is relatively new and I would like to add another: one is consortia and the other the so-called consultative group. They have become increasingly popular and my own feeling is that in the future they will probably be the way in which a good deal of development is channeled.

The Bank participates in about a dozen of them. It is a member of the ones you mentioned, those concerning Greece and Turkey. Those, I think, are chaired by OECD. The word consortia has come to mean something different from consultative group. A consortium is a group of countries which sit together and examine the development plans of a country; they then expect to end up agreeing to finance a certain portion of the development needs of that country. Consultative groups are somewhat more informal and they do not have what they call pledging sessions. I think probably the most important of these has been the Indian consortium. This is a fairly old one and is chaired by the Bank. It is most important because it involves India which is such a tremendous problem all by itself. They do basically two things: one is, as Mr. Elkin said, to examine the plans of a country and comment on them and prepare reports. As far as the secretariat is involved, it may have the duty of assembling the information and possibly commenting critically on it, which is what the Bank does. The role of the chairman of these consortia varies, some do this and others do not. This is one of the more important things the Bank does when it acts as chairman, namely, in the case of India, getting the information, analyzing the plans, making judgments as to what it thinks about the plans and then concluding, hopefully, with a joint agreement among the members of the consortium and the country concerned as to how the plan can be implemented and how much money will be forthcoming from the different members. I may say that in regard to India, we have just done something which is unique in our own experience. The Indian debt situation is very serious, and has been serious for a long time. We have been working with the members of the consortium on a plan to try and settle in some way India's debt problems. What we have done is to take 50 million dollars that we are to receive this year from India and put it into a special account with the reserve bank of India so that the foreign exchange will still be available to India. In other words we are taking money they pay us on loans and are depositing it with another agency of the Indian Government, so that that foreign exchange will not be lost by India. This is a short term arrangement—in banking terms, it is an interest-bearing, time deposit-account. And the idea is that the consortium will agree on more permanent arrangements whenever it can.

472

Mr. Arnold:

What Mr. Nurick has said on the World Bank applies in general terms also to the IDB. But there are some points where I would like to draw a comparison.

First of all, I would like to say that, in my recollection, the guarantee power of the International Bank was thought of as being one of the primary means of its operation. It has to be said that this expectation was immediately disappointed, because neither the World Bank nor the IDB has found it desirable or even feasible to guarantee loans.

I think it is rather significant that the term management is used for the "secretariat" in the World Bank. The same term is now used in the IDB; it does imply that the executive branch has a considerable importance in the institution. It might be of interest to add, however, that the power of management of the World Bank not to submit proposals to directors was carefully observed by the Latin American representatives when drafting the charter of the IDB. They did provide that the Board of Directors might request a proposal to be submitted but so far the power has never been exercised. I do want to stress that the relationship between the management and the Board of Directors in the Bank is very close. Moreover, the financial institutions do not interpret their charters strictly; convenient practice has evolved against the background of the charter. Naturally, no institution can be stronger than what its constituency is willing to support. The IDB follows nearly all the principles that Mr. Nurick mentioned, though they may not be applied with quite the same determination as in the World Bank. By saying this, I do not want to indicate that our institution is loosely run; I do not think it is. Nevertheless there may be some difference of atmosphere. I believe this will be interesting to observe as the African and Asian banks develop because the African Bank has no creditor nations and the Asian Bank has a very substantial sprinkle of them. For an example of the kind of thing I have in mind, our Bank has exactly the same policy on countries not paying debts promptly. On the other hand, expropriation matters are delicate. We have no graduate members as does the World Bank, all our borrowers are still borrowers.

We do try to pay a great deal of attention to disbursement and to working with the borrower country as it draws funds. We have not formally suspended loans but we have let it be known from time to time that we expect that something should be done before further funds could be received, and again this is an example of the technique of not working rigidly. You work flexibly and according to what judgment produces the best result without undue strain. But I do stress that we have a very great interest in this matter, our contracts typically contain an extraordinary circumstances clause, and we have not hesitated to mention that these clauses are in the contracts.

On the question of callable capital, we are in a similar position to the World Bank. In fact, we are in a more restrictive position because we agreed in our first borrowing to a limit which will be effective for a long time, if not forever after, to an amount not in excess of the subscription of the United States. This means that about two-thirds of our callable capital is really of no significance in our borrowing and will not be so for many years. I can only mention the position the African Bank is in, which has no callable capital at all and which has very great difficulty in raising any money in normal markets; it has to rely on government loans.

On the question of profits, we are still engaged in building up our reserves to make our position more attractive to lenders, though we have always obtained funds on very favorable terms.

I would like to comment on standards in relation to other organizations: we do follow the standards of other organizations in the sense of physical standards, for example we keep up very close consultation with the Pan American Health Organization on water supply and sewerage loans.

Like the World Bank, we do not pay direct attention to social standards. However, there is an interesting development in the field of general performance of member governments. This is always a delicate topic in our Bank. Naturally we strive to ensure that our member governments should improve their general performance but we cannot really insist on it. Now there is the Inter-American Committee for the Alliance for Progress (C.I.A.P.) set up as part of the OAS, which is supposed to review the progress of the members of that system. Their findings will unquestionably be of great interest to the IDB.

On the other hand, like the IBRD and the Fund, we insist on independence in our own final judgments.

Mr. Dobbert:

About the consortia: Mr. Nurick said that one was presided over by OECD and the other by the Bank but then he mentioned individual countries not only a subject of inquiry but, also, as sitting on the consortia. I am not entirely clear on the composition of these consortia: does their membership comprise governments or only interested international organizations that contribute basic information in the economic field or participate in financing? Are they mainly deliberative, the action then being taken individually by each of the participating countries and organizations, or are there joint decisions which in a way bind the members, member organizations and/or member countries?

Mr. Nurick:

In a legal sense, they are informal, they do not bind anybody. What they do end up with is a statement by the government representative regarding the government's intention to finance this or that project with a certain amount of money. Now at that point they may still have to go through their own legal processes to get that done.

Professor Stein:
Is there an instrument signed by the members of a consortium?

Mr. Nurick:
No. The composition of these consortia, at least the ones I am familiar with, include both governments and international organizations, but the composition changes. The Indian consortium, for example, consists only of the Bank, the IDA and member governments. The Turkish one is broader, it consists of governments, OECD and other international organizations. The country itself is not regarded as a member of the consortium.

Mr. Gold:
There are also debt reorganization arrangements. These consortia are not devoting themselves exclusively to raising new money. They are increasingly taking on other duties connected with the rescheduling of existing debts.

THE UNITED NATIONS DEVELOPMENT PROGRAM, UNCTAD AND REGIONAL COMMISSIONS

Mr. Schachter:
We would be incomplete if we did not mention at least another active participant in the U.N., which is very much involved in the same sort of thing. It is the largest section of the U.N. (in terms of personnel) which is concerned with the kind of problems involved in capital assistance and related matters. In the U.N. there is on the one side the roughly 100 million dollar U.N. Development Program now projected to 300 million dollars within the next few years. This involves a good many of so-called pre-investment grants, which in one way or another tie in with a bank or private investment development.

Secondly, the U.N. has the same sort of role that Mr. Gold referred to as multi-lateral surveillance. Many U.N. missions cover the same area as the Bank and the Fund, but with different groups in the government. This leads in many cases to a complaint of too many missions. On the other hand, the duplication involves an element of competition which may have some useful effects in the opinion of many people. This is a subject which has been given a good deal of attention by those concerned.

Thirdly, is the fact that in a great many ways, the U.N. machine operates as a pressure group or as a series of pressure groups directed towards lending or other types of financial institutions. This happens either through U.N. committees or bodies criticizing the Bank and the Fund and being answered, or probably more significantly, through joint committees which often involve people from the financial community who take part in the Bank and Fund also. For example, the U.N. has had committees on liquidity and on compensatory financing for short-term balance of payment deficits. I would guess that there have probably been about 50 such groups operating within the last few years which move in and around the subject matter covered by the IBRD and the IMF. So you have another interest group, largely of course representing the poor countries. It is a pressure group more than anything else, and some of the other U.N. organizations like UNCTAD and some of its subsidiary bodies are particularly active in that kind of activity. This is an important element in seeing how complex this whole picture has become today. Mr. Elkin mentioned the regional commissions. It is not only the ECE which has a role in this but the under-developed countries regional commissions. Economic Commission for Latin America personnel have pointed to changes which they have initiated or instituted in some of the economic fields. The Commission for Africa and Asia continue to push on these fronts. They are all part of the scene of the financial institutions.

MORE ON FINANCIAL INSTITUTIONS

Mr. Stevenson:

Before leaving the area of financial institutions, we have one area we have not touched upon which was mentioned in two papers that stressed the success of informal methods as far as relationship with members is concerned. This is the internal legal effect of their decisions. There has been a great deal of resort to judicial decisions (resort may have been made by counsel for private parties) with respect to interpretation of the Fund and World Bank agreements. So in this area at least there has been a use of formal procedures.

The question that I have in that connection is whether the power of the Bank and the Fund to interpret their constituent agreements is non-reviewable. Has this ever been questioned? In the one court decision which Mr. Nurick mentioned, the court did indicate that, if the interpretation had amounted in its opinion to an amendment of the agreement, it might not have given effect to it. I wonder if this is something you could briefly comment on.

Mr. Gold:

The Fund's power to interpret its Articles is a final power. The United States has indicated its view that that interpretation cannot be reviewed

476

by U.S. Courts. This leads to the interesting question of the review interpretations inside the institution.

Mr. Nurick:

I think that this case is of the most interesting ones in this whole field in the U.S. and I must say I have been surprised that not more attention has been paid to it; it is a very valuable case in a sense, because what it does is to say that an interpretation by an international body with interpretative powers is binding on a U.S. court as against private persons. And that is really what the Federal Communications Commission did. Not only that, but the interpretation was made after the law suit was brought. The interpretation answered the law suit, answered the point made in the complaint of the Bank and that was regarded by the Commission sitting as a court as final. Constitutional questions and others were raised, and the FCC wrote a very long opinion dealing with them.

Professor Sohn:

Are people upset by the case, because the Bank and the Fund judged in their own cause? The thought is rather uncomfortable.

Mr. Nurick:

I am sure that we will be careful in cases of this kind. The other interpretations we made were interpretations of the powers of the Bank as between itself and members but they do not affect private persons.

Professor Stein:

May I add for the purpose of completeness as far as financial organizations are concerned that there are two important bodies on the European continent: the European Investment Bank, which is organized in the image of the International Bank, and the European Development Fund used for financing development in the associated African countries.

Mr. Nurick:

My own experience has been that the EIB concentrates much more on the financial aspect of a project. Their agreements are much more like those of a private commercial bank. They are not particularly interested in general economic problems of a country; nor are they particularly interested in the general economic aspects of particular projects. They are more interested in getting paid back and in getting security; in that sense they are tougher than we are.

Professor Sohn:

One point Mr. Schachter raised indirectly relates to the relationship between the U.N. and the regional organizations. The unfortunate fact is that the Specialized Agencies are closely connected to the U.N. by various provisions of the Charter but there is no effective provision in the Charter, nor has any procedure been really developed in practice, for bringing the regional organizations more or less to the same level.

Mr. Elkin:

I believe that one notable difference between the EIB and the World Bank is that the loans of the European Investment Bank are governed by the law of the borrower—for example, Italian law—while in the World Bank they are governed by international law.

Mr. Gold:

I should like to say in connection with informality, the avoidance of formal sanctions and voting, and the evolution of new techniques, that I did not want to give the impression that the Fund feels it has free hand. There are legal limits to this flexibility.

A second comment I would make is that, as Professor Sohn has said, distinctions can be made among decisions. Decisions with respect to the obligations of the Articles and their interpretation can be distinguished from decisions laying down policies. In addition, there are decisions with respect to bilateral financial relations. Much of the enforcement mechanism of the Fund works through its financial operations.

I should like to comment on some aspects of compliance with obligations. These comments I base on the Fund's experience. First, the Fund tends to have a much more patient attitude towards a member violating its obligations if it remains in close contact with the Fund and tries to work toward compliance.

Secondly, I have noted the mention here of a principle of reciprocity in the observance of obligations, a principle whereby the other parties can police obligations by retaliating. I would like to say very firmly that is not the case in the Fund. We take the view that there must be an objective monetary order, an international order established by the Fund. Breach of an obligation does not entitle the other countries to retaliate. The best example is the case of France which adopted an unauthorized par value in 1948. The Fund then said that although the old par value was no longer legally binding, other members could not establish their own rates of exchange in connection with the franc. They would have to come to the Fund to agree on rates of exchange between their currency and the franc and the Fund gave advance approval if they would base the rate on the unauthorized change of the par value made by France. This was done in order to promote maximum exchange orderliness. Retaliation is not a principle of the organization. My last point is that we have a tendency to regard the obligations of the Articles as legal absolutes. We have resisted efforts to qualify those obligations, for example, by reference to such principles as self-preservation. Similarly, it has been decided that, even though the Fund is an economic institution, a member introducing exchange

478

restrictions for reasons of national or international security is nevertheless subject to the jurisdiction of the Fund and must get its approval under the Articles.

I want to say a few last words on why informality is so marked a feature of the Fund. One is the experience of the earlier years of the Fund in which a more rigid approach, including sanctions, was followed, with less than optimum results. The lesson learned was that collaboration and conviction were better than compulsion.

Another consideration is the need for adaptability in the constantly changing world of monetary matters. Some of the assumption of the Articles about the postwar world were not confirmed, and in many respects we have a very different world. We had to transform the Fund to meet those circumstances, and this has been done on the basis of consensus and without voting; and often without determination that there were legal obligations to act in accordance with the consensus.

COMPLIANCE WITH UNITED NATIONS DECISIONS

Mr. Stevenson:

It seems to me that we ought to devote some more time to the question of the extent to which informal, non-binding techniques which the functional international organizations are utilizing are applicable to the U.N. We could proceed from that to a discussion of a number of the questions raised in Mrs. Higgins' paper. What compliance techniques have been useful and effective in the U.N. as compared with those which have been useful and effective in the functional international organizations? Perhaps by way of contrast, the experience of the EEC should also be taken into account, for this represents in a way the other alternative, that of increasing the legislative and executive competence of the U.N. I think Mrs. Higgins has prepared the only paper which we have before us in this area and I should ask her to lead off this discussion.

Mrs. Higgins:

Most of the questions which I would like to see discussed were laid out in my paper. But we have had the benefit of hearing about the various techniques employed by the various agencies. It does seem appropriate to try and focus these on the U.N. experience, to see just how applicable they are. Basically I suggested in my paper that we could divide the U.N. decisions requiring compliance into four major groups:
(1) internal or housekeeping decisions; there I already suggested the compliance problem is not a very great one;
(2) decisions which set standards;
(3) decisions to control situations which would be incompatible with the obligations of the Charter;

(4) decisions to try to secure change in behavior of states, members or occasionally non-members.

I would like to return to my four clusters of decisions at the U.N. as far as the field of peace and security is concerned. Insofar as internal decisions are concerned, basically there has been no real problem here except for the Article 19 case.

As far as standard setting decisions are concerned, these are, within the U.N. experience, largely done in two major formats, by two major techniques: firstly, the treaty and there one runs immediately into the technical question of the possibility of reservations. One can note here, in contrast with the EEC experience, the growing tendency to omit any reference in adjudication clauses to the International Court of Justice. This is becoming a less and less common practice undoubtedly due to the disparity of views between member states in any of these organizations as to the desirability and the appropriateness of both the composition of the International Court and the role it should play in adjudication. There are also questions as to the number of states required to bring about such an effect in the protocol technique, such as used in one draft Covenant on Human Rights. Secondly, the other major technique in this area is "the declaration". We have already in discussion touched on the question that certain states will make every effort, if at all possible, to join in with declarations and not be isolated. The difficulties are that detailed courses of action are not usually required from such standard setting declarations, which in turn makes it difficult to provide adequate follow-up techniques to see whether compliance is manifest. Yet one can contrast the ease with which such declarations are passed and come to the inability of the General Assembly to pass a substantive resolution on the Arab Israel conflict in June and July of 1967. Here, everyone knew that compliance was going to be a very real, a very immediate, issue, and consequently getting a resolution on the books was a very much harder process altogether.

So far as the control of situations is concerned, I would mention specifically orders of requirements to cease-fire, to end hostilities, as good examples for discussion. Here of course, the U.N. positions are usually not taken until it is known that the parties are *ready* to comply, at least to a large degree. This of course is because such decisions are normally taken in the Security Council. Either the big nations are involved themselves or else they have client states or states involved which have a close relationship with them. Of course, this has been a major factor in the last round of fighting in the Middle East, where the cease-fire order only came at a stage when it was known there was some possibility of compliance. This is of course not always true, it is not true when the client relationship is not involved. In the Middle East in 1948 cease-fire orders were passed by the Security Council under Article 40 before there was any reasonable expectation of immediate compliance and the same is true of the Kashmir question, in 1948-1949. The reference to specific Charter authority has been a useful initial technique because it emphasizes community interest, together with, occasionally, the veiled possibility of further action by the Security Council, if compliance is not forthcoming. This occurred both in the order to cease fire in Kashmir in 1965 and in Palestine in 1948. I am interested here in the idea of our carrot-and-stick relationship. The experts within the ILO system perform this dual function, they make the shame by pointing to standards not being complied with, but they also offer technical inducement to the countries concerned—technical assistance—to enable them to reach the standards concerned. I think, within this area, the U.N. has also had some experience in using experts as "carrots", for example, the conciliation committees which have been set up in Kashmir. When the U.N. representative in Kashmir replaced the previous U.N. Commission in India and Pakistan, he drew up lists of points of difference between the two parties and then he worked his way systematically through these points of differences. Eventually they were reduced to a comparatively small list of nine points or so. The use of an expert in the field giving his assistance on a diplomatic level was employed as inducement to comply with resolutions already passed by the Security Council.

In this context, the first requirement was the cease-fire; the second, a plebiscite; and the third, demilitarization. The U.N. representative played a very active role in attempting to secure compliance through technical and diplomatic assistance however unsuccessfully on the second point.

I would like to say a word about peacekeeping as a compliance technique, once a decision has been taken by the Security Council. It does seem that a U.N. peacekeeping or peace observation group can in fact be its own technique for securing compliance. The placing of the U.N. presence in the field is, as such, an element in securing compliance with U.N. decisions. This may be done in respect of the U.N.'s own decision, such as in the case of UNEF in the Middle East in 1956 or even by a decision of parties between themselves which is in conformity with U.N. objectives, either explicitly stated objectives in previous resolution or implicitly stated ones. I had in mind the Karachi agreement which saw the sending of the U.N. military observer group into the field, but its functions in the field were to uphold the cease-fire which the U.N. had required under a previous resolution.

Again the U.N. Truce Supervision Organization in the Middle East had its functions elaborated under the U.N. armistice agreements, which were inter-state arrangements, but in conformity with U.N. objectives. Equally, one can do it by the informal, consensus method, as we have seen the extension recently of UNTSO's functions to the Suez Canal area where no formal vote of the Security Council was taken. Instead there was the interesting method of a suggestion being made by the Secretary General and, after heated debate and opposition in the Security Council, it was actually allowed through without a contrary vote. Paricularly interesting

481

are the quasi-judicial functions which are sometimes given to these peacekeeping and peace observation bodies in the field: the given order to check that compliance is taking place in accordance with a U.N. resolution by which the parties are either bound or on condition of which they agreed to have these U.N. operations in the field. The chief observer of the U.N. military group in India and Pakistan had a very active quasi-judicial function in passing decisions of "compliance" or "non-compliance" with particular charges and so does the chief of staff or his designated representative on the mixed armistice commissions in the Middle East.

I believe that "inherent sanctions" such as those of ICAO and the Bank are inapplicable to the U.N. experience, at least in this sort of decision. As far as the mobilization of shame is concerned, there is of course the technique of notification of a violation to the Security Council or other appropriate organ. This notification of a violation might be done by the parties themselves or perhaps more effectively by the commander or the chief of staff of the operation in the field, or, when hostilities have reached a fairly high level of violence, by the Security Council itself. One has seen all three of these levels in seeking to mobilize shame. It has been carried out, for example, in the Middle East, through the U.N. presence there. But it does give rise to the question of how one balances this mobilization of shame against the advantages to be gained from non-publication of such instances. Kashmir alone of all the areas where the U.N. has been operational in the peacekeeping sense has not had publication of reports, neither from parties about particular claims of violations across the cease-fire line nor by the chief observer who reports back to the Secretary General. The Security Council has, other than with major violations in 1965, had little occasion to pronounce on cease-fire violations. (It has of course passed many resolutions on the questions of the plebiscite and demilitarization.) The period of years over which this operation has been successful in complying with cease-fire provisions does lead one to wonder whether we should not have some discussion of the counter effects of the mobilization of shame technique in terms of recalcitrant positions and counter-charges which may flow from it when you do not have a committee of experts, which the U.N. of course does not have.

Now a few words on the final category of decisions, those which alter behavior patterns of nations. I feel that the U.N. practice has been far from satisfactory in matters of security compliance; it is here of course that the really hard core of non-compliance cases occur. The technique of progressive movement towards achieving compliance in a particular individual state by passing only "general" resolutions and then "specific" ones, has not led to the desired results in terms of compliance. The "carrots" that can be offered when this stage has been reached are essentially within the U.N. system (I am now talking about peace and security matters). They are negative, i.e., the possibility of the full resumption of normal participation in the organization. It is not positive in the way of a loan

482

forthcoming for a project within one's own territory. In the South African case, one has virtually run through the whole range of techniques that can be readily thought of, including committees to investigate initially, then committees to recommend sanctions to be taken if necessary, and individual direct negotiations which Hammarskjöld was engaged in with the South Africans shortly before his death. The facts are that the ultimate sanction—expulsion—requires a Security Council vote, and South Africa has certain protectors, at least insofar as the question of expulsion is concerned; that "naming" her in hostile resolutions had lead to a greater recalcitrance; that expert committees have certainly not been regarded as non-partisan as the ILO ones have; and there has not been the opportunity to mobilize home shame. The Committee of Twenty-Four, even the specific committees which have dealt with South Africa, have not yet been portrayed within South Africa territory as committees of high repute. Given all of these facts, I think, one ought to wonder whether there could have been greater use of the "carrots" side, the inducement side in a positive sense, not just the promise to drop the charges against South Africa but in offering positive advantages in exchange for taking the very difficult step of reorganizing her whole domestic system in accord with an international standard.

Mr. Schachter:

I just have a few points that I think might supplement Mrs. Higgins' comments:

First, your question, Mr. Chairman, was whether the compliance techniques that have been used in the Specialized Agency field and the other organizations are useable in the U.N. I think the simple answer is that all of them except for the judicial enforcement that the Community has, have in fact, been used. For example, the submission and examination of reports technique of the ILO has been used significantly and presumably with success under Article 73 of the Charter with respect to the non-self-governing territories. This did not require a treaty and is based on the Charter. It certainly had its inspiration in the ILO procedures. I think one can go through every one of the points made by the Fund, the Bank and the others, and find in each case appropriate parallels in the U.N. experience where the situations were somewhat similar as in the economic areas.

U.N. CARROTS AND STICKS

Mr. Stevenson:

As far as the "carrot" technique is concerned: is there really as much opportunity as in the Bank and the Fund for the U.N. to offer something positive? And have they really used it?

Mr. Schachter:

Before coming to that, it just occurred to me that, with reference to Mr. Lauterpacht's metaphor of the cookbook, I think the U.N. experience shows that the cookbook is not quite as applicable because generally one does not choose techniques as one does recipes from a cookbook. I think that is too simplified a view in cases of human rights or peace and security or economic matters. The situations are normally so difficult or range over such a large area of cases that one could not just employ a single recipe. The search for the levers of control call for the simultaneous or phased use of many instruments, so that an orchestra rather than a cookbook could be our metaphor.

Secondly, I suggest that, to a large extent, the lawyers are out of that endeavor. I think that their activity is considered, I submit, secondary, peripheral, marginal, by the people who make the decisions about methods of ensuring compliance. It is true that the lawyers properly show concern about the possible effect of general rules and such rules may be referred to in resolutions that are involved to bring about compliance or to condemn violations. However, I would suggest that that really does not make very much difference in effecting compliance. When you sit in the political scene and are evaluating effectiveness of pressures, you do not really worry about resolutions as much as interests and alliances. I do not think that we ought to be unrealistic about this aspect. Power and interest are very much part of the U.N. compliance problem. They did not receive much attention in the Specialized Agencies' discussion because we were concerning ourselves with rather explicit techniques rather then with the political means of achieving the desired results. Just one point where I might make some reservations about what Mrs. Higgins said about inherent or natural sanctions. Contrary to what I think she suggested, I would say that they are the main U.N. sanctions. What I mean is that states generally do not want to get into a war, particularly a nuclear war, and so compliance derives largely from that in cases where the alternative to compliance is the escalation of violence. Also, compliance may be a function of a perceived interest in reciprocity. These are both "natural" sanctions, as I understand that phrase.

Mrs. Higgins:

The agreement between superpowers that they do not want to get into a nuclear situation seems to me to leave a great deal of mobility for the smaller powers not to comply.

Mr. Schachter:

That is a relevant fact. On the other hand, the fear of escalation is an important factor for small powers who do not wish to risk proxy wars.

484

Professor Stein:

There is also a danger that the two superpowers may go beyond the very elementary agreement of avoiding nuclear war—that they agree upon too much and seek to impose their national will and national interest upon the organization. That too would be another danger for the U.N.

Mr. Schachter:

To come to Mr. Stevenson's earlier point about the "carrot-and-stick" procedure, I think he is right in suggesting that there are not enough incentives. This is so because the U.N. in many of the cases—for example, in a case like South Africa— is trying to deal with a problem that is at the very heart of a country's policy so that one cannot think of a monetary incentive as decisive. If the U.N. had all the money of the International Bank, it could not change national policies in that way. On the other hand, I would put much more stress than has previously been put by anybody on the need for incentives and not merely deprivations and threats. We ought in a great many crucial situations see what are the "quid pro quo" that might be worked out to move a situation in the desired way. It is important to see the U.N. problems in terms of carrots as well as of sticks. While the resources of the U.N. are of course less than those of the Fund and the Bank, they extend over a greater range of "resources" in that political agreements could affect all types of assistance.

Mr. Elkin:

A few words about the position of the lawyers, where Mr. Schachter is more skeptical than Mr. Lauterpacht was. I would agree that when it comes to standards in political cases the role of the lawyer is limited. But in the process of unconscious or conscious cerebration in organs of international organizations, I have found that the experience of techniques that a lawyer has at his disposal is of immense value in shaping procedure, in pointing out the necessity of including escape clauses, in institutionalizing decisions. If a president is open to the advice of the legal advisor, considerable influence is exercised by the latter. This is again why our exchange of views is so useful.

Professor Stein:

The U.N. function of legitimation has not been properly explored. If you look at the United States, there is today an intense need for this type of legitimation by the U.N. of what the U.S. has been doing in Vietnam, as at the time of Korea, and yet this legitimation of the Vietnam action is obviously not forthcoming. It is an extremely important function for the U.N. to say that an action is right, and there is an evident relation between what we have said about the mobilization of shame and this legitimation function. Again, I can see clearly the relationship between the legitimation function and the lawmaking function exercised in a series of

485

declarations by, say, the General Assembly, that is, where the United Nations becomes an agent in the making of customary international law through stating or restating or confirming new rules which eventually may be codified in new treaties. Going back to the mobilization of shame function, only a rather narrow élite responds to such things as the ILO statement that a certain national practice is wrong. It is a very small group of people that takes note, it is not really all over the newspapers. On the other hand, certain United Nations resolutions at any rate reach a wider constituency, beyond the small coterie of diplomats and officials.

I would draw a clear distinction between the role and importance of international law and the role and importance of the lawyers. The impact of international law may be quite limited, and I realized this in our investigation of the Test Ban negotiations. On the other hand, in my nine years of experience in U.N. work, I found that there was practically an unlimited scope for a lawyer. He is extremely helpful at any stage of the decision-making machinery. It is the lawyer who can point out a variety of options and say if you draft a resolution this way you will get this result, whereas if you do that, you will get a different result. He would and he should also, of course, point to a policy that is better suited to the long-range interest in the development of the organization. So we do have to make the distinction between the role of the law and the role of a lawyer.

Mr. Schachter:

All I was trying to say was, when it comes to the problem of getting effective action, references to legal texts and standards seem to me to be substantially discounted by the people who make decisions. Of course, there are cases such as the Cuban missile case in which concern was expressed for a solution compatible with legal principles. I was trying to make a different point; I was trying to stress that there is little expectation that the assertion of a resolution or of a provision of the Charter will bring about a change in a difficult situation. Nonetheless, lawyers may still have a significant role in other aspects.

Professor Stein:

We have seen situations where law and lawyers could ruin an organization if they are left too much scope and I think the Coal and Steel Community comes awfully close to that. The political steam which backed that organization has pretty much run out. You had a situation where the policy-making body, the High Authority, felt that it did not have enough support from governments of the member states. Accordingly, it would simply take the position, every time a proposal was made, of calling in the lawyers and asking them: does the Treaty require us to do this, and the lawyers would say, well, now the Treaty says that you can do this but it does not say that it requires you to do it. The High Authority would then say: nothing will be done because the lawyers say we are not obliged to do anything. This is of course an extreme situation and an oversimplification but the lawyers were put into the position of providing an alibi for non-action.

Mr. Nurick:

Mr. Schachter has made an analogy between the techniques of the Bank and Fund and those used by the U.N. and has pointed out that those of the Bank are essentially the same as those which can be found in the U.N. I just would like to explore this a bit further. I think that there is a basic difference in the institutions, but I think there is also a basic difference in the way they go about trying to effect compliance and I think it is a lot easier for the Bank and the Fund to effect compliance for many reasons. They do not operate in an area of publicity, the meetings are not open to the public, there are no political questions involved, and when the Bank and Fund call on their members to take action, they do expect their members to comply and they have every reason to expect that they will. On the other hand the U.N. very often, for political reasons, will adopt resolutions with which they do not expect compliance. Meetings of the U.N. do this fairly regularly. In this area, I think there is a very big difference between the institutions. If this is right, I wonder whether if the adoption of political resolutions does dilute the legal significance of resolutions generally. Can the problem be reduced by reducing the number of resolutions that are passed?

Mr. Schachter:

What is the function of a political resolution? That is the way you have to look at it. They have different functions. They may, for example, support positions among domestic or allied or other groups. Compliance by the target state need not be the only objective. Perhaps the standard-setting function ought to be continued regardless of compliance. I think arguments could be made on both sides. It may be desirable in some cases for the U.N. to continue to pass resolutions on human rights and also on many other subjects, even though the expectancy of effectiveness is rather low. For, in a sense, these resolutions are aiming at a better future by setting goals to be achieved. The situations vary widely and in many cases we would not wish to reduce the value of resolutions by passing those which would be disregarded. Admittedly, that would not be conducive to respect for such resolutions. That is why, as Mrs. Higgins said, the U.N. organs sometimes wish to make sure of compliance before they act.

Mr. Gold:

In the case of the Fund, decisions comparable to these resolutions of the U.N. would be general policy-making decisions, such as declarations against discrimination in payments or complicated multiple currency systems. In making this sort of general declaration, the Fund is careful to avoid premature action. It ascertains that the membership has been convinced of the rightness of the policy. It could endanger international cooperation if the Fund sought to enforce policies not supported by this conviction.

Mr. Schachter:

Would you recommend that for all other cases? And would you not be interposing a substantial block to the development of, let us say, more progressive measures if you impose that requirement in certain fields?

Mr. Gold:

I would not want to generalize from Fund experience, but perhaps the U.N. *should* be more cautious, and perhaps it should not make these general declarations without any real expectation of observance of them.

Mr. Schachter:

I share that view.

Professor Stein:

To what extent can law or a legal instrumentality such as a decision of an international organization be used effectively to change the behavior of states? You really do not conceive of IMF decisions as designed to modify the behavior of states. You try to persuade them.

Mr. Gold:

A lengthy process of talking to states may be involved. It may take years to convince them but I would not reverse the process, adopt a declaration knowing that they might not observe it and then expect the to follow it.

THE ROLE OF LAWYERS AND LEGAL RESOURCEFULNESS

Professor Sohn:

First, one comment on Mr. Schachter's point on the role of lawyers. I think that the most important role of the lawyers in an international organization is to invent new techniques for doing things when old techniques seem to be wearing out, trying to find new ways of doing things better than before, and anticipating problems rather than having to solve them later on. Precautionary, preliminary work is also of the greatest importance. I would say that in some U.N. areas this could be done very well; in others, because of political reasons, it does not work. The peacekeeping system certainly was helped by the lawyers who invented what people call the "Chapter VI and a half" of the Charter. There is much space in the Charter to develop new measures, new ways. If you were to read the reports of the Secretary General on what UNEF accomplished and what the Congo force did, you would see in how many places new departures have been accomplished through new devices. For instance, somebody decided that UNEF and the Congo force are subsidiary organs of the U.N. Therefore, as Egypt had ratified the Convention on Privileges and Immunities of the U.N. which gave the subsidiary organs a certain status, this status was given to the U.N. force as a whole. This is where a lawyer has helped to solve a very important problem very quickly.

But as most people concentrate too much on the political peacekeeping area, it is less known how much the U.N. has accomplished in the other areas. The sociologists and the behavioral scientists might maintain that there is no cause-effect relationship, but certainly the U.N. proved very successful in the area that Mr. Schachter mentioned, colonialism. The only thing the Charter had in Article 73 was a declaration saying that the colonial powers were going to keep their territories, though would consider them as a "sacred trust." If you read the statement by Churchill in Yalta and other statements of the colonial powers, you will find very clearly that they did not mean to give any powers to the U.N. to deal with the problem. They made, however, a little mistake. They agreed at one point that the U.N. could receive some reports on the subject provided they were technical, economic etc. When the first reports were submitted, the U.N. said that they were very interesting and that it should do something about them. It decided to appoint a special committee to discuss them, and the committee first asked for more information, and then it started complaining that it really did not get enough information and that it could not really discuss economic information without relevant political information. It asked, therefore, for the submission of more political information. A few states, such as Denmark, the United States, Australia, and New Zealand surrendered and gave the committee some information and the committee started pressing the others, especially the United Kingdom and France, to give it political information. Here again one of those legal devices helped. Some states stopped submitting information, and the committee said that it had at least the right to decide whether the obligation under the Charter to submit information had ceased and, therefore, it devised a whole list of factors relating to the question when a territory ceases to be non-self-governing.

Then, in connection with the Portuguese territories, the committee devised another list of standards helping it to decide when something is a colony with respect to which a country must submit information. So in this whole area, step by step, the U.N. went further and further. Maybe it was not due to U.N. pressure and its interest in the matter, but the fact is that most colonial territories are now independent or self-governing. The business was aired every year by the U.N. and the special committee pushed the governments. All those things show that we can go so far even on a very limited basis in the Charter. Of course, one day this power under

Article 73 more or less reached its limit and no one knew how to get any further.

Then someone discovered that there was another article of the Charter that spoke about the right of self-determination, and, just out of that one word, like Mr. FitzGerald's "airworthiness," the U.N. again built a whole system about (1) a declaration on what were the rights of self-determination; (2) the bigger declaration on colonialism; (3) a special committee; (4) the right to receive reports; (5) the right to receive petitions; (6) the right to hold hearings; and (7) the right to send visiting missions. All this developed out of one word in the Charter. So when there is the will there is a way for the lawyer. Of course, the lawyer looks at precedent. There was, for instance, a beautiful document compiled on the non-self-governing territories about reporting by the other agencies, and all the agencies submitted reports on how *they* did it—and the committee on information on non-self-governing territories accepted it with pleasure, and started using as many of these devices as possible. So, there was a clear application of techniques of other organizations in the U.N. Of course, one might say this was one-sided, that this applied only in one direction. How about the other areas? We saw a similar development in the general area of human rights, even before the Covenants.

All the way back, in 1956, the U.S.—to everybody's surprise—proposed that a system of periodic reports be started with respect to the Human Rights Declaration. The U.S. was the one that in 1948 had said that the Declaration was not binding. It said that the Declaration did not create obligations and that it did not require any follow-up procedures. France and other countries maintained that the Declaration did create obligations and that they required follow-up procedures. In 1956, when the U.S. decided to get out of covenant drafting, and announced that it would not ratify any new obligations, it was looking around for a substitute and said that the U.N. should at least strengthen the Declaration process. The U.N. proposed periodic reports, the Soviet Union objected a little, but later accepted the idea and then submitted pretty exhaustive reports pointing out the great development in human rights in the Soviet Union. Here again, we started simply with periodic reports, but immediately the next step came, and it was decided that somebody ought to evaluate the reports. The Commission on Human Rights persuaded all the Specialized Agencies to submit papers on how they did it and then established a special committee to evaluate the reports, in a general, objective fashion. Then it decided that government committees were not good enough and that a committee of experts should consider the reports instead. The Commission had already two committees of experts—the Commission on the Rights of Women and the Subcommission on Minorities and Discrimination. The Commission on Human Rights decided that these two committees of experts should do the preliminary sifting. The Commission on the Rights of Women did a very good job, the Subcommission on Minorities and Discrimi-

490

nation broke down in technicalities and never finished its work. So the Commission on Human Rights agreed to take it over, appointed a rapporteur, and adopted his report. This report went further; it started criticizing certain things, though in a general fashion. At its last meeting, the Commission, taking a cue from the proceedings on apartheid and other problems of South Africa, asserted the right, which the Economic and Social Council later confirmed, to consider not only general, objective observations, but cases of grave violation, such as apartheid. So a hole in the dike was made, because apartheid came up and everybody was interested. Until that time the Commission could not consider any such violation whatever.

Another point may be made with respect to the importance of the non-governmental organizations. Especially in the field of human rights, there are a number of non-governmental organizations which are pursuing the attempt to obtain a bigger role in the U.N. structure. The U.N. Charter, apart from the ILO, is the first document which gives to non-governmental organizations some role in a public international organization. Again slowly, by small concessions here and there, they are increasing their role. One role they are now trying for is the right to comment on these national reports on human rights. First, they could not comment at all. Then they were allowed to comment, provided they kept the comments general. It was very soon discovered that the rights of the Jews in the Soviet Union were being violated, or that there existed a problem of apartheid in this place or that place, or discrimination against one minority or another. Again, slowly, the Commission on Human Rights and the Economic and Social Council are assigning a slightly bigger role to non-governmental international organizations. If this continues over a number of years, their role may become very important. We are reaching the point, even apart from the Covenants, of breaking the barrier to U.N. consideration of violation of human rights. This is again a development which was made possible by the Specialized Agencies. It was the success of the Specialized Agencies, especially of the ILO, in dealing with this kind of a problem, which was the beacon that was followed by the U.N. But the U.N. is applying these techniques to a much broader area. While in certain political areas, perhaps, the U.N. has not done so well with respect to some problems of greater importance, in the area of human rights, to the surprise of many and despite rear-guard action of the Soviet bloc, these things seem to be getting through. Another encouraging fact is that this is not simply a Western effort but that quite a number of Afro-Asians and Latin Americans are taking a very active part. So here is another side of the picture where the U.N. has followed the Specialized Agencies with some measure of success.

Mr. Dobbert:

I think we are moving a bit into the field of political science and I suppose this is an extremely useful exercise, because the awareness of the political motivations and powers is most important to enable the lawyers in any organization to face their tasks realistically, and give realistic advice.

The lawyers can help to devise new techniques, where techniques so far used have proved to be obsolete. This is true not only for standard setting, encouragement of implementation and possibly enforcement, but also for devising new means for helping situations to "move along"—to use Mr. Schachter's term—in the direction which we believe will help the world. In this connection, I would like to refer not so much to the hard core cases: here the political positions are as a rule so strongly engrained that it is very difficult for the lawyers and international organizations generally to help in bringing about a change in policies. I would leave aside such situations. However, in the field of conflict and conflict resolution, I have been wondering whether it would not also be possible for the international organizations to prevent potential conflicts from coming to a point where they join the small nucleus of hard core situations. As an example I should like to deal very briefly with the question of river basins.

This may seem very far removed from subject matters of our discussion. As you know, international rivers run through, or along the borders of, various countries. They are therefore the potential source of both a community of interests and a conflict of interests. I think that some examples have shown that an initial tendency to stress competing interests could eventually be transformed into a community of interest by economic and institutional techniques. I do not want to deal with the old problems that are well known to American lawyers, such as the conflict between Canada and the United States that was largely resolved by the Joint International Commission, nor with the Mexican situation concerning the Rio Grande basin, but I would like to go to more recent examples. You have the Indus waters dispute which, I think, has helped to a large extent to show how this river, which was a constant source of conflict between India and Pakistan, could be used by treaty measures to the mutual benefit of these countries. Here we have a piece of a "carrot"—the treaty illustrates this very interesting combination of a fundamentally bi-lateral treaty which is co-signed by an international organization, like the Bank with its bags of money. As a further example, I would mention the Mekong: the role that the Mekong committee has played in the relations between three or four nations. It seems that in spite of the numerous conflicts of interest both between and within the various participating countries, the Mekong committee has been able to operate almost without any disturbance and to move between conflict areas because the countries or parties concerned knew that this was a catalyst of the development which was in everybody's interest once it started. I think that the Niger and Senegal rivers bear no open conflict situations of any kind, but there may be potential ones. The establishment of a machinery which enables the riparian States to exploit the river in common and sets rules and standards for the countries concerned can be of very great importance in preventing conflicts. Perhaps also (but here I am not too sure) when the bushfire has been extinguished with the help of the political organs of the U.N. or a regional organization, it may also be possible to avoid a recurrence by appropriate economic and social assistance. I am not too sure whether much has been done in practice but I believe that in the Congo various attempts have been made in this direction which may have contributed to taking some of the venom out of a conflict situation.

DOES THE GENERAL ASSEMBLY MEAN TO MAKE LAW?

Professor Schwebel:

To return to this shame element for a moment, I think that there is an aspect of it which is reflected in a somewhat different manner in the U.N. context, in the desire of delegations not to be isolated, at least on many issues. This is a definite factor in the voting pattern of some states; they do not like to be the only ones voting against a resolution or being in a company which is regarded as somewhat dubious, especially as regards racial and colonial issues. States will really strain to swallow something which they do not like in order not to be put in that spot.

I would like also to add a word to our discussion of standard-setting declarations and law-making declarations. Much of these declarations is cast on such a high level of generality or ambiguity as to mean little or to mean everything, depending on who is doing the interpreting. If one looks at these declarations in terms of the criterion which Mr. Schachter earlier advanced for a decision of a legal character—community expectations— I wonder whether one can assign much of a legal character to these declarations. Certainly it is not the expectation of the community that these declarations are, for the most part, going to be taken seriously or that they are really going to be implemented. This is not always the case. Surely it is the case though, with the more pretentious declarations; take, for example, the one which has been adopted on non-intervention. I do not think that it can seriously be suggested that it is thought that the states of the world and particularly those who primarily intervene are going now to be guided in a meaningful way by this resolution, and that it is the expectation of the community that they are really obliged by it since it is expressive of the pattern of behavior which governments implement. Even if one could implement certain parts of the resolution, as Sir Kenneth Bailey pointed out, it is manifestly impossible, if interpreted literally, to implement all elements of it, since it would seem to debar the most normal diplomatic activities as intervention.

As for the point of aiming at unanimity and not passing resolutions where there is a powerful and recalcitrant state which is not likely to apply them: it is again an appealing principle, which, however, should not be carried too far if the U.N. is to achieve its purposes. The U.N. has certain purposes which assume recalcitrance. It would plainly not be desirable to debar the U.N. from taking action against those states which violate its basic purposes and obligations. The essential meaning of collective security is that some states collect against the aggressor. If one made action conditional on unanimity, one would exclude, *a priori,* the concept of collective security. It seems that the design of the Security Council does indeed tend to exclude it since it depends on the unanimity rule, but, with that reservation, at least I do not think that unanimity is the fundamental U.N. concept. On the contrary, the idea is that majorities can take decisions—qualified majorities of various kinds.

As to measures of implementation, particularly in the human rights field, there seems to be a dichotomy between bold talk and timid action. There has been a great push on the part of many states for making the most extreme assertions of human rights, coupled with the absence of implementing machinery. Yet, those who have been more cautious in the assertion of human rights often have been more disposed towards measures of implementation to back up those they maintain. The one exception has been on racial matters, where there has been a tendency in many of those states who otherwise prate all the time about their sacred sovereignty to admit measures of implementation which could have considerable bite.

One more point. I think that at least in the case of the United States, and, I suspect, in the case of many other countries, resolutions may be voted for in the U.N. blithely, one might say, irresponsibly, because key decision-makers, normally not lawyers, having it fixed in their skulls that the General Assembly has no decision-making, no law-making authority, will vote for almost anything of transient political advantage, unaware that such votes may have a law-forming character. It is not the law, but simply an enunciation of a political objective, so what does it matter? This naiveté, this lack of legal sophistication, is very much part of the voting pattern in the General Assembly by some states. It is a reality which should give pause in the appreciation of what Mrs. Higgins has so ably drawn attention to: the cumulative impact of these resolutions. Consider the principal resolution of 1960 on colonialism. There is an extreme declaration, which plainly has some screwball provisions. But is is regularly cited now in the U.N. as holy writ. It has had a certain impact. In fact, U.N. declarations should be taken more seriously, though I would not favor investing resolutions which those who vote for them do not intend to have legal impact, with law-making effect. I am baffled by this problem of bringing home to the political decision-makers the seriousness of what they do in the General Assembly.

Mr. Valticos:

We should now be coming a bit closer to our subject matter, that is the extent to which the techniques of various organizations can be a source of experience. As we have said already, this depends to a great extent on both the subject matter and the constitutional set-up. My impression is that we should not so much differentiate between the political organizations, such as the U.N., and the technical organizations, but rather classify according to the subject matter considered in each organization. For instance, the main distinction which we have to keep in mind when we discuss the choice of techniques and the question of implementation in the U.N. might be between the decisions dealing with particular political situations like those of South Africa, the Middle East, on the one hand, and the standard-setting decisions, on the other. Different sorts of decisions and different methods of compliance can be envisaged for each of these two categories: the individual and political field on the one hand, and the general and standard-setting field, on the other. Another distinction which is also necessary is as to the sort of action which is required in the various cases; you have a certain number of decisions which aim at immediate action and you have a certain number of decisions which start a long process, let us say many provisions of the Covenants on Human Rights, where nobody expects any immediate and general action.

Of course it is mainly in relation to the general standard-setting activities of the U.N. that we could more usefully discuss the techniques of other organizations and see to what extent some of these can be taken into account, in this sort of progressive development which Professor Stein explained to us. I quite agree that the U.N. has used a wide range of methods, for instance this sort of innovation which was the examination by the committee on non-self-governing territories of government reports. In fact, this system made Professor Van Asbeck very unhappy because he compared it with the League of Nations Commission and considered it a serious drawback not to have an independent body, as was the Mandates Commission, examining the government reports and passing judgment on them, rather than having these reports examined by political bodies. But one has to be fair and say that it was not the same legal situation, that the mandates case was one where there were clear obligations on the part of member states of the League while the reporting procedure in the U.N. was itself already a development. However, this does not mean that we could not perhaps consider to what extent such a reporting procedure could be developed in the future, for instance in the case of the Human Rights Covenants, in such a way to ensure the high standards of thoroughness and objectivity which would be necessary to command the respect of the people to whom these evaluations of the report are addressed. As they stand now, the Covenants provide merely for a general appraisal of the progress made and only exceptionally, when this is formally accepted by the state concerned, for the examination of particular cases. But this may be only the beginning. We have to wait for sufficient ratifications to come in; we will have to consider whether these are accompanied by serious or less serious reservations which might limit the scope of the ratification. And then we may also expect the conference on human rights which will take place next year in Teheran to attempt to reinforce this general machinery of supervision which is established in the Covenants. No solid system of supervision is provided in the text of the Covenants but we have seen from previous examples that procedures sometimes have been established and developed without being formally provided for in texts. And we have also in mind the fact that, as at the end of 1965, the Economic and Social Council asked the various international organizations to report on their own system of implementation in the field of human rights. We have also seen the discussions on the proposed creation of a High Commissioner. The outcome is uncertain, but we should be aware that, in the process of development in the U.N. and elsewhere, there will certainly be political difficulties in procedures of implementation of general, standard-setting decisions.

There is another factor which might be interesting in this discussion: the Covenant on Economic, Social and Cultural Rights provides for the possibility for all the Specialized Agencies to make comments in the fields which come within their competence, to receive copies of the governments' reports and comment on them. We shall reach a stage of possible collaboration for which arrangements will have to be made and, while of course each organization will have to prepare its comments in accordance with its own methods, this sort of collaboration of the various organizations of the U.N. family might perhaps add something to the procedure which is established in the Covenants themselves, perhaps not formally, but informally, as a process of mutual information and collaboration. This also might be an interesting development.

Now I should say a few words about the "mobilization of shame" which I launched, and maybe I should clarify slightly about the idea of the "carrot" and the "stick". I should not like to give the impression that I attach undue importance to this idea. First, it cannot apply in all cases; it can only apply to cases which are likely to arouse public opinion at home or in other states within the international community which would attach great importance to the matter. It cannot be used for all standards, but only for very important matters. Secondly, it is not a question of raising the "stick" at the first possible opportunity. It should be kept as a sort of ultimate remedy. The ILO does something which could be considered as a sort of mobilization of shame. But it does so only after all the methods of persuasion, of understanding, of granting delays have been exploited. I do not want to give the impression that our committees of experts or other supervisory bodies are very severe watchdogs who do not

496

pay great attention in the first stages to raising the matters with all the necessary tact, care and sympathetic understanding of the problems in the member countries.

As regards the second element of the "carrot" and, in particular, in the South African case, there, of course, we are in a much more difficult, if not desperate, position. Since the declaration which was adopted by our conference in 1964 concerning apartheid in employment matters, we are requested every year to present to the conference a report on the progress or lack of progress in the situation. But we do not limit ourselves by merely making virtuous condemnations. Very strong words have been said, of course, but we have also tried to provide a sort of positive program of possible peaceful change, an economically orderly change, from a system based on racial discrimination to a system based on a multi-racial equality. We have done this in order to explain to the government of South Africa that abolition of apartheid would not bring chaos—on the contrary, in the report submitted last year we tried, by the economic information which we found in reports from big firms in South Africa themselves, to show how economic progress has even now been hampered and how they find operation more and more difficult because they cannot use African labor in more responsible positions. So we tried to explain that it is also in their own economic interest to change their system. But here we are faced with the vital conception of the social organization of a country, and we come up against the basic difficulty that even persuasion is stopped by political fundamentals.

Mr. FitzGerald:

As the debate was going on, I felt that we were straying away somewhat from compliance techniques although they have been coming back into the picture from time to time. Mr. Schachter has pointed out the relatively small extent to which the advice of the legal people was involved in certain decision-making activities and in the techniques of compliance. I have indicated to a number of you in private conversation the fact that very few of the compliance techniques in regard to the technical regulatory material in ICAO have been developed on the advice of lawyers. From time to time the lawyers may be called upon to solve difficult problems, but to my knowledge nobody in ICAO ever came to the Legal Bureau and asked how to go about implementing particular standards. ICAO standards have been developed and brought up to their present stage through a pragmatic exercise. This may well be true in many of things that occur in the U.N. One could pose the question, "Should the lawyers try to get a greater role in the development of compliance techniques in respect of decisions"? As we know, the lawyer has the ability to digest and to systematize a wide range of facts. This is something the technical people cannot always do when they have gone outside the confines of their slide rule. Professor Stein has pointed out the danger that in one organization the political people became legal prisoners. We are all familiar with the situation that the technical people will shy back from seeking legal advice because they do not want to be made prisoners. I do not blame them. Sometimes they prefer to turn a blind eye to the legal telescope which will show legal confines at the other end. They do see a much broader technical field outside the legal fence that we may build around them. This is a consideration to be borne in mind. Nevertheless we are aware of the conflict-prevention role of the lawyer, whereby, if he is asked for his advice in time, he will prevent a whole pyramid of difficulties from arising. This also is an important consideration.

This leads me to my last point in regard to the role of the lawyer. I think of a specific case in the development by accretion of practice in relation to Article 73 of the Charter. How much of what Professor Sohn said is a kind of an *ex post facto* lawyers' law whose development was shaped by government representatives sitting on U.N. committees, rather than by legal advice constantly given? To what extent, for example, would the U.N. Office of Legal Affairs have shaped the development of what happened in relation to Article 73? Or is it possible to say that, because the various U.N. organs have some rather good lawyers sitting as national representatives, you have available some advice which helps to shape developments? Much of what happens in the field of international organization is done by people who are not lawyers or who are not sitting as lawyers. Afterwards, lawyers and political scientists systematize the material and put rather more convenient labels on it for the purposes of study. Then the student, who is not aware that the clever lawyers and political scientists stepped in afterwards, thinks that the material was consciously developed in the light of constantly given legal advice, when this is just not so, in relation to a great mass of material. Therefore, I raise these questions with Professor Sohn and Mr. Schachter.

Mr. Schachter:

I wish the lawyers could take credit for it but I think we have nothing whatsoever to do with it. It is a complex story, but if there is to be anybody who is given credit for Article 73 development, it is a man, now dead, named Wilfred Benson. Benson had been an ILO official, very able and admirable as an international civil servant, who was very much devoted to the elimination of colonialism. He was the first director of that division on "information from the non-self-governing territories" and that is why I said earlier that the procedure had been inspired by the ILO procedure.

Mr. Benson was not a lawyer, he had been a British civil servant, and he is due a tremendous amount of credit. I would not venture now to say what would have been the case had the lawyers been asked about this constitutional possibility. But I believe that a great number of lawyers would have taken a conservative position and would have opposed what took place. And probably even today many people deplore that this procedure

498

was used to bring about the too rapid end of colonialism. I think that we might well have had the opposite situation had this been subject to a vote by a legal organ.

Professor Sohn:

I agree that this is what happens. The other part of the question is about the role of lawyers in national delegations and I think the fact that there are some lawyers among them sometimes helps and sometimes hinders. You have to remember that, in the major delegations, there may be a legal advisor who may be positively or negatively minded. We see here an interaction of many people from different countries, with various backgrounds, and different attitudes. It is seldom possible to pinpoint that this is a lawyer of that particular view or this. For example, if we take the "Uniting for Peace" Resolution, one could say that that was the work of two lawyers, Dean Acheson and John Foster Dulles, but many other people contributed too.

Mr. FitzGerald:

I think we ought to distinguish the lawyer who is sitting as a national representative; he is bound to take his country's vital interests into account.

Mr. Schachter:

My earlier point, if I just may restate it very briefly again, is a little different. It is that legal committees and legal advisors place emphasis on standard-setting and norm-creation. That interest is not shared naturally by the political people even when they are lawyers by training. In the international field far more than in the domestic field, the lawyers tend to promote highly abstract formulations of requirements. This does not mean all lawyers do so. I am talking about committees and other U.N. bodies made up of legal people. I think it is good to have standards, it helps to know what you are after. I think you get better support when standards are formalized in treaties, or solemnized in other ways. I would go along with all that, but I still feel that these points are less significant than other aspects. If you were a lawyer advising a corporation about matters of this kind you would normally be taking into account elements of cost, who has power, and many other things like that; they would in fact be uppermost in your mind.

HAVE GENERAL ASSEMBLY DECISIONS ON COLONIALISM MADE LAW?

Sir Kenneth Bailey:

In respect of compliance with decisions of international organizations, I was enormously struck by the contrast between the homogeneous charac-

499

ter of the European Communities and the enormously disparate character of the international community represented in a body like the U.N. The observations which I made earlier on the legal character of U.N. resolutions perhaps indicated sufficiently the reluctance on the part of the countries like my own to accept the duty of compliance with U.N. General Assembly resolutions in legal or even in political terms. This does not spring from an unenlightened policy or a policy of reaction but rather from the awareness of the distinction between acceptance of community standards as in the EEC, where the Community judgment is very closely comparable with national conditions, systems, and legal principles on the one hand, and the extraordinary variation in standards which govern the world community in the U.N. on the other. A democratic government like that of Australia is not likely to accept the decisions of delegates representing unrepresentative governments.

The view I would express is that the U.N. General Assembly has completely moved away from its lawyers. Partly also, its lawyers have moved away from the law. I think what Mr. Schachter said was right: that, if the great structure that Professor Sohn so deftly and quickly described as built on, but spectacularly departing from, Chapter XI of the U.N. Charter had been shaped by the hands of the lawyers, the structure might never have been built or would have been built on a less sweeping pattern and might have had very different effects.

I would like to develop a little the point about the General Assembly getting away from its lawyers, in relation to the anti-Western position of the U.N. General Assembly nowadays. The series of resolutions that draw upon the Declaration on the Granting of Independence to Colonial Countries and Peoples [1514(XV)], of 1960 have reached their apogee over the last couple of years. The Committee of Twenty-Four was established in 1961 to investigate and report on the degree of compliance with Resolution 1514. The duty to comply with it was assumed by the General Assembly and that Committee has had a pronounced effect on the speed of decolonization in some cases. Whether this is a good effect or a bad one is an open question.

But the anti-colonial position of the General Assembly had not yet reached the full stage that I am now about to describe because the report of the Special Committee on Principles of International Law concerning Friendly Relations and Cooperation Among States had not yet gone to the General Assembly and the legal position expounded in two or three texts which were tabled in the Special Committee and supported—I regret to say—by lawyers of some repute was this:
(1) by reason of the references in the Charter of the U.N. to self-determination, the relation of the administering authority to colonial territories is now illegal. (If you say what *were* the references to the self-determination in the Charter, they are found in two places only. One of them describes the purposes of the U.N., namely, to develop friendly relations be-

tween nations based on the principle of equal rights and self-determination of peoples. The other is in Article 55, where, with a view to the creation of conditions necessary to peaceful and friendly relations based on the principle of equal rights and self-determination of peoples, various human rights are to be promoted. You would think neither a very safe legal foundation for the proposition that the colonial relation is now illegal and a violation of international law. But, having regard to the representation issue at the U.N. and the disparity between the narrow base of power and responsibility and the great superstructure of asseveration, it is not surprising.) Moreover,

(2) the rights given by international law to states apply also to peoples, particularly those in colonial territories.

(3) A dependent colonial territory cannot legally form part of the territory of the administering state.

(4) Hence the use of force by other states to support independence movements in a dependent territory is not contrary to the Charter.

These conclusions will eventually take their place in the resolution structure of the General Assembly because they will find a tremendous majority; the entire non-aligned group will support them and the Eastern Europeans as well. Whether the Latin American group will is a question —some did in the Special Committee. The one point on which the Special Committee was in agreement was that it was a principle of universal application and was not limited to colonial peoples.

This record on self-determination underlies the suggestion I made that, in that field at any rate, the U.N. General Assembly got away from its lawyers and that the lawyers have got away from the law. This perhaps illustrates the basic problems of compliance with the U.N. General Assembly resolutions in its present phase. I do not know whether Mrs. Higgins would classify Resolution 1514(XV) as setting up standards to control the situations it stimulates. The contrast between the proceedings of the Committee of Twenty-Four on the one hand, with the League Mandates Commission and its experts on the other, and with the latter's independent, detached examination of colonial situations and colonial policies, is completely relevant.

There is of course a case to be made and I am not so partisan as not to realize that a case can be and *is* sincerely made by those who sponsor resolutions of the Special Committee and the Committee of Twenty-Four. It is based on the principle of the mobilization of shame. They say you must not escape the value of sweeping political exaggerations in the mobilization of public opinion in support of policies of colonial emancipation, or human rights and so on. The effect of this differs very greatly from one country to another, as was said earlier.

A last comment: on the peacekeeping questions which Mrs. Higgins raises in her paper: my answer to question 1, (do conference participants agree with the preceding identification and interpretation of the variables relevant to compliance with this category of U.N. decisions?) is decisively yes. Question 2, (are there other important factors which have been omitted?) I was just wondering whether the presence or absence of a vigorous national press should be stated among the factors for or against compliance. Question 3, (would the gathering and appraising of such factors, in a systematic way and in relationship to the entire membership, be of assistance to the U.N. Secretariat?) I think it would be of assistance to the U.N. Secretariat. You could really make a marvellous supplement to the Repertory of Practice and an invaluable book for every school of international law and international relations in the world. How much the Secretariat would be able to profit by it, I do not know. Question 5, (what is the scope of legal advisor's role in this relationship?) I think I have said enough about the role of legal advisors.

VARIABLES AND THE CHOICE OF COMPLIANCE TECHNIQUES

Mr. Stevenson:

It may be useful if we underline the question here: whether this process of identification of these variable produces compliance in one situation and non-compliance in another. Is it of any value in the selection of the particular compliance device that is used in a particular instance? Or is the situation to a certain extent as Mr. Schachter related it: that a great number of these compliance devices are used simultaneously and will be used anyway. He did talk about an orchestration of a number of different techniques. Now, how discrete can you be? Here we are going back to Mr. Lauterpacht's original formulation of the recipe for a particular case.

Mrs. Higgins:

Or, if we may use the orchestration analogy, have we really studied the score sufficiently in advance to decide which instruments we do want coming in when?

Mr. Schachter:

It may be useful to look at the problem in terms of the different roles which the U.N. or, for that matter, the other organizations, play. I shall try to list these different roles: (1) the role of a regulator of conduct. The U.N. and the agencies seek to regulate, apart from simply setting standards. (2) The U.N. and to some degree the other agencies play a role in effectuating the agreements of certain states, particularly the U.S. and the Soviet Union. This remains a principal strand of the Organization. It underlies the veto and the principle of major power responsibility. Obviously, compliance is often dependent on Soviet/American agreements. What is not so often realized is that the Organization may be a vehicle for giving effect to such agreements. There are many such cases: Suez, Kashmir,

Berlin, the treaty on nuclear proliferation. (3) There is a role in bringing about changes in the world. The idea of peaceful change, of revision of treaties or changing the distribution of resources is a major function of the U.N. (which may run counter to the one which I have just mentioned). The demand of a majority in the U.N. to change things in some ways has been particularly strong in the area of colonialism and in pressure for economic aid. The analogy would be to a trade union pressing for changes by those who have authority to make such changes. Compliance has a different meaning in this context than in that of regulation, for example. (4) The role of the U.N. in creating long term conditions of stability, which is something like the Fund's role. (5) The role of generating and formulating standards and norms. (6) The use of the U.N. as a political tool. Resolutions emerge, but the compliance problem here is different. (7) One might include bailing-out as a role. It is a U.N. operation which has rather a high degree of effectiveness for those who are being bailed out though not always successful from a general standpoint. A prime user of that function has been the U.K., for example, with Palestine: let the U.N. carry the bag. The U.S. did that in the Lebanon as well. Compliance has another dimension. Once again, it may be convenient for a national government to get U.N. legitimation of an action. The U.N. often is stuck with a problem too late. The Congo was a case like that. One can list many cases, when everything else has failed and the governments do not know what to do; then they turn to the U.N. This fact clearly has a bearing on the effectiveness of U.N. decisions.

Professor Sohn:
Isn't one of the basic functions of the U.N. to be the last resort?

Mr. Schachter:
I am not disputing that. I am just stating the type of role. I think there are seven compliance problems in those seven categories and I am sure one can extend the list to eight or nine. Technical assistance comes partly into this too. There is the fact that most of the organizations—and the U.N. notably—have shown a great shift from a concern with East/West questions to North/South questions. That is an element of importance with regard to how you carry out things, how you get support and so on.

Another general point is the fact that at this time we see, as you all know, a breakdown of some territorial states and the emergence of others. And it seems to me that, here again, we are coping with new forms which bear upon compliance and effectiveness. I would draw attention to the regional organizations which I think are extremely weak. Nonetheless, the regional organizations may have a specific role in achieving effectiveness. Also one can envisage other new institutions playing a bigger role in compliance, such as consortia.

Mr. Dobbert:

I would like to ask an indirect question about what Mr. Gaudet's statement concerning reciprocity as a measure of indirect compliance. It would seem that his concept of reciprocity is based more on the assumption that there might or might not be reciprocity between the *organization* on the one hand and the *member state* or states on the other.

However, with particular reference to norms established in the field of international trade, there are reasons to assume that non-compliance by a particular country will consequently entail either non-compliance or perhaps some other retaliatory measure on the part of other countries vis-à-vis that particular country. I might illustrate this by an example taken from FAO's field of activities: certification of plants for sanitary purposes. If a particular country does not certify the plants according to the procedure and criteria outlined in the International Plant Protection Convention, it will find that its plants will not be accepted in other countries and its trade made more difficult. There may be more convincing evidence, but the example does show that the idea of reciprocity can be built into multilateral arrangements, together with "sanctions" in the event of non-compliance. You have similar criteria for trade in meat and various other animal products, and they may also apply in the fields covered by GATT or EFTA; there, the mechanism may be more complicated because of the special procedures established by the organization to deal with alleged non-compliance. I think that this is quite an important aspect and it could well be worth exploring from that particular angle and not from the angle of relations between the organization as such and the member states.

Mr. Gold:

An important element in the observance of the rules and policies of the Fund has been a sense of equal or equivalent treatment among members large and small. Let me give some examples. In the liquidity exercise, some major financial powers thought of setting up a facility for themselves. The intention was that they would create reserves for themselves by convention and let the rest of the world earn supplements to their reserves by having surpluses in their balance of payments. All kinds of arguments were put forward to justify this. It became clear that this would incur the resentment of the rest of the world. In addition, it began to be feared that the structure of monetary discipline which the Fund had patiently built up over the years would be undermined and that the rest of the world might not be willing to continue to observe the rules and standards of the Fund if they felt they were being discriminated against. The next step was a search for a solution which would enable some countries to have an exclusive plan among themselves while at the same time conceding some provision for the rest. For example, 25 per cent of the created reserves would be granted to the rest and the Fund would administer that amount for them. Even this did not make any impression. Countries continued to feel that this was a discrimination against them. They were not thinking about profit because everybody knew the amount of the allocations would probably not vary with their form. The amount would depend on some international norm, such as quotas in the Fund. But that was not the point, countries wanted to *appear* to be treated with equality. In the end it was agreed that a system even of apparent discrimination only would not be acceptable, and might mean erosion of that compliance with the obligations and standards that is necessary for the success of the international monetary system. That is one example of what has been called a variable in the discussion that has played a part in the creation of a new international instrument.

Equal treatment is not necessarily the same treatment. In the example I have given, it did mean that, but sometimes it may mean equivalent treatment. The Fund's Arrangements to Borrow are an example. These are very large stand-by arrangements that the Fund has with ten members for the purpose of supplementing the Fund's resources to take care of the Fund's transactions with those ten members. They were set up with the adoption of the convertibility of European and other currencies in connection with capital outflow. This outflow would not go to the rest of the world, and therefore it was felt there was some justification for setting up special arrangements to augment the Fund's resources for the purpose of these ten countries. Although there was a justification, it produced disquiet on the part of some other countries because of the exclusive character of the arrangements. They argued that whatever the justification, the arrangements should have been made in some other way. It is very likely that this reaction was an influence in facilitating the establishment in the Fund of what we call the compensatory financing of shortfalls in export proceeds. This is a facility for the benefit of the less developed countries, the producers of primary products. Countries are willing to accept disproportionate voting strength in a weighted voting system and abide by the rules and standards of the institution but it is dangerous to follow a course which suggests that either in form or substance they will not all get equal or equivalent treatment as they see it.

Professor Schwebel:

On the question of the spiral of compliance breeding compliance and non-compliance breeding non-compliance, it is perhaps worth mentioning the declaration of the U.S. made at the time of the collapse of its efforts to uphold U.N. assessments and the application of Article 19 of the Charter. There was a statement that, as long as certain members did not pay assessments they chose not to pay, and as long as the General Assembly accepted that position without application of the sanction which was supposed to flow from that position, the U.S. reserved to itself the right not to pay assessments *it* did not wish to pay. It has never exercised that right and it may be assumed that it will not exercise it lightly, but the U.S. treats itself as having this right. In that connection, I should like to revert to the point Mr. Gold made of the objective legal order and the idea of one state taking a breach of treaty obligation vis-à-vis an international organization or another state as justification for its so-called right not to comply with an obligation, otherwise binding upon it. I think here the key to the U.S. legal analysis and one which distinguishes this case from the principle set forth by Mr. Gold, is that the General Assembly itself was party to the breach; it ratified the breach by declining to apply the sanction which it was required to apply in the case of non-payment of assessments. Therefore, the U.S. is justified in not paying assessments of the U.N. she pleases not to pay—or so it may be argued.

Mr. Nurick:

A point affecting compliance in the field of economic development institutions is that there are many of them: the World Bank, the IDB, the Asian Bank, the African Bank, the UNDP, the European Investment Fund, the European Social Fund and then the national institutions. I think the effect of this has been that there has grown up a segment of the bar which is very conscious of the difference in treatment which they can expect to get between one international organization and another and between an international organization and a domestic one. The impression has been created that there may be competition among these institutions for business. What that means is that there may be a point when a particular customer of one of the institutions may feel that he does not have to comply with a decision of that institution simply because he can go around the corner and get something just as good from somebody else without having to worry about a particular measure of compliance.

THE CENTRAL AMERICAN COMMON MARKET

Mr. Garcia-Amador:

The Central American Common Market is not a Common Market in the European sense. The Common Market in the Central American Economic Council is composed of economic ministers and meets once a year and the Executive Council, composed largely of economic under-secretaries, meets once a month. The special powers conferred upon the organs of the Central American Common Market are regulatory powers. The two Councils, particularly the Executive Council, are empowered to adopt regulations for the implementation of decisions, including many provisions of the General Treaty. The Executive Council adopts decisions by majority rule and the member states are only left with the power to put those decisions into effect. So you really have a sort of supranational competence.

So far as SIECA is concerned, although it is merely an organ like the general secretariat, it has two very important functions: one, the power of interpretation of any instrument or treaty dealing with the Common Market; secondly, it has the power, explicitly provided, to watch over the application and execution of observance by the states of the General Treaty as well as any other treaty. In practice, SIECA has been rather cautious in exercising this power.

I wanted to mention too that there is also a power to settle disputes through the Council; they do not have a court of justice like the European Common Market.

IMPLEMENTING INTERNATIONAL DECISIONS THROUGH MUNICIPAL COURTS

Mr. Lauterpacht:

To what extent and in what circumstances is it possible to use recourse to municipal courts to secure compliance with decisions of international organizations? So far we have been talking exclusively in terms of international sanctions or international means of persuasion, but there are contexts in which it is worthwhile to consider whether one could use national litigation: for example, in the cases of Rhodesia and South West Africa.

The principle is the same for both, but let me begin with the Rhodesian situation. We start from the proposition that the objective of the U.N. in Rhodesia is an effort to reduce Rhodesian exports of certain key commodities. The way this has been done, as I recollect, is by a resolution of the Security Council calling upon members not to purchase the named commodities and leaving it to the U.N. members to secure the implementation of that resolution. Now it has become increasingly apparent that these prohibitions are not being complied with, and that certain countries, members and non-members of the U.N., have made considerable purchases of the prohibited material. The most striking example is the alleged recent purchase by Japanese metal concerns of 20,000 tons of chrome ore at a price which is considerably below the world market prices.

Would it be open—in this case to the U.K., as the prime instigator of the sanctions—to sue in the Japanese courts such purchasers of prohibited Rhodesian chrome? Of course one asks the question how one could possibly do this. There must be a cause of action in terms of Japanese law as between the British Government and a purchaser of a product from Rhodesia. So then you have to consider whether in some way it is possible to introduce the necessary linkage to create the cause of action. And then one gets more closely into the terms of the U.N. resolution. It has occurred to me that the U.K., having regard to its retained sovereign powers over Rhodesia, would be entitled to pass legislation vesting in the Crown title to all Rhodesian prohibited commodities at the moment that they are shipped for export contrary to the prohibition. Title to the commodity would pass to the U.K. while the commodity was still in Rhodesia and was therefore still subject to British sovereignty. The commodity would arrive at a Japanese port and there the British Government would sue the Japanese purchaser to recover the commodity or its value. Now, there are two possibilities, the British Government might win, or it might lose. If it wins —object achieved; if it loses, object not completely defeated because of the possibility that this would create a certain amount of uncertainty in the market. Purchasers will not want to purchase law suits.

Professor Stein:

There is a certain parallel to this in the situation that developed during the Second World War when the Dutch Government-in-Exile adopted a decree vesting protective title in the State of the Netherlands to all securities belonging to individuals and corporations domiciled in the Netherlands. The question was raised in an American court whether this decree can be held applicable to bonds seized by the Germans in occupied Netherlands. The Federal Court of first instance said that because of the German occupation and *de facto* control, the Netherlands decree could not be held to apply to bonds in occupied Netherlands. However, the Court of Appeals reversed the decision.*

Mr. Lauterpacht:

Let me consider the South West African case. There the idea might be applied in an even more intriguing way. Our starting point here is that the General Assembly has declared that the mandate is terminated. So South Africa's administration over South West Africa is in United Nations terms ended. Now the question arises, who has sovereign rights over South West Africa? Could one assume for a moment that somehow there has vested in some non-South African body a legislative power relating to South West Africa? Could not the same principle be applied here as in the Rhodesian example already considered, so that the title to any South West African commodity vests in the U.N. authority responsible for the government of South West Africa at the moment of export, while the commodity is still in South West Africa and therefore within the jurisdiction of this U.N. body? So, the U.N. could sue to receive such property in the courts of whatever country that commodity reaches.

Mr. Gold:

A number of countries have imposed restrictions on payments and transfers to Rhodesia and these have been approved under the Fund's Arti-

---

* The reference is to State of the Netherlands v. Federal Reserve Bank, 99 F. Supp. 655 (1951), reversed in 201 F. 2d 455 (2d Cir. 1953).

cles. Presumably, Rhodesians would not be able to recover in a member court if there were non-payment as a result of these restrictions.

Professor Stein:

Do you contemplate a U.N. resolution that would say that every member shall adopt legislation to the effect that, on export from Rhodesia, title to chrome is vested in the U.K.?

Mr. Lauterpacht:

No, once the United Kingdom has passed the necessary legislation, all that other countries need do is to permit their courts to give effect to it.

Mr. Elkin:

In the South West Africa case, you propose to transfer title to the U.N. and you assume therefore that the U.N. has powers to expropriate citizens of member countries. Would you mind explaining that?

Mr. Lauterpacht:

In my eyes there is no compensable asset. This is the starting point. What one is trying to do is to deter the foreign purchaser from breaking the prohibition. We are starting from the proposition that the export of these commodities, as in the case of Rhodesia, is prohibited, in order to act as a sanction on a rebellious territory.

In effect one is expropriating the property of the Rhodesian seller or the foreign purchaser depending on when the title passes within the territory.

I can see the argument being raised in a foreign court that to recognize that the British legislation has effected the transfer of title in this way is contrary to the local public policy. Now that is just where the terms of the U.N. resolution come in: to negative the "public policy" aspect.

Mr. Stevenson:

Can the technique Mr. Lauterpacht suggests be applied in a case where there is not an anterior colonial or mandatory status?

Mr. Schachter:

I think you could find other situations where some doctrine could be advanced if one had Mr. Lauterpacht's ingenuity. My only comment is one of admiration for his approach. I have listened to discussions of this subject since 1951 and to my recollection no one has made a proposal of this kind. The heart of his point is that introducing some uncertainty into prohibited trade with Rhodesia may be a rather telling practical weapon.

Professor Sohn:

A more natural course of action for the U.N. would be to do what they have already done with respect to the ship that was coming into Mozambique. The Security Council, acting under Chapter VII of the Charter, might authorize the U.K. to stop any ship coming from Rhodesia or Mozambique or South Africa if there were reasonable grounds to suspect that it contained goods exported from Rhodesia in violation of the U.N. prohibition. Were they to discover such goods, they should be authorized to confiscate them in the name of the U.N.

Mr. Elkin:

This type of expropriation looks to me like a penal act, and I wonder whether the Japanese judge would recognize this and answer: "I am not going to apply U.K. penal law."

Mr. Lauterpacht:

My understanding of Japanese law is that he would not in fact be excluding U.K. law on the ground that it is penal but on the ground that it is against Japanese public policy. And my hope is that the U.N. resolution would be sufficiently explicit to require members to exclude from their legal system any hindrance to the application of the U.K. legislation. Then it becomes a matter of Japanese law, either self-executing or specially enacted, to give effect to the resolution.

What intrigues me about this idea is that it places everybody on the spot. You say to the states in the U.N.: are you really serious about sanctions? If yes, then you must put your legislation in order, so as to assist in the application of the U.N. sanctions.

Mrs. Higgins:

I think that the variety of difficulties here in securing compliance are very obvious. I think there is probably a confusion of objectives in the case of Rhodesia between, on the one hand the U.N. as a whole and, on the other hand, the U.K. Until the Unilateral Declaration of Independence, of course we had always declared that resolutions passing upon matters concerning Rhodesia were outside the competence of the U.N., and only within Southern Rhodesia's (not the U.K.'s) jurisdiction, and it is now through the waiver of our resumed competence that the matter comes before the U.N. Britain was at great pains to emphasize that the U.N. was acting at our behest in order to help us end the rebellion when the image from the U.N. end has certainly been that it is now rightly in business in Rhodesia in the human rights field.

These matters are not irrelevant legally. Should we wish to end sanctions, have we the unilateral authority to do so? And this does depend very much on whether you think that the U.N. is in this respect helping us to end the rebellion or achieve certain human rights, self-determination and other objectives within Rhodesia.

The very gradualist approach employed in the imposition of sanctions on

Rhodesia has been overdone. The very limited number of commodities covered and the fact that the first resolution was generally agreed upon by way of recommendation under Chapter 6 rather than Chapter 7 are examples. There was some ambiguous talk about "Chapter 6 and a half" in the British Parliament but countries did say that they did not regard themselves as bound by the first resolution. I feel equally about the domestic measures taken in Britain, particularly the tardiness with which we enacted our financial sanctions and the fact that they may even have amounted to assistance to the Rhodesian regime, which is, in terms of compliance, unfortunate.

I think there has been the additional difficulty of the question of *who* is your addressee. The U.N. here has been passing resolutions which are not addressed to the nation they wish to comply. The people who are required to comply with the sanctions are the other major trading partners of Rhodesia—there is nothing *Rhodesia* is required to do by the U.N. resolution, except, from her perspective, to stick it out and find ways of avoiding it. But she is in no direct legal relationship herself with the U.N. as a result of the resolution. And this of course arises because of her peculiar non-member and non-self-governing status.

There have of course been arguments about whether the measures taken have been in accordance with both Charter provisions and general international law—whether it is proper to allow one country to interfere with the ships of another country on the high seas when that country maintains trade with a territory which has been penalized for rebellion which in turn is not incompatible with general international law. That argument was heard about the Beira oil resolution. There have been arguments as to the legality of the Security Council's voting procedures. The dissenting nations have been able to latch onto the question of how is the U.N. entitled to act in a mandatory manner under Chapter 7 without there being a threat to peace. And this turns upon the authority of the Security Council finally to determine for itself whether there has been a threat to peace—whether it is a reviewable competence or not, and the ability of dissenting nations to say that they do not agree with this analysis of the factual situation. Of course the dissenters have been able to point to many other situations where a great degree of violence had occurred and no threat to peace has been found.

There has been the secondary level of compliance problem going on at the same time. Not only how you get Rhodesia to act but how do you get countries such as Portugal and South Africa to act if you are not willing to contemplate the use of sanctions against them? We in Britain have certainly made it clear that, while we may be willing to send a boat or two to stop the Joanna V out of Mozambique, we are certainly not willing to contemplate more generalized measures.

Well, the mobilization of shame has certainly not been very effective here. Some of the reports required are still unanswered, others contain information which is obscure, others still give certain information and turn blind eyes where their nationals behave otherwise. I suppose it is arguable that the U.K. has been dragging its own feet, for each time it has gone to the U.N., apart from the Biera instance, it has done so under pressure. All of these factors have made compliance extremely difficult, but obviously the core of the problem is South Africa.

Professor Sohn:

I would like to supplement one point. One of the resolutions on South Africa says that apartheid and racial discrimination constitute slavery, and therefore one could argue that goods produced in Rhodesia are slave-produced goods. You could base Mr. Lauterpacht's suggestion on that assumption. There is no question of expropriation because slave-produced goods are prohibited in international trade.

Mr. Elkin:

I am interested in the second proposition where the U.N. has the title. Can the U.N. acquire title to goods by expropriation? Can it become owner of such property?

Mr. Schachter:

In the U.K./Rhodesia case it is clear that the U.K. is generally regarded as having sovereign authority over the territory. In the other case, there is a position certified by a number of states but certainly not unanimously accepted that the U.N. acts as a kind of temporary trustee for the administration of South West Africa in view of the termination of the mandate and the lack of the establishment of a successor government. The basis of the U.N. claim to pass this kind of legislation would be authority over that territory; it stands in the shoes of a sovereign state in regard to this particular territory.

Mr. Stevenson:

I think you could avoid some of the confiscation implication by the same technique that the Dutch Government used—taking as trustee.

THE SANCTION OF EXCLUSION

Mr. Schachter:

There was reference to expulsion and suspension but there was virtually no reference to what is probably now the most common form of sanction procedure against recalcitrant governments, namely exclusion not through formal expulsion or suspension, but exclusion from committees and from activities in the organization. This has been done against South Africa more than any other country, although several others are now in the same

512

jeopardy. I would also include in the same broad area the increasingly common use of non-recognition, either through credential procedures or through other means; and I think whether we like it or not the U.N. has certainly acted with considerable effectiveness in excluding certain governments from any participation whatsoever—East Germany, North Vietnam, Mainland China and North Korea. Of course all of them share certain characteristics but the point is that this has been a rather effective means in an immediate sense, if not of bringing about compliance. It has been suggested that similar action through credentials be taken against South Africa. Action of that kind could be taken against unpopular governments wherever the issues of choice of government and recognition of government have come before the organization. Realistically it is the easiest "stick" to pick up today but it is debatable whether it is basically conducive to greater effectiveness.

Mr. Lauterpacht:

Strictly speaking, the examples which you mention do not give rise to problems in compliance technique because the states concerned did not actually disobey some order of the organization.

Mr. Schachter:

It is charged that they are not peace-loving.

Mr. Lauterpacht:

The problem is more general. Take the example of the ILO in 1956 when the Kadar regime was excluded. They were not excluded because they violated undertakings towards the ILO but simply because they executed Nagy in rather revolting circumstances. There was an upsurge of feeling in the ILO. There followed an interesting division of opinion in its Credentials Committee. The chairman took the view that there was no justification for not recognizing their credentials, but the mass of the organization felt the other way.

Mrs. Higgins:

Exclusion has not been at all successful in securing compliance by those excluded with standards of the organization.

Professor Sohn:

Then one has to say that this is not really a useful sanction.

Mr. Valticos:

Well, to a certain extent this sanction is an inducement to change behavior in some cases.

Mrs. Higgins:

Is there not a fundamental difference between this technique operating against a party which is already a member and not permitting membership to a party which is not yet a member? There is a very much more real compliance technique in the former case.

Professor Schwebel:

Not if in the latter case the state wants to get in and is being denied something.

Mr. Lauterpacht:

If one is talking about compliance technique, it is interesting to record the reaction of IMCO when the traditional shipowning nations tried to impose their standard of proper shipowning on the non-traditional "flags of convenience" nations. At the very first assembly of IMCO, the traditional shipowning states sought to exclude the non-traditional states from the Maritime Safety Committee. The election was subsequently the subject of an advisory opinion of the International Court. The Court held that the election had not been properly held.

Mr. Vignes:

Mr. Schachter spoke about exclusion, but in WHO we have another type of sanction: suspension.

Mr. Dobbert:

In 1963, Ghana proposed an amendment to the Constitution which would have allowed the expulsion of a member which persistently violated its obligations under the Constitution; it was of course aimed at South Africa. There was a very long debate and when the vote was taken the amendment failed to obtain the majority required. The Conference did, however, pass a resolution by which South Africa would be prevented from participating in the regional activities and from attending African regional conferences. There was one additional point, which would have precluded the Republic of South Africa from attending regional meetings outside Africa. The intention was to prevent the possibility of a transfer of the Republic of South Africa to another region, which theoretically might have been possible. It was because of this resolution, which South Africa considered illegal, that, a month or two after the Conference, she withdrew from FAO membership, in accordance with the withdrawal clause of the Constitution. However, in that resolution there was also a general clause to the effect that any country whose presence might defeat the program in Africa could be excluded from African regional meetings: that was probably aimed at Portugal. In the FAO Constitution, there is a provision to the effect that regional commissions under Article VI(1) are open to all member nations that have territories in the region, and the FAO Secretariat, which issues the invitations, would not have been in a position to exclude Portugal from those regional meetings without an amendment of the Constitution. Therefore the convening of meetings of African regional commissions became problematic.

Mr. Elkin:

I just wanted to point out that the snowball effect I was referring to in the economic field really applies in the examples given now. I remember that when, several years ago, the Committee for Technical Cooperation in Africa South of the Sahara wanted to exclude Portugal, the resulting risk would have been that certain animal diseases would spread to member countries because Portugal would stop certain services. So again you cannot always consider this particular technique as invariably effective.

SUMMARY COMMENTS

Mr. Stevenson:

May I endeavor to summarize some of the questions which have been discussed here and some of the unsettled issues.

The first general question we discussed was the choice of techniques to carry out an agreed course of action. As far as the functional agencies were concerned, there seems to be considerable diversity based on the nature of the institution and, more important, the subject matter dealt with and also to a certain extent, what the membership of a particular agency would accept. The traditional treaty-making procedures creating binding obligations through conventions recommended by international organizations seem still to be the most important legislative techniques of a number of the non-financial functional organizations, particularly the ILO and UPU. These conventions also still seem to provide the basic structure for implementing regulations and rules of other agencies such as the FAO.

The tendency in a number of other agencies seems to be to act through recommendations and other less binding or indeed non-binding means; this is true even where, as in the case of WHO, the agency does have a power to establish binding regulations, subject to contracting out.

In practically none of these agencies is there a desire for increased legislative power being vested in the agency as such.

As far as the EEC is concerned, we were told that the Communities were utilizing the full gamut of decisions to recommendations and opinions. There does not seem to be any predisposition to favor the non-binding as opposed to the binding type of technique.

The World Bank and Fund have done a good deal of legislating in a very broad sense, at least in establishing norms in connection with bi-lateral agreements: in the case of the Bank, the loan agreements, and in the case of the Fund, their stand-by arrangements, or, even in the absence of such

515

agreements, though the consultation process. Moreover, the Fund does seem to enforce a code of obligation and has passed a limited number of implementing regulations.

The U.N. seems to be using all forms of these techniques although there appears to be an increasing use of resolutions, and increasing concern about this.

As far as the legal effect of member states' approval of recommendations is concerned, it seemed to be almost the unanimous consensus of the functional agencies that because a member voted for a particular recommendation, it did not mean that it was legally bound by it, or would have to carry it out.

As far as the U.N. is concerned, there seemed to be a sharp difference of opinion—although it was explained in part by semantics. Some were talking about recommendations which were really interpretations of an existing obligation or were accompanied by contemporaneous statements of the legally binding nature of the recommendations.

We did not discuss internal legal effects except in connection with the EEC, the Central American Common Market, and in connection with the effect given to the IMF and World Bank interpretations of their constituent instruments.

Perhaps international lawyers have not taken into account as much as they should the possible efficacy of domestic courts in carrying out international law. Mr. Lauterpacht's suggestion in this area was certainly most stimulating.

As far as compliance is concerned, we devoted most of our time to discussing the variety of techniques of compliance and the reason why states comply or do not comply. It seems to make a very real difference what the purpose of the agency is or even more what particular role a general agency is playing and what it is in fact that we are trying to have complied with.

As far as the compliance techniques are concerned, there seemed general agreement that there was an unwillingness to use ultimate coercive sanctions and the view was that they were effective if at all, simply as a threat which in fact was not used.

There was a difference of opinion on mobilization of public opinion, although I am not sure whether the difference is more apparent than real, because I think that, even in the case of the ILO, the mobilization of opinion is only the last resort. The ILO feels it is necessary to have this final resort in order to make credible its attempt to arrive at some other solution first. Certainly the International Monetary Fund and the World Bank have indicated that the last thing they want to do is to resort to public opinion in their particular areas. Apparently the U.N. has used the resort to public opinion in some cases but designedly not in others.

Everyone seemed to feel that technical assistance was desirable both as a means of enabling countries to comply with resolutions and also as a

516

means of making decisions understandable to the people who have to administer them.

Other techniques were mentioned as applicable in some situations, such as the use of committees of experts. Natural sanctions were also referred to, particularly in the international aviation field ("avoiding collisions") and in peacekeeping ("avoiding atomic wars").

There was a great deal of discussion about possibilities of applying the "carrot" as well as the "stick" technique. This is perhaps the principal area where a great deal of more thinking needs to be done. The utilization of other agencies in cooperation with the U.N. might have been more fully discussed. The consortium approach was mentioned.

A further question which we discussed was the extent of study and knowledge of the reasons why states comply. Would a study of the reasons why states comply or do not comply help in selecting compliance techniques? Naturally, as pointed out, such a study to a certain extent would be in the realm of social psychology and political science as well as law.

One thing we did not refer to at length was whether there was any necessity for structural changes in international organizations. We discussed the possibility of increasing legislative powers of the Specialized Agencies, but not changes in the U.N., perhaps because this is regarded as politically impossible.

After a discussion of topics which future gatherings of legal advisors of international organizations might usefully discuss, the Chairman adjourned the meeting.

INDEX

Acheson, Dean
499

Aggression
387

Ago, Roberto
150

Apartheid
12, 136, 491, 497
I.L.O. Constitution and, 136
U.N. Resolutions on, 12-13, 35, 47
U.N. Special Committee on Apartheid,
56

Arab-Israeli conflict
32, 37, 40, 44, 50, 480, 481

Australia
Non-Intervention Resolution and, 390

Austria
constitutional practice with respect to
treaties, 423
Council of Europe and, 349-350, 423

Belgium
European Convention on Human Rights,
347-348

Benson, Wilfred
498

Brazil
I.L.O. and, 150

Bretton Woods Conference
469
See also **G.A.T.T.; I.B.R.D.; I.M.F.**

Central American Common Market
351-354, 506-507
dispute settlement, 507
Economic Council, 352
individuals, obligations under, 353-354
powers of, 352-354, 506
Secretariat, 507
supra-national competence, 506

Central American Integration Treaties
68, 352
self-executing provisions, 68

**Choice of techniques to carry out an
agreed course of action**
209, 359, 366, 379, 395, 405-408,
432-433, 444-447, 515-516
Council of Europe, 340-343, 422-423
determined by subject matter of decision,
495
European Communities, 309-314, 395
F.A.O. 212-227
informal means, 395
I.B.R.D., 103-105
I.C.A.O., 163-165, 186-191, 451
I.L.O., 134-139
I.M.F., 72-83
summary, 515-516
United Nations, 480, 495
W.H.O., 281, 284

Churchill, Sir Winston
489

**Committee for Technical Co-operation
in Africa South of the Sahara**
515

Compliance
32-49, 52-56, 360, 366, 367, 372-375, 378,
412-421, 431, 495-499, 516
See also **Internal Legal Effects of
Decisions of International
Organisations; Reports; Sanctions**
community expectations and, 372-375,
380, 381
Council of Europe, 424
diplomatic assistance, 481
domestic pressures for, 38, 39-40, 41
effectiveness, distinguished from, 32, 207,
219, 387-390, 401, 447
encouragement of, 443, 447-448
European Communities, 326-332,
412-421
factors operating in favour of, 37-38,
39-40, 49-50, 283, 372
F.A.O., 219
formal techniques, 412, 413
functional organisations, in, 186, 283, 412

G.A.T.T., 306
informal means, 90-94, 116-117, 132, 153, 326-329, 370, 412-421, 434, 435, 443
informal persuasion, 75-76, 283, 306
inspection, 287
I.A.D.B., 132-133
I.A.E.A., 286-287
I.B.R.D., 114-117, 487
I.C.A.O., 168-186, 201-202, 412, 442, 497
I.L.O., 52, 54, 55, 144-153, 434-436, 441-442
I.M.C.O., 514
I.M.F., 75, 90-94, 478, 487
judicial procedures, 329-332
mobilisation of shame, 434-435, 442, 447-456, 482, 496, 511-2, 516
peacekeeping and, 481-482
problems, 367, 368
reasons for non-compliance, 41-48
reciprocity, relevance of, 48-49, 161, 504-506
sanctions, use of to effect, 31, 40, 46, 75, 160-161, 375
summary, 516
technical assistance and, 432, 443, 453-454, 481, 516
variables, dependent upon, 33-50, 157, 207, 366, 386, 502-503
with United Nations decisions, 33-48, 50, 367, 388, 479-488, 502-503
W.H.O., 283, 412

Congo
36, 488, 493
O.N.U.C., 488

Contracting-out
See **International Legislation**

Council of Europe
67, 340-345, 421-428
Agreements, 340, 341-343, 422
  implementation, 343-345
  internal legal effects, 423
  legal nature, 341, 342, 422
  opening to signature, 342, 422
  ratification, 341, 422
aim, 340
choice of techniques, 422-423
Committee of Deputies, 421
Committee of Ministers, 340, 342, 421
  Committee on Legal Co-operation, 344
  examination of Annual Reports, 344
  resolutions, 340

voting, 341, 342-3
complaints procedure, 425
compliance, 424
Consultative Assembly, 342, 344-345
  national parliaments and, 344-345
  recommendations, 421
Conventions, 340, 341-343, 422
  accession to, 341, 342
  implementation, 342, 343-345, 427
  internal legal effects, 423
  legal nature, 341, 342, 422
  opening to signature, 342
  ratification, 341, 422
  submission to signature, 342, 422
decisions, types of, 340-343, 421
government representatives, 422
implementation of decisions, 343-345, 425-428
national parliaments, 428
Partial Agreements, 343
Recommendations, 340-341, 422
  adoption, 340-1
  implementation, 341, 343
  legal effect, 341, 422, 423
Records of the Minutes, 422
Reports by members, 343-344, 424-427
Resettlement Fund for Refugees and Over-population, 421
Secretary-General, 342, 427

Court of Justice of the European Communities
See **European Economic Community**

Covenants on Human Rights (U.N.)
364, 365, 375, 397, 435, 480
compliance problems, 365, 435, 495-496
ratification, 364

Cuba
missile crisis, 14, 486
O.A.S. and, 351, 429-430

Customary Law, International
12, 21, 371
development of, in U.N., 38
establishment of, 13
opinio juris, 20, 21, 22

Decisions of International Organisations
See also **Implementation of International Decisions; Internal Legal Effects of Decisions of International Organisations;** separate headings of international organisations

basis of obligation under, 372, 373, 392, 395
binding nature, 157-158, 208, 211, 351, 388, 395, 399-402, 429
classification, 157-158, 209-211, 378, 379, 385, 388, 417
context of, 275-276, 397
definition, 48 n.32, 207, 366, 367, 368, 370, 372, 374-375, 380-381, 382, 385, 386, 388, 394, 402-405, 407
forms, 208, 366-367, 373-375, 375, 380, 394-395, 416
hierarchy, 390-393, 397, 405
legal nature, 208, 393
recommendations, 388-389, 392, 396-397, 398, 405
scope of, 208
terminology, 158-159, 211 n.9, 388, 397, 405
treaties and, 395-398

Declaration on Human Rights
See **United Nations**

De Visscher
23

Dependant Territories
compliance problems, 95-96
I.M.F. provision for, 95-96

Developing Countries
See **Less Developed Nations**

Dillard, Hardy
15, 28, 30

Domestic Jurisdiction
12
anti-colonialism and, 14

Dominican Republic
O.A.S. and (1960), 351, 429

Economic Commission for Europe
476
Report of Executive Secretary, 471

Economic and Social Council of the United Nations
Extended Technical Assistance Programme (E.P.T.A.), 224
I.L.O. and, 150
World Food Programme and, 226

Effectiveness of International Decisions
218-219, 385, 386, 388, 403, 431, 433, 446, 488
See also **Sanctions**
compliance and, 32, 207, 219, 387-390, 401, 447
meaning of, 32, 72-73, 207, 404
sanctions and, 160-161
technical assistance and, 433

Euratom
Directives, 68
Treaty
  Art. 161, 68, 69
Regulations, 68

European Coal and Steel Community
309-346, 418-419, 486-487
amendment of treaty, 335-338
Court of Justice, 335, 336-338
High Authority, 335-338, 418, 419
Treaty
  Art. 70, 317
  Art. 92, 318
  Art. 95, 335-338

European Commission of Human Rights
56, 67
See also **European Convention on Human Rights**

European Communities
68, 500
defined by Court of Justice, 68

European Convention on Establishment
343

European Convention on Human Rights
56, 67, 346-350, 423
Belgian linguistic legislation, 423
Commission of Human Rights, 347-350
Committee of Ministers, 346, 347, 349
De Becker v. Belgium, 347-348
implementation of, 343, 346
mobilisation of shame, 455-456
national courts and, 67, 346
Ofner, Hopfinger, Pataki, Dunshirn v. Austria, 349-350
reports under Art. 57, 424

European Convention on the Establishment of Companies
343

European Convention on the International Classification of Patents for Invention
344

European Convention on the Punishment of Road Traffic Offences
343

European Court of Human Rights
56, 67, 69, 346, 348, 422

European Cultural Convention
344

European Development Fund
477

European Economic Community
40, 309-345, 363, 364, 365, 408-421
See also **Rome, Treaty of**
Agreements,
  with international organisations, 310
  with non-member countries, 310
Association Conventions, 314
cereals, 312
character of, 415, 416, 430
choice of measure, 311-312
Commission, 311, 312, 314, 315, 316,
  400, 413, 414
  binding nature of measures, 314
  consultation process, 414
  co-operation with Member States,
    328-329, 413
  power of initiative, 413
  proceedings under Art. 169, 329-330,
    411
  proceedings under Art. 170, 331-332,
    411
  proposals of, 415
Committees, 327-8
community law, 317
  application, 323
  development, 418
  implemented by executive procedure,
    322
  interpretation, 322-325
  primacy of, 325, 418
  role of Commission, 413
compared with other international
  organisations, 415
complaints procedures,
  under Art. 169, 329-331, 332
  under Art. 170, 331-332
compliance machinery, 326-332

Advisory bodies, 327-328
co-operation, 326-327, 328
judicial procedures, 329-332
obtaining information, 326-327
Conventions, 313, 400
Costa case, 321, 324
Council, 311-316, 409-410, 414
Court of Justice, 68-69, 314, 316, 319,
  411, 418-421
  domestic courts and, 323-325
  Grundig/Consten case, 401-402
  jurisdiction under Art. 177, 324-325,
    419-420
  nature of judgments, 420
  proceedings under Art. 169, 330-331
  proceedings under Art. 170, 332
  task, 317, 318, 420, 421
  Van Gend and Loos case, 317
Decisions, 310, 368
  addressed to individuals, 310, 318
  addressed to Member States, 310, 319
  direct applicability, 318, 319
Decisions of the Representatives of the
  Governments of the Member States
  meeting in the Council, 313-314
Directives, 68, 310, 311, 408-409
  adoption, 311
  binding nature, 311
  characteristics, 310, 319
  when used, 311-312, 409
federated states, 333-334
  Germany, 333-334
  Italy, 334
France
  "empty chair" policy, 409-410
individuals, 309, 310
  directly affected by E.E.C. measures,
    317-318, 319
  judicial protection of, 324
informality in, 412-421
legal effect of measures, 316-325
Luxembourg Agreement, 414
Member States
  co-operation with E.E.C., 326-329, 414
  permanent representatives, 410-414
national courts, 68
  Court of Justice and, 323-324, 325, 419
  interpretation of community law, 321,
    323-325
Opinions, 310, 419
  adoption, 311
  nature, 310, 319, 419
Recommendations, 310, 400
  adoption, 311
  nature, 310, 319

522

Records in the Minutes, 312
Regulations, 68, 309
  adoption, 311
  binding nature, 311
  characteristics, 310
  direct applicability, 318
  when used, 311, 312
Resolutions, 312, 409
Timetable, 409, 410
Transitional period, 411
voting, 314-316
  abstention, 315
  qualified majority, 315, 316
  simple majority, 315, 316
  unanimity, 315, 316
  weighting system, 315

European Investment Bank
472, 477-478
I.B.R.D. compared, 478
loans, 478

European Recovery Program
78, 257

European Social Charter
reporting system, 343, 425-427

Expropriation
14, 462, 473
foreign expropriatory legislation, 64-65,
  510

Federal Communications Commission
87, 123-126, 477

Federated States
360
provisions for, in
  European Communities, 333-334
  F.A.O., 235
  I.B.R.D., 117-119
  I.C.A.O., 200
  I.L.O., 153-155
  I.M.F., 94-96

Food and Agriculture Organisation
206-276, 439-440
Article XIV Agreements, 217, 217 n. 26,
  218-221, 439
  approval, 218
  directly regulatory provisions, 220-221
effectiveness of, 218
  obligations under, 219-221
Article XIV Bodies, 219

Article XV Agreements, 222-223
  F.A.O. functions, 223
  nature of, 222
  reports, 223
  subject matter, 222
Code of Principles concerning Milk and
  Milk Products, 227-238
  acceptance, 230, 234
  adoption, 228
  application, 230
  Codex Alimentarius and, 228, 229, 230
  Committee of Government Experts,
   228, 229, 232, 235
  composition of Standards, 229, 230,
   231, 236
  contents, 229
  dispute settlement, 235
  federated states, 235-236
General Standard for Cheese, 231
  implementation, 233
  International Dairy Federation and,
   227-228
  International Standards Organisation
   and, 227
  interpretation, 229
  participation in, 232
  scope, 229
  standards adopted, 228
See also Stresa Convention
Codex Alimentarius, 69, 238-256
  acceptance of Standards, 250-257, 440
  Code of Principles and, 228, 229
  Codex Committees, 241-242, 248-249,
   250
  Codex Standards, 240, 242-257
  establishment of, 238
  "General Principles", 242-244
  implementation, 255-256
  institutional framework, 239-242
  purpose, 243
  sanctions, 256, 450
  sources, 238
  withdrawal, 256
  W.H.O. and, 242, 243, 248-249
Committee on Commodity Problems,
  259, 264-275 passim
  Guiding Lines on Surplus Disposal,
   260, 262
  Working Group, 267-268
compliance, 219, 221, 451-452
  problems rare, 219, 221
Conference, 214, 215
Constitution,
  Preamble, 212
  Art. I(2), 212

Art. I(3), 213
Art. VI, 215
Art. VIII(4), 213, 214
Art. XI, 214, 215, 216
Art. XIV, 215, 217-221
Art. XV, 222-223
Art. XVI(2), 213
Art. XVIII(2), 216
Art. XVIII(5), 216
Consultative Sub-Committee on Surplus
Disposal
appraisal of, 269
developing countries and, 270
effectiveness of, 275
forum for consultation, 275
functions, 264-267, 272-275
G.A.T.T. and, 268, 271
membership, 264
reciprocity, 270
relationship with other international
organisations, 271, 273-274
"Usual Marketing Requirements",
271-272, 273
Working Group, 267
Conventions, 217, 218-221
decisions, forms of, 212-227
Director-General, 214, 220, 222, 223, 260
Emergency Measures, 219
E.P.T.A., participation in, 224
financial obligations of members, 212,
216-217
functions of, 212-213
headquarters agreements, 213, 223
legislative process,
adoption of standards, codes of
principles . . . 227
Codex Alimentarius, 250-254, 257
contracting-out system, 227
nature of, 227
obligations of members, 212, 213-217
under Code of Principles, 231, 233
under Codex Alimentarius, 255-256
under Conventions and Agreements,
219-221
under technical co-operation
agreements, 225
Stresa Convention (1951),
Annexes, 231-232, 236
"Appellations d'Origine", 231, 233, 237
Code of Principles and, 232, 235,
236-238
contents, 231-232
dispute settlement, 235
objective, 231
operation of, 233

participation in, 232-233
Permanent Council, 233
"Principles and Procedures which should
Govern Conventions and Agreements",
217-218, 222
"Principles of Surplus Disposal",
257-262, 457
acceptance, 260
background, 257-260
consultative machinery, 264-275
influence, 263
structure, 260
See also Committee on Commodity
Problems; Consultative Sub-Committee
on Surplus Disposal
privileges and immunities, 212, 213-214
reports procedure, 53, 212, 214-216,
451-452
under Article XI, 451-452
under Article XV Agreements, 223
sanctions, 216, 221
Codex Alimentarius, 256
element of reciprocity, 504
natural, 221
technical assistance, 440
Technical Co-operation Agreements,
224-226
U.N.D.P. and, 219, 224-225
U.N.S.P. and, 224
World Food Programme and, 219,
225-226, 257-258, 263, 266

Force, Use of
11, 13

France
constitutional practice with respect to
treaties, 67, 142, 320, 324
E.E.C. and, 323, 409-410
I.M.F. and, 478

General Agreement on Tariffs and Trade
304-308, 469
accession to, 305
administration of, 304, 306
amendments to, 304-305
Art. XXIII, 307
Art. XXV, 304
Art. XXV(5), 307
Art. XXXV, 305
binding provisions of, 304
complaints,
non-signatories, 305
procedure, 307
compliance, 306, 307

524

concessions, 304
Contracting Parties, 304, 305, 306, 307
  Chairman of, 305
decisions under, 305-306
Director-General, 305
dispute settlement, 307
F.A.O. and, 257
I.M.F. and, 92, 469
interpretation of, 305
most-favored-nation clause, 304
national legislation and, 304
nature of, 304
obligations of members, 304, 307
precedent, use of, 305-306
sanctions, 308
Supplementary Agreements, 305
voting, 306
waiver, 307
withdrawal, 308

General Assembly of the United Nations
11-13, 18, 42-43, 391-392, 493-494
decisions, 391-392
Declarations, 37, 493
  Approval of the Nuremberg
    Principles, 37
  Granting of Independence to Colonial
    Countries and Peoples, 500
  Offences against the Peace and
    Security of Mankind, 37
  Racial Discrimination, 391
Fourth Committee, 56
movement away from law, 500-501
quasi-legislative activity, 11, 12-13, 34,
  38, 493-494, 499-502
recommendations, 68, 389, 390, 391-392,
  396-397, 407
replacing Security Council, 42-43
resolutions, 160, 283, 500
sanctions, 160
Special Committee on Principles of
  International Law Concerning Friendly
  Relations and Co-operation among
  States, 500-501
Special Committee on the Situation with
  regard to the Implementation of the
  Declaration on the Granting of
  Independence to Colonial Countries
  and Peoples, 56
Uniting for Peace resolution, 48, 391, 499

Gentlemen's Agreements
373, 375-377, 388, 394, 405, 407
Security Council representation, 33,
  375-376, 382

Germany
constitutional practice with respect to
  treaties, 67, 122, 320, 321, 324
Council of Europe and, 341
E.E.C. and, 321, 323, 333-334

Ghana
F.A.O. and, 514
I.L.O. and, 149
Volta Dam project, 107

Great Britain
colonial issues, 42
constitutional law, 58-59
constitutional practice with respect to
  treaties, 67, 122, 166
parliamentary question time, 38
Rhodesia, 36-37, 43, 44, 45, 58-63, 391,
  507-512
Southern Rhodesia Act, 1965, 59
Suez, 42

Greece
I.L.O. and, 142, 150

Hart, H.
27, 28

Henkin, Louis
33

Higgins, Rosalyn
160

Human Rights
32, 37, 52, 53, 56, 391, 435, 487, 490-491,
  494, 496
See also **European Commission of
  Human Rights; European Convention
  on Human Rights; European Court of
  Human Rights; Inter-American
  Commission on Human Rights;
  United Nations**

**Implementation of
International Decisions**
57-65, 193, 366, 372-373, 378, 424-428
See also **Compliance; Internal Legal
  Effects of Decisions of International
  Organisations; Reports; Sanctions**
at individual level, 57, 58, 317-318, 353
at national level, 62, 64, 66-70, 73, 86-90,
  134, 139-140, 141-144, 165-167,
  173-176, 193, 194-195, 197, 219, 233,
  255-256, 279, 286, 295-296, 304, 318,

319-320, 321-323, 341, 344, 347-350, 364, 451
informal means, 363, 412-421
technical assistance and, 432
through national courts, 57-65, 141-142, 323-324, 346, 420, 507-512
through other international organisations, 456-460

Individuals
bound directly by international decisions, 166-167, 353
compliance with international decisions, 57, 58
Central American Common Market and, 353
European Communities and, 309, 310, 317, 324
I.C.A.O. and, 166-167, 195-196
petition,
European Commission of Human Rights, 56
United Nations, 56
Rome Treaty, rights under, 68
U.N. resolutions addressed to, 36
U.P.U. and, 293

Indonesia
withdrawal from U.N. over Malaya, 33

Inter-American Commission on Human Rights
56

Inter-American Committee of the Alliance for Progress
129

Inter-American Social and Economic Council
129

Inter-American Development Bank
129-133, 383-384, 473-475
Articles of Agreement, 383
    Art. II(4)(b), 130, 131
    Art. IV(3)(e), 130, 131
    Art. V, 129, 130
    Art. V(3)(a), 131
Board of Executive Directors, 129, 130-132, 133, 383, 473
Board of Governors, 384
callable capital, 474
compliance, 132-133

co-operation with Inter-American system, 474
flexibility in, 473
formal procedures, use of, 415
functions, 129-130, 383
headquarters agreement, 383
I.B.R.D. and, 130, 384, 473
international law and, 384
I.M.F. and, 130
interpretation, 384, 473
loan contracts, 132, 384
"Management", 473
members, 473
planned economies, 133
powers, 129-130
reports,
    Socio-Economic Progress in Latin America, 129
sanctions, 132-133, 384, 473
Social Progress Trust Fund Agreement, 129

Internal Legal Effects of Decisions of International Organisations
62, 64, 66-70, 73, 187-190, 360, 476-477
See also **Implementation of International Decisions; National Courts**
constitutional provisions, see **Treaties**
Council of Europe, 423
European Communities, 316-325
F.A.O., 233
I.A.E.A., 285, 286
I.B.R.D., 104, 106-114, 120-126
I.C.A.O., 165-166, 194-198
I.L.O., 140-144
I.M.F., 86-90, 476
U.P.U., 291-292, 294, 302-303
W.H.O., 279

International Air Transport Association
442

International Atomic Energy Agency
285-289
Board of Governors, 285, 286, 288
functions, 285
inspections, 287, 288
no legislative power, 438
Safeguards System, 286-288,
    Agreements under, 287
    compliance machinery, 287
    meaning of, 286
    prior consent necessary, 287
    reports, 287
    violations, 287

Safety Standards, 285-286, 438
sanctions, 288
Statute,
Art. III(A), 285
Art. XI, 285, 287
Art. XII, 287, 288
Transport Regulations, 285-286
formulation, 285-286
influence of, 286
review of, 286

International Bank for Reconstruction and Development
55, 100-128, 363, 458-467
Agricultural Credit Loans, 109
Articles of Agreement, 101,
amendment, 119-120
Board of Governors, 119-120, 462
borrowing operations, 120-121
capital, 100-101
compliance, 114-117
formal procedures, 114-115, 117
informal procedures, 116
Czechoslovakia, expulsion, 465
decisions, 103, 368, 370, 379
form of, 103-105, 379
development of, 461
dispute settlement, 115
economic reports, 461
Executive Directors, 119, 124, 126, 461
Federal Communications Commission
Case, 123-126, 477
federated states, 117-119
F.A.O. and, 219, 460
Guarantee Agreements, 104, 105, 107,
110-111, 113, 114-115, 126-8
informal understandings, use of, 103-104,
370
International Development Association,
102, 111, 118, 119, 467
International Finance Corporation, 102,
120
I.M.F., compared, 105, 460-461
interpretation of Articles of Agreement,
55, 419, 466, 476-477
effect in local law, 123-126
Letters of Representation, 104, 463
Loan Agreements, 105, 106, 110-111,
113, 114-115, 119, 126-128, 459
Loans, 101-102, 106-108, 461-463
administration of, 108-110
Australia, Loan No. 156 AU, 119
conditions, 101, 103, 105, 106-108, 462
default, 114-115, 462
further funds, 110

governmental obligations, 110-114, 462
Kenya Tea Development, Credit
No. 64 KE, 111
Malaysia, Loan No. 500 MA, 108
Pakistan Education Credit, Credit
No. 87 PAK, 107
pre-loan enquiries, 461
prematuration, 114-115, 117, 464, 465
suspension of disbursements, 114-115,
117, 464, 465
Volta Dam in Ghana, Loan
No. 310 GH, 107, 465
local law, impact upon, 103, 105,
106-110, 110-111, 112-113, 120-126
members, 100-101
informal understandings with I.B.R.D.,
103-104
obligations under Loan Agreements,
102, 105, 106-110, 110-111
Missions of Experts, 101
nature, 100-102
President, 461-462
privileges and immunities, 120-126
Procurement Guidelines, 112
Project Agreement, 104
Projects, 101-102, 108-114, 462
economic considerations, 106-108
evaluation, 102
financial considerations, 110-111
governmental assurances, 106, 108-110
supervision of, 116,
technical considerations, 112-114
profits, disposition of, 466-467
purposes, 100, 466
sanctions, 114-117, 126-127, 463-467
expulsion, 464-465
informal, 116-117
technical assistance, 463
Unesco and, 460
unpaid subscriptions, 466

International Civil Aviation Organisation
55, 156-205, 363, 431-432
Air Navigation Commission, 170, 172,
173, 188
Air Traffic Control Services, 197
"airworthiness", 381, 386, 391
Annexes to Chicago Convention, 156,
160, 165, 172, 180, 188, 190, 193
adoption, 169, 171, 190, 193
amendments, 172, 188
notification of differences, 171, 188,
203-204
Assembly, 162, 176

policy statements on implementation, 177-178, 184-186
Aviation Development Fund, proposed, 186
carriage by air, contracts of, 195-196
Certificates,
  endorsement, 163
  of airworthiness, 162, 195
  of competency, 162
  recognition of, 195
Chicago Convention (1944),
  Art. 5; 159
  Art. 12; 167, 189, 193, 195, 431-432
  Art. 28; 168
  Art. 29; 201
  Art. 33; 162, 195
  Art. 34; 201
  Art. 37; 168, 169
  Art. 38; 169, 188, 197, 204
  Art. 39; 163, 167
  Art. 40; 163, 167
  Art. 50; 192
  Art. 51; 192
  Art. 54; 168, 169
  Art. 62; 162, 192, 193
  Art. 77; 191
  Art. 84; 163, 199
  Art. 85; 163, 199
  Art. 87; 163, 192, 193, 194, 199
  Art. 88; 163, 199
  Art. 90; 168; 169; 173; 190
  Art. 91; 191
  Art. 92; 191
  Art. 93; 191
  Art. 93(bis); 189
  Art. 94; 189, 200
  amendments, 189, 199, 200-201
compliance, techniques, 168-186, 198-199, 200-201
consensus process, 164-165, 190, 191
consultation, 170, 172
contracting-out, 162, 188-189, 193, 196, 201
conventions, 163-164, 194-195
  ratification of, 187
Cooper, John, 431
Council, 156, 159, 162, 166, 169, 171, 173, 176, 188, 189, 192, 193, 392, 417, 431
  Air Transport Committee, 180
  President, 188
Danish/Icelandic Joint Financing Agreements (1956), 189, 197
decisions, 158-160, 164, 166-167, 168, 186-191, 192, 193-194, 392, 393

dispute settlement, 163, 199, 392
Facilitation of International Air Transport, 172, 180
  national facilitation committees, 180-181
  regulatory material on, 172, 180
federated states, 200
functions, 156, 162
Headquarters Agreement, 380
high seas, 167, 189, 193, 431-432
International Standards and Recommended Practices (SARPS), 165, 168-169, 190
  adoption, 169, 171
  development of, 170-171
  expectation of compliance, 190
  implementation, 173-176, 179
  notification of differences, 170, 171, 176, 177-178, 199, 203, 204
  publications, 179
interpretation of constitution, 55, 163, 199, 392
judicial control, 417
legislative process, 162, 168-186, 187-191, 277, 431
  contracting-out, 162, 188-189, 193, 196
Licences,
  endorsement, 163
  of personnel, 162, 167
  recognition of, 195
mobilisation of shame, 450
municipal law and, 165-166, 174, 194-198
nature, 156 157
Observers, 442
Prague, 198
privileges and immunities, 198, 200
Procedures for Air Navigation Services (PANS), 165, 169
  approval, 169, 171
  development of, 170-171
  expectation of compliance, 190
  implementation, 173-176, 179
  verification of differences, 169, 171, 176, 177-178, 189, 199, 204
  publications, 179
Quebec Province, 198, 380
recommendations, 164, 190
Regional Air Navigation Plans, 170, 171, 173
  approval, 171
  development of, 171
  implementation, 181-186
  review, 173
  Special Implementation Panel, 173, 181
  Standing Group of the Council on

Implementation, 173, 184
Regional Supplementary Procedures
(SUPPS), 169-179, 380
amendment, 188
approval, 171, 188
development of, 170-171
expectation of compliance, 190
notification of differences, 171, 188,
204
regions, 169, 170, 173
regulations, 69
reports, 173, 176, 178, 198-199, 203-205
resolutions, 159-160, 164
Romania, 190
sanctions, 161-163, 201, 416-417, 450
secretariat, 176
Secretary-General, 188
voting, 189-191
affirmative, effect of, 191-192

International Coffee Agreement
361

International Court of Justice
I.L.O. and, 149
interpretative role, 53-54, 55
judgments of, 69
judicial opinions in, 12-13
movement away from, 480
Statute of, Art. 38, 9, 12-13, 368, 371,
381

**International Federation of Airline Pilots'
Associations**
442

International Grains Arrangement (1967)
263, 271
Wheat Trade Convention, 263, 271

International Labor Organisation
52, 54, 55-56, 134-155, 366, 433-436
amendment of constitution, 155
Commissions of Inquiry, 143, 149, 150,
152, 434, 435
Committee of Experts, 52, 142, 145-147,
149, 448-449
comments, 146-147, 448
composition, 146, 448
report, 146, 448
requests, 147
terms of reference, 146
Committee on Freedom of Association,
150-151, 152

complaints procedure, 54, 55-56, 143,
149-153, 425
against Brazil, 150
against Greece, 150
against Italy, 150
against Japan, 151
against Liberia, 54, 143, 149
against Portugal, 54, 149
Constitution, 54, 137, 155
Preamble; 135, 140, 150
Art. 19; 134, 138, 139, 141, 145, 153
Art. 22; 144
Art. 23(2); 145
Art. 26; 152
Art. 36; 155
Conventions, 52, 69, 134-140, 379, 381,
434, 440-441
adoption, 137, 139-140
effect of ratification, 141-144
flexibility clauses, 138-139
interpretation, 392
modification, 137
national authorities, 139-140
reservations, inadmissibility, 137-138
revision, 139
supervisory machinery, 135, 140,
141-142, 144-153
total, 136
unratified, 140, 145, 441
Declaration of Philadelphia (1944), 135,
140, 150
Director-General, 139, 145, 433
Employment Service Convention (1948),
150
"equal opportunity", 135-136
Fact-Finding and Conciliation
Commission on Freedom of
Association, 151, 152
federated states, 153-155
Forced Labor Conventions, 143, 149
"freedom of association", 135, 150-151
Freedom of Association and Protection of
the Right to Organise Convention
(1948), 150, 151
functions, 134
Governing Body, 52, 134, 140, 141, 145,
149, 150
Hungary (1956), 513
internal legal effects of decisions,
140-144
International Labor Conferences, 52,
137, 139, 145
International Labor Office, 54, 137,
140, 392
interpretation of constitution, 54, 392

Labor Inspection Convention (1947),
150
legislative process, 433, 434
mobilisation of shame, 442, 447-449, 496
obligations of national authorities,
193-140, 141, 144-145
Official Bulletin, 54, 392
Promotional Programme, 153
Recommendations, 52, 69, 134, 139, 278
adoption, 139
national authorities, 139-140
supervisory machinery, 145-153
total numbers, 136
reports procedure, 52, 140, 141, 144-149,
425-426, 434-435
ratified conventions, 144-145, 146-147
unratified conventions, 145, 147, 441
seminars, 153
South Africa, 136, 497
supervisory machinery, 144-153
technical assistance, 153, 433, 434, 436,
453-454

International Law
9-31, 48-49
See also Customary Law, International;
International Legislation; Practice of
States; Treaties
community expectations, relevance of,
22-27, 28, 29, 158, 161, 162, 370-375
compliance with, 48-49
conceptual, 386, 387
dualist theory of, 66, 324
enforcement through national courts; see
National Courts
formulation of, 18
law of international organisations and,
368, 379, 381, 393-394, 395, 404
legitimacy and effectiveness in, 20, 22
monist theory of, 66, 320-321
normative processes in, 12, 18, 28 n. 77,
29, 161
obligation in,
basis of, 9, 20, 21
definition of, 16, 28-31
indeterminacy of, 11-12
recognition of, by states, 21
tacit, 13-14, 19
theories of, 15-16
obligatory legal norms in, 16-20, 21-22,
28
primacy over domestic law, constitutional
provisions, 320-321, 324
psychological factors in, 20-27
sources of, 10, 12, 23, 368, 370

International Law Commission
18, 19, 137

International Law Reports
393

International Legislation
11, 189, 208, 226-227, 277, 284, 381,
430-447
See also Treaties
adoption of standards, codes of principles,
regulations etc.,
E.N.E.A., 438
Euratom, 438
F.A.O., 227, 439-440
I.A.E.A., 438
I.B.R.D., 443
O.A.S., 443
United Nations, 443, 444, 493-494, 495
W.H.O., 277, 278, 281, 438
contracting-out system, 211
F.A.O., 226-227
I.C.A.O., 162, 188-189, 192, 193, 196,
201
W.H.O., 277-278, 439
European Economic Community, 418
I.A.E.A., 438
inter organisation co-operation, 456-460
legislative techniques, 434, 436-439
operational techniques and, 433

Inter Governmental Maritime
Consultative Organisation
286, 514

International Monetary Fund
55, 71-99, 160, 363, 458, 467-472,
478-479, 504-505
Articles of Agreement,
Art. I; 76, 97
Art. III(2); 85
Art. IV; 74, 95
Art. V(3)(a); 74
Art. V(3)(d); 97
Art. V(5); 74
Art. V(8)(d); 74
Art. VI(1); 74
Art. VII(3); 73
Art. VIII; 91, 94
Art. VIII(2)(b); 67, 73, 86, 88, 89
Art. VIII(5); 90
Art. XI; 95
Art. XII(2); 83
Art. XII(3); 83, 85
Art. XII(5); 83

530

Art. XII(8); 73
Art. XIV; 90-94, 468
Art. XIV(4); 73, 74
Art. XV; 74, 75
Art. XVIII; 86-90, 97
Art. XX(2)(a); 87
Art. XX(2)(g); 95, 96
Art. XXV; 97
Art. XXVII(a); 97
Art. XXIX(2); 97
balance of payments, 71, 78
Board of Governors, 72, 75, 83
code of obligations, as, 71, 77
complaints procedure, 76
compliance with obligations of, 90-94, 478
Consultative Groups, 472
consultations,
    under Art. XIV, 90-94, 98, 99, 468
    under Art. XVI, 94
currency,
    change in par value, 74
    convertibility, 90-91, 93
    establishment of par value, 77
    "scarce", 73
decisions, 367, 368, 379, 478, 487-488
    effect upon domestic law, 73
    form of, 72, 379
    nature of, 71-72, 84
    reached by consensus, 85
exchange contracts contrary to exchange
    control regulations, 67
exchange restrictions, 73, 74
exchange transactions, 74, 77
Executive Directors, 72, 75, 76, 79-80,
    83-86, 92-93, 97
    annual report, 72
    decisions, 84
    relations with members, 85
    status, 84
    voting, 83-84
federated states, 94-96
financial and regulatory agency, as, 71,
    467
Financial Consortia, 468, 471-472,
    474-475
    Debt Reorganisation Arrangements,
    475
    Greek, 471
    Indian, 472, 475
    Turkish, 471, 475
flexibility, limits to, 478-479
France (1948), 478
General Account, 96-97
G.A.T.T. and, 92, 469

General Arrangements to Borrow, 71,
    468, 505
Gold Tranche rights, 470
income, use of, 470
informal persuasion as means of effecting
    compliance, 75, 449-450, 479
I.B.R.D. compared, 462, 467-468
interpretation of Articles of Agreement,
    55, 72, 86-90, 419, 476
Managing Director, 75-76, 79, 84
members, 71
    equivalent treatment of, 504-505
    legal effect of approval of decisions,
    83-86
mobilisation of shame, 449-450
multilateral surveillance, 467
obligations of members, 77, 478
    as legal absolutes, 478
    implied, 77-78
    under stand-by arrangements, 79-80
Performance Criteria, 79-80, 97
Post-War Transitional Period, 90-91
privileges and immunities, 87
purposes, 71, 76-77, 467
Quotas, 71, 84-85
reports, 73, 75, 92, 468
resources, 71-72, 78
    relationship with members' obligations,
    77
    use of, 73, 77, 458
sanctions, 72-76, 97, 160-161
    performance criteria and, 79-80
    rarely used, 75
Special Drawing Account, 96, 97
Special Drawing Rights, 96, 97
Stand-by Arrangements, 78-83, 97, 363,
    367, 368, 405, 469
    legal character of, 82-83, 97, 367, 368,
    399
    period, 81
    practice, 79-80
    prior notice clause, 469-470
    reasons for success of, 79-82
technical assistance, 454, 458
Tranche policies, 78, 97
Transitional Arrangements, 73, 90-94, 98
United States Federal Communications
    Case, 87
voting, 83-85, 417
withdrawal, 75

International Organisations
constituent instruments, 364, 446
See also **Interpretation of Constitutions
    of International Organisations**

co-operation between, 209, 224-226, 276,
456-460, 517
delegation of national powers to, 67, 320
economic, 369
financial, 76, 446, 458-475, 476-479, 506
functional, 156, 157, 207, 363, 365, 378,
381, 387, 389, 430-431, 446
implied powers, 351, 363, 364
integrated, 365
kinds of, 67-68, 208, 227, 365, 366
national parliaments and, 369
nature of, 276, 394
law of, 202, 370-371, 381, 382, 393-394,
404
See also **Treaties; Decisions of**
International Organisations
conflict with municipal law, 197
enforcement through national organs,
68-70
non-self-executing provisions, 68
relationship with international law,
368, 379, 381, 393-394, 395
self-executing provisions, 67
sources, 393
political, 363, 365, 366, 378, 389
practice of, 208-209
secretariats, 381, 382

International Rivers
492

Interpretation of Constitutions of
International Organisations
53-55, 208, 364, 393, 401, 405-406, 408,
419, 473
administrative procedures, 54, 55, 411
by national organs, 69
compared with treaty interpretation, 364
constitutional law methods, 404
E.E.C. 400, 401, 413-414, 419
G.A.T.T., 305
I.A.D.B., 384, 473
I.B.R.D., 55, 419, 476-477
I.C.A.O., 163
I.C.J., role of, 53-54
I.L.O., 54, 392
I.M.F., 55, 86-90, 419, 476
judicial interpretation, 54
W.H.O., 54

Israel
Jerusalem, 41-42, 455

Italy
constitutional practice with respect to

treaties, 67, 142, 320, 321, 324
E.E.C. and, 321, 325, 333, 334
I.L.O. and, 150

Japan
I.L.O. and, 151

Jerusalem
41, 455

Jus Cogens
24

Kashmir
U.N. and, 480, 481, 482

Kelsen, Hans
22

Kenya
I.M.F. project, 111

Korea
U.N. and, 485

Lawyer, Role of
26, 484, 485, 486, 488-493, 497-499, 500

Legal Advisor
32, 33, 35, 66
of international organisations, 32, 375,
386, 387, 394, 404, 406-407, 408

Legal Effects of Approval of Decisions
by Member States
359, 398-399, 516
community expectations and, 399
Council of Europe, 342
European Communities, 314-316
I.C.A.O., 191-194, 399
I.L.O., 139-140
I.M.F., 83-86
summary, 515
U.N., 38

Less Developed Nations
14, 443, 453, 463
F.A.O. and, 270
I.B.R.D. and, 463
I.M.F. and, 505

Liberia
I.L.O. and, 143, 149

Luxembourg
constitutional practice with respect to treaties, 320, 324

Middle East
480-481
See also **Arab-Israeli conflict**

Mobilisation of Shame
See **Compliance;** separate international organisations

McDougal, Myres
15, 22, 27, 37, 387

National Courts
57-65, 73, 507-512
act of state doctrine, 62
Council of Europe and, 346
E.E.C. and, 317-319, 419, 420
I.B.R.D. and, 123-126
I.L.O. and, 141-142
I.M.F. and, 73, 87-89
implementation of international decisions through, 57-65, 73, 346, 507-512
proposed solution to Rhodesian question, through, 57-63, 507-512
proposed solution to South West Africa question, through, 507-512
public policy of lex fori, 60-61, 62

Netherlands
constitutional practice with respect to treaties, 66-67, 122, 320, 324, 423
Dutch Government in Exile, 508, 512

Nigeria
I.D.A. education project, 118

Non-Governmental Organisations
206

Non-Self Governing Territories
reports on, 40, 53, 483, 489-490, 495

Nuclear Non-Proliferation Treaty
364

Nuclear Powers
50, 484-485

Organisation of American States
129, 351, 365, 429-430
Cuba and, 351, 429-430
decisions, 351, 429-430

Dominican Republic (1960), 351, 429
Organ of Consultation, 351, 429-430
Rio Treaty, 351, 429

Organisation for Economic Co-operation and Development
Code of Liberalisation, 369
Council, 68
decisions, 385
mobilisation of shame, 455
reports, 471
treaties, 369
Working Party No. 3, 468

Organisation for European Economic Co-operation
471
Marshall Aid, 471
U.S. ratification of, 364

Outer Space
U.N. Declaration on (1963), 371, 373
Treaty on (1966), 371-372, 373

Pakistan
I.M.F. education project, 107, 109

Participants in Bellagio Conference
357

Petitions
European Convention on Human Rights, 56
Trusteeship Council, 56

Portugal
I.L.O. and, 143, 149
response to Rhodesia sanctions, 41, 43, 46

Practice of States
17, 18-20
accepted as law, 20, 21, 23, 371, 375-376
evidence of opinio juris, 22
importance of, 23
national decision-makers and, 24-25
obligatory effect of, 24

Prize Law
63

Publicity
avoidance of, to bring about compliance, 76
Council of Europe, in, 424
I.L.O., in, 442
reporting system and, 424, 442

533

Ramadier, Paul
150

Ratification
See **Treaties**

Reciprocity
49, 382, 386
as basis of compliance with international
 norms, 49, 478, 504-506
operation of, in international
 organisations, 49, 381, 386, 387
state-to-state level, 387
U.N. and, 387, 484, 505-506

Reports
Council of Europe, 343-344, 424-427
economic reports, 471-472
F.A.O., 53, 212, 214-216, 451-452
G.A.T.T., 307
I.A.E.A., 287
I.C.A.O., 173, 176, 178, 198-199, 203-205
I.L.O. 52, 134, 140, 144-149, 425-426,
 434-435
I.M.F., 73, 75, 92
need for publicity, 424
upon compliance, 38, 40, 44, 144-145,
 148-149
U.N., 40, 44, 52-53, 483
UNESCO, 53
W.H.O., 52-53, 279, 452

Rhodesia
32, 34, 35-37, 40, 43, 46-47, 48, 57-63,
 367, 391, 507-512
economic sanctions, 46-47, 510-511
 responses to, 35, 36-37, 43, 44 n.21, 45
mandatory sanctions, 36, 40, 41, 45, 57
military solution, 48, 50
Security Council Resolution 232(1966),
 36, 40, 41, 57
Tiger settlement, 45
Unilateral Declaration of Independence,
 43, 46, 510

Romania
I.C.A.O. and, 190-191

Rome, Treaty of
amendment, 335, 338-339
Art. 2; 316
Art. 5; 326
Art. 12; 317
Art. 16; 317
Art. 20; 313

Art. 31; 317
Art. 37; 317, 400
Art. 48; 323
Art. 53; 318
Art. 56; 323
Art. 85; 312, 317, 324, 413
Art. 86; 312, 413
Art. 93; 327
Art. 95; 318
Art. 102; 327
Art. 103; 327
Art. 105; 327
Art. 148; 315
Art. 155; 326, 329
Art. 169; 329-331, 411, 412
Art. 170; 331-332, 411
Art. 171; 332
Art. 177; 324-325, 419, 420
Art. 189; 68, 69, 309, 311, 316, 405, 408,
 409
Art. 191; 309, 310
Art. 192; 318
Art. 213; 326
Art. 220; 313
Art. 235; 335, 338-339
constitutionality, 321
provisions directly affecting individuals,
 317-318
national law, effect upon, 68, 317, 321

Sanctions
14, 34, 45-48, 49, 160-161, 382, 387,
 513 515
See also under separate international
 organisations
effectiveness of decisions and, 72-73,
 160-161
exclusion, 513-515
expulsion, 47
legal, 161, 202
military, 48
natural, 161, 202, 211 n.8, 221, 450, 482,
 484, 516
nature of, 34, 46, 160-161, 382
non-recognition, 513
suspension, 514
target state, 46

Schachter, Oscar
39, 49

Security Council of the United Nations
42-43, 48, 391
decisions of, 36-37, 41, 68, 391, 480
recommendations, 36-37, 44, 68

seating, 33
unanimity, 494
veto, 391
voting, 43

Self-Determination
anti-colonialism and, 14, 490, 500-501

South Africa
12-13, 34, 42, 47, 50, 455, 512, 513, 514
F.A.O. and, 514
Indians in, 390-391
I.L.O. and, 136, 497
Mandate over South West Africa, 13, 43,
    63
U.N. decisions and, 12, 13, 42, 45, 47,
    48, 63, 64, 483, 485

South West Africa
63-64, 507-512
authority over, 64, 508
General Assembly Resolutions, 63, 64

Spain
Civil War, 455

**Specialised Agencies of the
United Nations**
365, 403, 406, 407, 478, 483, 517
acts of, transformation into national law,
    69
Convention on Privileges and Immunities,
    213, 214, 406
co-operation in standard setting, 445-447,
    456-458
example to U.N., 490-491
South Africa, 47

Sugar Agreement (1968)
271

Switzerland
neutrality and application of sanctions,
    35-36

Technical Assistance Programmes
367, 368

Treaties
12, 66-70, 210, 226, 284, 364, 393, 396
concluded within international
    organisations, 210, 341, 366, 369, 379,
    395-398
constitutional practices with respect to
    application of,

Austria, 423
Belgium, 142
France, 67, 142
Germany, 67, 122
Greece, 142
Italy, 67, 142
Mexico, 142
Netherlands, 66-67, 122, 423
United Kingdom, 67, 122, 166
U.S.A. 67, 122, 142, 166
delays in treaty making process, 416, 430
establishing international organisations,
    66-70, 364
E.E.C. practice, 313
I.C.A.O. practice, 163
I.L.O. practice, 139-140, 141-144
movement away from, 284, 416, 432, 436
non-self-executing provisions, 68-69, 142
ratification, 43, 389
    I.C.A.O. 187
    I.L.O. 141-144
    U.P.U., 295-296
recommendations, compared with,
    396-397, 398
self-executing provisions of, 66-68, 142,
    341
signature, 43, 389
Triple Option Clause, 44 n. 20
value of, 369

**Treaty for the Prohibition of
Nuclear Weapons in Latin America**
288

Trusteeship Council
Petitions, 56

Trusteeship Territories
Reports on, 53

Tunkin, Professor Grigori
21, 27

United Kingdom
See **Great Britain**

United Nations
See also **General Assembly of the United
    Nations; Security Council of the
    United Nations; Specialised Agencies
    of the United Nations**
"Chapter VI and a Half", 488, 511
Charter,
    Art. 2(7); 43
    Art. 6; 47, 49

Art. 19; 47, 49, 480, 505
Art. 25; 36, 39, 44
Art. 27(3); 41
Art. 39; 37
Art. 40; 39, 480
Art. 41; 44, 49
Art. 42; 48, 49
Art. 50; 45-46
Art. 55; 501
Art. 73; 40, 483, 489, 498
Art. 97; 382
Art. 98; 382
Art. 99; 382
Art. 102; 83
Art. 104; 67
Art. 105; 67
colonialism, 489-490, 494, 499-502
Committee of Twenty Four, 483, 500, 501
complaints procedure, 56
consensus process, 191 n.99
credentials, 513
decisions,
    addressees of, 35-36, 511
    binding nature of, 48, 381
    compliance with, 479-488
    effectiveness of, 32
    form of, 37
    internal, 37-38, 480
    kinds of, 479-480
    non-compliance with, 42-48, 482-483
    purposes of, 33-35
    standard setting, 34, 47, 38, 480
declarations, 480, 493, 494
    on Human Rights, 365, 391, 397, 398, 435, 490
    on Non-Intervention, 389, 390, 493
law-making function, 485, 486
legitimation function, 485
membership, 500
mobilisation of shame, 482, 485
peacekeeping, 32, 37, 48, 50, 387, 391, 480-482, 488-489, 501-502
privileges and immunities, 67, 489
Regional Commissions, 475-476, 478
resolutions,
    addressees of, 35-36, 39
    effect of affirmative vote, 38
    legal character of, 500
    political, 487
    reference to specific obligation, 39, 40
See also decisions
roles of, 502-503
sanctions, 34-37, 40, 45-48, 49, 160, 482, 483, 484

Secretary-General, 40, 44, 382, 391, 427
treaties, 480
voting, 493

United Nations Council for South West Africa
64

Unctad
476
Committee on Preferences, 376
standard setting in, 443

United Nations Development Programme (UNDP)
475
F.A.O. and, 219, 224
I.C.A.O. and, 156
W.H.O. and, 279

United Nations Educational Scientific and Cultural Organisation (UNESCO)
reports procedure, 53

United Nations Emergency Force (UNEF)
382, 481, 488

UNICEF
257

UNKRA
257

United Nations Program of Technical Assistance
I.C.A.O. and, 177

United Nations Relief and Works Organisation (UNRWA)
257

United Nations Relief and Rehabilitation Organisation
See **World Health Organisation**

United Nations Special Fund
213, 440, 444
F.A.O. and, 224

United Nations Truce Supervision Organisation (UNTSO)
481
Mixed Armistice Commission, 44

Union of Soviet Socialist Republics
budgetary obligations in U.N., 47-48
Jews in, 491
Rhodesia and South Africa policy, 48

United States of America
Agricultural Trade Development and
  Assistance Act (1954), 257
Bretton Woods Agreements Act (1945),
  85, 122, 125
constitutional amendment in, 364
constitutional practice with respect to
  treaties, 67, 122, 142, 166
European Recovery Programme, 257
Hickenlooper Amendment, 462
I.A.D.B. and, 129
I.B.R.D. and, 120-121, 122, 124-126
I.L.O. and, 140, 440-441
Interest Equalisation Tax Act, 123
International Organisations Immunities
  Act, 122 n.12
Lend-Lease, 257
National Advisory Council on
  International Monetary and Financial
  Problems, 85
O.E.E.C. and, 364
proposes reports under Declaration of
  Human Rights, 490
Securities Act (1933), 121
Securities Exchange Act (1934), 121
U.N. assessments and, 505-506

Universal Postal Union
290-303, 407, 431, 455
activities of, 290 n.1
Acts of the Union, 291-300
  amendments, 298-299
  approval at national level, 295-296
  enumerated, 292
  legal nature of, 291, 293-294
  Regulations, 293
  reservations, 296-297, 455
  structure of, 292-293
  tacit ratification of, 291-292, 294, 295
Congress, 290, 291, 293, 296, 298, 300,
  301
Constitution, 292
  amendment, 299-300
continuity of, 292, 294
decisions,
  approval, 295-296
  binding nature, 302-303
  classification of, 290, 407
  other than legislative Acts of the
    Union, 300-303

Executive Council, 299, 302
Expanded Executive and Liaison
  Committee, 295-296
International Bureau, 302
interpretation of decisions,
  judicial, 54
  non-judicial, 300
legislative process, 291-302, 431, 433, 438
mobilisation of shame, 455
national postal administrations, 291, 293,
  298, 300, 302, 438
obligations of Member States, 293, 294,
  302-303
Universal Postal Convention, 292, 293
Vienna Congress (1964), 292, 293, 294,
  301

Vietnam
485

World Food Programme
263, 440, 456-457
ECOSOC and, 226
establishment of, 225 n.56
example of inter-agency co-operation, 457
F.A.O. and, 219, 225-226, 257-258, 263,
  266, 457
sanctions in, 226

World Health Organisation
277-284, 430
activities, 281
Brussels Agreements (1906, 1929),
  abrogation of, 282
Committee on International Quarantine,
  54
compliance by Members, 283
constitution, 279
  Art. 19; 439
  Art. 21; 277, 281, 282
  Art. 22; 277, 281
  Art. 23; 279
Director-General, 53, 54, 277
Executive Board, 278, 282, 283
Expert Committees, 283
Health Statistics, 280
International Health Conference (1946),
  277, 278
International Sanitary Regulations
  (1951), 54, 279-280
  adoption, 279-280
  reservations, 280
  revision, 280-281
International Statistical Classification of
  Diseases etc., 280

legislative process, 277-278, 282, 284,
    433, 436-437, 441
    contracting-out, 277-278, 439
    recommendations, 282
Nomenclature Regulations (1948),
    280-281
recommendations, 279, 281, 437, 441
    reasons for greater use of, 281-282
Regional Arrangements, 284
Regulations, 277, 278, 437, 441
    adoption, 277-278, 280, 281
    rarity of, 281, 283
reports procedure, 53, 279, 452
    under recommendations, 279

sanctions, 450, 514
Technical Assistance Program, 279,
    Regional Offices and, 284
United Nations Relief and Rehabilitation
    Organisation,
    succession to, 279, 282
World Health Assembly, 277-284 passim
    Committee on Administration and
        Finance, 278
    powers, 278, 279

Zambia
45-46

538